CAIRNS, FIELDS, AND CULTIVATION:

ARCHAEOLOGICAL LANDSCAPES OF THE LAKE DISTRICT UPLANDS

Jamie Quartermaine and Roger H Leech

Contributions by
Richard Bradley, Paul Gajos, Melanie Hall, John Hodgson, Elizabeth Huckerby,
Bob Middleton, Colin Wells, and Guy Wimble

Illustrations by
Emma Carter, Andy Croft, Adam Parsons, Anne Stewardson, and Mark Tidmarsh

2012

LANCASTER
IMPRINTS
19

Published by
Oxford Archaeology North
Mill 3
Moor Lane Mills
Moor Lane
Lancaster
LA1 1GF
(*Phone:* 01524 541000; *Fax:* 01524 848606)
(*website:* http://thchumanjourney.net)

Distributed by
Oxbow Books Ltd
10 Hythe Bridge Street
Oxford
OX1 2EW
(*Phone:* 01865 241249; *Fax:* 01865 794449)

Printed by
Information Press, Oxford, UK

ISBN 978-1-907686-07-8
ISSN 1345-5205

Series editor
Rachel Newman
Indexer
Adam Parsons
Design, layout, and formatting
Adam Parsons and Marie Rowland

Front cover: *The Mickleden Valley, surrounded by the Langdale mountains*
Rear Cover: *Partially reconstructed roundhouse TB 750, on Town Bank*

LANCASTER
IMPRINTS
Lancaster Imprints is the publication series of Oxford Archaeology North. The series covers work on major excavations and surveys of all periods undertaken by the organisation and associated bodies.

Contents

List of Illustrations

Figures

Plates

Tables

Abbreviations

BP   Before Present. In terms of radiocarbon dates, present is defined as AD 1950

EDM   Electronic Distance Meter; survey equipment measuring distances between it and a reflecting prism by computing phase differences between the outgoing and returning signal of a beam of infra-red radiation

HER   Historic Environment Record, which is held by the Lake District National Park Authority, Murley Moss, Oxenholme Road, Kendal, Cumbria, LA9 7RL

LDHER   Lake District Historic Environment Record

LDNPA   Lake District National Park Authority

LDNPS   Lake District National Park Survey

OD   Ordnance datum

OS   Ordnance Survey

RCHM(E)   Royal Commission on the Historical Monuments of England

SM   Scheduled Monument

SMR   Sites and Monument Record, now HER

Archaeological Date Ranges

The dates for the primary archaeological periods are based on national radiocarbon dating and known historical dates; they consequently have a varying degree of accuracy.

Mesolithic Period	10000-4000 BC
Neolithic Period	4000-2200 BC
Bronze Age	2200-700 BC
Iron Age	700 BC-AD 43
Roman Period	AD 43-410
Early Medieval Period	AD 410-1066
Medieval Period	AD 1066-1600
Post-Medieval Period	AD 1600-1900+

Contributors

Richard Bradley
Department of Archaeology, School of Human and Environmental Science, University of Reading, Whiteknights, PO Box 217, Reading RG6 6AH

Paul Gajos
Associate Director, CgMs Consulting, Newark Beacon, Beacon Hill Office Park, Cafferata Way, Newark NG24 2TN

Melanie Hall
(formerly of) Department of Archaeology, Reading University

John Hodgson
Senior Archaeologist, Lake District National Park Authority, Murley Moss, Oxenholme Road, Kendal, Cumbria, LA9 7RL

Elizabeth Huckerby
OA North, Mill 3, Moor Lane Mills, Moor Lane, Lancaster LA1 1GF

Roger H Leech
Department of Archaeology, University of Southampton, Avenue Campus, Highfield, Southampton SO17 1BF

Bob Middleton
Project Manager, Catchment Sensitive Farming, Natural England, Renslade House, Exeter EX4 3AW

Jamie Quartermaine
OA North, Mill 3, Moor Lane Mills, Moor Lane, Lancaster LA1 1GF

Colin Wells
(formerly of) Lancaster University Archaeological Unit

Guy Wimble
Ironside Farrar Environmental Consultants, 111 McDonald Road, Edinburgh EH7 4NW

Foreword

The Lake District National Park has a rich and distinctive prehistoric archaeology, which has been relatively understudied in comparison with other upland areas of England. Before the 1980s, research into the prehistory of the Lake District had been carried out by a small number of dedicated amateur archaeologists and an even smaller number of university-based academics. Various reasons can be cited for this, including a widely held view of the north of England as a backward area in prehistory, and the lack of a local university department of archaeology (except for a brief period at Lancaster University).

The exceptions to this general picture include the research by Clare Fell and others into the Neolithic stone axe-production sites in the central fells, the extensive fieldwalking activities of the Cherry family, and Winifred Pennington's work on the palaeobotany of the area. However, it was not until the creation of the Cumbria and Lancashire Archaeological Unit (later renamed the Lancaster University Archaeological Unit, now Oxford Archaeology North), and its subsequent programmes of fieldwork, that the extent and significance of the prehistoric resource in the Lake District was more widely appreciated.

The most important of the Unit's projects in this regard was the Lake District National Park Survey (LDNPS), which was designed to enhance the Sites and Monuments Record (now Historic Environment Record) for the area. The immense value of this work is rooted in its adoption of a landscape approach to recording the archaeological resource, seen particularly in the ground-breaking survey of the Neolithic stone axe-production sites (published separately) and the recording of the extensive prehistoric cairnfields, settlements, and ritual monuments over wide areas of the Lake District fells.

Some of the results of the LDNPS have already been used to good effect, both for further research and for conserving this important archaeological resource. In addition, many of the important prehistoric sites that were recorded for the first time were designated as Scheduled Monuments through English Heritage's Monuments Protection Programme in the 1990s.

Publication of this important work will bring the rich prehistoric archaeology of the Lake District to a wider audience, including local residents and visitors to the National Park. All who have been involved in this work, including the English Heritage and National Park officers who commissioned the survey in 1982, the Unit staff who laboured in the fells, and the authors of this volume, are to be congratulated in taking forward our understanding of the Lake District's prehistory and providing a solid foundation for future research and management.

John Hodgson
Senior Archaeology and Heritage Adviser, Lake District National Park Authority

Summary

The detailed archaeological survey undertaken throughout the Lake District between 1982 and 1989 recorded some of the most remarkable field systems and settlements in England, mainly of later prehistoric date. The recording programme was set up primarily to provide for the management of these upland landscapes, and to ensure their preservation in the future. A secondary aim was to seek a greater understanding of the character of the occupation of the marginal lands of the Lake District and how this developed over an extended period.

The survey programme was targeted on areas of known archaeological potential, particularly the South-West Fells and the Western Fells of the Lake District, but, in addition, several other areas were examined within the Northern Fells, the Eastern Fells, and the Southern Fells. The survey involved the detailed recording of the landscape by means of instrument survey, and examined 78 square kilometres of uplands, recording over 10,300 monuments.

This, and subsequent surveys, have demonstrated that the greatest concentration of prehistoric landscapes within the Lake District is on the marginal uplands in Western Cumbria, adjacent to the Cumbrian coastal plain, which has been shown, as a result of extensive fieldwalking (*eg* Cherry and Cherry 1986), to be an area of Mesolithic and Neolithic activity. This survey programme, however, was geared to recording upstanding monuments, rather than artefacts, and thus it is not surprising that the majority of the remains identified in this programme would appear to be of Bronze Age date and reflect an expansion out from the coastal plain during a period of good climatic conditions. The most common physical expression of this activity was the cairnfield, which reflects the clearance of stone as part of a programme of land improvement. A typological development of the cairnfield could be discerned, which began with a localised sub-circular cluster of cairns, perhaps implying the exploitation of a small forest clearing. From these simple beginnings, the rationalisation of the cairns into lines, reflecting the beginnings of a field system, could be traced. The more advanced stages concerned the formation of complex field systems, some of which incorporated substantial lyncheted boundaries, indicating the cultivation of the marginal lands.

There was not the same density of prehistoric cairnfields and field systems in the southern, central, and eastern parts of the National Park, but some significant landscapes have been identified. On Heathwaite Fell, a medieval settlement had clearly developed over earlier agricultural activity, and in the Mickleden Valley, landscape development could also be recognised. The most notable ritual landcape is on Askham Fell, where an alignment of sepulchral monuments and a stone avenue extending across a natural col between two valleys have been recorded.

There was a general dearth of Iron Age-type monuments on the marginal lands which, coupled with palynological evidence indicating some forest recovery during that period, suggests a degree of abandonment of these areas, possibly in response to a climatic decline in the earlier part of the Iron Age. At several sites, particularly on the South-West Fells, there was clear evidence of a reoccupation of the uplands during the Roman period, which may have continued into the early medieval period. At several sites across the Lake District, localised medieval settlement was also found, in some cases developing out of shieling sites, and quite often this activity was superimposed upon earlier prehistoric or Roman landscapes. Post-medieval activity within the extent of the study areas was primarily unintensive pastoral farming, represented by stock shelters and extensive Parliamentary enclosure, but also by localised industrial extraction.

The surveys have demonstrated that a series of nationally important archaeological landscapes survive on the marginal uplands of Cumbria, which form a palimpsest of many periods of activity, and provide a remarkable opportunity to understand the development of the land and its people. As a result of this programme, the archaeological landscapes are now subject to improved management and conservation, and have a significantly greater potential for survival beyond the twenty-first century.

Résumé

L'étude topographique des vestiges archéologiques effectuée dans l'ensemble du Park national de Lake District entre 1982 et 1989 a permis le relevé des plus remarquables parcellaires et habitats d'Angleterre, datant principalement de la préhistoire récente. Initialement, ce programme de relevé a été mis en place pour garantir la gestion des paysages de ces hautes terres, et pour assurer leur conservation future. Un deuxième objectif a été de mieux comprendre les caractéristiques de l'occupation de terres marginales du Lake District et la manière dont cela s'est développé sur le long terme.

Le programme d'étude ciblait des zones de potentiel archéologique, tout particulièrement les collines de South-West Fells et de Western Fells du Lake District, mais aussi plusieurs autres secteurs ont été étudiés sur les monts de Northern Fells, Eastern Fells et Southern Fells. L'étude topographique a impliqué le relevé détaillé du paysage grâce à des instruments électroniques et a examiné 78 kilomètres carrés de hautes terres permettant de répertorier 10 300 monuments.

Ceci, et les études subséquentes, ont démontré que la plus grande concentration de paysages préhistoriques dans le Lake District se trouve sur les hautes terres marginales de l'Ouest de Cumbria, adjacente à la plaine côtière cumbrienne qui, grâce à la prospection pédestre (voir Cherry and Cherry 1986), s'est avérée être une zone d'activité mésolithique et néolithique. Le programme d'étude topographique était toutefois destiné à relever les monuments en élévation, plutôt que les artefacts. Il n'est donc pas surprenant que la majorité des vestiges mise au jour dans le cadre de ce programme semble dater de l'Age du Bronze et traduise une expansion à partir de la plaine côtière à une période climatique clémente. Celle-ci se manifeste le plus souvent sous forme de cairnfield (ensemble de cairns) qui atteste le dégagement de pierres au cours d'un programme d'amélioration de la terre. On pouvait discerner un développement typologique de cairnfields, qui débute avec un regroupement de cairns quasi-circulaire, laissant peut-être supposer l'exploitation d'une petite clairière au cœur de la forêt. A partir de ces simples origines, la rationalisation des cairns en alignements qui marquent les prémices d'un parcellaire, pourrait être retracée. Les étapes les plus avancées concernent la formation de parcellaires complexes, dont les limites de certains sont matérialisées par des rideaux, indiquant la culture de terres marginales.

La même densité de cairnfields et de parcellaires préhistoriques n'existe pas dans les parties sud, central et est du Park National, mais des paysages d'un grand intérêt ont été identifiés. Sur Heathwaite Fell, il subsiste des traces nettes d'aménagement d'un habitat médiéval, surimposé à une activité agricole antérieure ; et dans la Vallée de Mickleden, on reconnaît le développement paysager. Le paysage rituel le plus remarquable se trouve sur Askham Fell, où un alignement de monuments funéraires et une allée de pierres s'étendant sur un col naturel entre deux vallées ont fait l'objet d'un relevé.

Le manque général de monument de type Age du Fer était notable sur les terres marginales qui, conjugué au témoignage palynologique indiquant quelque recouvrement de la forêt à cette période, suggère un degré d'abandon de ces zones, réponse possible au déclin climatique au premier Age du Fer. Sur plusieurs sites, particulièrement sur les South-West Fells, une nouvelle occupation des hautes terres est évidente durant la période romaine, et s'est peut-être poursuivie jusqu'au haut Moyen Age. Sur plusieurs sites de l'ensemble du Lake District, un habitat médiéval localisé a également été découvert, qui s'est développé, dans certains cas, à partir de « shieling sites » (campements saisonniers) et, assez souvent, cette activité supplantait des paysages préhistoriques ou romano-britanniques anciens. L'activité post-médiévale dans l'emprise des secteurs d'étude était principalement l'élevage peu intensif, représenté par des abris pour animaux et une importante cadastration, mais aussi par une extraction artisanale localisée.

Les études topographiques ont démontré qu'une série de paysages diachroniques d'importance nationale subsistent sur les hautes terres de Cumbria, opportunité remarquable de comprendre l'évolution de la terre et de ses peuples. Grâce à ce programme, les paysages archéologiques font à présent l'objet d'une gestion et d'une conservation améliorées et jouissent d'un potentiel de survie beaucoup plus important au-delà du XXIème siècle.

Zusammenfassung

Die detaillierte archäologische Untersuchung, die zwischen 1982 und 1989 im Lake District durchgeführt wurde, dokumentierte einige der bemerkenswertesten Feldsysteme und Siedlungen in England, welche vor allem aus der späten prähistorischen Zeit datieren. Das Dokumentationsprogramm wurde in erster Linie aufgestellt, um die Verwaltung dieser Hochebenen sicherzustellen, und deren Erhaltung für die Zukunft zu gewährleisten. Ein weiteres Ziel war, ein besseres Verständnis für die Charakteristik der Besiedlung der Randgebiete des Lake District zu erhalten, und festzustellen, wie sich diese über einen längeren Zeitraum entwickelten.

Das Programm dieser Untersuchung war auf Gebiete von bekanntem archäologischen Potential ausgerichtet, vor allem in den South-West Fells und den Western Fells des Lake District, jedoch wurde zusätzlich eine Anzahl weiterer Gebiete in den Northern Fells, den Eastern Fells, und den Southern Fells untersucht. Die Untersuchung umfasste die detaillierte Dokumentation der Landschaft durch Vermessungstechnik, wobei 78 Quadratkilometer Hochland untersucht, und über 10.300 Monumente erfasst wurden.

Diese, sowie nachfolgende Untersuchungen, haben bewiesen, dass sich die größte Konzentration prähistorischer Landschaften in den äußeren Hochebenen von West Cumbria befindet, und zwar direkt an die Küstenebene Cumbrias angrenzend, welche sich durch extensives Begehen (z.B. Cherry und Cherry 1986) als ein Gebiet hoher mesolithischer und neolithischer Aktivität erwiesen hat. Dieses Untersuchungsprogramm war allerdings gezielt auf stehende Objekte statt auf Fundplätze ausgerichtet, und daher ist es nicht überraschend, dass die Mehrzahl der im Rahmen dieser Untersuchung identifizierten Überreste in die Bronzezeit zu datieren scheinen, und somit eine Ausdehnung aus der Küstenebene während einer Periode guter Klimabedingungen widerspiegelt. Der häufigste physische Ausdruck dieser Aktivität ist das so genannte Cairnfield (Cairn = Steinhaufen, Cairnfield = Gruppe von mehreren Steinhaufen, räumlich identifizierbar), welches die Abräumung von Steinen als Teil eines Programms zur Bodenverbesserung widerspiegelt. Eine typologische Entwicklung des Cairnfield konnte mittels einer lokalisierten sub-kreisförmigen Ansammlung von Steinhaufen, ermittelt werden, die vielleicht die Nutzung einer kleinen Waldlichtung widerspiegelt. Von diesen einfachen Ursprüngen konnte die Anordnung der Steinhaufen in Linien verfolgt werden, was die Anfänge eines Feldsystems beweist. Die fortgeschittene-ren Stadien umfassten die Bildung komplexer Feldsysteme, von denen einige substantielle Begrenzungen mit Feldrainen aufwiesen, was auf die Kultivierung der Randgebiete hindeutete.

Die südlichen, zentralen und östlichen Teile des Nationalparks wiesen nicht die gleiche Dichte an prähistorischen Cairnfields und Feldsystemen auf, jedoch wurden einige bedeutende rituelle Landschaften identifiziert. Auf Heathwaite Fell, hatte sich eine mittelalterliche Siedlung deutlich von früherer landwirtschaftlicher Tätigkeit fortentwickelt, ausserdem war eine Entwicklung der Landschaft im Mickleden Valley erkennbar. Die bemer-kenswerteste Rituallandschaft liegt auf dem Askham Fell, auf welchem eine Ausrichtung der Grabmäler sowie eine Steinallee, die sich über einen natürlichen Pass zwischen zwei Tälern erstreckt, nachgewiesen werden konnte.

Ein allgemeiner Mangel an eisenzeitlichen Monumenten in den Randgebieten wurde festgestellt, welcher zu-sammen mit palynologischen Hinweisen auf eine Wiederbewaldung während dieser Zeit hinweisen könnte. Dieser deutet auf eine teilweise Aufgabe dieser Gebiete, möglicherweise als Reaktion auf einen klimatischen Verfall in der ersten Hälfte der Eisenzeit, hin. An mehreren archäologischen Stätten, besonders auf den South-West Fells, gab es eindeutige Hinweise auf eine Wiederbesiedlung des Hochlands während der römischen Periode, welche sich bis ins frühe Mittelalter fortgesetzt haben könnte. An mehreren Stätten im Lake District wurden ebenfalls lokalisierte mittelalterliche Siedlungen festgestellt, die sich in einigen Fällen aus Hütten-siedlungen entwickelt haben, und häufig überlagerte diese Besiedlung frühere prähistorische und römische Landschaften. Nachmittelalterliche Aktivität in den Untersuchungsgebieten ist in erster Linie durch wenig intensive Weidewirtschaft, Tierunterstände und umfangreiche Einfriedung repräsentiert, aber auch durch lokalisierten industriellen Abbau.

Die Untersuchungen haben erwiesen, dass eine Reihe von national bedeutenden archäologischen Landschaften in den Randgebieten des Hochlandes von Cumbria überdauern und ein Palimpsest vieler Aktivitätsperioden bilden, und eine ausgezeichnete Gelegenheit bieten, die Entwicklung des Landes und seiner Menschen zu verstehen. Als Ergebnis dieses Programms unterliegen diese archäologischen Landschaften nun verbesserter Verwaltung und Erhaltung, und haben eine beträchtlich größere Chance jenseits des 21. Jahrhunderts zu überleben.

Acknowledgements

This volume is a product of many years of intensive survey by many survey staff, too numerous to list individually here, but without whose unstinting and enthusiastic support the surveys could never have been completed. We would like to single out those supervisors and assistants who have provided particular help. Valerie Turner, who directed many of the earlier surveys and assisted with the Ulpha Fell survey, provided an invaluable insight into the recording of these upland landscapes. We are also indebted to Philip Howard, Brian Bentham, Bob Middleton, Ken Robinson, Martin Brann, Pippa White, and Fiona Pitt, whose support and humour made the sometimes inclement conditions on the fells that much more bearable. The publication and archive illustrations were for the most part drawn by Dick Danks, and the electronic illustrations were generated by Andy Croft, Emma Carter, Adam Parsons, Anne Stewardson, and Mark Tidmarsh. Adam Parsons also edited the drawings to make them suitable for publication. Jo Dawson is to be thanked for researching the history of Crosbythwaite.

The authors would like to thank the many landowners and tenants who allowed survey on their land. We would also like to thank the National Trust for their continued support for the project, and for enabling access to their properties at Town Bank, Stockdale Moor, Burnmoor, Mickleden Beck, and Hesk Fell. In addition, the Lowther and Muncaster Estates are to be thanked for allowing the surveys to be undertaken across their land on Askham Fell and on the South-West Fells. In particular, we would like to thank Philip Claris, who co-directed the survey of Mickleden Beck and provided much inspiration for its survey and that of the adjacent Langdale Neolithic axe-production sites.

Many people assisted our studies and provided invaluable data on sites. Elizabeth Huckerby and Colin Wells provided considerable advice and assistance with the palaeoecological context for the archaeological landscapes. We would particularly like to thank Angus Winchester for making available the results of his work on the history of the Bootle Fell medieval settlement, for generously sharing his knowledge of the fells in medieval and later times, and also for many valued discussions, some on the memorable May Fell Walks organised for the Cumberland and Westmorland Antiquarian and Archaeological Society. We would also like to thank Nick Higham for providing access to the results of his unpublished survey work on Heathwaite Fell. Tom Clare, the former Cumbria County Archaeologist, is thanked for permission to use his oblique aerial photographs of the main survey areas, and for his invaluable advice in the planning of the survey programmes; the late Mary Higham provided valued assistance in researching the place-name evidence for the Whin Garth settlement and advice on medieval enclosure practices. Guy Wimble is thanked for making available the results of his PhD thesis on the palaeoecology of the Duddon Valley, and for allowing the publication of his pollen core from beneath a clearance cairn near Devoke Water (excavated in 1985 by Adrian Olivier) and from the adjacent Tewit Moss. Adrian Olivier is to be thanked for allowing us to present the results of the Devoke Water cairn excavation, as is Paul Gajos for writing up the results. We must also thank Bette Hopkins, then Cumbria SMR officer, for providing access to SMR information held by Cumbria County Council. Mark Edmonds and Richard Bradley are thanked for making available the results of the Reading University project undertaken around Great Langdale and the Mickleden Valley in 1987. Peter Fowler, then Secretary of the RCHM(E), is also to be thanked for visiting the project while in progress in the Devoke Water area, and for his various helpful suggestions.

The project was undertaken by the Lancaster University Archaeological Unit (LUAU; now Oxford Archaeology North) and was funded by English Heritage and the Lake District National Park Authority. We would like to thank all those at English Heritage who have provided so much support, over the years, to the survey programme, in particular, Geoffrey Wainwright in the setting up of the project, and David Fraser, Bill Startin, Gerry Friell, and Tony Wilmott, who have in their time provided much guidance and support. We would particularly like to show our appreciation to Pamela Leech and the late Brenda Capstick, successively the English Heritage Field Monument Wardens for the area, who were constantly following in our footsteps to monitor the Scheduled Monuments within the study areas; they provided an immense source of enthusiasm for the archaeological landscapes of the fells, as well as providing scheduling details for the survey areas.

For the Lake District National Park Authority, we thank Andrew Lowe for his support during the earlier years of the project, and John Hodgson more recently for providing support during the preparation of the publication, and for contributing to *Chapter 9*. Finally, we would like to thank Richard Newman, Rachel Newman, John Hodgson, Tertia Barnett, Richard Gregory, Andrew Fleming, and Richard Bradley for their comments on drafts of this volume, and Richard Gregory and Rachel Newman for editing the final draft.

The programme was originally set up by Roger Leech, then director of the Cumbria and Lancashire Archaeological Unit, who undertook the earlier surveys of Birkby/Birker Fell, Ulpha Fell, Corney Fell, Thwaites Fell, Whitrow Beck, and Burnmoor. In 1984 and 1985, Valerie Turner undertook the surveys of Shap/Askham and Caldbeck Fells (Turner 1987; 1991). From 1985 onwards, the survey programme was led by Jamie Quartermaine, who directed all the subsequent surveys (Hesk Fell, Stockdale Moor, Town Bank, Bootle Fell, Heathwaite Fell, Askham Fell, Stainton Fell, Barnscar, Whin Garth, and Charlesground Gill). The axe-production site surveys (Langdale, Scafell Pike, and Mickleden) were jointly directed by Jamie Quartermaine and Philip Claris (Claris and Quartermaine 1989).

Dr Richard Chiverrell of Liverpool University is to be thanked for the image of the glacier at Ladalsbreem, Josteldal, Norway, used as Plate 3. Plate 8 is reproduced from *Transactions of the Cumberland and Westmorland Antiquarian and Archaeological Society*, New Series Volume 93 (1993), and the Cambridge University Collection and Bob Bewley are thanked for permission to use this image. Plate 13 is reproduced from the *Transactions of the Cumberland and Westmorland Antiquarian and Archaeological Society*, Old Series Volume 12 (1893). The Lake District National Park Authority is thanked for permission to reproduce photographs from a number of sites (Pls 17, 165, 166, 172, 190, 192, 194, 196). Plates 45 and 51 are reproduced from the personal collection of the late Bill Fletcher. Thanks are also due to the University of Birmingham for permission to reproduce the image of bracken at Tonguesdale Moss (Pl 193). The Cumbria Historic Environment Record is thanked for permission to use the aerial photographs taken by Tom Clare (Pls 25, 26, 40, 42, 44, 47, 54, 68, 74, 79, 105, 148, 185, and 189).

The figures contain contour data which is Ordnance Survey data © Crown copyright and database right 2011. Figures 162 and 164 contain Ordnance Survey mapping with the permission of the Controller of Her Majesty's Stationery Office Crown Copyright, Oxford Archaeology Licence No AL 100005569 (January 2012).

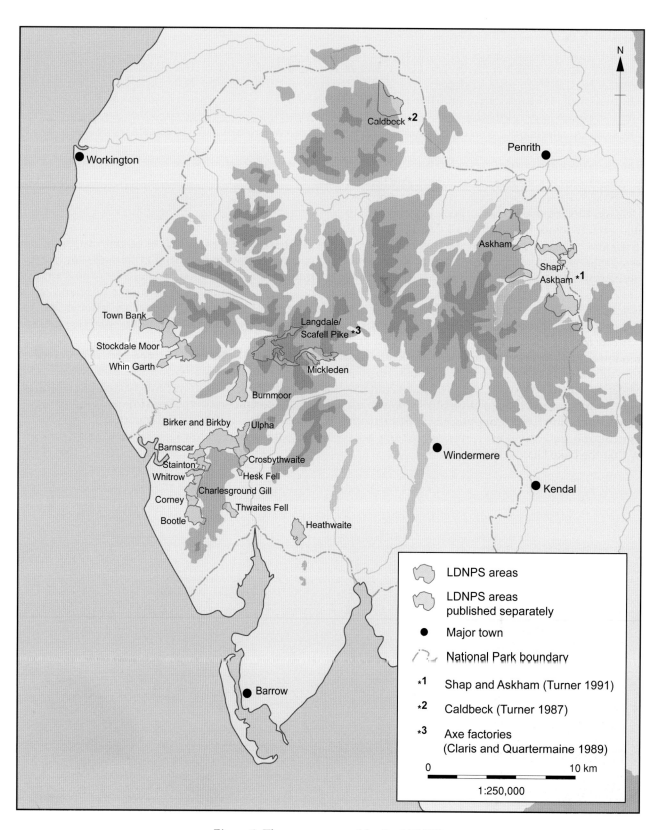

Figure 1: The areas surveyed by the LDNPS

1

INTRODUCTION

A programme of survey, called the Lake District National Park Survey (LDNPS), recorded (between 1982 and 1989) the abundant archaeological landscapes that extend across the uplands of the Lake District. The survey targeted areas that contained a known significant archaeological resource, but one that had not been recorded in any detail, and which are some of the most important archaeological landscapes within Northern England. These areas are for the most part found on the western side of the Lakeland massif, adjacent to the coastal plain (Fig 1). The archaeological monuments recorded date from the neolithic period through to the present, although the majority were of prehistoric date. Most of the monuments indicate agricultural use of these marginal lands, and the survey thus provided the opportunity to examine the agricultural development of these particular areas within the Lake District through time.

The Lake District

The Lake District is a region of contrast, from the still waters of its long, radial lakes to the craggy pinnacles of its mountains (Pl 1). Its topography is one that has largely been created by fire and ice; a central volcanic dome was cut by glaciers, which gouged their way down from the summit, leaving behind massive, steep-sided valleys (Pennington 1978, 207-8). When the ice melted, the gouged-out valley bottoms filled with water and the resultant lakes and rounded hills have become the familiar Lakeland landscape of today (Pl 2).

In scale and altitude, the Lake District cannot compete with many other mountainous regions of the world,

Plate 1: The classic glacially cut radial valley of Wasdale, in the central Lake District

Plate 2: The view across Scafell and Bow Fell, at the centre of the Lake District

or even Britain, but its natural, rugged beauty has made it a focus for poet and visitor alike. Since the eighteenth century (West 1780), travel guides and the lyrical writings of romantic poets, such as Coleridge, Wordsworth, Southey, and Tennyson, have attracted the visitor (Wordsworth and Coleridge 1798; Tennyson 1830). The first travellers were few and far between and it was indeed possible to 'wander lonely as a cloud', but with the construction of the railway to Windermere in 1847 (Rollinson 1996), and then the expansive influx of the motor car, the Lake District has become sated with this transient population. The character of much of the land has changed from one predominantly of marginal hill farms, to one dominated by tourism.

To the visitor, the Lake District is presented as a remote, natural wilderness, a land unspoilt by humans, and characterised by those romantic writings of William Wordsworth (Wordsworth and Coleridge 1798), and the works of Beatrix Potter (1903) and Alfred Wainwright (1955). The reality, needless to say, is very different. Humans have manipulated the landscape at least since the neolithic period, when they started the deforestation of the extensive, Holocene upland forest, notably in the centre of the Lake District, near Great Langdale (Pennington 1964). At the same time, they began an extraction for axes on an industrial scale around the

central peaks (Claris and Quartermaine 1989). From the Bronze Age onwards, deforestation was started in earnest as a result of an agricultural expansion onto the marginal fells, around the periphery of the Lake District. The land has been farmed ever since, at varying levels of intensity, reflecting, in part, the ebb and flow of settlement onto the marginal fells as a result of the differing climatic and population pressures. The treeless, exposed, grass-covered fells of today are more a testament to the hands of humans than they are to nature. It is primarily the extent to which humans have exerted their influence on the natural landscape that this volume seeks to address.

Formation of the Landscape

The Lake District has one of the most varied and scenic landscapes in England, comprising the highest and most concentrated range of mountains. This range is bounded on three sides by coastal fringes with extensive deposits of lowland peat (Hodgkinson *et al* 2000). To the east, away from the coastal plains, the topography gives way to the more rounded relief of the Howgill Fells to the south, and to the north, east of the Eden Valley, to the Pennine Chain (Moseley 1978).

Plate 3: A Norwegian glacier, surrounded by deposits of moraine. Similar glaciers created the radial valleys of the Lake District

Geomorphology of the Lake District and its environs

The distinctive topography of the Lake District principally comprises an uplifted mountain chain, formed during the Caledonian orogeny, which was then exposed to consecutive folding and uplifting processes to produce a complex, central dome. Extensive, subsequent, denudation and deep erosion of younger, superficial rocks created the radial-drainage pattern that characterises the Lake District landscape (Moseley 1978). This basic structure was established by the end of the Tertiary period, after which the Lake District was sculpted into the landscape with which we are familiar today by successive Quaternary glaciation events. Glacial action (Pl 3) carved the lasting, distinctive relief of the lakes, fells, and dales. It scooped out corries, created hanging valleys and waterfall ravines, and deposited morainic material on many valley floors and mountain slopes. It has also left great swathes of drift over lower-lying areas and led to the accumulation of alluvial and marine sediments (Hodgkinson *et al* 2000, 5).

The majority of the areas examined by the LDNPS lie on the fringes of this distinctive topographical area and include the Western (*Ch 3*), South-West (*Chs 4* and *5*), Southern (*Ch 6*), and Eastern Fells (*Ch 7*). Of these areas, the Western Fells are characterised by mountainous terrain, with lower tracts of landscape situated to the west, above and adjacent to the coastal plain, whilst the South-West Fells comprise a narrow range of hills, similarly bounded by the coastal plain, to the west and south, but also by the Duddon Valley to the east. To the east of this latter area lie the Southern Fells, bounded to the west by the Duddon Valley, and to the east by Coniston Water, and the valley of the River Crake. These include mountainous terrain and also tracts of lower, more undulating, landscape. Similarly, the Eastern Fells, which are bounded by the Troutbeck and Ullswater valleys, comprise tracts of mountainous terrain to their west, with lower, undulating, landscape to the east. In addition to these four areas, the LDNPS also considered a small section of the Central Fells, focusing on the Mickleden Valley (*Ch 6*). This area, close to the centre of the Lake District massif, is dominated by a classic U-shaped glacial valley, associated with deposits of scree on its sides, and morainic drift situated at its extreme north-western valley head.

Beyond the survey areas, to the north and west of the Central Lake District massif, lies the Cumbrian Plain, which is dominated by younger sedimentary rocks. These are arranged in a series of low ridges, which forms a gently undulating terrain, giving

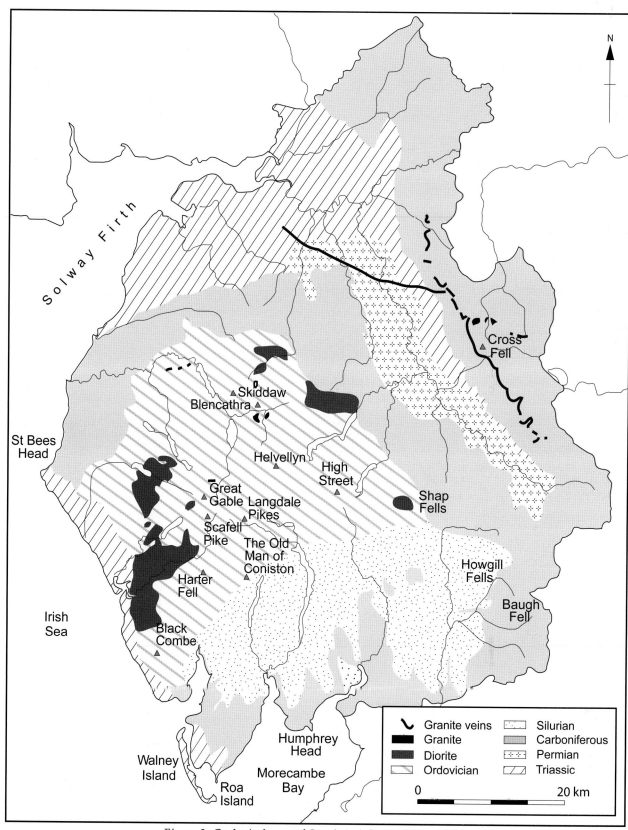

Figure 2: Geological map of Cumbria (after Halliday 1997)

Legend:
- Granite veins
- Granite
- Diorite
- Ordovician
- Silurian
- Carboniferous
- Permian
- Triassic

0   20 km

Map labels: Solway Firth, Cross Fell, Skiddaw, Blencathra, St Bees Head, Helvellyn, High Street, Great Gable, Langdale Pikes, Shap Fells, Scafell Pike, The Old Man of Coniston, Howgill Fells, Harter Fell, Baugh Fell, Irish Sea, Black Combe, Humphrey Head, Walney Island, Morecambe Bay, Roa Island, N

way to a variety of wetland and coastal landscapes, comprising intertidal mudflats, estuarine and lagoon formations, sand dunes, marshes, and seacliffs at St Bees Head (Hodgkinson *et al* 2000, 3). However, this contrasts with that area situated beyond the north-eastern and eastern perimeter of the Lake District massif, where a band of limestone has created an upland landscape, dominated by rolling hills and expanses of open moorland, mixed with localised pasture land. Similarly, to the south of the central massif lies an undulating terrain of low ridges and fells, which now support extensive woodland. This area is defined at its southern extremity by the broad sweep of Morecambe Bay and the surrounding limestone lowlands.

Geology and soils

Cumbria has a complex geology (Fig 2) and hence a varied landscape and flora (Halliday 1997). The central massif of the Lake District principally comprises the most ancient, Ordovician and Silurian, rocks. These are surrounded by a ring of Permian, Triassic, and Carboniferous formations, with the latter rising to the east into the northernmost part of the Pennine Chain (*ibid*).

The oldest rocks are the Skiddaw Slates, which form the Skiddaw fells and most of the Northern Fells. The relative softness of the Skiddaw Slates has allowed the landscape of this area to be shaped into immense, smooth slopes, rising to peaks and domes, with steep, flanking screes, while the acidity of these rocks has produced poor soils and an impoverished flora (*ibid*). In the Central Lake District, the Borrowdale Volcanic Series is the most extensive of the Ordovician formations (Moseley 1978; Pl 4). The different hardnesses of these rocks has produced the irregular, rugged character of the central fells, and its harder, finer-grained rocks were exploited in the neolithic period on a massive scale to create axes (Claris and Quartermaine 1989).

Mudstones, grits, and shales of the Silurian period form the Coniston Limestone Series, and the rocks of the southern part of the Lake District (Moseley 1978), which extend eastwards into the Howgills, and Middleton and Barbon Fells of the Cumbria/Lancashire border. The varying softness of these rocks has given rise to a tamer landscape than that of the Northern Fells, with its characteristic low, irregular topography of hillocks, hollows, and tarns, and the larger lakes of Windermere (Pl 5) and Coniston Water. The more favourable terrain and relatively fertile soils of this region, with greater nutrient run-off into the surrounding drainage basins, have encouraged woodland formation and more intensive agricultural exploitation than in other parts of the Lake District.

Mountain-building processes during the Devonian period caused localised metamorphosis of the existing geology, including the Skiddaw Slates and Borrowdale Volcanic Series, forming metal- and mineral-bearing rocks, that have had implications for later mining and extraction activities (*ibid*). In the Carboniferous period, a mantle, principally of limestone, was deposited over the entire Lake District. This stratum has subsequently been completely eroded from the central massif, and survives only as a peripheral ring around the older rocks, principally seen as limestone outcrops, pavements, and low scarps. In these areas, the geology has produced calcareous

Plate 4: Exposed outcrops of the Borrowdale Volcanic Series at the summit of Scafell Pike

Plate 5: Windermere, looking north

soils, which support important lime-rich habitats. Outside the northern part of this limestone ring, and parallel to it, is a band of Coal Measures containing grits and shales. Encircling the north and east of this peripheral limestone ring, and also defining the south-west of the central massif, are younger Permian and Triassic rocks, which collectively form the New Red Sandstone. Much of this region was subsequently overlain by more recent glacial deposits, and today it predominantly comprises low-lying farmland with large, raised peat bogs (Halliday 1997).

The Vegetational and Climatic History of the Lake District During the Holocene

The Holocene refers to the period beginning *c* 10,500-10,000 cal BC, when temperatures began to rise from glacial coldness to the more equable levels that are still enjoyed today (Hodgkinson *et al* 2000, 174). However, the 12,000 years or so since the end of the Devensian ice age have not seen a constant 'warm' climate in the Lake District and North-West Europe, but rather a series of fluctuations, during which the area has experienced periods with both warmer and colder average temperatures than that of today. The erratic nature of the climate during the Holocene has, therefore, influenced the development of the vegetation and ecology of the region, which, in turn, has affected human activity.

Palaeolithic period (*c* 2,600,000 - 10,000 cal BC)

The transition from the glacial period to the beginning of early post-glacial conditions did not occur smoothly, and it is apparent that there was a tripartite division of the last stages of the Devensian glacial period (Goudie 1983). A cold phase terminated with the first herald of warmer conditions, which began *c* 12,000 cal BC; however, sometime around 10,850-10,600 cal BC there was an abrupt return to a near-glacial regime. By *c* 10,500-10,000 cal BC, temperatures again rose, this time on a long-term basis, and the true post-glacial era was initiated. Evidence for this sequence is recorded in the Lake District in the form of pollen from contemporary vegetation trapped and preserved in the sediments of lakes existing at the time, and since sealed under many metres of overlying material. The pollen evidence from places like Blelham Bog and parts of Windermere (Pennington 1970) shows that, during the twelfth and eleventh millennia BC, the climate became warmer during the 'Windermere Interstadial', allowing the spread of juniper scrub in the Lake District valleys, and the colonisation of southern areas by birch trees. On the basis of the study of organically rich lake muds, dating from this period, it is now thought probable that all ice and permanent snow had disappeared from the district. Soon after *c* 11,000 cal BC, however, a return to much colder conditions enabled the repossession of the landscape by tundra plants (*ibid*). The stratigraphical sequence in lakes and tarns containing deposits of this age also retains a climatic signature from this event, in the form of laminated or layered clays laid down by glacial outwash from reinvigorated snowfields and corrie glaciers. More substantial physical evidence from this period (known as the 'Loch Lomond Stadial') can still be seen in places like the head of Mickleden in Langdale, where hummocky moraine marked the dumping ground of debris from the last Lake District glaciers (Walker 1965a). This cold 'snap' (on a geological timescale), which interrupted the trend to a warmer climate, lasted perhaps 500 years or so, and is likely to have caused widespread disruption to the fragile immature soils and stabilising vegetation cover, which had gained a precarious toehold in the area. It is possible that many of the screes and alluvial delta-fans of the area's lakes are a result of this episode.

Mesolithic period (10,000 - 4000 cal BC)

After *c* 10,500-10,000 cal BC, prolonged and extreme cold conditions effectively ended for good, temperatures rose rapidly, and forest cover began its inexorable spread across the raw soils of the Holocene landscape, which was to culminate in continuous tree cover up to 800 m OD. The beginning of this phase was marked by the rapid and widespread expansion of juniper, which has been dated in the north of Cumbria to *c* 9000-7000 cal BC (Walker 1966). This 'juniper maximum' was followed swiftly by an expansion of birch forest. The dominance of birch was ephemeral, however, as the warm temperatures of the early Holocene enabled the establishment of closed mixed forest over the whole area, probably up to the very summits of the mountains in some places. The forest was largely dominated by hazel, elm, and oak, although in some areas pine formed an important component. Lime was a significant tree in the extreme southern part of the Lake District, particularly in the southern limestone areas fringing Morecambe Bay, but it appears to have reached its climatically controlled northern limit of distribution in this area, and did not advance further to dominate the woodland canopy, as in many other parts of England (Rackham 1980).

The first part of the mesolithic period probably enjoyed a more continental climate, being warmer and drier than today (Huntley 1993, 214). A shift to wetter conditions followed, which would have encouraged a rise in water tables. This may be reflected in the vegetational record, as it appears that the nature of the woodland cover changed subtly as the Holocene progressed. Although oak and elm still dominated the drier soils on hillsides, alder began to occupy large areas of the less well-drained valley floors.

The effects of human activity on the vegetation become noticeable in the palaeoecological record of

the time, particularly in the fringe areas of the region. There is good evidence from lowland Lonsdale, on the southern limestone fringe of the Lake District, for small-scale anthropogenic clearance of woodland cover, which was taking place towards the latter part of the period (Taylor *et al* 1987; Middleton *et al* 1995, 188-9). Charcoal is also common in the mesolithic stratigraphy of the lowland raised mires surrounding the uplands, although it is not known for sure whether this burning was directly associated with human activity (Huckerby and Wells 1993).

The archaeological evidence for contemporary settlement is patchy, and partly reflects the areas within which fieldwork has been concentrated. Scatters of mesolithic assemblages are concentrated along the coastal plain, having been found from Walney Island (Barnes and Hobbs 1950), via Eskmeals (Bonsall *et al* 1986; Cherry and Cherry 1986), to as far north as St Bees (Cherry and Cherry 1973). However, a few scatters of late mesolithic artefacts have also been identified from the limestone uplands of east Cumbria (for instance, Wickers Gill, Howes Plantation, Tarn Moor 1 and 5, and Rayseat 1, 6, and 7; *cf* Cherry and Cherry 1987).

The Eskmeals sites were ranged along the edge of the old coastline and, on excavation, occupation was found to be both fairly small and structurally simple. For example, the Monks Moors 1 flake scatter covered an area measuring some 35 x 15 m, within which there was an elongated oval arrangement of hearths and stakeholes that was only 7 x 24 m (Bonsall 1981). The chronology of the sites falls within the later mesolithic period, as a radiocarbon date from Monk Moors 1 suggests occupation *c* 6000-5400 cal BC (5986-5384 cal BC; 6750±155 BP; B-1216), whilst those from Williamson's Moss suggest that the earliest occupation ranged from *c* 4500 cal BC to 4300 cal BC (4460-4338 cal BC; 5555±40 BP; UB-2545; 4224-3355 cal BC; 4925±165 BP; UB-2711; Bonsall *et al* 1986, 26). This is consistent with the less precise dating of artefact scatters, which generally show later mesolithic affinities.

In addition to the coastal sites, a programme of excavation in 2009, ahead of the Carlisle Northern Development Route, has also identified a very large mesolithic flint scatter, and associated activity, on a Holocene terrace of the River Eden (Pl 6). In addition, palaeoenvironmental assessment has shown that, although charred plant remains associated with the flints are not abundant, well-preserved pollen is present in the organic deposits found in a nearby palaeochannel, immediately adjacent to the site, which radiocarbon assay indicates date from the late mesolithic period to the Bronze Age (OA North 2011a). Once analysis is complete, this

Plate 6: Mesolithic to Bronze Age features excavated prior to the construction of the Carlisle Northern Development Route

site, with its finds and pollen in close association, will undoubtedly provide an excellent record of anthropogenic activity, forming the earliest prehistoric occupation of northern Cumbria.

Neolithic period (*c* 4000 - 2000 cal BC)

The first significant human interference with the natural vegetation cover occurred at around 4000-4500 cal BC in north, west, and south Cumbria, where pollen evidence indicates small reductions in the cover of tree species, particularly elm, along with the presence of weeds associated with human activity, such as plantains (Pennington 1970). However, this activity, which may represent small-scale clearances, was soon to be totally eclipsed by the first large-scale deforestation in the region, which began *c* 4000 cal BC in the west Cumbrian coastal areas. During the first part of the third millennium BC, large-scale clearances of forest took place there, associated with cereal cultivation, identified within sediments contained in Barfield Tarn (*ibid*). The west Cumbrian coastal strip was therefore perhaps one of the earliest areas to become permanently deforested in the country, as a result of this intensive activity. Around the same time, initial small-scale clearings were being made at the upper edges of the fellside forest cover around the head of Langdale, which was almost certainly associated with the initial workings of the Langdale axe-production sites (Hedges *et al* 1994, 360). Deforestation activity there intensified in *c* 3000 cal BC and continued for several centuries.

Studies of the sediments from Blea and Angle Tarns have also indicated increased soil erosion contemporary with this activity, and wood charcoal has been identified stratified in muds at Langdale Combe, which was associated with the clearance levels (Walker 1965a). All the evidence, therefore, points to the current largely treeless and leached nature of the landscape above *c* 500 m OD, in this area, as having been initiated during the neolithic period (*ibid*).

To an extent, neolithic settlement in Cumbria continued the earlier, hunter-gatherer, tradition, and many of the later mesolithic flint scatters also include neolithic material (*eg* Wickers Gill, Kemp Howe 5, Windrigg Hill 6, and Gaythorn 3; *cf* Cherry and Cherry 1987). Similarly, radiocarbon dates, ranging between *c* 4200 cal BC and 3300 cal BC, from the Williamson's Moss excavation showed that this site continued to be utilised during the neolithic period (Bonsall *et al* 1986, 26). There was also, however, an expansion of more permanent settlement across the west Cumbria coastal plain, typified by sites such as Ehenside Tarn (Darbishire 1873). This is complemented by the evidence of extensive forest clearance and cultivation from the area of the coastal plain, indicating considerable neolithic farming activity in this area (Pennington 1975). There is also evidence of a certain amount of neolithic activity within the upland interior, but this does not necessarily reflect settlement. Early

*Plate 7: The axe-production sites in Great Langdale,
exploiting a band of fine-grained tuff outcropping just
below the summits*

stone circles, such as Castlerigg and Swinside, are distributed around the marginal, peripheral areas of the Lake District, but are not associated with clearance activity (Burl 1976). Around the summits of the central massif (Scafell and Langdale Pikes) are the remains of very large-scale axe production (Pl 7), which was at its most intensive around the end of the neolithic period. The forest clearance in the vicinity of the sites, however, is not necessarily an indication of agricultural activity. For example, there is no evidence of any settlements apart from very small, temporary camp sites on the main communication routes (Claris and Quartermaine 1989, 12), and the clearance is more likely to relate to the industrial processes.

On the basis of the limited number of excavated neolithic settlement sites from the region, which include Ehenside Tarn (Darbishire 1873) and Plasketlands (Bewley 1993), both outside the Lake District proper, neolithic settlement appears to have been more permanent in character than its mesolithic counterpart, reflecting a partial economic dependence upon farming. Ehenside Tarn, on the Cumbrian coastal plain, was excavated in 1871 (Darbishire 1873), but the basic recording techniques did not identify any structures, apart from a large central hearth (*ibid*). However, considerable quantities of domestic tools and furniture were uncovered, including stone axes (and a hafting), axe-polishing stones, quern stones, wooden paddles, wooden bowls, and ceramic vessels. This artefact assemblage suggests a substantial, permanent settlement with a

mixed economy that included hunting, fishing, cereal production, and industrial processing.

The pollen cores taken at the time of excavations in 1957 at Ehenside Tarn have now been resampled and subjected to AMS dating. The results of these analyses provide a record of human activity in the local landscape, which has modified the vegetation from the early neolithic to the Roman periods, and possibly also the early medieval period (Walker 2001).

*Plate 8: The neolithic enclosure at Plasketlands on the
Solway Plain*

At the site of Plasketlands, on the Solway Plain (Bewley 1993), a sub-rectangular ditched enclosure was revealed, which was initially considered to be of Iron Age/Roman date (Pl 8). However, three radiocarbon dates, of 3958-3535 cal BC (4940±90 BP; GU-3573), 3706-3379 cal BC (4810±60 BP; GU-2571), and 3985-3712 cal BC (5090±60 BP; GU-2572), indicated that this site was, rather, a neolithic creation. Excavation in 2009, ahead of the construction of the Carlisle Northern Development Route, has also

*Plate 9: The head of a neolithic wooden trident from the
Carlisle Northern Development Route*

recovered neolithic wooden artefacts, along with pieces of elm, from an organic deposit found in a palaeochannel of the River Eden (Pl 9; OA North 2011a). Moreover, pollen assessment suggests that evidence for the elm decline is likely to be present in these deposits, with high values of elm pollen recorded in the lower contexts, and much reduced ones higher up the sequence (*ibid*).

Bronze Age/early Iron Age (*c* 2000 - 400 cal BC)

The southern lowlands of Cumbria, around the fringes of Morecambe Bay, provide some evidence for the influence of human activity on the natural vegetation, and some details of the early agricultural regime, during the Bronze Age (*c* 2000-800 cal BC). In these areas, the available evidence suggests that small-scale, short-lived clearances occurred from *c* 1500-1000 cal BC, which were then followed by more extensive and prolonged episodes of clearance, with some small-scale cereal cultivation (Wimble 1986; Wimble *et al* 2000). In tandem with this, earlier Bronze Age settlement appears to have expanded in the Cumbrian lowlands (Hodgkinson *et al* 2000), as evidenced, for instance, by the Bronze Age roundhouses and ditches recently excavated close to the River Eden (OA North 2011b).

Significantly, during this period, Bronze Age communities also appear to have begun to exploit, and expand into, the uplands, particularly those areas in south-west Cumbria lying between 230 m and 300 m OD, adjacent to the coastal plain, and this may have been stimulated by a concomitant expansion of settlement in the lowlands. It is these upland areas, for instance, that are often littered with cairnfields, burial cairns, and field systems, which would appear to reflect Bronze Age activity and expansion into more marginal areas. During this time, oak forest decreased and grassland expanded in its wake, but given the lack of evidence for cereal cultivation, this change has been interpreted as indicating pastoral activity, with grazing animals preventing the regeneration of woodland (Pennington 1970, 72). In addition to this evidence, major clearance episodes are recorded in the pollen diagrams from Burnmoor Tarn, Devoke Water, Seathwaite Tarn, and Ennerdale Water (Pennington 1964; 1981; 1991; Chiverrell 2006), which date to the period 1608-920 cal BC (3030±140 BP; NPL-124; Pennington 1970). However, in contrast, although the south-western Lake District may have witnessed extensive woodland clearance, Bronze Age clearance continued to be less widespread and more temporary in nature in the Central Lake District (Chiverrell 2006).

The loss of the trees in the Bronze Age also made the land more susceptible to leaching and erosion, and this is recorded in the Lake District by an increase in sediment accumulation at around 2461-2043 cal BC

(*ibid*). Indeed, climatic deterioration, starting perhaps in the period *c* 1200-1600 cal BC, may have exacerbated this trend (Pearsall and Pennington 1973). This deterioration resulted in a colder and wetter climate, whereby mean temperatures dropped by up to 2° C, which is likely to have reduced the growing season by as much as five weeks (Lamb 1981, 55). Such a climatic decline would have made agricultural exploitation of marginal areas unviable, and there is evidence that many Bronze Age settlements on Dartmoor were abandoned at about this time (Burgess 1985, 201).

In Cumbria, evidence for a decline in agricultural activity dates to the later Bronze Age and early Iron Age, when the pollen evidence obtained from several sites around Morecambe Bay suggests that there was a regeneration of woodland (Wimble *et al* 2000; Coombes *et al* 2009). This regeneration is also associated, around 1446-1052 cal BC (3055±65 BP; CAR-552), with a decrease in the amount of sediment accumulating in the lakes of the area, suggesting, in turn, more stable vegetation cover, and less clearance activity (Chiverrell 2006). This episode of woodland regeneration may also imply that the more marginal, upland areas were abandoned, an action that may have been driven by the suspected shift to cooler and wetter climatic conditions, during the late Bronze Age / early Iron Age (Wimble *et al* 2000; Coombes *et al* 2009).

Although the chronology of northern upland settlement is more uncertain, it is possible that this episode of climatic deterioration may explain the limited numbers of known settlements, dating to this period, found in the Lake District. Moreover, some of these settlements might be represented by the hillforts of the area, such as those at Carrock Fell, on the Caldbeck Fells (Turner 1987), and Castle Crag, beside Haweswater (LUAU 1998a; Pl 10), and it may well be that, in this instance, defence rather than agriculture prompted upland settlement. The implication is that there was an extensive retreat from the marginal uplands at this time, which approximately coincided with that of the climatic decline evidenced by palaeobotanical data.

Later Iron Age-Roman period (*c* 700 cal BC - AD 410)

The late Iron Age saw a renewed period of extensive woodland clearance in the Cumbrian uplands, the lowland valleys, in some parts of the Central Lake District, and also in the coastal fringes (Pennington 1997; Wimble *et al* 2000; Chiverrell 2006; Coombes *et al* 2009). In the uplands, this clearance was possibly more sustained than in the lowlands, and may have led to soil acidification and the development of moorland, which prevented widespread regeneration of woodland, as seen in the Cumbrian lowlands at the end of the Iron Age and during the Roman period (Pennington

Plate 10: Castle Crag hillfort, beside Haweswater

1970; Dumayne-Peaty and Barber 1998; Wimble *et al* 2000; Chiverrell 2006). At Coniston Water, a long pollen sequence records a major period of clearance activity commencing before *c* 88 cal BC-cal AD 270 (Pennington 1997; Wimble *et al* 2000). Similar clearance episodes dating between *c* 700 cal BC and *c* cal AD 270 are recorded from the coastal mires of the Lyth Valley and the Duddon Mosses (Wimble *et al* 2000), and from Deer Dyke Moss (Coombes *et al* 2009). Furthermore, the pollen diagrams from Deer Dyke Moss suggest a more intensive and prolonged period of agriculture (*ibid*). Studies of hill-slope gullying, sediment accumulation in lakes, and fluvial instability also suggest an increase in landscape instability after *c* 165 cal BC-cal AD 75 (Chiverrell 2006).

Towards the end of the Iron Age, at the transition with the Roman period, there were, however, variations in the level of anthropogenic activity witnessed in Cumbria. A period of woodland recovery occurred, although there were inexplicable local variations in its timing between the Duddon Mosses and those of the Lyth Valley and north Cumbria (Wimble *et al* 2000). Woodland regeneration took place earlier in south-west Cumbria, at the end of the Iron Age (*c* 345 cal BC-cal AD 69 (2065±60 BP; CAR-695)), whilst in the south-east of the county and within the Carlisle lowlands this regeneration occurred later, between *c* cal AD 680 and *c* cal AD 835 (Dumayne-Peaty and Barber 1998; Wimble *et al* 2000; Chiverrell 2006).

In southern Lakeland, there was a period of reoccupation of the fells from the end of the Iron Age, and throughout the Roman period. Elsewhere, however, the same resurgence of activity on the marginal uplands did not occur until later in the Roman period and was associated with the cultivation of cereals, as the climate took a turn for the better (*c* AD 300-600). Warmer and drier conditions (detectable by indications of a slow growth rate at this time in many lowland bogs surrounding the mountains) enabled such activity to take place in the uplands, and led to the complete deforestation of these areas, along with major soil changes (Pennington 1973, 232). The environmentally damaging exploitation, which was begun in the Bronze Age, was therefore compounded during the Roman period, and allowed the severe erosion of soils to accelerate, leaving the desolate, rushy, cairn-strewn moors we know today.

Early medieval period (*c* AD 410 - 1066)

The climate of North-West Europe, *c* AD 800-1100, seems to have been warmer and drier than today (Lamb 1977), and this may have had some influence on settlement and the exploitation of the Cumbrian landscape during the early medieval period. For example, palynological research at the turn of the twenty-first century points to extensive woodland clearance and agricultural exploitation during the early medieval period (*c* AD 700-1000) in the lowlands of Cumbria (Pennington 1997; Wimble *et al* 2000; Chiverrell 2006; Coombes *et al* 2009), which followed

11

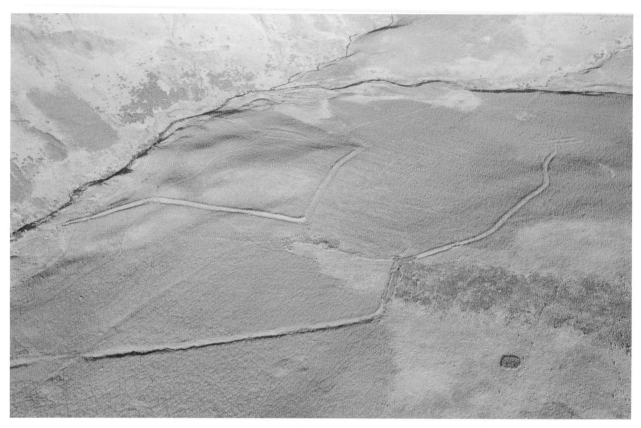

Plate 11: The characteristic open fell of Lakeland, with the former enclosures of Grassoms, on Bootle Fell

a brief period of woodland regeneration in the Roman period (*above*). In addition, the pollen record from several of the coastal raised mires suggests that during this period pastoral farming was now more important than arable cultivation.

In the Cumbrian uplands, a pollen core from Littlewater, near Haweswater, revealed an episode of agricultural activity, including evidence of cereal pollen, as well as flax (*Linum usitatissimum*) and hemp (*Cannabis/Humulus*) retting, which was dated to *c* cal AD 440-690 (LUAU 2000a). In addition, Pennington (1964) argued that there was no evidence for woodland regeneration dating to the early medieval period, though the low resolution of these early pollen diagrams may have precluded the identification of small changes in the pollen record (Chiverrell 2006). In contrast, Chiverrell suggests that lower levels of mineral sedimentation in the lakes of this area may represent a reduction of anthropogenic activity in the uplands (Pennington and Lishman 1984). This does not seem to be the case at Devoke Water and Tewit Moss, however, where, after the Roman period, there was probably only a slight and brief regeneration of the woodland, which seemingly dates to the seventh or eighth century AD (*Ch 5, p 204*). It is perhaps also of note that the many 'thwaite' names of the Central Lake District, which are of Norse origin (Armstrong *et al* 1950), also imply that there was an expansion of clearances

into areas of woodland, which had not been affected by Bronze Age or Roman activity, perhaps from the tenth century onwards.

Medieval-early post-medieval period (AD 1066 - 1700)

The episodes of early medieval clearance were followed by a marked regeneration in woodland cover around AD 1000, which has been interpreted by some authors as being a result of the 'Harrying of the North' by William the Conqueror in AD 1069 (Oldfield 1969; Wimble *et al* 2000). At Deer Dyke Moss, this woodland recovery continued until *c* AD 1100 (Chiverrell 2006), although, more generally across the region, major and more permanent decline in tree pollen took place after *c* AD 1000.

This decline in tree cover was exacerbated further in the late medieval period, when monastic estates, such as those of Furness Abbey, were established in the uplands, to undertake large-scale sheep farming (Winchester 1987, 42). This provided the final blow to what would have otherwise become a patchy and much disturbed mosaic of regenerating scrub and grassland in the uplands, and led to the largely open fell country which is so characteristic of central Lakeland today (Pl 11). Indeed, in the Central Lake District, tree pollen was at its lowest level in *c* AD 1600, with the native oak woods replaced at first by dwarf-shrub heath dominated by heather (*Calluna*) (Pennington 1997). Furthermore, in some areas, such as around Coniston Water, there were also peaks in *Ilex* (holly) pollen, which have been interpreted as evidence for 'Hollins', areas of holly trees maintained for winter feeding (*ibid*).

The late medieval period was also marked by a climatic deterioration, the so-called 'Little Ice Age', which saw colder and wetter conditions established in the period *c* AD 1200-1700 (Lamb 1977). This would undoubtedly have aided the expansion of degraded floral communities and the spread of mire and acid grassland. There is also evidence for the large-scale erosion of sediment into the lakes, and hill-slope instability, in the late medieval period, which may be another outcome of the climatic downturn associated with the 'Little Ice Age' (Chiverrell 2006).

Late post-medieval-modern period (AD 1700 - to the present)

Today, only a few patches of upland sessile oakwood survive, such as those at Keskadale in the Newlands Valley. These are perhaps all that remain of the 'wildwood', the natural, formerly dominant, 'pre-sheep' vegetation. Centuries of overgrazing have led to the impoverishment of the flora and grazing quality of the land so that many acres are now occupied by rushy slacks and matt-grass swards (Pearsall and Pennington 1973, 133-8).

The more recent history of vegetation is reflected, to some degree, in Pennington's (1997, 50) pollen diagram from Coniston Water, which provides a summary of the history of woodland and possible management regimes in this area, for the past 500 years. At this site, the lowest pollen levels for oak date to between AD 1600 and 1800, and are probably associated with high levels of subsistence farming and also increased coppicing of the woodland for charcoal production. However, charcoal production is thought to have declined from *c* 1900 and, at Coniston, this may have resulted in a reduction in hazel pollen, which was out-competed by other woodland species. These species, as recorded in the Coniston pollen diagram, included pine and beech, which are also known from documentary evidence to have been planted from the eighteenth century onwards (*ibid*).

Other studies from the uplands of the western Lake District, which also provide evidence from the last 2-300 years, are of (sub)-fossil diatoms, aquatic macrophytes (higher plants), and lake chemistry (Whitehead *et al* 1997; Bennion *et al* 2000; Tipping *et al* 2008). This research has shown that, since the mid-1800s, levels of eutrophication have risen in Bassenthwaite Lake, and more markedly in Esthwaite Water, with levels rising more sharply since the 1970s, although they have remained constant in Wastwater (Bennion *et al* 2000). This has resulted in an increase in aquatic flora, an increased frequency of algal blooms, and a reduction in the depth of light penetration. Since the 1960s, levels of nitrates in both Buttermere and Wastwater have also risen, and this seems to be correlated with the use of fertilisers to improve pasture, and increased levels of soil leaching, which reflect changes in nearby land use (Tipping *et al* 2008).

Peat Inception

Peat is an organic sediment, composed of partially decomposed vegetation, which forms *in situ* in mires and fens where conditions are anaerobic, acidic, and where drainage is impaired. The mires, where peat is found, are categorised as raised, valley, basin, or blanket mires. However, in the uplands these generally take the form of valley, basin, or blanket mires, with blanket mires being the most widespread (Pl 12). Blanket and raised mires depend entirely on rainfall for their nutrient supply, although basin and valley mires have at some point in their succession received nutrients from ground water (Moore *et al* 1991, 14-15).

Determining and understanding the relationship between the archaeological record and the date of peat inception, especially that forming blanket mires, in some parts of Central Cumbria is important. For

Plate 12: Blanket moss on the Langdale Fells

example, the expansion of blanket mire, on the gentler slopes of this area, led to a gradual covering of the landscape, burying earlier archaeological features. Fortunately, the date of peat inception in two areas of Central Cumbria, the South-West Fells and the Langdale Fells, was investigated as part of the English Heritage-funded *Upland Peats* survey (OA North 2009a). This survey concluded that, in the South-West Fells, peat inception has a relatively narrow timespan, extending from the neolithic period to the Bronze Age. No correlation with altitude was identified, but the western, and therefore the wetter, side of the ridge forming the South-West Fells demonstrated earlier peat inception, than that to the east. On the lower slopes, ranging between 150 m and 310 m OD, peat inception occurred in the neolithic period (*c* 3370-3000 cal BC), but at a higher altitude (*c* 400 m OD), it occurred approximately 1500 years later, in the Bronze Age. The cause of this latter peat initiation is unclear, but it seems to have occurred at a time of a general acceleration in peat growth in Central Cumbria (Pearsall and Pennington 1973; Pennington 1997). On the lower slopes, the peat appears to have remained constrained in, and around, a stream and in two basins, but at the greater altitude blanket bog developed, which had a depth of 3 m (OA North 2009a).

In the Langdale Fells, extensive, but localised, clearance in the neolithic period is recorded in many of the pollen records (Pennington 1965a; 1965b; 1975, 1981, 1991; 1997; Walker 1965a; Chiverrell 2006). Pennington (2003) suggests that soil changes, associated with the replacement of forest by heather after *c* 3000 cal BC, led to increased acidification of the soils, which in many places, such as in areas of impeded drainage, led to the development of peat. The *Upland Peats* survey (OA North 2009a) dated peat inception at three sites in the Langdale Fells, with two samples taken near the Langdale Pikes and a third near to the summit of High Raise. The inception dates have a relatively narrow range between the late neolithic period and the late Bronze Age; again, there is no correlation between altitude and peat inception.

The base of the peat at the two sampling sites near the Langdale Pikes has been dated to the early Bronze Age, but by about 1000 years later, peat development in the Langdale Fells had moved northwards as far as High Raise, at *c* 675 m OD (NY 27837 09020; OA North 2009a). Although the pollen evidence from the three sites suggests that peat developed in a relatively open, possibly cleared, landscape, the shift from the basal mor-humus to peat itself took place under relatively stable conditions (D Robinson *pers comm*). The base

of one of the cores was on top of a neolithic axe-production site (OA North 2004a) and the results reinforce the emerging picture that peat inception on the high fells around Great Langdale took place following a long history of human modification of the landscape. The reason why peat inception took place at the three Langdale sites is not entirely clear, but its date is broadly consistent with a number of other dates from the *Upland Peats* survey (OA North 2009a).

Background to the LDNPS

The survival of the archaeological landscape

The marginal uplands of Britain are a remarkable archaeological treasure trove, for they retain the fossilised relict landscapes of whole agricultural communities and provide an insight to our past. Within the Lake District, these surviving landscapes demonstrate human attempts to control and exploit their environment; the axe-production sites of Great Langdale (Claris and Quartermaine 1989) provided the raw material to make the tools for deforestation during the neolithic period, and the extensive Bronze Age cairnfields of the lower fells reflect the successful clearance of this forest. This remarkable survival of archaeological landscapes is primarily attributable to the marginal nature of the land. When the land was farmed, particularly during the earlier Bronze Age, the climate was significantly warmer than at present, and this enabled the establishment of farms and settlements on the uplands. With the climatic deterioration of the late Bronze Age / early Iron Age (*p 10*), the land became viable for only unintensive pastoral farming practices, and many of the upland settlements appear to have been abandoned during this period. Although there were limited reoccupations of the fells in subsequent periods (*eg* Wells 2003; Dickinson 1985; OA North 2009b), these were not sufficiently intensive to obscure, or remove, the traces of earlier activity, and these in turn have added to the palimpsest of landscape development. Significantly, exclusion from intensive land use during the subsequent millennia has also ensured the fossilisation of complete archaeological landscapes.

Other northern uplands, such as the Forest of Bowland and parts of the Yorkshire Dales, have also been subject to similar unintensive farming practices, but they often do not display the same wealth of archaeological landscapes (LUAU 1997a; 2000b). To an extent, this is attributable to extended peat development, which has obscured or inhibited such activity, whereas in the Lake District there is relatively little peat formation at lower altitudes, and consequently a greater exposure of early monuments (OA North 2009b).

Previous archaeological work

Although the Lake District Fells have been the subject of considerable antiquarian attention, until recently this was largely concentrated on the excavation of funerary monuments, which were often inadequately recorded and published. A limited number of individuals did also examine the landscape and produced some surveys that were of a high quality for the period, particularly that of the large Barnscar settlement (Dymond 1893; Pl 13); however, even this survey only recorded the central section and omitted much of the settlement and cairnfield remains. Swainson-Cowper (1893) undertook some localised survey work around the Furness peninsula, which included elements of the Heathwaite Fell complex. Some of the most extensive landscape-recording work was undertaken by Joseph Spence (1934; 1935a; 1935b; 1937; 1938; 1939) on various sites around the Lake District (Askham Fell, Whin Garth, Stockdale Moor, and Town Bank). However, these surveys again concentrated on specific elements within the overall landscape. In 1936, the Royal Commission on the Historical Monuments of England published an inventory of historical monuments within the old county of Westmorland (RCHM(E) 1936); this included the localised mapping of significant archaeological monuments, some of which were on Askham Fell.

In the post-war period, some significant archaeological research was undertaken in relation to archaeological landscapes. For instance, Jim Cherry (1961) undertook a number of identification surveys around the South-West Fells, highlighting the archaeological potential of the area. In addition to this, Donald Walker (1965b) excavated and undertook palaeobotanical analysis of cairns from the Barnscar area, and his results provided a dramatic insight into the origin of these clearance mounds. Then, in the early 1980s, Colin Richardson (1982) undertook excavations of a cairnfield at Birrel Sike (NY 072 074), an area of moorland between Stockdale Moor and Town Bank above the west Cumbrian coastal plain. The project provided some useful radiocarbon dates for Cumbrian cairnfields, which demonstrated Bronze Age activity at the site.

Winifred Pennington's contribution to the palaeobotany of the Lake District has been enormous. She undertook a major programme of pollen analysis from coastal and upland sites throughout the National Park (*inter alia*; Pennington 1964; 1965b; 1970; 1973; 1975), which put the Lake District at the forefront of palaeobotanical research. Indeed, the vegetational history of the area is still one of the most comprehensively recorded in the country, although it has only recently been linked to scientific dating.

Plate 13: Dymond's 1893 survey of Barnscar

The result of all this sporadic survey work was an archaeological record which, in 1982 (at the start of the LDNPS), was at best patchy. Moreover, for most of the settlement areas, the only entry recorded within the then Cumbria Sites and Monuments Record (SMR; now the Historic Environment Record (HER)) was 'Cairns', a term which had been derived from Ordnance Survey (OS) record cards, and significant proportions of these sites had also never been recorded.

The Origins of the LDNPS Programme

The Cumbria and Lancashire Archaeological Unit (CLAU), which was renamed the Lancaster University Archaeological Unit (LUAU) in 1989, and then became Oxford Archaeology North (OA North) in 2001, was established by the Directorate of Ancient Monuments and Historic Buildings at the Department of the Environment (DoE, the predecessor of English Heritage) within the Department of Classics and Archaeology at Lancaster University in April 1979. The purpose of the unit was to advance the understanding of the archaeology of north-west England by undertaking excavations and surveys directed at sites and monuments threatened with destruction. In the first three years of the unit's existence, several such projects were undertaken, all of which had been identified as priorities in 1979. By 1982, however, it was clear that a longer-term strategic review of priorities in the North West was needed. With this in mind, the Directorate of Ancient Monuments and Historic Buildings commissioned the unit to undertake 'an assessment of the Sites and Monuments Records for Cumbria and Lancashire', the purpose of which was to determine the quality of the existing database for the two counties, and to make recommendations for future work (Leech 1982).

In looking at the Bronze Age sites of the two counties, the SMR assessment identified serious deficiencies in the existing database. For areas of upland settlement of the Bronze Age, only 6% of the groups of small cairns were scheduled as Ancient Monuments. From a sample survey of parts of Birkby and Birker Fells in the Lake District, undertaken during Easter 1982 (Leech 1983), it was established that approximately 30% of the small cairns seemed to be unrecorded, even in the best-studied upland areas. The sample survey also provided data for the logistics of surveying upland areas for SMR enhancement.

The wider analysis of the SMR assessment indicated that there were considerable areas within the Lake District National Park in which survey would add much data to the existing SMR; these approximately corresponded to the fells, between the 170 m and 330 m contours. It was observed that the later prehistoric landscapes of the peripheral fells of the Lake District, and of the Pennine Edge, were as well-preserved and as extensive as those of south-west England, although this was not generally recognised within the archaeological community. These observations were very much in accord with those of the Prehistoric Society which, in its own assessment of national priorities, had also highlighted the need for 'surveys, for expansion of Sites and Monuments Records particularly in the north of England [and Scotland]' (Prehistoric Society 1981).

It was therefore recommended that the unit's strategic programme should include a five-year survey project directed at the later prehistoric landscapes of the Lake District National Park (Fig 1). A project proposal for the Lake District National Park Survey programme was submitted by the unit to the Directorate of Ancient Monuments and Historic Buildings in 1982 for funding, and was approved, enabling a programme of survey to commence from Easter 1983. The project design, at that stage, envisaged that five areas would be selected for survey from different parts of the National Park, encompassing a total of 80 km². The areas selected were ones within which it could be predicted that unmapped monuments existed, and where there was a potential for extracting data for analysis of site distribution, land use, territories, and so on. Initially, these were centred on the South-

Plate 14: Surveying in the Langdale Fells

16

West Fells, where there were extensive landscapes identified, but the programme was later expanded to encompass most parts of the Lake District (see *Appendix 1* for the methodology used).

The survey project was established in collaboration with the Lake District National Park Authority,

which part-funded the programme. In 1984, the programme was expanded to enable the recording of the neolithic axe-production sites around Langdale and Scafell Pike (Pl 14), which are on land leased to, and managed by, the National Trust. This element of the survey programme was undertaken jointly by the unit and the National

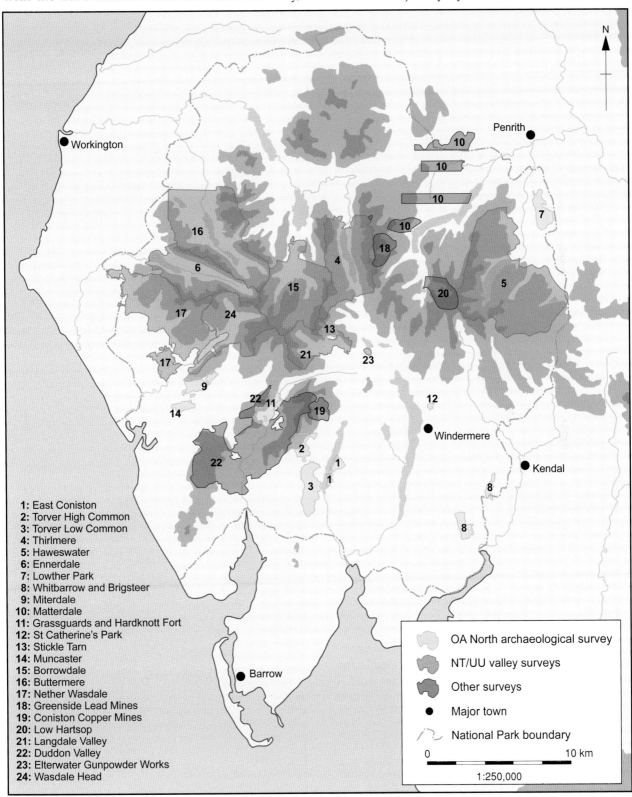

1: East Coniston
2: Torver High Common
3: Torver Low Common
4: Thirlmere
5: Haweswater
6: Ennerdale
7: Lowther Park
8: Whitbarrow and Brigsteer
9: Miterdale
10: Matterdale
11: Grassguards and Hardknott Fort
12: St Catherine's Park
13: Stickle Tarn
14: Muncaster
15: Borrowdale
16: Buttermere
17: Nether Wasdale
18: Greenside Lead Mines
19: Coniston Copper Mines
20: Low Hartsop
21: Langdale Valley
22: Duddon Valley
23: Elterwater Gunpowder Works
24: Wasdale Head

OA North archaeological survey

NT/UU valley surveys

Other surveys

Major town

National Park boundary

0   10 km

1:250,000

Figure 3: Areas of survey subsequent to the LDNPS programme

17

Trust, and was funded by English Heritage and the National Trust. The surveys of the axe-production sites were distinct in aim and character from the main component of the LDNPS programme, and were consequently published independently (Claris and Quartermaine 1989).

Subsequent Archaeological Work in the Lake District

Following the completion of the LDNPS fieldwork in 1989, archaeological research in the Lake District has continued both in the form of landscape surveys and more intrusive investigations. While it is beyond the scope of this volume to present in detail the results of this research, reference will be made to those studies which have particular relevance to the LDNPS.

Surveys
A considerable amount of landscape survey has been undertaken subsequent to the LDNPS programme, covering a substantial proportion of the Lake District (Fig 3). These surveys encompass much larger areas than that covered by the LDNPS programme (Fig 1), and this in part reflects the introduction of Global Positioning System (GPS) technology, which has allowed the recording of archaeological sites without the need for established survey control points. This freedom has enabled very rapid identification survey, which can cover large areas in a short amount of time, although the level of recording for each site, or monument, has been at a very basic level (Pl 15). For example, sites tend merely to be shown as a dot on a map, or whole cairnfields may be shown as a line defining their extent. However, even though these rapid identification surveys do not provide enough detail to understand fully the development of individual relict landscapes, they have been an extremely effective management tool used in the long-term conservation of the archaeological resource. More detailed survey programmes, such as those undertaken as part of the LDNPS, remain limited, with only a few other surveys, such as those of the High and Low Torver Commons (LUAU 1994a; 1995), which allow a detailed analysis of landscape form and development.

The major surveys undertaken following the LDNPS (Table 1) include the rapid identification surveys on behalf of the National Trust, which examined the archaeological resource throughout each of the major radial valleys of the Lake District, such as Borrowdale, Buttermere, Ennerdale, Wasdale, and Langdale (Fig 3). In addition, these surveys incorporated detailed documentary studies, boundary surveys, and a level of holistic landscape analysis. Whilst this approach has allowed a remarkable insight into the formation of these valleys, its rapid form means that they do not provide a detailed assessment of the development of individual landscapes. Other, more recent surveys, include the *Upland Peats* project, which examined the archaeological potential preserved within and beneath the peat in, amongst other areas, the South-West Fells and the Langdales, to determine the threats to the archaeology and, ultimately, to propose guidelines and recommendations for the management of the archaeological and peatland resource (OA North 2009a).

Intrusive investigations
As well as the extensive surveys within the Lake District, there have been a few projects that have entailed intrusive investigations. Although these were generally small-scale in scope, they have made an enormous contribution towards an understanding of the upland landscape.

Langdale axe-production sites
The Langdale axe-production sites represent some of the most important archaeological landscapes in the Lake District, if not nationally. During the LDNPS programme, several excavation programmes were

Plate 15: A GPS survey in progress

18

Survey Name	Date of Survey	Survey Extent (Sqkm)	Survey Level	Source
Coniston Copper Mines	1985, 1997, 2007	4.5	2	Middleton 1985; Lofthouse 1997; OA North 2007a
Low Hartsop	1986	9.3	2	RCHME (now English Heritage) Archives
Langdale Valley	1990s	22	1	Lund and Southwell 2002
Wasdale Head	1990s	30	1	National Trust 2000
Greenside Lead Mines	1992	6.5	2	RCHME (now English Heritage) Archives
Torver High Common	1994	4.5	2	LUAU 1994a
Torver Low and Blawith Commons	1995	9.8	2	LUAU 1995
Thirlmere	1996, 1998	48	1/2	LUAU 1997b; 1998b
Haweswater	1995-7	97	1/2	LUAU 1997c; 1998a
Ennerdale	1995-7, 2003	38	1/2	LUAU 1998c; OA North 2003a
Lowther Park	1996, 1997, 2007	5.5	1/2	LUAU 1997d; 1997e; OA North 2007b
Whitbarrow and Brigsteer	1999	6	1	LUAU 1999
Miterdale	2000	4.3	1	LUAU 2000c
Green How Causewayed Camp	2000	2	2	Horne and Oswald 2000
Matterdale	2000-3	98	1	Hoaen and Loney 2003
Elterwater gunpowder works	2001	1	2	Jecock et al 2003
Grassguards and Hardknott Forest	2002	5.2	1	OA North 2002
St Catherine's	2004	1	1	OA North 2005a
Stickle Tarn	2005	1.5	1	OA North 2005b
Muncaster	2005-6	2	1	Eskdale and District Local History Society 2008
Upland Peats	2003-6	13	2	OA North 2009a
Borrowdale	2006	52	1	OA North 2007c
Duddon Valley	2006	73	1	Duddon Valley Local History Group and Lake District National Park Authority 2009
Buttermere	2008	53	1	OA North 2009b
Nether Wasdale	2009	65	1	OA North 2009c
East Coniston	2010	2.3	1	OA North 2010a

Level 1: rapid identification surveys only
Level 2: detailed survey of the landscape
In Level 1/2, the survey was undertaken at Level 1, with smaller elements of the landscape subject to more detailed, Level 2, survey. Small or unsystematic surveys have not been included

Table 1: Major surveys undertaken in the Lake District following the LDNPS

initiated in order to investigate these important prehistoric landscapes. One of these, in 1987, led by Reading University, entailed extensive test pitting across the peat-covered area of Langdale Combe (Bradley and Edmonds 1993). This area is at the back (northern side) of the craggy Langdale Pikes, and the test pitting was intended to establish the northernmost extent of the axe workings.

The programme also involved excavation of selected sites, which included quarry workings and dispersed axe-working sites. This, in turn, demonstrated a broad diversity of production techniques and provided radiocarbon dates, which spanned the period 3772-3530 cal BC (4870±50 BP; BM 2625) to 3517-3103 cal BC (4590±50 BP; BM 2627; *ibid*).

Other excavations in the Langdale area have focused on the shoulders of Harrison Pike and Thorn Crag, and were in advance of footpath repair work; significantly, these provided dates for pre-axe-working horizons (Hedges *et al* 1994, 360–1). A further programme of excavation on a footpath at Harrison Combe (Site 123; Pl 16) demonstrated multiple episodes of working and also produced a mesolithic radiocarbon date for a horizon found immediately beneath the axe-working debitage (OA North 2004a).

Stephenson Ground

Between 1986 and 1998, a programme of survey and excavation was undertaken at Stephenson Ground, in the Lickle Valley (Pl 17), in the southern Lake District (Duddon Valley Local History Group and Lake District National Park Authority 2009; Thorpe and Ball 1994). It revealed a palimpsest of activity dating from the Bronze Age to the medieval period. Notable features included a Bronze Age roundhouse, a medieval longhouse, dated to the twelfth to fourteenth centuries, and also later medieval shielings.

Baldhowend and Glencoyne Park

In conjunction with a wider survey examining the Matterdale and Hutton parishes of the Lake District, a programme of excavation was undertaken at an unenclosed settlement, at Baldhowend, and at a

simple enclosed settlement (GP6), in Glencoyne Park, beside Ullswater (Loney and Hoaen 2000; Hoaen and Loney 2004). At Baldhowend, three roundhouses were excavated, one of which (House A) was subsequently dated to 375 cal BC-cal AD 65 (2120±80 BP; Beta-123084) and cal AD 179-408 (1745±40 BP; GU-9336). Similarly, at the Glencoyne Park enclosed settlement, a roundhouse was excavated, which was occupied from the pre-Roman through to the post-Roman period, whilst a cut identified beneath the enclosing wall of the settlement was dated to 1105-835 cal BC (2810±50 BP; Beta-171115).

Duddon Valley

As part of a wider programme of archaeological study in the Duddon Valley, three ring cairns at Lead Pike, Seathwaite Tarn (Pl 18), were excavated in 2003 and 2007 (Duddon Valley Local History Group and Lake District National Park Authority 2009). The initial identification of the monuments had been made by Peter Rodgers (former Area Manager for the Lake District National Park Authority), who had been researching this monument type in the Lake District for a number of years. The largest of the cairns (Cairn 1) was 9.1 m across, the stone bank of the ring being up to 2.8 m wide. In the event, no burials were identified, within those parts of the cairns that were subject to excavation, and only two sherds of prehistoric

Plate 16: Excavation in progress at Site 123, a Langdale axe-production site

Plate 17: Excavation in progress at Stephenson Ground

pottery were recovered. Radiocarbon dates indicated a broad date range of 1540-1250 cal BC for the construction of the cairns (1540-1400 cal BC (3180±30 BP; POZ-24044); and 1430-1250 cal BC (3070±35 BP; POZ-24036); *op cit*, 106).

Burnt Mounds

A study (Hodgson 2007) has compiled evidence for burnt mounds within the Lake District National Park, part of which included new survey work. This study identified 17 of these monuments within the

Plate 18: The Seathwaite Tarn ring cairns (centre) within the rocky landscape

Park, or its immediate environs, although at least seven new burnt mounds have subsequently been discovered, notably in the Nether Wasdale area of the western Lake District (OA North 2009c). Several of the burnt mounds have been excavated, including one on an eroding cliff face at Drigg (Pl 19), which has produced late neolithic dates, ranging from 2460-2230 cal BC (3900±50 BP; GU-5884) to 2480-2280 cal BC (3960±50 BP; GU-5885; OA North 2010b). A further mound has also been excavated at Sparrowmire Farm, just outside the Park, near Kendal, which was found to contain a timber trough. Material associated with this burnt mound was radiocarbon dated to 1678-1410 cal BC (3240±50 BP; AA-34789/GU-8449) and 1408-1126 cal BC (3020±50 BP; AA-34791/GU-8447; Heawood and Huckerby 2002).

Aims of the LDNPS

Management aims

The principal reason for the establishment of the LDNPS was to address the enormous imbalance between the acknowledged wealth of archaeological survival and the limited recognition of it within the Cumbria SMR. The survey was intended to provide data to enhance both this record, and also the National Monuments Record, and thereby enable the better management of the upland archaeological resource.

It was also recognised that enhancement of the existing records was required in order to allow the appropriate scheduling of these nationally important landscapes, which were inadequately protected by law. The level of survey detail employed was also, in part, intended to provide an adequate basis for this process, and as a consequence the scheduling of most of the identified landscapes has now been reappraised by the English Heritage Monuments Protection Programme (Darvill and Fulton 1998). The surveys were also intended to facilitate the English Heritage Field Monuments Warden Scheme, through the provision of maps for monuments already scheduled, and to provide data for the production, by the Lake District National Park Authority, of an archaeological management plan, which would evaluate strategies for the conservation of these important archaeological landscapes.

The LDNPS programme also provided a mitigation record of the archaeological landscapes in the event that any damage or decay might occur to the monuments contained within them. In particular, the survey was extended to encompass the Langdale/Scafell Pike neolithic axe-production areas, as it was recognised that there was an immediate threat to these important sites. In this instance, there was a need to provide a detailed record as mitigation, but also to inform the production of a management plan by the National Trust, which would enable the protection, monitoring, and stabilisation of the fragile sites associated with axe production (LUAU 1994b). The resultant survey was also designed to provide the basis for the statutory protection of the archaeological resource, as an earlier application for scheduling had been rejected because of the insufficient precision of the mapping. Unfortunately, a subsequent application was also rejected because of the legal difficulties of scheduling large areas of Langdale. A further proposal for scheduling was developed in 2005 in anticipation

Plate 19: The burnt mound at Drigg, visible within an eroding section of cliff face

of the enactment of the Heritage Protection Bill. The bill, however, has yet to be put before Parliament, so after nearly 30 years, these internationally important monuments are still without statutory protection (K Robinson *pers comm*).

Academic aims

The secondary aim of the survey was to address the enormous academic potential of the upland landscapes. Although upland settlements and cairnfields are documented from other upland regions, the extent to which the Cumbrian examples have survived, and are not obscured by peat, provided a remarkable opportunity to study the development of agricultural landscapes and settlement. It was therefore recognised at an early stage that there was a need to record the monuments in sufficient detail to be able to analyse the form and development of the upland landscapes. As such, this markedly contrasts with the many identification surveys for management purposes that have followed the LDNPS programme, both in the Lake District and elsewhere in the North West, which were required only to record the extent of site groups and not the individual monuments (*p 18*).

At the same time, it was realised that there was a need to record and interpret the overall landscapes rather than allow an over-emphasis on individual monuments or monument types. As a consequence, the programme was designed to provide a record of the landscapes at a consistent scale of 1:1000. This enabled an assessment of the wider landscape and also allowed for the recording of an individual monument, and in

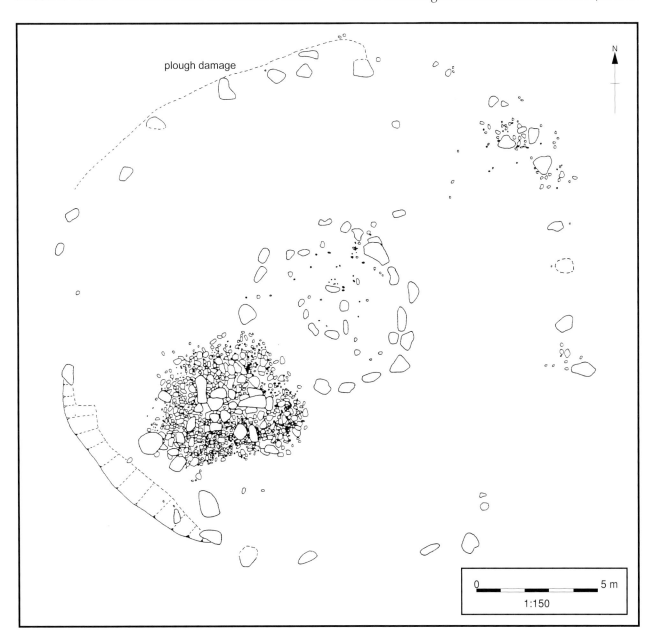

Figure 4: Plan of Shapbeck stone circle (after Turner 1986)

23

some cases their internal detail. Only two monuments (The Cockpit (*AF 86*; *Ch 7, p 302*) and Shap Beck stone circle (Turner 1986)) were surveyed and reproduced at a greater scale (Fig 4), reflecting their archaeological importance and their complexity of internal detail. As part of this more holistic approach, the survey also aimed to examine the identified landscapes within a wider environmental context. As such, the archaeological landscapes were assessed in conjunction with the large body of palaeoenvironmental data that was available for the Lake District, as a result of the extensive work of Pennington (1970), Walker (1965a), and Wimble (1986). Finally, it was recognised that relatively little detailed work had been undertaken within the upland landscapes of the North West, and that there was a pressing need to set the archaeological landscapes from this area within the broader context of Northern England.

During the eight years of fieldwork (1982-9), the LDNPS programme recorded over 10,300 discrete monuments from *c* 78 km² of unimproved upland (Fig 1). The work was undertaken within 18 individual

Survey	Prefix Code	Area of Survey km²	No of Site Groups	No of Monuments
Western Fells (*Ch 3*)				
Town Bank	TB	3.2	15	893
Stockdale Moor	SM	4.6	9	838
Whin Garth	WG	4.8	10	695
Burnmoor	BM	5.5	16	498
South-West Fells (West) (*Ch 4*)				
Bootle Fell	BF	3.5	11	918
Corney Fell	CF	1.2	5	324
Charlesground Gill	CG	2.6	9	281
Whitrow Beck	WB	0.9	5	280
Stainton Fell	SF	2.6	9	514
Barnscar	BS	1.8	6	875
South-West Fells (East) (*Ch 5*)				
Birkby / Birker Fell	BB	6.7	18	1038
Ulpha Fell	UF	3.5	13	299
Crosbythwaite	CT	1.2	2	370
Hesk Fell	HE	0.3	1	69
Thwaites Fell	TF	1.4	7	327
Northern Fells				
Caldbeck Fell [+]	CA	4.1	14	190
Southern and Central Fells (*Ch 6*)				
Scafell Pike [*]	SP	4.4	17	371
Langdale Pikes [*]	LP	3.7	18	244
Heathwaite Fell	HF	3.7	13	530
Mickleden Beck	MB	1.0	6	144
Eastern Fells (*Ch 7*)				
Shap and Askham [†]	SA	12.2	65	388
Askham Fell	AF	5.5	12	221
Total		**78.4**	**281**	**10,307**

+   Turner 1987
*   Claris and Quartermaine 1989
†   Turner 1991

Table 2: Monument number for, and size of, each survey area

surveys, spread over five areas of the Lake District. These included the Western Fells, comprising the survey areas of Town Bank, Stockdale Moor, Whin Garth, and Burnmoor (*Ch 3*); the South-West Fells, comprising the survey areas of Bootle Fell, Corney Fell, Charlesground Gill, Whitrow Beck, Stainton Fell, Barnscar, Birker and Birkby Fells, Ulpha Fell, Crosbythwaite, Hesk Fell, and Thwaites Fell (*Chs 4* and *5*); the Southern and Central Fells, comprising the survey areas of Heathwaite Fell and Mickleden (*Ch 6*); and the Eastern Fells, comprising Askham Fell (*Ch 7*). The survey areas often bordered each other, particularly on the Western and South-West Fells, where there are intensive settlement remains across all the marginal slopes. In some instances, their common boundaries are therefore administrative rather than indications of original prehistoric land divisions; hence there can be a single cairnfield on both sides of a survey area boundary (for instance, the Bootle Fell/Corney Fell boundary; *Ch 4, p 119*).

The topographical extent and quantity of archaeological monuments for each survey area varied (Table 2). Each survey area has a prefix code (*eg* TB for Town Bank) to enable a clear-cut designation of individual monuments and groups to the relevant survey area. They have been grouped in the order they appear in the text.

Reports for five of the surveys have been published separately. These include Birkby/Birker Fell (Leech 1983); Stockdale Moor and Town Bank (Quartermaine 1989); Langdale and Scafell Pikes (Claris and Quartermaine 1989); Shap and Askham (Turner 1991); and the Caldbeck Fells (Turner 1987). The earlier publications for the Birkby/Birker Fell and the Stockdale Moor/Town Bank surveys were only interim publications and these are reproduced in full within this volume.

Organisation of the Volume

The compilation of the text has been split between the principal authors, Jamie Quartermaine and Roger Leech. *Chapter 1* was written by Jamie Quartermaine and Colin Wells, with contributions by Roger Leech and Bob Middleton. *Chapter 2* was written by Jamie Quartermaine, summarising the characteristics of the principal types of monuments encountered within the survey, which are referred to in the subsequent descriptive chapters. The structure of the descriptive section of the volume (*Chs 3-7*) reflects the principal areas of the survey and describes and discusses the principal, clearly definable, site groups. *Chapter 3*, written by Jamie Quartermaine and Roger Leech, examines the archaeology of the Western Fells; *Chapter 4*, written by Jamie Quartermaine and Roger

Leech, examines the western part of the South-West Fells; and *Chapter 5*, also written by Jamie Quartermaine and Roger Leech, examines the eastern part of the South-West Fells. The palaeoenvironmental section of the Birkby/Birker Fells was compiled by Guy Wimble and Elizabeth Huckerby, and the excavation report on the Devoke Water cairn was prepared by Paul Gajos, from an archive compiled by Adrian Olivier. *Chapter 6* examines the Southern and Central Fells and was written by Jamie Quartermaine, with contributions by Melanie Hall and Richard Bradley on the palaeobotanical survey in Mickleden Beck; *Chapter 7* examines the Eastern Fells and was written by Jamie Quartermaine; *Chapter 8*, written by Jamie Quartermaine, is a discussion examining the development of the agricultural exploitation and settlement of the marginal landscapes of the Lake District; whilst *Chapter 9* was written by John Hodgson and Jamie Quartermaine, and examines the threats to, and future of, the archaeological landscapes discussed in this volume. *Appendix 1* presents the methodology for the survey, whilst *Appendix 2* lists the more distinctive monuments (unenclosed roundhouses, ring cairns, and long cairns) recorded during the course of the survey. Finally, *Appendix 3* lists the radiocarbon dates referred to in the text.

Site plans

The survey plans with the main text are selective and show only the more significant areas of archaeological remains. They are at a reduced scale and some internal detail of the features has been lost as a result. However, all of the archaeological remains identified during the survey are depicted on a set of archive plans (drawn at 1:1000). The main groups and sub-groups are identified on all location and site plans within the volume, and also in the archive plans. All individual monument numbers are shown on the archive plans, but only the more significant monuments are numbered on plans within the text. In the course of the surveys, all possible archaeological monuments were recorded and were incorporated within the primary archive. Very small numbers of these were indistinguishable from natural brash deposits and were subsequently omitted from the final archive plans; however, these have been ascribed survey numbers and remain in the site catalogue, although labelled as natural features.

All the archive plans have been digitised; the resultant data have been incorporated into the GIS of the Lake District National Park Authority's Historic Environment Record (HER), where they are available on application. This digitised dataset has been used to create selective distribution maps within this volume, a complete set of archive drawings being reproduced on an accompanying CD.

Site Descriptions

Site grouping format

Although within each survey area there were upward of 1000 individual monuments, most of these fall within clearly defined spatial clusters or groups, referred to in the description and on the site maps as main site groups. These main site groups are denoted through the use of upper case Latin numerals (for instance, SF IX refers to Stainton Fell monument group 9). In many cases, these main groups have been further divided into sub-groups (for instance, SF IXA refers to sub-group A within Stainton Fell monument group 9) for ease of description, on the basis of observed similarity of form or an identifiable clustering of monuments. These groups have been denoted by a light yellow toned line around the extent of each group. In addition, in some survey areas, individual fields and plots are also identified through the use of lower case italicised Latin numerals (for instance, SF IX*iii* refers to plot 3 in Stainton Fell monument group 9), whilst individual monuments within the monument groups are denoted by italicised Arabic numerals (for instance, *HF 123* refers to Heathwaite Fell monument 123). A faded red tone has been used to highlight significant alignments in each group, a blue tone for plots, and a green tone to highlight significant groups of features within the larger monument groups.

Monument descriptions

In the descriptive sections of the volume (*Chs 3-7*), the individual monuments within these groups are not specifically described unless they are of particular archaeological significance, and any isolated monuments outside the groups are not discussed at all, unless of particular significance. A full description of each monument is held within the Historic Environment Records held by Cumbria County Council (Cumbria Historic Environment Record (CHER), Planning Department, Cumbria City Council, County Offices, Kendal, Cumbria, LA9 4RQ) and the Lake District National Park Authority (Lake District Historic Environment Record (LDHER), Lake District National Park Authority, Murley Moss, Oxenholme Road, Kendal, Cumbria, LA9 7RL). The LDHER is the official database of archaeological and historical sites in the Lake District, and also the source of information for advice and decisions on planning and land management in the National Park (http://www.lakedistrict.gov.uk/index/learning/archaeology/archaeologydiscoveryzone/archaeologyldher.htm). Descriptions of the monuments can also be found within copies of the project archive held by the Cumbria County Record Office (Cumbria County Council, County Offices, Kendal, Cumbria, LA9 4RQ); the National Monuments Record (National Monuments Record Centre, Kemble Drive, Swindon, SN2 2GZ); and Oxford Archaeology North.

2

MONUMENT TYPES

Of the 10,300 individual archaeological monuments recorded by the Lake District National Park Survey (LDNPS), the great majority (about 98%) were characteristic of a limited range of only 17 monument types, and the remaining 2% were either rarer types of monument or could not be reliably classified. The fact that such a limited range of monuments was identified stems from the surveys being targeted on areas of cairnfield, and only a limited range of monument types are associated with these landscapes. In order to provide a better understanding, and broader context, for the descriptive text that follows (*Chs 3-7*), a summary of these 17 monuments has been compiled. This summary highlights their form, their distinctive characteristics, their date range, and sets them within a national context. However, the categorisation of observed monuments into recognised types can, on occasion, be a matter of some difficulty as, for example, a simple ring feature could potentially be a clearance cairn, a ring cairn, or even a roundhouse. To this end, the monument-type descriptions outline the principal criteria used for interpreting the function and classification of an observed feature.

The monument types are common features within many upland landscapes in the UK and have been discussed on many occasions within the archaeological literature. The present descriptions, however, specifically relate to those monuments identified within the LDNPS, and are not necessarily indicative of generic types found in other regions. At the same time, an attempt has been made to show how these Lake District monuments vary from those found in other parts of the UK. The monument types discussed are also categorised according to their broad function. Firstly, there are agricultural monuments, such as field boundaries and cairns; secondly, domestic structures are described, such as houses and enclosed settlements; and finally, there are funerary/ritual monuments.

Agricultural Monuments

Clearance cairns

The ubiquitous small cairn is a common component of the archaeological landscapes in most upland areas

Plate 20: A localised cairnfield at Charlesground Gill

of the UK (see, *inter alia*, Yates 1984a, 218-19; 1983, 341-2; Fowler 1981, 16-20; Ward 1977; Fleming 1971, 4-5; Jobey 1968, 46-50). It is normally found in well-defined groups (called cairnfields; Pl 20), although it can also be found in relative isolation. Cairns of this type may have been formed through the clearance of unwanted stone from adjacent agricultural land, and the practice of dumping unwanted stone, raised by the plough, into piles has happened within living memory in the Western Highlands (Graham 1956, 23); it is also a process that still occurs in some of the more remote parts of Turkey (as seen by the author in 1989). However, the earliest cairn construction was not necessarily linked to arable farming, and there is evidence from the excavated cairns at Barnscar (Walker 1965b) that some cairnfields may have been a result of deforestation and associated intensive land reclamation. For example, beneath the Barnscar cairns there was evidence of burning, the partial stripping of the original ground surface, and the excavation of pits, possibly to remove tree stumps (*ibid*). Following this, the final construction of the cairn consumed the unwanted stone produced by these processes.

The individual small cairns are very varied in form, although the majority are between 3 m and 4 m in diameter, with irregular, often ill-defined, edges. There are also examples that are large and prominent, with very well-defined edges, which can be confused with funerary round cairns (*pp 44-5*), but they are typically not as large and do not have such regular edges as their sepulchral counterparts. The larger clearance cairns are also invariably found in groups and are association with a field, or an area of improved ground. Although small cairns come in a broad variety of shapes, reflecting their haphazard formation, they are most commonly round or slightly oval. Elongated cairns are also significant, because they reflect the need to deposit unwanted stone in as narrow an area as possible, either at the edge of agricultural plots, or along lines of ridge and furrow (*eg WG 261; Ch 3, pp 90-1*; and *HF IXC; Ch 6, p 276*). Although cairnfields are usually located in areas of better-quality land, and the edge of the cairnfield will often coincide with an interface between land of different qualities, the individual cairns are often placed on localised islands of unusable ground. These areas include small outcrops, or earthfast boulders, which were selected in order to maximise the better land, between the cairns, that was presumably used for agriculture.

Simple cairnfields are typically small and isolated within the wider landscape, and are not associated with identified domestic structures or settlements. In contrast, the more complex cairnfields exhibit some form of rationalisation into fields and, at the same time, are often associated with domestic structures, typically house platforms or stone-founded roundhouses (*pp 32-3*). In these instances, the cairnfield appears to be an integral part of permanent settlement. The apparent absence of domestic structures associated with the simple cairnfields may therefore indicate that these were isolated farming areas, which were remote from the principal settlements. Alternatively, the simple cairnfields may have been associated with timber structures, that do not survive as surface monuments, which would not be visible unless they were set on a terraced platform (*pp 33-4*). It is also likely that the earliest occupation of an upland area was undertaken seasonally, during the summer months, mirroring the later transhumant practice of shielings in the medieval period (Winchester 1987). Such impermanent occupation may only have been associated with temporary structures, such as tents, which may have left an extremely ephemeral record.

Date
The practice of building clearance cairns, in association with agriculture, is not unique to any particular period of time. Given this, an isolated cairn is inherently undatable. However, when cairns are set within cairnfields these are, at times, associated with typologically datable monuments. For example, quite often the cairns are associated with funerary round cairns, or roundhouses and, in these instances, a Bronze Age or early Iron Age date can be inferred. Limited numbers of small cairns have also been excavated and dated within the Lake District. Notably, these include

a small cairn excavated at Birrel Sike, between Town Bank and Stockdale Moor (Richardson 1982), which produced a date of 2299-1740 cal BC (3640±100 BP; BIRM-1063), thus reinforcing the general Bronze Age dating for this class of monument. Small cairns are also found in medieval contexts, notably at Heathwaite Fell, where there is a group of very large cairns, within the area of a medieval settlement (HF IX; *Ch 5, p 272*), which is closely associated with ridge and furrow. While these cairns may have their origins prior to the medieval settlement, they were undoubtedly built up during the medieval period. This is also confirmed by a pollen core taken from beneath a small cairn, excavated at Devoke Water by Adrian Olivier and Guy Wimble, which had a humin fraction dated to cal AD 663-963 (1230±70 BP; CAR-911), indicating that parts, or all, of the cairn were constructed in the early medieval period (*Ch 4, p 201*). Small cairns thus do not typologically belong to any particular period, but in many instances they can, by association, be ascribed to broad date ranges. In particular, many of the cairnfield groups in the Lake District are associated with Bronze Age funerary monuments, and are likely to date broadly to the second millennium BC.

Boundary markers
Three basic forms of boundary marker were observed during the survey: walls, stone banks, and lynchets. These to an extent reflect differing intensities and types of activity within the areas defined, and it is not unusual to find boundaries made up of more than one type of marker. The significance of this type of site is that they define, either deliberately or even inadvertently, the extent of agricultural plots or fields. The development of boundary markers, in an otherwise random cairnfield, denotes an attempt to rationalise the agricultural landscape. The form and character of these markers provide an indication as to the form of the agriculture within the field/plot, and the length and height of the marker provide some indication of the intensity with which this agriculture was practised.

Walls
Decayed walls are most common in settlement areas where there is evidence of Romano-British or medieval activity, such as at Heathwaite Fell and Barnscar (*Ch 6, p 264; Ch 4, p 178*), though they are also occasionally found associated with some prehistoric-type cairnfields. Depending on the state of decay, they often display evidence of dry-stone structure, either as a kerb or as intact facing stone. The more decayed walls survive as prominent turf-covered banks, with substantial quantities of protruding stone, usually a mixture of medium to large facing stones, with smaller stones forming the wall core. Because of the general abundance of stone on the fells, there was little subsequent need to rob these earlier walls, and so,

Plate 21: A decayed dry-stone wall on Heathwaite Fell

when decayed, they will often comprise continuous banks of stone, substantial in volume, with a regular width/height (Pl 21). This is in marked contrast to the typical form of stone banks (*see below*).

Some of the walls completely enclose fields, as, for example, the walls within the Whin Garth field system (*Ch 3, p 81*). However, there are many, particularly those associated with cairnfields, which do not enclose land and which were probably not, by themselves, originally used to control the movement of stock. An example of this is the field system around the Heathwaite farmstead (HF IX; *Ch 6, p 272*), which has boundaries that are partly marked by walls and partly by stone banks. These boundaries include sections of standing walls, which are very wide (*c* 2.5 m thick), contain large amounts of stone, and which were evidently used to absorb stone cleared from the adjacent fields. As those sections of these boundaries built as stone banks (*see below*) could not have controlled stock, there was either an additional fence, which no longer survives, or these boundaries were not intended for such purposes. If they were not intended to control stock, then it is to be presumed that their primary purpose was to absorb cleared stone.

Stone banks/cairn alignments

Within cairnfields, the most common type of boundary markers recorded by the survey are stone banks (Fig 5). These are low, discontinuous turf-covered banks with stone sporadically protruding from the turf (Fig 6). They are irregular in width and height, often with minimal quantities of stone, and in some instances are defined only by alignments of cairns. In these instances, there is no evidence that there has been any robbing of stone from a continuous bank, which suggests that this was also their form in antiquity. The generalised form of the stone bank is in marked

contrast to that of even the most decayed walls, which display greater uniformity throughout their length. In addition, even the more substantial stone banks do not display any evidence of dry-stone structure (Crone and Mills 1988).

Despite the erratic, discontinuous form of stone banks, they clearly mark former boundary lines, as they often define the edges of cairn groups. Their form is consistent with the random deposition of unwanted stone, along boundaries at the edge of plots, and they appear to be an alternative form of stone clearance to the discrete small cairns. Thus, the continuation of a stone bank on Stockdale Moor (SM I; *Ch 3, p 70*), for example, is represented by an alignment of five elongated clearance cairns (Fig 5). It is also quite common to find boundaries defined only by clearance cairns, as at Little Grassoms on Bootle Fell (BF X; *Ch 4, p 131*), where a series of regular, adjacent plots is marked almost entirely by parallel alignments of clearance cairns.

Identifying boundaries marked by cairn alignments can be problematic, particularly as within any random cairnfield some cairns will undoubtedly appear to be aligned. It became necessary, therefore, during the survey, to establish criteria to discriminate between

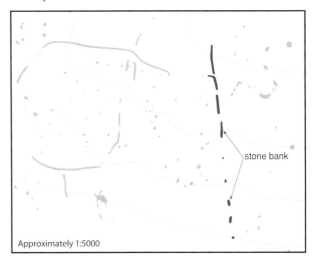

Figure 5: A discontinuous stone bank on Stockdale Moor

Figure 6: A stone bank surviving as a low, turf-covered mound

29

Plate 22: Cultivation lynchets at Austwick, near Settle, North Yorkshire

random and deliberate cairn alignments. An alignment was regarded as significant if it included elongated clearance cairns orientated along the alignment; stone banks were incorporated into the alignment (following the same orientation); it defined the edge of a cairn group; and/or the line of cairns was remote from all other cairns.

Although cairn alignments/stone banks were often the only surviving markers of boundaries, it is probable that in antiquity there were other forms of marker, against which the clearance stone was piled. For example, within the Stockdale Moor cairnfield (SM V; *Ch 3, p 75*) a long, artificially straight alignment of six cairns was identified, following the line of the slope. In this alignment, the cairns are up to 70 m apart, yet when there was thick vegetation on the ground it was difficult to see the cairns from as little as 25 m away. The cairns are too widely spaced to define the boundary and it is likely that originally there were supplementary markers, such as hedges, to define it. This said, however, excavation of a stone bank at Hallshill, near Bellingham, Northumberland (Gates 1981), produced no evidence for postholes or ditches, and it may be that any putative marker had a very ephemeral nature.

Lynchets

Lynchets are found on the break of slope, along a boundary, and form as a result of soil slippage and creep during cultivation (Pl 22). They usually comprise two distinct components (Fig 7): a negative lynchet, representing an area where soil has been

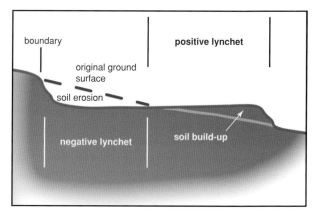

Figure 7: Schematic section through a positive and negative lynchet

eroded from the original ground surface; and a positive lynchet, which is the corresponding area of soil accumulation. Boundaries marked by lynchets are almost always also marked by stone banks, an indication that the loss of soil by slippage has resulted in bringing stones to the surface, which were then cleared. Lynchets are mostly associated with the more complex field systems, and settlements, rather than simple cairnfields (*Ch 8, pp 327-32*), and those within cairnfields are more commonly associated with very small plots rather than more extensive fields.

Ridge and furrow

Lynchets can also be associated with ridge and furrow, which is the formation of parallel ridges and troughs through repeated ploughing. These very characteristic earthworks are caused by the

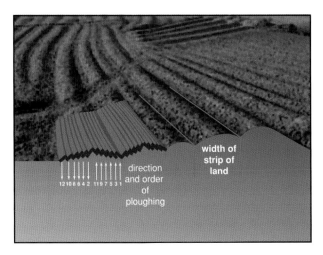

Figure 8: The development of ridge and furrow through ploughing

use, on long narrow strips, of ploughs with a fixed mould board. The movement of the plough, on one side of the strip, will turn the soil over in the direction of the centre, and the return journey, down the other side of the strip, will similarly move the soil towards the centre (Fig 8). Over time, this results in a pronounced build-up of soil in the middle of the strip (ridge), whilst linear hollows (furrows) form at the edges of the strip. The practice of creating ridge and furrow was a deliberate agricultural strategy, as it formed a self-draining seedbed and also created an open drain between the ridges (Hall 2001).

The strips were farmed by individual families, mostly within large, open fields, and are typically medieval in date. The medieval ploughs were pulled by teams of oxen, and the combination was invariably quite long, and correspondingly difficult to turn. The result of this was a wide turning circle and a tendency to twist the end of each furrow to the left. This, in turn, left wide strips (over 4 m ridge to ridge), which had a characteristic reverse S-shape morphology (Eyre 1955). As horse ploughing was introduced in the post-medieval period, so the turning circle required was reduced, which resulted in narrower and straighter ridge and furrow. Ridge and furrow has been identified at several sites examined by the LDNPS, and these typically reflect episodes of medieval cultivation. This is most notable on Heathwaite Fell (*Ch 6, p 264*), where the ridge and furrow is superimposed upon an earlier cairnfield.

An earlier, pre-medieval, form of ridge and furrow cultivation is termed cord rig. This is narrower than medieval ridge and furrow, being between 0.7 m and 1.5 m wide, and facilitated drainage; it has been commonly found on the Northumberland uplands (Topping 1989a; 1989b). Cord rig tends to be dated to the Iron Age and examples have been identified

beneath Hadrian's Wall, for instance, at Tarraby Lane (Smith 1978). In similar circumstances, cord rig has been ascribed an Iron Age date at the Roman fort at South Shields, and is suspected to date earlier than the second century BC (Hodgson *et al* 2001, 153). Cord rig was not, however, identified during the LDNPS programme.

Pastoral enclosures

The LDNPS identified a few distinctive large enclosures, which were up to 116 m across (*eg HE 46; Ch 5, p 251*). Their outer banks invariably displayed some limited evidence of dry-stone masonry, but were usually very decayed, seemed earthfast, and contrast with post-medieval stock enclosures, which often have up to four or more extant courses of masonry. The interior of these enclosures is typically featureless, and seemingly empty, although some incorporate one or two small structures, which are set into the outer walls, either in the corners of the enclosure or butting onto the outside. Although there is often internal terracing within these structures, terracing was absent from the interiors of other, associated, enclosures. Their function would appear to be for the control and corralling of stock, and the associated roundhouses, where present, probably provided accommodation for the stockmen. The classic example of this type of enclosure is found on Hesk Fell (*HE 46; Ch 5, p 251*), where its 'D' shape resulted from the construction of a semi-circular enclosure against a land boundary (Fig 9; Pl 23). Others were identified on Town Bank (*TB 6, TB 72-82,* and *TB 649-51; Ch 3, pp 50-60*), Heathwaite Fell (*HF 530; Ch 6, p 280*), Ulpha Fell (*UF 54; Ch 5, p 228*), and Crosbythwaite (*CT 344; Ch 5, p 237*). These pastoral enclosures have upland parallels on Dartmoor (for example, the Cholwichtown main enclosure, the Penn Moor/Rook Reave enclosure, and the Hurston Ridge D-shaped enclosure), which were built against, or formed part of, reaves, long territorial boundaries found on Dartmoor, which typically date to the Later Bronze Age (Fleming 1988, 5 and 39).

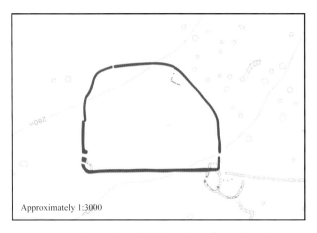

*Figure 9: The Hesk Fell (*HE 46*) D-shaped enclosure*

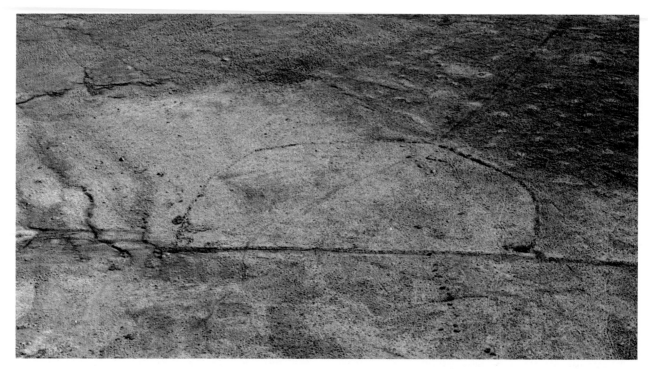

Plate 23: The Hesk Fell D-shaped enclosure (HE 46)*, looking south-east*

Dating

Significant numbers of these enclosures are associated spatially with cairnfields in the Lake District and may therefore be of contemporary date (*eg HE 46; Ch 5, p 251*). Enclosure *TB 649-51* (*Ch 4, p 59*) is part of a settlement complex, which is integral with a linear, cultivated, field system, and is also associated with stone-founded roundhouses. Although the chronology of the field system has not been established reliably, it would appear to pre-date an Iron Age type of enclosed settlement on the same site, and could potentially date to the later Bronze Age or early Iron Age. However, it is important to stress that the use and construction of a pastoral enclosure is not unique to any particular period, and there are alternative examples (albeit somewhat smaller) linked to longhouses (Coggins *et al* 1983; OA North 2003a, site EF 398). In these instances, these particular enclosures seem to be early medieval or medieval in date.

Domestic Structures

Unenclosed settlements

Associated with some cairnfields and field systems are domestic structures, either in groups, or more commonly in isolation, which are not enclosed by defensive banks; as such, these represent the most basic form of settlement identified. Two basic types of unenclosed circular structures, presumably serving a domestic function, were identified during the survey. These include stone-founded roundhouses, and house platforms, which served as the terraced base

for a timber structure that has not survived as visible evidence on the ground surface.

Stone-founded roundhouses

Stone-founded roundhouses are by far the most common form of circular dwellings identified by the LDNPS, with 52 possible examples, in contrast to only 13 house platforms. These structures often form clearly defined settlement groups of up to six houses, but are more typically found singly. Two settlements (TB VIII and TB XI; *Ch 3, pp 55-60*) had both platforms and stone-based roundhouses in close association, and hence the two types do not necessarily represent diverse traditions of house construction.

Plate 24: A roundhouse in the enclosed settlement at Barnscar

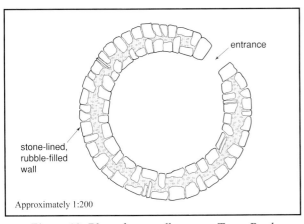

Figure 10: Plan of a roundhouse on Town Bank

The roundhouse in its simplest form is a ring bank (Pl 24) which, in its unexcavated state, can be confused with other monument types. The ring cairn, an annular funerary monument (*p 41*; Lynch 1972, 61-2), for example, can be of comparable size, can incorporate an entrance, and can be associated with cairnfields. Although it is possible to apply some typological criteria to discriminate between them, in many instances a reliable interpretation of function can only be determined by excavation. The classic form of stone roundhouse has a terraced interior, a prominent, though sometimes irregular, external bank, an entrance, and is in direct association with a field system (*eg TB 238* and *TB 241*; *Ch 3, p 52*; Fig 10). However, roundhouses built on flat ground do not have internally terraced interiors and there are many examples that are remote from field systems (Harris 1984). In addition, not all roundhouses have obvious entrances. For instance, on Town Bank, there are four classic roundhouses incorporated into the boundaries of field systems (*TB 73, TB 76, TB 462,* and *TB 475; Ch 3, pp 50-7*), but none of them display evidence of an entrance. In these examples, the implication is that the original entrance has become obscured by subsequent collapse.

Roundhouses exhibit a broad variation in size, but are usually about 4-15 m in diameter, with an average diameter of 9 m. When compared with similar examples from the North East, these are larger than those in Northumberland, which have an average diameter of 7.8 m (Gates 1983, 130). The Cumbrian structures do not appear to display any consistent orientation for the entrance, which is in marked contrast to the examples from Northumberland (*op cit*) and south-east Perthshire (Harris 1984, 202), where there was a preponderance of south-easterly orientated entrances.

Although the Lake District settlements were on occasion of sufficient size to include seven houses (*eg* TB IV; *Ch 3, p 52*), for the most part the settlements comprise a single roundhouse (Fig 11). The sample of houses recorded is small by comparison with

that from Northumberland, although the range of settlement sizes appears comparable (Gates 1983, 132). The majority (63%) of the houses are also associated with field systems, which is remarkably similar to the percentage (66%) of similar sites from south-east Perthshire (Harris 1984, 209-10).

House platforms
On the basis of size, the house platforms recorded by the survey form two distinct types. The smaller platforms are only large enough to accommodate a single structure, whereas the larger platforms could potentially accommodate up to three or four buildings.

Small platforms
Only a few small platforms were found in the course of the survey, and most of these were from two groups located on Heathwaite Fell (HF IXD and HF XI; *Ch 6, p 272*). They comprise oval or circular platforms, cut partly into the slope, which have front aprons built using material excavated from the rear. The net effect was a level circular terrace of sufficient size to accommodate a timber structure, the remains of which do not survive as surface evidence (Fig 12). If the ground was relatively level, and in antiquity there had not been a need to terrace, then there may not be any surface indication of a structure. It is, therefore, significant that, during excavations at Stephenson Ground, in the Duddon Valley, a Bronze Age timber roundhouse was discovered in association with a cairnfield, although prior to the excavation, there had been no surface indications of the building's existence (Thorpe 1994).

The recorded platforms have, on average, diameters of about 5.8 m, which is small by comparison with examples from Peebleshire/Lanarkshire (Jobey 1980, 13), although they are similar in form and size to charcoal-burning platforms (Bellhouse 1991). Indeed, the only significant morphological difference is that the latter type often has charcoal either exposed on the surface, or in localised areas of disturbance. In addition, charcoal platforms are normally found grouped in areas which have a

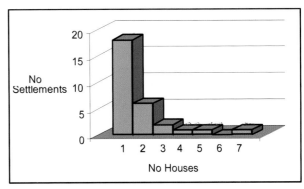

Figure 11: Numbers of settlements with one or more houses identified during the LDNPS

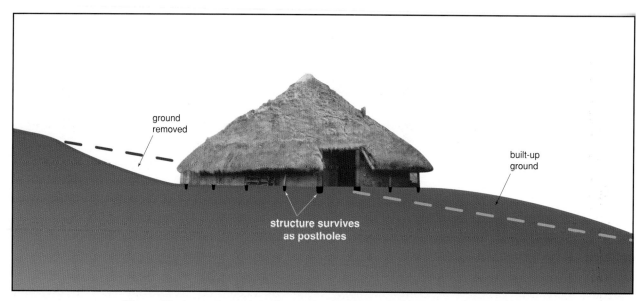

Figure 12: A reconstruction of a timber roundhouse set on a terraced platform

tradition of iron or lime working, and are on ground which was woodland within the last few hundred years. They are also normally found in close proximity to tracks (Lambert 1989).

Large platforms
Only five large platforms were identified during the LDNPS, but they are sufficiently distinctive to warrant a separate description. These platforms do not have any consistent shape. For example, one is rectilinear (*BS 213*; *Ch 4, p 184*), two are oval (*TB 82* and *TB 636*; *Ch 3, pp 50-60*), one has a regular, circular, shape (*SF 90*; *Ch 4, p 173*), and one is D-shaped (*TB 291, Ch 3, p 55*). Their sizes range from 25 m to 28 m along the longest axis, and the top of the front apron can be as much as 2.5 m above the downslope ground surface. The surface of the platform is usually remarkably level and, apart from one large orthostat within *TB 82* (*Ch 3, pp 50-1*), no internal features were recorded. In two examples (*TB 636*; *Ch 3, pp 59-60*; and *SF 90*; *Ch 4, p 173*), the volume of the front apron appears to be much larger than that cut back from the rear scarp slope, and in consequence much of the structure was proud of the slope, hence improving the drainage on the platform. To construct the platform in this way would have necessitated importing substantial volumes of spoil to the site. All of these platforms are associated with field systems, and *TB 636, BS 213,* and *SF 90* (*Ch 3, pp 50-60*; *Ch 4, p 184*; *p 173*) have cultivation plots extending away from them, which were clearly related elements. The size of the platforms suggest that they were either for a single large building or a series of smaller structures.

Dating
Only limited numbers of excavated, unenclosed roundhouses from the North West have generated radiocarbon dates, and none of these are from the LDNPS

dataset. Larger numbers, though, have been dated in the North East, and these span the period *c* 1500-100 cal BC. This date range significantly overlaps that for enclosed settlements (Jobey 1985, 180-4; Haselgrove 2002, 61).

Enclosed settlements
Two distinctive types of enclosed settlement were identified by the survey. The first is a simple form, comprising independent roundhouses, surrounded by an unconnected enclosing boundary. The second type is a more complex homestead, whereby the roundhouses and enclosures merged into each other to form an outer boundary.

Simple enclosed settlements
Only two examples of simple enclosed settlements were found during the LDNPS. The first, from Whitrow Beck (*WB 163*; *Ch 4, p 164*), has a single definite roundhouse, and the second, from Town Bank (TB IIID; *Ch 3, p 64*), has three houses in the centre of a sub-circular, enclosing, bank (Fig 13; Pl 25). The Whitrow Beck enclosure is 46 m in diameter,

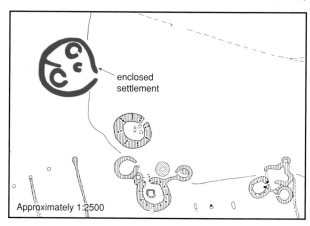

Figure 13: Plan of the simple enclosed settlement at Town Bank (TB IIID)

34

Plate 25: The simple enclosed settlement on Town Bank (TB IIID; foreground)

whilst the enclosure at Town Bank measures 37 m across. The roundhouses on Town Bank are *c* 11 m in diameter and that from Whitrow Beck measures 8 m across. The entrances of both enclosures, and those of their respective houses, are all orientated towards the east.

The emphasis of these enclosures appears to be on defence. For example, they typically have a single entrance and the external banks were probably, on the basis of examples from the North East, reinforced by palisades (*eg* Alnham, Northumberland; Jobey and Tait 1966; West Brandon, Durham; Jobey 1962). The external enclosure tends also to have large orthostat-edged walls (Spence 1937; Hoaen and Loney 2004), although their original height is often unknown, nor is there evidence for any timber superstructure. This presumed emphasis on defence is reinforced by an example from Banishead, near Coniston Old Man, which is D-shaped and has been positioned so that the long side of the enclosure coincided with a natural sheer crag, thus providing an effective line of defence (LUAU 1994a).

Although these monuments are relatively rare within the areas surveyed, there are other notable examples, including some located just outside the boundaries of the LDNPS study areas. One has been found at Thornholme Farm, on the opposite side of the gill to Town Bank (Crawford and George 1983, 27), which

contains seven roundhouses. A further example has been found at Bolton Wood (Spence 1937), close to the Whin Garth survey area, and this contains a single, irregularly shaped, 'roundhouse'.

Dating
Only one example of a simple enclosed settlement from the North West has been subject to modern excavation, Glencoyne Park 6, at Matterdale, which is associated with three roundhouses (Hoaen and Loney 2003; 2004). One of these houses was excavated, and proved to have three phases of occupation. These consisted of two aceramic phases, sandwiching a phase associated with a rich assemblage of Roman fine wares (Hoaen and Loney 2004, 50). Excavation indicated that the external boundary was similarly multi-phased, of which the earliest phase comprised a ditch, dating to 1105-835 cal BC (2810±50 BP; Beta-171115). This feature was overlain by a large orthostatic wall that pre-dated the Roman period (*ibid*). The indications are that this settlement had its origins in the early Iron Age, and was subsequently occupied for a protracted period of time.

In the absence of other dated Cumbrian examples, there are numerous dated parallels from the North East. These examples employed both timber (Alnham; Jobey and Tait 1966; West Brandon; Jobey 1962) and stone construction (Middle Hartside

Hill; Jobey 1964), the simple timber-enclosed settlements usually dating from the later part of the first millennium BC (Ritchie 1970, 52-5; Jobey 1985, 183). However, there is one example from Wolsty Hall, Cumbria (Blake 1959, 7-10), which may have continued to be occupied into the Roman period. In contrast, the stone-built examples from Northumberland have a more consistent Roman date (Jobey 1964). In the absence of more local, and comparably dated, examples, the conclusion must be that the two examples from the LDNPS dataset broadly date to the Iron Age/Roman period.

Complex enclosed settlements

The complex form of settlement seems to have been a development from the simple enclosed settlement and, on the evidence of excavated examples from the eastern side of the Pennines, incorporated both buildings and stock pounds. There, both forms of enclosed settlement overlap chronologically and, indeed, the more irregular, complex enclosed settlements may reflect expansion and adaptation of the simple form over a period of time (Jobey 1966).

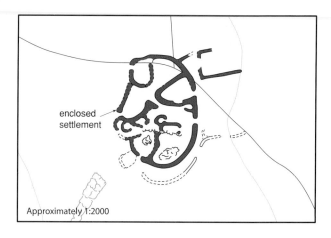

Figure 14: Plan of a complex enclosed settlement (AF 203) on Askham Fell

Characteristically, the interiors of these settlements are filled with roundhouses and more irregular enclosures, often sunken, which merge into each other and the enclosing bank (Fig 14; Pl 26). In some, the enclosing bank is no more than the exposed sections of a series of merged enclosures. Many of

Plate 26: The complex enclosed settlement at Broadwood, near Ingleton, North Yorkshire

these are circular, or oval, but there are also substantial numbers with square or rectangular shapes.

Only two examples of this form of enclosed settlement were recorded by the LDNPS (*BS 477*; *Ch 4, p 188*; and *AF 203*; *Ch 7, p 309*), but they are relatively common on the eastern side of the Lake District. There are similar examples located just beyond the extent of the Askham Fell survey (*eg* Highfield Plantation, near Askham; RCHM(E) 1936, 24-6; and Greatholme Plantation, in Lowther Park; LUAU 1997e). All examples, both within and outside the present dataset, display a wide variety of internal forms. *AF 203*, for example, has a communal character, whereby all the buildings are grouped together in the central section, with the stock pounds kept separate on either side (Fig 14). By contrast, the *BS 477* settlement has an individual character, with three separate, semi-discrete units, each comprising a house with one, or more, enclosures, yet all contained within a single, albeit irregularly defined, enclosure. Both examples have many entrances through the outer enclosure bank, and those of *AF 203* often only lead into the stock enclosures, there being separate entrances to gain access to the houses. While this is a very sensible solution for managing the different elements of a working farm, it is a defensive liability, and would suggest that its inhabitants had little fear of attack, or robbery. However, its clearly defined nucleated, and enclosed, form may reflect earlier types of enclosure, which were constructed with defence in mind.

One of the other common characteristics of the complex enclosed settlement is that the stock pounds often have a floor which is sunken below the adjacent ground level. While not proven, the lowering of the floor level within these pounds was probably the result of keeping stock in them, in wet conditions, and repeatedly removing churned up manure and mud from their interiors, in order to fertilise the adjacent fields.

Dating
This type of farmstead is common in the North West (*eg* Holborn Hill and Muddy Gill Farm settlements near Asby, and the Crosby Garrett settlements; RCHM(E) 1936, 17-18 and 74-7). They are typically dated, on the basis of a limited number of excavations, to the Roman period (*eg* Ewe Close, Crosby Ravensworth; Collingwood 1908; and Waitby; Webster 1972). Moreover, the finding of a Romano-British brooch, during excavation by G de G Sieveking (C Richardson *pers comm*), within monument *BS 477* would appear to confirm that the Barnscar settlement was in use during this period (*Ch 4, p 188*). In addition, recent excavation of a complex enclosed settlement at Ingleton, North

Yorkshire (Pl 26), recovered Roman ceramics from above the floor of a roundhouse (Johnson 2004). A radiocarbon date of 88 cal BC-cal AD 66 (2010±28 BP; KIA-22910) was also gained from the enclosure bank, indicating an apparent origin for the settlement in the late Iron Age (*ibid*).

Rectilinear houses
Significant numbers of elongated, rectilinear houses (Pl 27) were identified during the survey, sometimes in isolation but commonly in association with a field

Plate 27: Upstanding remains of a typical longhouse

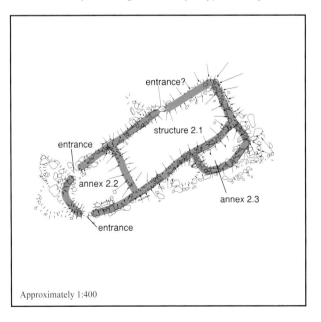

Figure 15: Plan of a typical longhouse with an internal partition, at Green How, Muncaster

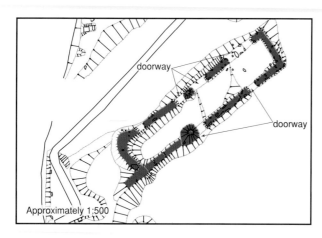

Figure 16: Plan of the cross-passage house at Bank End Farm, Muncaster

Plate 28: A typical shieling (hafod) in the Tanat Valley, North Wales

system, or grouped into a settlement. Within the LDNPS dataset, these structures vary in size, with the largest being 24 m long and the smallest only 7.5 m long. However, the average length of these structures is 11.5 m. In contrast, they display much greater conformity of morphological form. For instance, the average building has a proportion of 2:1 between the long and short sides, and the majority do not have an internal partition, though where these do occur they are invariably within the larger houses (Fig 15). The majority of the rectilinear houses have a single entrance, positioned in a long side, although lesser numbers have opposing entrances on both sides, characteristic of the cross-passage type of house (Brunskill 1974, 50). If they have been set on a slope, they are also invariably internally terraced. The houses vary in complexity, the simplest form being

a single-celled structure, with a single entrance, but there are also numerous examples of multi-celled structures (up to three cells), with multiple entrances (Fig 16). In general, the more complex houses are often associated with field systems.

Shielings

Upland rectilinear buildings have the potential to be shielings (Pl 28), which were the temporary dwellings used during the summer months by transhumant herdsmen and their families (Ramm 1970). This was a practice that was prevalent throughout the medieval period and has been documented as late as the mid-seventeenth century in northern Cumbria (Winchester 1987, 92). Place-name evidence can provide an indication of such transhumant buildings, and in Cumbria the name 'Scale', deriving from the Old Norse element *Skali*, meaning 'a hut', normally refers to a shieling site (Field 1993, 118). However, it is also a name that continued to be used for remote structures, in upland areas, and is not necessarily a diagnostic indicator of a shieling. Many of these names are now associated with established settlements, and the potential exists that these developed from medieval transhumant structures. A case in point is Scale Farm at Whin Garth, which is a decayed seventeenth-century farm with a typical 'longhouse' arrangement (Brunskill 1974, 78). Within the associated farm land are the remains of at least one small rectilinear building (*Ch 3, p 91*), which was potentially the shieling referred to by the place-name, and hence Scale Farm may have developed from an earlier, temporary, settlement. Other Cumbrian place-names, such as Swinside, also incorporate the Scandinavian element *sætre*, meaning shieling (Field 1993, 118).

In the absence of documentary, or place-name, evidence, it is difficult to distinguish a transhumant structure from other types of building, on the basis of the physical evidence alone. Some shielings have associated enclosures or even field systems (Ramm 1970), and a small, short-lived, but not seasonally occupied, farmstead may have the same structural characteristics as a shieling. Because of the difficulty in determining the function of upland rectilinear structures, the term 'shieling' is not used in this volume unless clear documentary or place-name evidence exists.

Farms

Farms are defined as permanent settlements, and as such are distinct from shielings and shepherds' huts. Their characteristic form is a rectangular building linked to some form of field system, yard, or outbuildings (Pl 29). In their most simple form they can be a single-celled rectilinear structure, associated with a single field, but at their most complex, they comprise multi-celled, cross-passage, buildings that are the forerunner of post-medieval

Plate 29: A typical farm site, at Bryn-Llidiard in the Nantlle Valley, North Wales

farms. The best example from the LDNPS dataset is Scale Farm, located in the Whin Garth survey area (*Ch 3, p 91*). This is a three-celled structure, with outbuildings, yard, and a large and complex radial field system extending out from it (Fig 17), which in character seems to be post-medieval in date. However, the more typical farms identified in the LDNPS dataset are epitomised by that on Great Grassoms (*Ch 4, p 134*), which comprises two separate rectilinear houses, each with their own, albeit nested, field system. The first (*BF 897*) is a three-celled structure, with an associated yard, and the second (*BF 892*) is a two-celled, but larger, building, again with a yard.

Dating

The date range for rectilinear houses is fairly broad, extending from the early medieval period through to the post-medieval period. Early medieval examples include a 10 x 5 m longhouse at Bryant's Gill, Kentmere (Dickinson 1985, 86), in the central Lake District, which produced radiocarbon dates of cal AD 619-875 (1320±60 BP; RCD-434) and cal AD 691-997 (1170±70 BP; HAR-8067; Newman 2006, 98). Similarly, longhouses at Simy Folds, Upper Teesdale, in the North Pennines, have been radiocarbon-dated to cal AD 665-979 (1210±80 BP; HAR-4034) and cal AD 687-993 (1170±70 BP; HAR-1898; Coggins *et al* 1983). At Stephenson Ground, in the Duddon Valley, there is an oval-shaped longhouse which, excavation suggests, was associated with at least two phases of construction, as postholes were discovered underlying a stone wall (Thorpe 1994).

Dating from finds and radiocarbon assay implies activity in the twelfth to fourteenth centuries (*ibid*; Duddon Valley Local History Group and Lake District National Park Authority 2009), though it is possible that the earlier phase was pre-Norman. Post-medieval examples are found at Smithy Beck, Ennerdale (Fletcher and Fell 1987). At this site, excavation indicates that the rectilinear house was associated with ceramics dating from the late fourteenth/fifteenth century through to the late sixteenth century. The majority of those houses that have been dated, however, were occupied within the first half of the second millennium AD. A settlement at Great Grassoms (BF XI), Bootle Fell (*Ch 4, p 134*), has two longhouses, and there are documentary references to the site from AD 1252 (Wilson 1915, 364-5) and AD 1510 (CRO D/LONS/W/Millom Courtbook 1510-23, 64).

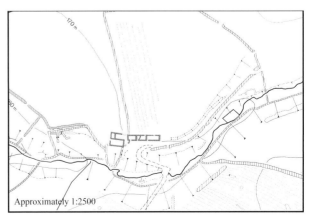

Figure 17: Plan of Scale Farm, Whin Garth

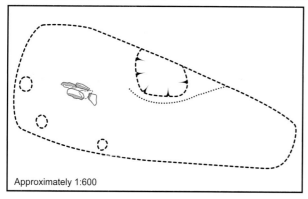

Approximately 1:600

Figure 18: A long cairn, at Pikestones, Anglezarke Moor, Lancashire

Plate 30: Engraving of Sampson's Bratfull long cairn (after Parker 1904)

Funerary and Other Monuments

Three main types of funerary cairn were identified during the survey. These include long cairns, ring cairns/stone circles, and round cairns. In addition to these, there is also a local variant form of funerary monument, which has been termed a star-fish cairn (Taylor 1886, 332-5; Parker 1904, 111).

Long cairns

The classic long cairn is a roughly trapezoidal or rectangular mound of stone (Fig 18), and is often chambered. It is usually between 15 m and 100 m long, and its length is at least twice the greatest width (Masters 1984). Long cairns are generally greater than 1 m high in their unexcavated state (Pl 30). The mounds typically cover the disarticulated remains of numerous individuals that were usually deposited in open chambers, of timber or stone (Pl 31), which were probably repeatedly accessed. It is uncertain, however, as to how the bodies were defleshed, whether by means of exposure, or initial burial (Bradley and Edmonds 1993, 26). Unfortunately, the most characteristic features of long cairns, the facade and the internal chambers, are rarely visible prior to excavation (Masters 1973). As none of the possible long cairns

from the present survey have been subject to modern excavation, the interpretation of their function rests on less diagnostic criteria.

The survey recorded 11 possible long cairns, which satisfy some of the relevant criteria, though only five are within the dimensional parameters set out above. Two are from Stockdale Moor and one of these, the Sampson's Bratfull cairn (*SM 435*; *Ch 3, p 71*), had previously been classed as a long cairn (Daniel 1950, 183). The other cairn on Stockdale Moor (*SM 739*) is long, has an oval shape, but has been disturbed by the possibly later superimposition of banks at its western, broader, end. A third long cairn was found in the Town Bank survey area (*TB 564*; *Ch 3, p 58*), and has a well-defined, trapezoidal, shape with evidence of a possible kerb set into its eastern side. In addition, a single, very large, boulder has been set on top of the cairn, which may be a marker stone. It is possibly significant that, in the vicinity of this cairn are four others, which satisfy some of the long cairn criteria (*TB 526, TB 536, TB 551,* and *TB 591*; *Ch 3, p 58*).

A further cairn, identified during the survey of Stainton Fell (*SF 363*; *Ch 4, p 175*), displays the shape and dimensional characteristics of a long cairn (27 x 13 m), and also has two large, upright, stones at the front of the mound, which are suggestive of a facade. However, there are natural outcrops protruding from the sides, and the eastern, butt end merges into the natural slope. Given this, it is possible that the facade was a natural feature adapted to form a part of the monument. The fifth long cairn, from Askham Fell (*AF 212*), is large (18.6 x 8.7 m), but not particularly prominent. The remainder are substantial elongated cairns, but these do not come within the size parameters of the classic long cairn, as defined by Masters (1984). This may either be an indication that the observed elongated cairns were not funerary monuments, or that earlier research into the long cairn has only focused on the very large examples, resulting in a biased view of their actual size range.

Plate 31: Stone cist within the Pikestones, Anglezarke Moor, Lancashire

40

Dating

The paucity of excavated examples from the western side of the Pennines means that an assessment of their potential chronology is reliant upon dated long cairns from elsewhere. Some of the best dating evidence derives from Wessex, where long cairns appear to have been constructed between *c* 3800 cal BC and *c* 3300 cal BC, after which they apparently ceased to be built (Bradley and Edmonds 1993, 28). Other radiocarbon dates obtained from Seamer Moor (3978-3652 cal BC; 5030±90 BP; NPL-73) and Skendleby (3516-2624 cal BC; 4410±150 BP; BM-191), both in Yorkshire, suggest that the cairns/barrows in this area date to the middle of the fourth millennium BC (Manby 1970, 18).

Ring cairns/stone circles (variant circles)

Ring cairns and stone circles are inter-related categories of prehistoric monument. At one extreme there are the true stone circles, which comprise only upright stones and have no associated bank. At the other extreme are the stone rings, which comprise a circular bank up to 25 m in diameter, incorporating small stones, but no upright stones or megaliths. Between these forms, however, is a considerable range of monuments, which are neither one nor the other. Traditionally, ring cairns and stone circles have been treated as disparate entities, and the net result is that some monuments have been categorised both as ring cairns and stone circles. The interrelationship between these monument types was highlighted by Frances Lynch (1972; 1979), who identified the diversity of these monuments, and categorised them as 'variant circles'. This term embraces all monuments with an annular bank (*ibid*). It also includes stone circles where the upright stones overshadow a low bank that links them together, as for example at The Cockpit on Askham Fell (*Ch 7, p 302*). Furthermore, many of the classic early Cumbrian stone circles, such as Long Meg and her Daughters, and Castlerigg (Burl 1976), include elements of an earthen bank, reinforcing the link between stone circles and ring cairns. Within the LDNPS dataset, there are seven basic forms of the 'variant circle', based on the classifications which have been applied both to stone circles (Waterhouse 1985) and ring cairns (Lynch 1972).

Free-standing stone circle

The free-standing stone circle is one of the archetypal forms of megalithic monument, which comprises a circle of stones without an associated bank. There are two basic forms of this circle: those with internal burial mounds, which have been classified as 'Encircled Cairns' (Lynch 1979, 7); and the open stone circle, which contains no evidence of burial (Pl 32). In Cumbria, the open stone circles are significantly

Plate 32: The north-east stone circle (BM 326), White Moss

larger than those which contain burial mounds, and include examples from Swinside, near the Duddon Estuary, and Elva Plain, near Cockermouth (Burl 1976, 40). Significant numbers of Cumbrian stone circles include internal burial mounds, notably the five stone circles on Burnmoor (*BM 220, BM 221, BM 325, BM 326*, and *BM 352; Ch 3, pp 109-13*), one of which (*BM 352* at Acre Hows) has five internal burial mounds (Fig 19). However, such burial mounds are not necessarily contemporary with the associated stone circle and may post-date them by a considerable period.

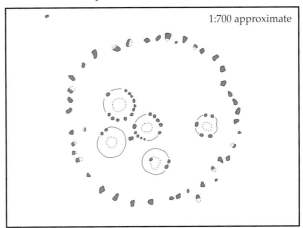

Figure 19: Brat's Hill stone circle at Acre Hows, Burnmoor (BM 352)

Concentric stone circle

The concentric stone circle comprises two rings of stones, and is a relatively rare form. The classic Cumbrian examples of this monument type are Gunnerkeld, near Shap, and the Druids' Circle on Birkrigg (Burl 1976). The Cockpit stone circle (*AF 86; Pl 33*), on Askham Fell (*Ch 7, p 302*), has a secondary ring of stones to the south of the main ring, and this is possibly continued around the northern side by an arc of small cairns. As such, this may be a further example of a concentric stone circle, though this monument also has characteristics of the embanked stone circle (*p 42*).

Embanked stone circle

The embanked stone circle has substantial upright stones set around the inner face of a low ring bank. The best example of this monument from the LDNPS is The Cockpit (*AF 86*) on Askham Fell (*Ch 7, p 302*; Pl 33). Other possible examples are the Castlerigg and Long Meg stone circles (*ibid*), which incorporate sections of bank around parts of the stone circumference.

Plate 33: The Cockpit stone circle on Askham Fell

Cairn circle

The cairn circle is a platform cairn with large uprights incorporated around the edge. Only one example was recorded by the present survey (*AF 117*; *Ch 7, p 305*).

Kerbed cairn

The kerbed cairn is characterised by its small size, being usually 3-5 m in diameter, and by its particularly prominent kerbed stones, in comparison with the size of the cairn. Also, the cairn material never rises above the kerb. The cairns are either circular or oval, although circular kerbed cairns predominate. The best example within the LDNPS dataset is from Mickleden Beck (*MB 12*; *Ch 6, p 288*).

Kerbed ring cairn

The kerbed ring cairn has an annular bank, edged by a kerb of larger stones. The difference between this monument and the kerbed cairn is that it has an open interior, as opposed to one which has been filled. There are two examples of a possible local variant of

Plate 34: Ring cairn SM 36 on Stockdale Moor

this type in the LDNPS dataset (*HF 113*; *Ch 6, p 269*; and *AF 115*; *Ch 7, p 305*). Of these, the example on Heathwaite Fell (*HF 113*) has, in addition to the normal kerbed bank, a single, very large monolith incorporated into the ring.

Stone ring

The stone ring is the simplest form of ring cairn (Pl 34). It comprises a bank of stones, which is sometimes retained by dry-stone walling, and sometimes incorporates an entrance. It is typically larger than the other classes, being as much as 25 m in diameter, and there are numerous examples from the LDNPS dataset (*eg SM 36*; *Ch 3, p 78*; and *AF 80*; *Ch 7, p 301*).

A sub-category of the conventional stone ring is the small ring, which was identified by the LDNPS. Although it is described here as a sub-set of the stone ring, it was not necessarily a funerary monument. It comprises an annular bank, no more than 7.5 m in diameter, with no evidence of a kerb, or an entrance, and is typically found in groups within a cairnfield. One excavated example is at Birrel Sike, between Town Bank and Stockdale Moor (*HC 1*; *Ch 3, p 128*; Richardson 1982), which is one of 39 similar annular banks distributed within a cairnfield containing a total of approximately 70 cairns. On excavation, it was found not to be a roundhouse, as had been originally suspected, and, as it had a regular, internal face, it was not a robbed cairn. It also did not reveal any evidence of a burial, although the excavator suggested that it may have been a ring cairn. It produced a radiocarbon date of 2396-1756 cal BC (3670±100 BP; BIRM-1018), and an adjacent clearance-type cairn produced a very similar date of 2299-1740 cal BC (3640±100 BP; BIRM-1063). In general, the size and association of this type of ring feature contrast with the more solitary and substantial funerary ring cairns, and there is a possibility that they were more directly associated with the adjacent stone clearance activity. Indeed, it is possible that these features were formed during clearance around a tree stump, which then subsequently decayed.

Within recent years, substantial numbers of the smaller stone rings have been identified by Peter Rogers (2000). These range in size from 3-14 m, and vary in form. Some also have distinct kerbs, and some incorporate large boulders within their perimeters, but most are formed from continuous stone banks, with no signs of an entrance. Some examples are also internally terraced or levelled, whereas others have irregular or sloping internal surfaces. A group of small stone rings was identified at an altitude of about 500 m near Stickle Tarn in Great Langdale, and these often seemed to be associated with banks, clearance cairns, or irregular enclosures. The presence of these associated features led to the tentative suggestion that they had a domestic or agricultural function, rather than a funerary one (OA North 2005b).

Peter Rogers discovered a further group of small stone rings near to Seathwaite Tarn, in the Duddon Valley, including two which were subsequently excavated (Duddon Valley Local History Group and Lake District National Park Authority 2009). The largest of these (Cairn 1) is *c* 10 m in diameter, standing on the top of a shallow knoll, and incorporates a number of very large boulders within its bank. Two quadrants of the cairn were excavated, demonstrating a roughly built stone bank, with larger stones at the edge, but no kerb *per se*. No burials were identified, but some charcoal-rich soil, indicative of burning, along with white quartz, was discovered within the bank. Radiocarbon dates for the cairn varied from 1540-1400 cal BC to 1430-1250 cal BC (3180±30 BP; POZ-24044; 3070±35 BP; POZ-24036). These cairns are not associated with agricultural features and, as such, were interpreted as having a ceremonial function (*ibid*).

Variant circles: setting and association

The open stone circles, and related monuments, are often situated, not in prominent locations but, instead, in areas where there is an emphasis on access (Burl 1976, 61); thus The Cockpit (*Ch 7, p 302*) and Grey Yauds are located on significant natural passes. Castlerigg lies on a gentle spur, overlooking the major east-west River Greta access route and the Derwent Valley, whilst Long Meg is within the major Eden Valley route. The open stone circles are also often found on lower ground and are frequently within present-day farmed land which has, in some instances, affected the survival of the monuments. There are at least 16 circles in Cumbria, which have been either completely destroyed or where only a few stones remain (Waterhouse 1985, 90-3).

Ring cairns, by contrast, are usually found scattered over the uplands; they are often on hill slopes, or on a plateau, and occasionally they are found associated with round cairns in cemetery groups, as at Monks Graves (SM VII) on Stockdale Moor (*Ch 3, p 78*). They are periodically found in the locality of a cairnfield and can thus be confused with roundhouses. However, generally the roundhouses are internally terraced into slopes and are often directly associated with field systems/cairnfields, which are traits that allow them to be discriminated from the ring cairns. In extreme cases (*eg SM 496; Ch 3, p 70*), though, the nature of the monument cannot be reliably determined without excavation.

Dating

This broad range of monument forms reflects the development and adaptation of annular monuments over a considerable period of time. The earliest form was the large, open stone circle, the chronology of which extends back into the late neolithic period, while the embanked and concentric stone circles are typically later generic forms (Burl 1976, 59; R Bradley *pers comm*). There are no reliably dated Cumbrian stone circles, although late neolithic 'Cumbrian' axes were found within the Castlerigg circle and the Grey Croft circle, near Sellafield (Burl 1976). Burl (*op cit*, 60) has attempted to provide a rough chronology for the Cumbrian circles on the basis of various traits, which have been determined from dated sites beyond the region. Early, essentially neolithic, traits are defined as a diameter exceeding 27 m, having over 20 stones, an entrance, stones over 1 m high, and a circular or flattened shape, whilst later, essentially Bronze Age, traits include concentricity, an oval shape, and embanked stones. On the basis of these criteria, Castlerigg and Swinside are likely to be late neolithic in date and the largest of the five Burnmoor stone circles (*BM 352; Ch 3, p 113*) is similarly relatively early, while the remaining four Burnmoor stone circles may be later in date. Depending on how the criteria are interpreted, The Cockpit (*AF 86; Ch 7, p 302*) is either relatively early, or very late, being a large open circle, but one which is also embanked.

The classic ring cairns, in contrast, have a significantly later chronology. The Totley Moor ring cairn, in the eastern Peak District, was found to have a middle Bronze Age date, on the basis of ceramics (Radley 1966), and Shaugh Moor (ring cairn 2) has provided dates of 1961-1513 cal BC (3430±90 BP; HAR-2220) and 1736-1321 cal BC (3240±80 BP; HAR-2214; Wainwright *et al* 1979). In addition, there are several excavated ring cairns from Northern Britain. Of these, the ring cairn at Manor Farm, Borwick, North Lancashire, probably dates to the early Bronze Age, based primarily on radiocarbon dates of 2466-1533 cal BC (3630± 170 BP, HAR-5626) and 1739-1399 cal BC (3270±80 BP; HAR-5658), the latter of which was obtained from inhumed bone (Olivier 1987). Similarly, the ring cairn at Weird Law, in the upper Tweed Valley, produced an early Bronze Age radiocarbon date of 1974-1523 cal BC (3440±90 BP; NPL-57; MacLaren 1967), whilst that at Levens Park, South Cumbria, had a primary burial associated with early Bronze Age ceramics (Sturdy 1972). At Hardendale, on Shap, excavation of a ring cairn identified a multi-phase use of the site, the date for the earliest inhumation being 1920-1524 cal BC (3430±80 BP; OxA-2127) and the latest (Phase 4), 1869-1515 cal BC (3360±60 BP; OxA-1834; Howard-Davis and Williams 2005). Finally, a cairn at Whitestanes Moor, Southern Scotland, generated a radiocarbon date of 1874-1414 cal BC (3310±90 BP; GAK-461; Scott-Elliot and Rae 1965). All these dates suggest an early to middle Bronze Age date range for the conventional ring cairn.

Plate 35: A large round cairn, at Cors y Carneddau, Snowdonia

The more variant forms of annular monument, such as the cairn circle and the kerbed cairns, similarly date to the Bronze Age. The Askham Fell cairn circle (*AF 117*; *Ch 7, p 305*), for example, produced a Food Vessel (Taylor 1886) of a type that typically dates to *c* 2050-1700 cal BC, a period which falls within the early Bronze Age (Needham 1996). However, excavated examples of a limited number of kerbed cairns have produced dates which are slightly later than those of the conventional stone ring. Cremated material from two kerbed cairns (1 and 3) at Claggan, Argyll (Ritchie *et al* 1975, 21-2), produced radiocarbon dates of 1297-980 cal BC (2925±50 BP; SRR-284; cairn 1) and 1386-1128 cal BC (3008±40 BP; SRR-285; cairn 3). The overall implication, therefore, is that this class of monument continued to be established in the later phases of the Bronze Age.

Function

It is evident that the form of these annular monuments developed over a considerable period. It would also appear that their function has undergone a similar transition, since the large open circles, displaying Burl's (1976) early traits, for the most part appear to have served a different function from the later stone circles, and ring cairns. The early stone circles, even when excavated, do not often display evidence of contemporary burial, and this has prompted the suggestion of alternative ceremonial or ritual functions. For instance, Thom (1967) proposed that megaliths and some stone circles served as astronomical observatories for determining the solstices and equinoxes. However, the significant astronomical alignments only appear to be valid for a limited number of the stone circles, of which one is possibly Castlerigg. The presence of items, such as stone axes, outside of a burial context may be evidence that the sites served, at least in part, as trading centres (Bradley and Edmonds 1993). Ultimately, however, these early stone circles may have served multiple functions, and were perhaps used for conducting rituals, for trading, for burial, and even, possibly, for calendrical purposes.

In contrast, the later forms of stone circles and variant circles display a greater emphasis on burial. For instance, the cairn circle, as typified by *AF 117* (*Ch 7, p 305*), comprises a stone circle set into a large burial mound, and there is no evidence of an alternative function. True ring cairns also typically have a funerary function, with urned or unurned cremated funerary remains being placed within pits and cists found within these monuments (Lynch 1979). It is interesting to note, however, that, in some instances, the funerary function of a ring cairn was probably not the initial one. For example, at the Brenig 44 ring cairn, North Wales, the central inhumation was interred only as part of second phase of activity, prior to which the cairn had existed for some considerable time, sufficient for its outer revetment to become degraded (Lynch 1993, 132). This may suggest that initially the cairn had a ritual function that was not strictly related to the interment of burials. Within the interior of some ring cairns are low mounds, which, in the Lake District, are usually formed of stone (*eg SM 38*; *Ch 3, p 78*) and may cover one or more burial pits. However, again, these are not necessarily contemporary with the construction of the ring cairn.

Round cairns

The round cairn is the most common type of identifiable funerary monument from the LDNPS. Many Cumbrian examples have been explored by antiquarians, as testified by the irregular depressions in the majority of the larger cairns. However, only a few of these early investigations have been published (*eg* Greenwell 1877) and even fewer have been recorded by sophisticated excavation methodologies. A greater number of round cairns have been properly excavated in south-west Scotland, and a comprehensive analysis of the total sample from Dumfries and Galloway has been undertaken by Yates (1984b), presenting a dataset which can be used as a comparison with that from Cumbria.

The round cairn has a simple form, which is basically a large circular mound, and as such can be similar to the clearance-type cairn. However, it normally has a large, regular, well-defined shape, and is very prominent, with a large height to width ratio (Pl 35), and it also has a uniform, rounded, profile (unless disturbed). It is typically much larger than the clearance equivalent and generally has a diameter of 7-26 m (*op cit*, 34). The disturbed form of the cairn can also be confused with other ring features (for instance, a ring cairn), although the internal hollow of a robbed round cairn typically has an irregular shape with a rounded bottom, which is often off-centre.

Although the funerary cairn usually has a kerb, because of subsequent collapse this is often not evident without recourse to excavation (*op cit*, 22). At two sites

Plate 36: Stone cist within the White Raise round cairn, AF 130, Moor Divock

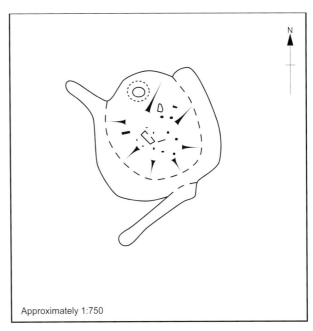

Approximately 1:750

Figure 20: Star-fish cairn AF 130, on Askham Fell

(BF 813 and SF 338; Ch 4, p 133; p 175), disturbance has exposed an outer bank, which has a different matrix from the main body of the cairn on top of it. The implication is that these were capped ring cairns, a similar form of construction being revealed during excavations of two ring cairns in the North West (Manor Farm, Borwick; Olivier 1987; and Hardendale; Howard-Davis and Williams 2005).

Occasionally, a stone cist is exposed (Pl 36) as a result of antiquarian excavations (eg BF 804; Ch 4, p 133; and AF 130; Ch 7, p 306). Within the LDNPS, the cist from AF 130 on Askham Fell was for an inhumation (Taylor 1886), in keeping with the round cairns from south-west Scotland, which have cists of a similar size (average 1.14 x 0.66 m) and were predominantly for inhumations (Yates 1984b, 25).

The funerary round cairn is typically placed in a prominent position, with a commanding aspect with respect to the local topography. This can be the summit of a hill, or any raised position. For example, within the LDNPS dataset, cairn BF 731 (Ch 4, p 131) lay at the forward edge of a natural terrace, and is visible from all around. Less extreme examples are found on the other side of Bootle Fell, where two cairns (BF 804 and BF 813; Ch 4, p 133) are situated on the back of a spur between two becks. Although they are not on a localised high point, they are visible from anywhere within the Grassoms and Crookley valleys.

Dating
There are examples of round cairns in Britain, which date to the neolithic period (Kinnes 1979), including one from Crosby Garrett in east Cumbria (Greenwell 1877, 389-91), and another from the Caldbeck Fells (Barker 1934). By the same token, there are round cairns that date to the Iron Age (eg Alnham; Jobey 1966), attesting to the longevity of this most basic form of funerary monument. However, of the datable cairns from south-west Scotland, 95% can be ascribed to the early Bronze Age, primarily on the basis of ceramic finds (Yates 1984b, 2-3), and the few datable cairns from Cumbria reinforce this chronology (Grinsell 1953, 240-7).

Star-fish cairns
There is a small sample of funerary monuments from the LDNPS dataset, which have short sections of prominent bank spiralling out from the cairn edge (eg SM 739, Ch 3, p 72; AF 119 and AF 130; Ch 7, pp 305-6; Fig 20), and also limited numbers of examples that have not been included within this dataset, for example a round cairn at Hollin Stump on Gaythorne Plain (NY 652 116; J Cherry pers comm). Because of their distinctive form, they have been termed 'star-fish' cairns (Taylor 1886, 332-5; Parker 1904, 111). However, it has yet to be established if the banks were a contemporary element of the funerary monuments, or later additions. The component stones of the banks have uniform lichen cover and seemingly merge into the mass of the body of the respective cairn; thus, they would appear not to be recent additions, although they may have been added in antiquity. It is also worth noting that there are examples of three-pointed burial monuments (tricorns) from pre-Christian Norse contexts, which are supposed to represent the concept of the world tree Yggdrasill, the three banks representing tree roots (Andrén 2005). Possibly conceptually linked to these are the tri-radial cairns found exclusively in Northumberland, which have a comparable form (Frodsham and Waddington 2004, 174). These examples, however, by definition have three banks, which extend directly out from the centre, whereas the examples identified from the LDNPS dataset have variable numbers of banks, and these extend tangentially out from the edge of the cairns. It is

Plate 37: Burnt mound to the west of Crag House, Buttermere

possibly significant that both cairns *AF 119* and *AF 130* (Fig 20) have banks that are orientated along an alignment of funerary monuments, and hence they may be associated features of the cairn group, suggesting a degree of contemporaneity. The sample is, though, too small at present to provide any reliable indication as to the relationship between the cairn and banks, and it is not possible to determine if this is a distinct form of funerary monument.

Burnt Mounds

Burnt mounds are anomalous features, comprising mounds of largely burnt stone, within a charcoal-rich matrix. They usually have kidney-shaped plans and are typically located adjacent to a watercourse or spring. At the time of the LDNPS programme, very few had been documented, but an improved awareness of their characteristic form has meant that they have increasingly been recognised across the Lake District. A study by Hodgson (2007) identified 17 burnt mounds within the Lake District, and subsequent surveys of Buttermere (Pl 37) and Nether Wasdale (OA North 2009b; 2009c) have identified a further eight examples. Within the LDNPS areas, two burnt mounds were recognised, one at Whin Garth (*WG 696*; *Ch 3*, *p 94*) and the other on Heathwaite Fell, although the latter was discovered subsequent to the main survey (Hodgson 2007, 209). A third has also been identified near to the Crosbythwaite survey area, at Winds Gate (SD 1848 9584) on Birker Fell (Hodgson 2007).

At one level, the function of these monuments appears relatively straightforward, as, where excavations have taken place, they have demonstrated that the mounds were constructed around troughs, often made of timber planks (Heawood and Huckerby 2002). The mounds are also invariably close to a water supply, and the stones forming the mounds are cracked from having been cooled rapidly. The implication is that the mounds comprise waste stone, which had been first heated up and then immersed into the water-filled trough in order to heat the water. The much-disputed question, though, is why there should have been a need to heat troughs of water, and there have been numerous theories revolving around cooking, saunas, or bathing (*cf* Barfield and Hodder 1987). The cooking theory is somewhat confused by the fact that, at least in the Lake District, the sites are typically remote from settlement sites, and excavations have not identified any marked deposits of animal bone (*ibid*; Heawood and Huckerby 2002). The bathing/sauna theory has yet to be reliably confirmed, and so it is anticipated that the function of these characteristic monuments will be much debated for some time to come.

Dating

In the past, these monuments were generally considered to be a product of middle to late Bronze Age activity, as the majority of sites date to 1600–1000 cal BC (English Heritage 1988; Heawood and Huckerby 2002). Indeed, this is typified by the example from Sparrowmire Farm, Kendal, which contained material dating from 1678-1410 cal BC (3240±50 BP; AA 34789/GU-8449) to 1408-1126 cal BC (3020±50 BP; AA-34791/GU-8447; Heawood and Huckerby 2002). More recently, however, excavated Cumbrian examples have extended this date range into the late neolithic/early Bronze Age. These include sites at Drigg (OA North 2010b) and Aldingham, Low Furness (SD 2780 7070), which has produced dates of 2290-2020 cal BC (3740±40 BP; SUERC-1855) and 2140-1910 cal BC (3640±35 BP; SUERC–1856; Hodgson 2007; The Morecambe Bay Archaeological Society 2006), and five at Stainton West, near Carlisle, the earliest of which produced a date of 2870-2570 cal BC (4110±35 BP; SUERC-32717). This was, however, typologically somewhat different from the others, which ranged in date from 2280-2020 cal BC (3720±35 BP; SUERC-32714) to 1630-1450 cal BC (3270±35 BP; SUERC-32715; OA North 2011a).

3

THE WESTERN FELLS

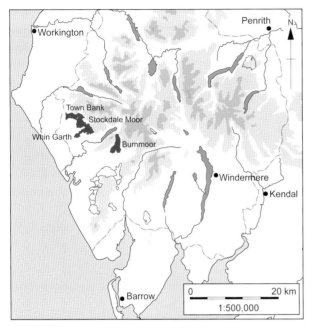

Figure 21: The extent of the survey on the Western Fells

The Western Fells of the Lake District comprise the remote, mountainous terrain between Ennerdale and Eskdale. The main area of archaeological remains is on the lower, marginal lands at the western side of the fells, immediately above and adjacent to the lowlands of the coastal plain. In total, the survey programme investigated 18.1 km² of marginal land within four survey areas, which comprised Town Bank, Stockdale Moor, Whin Garth, and Burnmoor (Fig 21). Three of the survey areas are in the northern section of the Western Fells, extending from Kinniside Common to Wasdale, a broad ridge with a progressive increase in altitude towards the east of the fells, culminating in the summit of Pillar at 892 m OD. Burnmoor, in the southern part of the Western Fells, is on a natural ridge between Wasdale and Eskdale, which is edged to the west by Miterdale, and to the east by increases in altitude, leading up to the summit of Scafell, at 964 m OD.

Town Bank

Town Bank is an extensive area of unenclosed moorland on the lower, southern slopes of Lank Rigg

(between NY 095 103 and NY 065 098). For the most part, it has a fairly moderate, uniform gradient, but it is edged to the south, west, and east by the steep slopes of the Worm Gill and River Calder (Fig 22). The deep and fast-flowing Worm Gill forms the boundary between the Town Bank and Stockdale Moor (*p 49*) survey areas and is potentially an ancient land division, which divides settlement areas of very different character (Pl 38).

Some large expanses of mire occur on the moor, and it is in between these, on the areas of well-drained land, that the settlements and cairnfields are generally located. Cairnfield boundaries occasionally coincide with mire edges, and there are only limited numbers of monuments within the mires; hence there does not appear to have been a significant change in the drainage pattern since the construction of the cairns.

Archaeological history

The earliest recorded monuments on Town Bank are the TB XIII enclosures (*pp 63-4*), which are shown on the 1867 First Edition 6″ to 1 mile OS map. By the time of the 1926 Second Edition 6″ to 1 mile map, settlements/cairnfields TB XI (*p 59*) and TB X (*p 57*), and part of TB III (*p 53*), are also depicted. The earliest descriptive record of the TB XIII settlement dates from 1877 (Clifton Ward 1878, 249), whilst Parker (1904, 114-17) produced a crude plan of the TB XIII settlement and mentions the cairns around Grey Crag (TB III). The results of another survey of the TB XIII settlement were published in 1938 (Spence 1938), along with a selective plan of the TB XI (*p 59*) complex. During this survey, a description of funerary cairn *TB 803* was made, which forms the most detailed record of the cairn prior to its subsequent destruction (*p 64*). This description notes that,

'the cairn is almost circular, measuring 62 ft by 58 ft [*c* 18.9 x 17.6 m] and is 6 ft in height [*c* 2 m]. It is composed of large river boulders and has two well-marked depressions, the result of disturbance, near the centre' (*op cit*, 64-5).

In 1956, Bill Fletcher, and the pupils of Pelham House School, excavated *TB 803* and roundhouse *TB 750* (W Fletcher *pers comm*). The former was

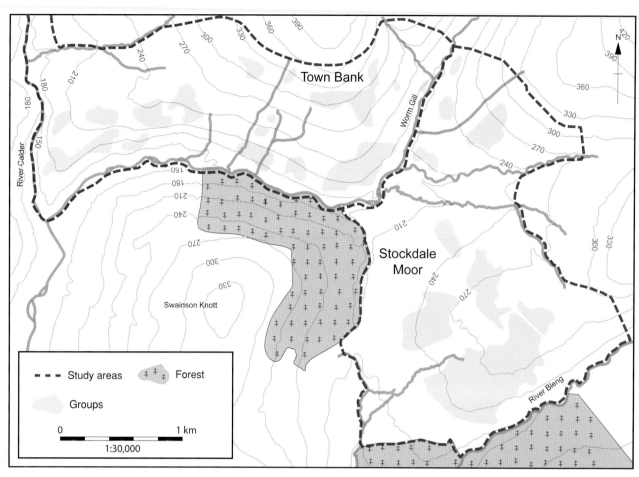

Figure 22: The Town Bank and Stockdale Moor survey areas

Plate 38: Town Bank, looking west towards the confluence of Worm Gill and the River Calder, with a very different agricultural regime beyond

48

completely excavated and the cobble spoil, which was estimated by Fletcher to have weighed 1000 tons, was deposited in a ring around the site of the cairn. The only extant records of the results are four photographs and a sketch plan produced from memory, years after the event (*pp 64-5*). The excavation of the roundhouse emptied the interior and clarified the lines of the walls, which were subsequently reconstructed; again, only a limited record of the results survives. Yet another survey of settlements TB XIII and TB XI was undertaken in 1984 by Carole Palmer (1985), who identified the main areas of the Town Bank cairnfields.

The survey area

The Town Bank survey was carried out between April and May 1986 over 3.2 km² of unenclosed moorland (Fig 23). In total, 893 monuments were recorded within 15 site groups (TB I-XV; Fig 24). These site groups vary in size from only three monuments at TB I to a field system and settlement at TB IV, which contained 207 monuments. The site groups extend in a broad band along the moderately sloping northern side of the Worm Gill valley, and range in increasing complexity from relatively simple cairnfields, at the eastern end of the study area (*eg* TB III), to the complex field system and

settlements (TB XIII) found at the western end of the study area (Fig 24). By comparison with other survey areas, including the adjacent Stockdale Moor, these site groups have an abnormally large number of buildings with associated field systems. These range in character from a pastoral enclosure, with attached building at TB II, unenclosed stone-founded roundhouse groups at TB IV, TB VIII, TB IX, TB XI, TB XIII, and TB XV, to a defensive enclosed settlement at TB XIII. The broad range of landscapes and the complexity of settlement/field systems make this one of the most important survey areas recorded by the LDNPS.

Just beyond the north-western limit of the survey area (NY 0640 1026) is a well-documented packhorse bridge (Parker 1904, 114-15), spanning the River Calder, called Monk's or Matty Benn's Bridge (Pl 39). It was the crossing point for a medieval/post-medieval drove road, which traversed Town Bank, crossed Worm Gill near Mountain Pinfold, and continued towards Scalderskew and beyond (Hindle 1984). The eastern section of the road on Town Bank is still clearly visible (Fig 24) and part of it is still in use. However, the line of the original road between TB XI and Monk's Bridge, an area of poor drainage, is no longer visible.

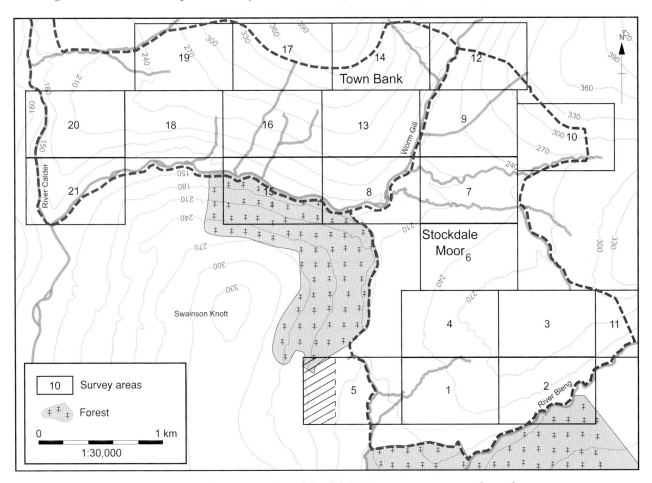

Figure 23: The Town Bank and Stockdale Moor survey areas as planned

49

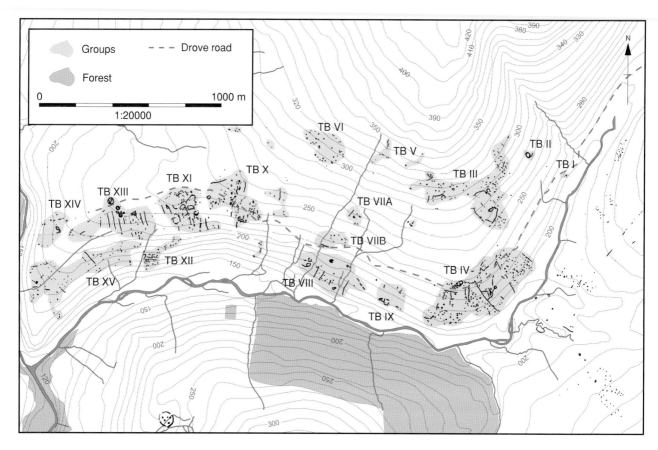

Figure 24: Monument distribution within the Town Bank survey area

Plate 39: Monk's, or Matty Benn's, Bridge, an early packhorse route over the River Calder, that leads from the Town Bank ridge

Town Bank I (Swarth Beck): monuments *TB 1-3*

A small ring feature (8.9 m in diameter) on an alluvial terrace of Worm Gill (Fig 24), between 220 m and 230 m OD, was associated with two small cairns. It appeared to be separate from the main Town Bank cairnfields, the closest (TB III) being 320 m away. It had a regular circular shape, and both the inner and outer edges were well defined. There was no visible entrance, but it had a slight internal terrace. Its function is uncertain but, given that it was internally terraced and was associated with two clearance-type cairns, it was potentially a roundhouse.

Town Bank II: monuments *TB 6-8*

A large, oval enclosure (*TB 6*; Pl 40), was located on the moderate slopes at the north-eastern end of Town Bank, at *c* 280 m OD (Fig 24). This comprised a well-defined, turf-covered bank (*c* 32 x 23 m), which had many protruding stones, with a short length of dry-stone masonry surviving at the southern end (*c* 7 x 3.5 m; Fig 25). A gap, visible in the northern section of the wall, coincided with a small rectilinear structure located on the inside of this wall. The land within the enclosure was unterraced, uniformly sloping, and well drained, and the size, shape, continuous perimeter, and unimproved land within the feature indicated its use as a pastoral enclosure (*Ch 2, p 31*). There was no apparent association with any of the cairnfield groups and it was morphologically distinct when compared with the other Town Bank enclosures. The advanced state of decay indicates that it was not of recent construction.

Town Bank III (Gray Crag): monuments *TB 9-137*

This field system and cairnfield comprised three groups of cairns, located on the moderate slopes at

Plate 40: Enclosure TB 6 (TB II)

the north-eastern end of Town Bank, between 255 m and 310 m OD (Fig 24). The cairnfields surrounded a probable field, and were associated with buildings (*TB 73* and *TB 76*; Fig 25) and a large terraced platform (*TB 82*).

The cairnfields

One of the cairn groups (TB IIIA; Fig 25) was found on moderately steep, well-drained land, which changed to poorly drained land on a line which approximately coincided with the lower edge of the group. The cairns were poorly defined, irregular in shape and profile, and their size varied substantially, with those at the north end of the group being significantly smaller and more ill defined than those at the southern end. Although there were short stubs of stone bank within the group, there were no significant cairn alignments, and their distribution was essentially random. A second cairnfield comprised a small group of moderately well-defined, low clearance-type cairns (TB IIIC), located immediately to the south-east of a partial enclosure (TB IIIB; *p 52*). The spread of cairns was restricted at the south-eastern edge by an area of poor drainage. The third cairnfield consisted of clearance cairns and stone banks (TB IIID), which were located on a well-drained, natural, terrace. The cairns were limited in number, but significantly larger and more prominent than those of TBIIIA.

The cairnfields also included three examples of a distinctive site type (*TB 60, TB 117,* and *TB 120*), comprising a semi-circular bank, with the open side facing downslope. Two of these sites (*TB 60* and *TB 120*) were semi-circular in shape, whilst one

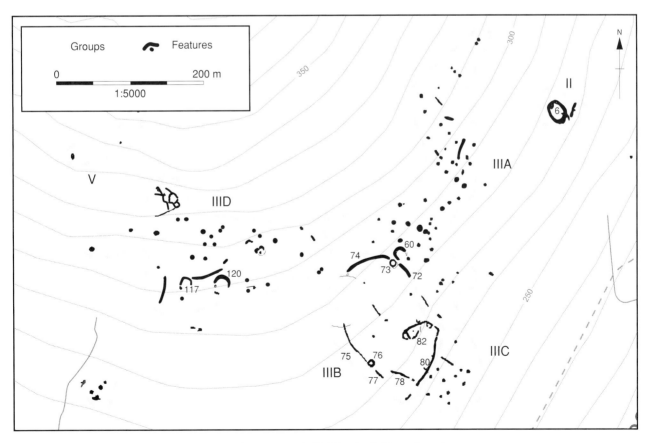

Figure 25: The TB II and TB III cairnfields and settlements

(*TB 117*) had a rectilinear form. The central parts of the banks had a lynchet-like profile and the gradient within the 'semi-enclosure' was similar to that outside. The profile of the bank was indicative of soil slippage, suggesting that these features may have been small, cultivated plots.

The enclosure/field, terraced platform, and buildings

In addition to the cairnfields, a group of monuments was identified (TB IIIB) which defined a semi-enclosed plot of land, the interior of which was generally well drained, had little surface brash, and was on a uniform slope. This plot was defined by a discontinuous perimeter boundary, with a marked gap on the eastern side. The north-western section of the plot had also been lost within an area of mire. Most of the sections of this perimeter bank were irregular in definition, width, and quantity of stone, and were probably stone banks. The exception was the southernmost section (*TB 80*), which appeared to form the relict remains of a wall, although it was not clear why this section alone should have been built, or rebuilt, in a more deliberate manner. This section had large quantities of stone, probably indications of a dry-stone structure (at NY 9078 9845), and a well-defined entrance near its northern end. There was a relative paucity of cairns within the partial enclosure, when compared to the cairn concentrations outside. In the case of TB IIIA and TB IIIC, the spread of cairns was bordered by the line of these enclosure boundaries.

Extending out from the south-eastern boundary of the enclosure was a substantially terraced platform (*TB 82*), which was subdivided into two enclosures. The western, smaller enclosure (9.5 x 6.5 m) was D-shaped, with a moderately defined entrance, while the larger, eastern part (19 x 16 m) had a slightly irregular shape and only an intermittent boundary to the south-east. The surface of the platform was featureless, with the exception of a large, prominent boulder in the centre. The larger enclosure was both too large and too irregular in shape to have been roofed, although it may have served as a platform for one or more timber structures.

In line with the field boundaries were two similarly sized ring features (*TB 73* and *TB 76*), both about 9 m in diameter. The associations with the field boundaries and their small, regular, shapes suggest that they were roundhouses, although the westernmost of these (*TB 76*) had no internal terrace (Pl 41), and that to the north-east (*TB 73*) had only a very ill-defined entrance. Another possible building was attached to the inside of the eastern boundary (*TB 80*; NY 9065 9850), immediately adjacent to the entrance through the wall. It comprised an ill-defined, rectangular enclosure with slight, internal, terracing on the inside.

Plate 41: Roundhouse TB 76, *set against a field boundary* (TB 75)

Town Bank IV (Worm Gill: monuments *TB 144-351*

This area lay between 190 m and 250 m OD and contained a large, complex field system (Fig 24), which had been subdivided into distinctive 'fields' (TB IVA-D; Fig 26) by a series of discontinuous stone banks, which were orientated downslope (Pl 42). Some of these fields contained dense concentrations of cairns, while others were largely devoid of cairns; associated with the field system were two settlement areas. One (TB IVB) was defined by two roundhouses, within one of the 'fields', whilst the other settlement area lay to the immediate north of one of the field systems (TB IVE) and was defined by possible roundhouses, and a possible house platform.

The field system and cairnfields

The north-eastern field (TB IVA) was on a steep, slightly undulating area of well-drained moorland, and was defined to the north-east and the south-west by stone banks *TB 146* and *TB 210* respectively (Pl 43). Within the field was a large concentration of ill-defined, clearance-type cairns, which were bordered on the south-east by a sharp break of slope, dropping to the Worm Gill flood plain.

A second field (TB IVB), defined by stone banks *TB 210* and *TB 247*, was positioned on a slightly undulating, moderately sloping area of moorland. It was generally well drained, although the lower end, to the east of *TB 250*, was very poorly drained. Bank *TB 247* was predominantly continuous, and well defined, but was also irregular in width and varied in its quantity of stone, all of which indicate that it was formed by stone clearance. The field had very few cairns within it, in contrast to the adjacent field (TB IVA), but it did contain two roundhouses (*TB 241* and *TB 236*) and a small rectilinear plot attached to stone bank *TB 247* (p 54). At the upper, north-western, end of TB IVB was another possible field, bordered by stone banks *TB 219* and *TB 220*, which were very poorly defined. Bank *TB 219* had

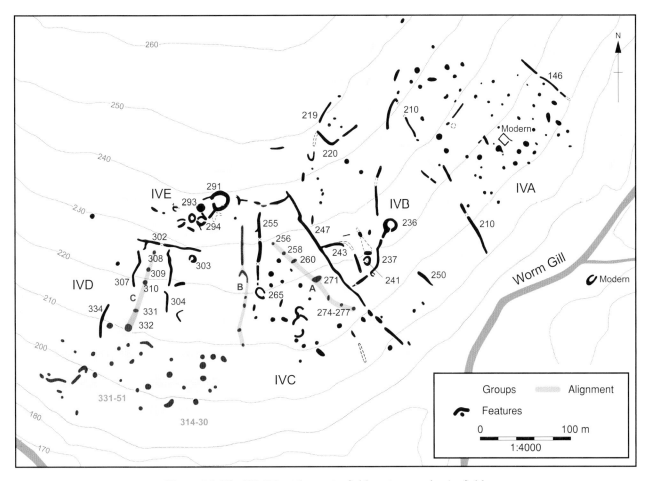

Figure 26: The TB IV settlements, field system, and cairnfields

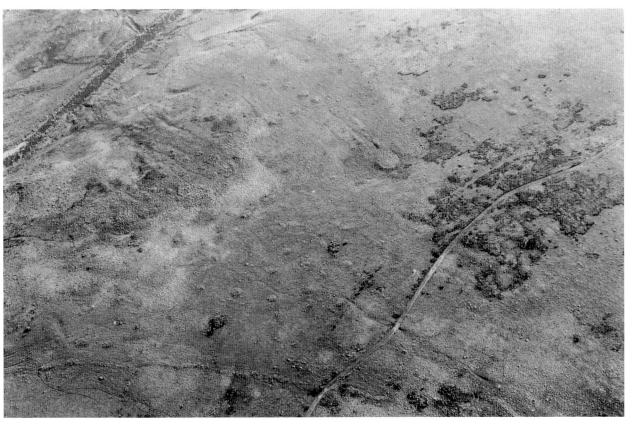

Plate 42: The TB IV cairnfield and field system, looking south-west (TB 247; bottom)

Plate 43: The area of the TB IVA cairnfield, around a later rectangular stock pound

what appears to have been a lynchet profile, which may imply soil slippage within this 'field'.

A third group of monuments (TB IVC) was identified as a field, forming a truncated 'V' shape, which was defined to the east by stone bank *TB 247* and to the west by a short bank (*TB 255*). The field contained many cairns, consistent with stone clearance, which were generally well defined and low-lying, but also irregular in shape and profile. The extent of the cairnfield did not precisely coincide with field boundary *TB 247*, and, instead, its eastern edge was defined by a significant alignment of cairns (A). There was, therefore, a possibility that these two putative boundaries belonged to different phases of the field system.

A fourth group of monuments (TB IVD) comprised a possible field, which lay immediately to the west of the field defined by banks *TB 247* and *TB 255* (TB IVC; *see above*). Although this field was devoid of cairns, it did contain a single roundhouse (*TB 303*), and was surrounded by a marked concentration of large cairns (*TB 314-30*). The field was defined intermittently to the west and north by stone banks *TB 304* and *TB 302* respectively, to the east by an alignment of cairns and stone banks (B), and to the south by the group of cairns. This small, partially enclosed area was well drained, but had an abundance of surface

brash. The large clearance cairns (*TB 314-30*) associated with the field were found at its southern limits, and were significantly larger, and more prominent, than a group of cairns to the west (*TB 331-51*). To the west of the field, a significant cairn alignment was also found (C), which was parallel to, but distinct from, the field boundary defined by stone bank *TB 304*. To the west of this was a further stone bank, *TB 307/334*, which defined the western edge of the site group.

The roundhouses, rectilinear plot, and house platform
Roundhouse *TB 236* was located within one of the fields (TB IVB; *p 53*) and was connected to the rectilinear field system by a substantial bank (*TB 237; Fig 26*). This bank was evidently a decayed wall, as it contained large amounts of stone, had a regular width, and in places was faced with large, prominent boulders, with an associated rubble fill. It followed an S-shaped alignment, which skirted around roundhouse *TB 241*, implying that it post-dated this, and that *TB 241* was possibly still in use at the time the walls were built. A small, rectilinear plot (*TB 243*) was also located within this monument group (TB IVB) and enclosed 974 m² of well-drained, smooth-surfaced land on a uniform gradient, at the western side of this field. At its upper end, it was bordered by a large, slightly irregular, negative lynchet, with a height of 0.8 m from its downslope base, while at the lower end was an irregular, ill-defined bank and an associated

positive lynchet. It was evident that considerable soil slippage had taken place within the field, which indicates past ploughing.

A small oval enclosure (*TB 265*; 14 x 10 m), potentially a house platform, was also discovered associated with the field with a truncated V-shape (TB IVC; *p 54*). This enclosure was positioned at the bottom of a bank (*TB 255*) associated with this field system, and had internal terracing, irregular outer banks, and a large ill-defined entrance.

The enclosures, banks, and cairns

A compact, complex system of enclosures, banks, and cairns (TB IVE) was also found above the cairn-free field (TB IVD; *p 53*). The largest enclosure (*TB 291*) was D-shaped, substantially terraced, and measured 21 x 20.5 m. Although the size and shape suggested that the enclosure did not represent a roofed structure, there is a possibility that it was a house platform. Adjacent to the entrance of this enclosure was a large, very prominent, round cairn (*TB 293*; 8.5 m in diameter) with a kerb to the north-west, implying that it had was a funerary monument. In contrast, monument *TB 294* was a small, poorly defined, circular ring feature, which was probably a roundhouse.

Discussion

Taken as a whole, TB IV forms an extremely important group of monuments representing a settlement and an associated field system, which in part incorporated cultivation. The evidence also suggests that this was, perhaps, a permanently occupied, well-developed, settlement, which may have had some degree of longevity, to judge by its complexity. The settlement groups were defined by at least five domestic structures, be they roundhouses or platforms, which were linked with the field system. The field system was divided by a series of discontinuous stone banks, orientated downslope, and linked into these boundaries was a series of related elements, cairnfields, settlement groups, and a cultivated plot. Significantly, there was an apparent relationship between the cairn groups and the boundaries, in particular in TB IVA, which demonstrates that the cairnfields were an integral part of the field system. Moreover, the presence of fields without cairns also demonstrates that the cairns fitted in with what appeared to be a deliberately designed arrangement, and that different fields were being put to different uses. For instance, those fields without cairns, for the most part, contained domestic settlement, and it is notable that a small plot (*TB 243*) was associated with one of these settlements (TB IVB). This small plot, which had top and bottom lynchets and had evidently been cultivated, was directly linked to the buildings, and its relative isolation may suggest that it was used for horticulture.

Town Bank V (Boat How): monuments *TB 354-67*

A small, scattered group of cairns and two short sections of stone bank were identified on the moderately sloping southern side of Boat How, between 310 m and 350 m OD (Fig 24). There were extensive brash deposits in the area and some of the cairns were also superimposed on natural rock outcrops, both of which made their definition difficult.

Town Bank VI (Boat How): monuments *TB 368-409*

This cairnfield was situated on well-drained, undulating land, between 290 m and 325 m OD (Fig 24), which had a thin turf cover and sporadic brash. The cairns were generally low, with angular stones, which had little lichen cover. The stone forming these cairns was found, through probing, to merge with the underlying natural brash. Given this, there is a possibility that many of the cairns are in fact natural features. However, some did have regular shapes and slightly rounded profiles, and it is therefore possible that areas of small outcropping stone were enlarged with stone cleared from the adjacent land.

Town Bank VII: monuments *TB 423-42*

This cairnfield comprised two small groups of cairns divided by an area of marsh, lying between 220 m and 235 m OD (Fig 24). The northern group (TB VIIA) was on an island of moderately drained land, while the southern group (TB VIIB; Fig 27) was on well-drained land. In general, the cairns were consistent with stone clearance, being small, ill defined, and low-lying. However, some of the cairns in the northern group were possibly natural, or enhanced natural features.

Town Bank VIII: monuments *TB 443-64*

A small field system was located on well-drained, moderately sloping land, lying between 170 m and 205 m OD (Fig 24). This field system also incorporated enclosures, roundhouses, stone boundaries, and occasional cairns.

There were three possible fields, defined by four parallel stone banks (*TB 450*, *TB 452*, *TB 458*, and *TB 464*; Fig 27), which were aligned downslope, although there was no evidence of soil slippage along the banks. They were edged to the south by the scarp slope that drops to the Worm Gill floodplain. A few cairns occurred within each of the fields.

Within the easternmost field was a small, ill-defined, roundhouse (*TB 462*; *c* 9.5 m in diameter), which was adjacent to a beck. It had a slight internal terrace, cut back into the slope, but lacked an

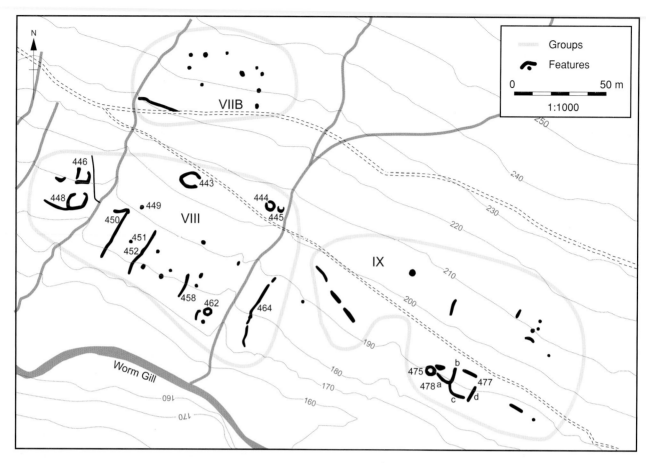

Figure 27: The TB VII-IX settlements, field system, and cairnfields

obvious entrance. Linked to the roundhouse was a small, rectilinear, enclosure (10 x 7 m). Two other roundhouses (*TB 444* and *TB 445*) were located further up the beck, but these were remote from the field system. *TB 444* had a substantial internal terrace and an entrance orientated north-west. Immediately adjacent was *TB 445*, which was a circular, terraced, platform, probably for a roundhouse, with no clear upslope edge.

Monument *TB 443* was a large, irregularly shaped, terraced enclosure, with a large, ill-defined entrance, and was remote from the field system, whilst monuments *TB 446* and *TB 448* were both rectilinear enclosures with ill-defined outer banks, and both exhibited soil slippage deposition against the lower banks. Extending east from these lower banks were lynchets, implying that cultivation was undertaken either within the enclosures, or in the areas immediately to the west.

Taken as a whole, these monuments form a small, seemingly self-contained, farmstead. It had a series of parallel, stone banks orientated downslope, which defined the extent of at least two fields, and within these were a few clearance cairns. Associated with the fields was certainly one roundhouse, with an attached enclosed yard, and

a further two houses were more remote from the fields, but within the immediate environs of the settlement. The two small adjacent enclosures (*TB 446* and *TB 448*) were open on the upper side and had down-slope lynchets, indicating that they were cultivated; given that they were relatively small, they may have been used for horticulture.

Town Bank IX (Worm Gill): monuments *TB 466-83*

The main part of this field system comprised a probable roundhouse associated with two possible plots (Fig 27). The putative roundhouse (*TB 475*; 11 m in diameter) had a regular, circular, shape, but lacked an obvious entrance, as this had probably been disturbed by the later construction of two stubs of dry-stone walling on top of the outer bank of the roundhouse. The site was for the most part located on a natural terrace, which lay between 185 m and 210 m OD.

The westernmost plot (*TB 478*) enclosed an area of *c* 158 m², and had a positive lynchet at the bottom of the plot, but no corresponding negative lynchet at the top. The easternmost plot (*TB 477*) was much larger (*c* 540 m²) and had possible lynchets at both the top and bottom. Though there was evidence of soil slippage within the plots, indicative of agriculture, some large boulders were also present, which would have impeded the movement of a plough, and may suggest hand cultivation.

Taken together, these monuments formed a small farmstead, composed of two small cultivation plots associated with a roundhouse, located on a natural bench above the flood plain of the Worm Gill. There were several stone banks and associated cairns elsewhere on the bench, sufficient to indicate that there were less intensive agricultural methods being practised in the vicinity of, though probably related to, the farmstead. The settlement was probably contemporary with TB VIII (*p 55*), found on the opposite side of an unnamed beck.

Town Bank X (Tongue How): monuments *TB 508-612*

A complex cairnfield lay on the gently sloping land of Tongue How (Fig 24), between 220 m and 260 m OD (Pl 44). It incorporated a number of significant alignments and there was a small, possibly cultivated, terrace at the lower end of the group. Within the cairnfield were at least two extremely large long cairns (*TB 591* and *TB 564*; Fig 28), which were possible funerary monuments.

The cairnfield was a mix of many small cairns, alongside a lesser number of large and prominent cairns. Many of these and some stone banks appeared to be aligned along three radial lines extending from a point to the north-east of the system (NY 0771 1003), although this was itself unmarked. The first of these comprised a stone bank (*TB 513*) and cairn (*TB 510*), whilst the second consisted of an alignment of at least seven cairns (Alignment A), possibly also incorporating feature *TB 515*. The third was an alignment of two stone banks and an elongated cairn (*TB 524*, *TB 547*, and *TB 548*), which may have continued after a dog-leg via cairns *TB 570-4*. These stone bank/cairn alignments appear to have defined the edge of activity areas. For example, between the first and second, there was a marked paucity of cairns, whereas the area between the second and third had a large concentration of cairns of all sizes. To the east of the third alignment was a small area devoid of cairns, and beyond that was a further concentrated cairn group. On the present evidence, it would appear that the alignments marked the lines of former field boundaries and, although not very clearly defined, this apparent alternating arrangement of fields with and without cairns compares with the radial field pattern observed at TB IV (*p 52*).

At the lower end of the cairnfield was a small, irregularly shaped terrace, in between a large straight bank/lynchet (*TB 590*), which had a sharp break of slope on the downward side, and a curved

Plate 44: The TB X (right), and TB XI, field systems, the latter overlain by the dry-stone stock pound (centre)

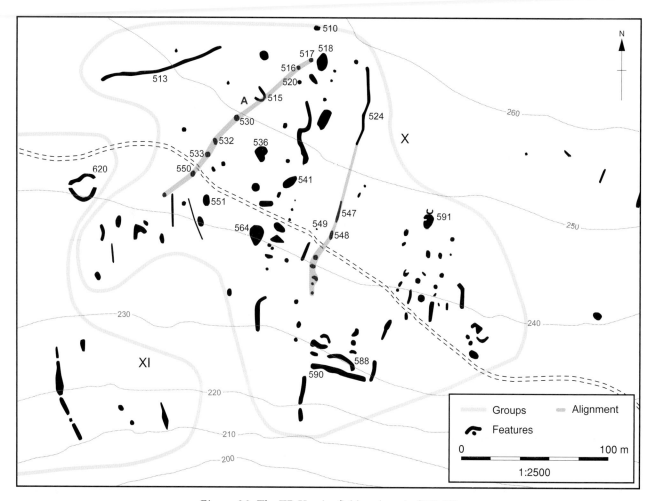

Figure 28: The TB X cairnfield and part of TB XI

irregular bank (*TB 588*). The amount of clearance stone around this feature, coupled with the apparent lynchet, would suggest that this formed a small, cultivated plot.

Within the cairnfield were also several cairns which had elements characteristic of funerary monuments (*TB 518, TB 536, TB 541, TB 551, TB 564,* and *TB 591*). *TB 518* was large (13.5 x 7.5 x 0.4 m), oval, well defined, and had two large boulders protruding from its centre. *TB 536* was large (11 x 0 x 0.7 m), very prominent, and pear-shaped, although its profile and shape were slightly irregular, particularly on the eastern side. *TB 541* was large (12 x 6 x 0.5 m), well defined, prominent, and oval, but it had been severely damaged by a parallel-sided cut which had been made through its centre. The appearance of this cut suggests the use of a mechanical excavator, and it would seem that the cairn had been robbed to provide metalling for the adjacent track. *TB 551* was well defined, large (8.5 x 4.5 x 0.8 m), prominent, and pear-shaped. It had a regular, rounded profile and there was a very large boulder placed on its top, which was possibly a marker stone. *TB 564* was very large (15 x 9 x 0.9 m), very prominent,

regular in profile, and pear-shaped, and had some large stones, possibly kerb stones, on its east side. Again, this cairn had a very large boulder set on its top, possibly representing a marker stone. *TB 591* was large (9.5 x 7.5 x 0.4 m), pear-shaped, and prominent. It had been truncated on its west side, and a later semi-circular, dry-stone structure had been constructed on top of its northern end, which would appear to have been a small bield.

Taken as a group, these possible funerary monuments had all been deliberately constructed and were distinct from the surrounding small, irregular, clearance-type cairns, having both marker and kerb stones. Although the cairns were elongated, only one of them (*TB 564*) was of sufficient size to fulfil the prerequisite parameters for a long cairn, as defined by Masters (1973), who indicated that such cairns should be between 15 m and 100 m in length. However, given that at least one of the cairns (*TB 564*) displayed all the characteristics of a deliberately constructed pear-shaped long cairn, it is possible that the remainder were also funerary cairns, grouped as a small cemetery, that could have pre-dated the field system and cairnfield.

58

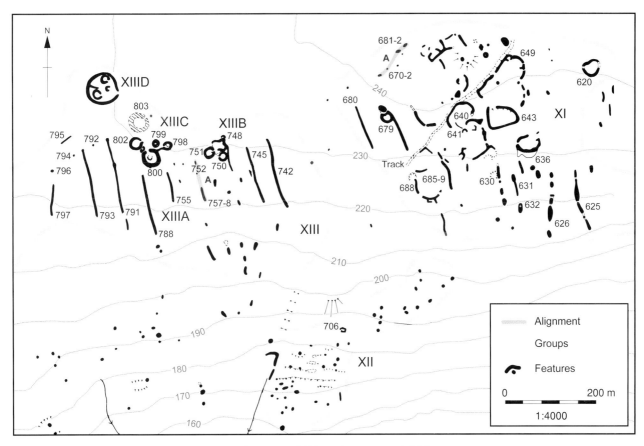

Figure 29: The TB XI-XIII settlements and field systems

Town Bank XI (Tongue How): monuments *TB 620-93*

An extremely complex area of banks, cairns, and inter-related enclosures lay on a moderately sloping, well-drained area of moorland, between 210 m and 245 m OD (Fig 24; Pl 44). This was in marked contrast to the area immediately to the north, which was flat and poorly drained, with peat cover. The cairns and banks were for the most part arranged in significant alignments that extended either across or downslope, and were evidently elements of an integrated field system.

In the centre of the settlement was a series of partial enclosures (Fig 29), none of which appeared to exhibit soil slippage, although in one case (*TB 636*) there was very clear evidence of terracing. The largest of these enclosures (*TB 649*) appears to have butted onto a smaller enclosure *TB 643*, suggesting that both formed the component parts of a double enclosure. The boundary of *TB 649* was very irregular in form and size. For instance, to the south-west it contained many large boulders, was prominent, and had a dry-stone structure, but further to the north-east there were sections in which it was ill defined, with small amounts of stone and no clear evidence of structure. The boundary also contained discontinuities and, although substantial sections of it were constructed

as a wall, there may have been sections where it had a more ephemeral form, comprising clearance stone placed along an impermanent boundary marker, such as a fence. A small roundhouse was incorporated into the northern corner of the enclosure, which is paralleled by the corner buildings found associated with the D-shaped enclosure on Hesk Fell (*HE 46d/c*; *Ch 5*, *p 251*). This roundhouse had a dry-stone wall around its northern side, an ill-defined entrance facing into the enclosure, and an approximately flat internal area. The southern part of the adjacent enclosure (*TB 643*) was decayed and ill defined, partly because a dry-stone shelter had been built on top of it, which is plotted on the 1867 First Edition 6" to 1 mile OS map. Internally, *TB 643* had a gentle slope as a result of extensive terracing up against the northern bank. Its entrance also led into the larger, adjacent enclosure (*TB 649*).

The other possible enclosures in this area were not as well defined. For example, the banks of *TB 685-9* represented a very incomplete enclosure, associated with a circular house platform (*TB 688*). *TB 640* was a further example of an incomplete enclosure, again associated with a circular platform (*TB 641*). These enclosures, with attached buildings, exhibited no evidence of soil slippage and probably had a function associated with stock control.

Enclosure *TB 636*, although also only partially enclosed, was a very different type of structure. It comprised a large platform (*c* 25 x 25 m), with an artificially flat internal area. The back of the terrace was set slightly into the northern slope, but the forward apron comprised a considerable volume of material, which was composed of soil and stone. The volume of the forward apron was far greater than could have been removed from the back of the terrace, suggesting that some soil and stone had been imported to build the platform. The surface of the platform was well drained by comparison with the adjacent moorland, being largely constructed of a porous material and being proud of the adjacent ground surface. Indeed, this may in part have provided a reason for constructing the platform in this monumental manner. The effort involved in building this platform would imply that it served a domestic, rather than agricultural, function, and it may have had timber structures built on it. The platform was paralleled at *SF 90* on Stainton Fell (*Ch 4, p 173*) and at *BS 213* on Barnscar (*Ch 4, p 184*).

Enclosure *TB 620* was an irregularly shaped enclosure (20 x 17.5 m), which was also terraced and had an approximately flat internal area. However, the terrace was largely formed by being cut into the slope and lay predominantly below the level of the surrounding moor; consequently, it was very badly drained and would have been an undesirable location for a domestic structure.

Unlike other Town Bank field systems (*eg* TB III, TB IV, TB VI, or TB X), there were no random scatters of cairns in this area. Instead, the cairns were generally aligned along field boundaries and related to a field system. On the southern side of the settlement area was a series of approximately parallel stone-banks/cairn alignments (*TB 625, TB 626, TB 630*, and *TB 631/2*). These contained large quantities of stone, but were very irregular in width, and probably reflect the deposition of clearance stone along the lines of field boundaries.

A further example of a cairn alignment was found at the north end of the settlement area (Alignment A), orientated towards the TB XIII settlement area (*p 60*). Stone banks *TB 679* and *TB 680* were also possibly related to the TB XIII settlement. They were parallel with, and very similar in form to, seven stone banks associated with TB XIII (Fig 29), and they may all have been part of a single field system. Stone bank *TB 679* had a lynchet-like profile, indicating soil slippage in the field between it and stone bank *TB 680*. Similarly, there were indications of cultivation on some of the banks (*eg TB 791* and *TB 793*) of the TB XIII settlement. At the top of bank *TB 679* was a prominent, well-defined, internally terraced, roundhouse, with no obvious entrance, which was linked into the field system. A

track ran through the centre of the settlement area, though this was probably not contemporary with the settlement and was perhaps part of a medieval route, which passes through this area towards Matty Benn's Bridge (Pl 39; NY 064 103).

Taken as a whole, the monuments found in this area formed a complex settlement, which included at least four possible domestic structures or platforms (*TB 636, TB 649, TB 688*, and *TB 679*). They were associated with a series of field plots defined by parallel stone banks (*TB 625, TB 626, TB 630, TB 631-2, TB 679*, and *TB 680*), some of which have lynchet profiles, suggesting cultivation. In addition, there was a series of partial enclosures, which also displayed evidence of soil slippage (*TB 643* and *TB 689*). The cairns were almost all aligned along plot boundaries and were generally very large and prominent, seemingly a product of very intensive and organised stone clearance. Together these features appeared to represent a broadly self-contained, agricultural settlement, the complexity and diversity of which may be indicative of an extended occupation.

Town Bank XII: monuments *TB 694-741*
This small group was situated on a naturally sloping terrace, lying between 160 m and 200 m OD, which was edged to the north and south by steep slopes (Fig 29). It included parallel lines of irregular, ill-defined, narrow strip-terraces, which were overlain by cairns. The cairns were irregular in form and would appear to have been cleared stone deposited along the terrace edges, to maximise the area of workable land in between. There were also some cairns away from the terracing. At the northern edge of the area was a small, rectilinear, dry-stone structure (*TB 706*), which was 7.1 x 5.2 m in size and survived to a height of 1.2 m. This type of rectilinear building was not found elsewhere in the survey area, but was closely comparable with the medieval type of simple farmstead, or shieling (Ramm 1970).

The terraces were components of a series of cultivation strips, with clearance stone deposited in mounds along their edges; these cultivation strips were distinct from other field systems noted elsewhere within Town Bank. It is probable that they were not only spatially associated with the rectangular building but were also contemporary with it, and this suggests that it was probably a small farming settlement, which may potentially have had a transhumant origin.

Town Bank XIII (Tongue How): monuments *TB 742-62* and *TB 788-812*
A complex area of settlement comprised a regular field system (TB XIIIA), associated with two farmsteads (TB XIIIB and TB XIIIC), with roundhouses and linked yards (Fig 30). Spatially associated with the

field system, but not necessarily contemporary, was an enclosed settlement, containing three roundhouses (TB XIIID). Also associated with this monument group was a large funerary round cairn (*TB 803*). The site group lay between 210 m and 230 m OD.

The field system

The field system (TB XIIIA) was in an area of uniformly sloping, well-drained land, and was defined by a series of parallel, ill-defined stone banks, which were orientated approximately downslope (*TB 797, TB 793, TB 791, TB 788, TB 755, TB 752/758, TB 745,* and *TB 742*). The field system probably also included field *TB 679/680*, which was parallel and broadly similar, but was spatially associated with TB XI (Fig 29). The stone banks were low, and contained irregular, but generally minimal, amounts of stone. There was no evidence of any dry-stone structure and they were consistent with the erratic deposition of stone clearance along the line of field boundaries. Small cairns (*TB 792, TB 794,* and *TB 796;* Fig 30) were aligned along the

top of the western section of the field system, two of which were incorporated into the termini of banks *TB 791* and *TB 793*. These were probably clearance cairns positioned beside the upper boundary of the two westernmost fields. Parallel to this was an extended alignment of short sections of stone bank (*TB 795, TB 806,* and *TB 809*), which may have represented the line of a further field boundary.

The fields defined by the stone banks were generally long, narrow, and had comparatively uniform widths, the fields between banks *TB 755* and *TB 793* being 28 m, 29 m, and 28 m wide respectively. The field to the east of *TB 755* had a probable eastern boundary marked by an alignment of stone bank and cairns (A), and its overall width was 32 m, which was in accord with the neighbouring fields. There was a marked paucity of clearance cairns within the fields, except between banks *TB 755* and *TB 745*, where the banks were less continuous. Such differences represented slightly varying stone clearance practices, and may

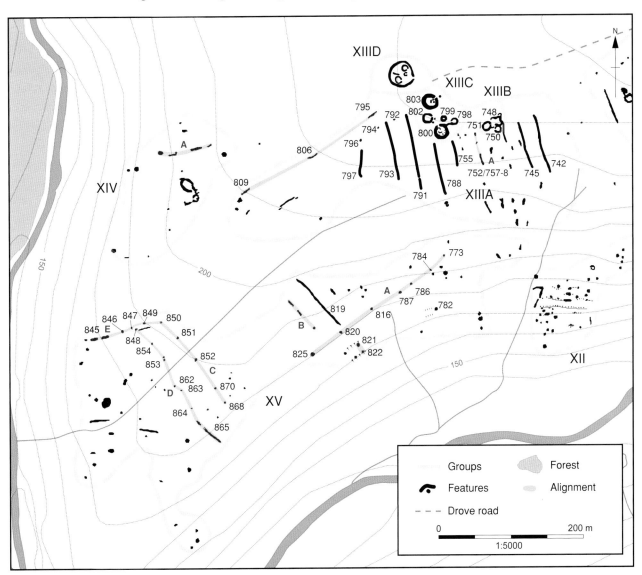

Figure 30: The TB XIII and TB XIV settlements, and TB XV field system

61

Plate 45: The excavation of roundhouse TB 750, *by Bill Fletcher,* c 1956

Plate 46: Roundhouse TB 750, *as reconstructed by Bill Fletcher, looking south*

be indicative of differing agricultural functions for the respective fields. Stone banks *TB 742* and, to a lesser extent, *TB 745*, had lynchet-like profiles, reflecting soil slippage on the western sides of the banks, probably as a result of ploughing, or ard cultivation.

The farmsteads

One of the farmsteads (TB XIIIB) found in this area was located adjacent to an area of cairns and patchy stone banks, and comprised three interconnected units. These were a roundhouse (*TB 750*), a sunken oval enclosure (*TB 751*), and an irregularly shaped enclosed area (*TB 748*) between the other two features.

The roundhouse (*TB 750*) was excavated and partly reconstructed by Bill Fletcher in *c* 1956 (W Fletcher *pers comm*; Pl 45), although it was not adequately recorded and remains unpublished (*p 49*). At the time of the survey, it comprised two to three courses of well-defined, dry-stone, masonry, in a regular, circular wall, with a well-defined entrance to the west, but precisely what form it had prior to Fletcher's work is not known. Fletcher, however, reported that he believed that the lines of the walls were genuine and that no excavation work or reconstruction was undertaken around the entrance (W Fletcher *pers comm*). The stone debris found within the structure was either used to build up the walls, or was dumped outside the structure. Narrow ditches around the outside of the wall were visible, which were presumably excavated in the 1950s but, because of these and the redeposited spoil, it is no longer clear how the roundhouse connected with the adjacent enclosures. The present plan of the structure is broadly similar to that produced by Spence (1938), which would suggest that the excavation and reconstruction did not seriously distort the original structure (Pl 46). However, Spence (*op cit*, 68) records that the entrance to the irregular enclosure (*TB 748*; *see below*) was via a 1.2 m-wide alley in between the roundhouse and the 'inturning of the east wall' of the irregular enclosure, whereas now any possible access has been obscured by spoil.

Monument *TB 751* was a very well-defined oval enclosure (14 x 11 m), which was sunk below the surrounding ground level by as much as 1.2 m. Around the edge was a bank of medium-sized stones and large boulders, with no evidence of structure; the internal area was irregular, but approximately flat. The rough construction of the banks, and the slightly irregular, elongated shape, would have made any building difficult to roof, and therefore it was more likely that it was unroofed.

The irregular enclosure (*TB 748*) was found to the north of the roundhouse and enclosure, and was defined by an outer bank containing a large amount of stone, but was irregular in width and quantity of stone and had no evidence of any dry-stone structure. The irregularity of shape would suggest that it was never roofed.

Taken as whole, the complex appears to have been a farmstead, comprising a small roundhouse with two ancillary enclosures, probably relating to stock control. The three enclosures were interconnected, such that access to enclosure *TB 751* was only through enclosure *TB 748*, whereas the access to the roundhouse was independent of the other two, so separating the domestic and agricultural functions of the farmstead. Although the elements of the settlement were interlinked, there was no attempt to incorporate any defensive function, and it was not an enclosed type of settlement.

The second farmstead (TB XIIIC) found in this area also comprised three principal interconnected, circular enclosures (Pl 47). Of these, *TB 802* displayed all the criteria of a roundhouse, in that it had a regular, well-defined, fairly prominent outer bank (13.7 x 13.2 m), and the entrance was narrow (1.5 m wide) and faced east, away from the prevailing winds. The area within the bank had been internally terraced and contained no obvious internal features.

Monument *TB 800* was a very different form of enclosure. It was large (21 x 19.5 m) and its internal area had been sunk considerably below the present ground level (*c* 1.8 m between the top of the outer bank and the floor; Pl 48); it was also crudely terraced, so that a slight slope remains towards the south. Within the enclosure was a small, three-sided structure with patchy lichen cover on the stones, which demonstrated that it was comparatively recent. This overlay a decayed, ill-defined curved bank, which may have been the remnants of an earlier structure. The outer bank of the enclosure was very prominent, with steep internal sides, and was slightly irregular, and including some large, jagged boulders protruding from the turf cover. To the north was a large entrance which, according to Spence (1938, 67), had large orthostats on either side of it; however, these were no longer visible. Although the bank was a little higher than the surrounding ground level, its volume was considerably less than that of the artificial hollow within, which would indicate that the material from within the enclosure was removed from the site.

Monument *TB 798* was linked to enclosure *TB 800* by a length of bank, and comprised an oval, well-defined, regular outer bank. Within it was a prominent, sub-triangular cairn butting onto the inside of the bank, which took up most of the internal space. This feature would have been an inconsistent element within a dwelling, and it was not necessarily contemporary with the outer bank.

Plate 47: The TB XIII field system, looking south, with TB XIIID (foreground) and TB XIIIC to the south-east

Plate 48: The interior of sunken enclosure TB 800, containing a later dry-stone bield

Monument *TB 799* was a large prominent mound (8 m in diameter), with a small, irregular, central depression. It had the appearance of a disturbed round cairn and appears to have been an incongruous element within the farmstead.

The enclosed settlement

A large (37 x 35 m) enclosed settlement (TB IIID) was identified on flat, poorly drained ground (Pl 47). The outer bank was generally well defined, prominent, and contained a regular quantity of stone, and it also displayed evidence of a dry-stone structure on its western side. The settlement contained three well-defined, circular structures, which would appear to have been roundhouses (Pl 49). Their entrances, as well as that of the enclosing bank, were all orientated towards the east, away from the prevailing winds.

The enclosure was slightly remote from the other settlements and field system, and was not necessarily contemporary with them. A very similar form of settlement was found on the opposite side of Worm Gill, at Thornholme Farm (Crawford and George 1983, 27), though it was considerably larger (*c* 70 m across) and contained seven roundhouses.

The funerary round cairn

Adjacent to monument *TB 799* (Fig 30) was a large, circular bank (*TB 803*), which represented a spoil tip from an excavation of a large round cairn, conducted by Bill Fletcher in 1956 (Pl 50). According to Spence (1938), the original cairn was 18.9 x 17.6 m in plan, and *c* 2 m high, with two approximately centrally located depressions, attesting to earlier disturbance. Nothing now survives of the cairn, but some buried elements of the site may survive, as Bill Fletcher (*pers comm*) claimed not to have excavated through the 'floor' of the cairn. There were, however, three small hollows in the present ground surface, which were probably attributable to his excavations. The excavation was not

Plate 49: Enclosed settlement TB XIIID, looking north

recorded but, from sketches that Fletcher produced after the event, it would appear that there was a small cist (0.9 x 0.61 m) on the eastern side of the cairn, comprising nine small uprights (Pl 51). There was also a 'scatter of charcoal' associated with it, but no skeletal remains were noted, which may suggest that a former cremation burial was beneath, or had been inserted into, the cairn. The only other finds recorded were a piece of deer antler and a sandstone 'rubbing stone' (W Fletcher *pers comm*).

Town Bank XIV (River Calder): monuments *TB 828-44*

A farmstead and associated scatter of cairns were recorded on a gently sloping, well-drained area of exposed fell, lying between 180 m and 205 m OD

Plate 50: The spoil mounds from the excavation, by Bill Fletcher, of round cairn TB 803

Plate 51: The cist exposed in the centre of round cairn
TB 803

(Fig 24). The farmstead was similar to those of TB XIII (*p 64*) and comprised a sunken, oval enclosure linked by a wall to a roundhouse (Fig 30). Large outer banks marked the edges of the enclosure, which had a wide, well-defined entrance orientated towards the roundhouse. The internal area was terraced, approximately level, and sunken to 0.4 m below the surrounding ground level. The surface of the enclosure floor was accordingly badly drained and would have been inappropriate for human accommodation.

The roundhouse was on higher, better-drained ground. It had a regular, circular outer bank with a small, well-defined entrance on the western side. The internal area was terraced into the hillside and was approximately level and flat, with no surface stone. The surrounding cairns were loosely scattered and there was a possible field boundary represented by the alignment of cairns / stone banks (A).

Town Bank XV (River Calder): monuments *TB 763-87, TB 813-27,* and *TB 845-93*

A patchy group of cairns and short stone banks was recorded along the gently sloping, well-drained south-west edge of Town Bank, lying between 210 m and 160 m OD (Fig 24). Although first appearances suggested that these sites were randomly distributed, closer examination showed a series of alignments of cairns and stone banks, which may represent the boundaries of an irregular field system.

At the north-eastern side of the group was an alignment of seven cairns (A; Fig 30), perpendicular to a north-west / south-east-aligned stone bank (*TB 819*). Taken together, these may represent a field system, particularly as stone bank *TB 819* had a slight lynchet-like profile, was parallel to an alignment of stone banks / cairns (B), and was possibly formerly one of the boundaries of a cultivated field. Moreover, this possible field was very similar to those found in the TB XIII field system (*p 61*), and the dimensions of the field were also similar: its width was 28 m, compared to an average width of 29.6 m for the TB XIII fields.

Given its character and size, it is possible that this field was broadly contemporary with the TB XIII field system.

At the western end of the group was a pair of parallel alignments (C and D), which were approximately perpendicular to a further significant cairn alignment (E). Together, these potentially represent the surviving elements of an extended field system.

At the north-western end of the group were several small 'terraces' associated with clearance-type cairns (*TB 782, TB 821,* and *TB 822*). They were too irregular to have been house platforms, and also had rounded bottoms; in consequence, they are more likely to have been the result of soil slippage rather than deliberate terracing.

Conclusions

The archaeological landscape of Town Bank is extraordinarily significant; not only does it display activity extending between the neolithic and medieval periods, but it demonstrates a complex development of probable Bronze / Iron Age settlements and field systems. Furthermore, these cairnfield and settlement remains are very distinct from those found on Stockdale Moor (*p 68*), with sites displaying a broad variation of character, from the simple, random type of cairnfield, such as at TB VII, to the complex farmstead, such as those within the TB XIII group. It is the latter type, however, which makes up the majority of the Town Bank sites, and it is these well-developed settlements that give Town Bank its notable character.

Neolithic/Bronze Age funerary activity

The earliest activity on Town Bank is represented by one, and possibly more, funerary-type long cairns in the TB X group (*p 57*). There are several large, and prominent, cairns that are distinct from the other much smaller cairns in the cairnfield, and one in particular, *TB 564* (Fig 28), is a probable long cairn, which may date to the neolithic period or early Bronze Age (Smith 1974, 128-36). This cairn, for example, is pear-shaped, very prominent, has a possible kerb, and also has a large marker stone on its summit. The remainder of the surrounding cairnfield was not physically related to this, or the other big cairns, and was not necessarily contemporary with them.

Funerary activity extending into the Bronze Age is implied by the large round cairn (*TB 803*) in the TB XIII site group (Fig 30). The cairn was very large, measuring *c* 18.9 x 17.6 x 2 m plan, and had an off-centre cist for a presumed inhumation. Round cairns, such as this, have a broad date range that extends throughout the Bronze Age (Yates 1984b, 2-4). However, despite its proximity to the rest of the TB XIII components (*p 60*), there is no direct relationship between these and the round cairn, and therefore this does not imply a similar date for the settlement.

Primary cairnfields
Town Bank demonstrates a broad development of settlement / agricultural systems, from the basic primary cairnfield, through to arable field systems and associated permanent stone-founded roundhouses. The recorded cairns are similar to those found at Stockdale Moor (*p 68*), and comprise a series of early, primary, cairnfields of randomly distributed cairns scattered across the area. Few, if any, vestiges of field boundaries, let alone a field system, are associated with these cairns, and they are also not typically associated with domestic structures. Examples of these primary cairnfields include those found in the TB VI and TB VII groups (Fig 24). The TB III group (*p 50*) is a further example of a random-type primary cairnfield, except that it has a seemingly later enclosure and farmstead superimposed on one end of it. Other examples of simple cairnfields have been found to be of Bronze Age date (*Ch 2, p 28*). Typologically, this is also the most basic form of agricultural activity exhibited at Town Bank, so in theory these cairnfields should be earlier in date than the other, more developed, field systems. However, in the absence of scientific dating evidence, such typological dating is inherently unreliable and needs to be treated with caution.

Development of field systems
Town Bank is characterised by a series of relatively sophisticated field systems, extending in a linear spread along south-facing, well-drained, sloping areas, each being associated with either stone-founded roundhouses, or house platforms. There is a degree of commonality, in that these field systems have field boundaries, comprising stone banks, that are, for the most part, orientated downslope, and there are relatively few cross-slope boundaries. TB IV, for example, has a slightly radial-shaped field system (Fig 26), reflecting the fact that it is located on a naturally curved spur. There are, however, some, possibly significant, differences in the character of the field systems at the eastern and western ends of Town Bank. At the eastern end were large, irregularly shaped fields, associated with large concentrations of randomly distributed clearance cairns (*eg* TB III and TB IV), whereas at the western end, the field systems (TB XI, TB XIII, and TB XV) had only a few randomly distributed clearance cairns, and the unwanted stone appears to have been piled into large, irregular alignments of stone banks (*eg* TB 625 and *TB 626*; Fig 29). The fields defined by the banks were often long, narrow, and small, but usually had regular widths (*eg* TB XIIIA; Fig 30).

It is probable that the differences between the various systems reflect the use of different agricultural practices across Town Bank. For instance, areas containing randomly distributed cairns are not conducive to the use of a plough, or an ard, and, as there were lynchet profiles exhibited on some of the TB XIII and TB XV field boundaries, the differences between the field systems probably reflect a change of emphasis from pastoral towards arable farming. They appear to represent different stages of agricultural development and, while it is possible that these two contrasting farming practices were in contemporary use, they would appear to have had a different overall historical development. The predominance of cairns at TB IV may reflect an extended development from a primary cairnfield, whereas the westernmost system (TB XIII) may imply newly established field systems, which were not constrained by the presence of earlier agricultural remains. So, on this basis, the two systems may have had contemporary use, though the eastern seemingly had earlier origins.

In between these two, somewhat distinct, types of field systems are other more transitional examples, such as TB XI (*p 59*), which appears to represent a transitional type between those settlements associated with a cairnfield (*eg* TB IV), and those settlements associated with narrow fields (*eg* TB XIII). As such, this transitional type included a mixture of features from both categories. It had a parallel field system, similar to that of TB XIII, but also a possible house platform (*TB 636*; Fig 29), similar to one (*TB 82*; Fig 25) from the TB III settlement. It is also extremely complex, with a diversity of forms of pastoral enclosure, and there was evidence of more than one phase of construction (*ie TB 649* appears to have butted *TB 643*; *p 59*). In addition, the transitional type of field system at TB XI appears to have had a more extended and complex development than the neighbouring TB XIII field system. The implied longevity of this field system, coupled with these transitional features, reinforces the idea of the progressional development of settlement form.

Farmsteads
A distinctive type of unenclosed farmstead was found at Town Bank, comprising a large sunken enclosure linked to a roundhouse with, in some cases, additional enclosures (for instance, within groups TB XIIIB, TB XIIIC, TB XIV, and TB IV; Fig 24). In some cases, the sunken pounds had well-constructed entrances and well-defined, regular, outer banks. Indeed, in the case of *TB 800* (TB XIIIC), the volume of spoil removed from the large, sunken, enclosure was far greater than that now held within its outer banks, which would suggest that a substantial part of the interior of the enclosure had been removed. In this area, the ground was not particularly well drained, and it is probable

that conditions were similar in antiquity. The sunken enclosures would therefore have been unsuitable for domestic accommodation, as they were below the adjacent ground level and would have thus been extremely damp. Given this, it is instead more likely that they served as byres for stock. A sunken floor was a common feature of stock pounds within complex enclosed settlements (*eg AF 203; Ch 7, p 309*) and almost certainly reflected the practice of the winter corralling of stock, and the subsequent removal of the manure and churned up mud for putting onto the fields. Over some time, this probably resulted in the characteristic sunken interior found at these farmsteads.

The uniformity of the farmsteads would suggest that they were broadly contemporary, although examples are associated with different types of field system. For example, the TB XIIIB and TB XIIIC farmsteads were linked to regular, narrow, field systems, whereas the TB IV farmstead was associated with a large, irregular, cairnfield type of field system. The TB XIIIB farmstead appears to have been contemporary with its adjacent field system, because a stone bank that extended from it formed part of the parallel field system, and was separated from its neighbour by a 24 m gap, which was a typical width for these fields. Conversely, the TB IV (*TB 291*; Fig 26) farmstead was not directly linked to the adjacent field system, and was very different in form from the unenclosed, ungrouped, roundhouses (*TB 236, TB 241,* and *TB 303*), which form an integral part of the field system. Thus, farmstead *TB 291* was not necessarily contemporary with the establishment of the field system, or the unenclosed roundhouses, and may reflect a later phase of the TB IV settlement.

The dating of these farmsteads is somewhat uncertain, given that none has been excavated or dated by other means, and there is also a scarcity of dated parallels within the North West. There are, however, some dated examples of unenclosed, stone-founded roundhouses from Northumberland, which are potentially comparable to the Town Bank examples (*eg TB 236, TB 241,* and *TB 303*). These Northumbrian examples span a broad period from about 1300 cal BC to *c* 100 cal BC (Gates 1983, 117; Jobey 1985, 180-4; Haselgrove 2002, 61), and suggest a late Bronze or early Iron Age date for the Town Bank farmsteads.

Simple Enclosed Farmstead
A later stage of activity at Town Bank is possibly represented by the simple enclosed settlement (TB XIIID; Fig 30) at the western end of the area. While this is in the general area of the TB XIIIA field system, there is no apparent relationship between the two. As such, it would appear to have been a later reoccupation of the site and, in the absence of a related field system, probably worked within a purely pastoral economy. There are other examples of this type of

enclosed settlement in West Cumbria, notably that near Thornholme Farm, on the opposite side of Worm Gill (Crawford and George 1983, 27). The Glencoyne Park 6 settlement is also similar, in Matterdale (Hoaen and Loney 2003; 2004), which probably, following its establishment in the early Iron Age, had an extended life. Northumbrian parallels (Jobey and Tait 1966; *Ch 2, pp 34-6*) with a similar plan, but of timber construction, suggest an Iron Age date, but could also date from the early Roman period.

Medieval activity
The latest phase of significant activity was represented by the small settlement, TB XII (Fig 29), which comprised a small, single-celled rectilinear building, associated with a series of parallel cultivation terraces. The simple, remote, character of the building is suggestive of a medieval shieling, which is a type of monument that is often associated with small-scale cultivation features (Ramm 1970, 44). Such monuments were also found elsewhere during the LDNPS (*Ch 2, p 38*). This settlement is, however, not in character with the other Town Bank settlements, and is likely to reflect an isolated reoccupation of the moor.

Stockdale Moor

Stockdale Moor is an extensive area of undulating, but generally low, unenclosed moorland positioned between the River Bleng and Worm Gill (Fig 22). It is an area containing extensive cairnfields, which are located across the gently sloping and typically well-drained moorland. The north-eastern limit of the area is defined by steep slopes leading to the summits of Cawfell and Haycock, while Swainson Knott and Ponsonby Fell mark the south-west limits. The fast-flowing Worm Gill divides the Stockdale Moor sites from the large and complex settlements on Town Bank. Deep peat deposits were also found around the highest point of Stockdale Moor, where the gradient was most shallow. As a consequence, the component cairns of a small cairnfield, SM II (*p 73*) on top of the moor were partly obscured and were ill defined. Although the gradient was not particularly steep throughout the area, there were no extensive mires found, and only occasionally were cairnfields edged by mire. The significant exceptions were a narrow mire on either side of a beck, which defined the north-western edge of cairnfield SM I (*p 70*), and small patchy mires around cairnfield, SM V (*pp 75-6*).

Archaeological history
The earliest cartographic record of the antiquities on Stockdale Moor is the 1867 First Edition 6" to 1 mile OS map, which depicts the approximate location of Sampson's Bratfull long cairn (*SM 435; p 71*) and a sheepwash (*SM 136*). However, all the major

cairnfields were shown, to some extent, on OS mapping dating to 1926, with the exception of Monks Graves (SM VII). Furthermore, parts of the SM I, SM II, and SM III cairnfields, and Sampson's Bratfull, have been scheduled as Ancient Monuments on the basis of the archaeological detail shown on this mapping.

The earliest descriptive record of the Stockdale Moor settlements dates from 1877 (Clifton Ward 1878, 248-9). Clifton Ward (*op cit*, 248) briefly described Sampson's Bratfull (*SM 435; p 71*) and the large round cairn on the summit of Stockdale Moor (*SM 436; p 71*), which he recorded as containing 'many small circular pits, about 2 yards across'. The other summit cairns (*SM 437* and *SM 438; p 69*) and the existence of many smaller cairns were also noted. Following this, Parker (1904, 110-11), in the early part of the twentieth century, published illustrations of the two large cairns (*SM 435* and *SM 436*), a circular structure (*SM 496; p 71*), which he described as a 'circular tumulus', and long cairn (*SM 739*), which he described as a 'star-fish cairn' (*p 72*).

The only archaeological mapping undertaken prior to the present survey was by Spence (1939), who produced a notional plan of the Monks Graves cairn group (SM VII; *pp 78-80*) and a more detailed plan of the Caw Gill enclosure (*SM 139; p 77*). Although there was evidence of antiquarian disturbance at most of the larger cairns, the only reported excavations were by Bill Fletcher, who dug a trench into the centre of Sampson's Bratfull in the early 1950s (Crawford and George 1983, 25). However, there are no published records of Fletcher's findings.

The survey area
The survey was undertaken between April and May 1985 on 4.6 km[2] of unenclosed moorland (Fig 23). The survey resulted in the discovery of 838 monuments, which were found within nine site groups (Fig 31). The remains comprised cairnfields, of varied levels of complexity. Of these, the most extensive was SM I, at the southernmost extent of the area, which incorporated several stone banks and cairn alignments, indicative of a simple field system. The other cairnfields were smaller, and had occasional banks and cairn alignments, which may again be indicative of simple field systems. Possibly the most distinctive aspect of the area was that it included a substantial number of very large funerary cairns, ranging from the large long cairn, Sampson's Bratfull (*SM 435; p 71*), to a line of three large round cairns on the high point of Stockdale Moor (*SM 436-8; pp 69-70*). In the northern part of the area, the sizable cairnfield of Monks Graves (SM VII) was also surveyed, possibly

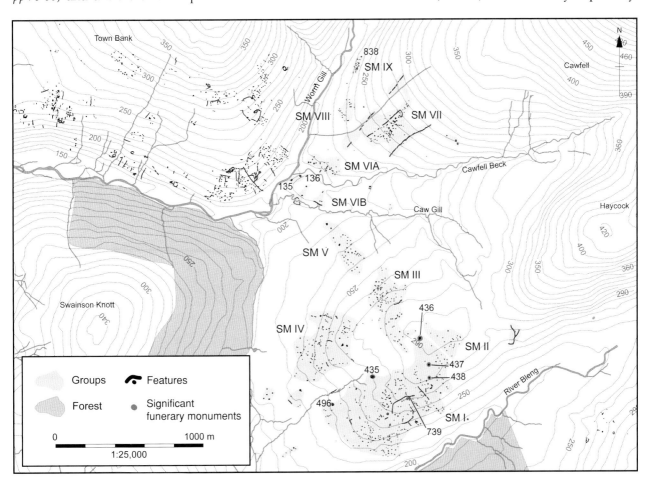

Figure 31: Monument distribution within the Stockdale Moor survey area

incorporating a Bronze Age cemetery, defined by a group of putative funerary round and ring cairns.

Stockdale Moor I: monuments *SM 436-52* and *SM 496-807*

This was the largest of the cairnfields (Fig 31), and comprised mainly randomly distributed small cairns. However, it also incorporated a series of stone banks and cairn alignments that were indicative of the development of a simple field system within an extensive area of improved land. This cairnfield comprised mainly small, ill-defined, cairns on a well-drained, gently sloping area of moorland. The main concentrations of cairns were towards the southern end, where they formed a wide band, which followed the contours, partly on a natural terrace. The north-western part of the cairnfield was also on moderately flat land, but in an area of natural stone outcrops, which confused the interpretation of some of the sites.

Field systems

The central part of this area was occupied by two possible fields (Fig 32), which were defined by discontinuous stone banks. The more obvious (SM IA), the westernmost of the two (*i*), had a large gap to the south-west, but otherwise was well bordered. It contained very few cairns, but did contain a natural gully, and an abundance of surface stone, which meant that it was generally unsuitable for cultivation. The other field (*ii*) was found immediately to the east (SM IB), and was bounded discontinuously on only three sides. In contrast to the adjacent field (*i*), it had a moderate concentration of cairns, which did not extend beyond the lines of its defining stone banks, suggesting that the cairns and the field boundaries were in contemporary use. The land within field *ii* was well drained, had a uniform, moderate, slope, and was better-quality agricultural land than that to the west. The differences between the two fields perhaps suggest that they were used for different agricultural functions.

To the west of field *i* was an area (SM IC*iii*) that was largely devoid of cairns, apart from a small, compact group (*SM 651-4*) at its centre. It was very poorly defined by a band of cairns to the south and west (*SM 535-79* and *SM 628-50*) and another smaller group of cairns to the north (*SM 580-90*). The area had a gently sloping, relatively well-drained topography that could be agriculturally viable, and thus, although poorly defined, it was possibly an agricultural plot.

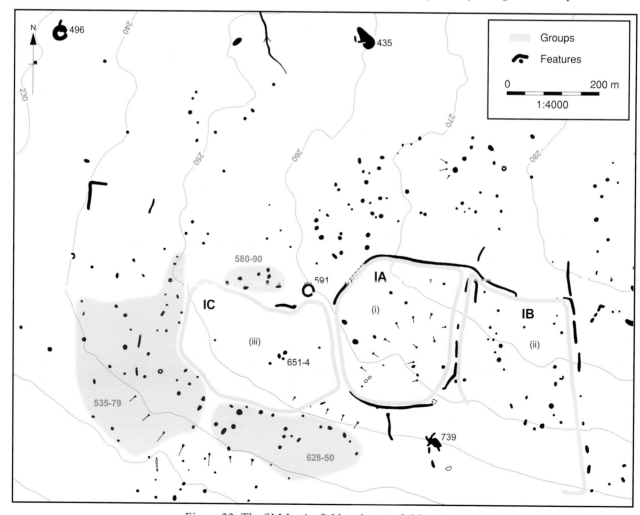

Figure 32: The SM I cairnfield and proto-field system

70

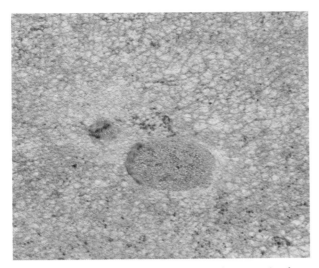

Plate 52: Round cairn SM 436, on the summit of Stockdale Moor

Adjacent to both fields *i* and *iii* was a ring bank (*SM 591*), comprising a regular, low, circular bank with an eastern entrance. However, it had no internal terracing, despite being on a gentle gradient. Its association with the adjacent field systems suggested that it might have been a domestic structure, but it also displayed similarities to some of the SM VII ring cairns (*p 78*).

Funerary monuments

Around the outside of the cairnfield were four large cairns which, because of their size and prominence, suggested funerary monuments. Three of these were aligned along the highest, and most prominent, part of the moor (*SM 435, SM 436,* and *SM 496;* Fig 31) and were not directly associated with the nearby cairnfields.

One of these aligned cairns (*SM 436;* Pl 52) had a diameter of 14.2 m and was up to 1.9 m in height (Pl 53). There were five sub-circular depressions within the body of the cairn, which each displayed to some extent evidence of a dry-stone internal revetment. These may have been deliberately constructed features, rather than the by-products of antiquarian investigations, since the earliest descriptive narrative (Clifton Ward 1878, 249) referred to them. Moreover, it was evident that the depressions were not recent and it is probable that they were created as bields to provide shelter to shepherds.

Another aligned cairn, known as Sampson's Bratfull (*SM 435;* Fig 32), was the largest of the funerary monuments (Ch 2; Pl 54). Although it was found towards the higher part of the moor, it was located in a slight hollow on poorly drained ground, and was spatially slightly remote from elements of the cairnfield. It is a very well-constructed, trapezoidal long monument (25 x 13.5 m) and its form is typical of a neolithic long cairn (*cf* Masters 1984). There were four sub-circular depressions (each *c* 1-2 m in diameter) set into the body of the cairn. Again, these were not a result of recent disturbance, as they were first reported in 1878 (Clifton Ward 1878, 249). The sides of at least one of the depressions were internally revetted with a very

Plate 53: Round cairn SM 436, looking east

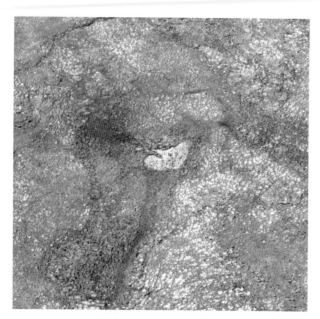

Plate 54: Sampson's Bratfull (SM 435; centre), a presumed neolithic long cairn

crude dry-stone structure, similar to that seen in cairn *SM 436 (p 71)*. The revetment stones were similar in size to those of the main body of the cairn and this depression appeared to have been a very basically designed feature; like those in *SM 436*, it is most probable that these features were bields. A trench had also been excavated into the main body of the cairn from the southern side, whilst an elongated mound of stone, extending outwards from the trench, probably represents spoil from this excavation. This feature was not mentioned in the descriptions from 1904 (Parker 1904) or 1950 (Daniel 1950) and was probably the results of Fletcher's unrecorded excavations during the 1950s (Crawford and George 1983, 25).

The third aligned monument (*SM 496*; Fig 32) was a well-defined, internally kerbed ring feature (Pl 55), which was prominently located on top of a small hillock, remote from any field system. The outer bank contained a large proportion of small stones, which is abnormal for dry-stone construction, and there was also an eastern-facing entrance, with orthostats on either side, and a bank extending out of the northern side. Although it has some similarities with the Moel Goedog complex ring cairn (Lynch 1979, 2-3), the entrance suggests that it was more probably a roundhouse.

On the opposite side of the cairnfield from Sampson's Bratfull was another large, pear-shaped cairn (*SM 739*; Fig 32; Pl 56). A bield had been set into its main body, which had patchy lichen cover on its component stones and was clearly a relatively modern feature. However, there were also four small stubs of 'wall' protruding from the body of the cairn, which had uniform lichen cover over their component stones. These were not modern features, but were not necessarily contemporary with the cairn. It had previously been

Plate 55: Entrance to probable roundhouse SM 496, looking south-west

Plate 56: Pear-shaped long cairn SM 739, with radiating arms, reminiscent of a star-fish cairn

described as a 'star-fish' cairn (Parker 1904, 111), and was reminiscent of round cairns on Askham Fell (*AF 130* and *AF 119*; *Ch 7, p 306*), which had similar radial banks.

Stockdale Moor II: monuments *SM 453-77*

A small group of cairns was recorded on the flat, peat-covered land on top of the moor, near the north-eastern limb of the SM I cairnfield (Fig 31). The cairns were ill-defined, low, turf-covered mounds, with no stones protruding, although stone was found under the surface during probing. The extent of peat growth over these cairns discriminated them from the neighbouring cairns of SM I, and it may reflect either chronological differences, or a faster rate of peat growth in this area.

Stockdale Moor III: monuments *SM 195-310*

This was a simple (primary) type of cairnfield without field systems, funerary monuments, or dwellings (Fig 31; Pl 57). It was divisible into two distinct sub-groups, the first (SM IIIA; Fig 33) comprising 32 cairns, being the southernmost of the cairn groups found on a flat plateau on top of Stockdale Moor. It had a low density of generally ill-defined cairns, and was divided from the second group of cairns found in this area by a sharp break of slope.

The second sub-group of cairns (SM IIIB) was located downslope and to the north-west of the first group, and was situated on a moderately sloping, well-drained area of moorland, on the northern side of Stockdale Moor. This area was also characterised by sporadic patches of outcropping brash. This group of cairns was relatively large, containing 78 cairns, which were very densely distributed. The cairns varied in size, with those at the northern side of the group being noticeably larger than those upslope, and to the south. The cairns had an essentially random distribution, and there were no significant alignments, although there was a short section of stone bank (*SM 275*) extending east/west at the northernmost edge of the cairnfield.

Stockdale Moor IV: monuments *SM 311-434* and *SM 493-94*

This was a large, low-density cairnfield, comprising 125 cairns and banks, on a moderately drained, gently sloping area of moorland (Fig 31). There was

Plate 57: The SM III cairnfield, looking west

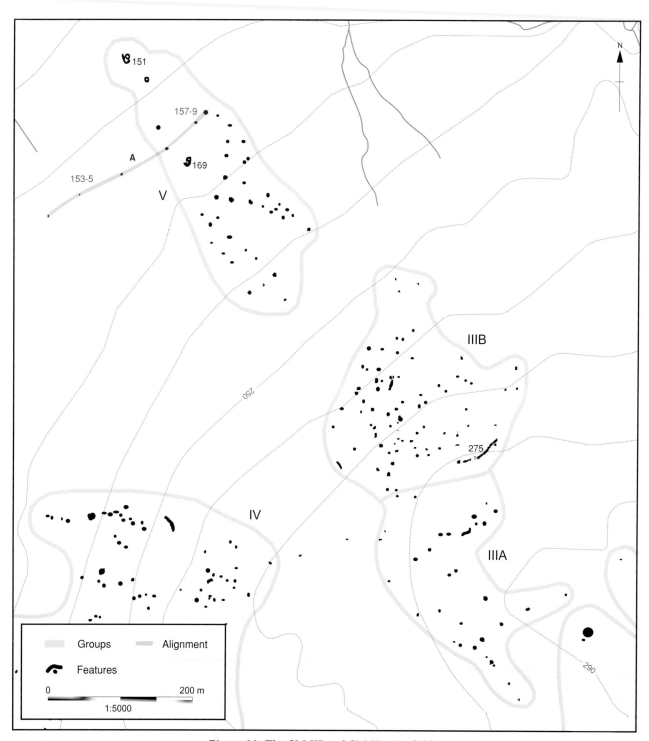

Figure 33: The SM III and SM V cairnfields

a sharp break of slope, approximately along the 260 m contour, which divided the north-westernmost from the north-eastern part, although, there was no significant change of the distribution pattern of cairns between these. The cairns were generally small, ill defined, and consistent with stone clearance.

A sub-triangular area, 170 x 126 m in extent, within the cairnfield was characterised by a very low density of cairns, although it was loosely bordered by short sections of stone bank (*SM 365, SM 424,* and *SM 434;* Fig 34), and by a significant cairn alignment (*SM 428-32*). Despite its poor definition, there is a possibility that this was a field.

Isolated from, and to the south-west of, the main part of the cairnfield was a ring feature (*SM 493*), which was located on a slight rise. It was 13.5 m in diameter, and the outer edge of the bank was well defined, although the inner edge was slightly irregular and in places poorly defined. There was no clear entrance associated with this monument. Its interpretation is uncertain,

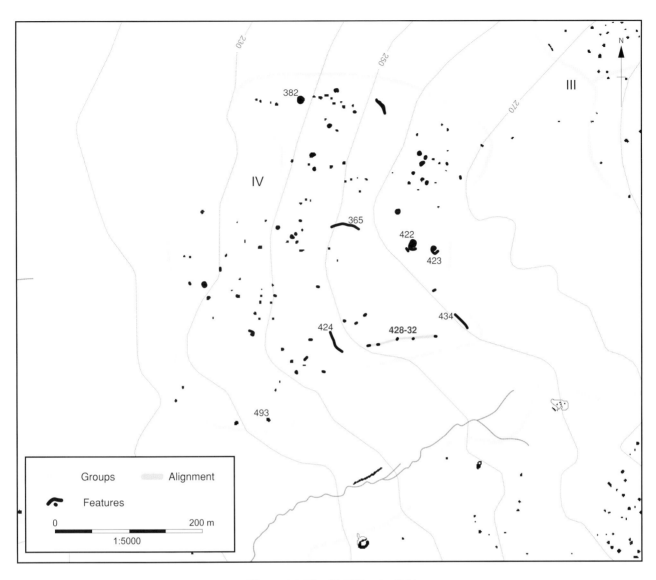

Figure 34: The SM IV cairnfield

but, given that it was set on a local high point and was remote from the nearest cairnfield, it is likely that it was a small ring cairn, rather than a roundhouse.

Within the cairnfield were three large cairns (*SM 382, SM 422,* and *SM 423*) which, in terms of their prominence, definition, and size, were distinct from the surrounding clearance-type cairns. Cairn *SM 382* was in the northernmost part of the cairnfield and was a very well-defined round cairn with a rounded profile (0.6 m high), a regular shape, and with a diameter of 9.3 m. Given its distinctive, prominent, and well-defined character, it is probable that this was a round funerary cairn. The two other large cairns (*SM 422* and *SM 423)* were together on a slight topographical high point, at the eastern side of the cairnfield, within an area that had relatively few cairns. *SM 422* was a 14.5 m-long, pear-shaped mound, with well-defined edges, and two linear hollows in its eastern side that possibly reflect structural

components (Pl 58). Cairn *SM 423* comprised a low round cairn with a partial semi-circular enclosure attached to its south-eastern side, and was 10.5 m in length (Pl 59). The function of these two very distinctive cairns cannot be determined reliably, but that they were for funerary purposes cannot be excluded.

Stockdale Moor V: Monuments *SM 151-94*

This was a small cairnfield of 43 cairns on gently sloping moorland on the northern slopes of Stockdale Moor (Fig 31). The area had small to medium depths of peat deposits and areas of poor drainage beyond the cairnfield, which may in part have dictated the extent of the land improvement associated with the cairns.

In general, the cairns were consistent with stone clearance, yet they were significantly larger, more prominent, and more widely spaced than those of the nearby SM III cairnfield (p 73). The lower, northernmost edge of the cairn distribution coincided

75

Plate 58: Cairn SM 422, looking south

Plate 59: Cairn SM 423, looking south-east

with a significant cairn alignment (A; Fig 33), which followed the line of the contours for 260 m. Each cairn was up to 55 m apart, yet they defined a very straight line. Such an alignment cannot be explained by chance, and they almost certainly defined the line of a former field boundary. While it is possible that the boundary was solely defined by these cairns, given that they were so far apart, and also that there was hardly any intervisibility, it is perhaps more probable that they were on the line of a more ephemeral type of boundary, such as a fence, which did not survive as surface evidence.

Within the cairnfield were two monuments which were similar and very distinctive (*SM 151* and *SM 169*). They were both slightly isolated from the main part of the cairnfield, and were well defined, fairly prominent, and both had an enclosure attached to the southern side of a sub-circular, or annular, cairn. The northernmost of these (*SM 151*) comprised a circular ring bank with an irregular enclosure butted onto its southern side. The ring bank was 7.8 m in diameter, 0.3 m in height, and had a possible entrance, but there was no evidence of an entrance through the bank of the adjacent enclosure. By contrast, the southern of the two monuments (*SM 169*) comprised a disturbed round cairn, instead of a ring bank, but this again had an irregular enclosure (overall 12.3 x 9.2 m in extent, and 0.4 m in height), with evidence for a possible entrance on its western side. It is, perhaps, significant that there was a similar monument (*SM 423*) in the SM IV site group, immediately to the south (*p 75*), which comprised a circular, low mound of loose stone, with a semi-circular bank extending from one side. Moreover, all three monuments displayed considerable similarity of form, and they were placed in relatively prominent positions, either on the summits of hillocks or at the edge of a scarp slope, and were only spatially associated with the adjacent cairnfields, or stone banks. Given this, they would therefore appear to form the same class of monument, and another comparable example was also found during the LDNPS (*BF 30*; *Ch 4, p 122*). Although the purpose of these monuments is at present equivocal, it is more likely to relate to a ritual/funerary function than a domestic one.

Stockdale Moor VI: monuments *SM 107-43*

This monument group contained a small cairnfield on the north side of Cawfell Beck and an unrelated, diverse group of monuments between Cawfell Beck and Caw Gill (Fig 31). The cairnfield (SM VIA) was small and contained 27 cairns and banks positioned on a gently sloping spur between Worm Gill and Cawfell Beck. The cairns and stone banks were ill defined, irregular in width and shape, and the cairns were of various diameters (1.9–7 m across). Taken as a whole, these features were consistent with stone clearance. A short length of stone bank was approximately aligned with a very long stone bank (*SM 26*) that has been grouped with SM VII (*p 78*), and it possibly represented a continuation of this linear feature.

The other group of monuments in this area (SM VIB) consisted of a widely scattered mix of seemingly unrelated monuments on, and around, a spur between Cawfell Beck and Caw Gill. The spur had steep sides, particularly around the western end, but had a gently sloping top. The monuments on the

Plate 60: Post-medieval sheepwash (SM 136), on the banks of Cawfell Beck

and had a distinct character in comparison with the other site groups on Stockdale Moor. Their form and condition suggested that they were of relatively recent date.

One of the structures (*SM 135;* Fig 31) was a small, elliptical enclosure on the fairly flat, albeit rocky, ground of the Worm Gill flood plain. It had an entrance on the northern side and was internally flat. At the base of the Cawfell Beck gully was a small walled enclosure (*SM 136*) standing to a height of 1.3 m, with one opening on the western side, and a funnelled entrance leading directly into a fairly deep part of the beck (Pl 60). It was therefore a typical sheepwash and was described as a 'washfold' on the 1867 First Edition 6" to 1 mile OS map. Its form, condition, and representation on nineteenth-century maps indicate a post-medieval date. A U-shaped, walled enclosure (*SM 139; c* 46 x 48 m; Pl 61) was also recorded in the Caw Gill valley. The open-ended section of this enclosure extended up to the top of the steeply scarped valley side, while the bottom extended across the gill and was revetted into the base of a natural bowl. It had first been surveyed by Spence (1939), who imaginatively interpreted it as a Roman amphitheatre. Its location and the condition of its walls suggests a more recent date. Indeed, it more probably served as a sheepwash in the post-medieval period, particularly as sheep driven into the top of the enclosure could only have got out at the bottom, by walking through the beck.

flat top of the spur comprised four diverse, scattered cairns and a stone bank. Around the bottom of the spur were three prominent, well-defined, walled structures, which were in a good state of preservation

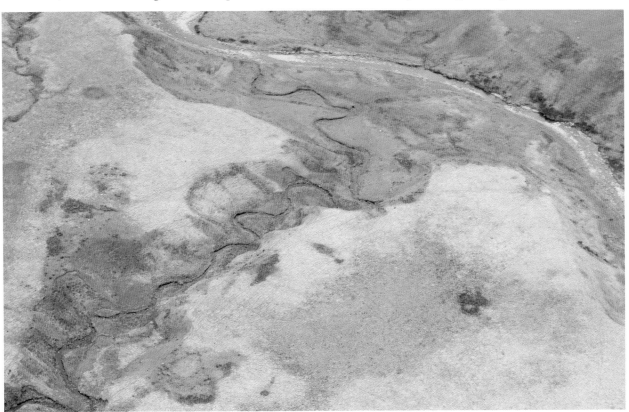

Plate 61: Caw Gill, showing enclosure SM 139 (centre left) set into a steep valley side

Stockdale Moor VII (Monks Graves): monuments *SM 26-102*

The Monks Graves cairnfield was a sizable group made up of both large and small cairns, the larger cairns being grouped, and these also displayed funerary characteristics that set them apart from their small clearance counterparts. The cairnfield was located on a moderate, uniformly sloping area of moorland (Fig 31), which was well drained, and was better agricultural land than many other parts of Stockdale Moor. The cairns were found between two very long, parallel stone banks, which broadly defined a field system (Pl 62).

The component cairns fell into two distinct types according to their size and height. The larger cairns (*SM 34-43* and *SM 87-97*; Fig 35) were grouped at the highest part of the field system (north-eastern end) and were very prominent and well defined. Included within the group were five funerary cairns, comprising three kerbed cairns (*SM 34*, *SM 39*, and *SM 41*) and two ring cairns (*SM 36* and *SM 38*). There is a possibility that some of the other cairns also had a funerary function.

The kerbed cairns were larger than the surrounding cairns, had clearly distinct kerbs, and were well defined and prominent (*SM 34*: 5.4 x 4.7 m; *SM 39*: 7 x 5 m; *SM 41*: 4.7 x 4.5 m). Ring cairn *SM 36* (10.2 m

in diameter) had a uniform-shaped bank, without an entrance, the interior being flat, with no internal features (Pl 63). Monument *SM 38* was also a kerbed ring cairn (8.2 m in diameter), comprising a uniform ring, with no entrance, but within the ring was a sub-triangular platform cairn which had a relatively flat top, that butted against the inside of the ring bank.

There were also two groups of smaller-sized cairns, one at the lowest part of the field system (*SM 31-3* and *SM 56-78*), and a smaller group (*SM 44-55*) to the north-east of the larger funerary cairns. The cairns of these two groups were small, irregularly shaped, generally ill defined, relatively numerous, and very distinct from the large cairns. They were consistent with stone clearance and indicate agricultural use of the area.

Two discontinuous stone banks (*SM 30* and *SM 99*) were also found, which reflected the line of field boundaries, and were probably two sides of a large rectilinear field. Bank *SM 30* was very well-defined at the north-east end, where it was adjacent to the group of large cairns, but was poorly defined and intermittent at the south-western end, where it was adjacent to the small cairns (Pl 64). An additional stone bank (*SM 26*) was also observed, which was extremely long, at over 620 m. It was not quite parallel to the other two banks, and was not necessarily an integral part of the field system.

Plate 62: Monks Graves (SM VII), showing the area of large cairns adjacent to elements of a field system (centre)

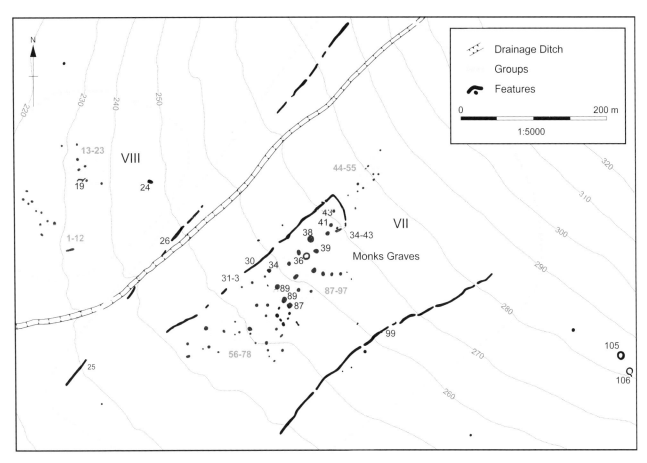

Figure 35: The SM VII (Monks Graves) and SM VIII cairnfields

Plate 63: Ring cairn SM 38, with a platform set within it

Plate 64: Large, patchy stone bank SM 30, *looking north-east, upslope*

Discussion

Ring cairn *SM 38* can be compared in form to an excavated example from Weird Law in Peebleshire (MacLaren 1967), which had four cremations beneath the central mound, and produced a radiocarbon date of 1974-1523 cal BC (3440±90 BP; NPL-57). This is in accord with the other dates for ring cairns, which chronologically places these monuments in the Bronze Age (*Ch 2, pp 43-4*). Furthermore, in terms of their spatial and typological association with the rest of the group in this area, there is a case for suggesting that the large cairns formed a Bronze Age cemetery. By contrast, the cairns at the southern end of SM VII were small, erratically defined, and were consistent with stone clearance. Although there was a slight merging of the two groups of cairns, they appear to have represented contrasting uses of the moor, and it is probable that the two elements were constructed in different phases of activity, with the funerary cairns perhaps pre-dating the clearance cairns.

Stockdale Moor VIII: monuments *SM 1-24* and *SM 86*

In this area (Fig 31), a small cairnfield was discovered on well-drained ground, which was associated with a limited area of sporadic stone outcrops. The cairnfield fell into two distinct groups (Fig 35; *SM 1-12* and *SM 13-23*). Both comprised small, very ill-defined, irregular cairns that were consistent with stone clearance. In addition, one cairn (*SM 24*), found some 64 m to the east of the northern group, was pear-shaped, moderately large (7.5 x 4.5 m), prominent (0.4 m high), and may have been a funerary monument.

Stockdale Moor IX: monuments *SM 815-38*

A small group of cairns was located on an alluvial terrace on the eastern side of Worm Gill (Fig 31). The cairns exhibited substantial variation in size and definition, but

in general were consistent with stone clearance. The only possible exception was an annular monument (*SM 383*; Fig 31) at the northern end of the group, which had a well-defined, slightly prominent ring bank (5 x 4.5 x 0.2 m). It had no surviving entrance but, nevertheless, could potentially have been a roundhouse.

Conclusions

Stockdale Moor was scattered with large and small cairnfields, which were generally simple in type and demonstrated no particular orientation or relationship between the various groups; they had random cairn distributions and only occasional stone banks. There were also some cairnfields (SM I, SM IV, and SM VII) containing stone banks and cairn alignments, which would appear to have delineated simple fields. These were generally within an extensive area of randomly distributed cairns, very different from the Town Bank cairnfields (*eg* TB IV; *p 52*), which were incorporated within regular field systems.

Although the remains attest to a great deal of agricultural activity, there was only one probable habitation (*SM 591* in SM I; Fig 32), which may be an indication that other domestic structures had been constructed in timber and did not survive as surface evidence. In addition to this simple roundhouse, ring features were identified (*SM 36*, *SM 38* (both SM VII), *SM 105*, and *SM 496* (*p 70-8*)), which usually had no entrances, no internal terracing, and were kerbed. In the absence of excavation, the visual information would suggest that most of these monuments were ring cairns, rather than roundhouses. Other types of funerary monument found on the moor included round cairns. There were also two large, pear-shaped long cairns (*SM 435* (*p 71*) and *SM 739* (*p 72*)), located on opposite sides of the SM I cairnfield. There were no particular vistas to be noted at either location, particularly as the larger of these, Sampson's Bratfull (*SM 435*), was in a poorly drained, gentle hollow, and this lack of prominence is largely in accord with other examples of long cairns recorded during the survey (*HF 60, HF 420; Ch 6, p 267-77; TB 564, TB 541, TB 536,* and *TB 518; p 57*). At Monks Graves (SM VII), a group of funerary-type ring cairns and round cairns was immediately adjacent to groups of clearance-type cairns (Fig 35). This cemetery and cairnfield were not necessarily in contemporary use, although it has not been possible to establish the relative chronology on surface evidence alone. There was a possible parallel for this cemetery at Town Bank (TB X; *p 57-8*), where a group of large elongated cairns within a field system / cairnfield was recorded.

The cairnfields were spatially associated with funerary monuments (ring cairns and round cairns), which can be dated broadly to the second millennium BC (*Ch 2, pp 41-5*), and there were no datable later prehistoric, or later, monuments in association, apart from post-medieval pastoral structures. This may imply that the cairnfields reflect a second millennium BC agricultural exploitation of the fell. Sampson's Bratfull, which was near the edge of the SM I cairnfield, was probably of neolithic date, and as there is no direct relationship between it and the cairnfields, this probably indicates earlier, pre-agricultural activity in this area, and does not necessarily imply that the cairnfield had a particularly early origin. There is also a possibility at Monks Graves (SM VII) that the funerary round cairns were earlier than the agricultural clearance cairns, which raises the possibility that in some areas funerary activity on Stockdale Moor preceded agricultural activity.

Whin Garth

The survey area (Fig 36) was on a large, gently sloping spur extending down from Seatallan mountain, between the valleys of the Rivers Bleng

and Wasdale. The extent of the survey area was defined to the south-west by forestry plantations, a ridge-top track (Guards Lonning), and a group of fields that were shown by aerial photographs to be archaeologically unproductive. At the eastern end, the survey area was defined by the steep, lower slopes positioned between Seatallan and the River Bleng. At the lower end of the spur, the ground was generally well drained. Further up was an area of gently sloping ground, adjacent to the steeper scarp slopes of the Seatallan peak, which receives the run-off from the adjacent mountain and, as a result, had substantial areas of mire. In this area, the cairnfield groups were found to be either on islands of better-drained land or were on the adjacent, steeper-sloping land.

Three distinct forms of modern land use were found in the area, according to altitude. At the lower, south-western end of the spur, below about 190 m OD, the land was enclosed, improved pasture. The middle section of the spur, between approximately 190 m and 280 m OD, had enclosed, unimproved land on

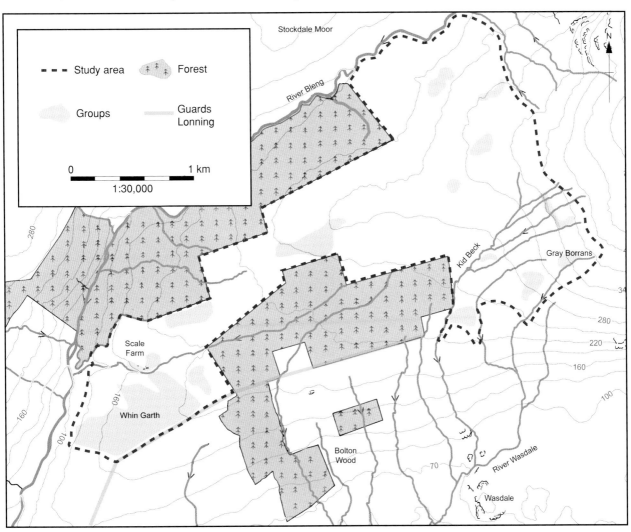

Figure 36: The Whin Garth survey area

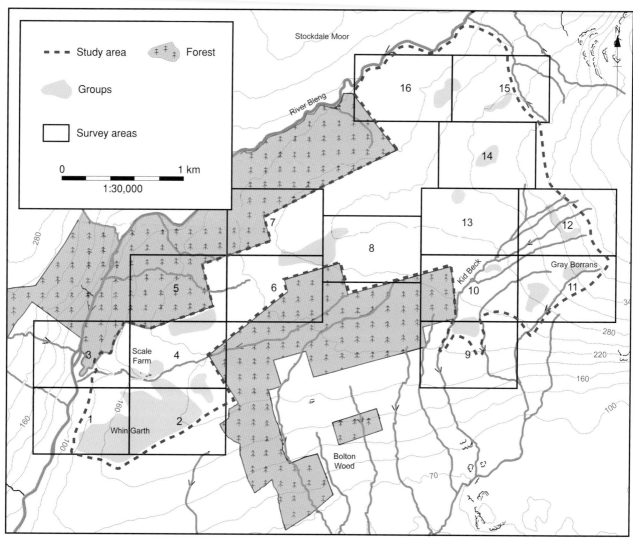

Figure 37: The Whin Garth survey area as planned

the spine of the ridge, although the sides were covered by forestry plantation. At the upper, north-western end of the survey area, on the lower slopes of Seatallan, the land was open moorland.

The character of the archaeological remains ranged from medieval settlement and field systems, on the enclosed land at the western end of the spur, to small cairnfields, probably of prehistoric date, on the eastern unimproved land, which were found up to an altitude of *c* 360 m OD. The archaeological wealth of the area extends beyond the limits of the Whin Garth survey, however; for example, just to the north of the River Bleng are the large, complex cairnfields of Stockdale Moor (*p 68*), and to the south is an enclosed settlement (Bolton Wood; NY 104 054) and associated cairnfields, some of which have been destroyed by the Losca forestry plantation (Spence 1937). The survey recorded that one of the site groups (WG III; *p 94*) had been truncated and partly destroyed by recent forestry plantation. Furthermore, given that there were nearly 2.5 km² of forestry plantation within this area that were not investigated, and that small cairnfields were

scattered throughout the adjacent areas of unimproved land, there was a reasonable possibility that other cairnfields have been destroyed.

Archaeological history
The 1867 OS First Edition 6" to 1 mile map showed Scale Farm (WG I; *p 91*) in ruins, and a large elliptical enclosure, but otherwise no indications of antiquities within the area. The earliest descriptive record of settlement dates from 1877 (Clifton Ward 1878, 249), which described the WG X cairn group near Yokerill Hows as 'cairns and an old wall of semi-circular form,' and the WG VI cairnfield at Gray Borrans as 'cairns'. By 1926, these cairn groups had been added to the OS 6" to 1 mile map.

The Gray Borrans and Yokerill Hows cairn groups were scheduled (CU 103 and CU 104) on the basis of the 1926 Third Edition 6" to 1 mile OS map. Unfortunately, the area of the Gray Borrans Scheduled Monument (CU 103) is of limited extent, lying between the cairnfields of WG VI, and does not contain a single cairn. The earliest reference to the complex field system

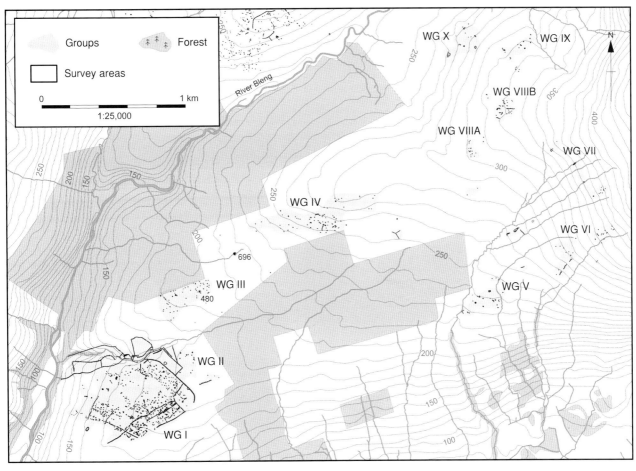

Figure 38: Monument distribution within the Whin Garth survey area

at WG I was by Spence (1937), who, on the basis of the excavation of a limited sample, suggested that the cairns were the result of stone clearance.

The only other independent reference to the WG I field system was by Ramm (1970, 42), who described three possible shielings (*WG 206*, *WG 219*, and *WG 283; p 83*) within the cairnfield. The identification of the structures as shielings was based upon the 'Scales' name of the nearby farm, which is one of the vernacular terms used to refer to such activity.

The present survey was prompted by oblique aerial photographs taken by the then County Archaeologist, Tom Clare, in the late 1980s, which revealed the extent of the WG I field system, and also showed extensive damage to the monuments caused by agricultural vehicles (*Ch 9, p 354*). Apart from these, of the ten site groups recorded during the Whin Garth survey, only three had been previously identified in the archaeological record, which illustrates the lack of antiquarian activity in this locality.

The survey area

The survey was undertaken in April and May 1989 over 4.8 km² of unenclosed and enclosed rough pasture land (Fig 37). In total, 716 monuments were

found within ten site groups (WG I-X; Fig 38). The archaeological landscapes varied from the extremely complex settlement and field system at WG I, to a scatter of smaller and more localised cairnfields, which were to be found on the better-drained, but gently sloping, land across the lower flanks of Seatallan mountain.

Whin Garth I: monuments *WG 2-446*

A complex, multi-phased settlement, field system, and cairnfield lay on the top of a broad, flat-topped ridge formed between the valleys of the Rivers Bleng and Wasdale (Fig 38; Pl 65). The land for the most part is gently sloping and well drained, just above and to the east of Gosforth, and consequently had been enclosed. The main part of the field system lies on a gentle gradient, with a significant increase in slope at the extreme western edge, where it drops down to the River Bleng. The land was improved grassland, and had a fairly uniform surface. Very little natural surface stone was found near the top of the ridge, but there was a steady increase in the quantity of stone downslope towards the western edge of the field system.

The main part of the settlement/cairnfield lay within five modern fields, which extend out from a track at the top of the ridge (Fig 39), the boundaries of which

Plate 65: The area of the WG I cairnfield, looking south

were numbered during the survey (*FB 1-5*). The condition of the monuments varied from field to field, as each had been subject to different degrees of land improvement. The archaeological remains in one of the north-eastern fields (Y) were in the best condition, where there was no evidence of modern stone or cairn clearance, and there were only two vehicular tracks running through the length of the field. The western three fields (V-X) had been subject to a limited amount of modern cairn and stone clearance, mainly in the north-western part of the larger of these modern fields (X), and there were very large mounds of recently deposited stone (*WG 11, WG 12, WG 115, WG 129, WG 153,* and *WG 196*) in them. Although there were a few depressions marking the positions of former cairns, the immense size of the modern clearance piles was an indication that many more cairns had been destroyed during this episode of land improvement. It would appear, however, that the dearth of cairns was not solely attributable to this improvement, particularly as a similar dearth was present in areas (such as field Y) which had not been subject to recent improvement.

There were some cairns, mainly from within modern field W, which had been hollowed out or levelled, but were not near one of the modern clearance cairns. These had possibly been robbed to provide stone for the adjacent dry-stone walls. Extensive damage had also occurred as a result of vehicular traffic, particularly within modern field V and around the field entrances. No consistent route had been followed by the agricultural vehicles, so there were numerous wheel ruts (up to 0.2 m deep), which had severely disturbed the underlying stratigraphy. Although the cairns and banks had been avoided, traffic was concentrated in between the cairns, and caused increased damage to the adjacent deposits.

The south-westernmost and north-easternmost fields (U and Z) had no surviving cairns, and the only intact sites within field U were an elliptically shaped enclosure and a continuation of a decayed wall (*WG 34*). According to local farmers, field U had recently been improved, and air photographs taken in the mid-1980s (*see Ch 9, pp 350-2*) show a large number of depressions resulting from disturbance. It is perhaps significant that the 1867 First Edition 6" to 1 mile OS map showed modern fields V-Y as being rough pasture, while modern fields U and Z were then improved ground, and it is possible that some cairns had been removed from those fields during an earlier episode of clearance. This may also partly explain why

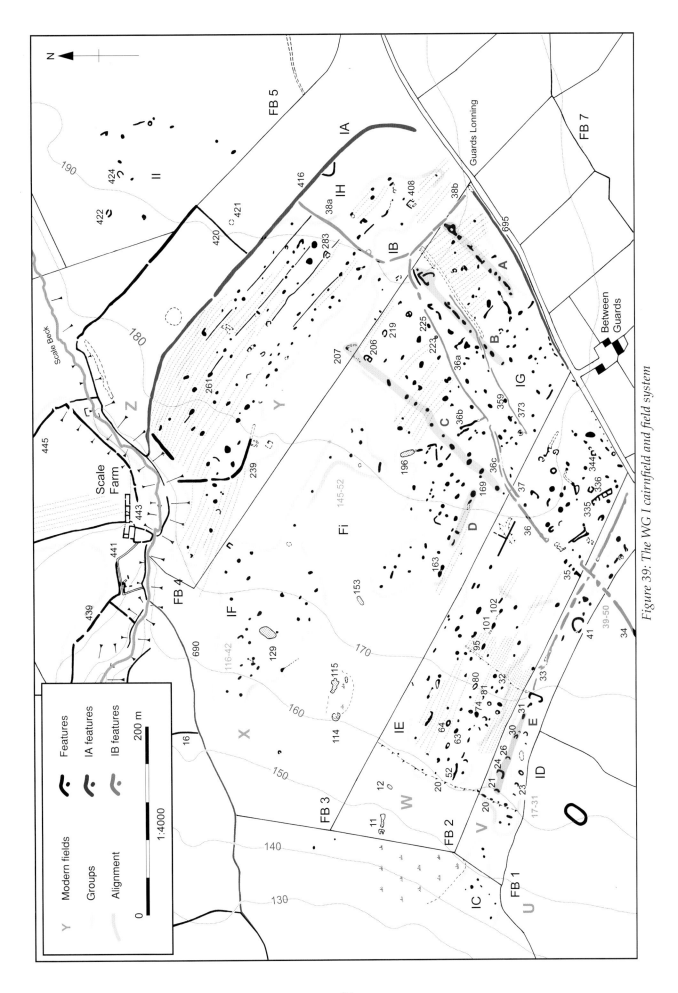

Figure 39: The WG I cairnfield and field system

85

Plate 66: WG I, with boundary WG 416 prominently dividing modern field Y from field Z, and Scale Farm in the foreground

a cairnfield survived in a relatively good condition in modern fields V-Y.

The site group was very complex. It comprised cairnfields with spatially associated shielings, superimposed on which were later field systems, which related to the nearby farms of Scale and Between Guards. For ease of description, this group is initially described in terms of the two main phases of field system that divide up the site, followed by a description of the most complex cairnfield group. This is then followed by descriptions of the remaining groups of cairns, and associated features, and finally the remains relating to Scale Farm.

The field systems

Monuments *WG 416*, *WG 690*, and *WG 695* comprised the earliest field walls within the field system (WG IA; Fig 39), and for the most part defined the northern, eastern, and southern extent of the site on the northern side of the Whin Garth ridge (Pl 66). They defined the extent of an early intake of the moorland and the boundaries formed by these monuments were butted by several decayed walls (*eg WG 38* and *WG 33*). Although walls *WG 416* and *WG 695* were orientated towards each other, they did not actually join, which may reflect subsequent disturbance or robbing. Two of these walls were still in use (*WG 416* and *WG 690*), but had a form which was distinct from the later

dry-stone walls, generically known as Cumbrian banks (LUAU 1997f). Walls *WG 416* and *WG 695* were broad, well built, and incorporated many medium, unworked stones within a turf-bonded fabric. There was a similar section of wall on the north-western side of the modern track, lying outside the survey area (between NY 0921 0505 and NY 0890 0499), which was very high and contrasted markedly with the wall on the other side of the track. It was on the same line as *WG 695* and was presumably a continuation of the same enclosure boundary.

Wall *WG 416* was aligned directly towards Scale Farm and, although the relationships were confused by the later rebuilding of the section adjacent to Scale Beck, it appeared to merge with wall *WG 445*, which defined the primary radial plot on the north side of the farm. This implied a relationship between enclosure boundary *WG 416* and Scales Farm, and may be an indication that they were broadly contemporary.

On the south-eastern side of the Guards Lonning track was a boundary (*FB 7*), though outside the survey area, which was similar to *WG 416/690*. It was butted by other boundaries and divided two areas of field system. On its north-western side was a series of straight cross walls which linked the boundary to the track, and the fields were all quadrilaterally shaped. On the other side (to the south-east), the walls were

86

Plate 67: Decayed wall WG 36

not straight and the plots were very irregular in shape. As with *WG 416/695*, this boundary also appeared to have defined the extent of an original intake. Between these two enclosure walls (*WG 416/695* and *FB 7*) was a very broad corridor (*c* 120 m wide) which is characteristic of an outgang, to lead stock from winter to summer pastures (M Higham *pers comm*). At the interface between the open fell and enclosed land, the boundaries curved inwards to funnel the stock down the corridor from the fell. Boundary *FB 1* overlay decayed wall *WG 34* (*see below*) of another field system and was clearly a later intake of unimproved pastureland.

In addition to these earliest field walls, later monuments *WG 33-8* and *WG 373* (WG IB) were also identified, which defined three former fields opposite, and to the north-west of, Between Guards Farm. These survived as prominent, regular banks and were generally continuous, with any gaps created either deliberately or as a result of disturbance. Although turf cover obscured evidence of dry-stone construction, it is highly likely that these originally were walls, rather than banks.

Wall *WG 34* extended south-west from wall *WG 33* and was, for the most part, regular and continuous. The section within modern field W was

discontinuous and irregular, possibly reflecting the extensive vehicular disturbance in this locality. A short stub of wall *WG 34* extended north-east from *WG 33*, parallel to the main north-east/south-west boundary (*WG 35-6*), and offset by *c* 6 m. This parallel arrangement was reflected further along the slope by wall *WG 37*, which closely followed wall *WG 36* (Pl 67) and was offset by only *c* 3 m. This was almost certainly the discontinuous south-eastern edge of a narrow track, though where it led, and what it related to, is uncertain. However, it will almost certainly have been in contemporary use with either the outgang, or a track on the approximate line of the present Guards Lonning, just beyond the south-eastern boundary of the plot, which has accommodated a communication route since before the *WG 36/38* fields were established.

Wall *WG 35* extended up to modern wall *FB 2*, but there was no surviving evidence of a continuation joining it to wall *WG 33*. It survived as a series of short banks orientated downslope, which would appear to reflect disturbance by ridge and furrow. There were three distinct sections of wall *WG 36*; the easternmost section (*WG 36a*) turned at approximately a right-angle into section *WG 36b*, and the westernmost section (*WG 36c*), along with *WG 37*, appeared to define a narrow track (about 3 m wide). The most prominent and uniform section was *WG 36c*, closely followed by *WG 36b*, although this was fairly short, and section *WG 36c* was markedly less prominent and more irregular in form. It had a slight lynchet-like profile, which would suggest that the ridge and furrow cultivation extended up to its north-western side. A small, circular, ill-defined structure appeared to have been incorporated into its south-western terminal. Wall *WG 36a* followed a line that seemingly diverted to avoid cairn *WG 223*, and to a lesser extent cairn *WG 225*, suggesting that it post-dated the cairns; it also butted onto wall *WG 38*.

Wall *WG 38* was very prominent and broadly continuous, the only gaps apparently being a result of later disturbance. It had a ditch to the south-east and a slight lynchet profile, suggesting cultivation to the north-west. Although there was no actual relationship between *WG 38* and two adjacent enclosure boundaries (*WG 416* and *WG 695*), in terms of alignment, it is probable that *WG 38* butted both. A small, rectilinear structure was also butted onto its southern face (at NY 09408 05316).

Wall *WG 373* was irregular in alignment and in the quantity of stone within it. In places it was relatively prominent and thus it was possibly a decayed wall. It was approximately parallel to *WG 36*, appeared to have butted onto wall *WG 38*, and hence was probably of the same broad stratigraphic phase as wall *WG 36*.

This feature cut through a cairn alignment (B; *see below*) and diverted to avoid cairn WG 359. It therefore post-dated both elements. Ridge and furrow extended up to it and there was a fairly well-defined headland adjacent. The same ridge and furrow passed through the cairn alignment (B; *see below*) and extended up to wall *WG 695*.

Linked to the field system, and extending out from the Guards Lonning/outgang route, was field boundary *WG 33*. This varied in form more than most other features, and at its eastern end, particularly to the east of *WG 34*, it was a continuous, prominent, and uniformly decayed wall. However, to the west it became increasingly discontinuous, irregular, lacked prominence, and had the characteristics of a stone bank (*Ch 2, p 84*). The implication is that this began as an early stone bank forming a field boundary, that had subsequently been modified when a later field system, represented by decayed walls (*WG 33, WG 35-8* and *WG 373; WG IB*), was established in this area. This modification appears to have been confined to the short section between *WG 34* and the Guards Lonning, where a wall was built, whereas that section to the north-west of *WG 34* was left as a stone bank.

The complex cairnfield

A cairn group was identified which formed a very complex site group (WG IG). It comprised a dense cairnfield, of fairly large and prominent cairns, which incorporated four phases of field system, with the latest being the modern, post-enclosure, field configuration. Ridge and furrow was found in close proximity to the cairns, though the evidence suggests that it avoided them. However, the cairns did appear to have been augmented by stone raised by the plough.

Of the four phases of field system on the site, the earliest appears to have been associated with the cairnfield, and comprised three well-defined, parallel cairn/bank alignments (A, B, and C). Although there was a fairly high density of cairns to the north of Alignment A, there were only two to the south, which would suggest that the edge of the cairnfield broadly coincided with this alignment. In the south-western part of the group, the cairns were seemingly edged by bank *WG 36* (*p 87*) to their north. However, this section of the bank was on the line of Alignment C and there is a likelihood that the bank overlay the alignment, in which case it is probable that the cairnfield related to the earlier boundary, considering that the north-eastern section of *WG 36* passed through the middle of the cairnfield. Similarly, towards the north-western end of Alignment C, there were only three cairns (*WG 197-99*) to the north of it, but a fairly high density to the south, implying a relationship between these features. Extending off

from Alignment C was another possible, though much shorter, significant cairn alignment (D), which defined the south-western edge of this complex cairn group. Alignment B was cut by decayed wall *WG 373* (*p 87*), and the ridge and furrow that extended between it and wall *WG 695* also cut through Alignment A, which passed between these two walls. Although Alignment A appeared to stop short of wall *WG 38*, this did not necessarily indicate a relationship, as the terminals of all three alignments defined a line, marked by *WG 207, WG 217, WG 218, WG 228,* and *WG 404,* that was perpendicular to their orientations, and extended far beyond *WG 38*. As such, the implication is that *WG 38* approximately adopted the line of part of a much older boundary. Given its positioning, this alignment may represent the north-eastern side of the rectangular field defined by the cairn alignments, which partly coincided with both *WG 38* and modern boundary *FB 4*. However, the orientation of this alignment differs by about 15° with these two field systems, and would appear to pre-date them both.

Two sub-rectangular structures (*WG 206* and *WG 219*) were also found within the cairnfield, which had previously been identified as shielings (Ramm 1970, 42, nos 168 and 167). The better-preserved of the two (*WG 206*) had prominent external banks, a well-defined entrance on its north-western side, and a possible internal division. *WG 219* was a simpler structure; it was single-celled, oval in shape, and, though it did not have prominent banks, had a surface level that was slightly raised above the adjacent ground.

In the southern part of the cairn group were several very ill-defined features, which were also possibly structures (*WG 335, WG 336,* and *WG 344*). *WG 335* was the best preserved of these, but nevertheless was both irregular and ill defined. It appeared to be a long, four-celled, sub-rectangular structure, and its three ill-defined internal divisions extended out from a common, relatively prominent, back wall. Adjacent to it was what appeared to be a small sub-rectangular structure (*WG 336; c* 7.5 x 6.0 m), with a gap or possible entrance on its south-eastern side, and a very ill-defined internal depression. Further to the east was the other small sub-rectangular structure (*WG 344; c* 6.7 x 5.8 m) which, like *WG 336*, had an apparent entrance on the south-eastern corner. There were also other somewhat similar structures with internal depressions, but which, in terms of their irregularities, were more in keeping with disturbed cairns. Their lack of prominence and regularity of form distinguishes them from other more credible shielings in this settlement group, but without excavation, it would not be possible to make a positive identification.

The cairnfields and associated monuments

A small group of cairns (WG IC) was identified in an area to the north-west of those monuments which defined the three former fields opposite, and to the north-west of, Between Guards Farm (*WG 33-8* and *WG 373*; *p 87*). This group of cairns was also cut by the boundary of the parliamentary enclosure forming the west side of modern field V. The ground was moderately sloping, particularly towards the western edge of the group, and was generally undulating. The ground surface was fairly rough and had considerably more surface stone than that within an adjacent group of cairns (*WG 17-31*, *WG 33*, and *WG 39-50*; *see below*); the change of terrain coincided with the line of lynchet *WG 20*. The cairns were fairly small, very irregular, generally ill defined, and were associated with surface brash.

In contrast, the adjacent group of cairns (WG ID) was better defined, larger, and more prominent. This small group was found within narrow modern field V, the extent of which was limited to the north-east by field boundary *WG 33* and to the south-west by the modern field wall (*FB 1*). The line of boundary *WG 33*, at its lower, north-western end, was continued by an alignment of cairns (E), which would suggest a relationship between the cairn group and the boundary. Field boundary *WG 34* passed through the group and there was no significant difference in the distribution of cairns on either side of it; hence it is probable that the distribution of these cairns pre-dated the boundary. Although it is clear that these cairns pre-dated the field boundaries defined by walls *WG 33-8* and *WG 373* (*p 87*), and also boundary *FB 1*, which overlay *WG 34*, the cairn distribution did not extend across *FB 1*. It would appear, therefore, that the ground within the later enclosure, edged by *FB 1*, had been improved, and any cairns associated with this cairnfield destroyed.

The size and definition of the cairns varied considerably, although generally they were not particularly prominent. They also did not have any consistent shape, though this may reflect the extensive disturbance within this area. A vehicle track had cut a section through a semi-circular bank, *WG 23*, which revealed an internally terraced profile. Although this had the appearance of a deliberately constructed platform, there were other structures in the area which looked similar, but seemed to be a product of robbing. In addition to the cairns, monument *WG 41* was identified, a relatively large (15 m across) D-shaped enclosure that had been internally terraced. It comprised a uniform, prominent, well-defined bank, except for the south-western section, which had been destroyed by a modern vehicle track. There was no evidence of an entrance in the broadly complete north-eastern section, but there may once have been

one in the disturbed section. The internal terracing was inconsistent with stock control, and there is a possibility that it had a domestic function.

At the lower, north-western end of the second group of cairns (WG ID) was a long, positive lynchet (*WG 20*), which extended across the slope and had some small piles of clearance stone deposited on it. It marked the lower edge of a third cairnfield (WG IE; *see below*), but only approximately defined the western edge of the cairnfield defined by the monuments forming WG ID, as three small cairns were recorded just to the west of it. It was clearly a product of cultivation, causing soil slippage immediately upslope of it, and though there was ridge and furrow in the upslope area, there was none surviving that extended right up to the lynchet. A marked change of terrain was seen downslope of the lynchet, where the ground was much more rocky and undulating, and was generally steeper; this in part reflected the effect of soil slippage and land improvement above the lynchet, but also the lynchet coincided with a natural break of slope. As both the edge of the cairnfield and the lynchet were linked to the break of slope, the coincident use of the same line does not necessarily indicate a contemporary relationship.

A third concentration of cairns was identified (WG IE), which formed a relatively coherent group within modern field W. A lynchet (*WG 32*) parallel to *WG 20*, which delineated the lower edge of WG IE, passed through the upper (easternmost) part of the group, and again was probably a later feature, particularly as a change of ridge and furrow configuration on either side of this lynchet suggested that it was a product of cultivation. Within the lower (north-western) part of the group, the ridge and furrow was focused on either side of the main concentration of cairns, but not within it, with some ridge and furrow diverting around cairns; this cultivation thus clearly post-dated the construction of the cairns. Some cairns were elongated in the direction of the ridge and furrow and/or were linked by narrow banks of clearance material (*eg WG 95*, *WG 101*, and *WG 102*) along that orientation. This was probably a result of the plough cutting the sides of round cairns and raising additional clearance stones, which augmented the earlier cairns. There was also a significant alignment of banks (*WG 52*) orientated downslope at the western end of the group, but no adjacent surviving ridge and furrow, and therefore this alignment may have related to the cairnfield. In addition, several small, semi-ring features (*WG 63*, *WG 64*, *WG 74*, and *WG 80*, and *WG 81*) were randomly scattered within the cairn group. Some had flat bottoms and were reminiscent of platforms (*eg WG 80*), whereas others were elongated cairns

Plate 68: The WG IH cairnfield, looking west

Plate 69: Scale Farm and its field system (WG 443), looking south

with the off-centre depressions that are characteristic of localised disturbance.

A fourth group of cairns (WG IF) was recorded, which spatially formed two small concentrations (*WG 116-43* and *WG 145-52*) positioned at the lower end of modern field X. The terrain at this end of the field was steeper, slightly more undulating, and had more surface stone, despite the modern clearance of stone and cairns that has been undertaken in this area (modern cairns *WG 115*, *WG 129*, and *WG 153*). The cairns were, in part, spread around the outside of a large, sub-rectangular area that was devoid of cairns

(field F*i*). The ground within this area was scrubby, generally ill drained, and was crossed by numerous natural water channels, and it is possible that the lack of cairns reflects the poor agricultural quality of the land, rather than recent disturbance. The cairns in this group were generally small, not particularly prominent, and irregular in form; some were associated with brash deposits and were ill defined. For the most part, the cairns were significantly less prominent and smaller than those of an adjacent group (WG IG; *p 88*) to the east, and there was a marked gap between the two groups. It would also appear that these two groups were distinct, both in terms of spatial separation and the form of the component cairns. Remote from this cairnfield was a circular, banked platform (*WG 114*), with an easterly orientated entrance, and a level internal surface. It was adjacent to a stream and displayed all the typical structural features of a sub-circular building, but was not directly associated with any field system or cairnfield. However, there was a modern clearance cairn nearby (*WG 115*) and it is possible that this had consumed the evidence for any associated features.

A fifth cairnfield (WG IH) contained some fairly well-defined cairns, many of which were prominent, but varied in size (Pl 68). Ridge and furrow ran between, and occasionally around, the cairns and, although this was evidently later, the cairns had also been augmented by clearance stone from this

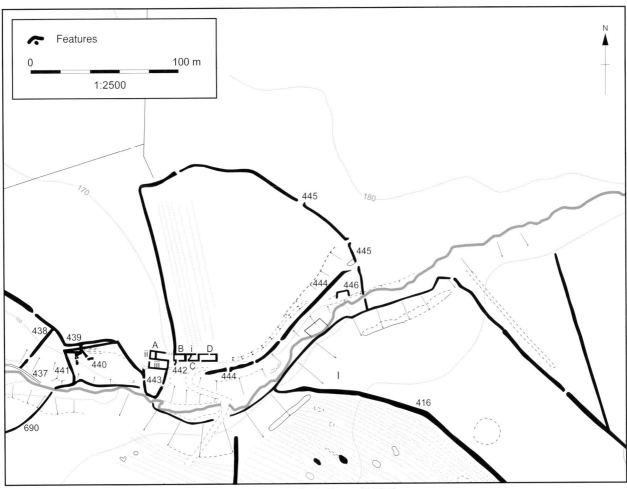

Figure 40: Scale Farm (WG I)

later episode of cultivation (*eg WG 261*). There was a similar distribution and form of cairns on either side of a wall (*WG 38a*) forming part of one of the field systems defined by monuments *WG 33-8* and *WG 373* (WG IB; *p 87*). This implied that the cairns pre-dated the field system. In addition, Bank *WG 239* extended out from Scale Farm, along with boundary *WG 416*, and it passed through part of this cairnfield, although, to the south, it turned to follow a line which corresponded to the south-western edge of the cairnfield. The relatively well-defined edge of this cairnfield may be an indication that there had once been a boundary there and, although this could not have been *WG 239*, there may have been an earlier boundary which *WG 239* partly followed. Although there was no evidence that this cairnfield extended north-east of boundary *WG 416*, this does not necessarily indicate that the boundary was the earliest component, because cairns may have been removed as a result of the land improvement within modern field Z. Two rectilinear structures in the cairnfield were possibly shielings (*WG 283* and *WG 408*), one of these (*WG 283*) having been identified as such by Ramm (1970, 42, no 166). Structure *WG 283* had a prominent, external bank, an internal division, and a south entrance; however, its plan from the present

survey did not entirely coincide with the uniform, rectangular arrangement shown by Ramm (1970, 37). *WG 408* comprised an almost level, rectilinear platform delineated by ill-defined, low-lying banks, with that on the south-western side being particularly indistinct.

Scale Farm
A monument sub-group (*WG 437-46*) was identified that comprised the buildings, fields, and enclosures that constituted Scale Farm on the northern side of Scale Beck (Fig 39). The stone-constructed farm buildings had a longhouse arrangement (Brunskill 1974, 78-80; Pl 69) and were divided into four cells (Cells A-D; Fig 40). Cells A and D were later extensions, the earliest element of the structure being two-celled (Cells B and C), with an internal division composed of poor masonry containing many relatively small stones (*WG 442*; Pl 70). There was no evidence of any roofing materials within the collapse and it had probably had a turfed or thatched roof. Room *i* butted onto cell B and appeared to have had a fairly broad, stock-type entrance. Butting on to the building's southern side was a slightly larger structure (*iii*), with poorly constructed walls, which may not have been strong enough to support a roof, and hence was probably a stock enclosure. Wall

Plate 70: The Scale Farm house (WG 442), looking west

WG 445 defined a primary 'arc' of a field that radiated out from the farm buildings. It was butted by other elements of one of the other field systems, defined by monuments *WG 416, WG 690, WG 695,* and *FB 7 (p 86),* and was probably an early feature.

To the west of the farm were three phases of field boundary; the earliest plot, *WG 443,* extended from structure *iii,* and butting onto this was boundary *WG 438* and *WG 439,* which incorporated a small rectilinear building set into a corner of *WG 439.* Both the building and the boundary wall were overlain by wall *WG 441.*

Phasing
The survey identified five horizontally stratified phases of field system and cairnfield, extending across the summit and sides of the ridge at WG I.

Phase 1
The earliest phase comprised the cairnfields (WG IC-IH) and the field system defined by cairn alignments found in the complex cairn group (WG IG). In places, the cairn alignments defined the edges of cairn groups, but on the present survey evidence it is not possible to sub-divide the phase. There was no evidence of a direct relationship with the later field boundaries (*WG 416, WG 690, WG 695,* and *FB 7;*

p 86), in part because intensive land improvement had destroyed the cairns beyond these boundaries. However, there was a 15° difference between the orientations of the field system defined by cairn alignments and the Phase 2 field system, which would suggest that the earlier field system was no longer in use when the Phase 2 field system was established. The relationship between the Phase 1 and the Phase 3 (*WG 33-8* and *WG 373; WG IB; see below*) field systems was more clearly defined, as the Phase 3 walls cut through the middle of cairn groups and across the cairn alignments, and hence clearly post-dated them.

There were limited numbers of small, sub-rectangular buildings within the cairnfields, which were possibly shielings (*eg WG 206, WG 219, WG 283,* and *WG 408;* Fig 39). One of these (*WG 206*) was spatially associated with cairn Alignment C, but none was directly associated with either of the field systems attributed to Phase 2 or 3. Whilst these buildings were found within an enclosure apparently associated with a permanent farm, it is unlikely that the two were contemporary features. Indeed, it is more probable that the shielings were the antecedents of Scale Farm (Phase 2) and were medieval in date, when transhumance was at its most prolific (Ramm 1970). Although there were no direct relationships between the shielings and the cairnfield, there was a broad spatial relationship, and thus they seem more appropriate as part of the Phase 1 episode of land use. While it is probable that some elements of the cairnfields pre-dated the transhumant occupation of the site, it is not evident whether these cairns had a prehistoric origin, or if this was simply an early phase of medieval activity.

Phase 2

The boundaries (*WG 416, WG 690, WG 695*, and *FB 7; WG IA*) forming a second phase of field system were butted by all the other dry-stone walls (*WG 16, WG 33, WG 38*, and *WG 420*) identified in this survey area. These boundaries appeared to define the extent of an original land enclosure. Walls *WG 416* and *WG 690* were orientated towards Scale Farm, having a direct relationship with its boundaries, and thus either post-dated it, or were contemporary with the farm. Another boundary that extended out from Scale Farm (*WG 239*) cut through an area of cairnfield (*WG IH*), and was probably contemporary with the boundaries, even though it had no direct relationship with them.

There were no evident internal divisions within the enclosure at the time of its construction, which would suggest that it was primary. Walls *WG 416/695* and boundary *FB 7* defined the funnelled sides of an outgang, which would have followed the high, predominantly unenclosed, and therefore unrestricted, ground between Gosforth and Wasdale. When the outgang was in use, the corridor would have been unimproved ground and there would have been no artificial obstructions. It is evident, therefore, that the farms of Between Guards and Guards End, which at the time of survey lay in the middle of this corridor, post-dated the use of the route, and by implication probably also the construction of Scale Farm.

The Scale Farm complex, which was undoubtedly occupied in the post-medieval period, itself had up to six sub-phases of construction. The earliest sub-phase (Phase SF1) comprised the cells of the farmhouse (C, B; Fig 40), and it is possible that it developed from a single-celled structure located at the heart of the farmhouse. Indeed, given the name of the farm, this has more in keeping with a small medieval structure, which may have developed from a shieling. Structure *i* (cell A), cell D, and field wall *WG 445* represent the second sub-phase (Phase SF2). In the third sub-phase (Phase SF3), structure *ii* and stock enclosure *iii* were added. The fourth sub-phase saw the addition of plot *WG 443*, which extended down the steep side of the Scale Beck gully. Field boundary *WG 439* butted onto plot *WG 443* (Phase SF5), and, finally, the sixth sub-phase (Phase SF6) was represented by wall *WG 441*, which partly overlay *WG 439*.

Phase 3

In Phase 3, three fields, defined by walls *WG 33-8* and *WG 373 (WG IB)*, were established, extending out from the south-eastern edge of the primary intake wall (*WG 695*). The earliest of the fields was within the eastern corner of the primary intake (Phase 3a) and its boundary, *WG 38*, appeared to butt walls *WG 695* and *WG 416*. It also cut through an area of cairnfield (*WG 1G*). The larger field (Phase 3b) was opposite Between Guards Farm and was defined by wall *WG 36*, which butted onto *WG 38*. A parallel and broadly similar boundary (*WG 373*) also butted against *WG 38* and cut across one of the Phase 1 cairn alignments (B).

The fields were strung in a line along the edge of the outgang, or track, and both their formation and the access was evidently from that south-eastern side. Moreover, the field system was probably linked to the Between Guards Farm, which stood within the former outgang corridor. The farm comprised a post-medieval structure, and the fact that it was constructed only after the outgang became redundant would suggest either a post-medieval, or evan a late medieval, date of origin.

Phase 4

Phase 4 comprised the ridge and furrow that was found in abundance across the whole survey area. The ridge and furrow avoided the Phase 1 cairns, its orientation was diverted by the Phase 2 field boundaries, whilst its headland was against all of the Phase 3 boundaries (*eg WG 373*). However, it was not confined to the area of the Phase 3 fields and so probably did not relate specifically to that phase of use. The ridge and furrow also related to a pair of lynchets at the western end of the field system (*WG 20* and *WG 32*), which were possibly also established during this phase.

Phase 5

Phase 5 was represented by the modern field boundaries (*FB 1-4*, and *FB 6*), which cut through the cairnfields, Phase 3 boundaries, and ridge and furrow found near Scale Farm (between NY 0905 0501 and NY 0949 0520). These field boundaries are shown on the 1867 First Edition 6" to 1 mile OS maps, and were clearly a product of the Parliamentary enclosure movement, in the eighteenth or early nineteenth century (Whyte 2003). Although this represented a dramatic change in the layout of the field system, the focus of activity was again from the south-eastern end of the survey area. The only access into fields V-X and Z was via gates from the ridge-top track.

Whin Garth II: monuments *WG 417-36*

This is a small irregular group of cairns and a bank in an area of unimproved but enclosed land, to the east of the WG I cairnfield and field systems (Fig 38). The component cairns were generally small, and were ill defined because of the dense matt-grass vegetation which covered them. In addition, there were two small, low-lying horseshoe-shaped features (*WG 422* and *WG 424*; Fig 39). However, the obscuring vegetation made it impossible to determine if these were structures or disturbed cairns.

Both the cairns and the bank extended up to the north-west/south-east-orientated modern wall, *FB 5*, beyond which there was a narrow, substantially improved field (Z) that contained only one surviving cairn (*WG 421*). The field was shown as improved land on the 1867 First Edition 6" to 1 mile OS map. If land improvement within field Z had removed clearance cairns, then it is possible that this small cairn group was originally a part of the Phase 1 WG I cairnfield.

Whin Garth III: monuments *WG 447-95, WG 696*, and *WG 700-19*
This group comprised a cairnfield on fairly flat, slightly undulating, unimproved but enclosed moorland, to the north-east of Scale Farm and the WG I cairnfield and field systems (Fig 38). Dense matt-grass vegetation throughout the area limited the definition of the cairns, but they generally had a regular, circular shape and, although they had no exposed stone, probing invariably revealed stone near the surface. There was a small horseshoe-shaped structure (*WG 480*) in the centre of the cairnfield, which had a slightly recessed interior and moderate-sized stones defining the external edges of the banks; this may have been a small building or a simple bield.

The cairns extended up to the edge of a modern forestry plantation and it is likely that part of the cairnfield had been lost when it was planted. To the east of the main group, beside a small mire-filled beck, was a burnt mound (*WG 696*; 15 x 14 m), which had a rounded profile (up to 1.8 m high) and kidney shape, with a U-shaped recess extending into the body of the mound, away from the stream edge (Pl 71). There were many, small, angular, fire-cracked stones exposed on the surface of the mound, and its form was typical of such monuments, which invariably have fire-cracked stones, are crescent-shaped, and are close to water supplies (Barfield and Hodder 1987). The numerous excavated examples predominantly date to the Bronze Age, although a small minority also date to the early Iron Age (O'Drisceoil 1988; Hedges 1975).

A watching brief undertaken in 1993, in advance of forestry planting, identified a very small assemblage of Bronze Age waste flakes (four flakes) from the area around the cairnfield (LUAU 1994c). Apart from a small number of twentieth-century finds, these were the only artefacts recovered.

There was no evidence of any significant cairn alignments and the cairn distribution was essentially random; its form is characteristic of the primary-type of cairnfield (*Ch 8, pp 328-9*). It is likely that the land was cleared of forest and farmed during the Bronze Age, resulting in the creation of a primary cairnfield, given the spatial association with the distinctive Bronze Age burnt mound and a small Bronze Age lithic assemblage.

Whin Garth IV: monuments *WG 496-556*
This site group comprised an area of cairnfield on the southern slope of the main ridge (Fig 38), where the ground was unimproved but enclosed, to the east of the WG III cairnfield. The cairnfield extended in a narrow band up the ridge, and all the constituent cairns were similar in size and form. Within the overall group were three concentrations that were distinct in terms of their distribution and their associated topography. One area was also found to contain a number of semi-circular banks, which did not coincide with the cairns. It is, therefore, possible that this anomaly reflected two independent episodes of activity, one relating to the cairns and the other to the semi-circular banks.

The first monument concentration (WG IVA; Fig 41), was a loosely scattered group of small, generally ill-defined cairns on undulating terrain, containing substantial amounts of outcrop and surface stone. The distribution and form of the cairns were similar to that observed in another concentration (WG IVC; *p 95*) found on the top of the ridge, about 300 m to the east, but was very different from the adjacent group of cairns (WG IVB), which had a greater concentration and variety of monuments.

This latter group formed the second concentration of cairns (WG IVB), which lay on a steeper gradient,

Plate 71: Burnt mound WG 696, set within an area of mire

but was more uniform, and was also positioned on generally well-drained, smooth, thin grass-covered ground. It comprised a relatively compact group of semi-circular banks, in association with a much smaller number of cairns and banks; the cairns were concentrated in the northern, upslope part of this area. There were also two very prominent, internally revetted grouse butts, which had a similar plan to the semi-circular banks, but a very different form. There was a marked uniformity to the semi-circular banks. They usually had their open end facing downslope and were of a fairly standard size (3.5-6.5 m in diameter), although *WG 509* had a diameter of *c* 10 m. They were often situated around an internally terraced platform (*eg WG 517-18, WG 522, WG 527, WG 539,* and *WG 543*), although some (*eg WG 542* and *WG 510*) contained no evidence of internal terracing. One of the semi-circular banks (*WG 527*) was associated with a rectilinear plot, defined by a stone bank, and the upslope end of the group was a prominent bank with a lynchet profile and a small semi-circular bield set into it. These distinctive monuments were spatially associated with a small, rectilinear plot and a possible lynchet and, unlike the associated grouse butts, they had an irregular distribution. Because of their generally small size and the ill-defined, sometimes unmarked, forward edge of the terracing,

they were not characteristic of house platforms and their precise function is uncertain. However, they were reminiscent of a series of semi-circular banks (*eg BF 221-2, BF 225, BF 228,* and *BF 229*) on the downslope side of the BF II ridge on Bootle Fell (*Ch 4, p 123*).

The third concentration of cairns (WG IVC) in this area was characterised by a loose scatter of monuments on well-drained, gently sloping ground on the top of the ridge. The cairns were small and moderately defined and there was only one semi-circular bank (*WG 549*).

Whin Garth V: monuments *WG 559-78*
This group comprised a small, irregular scatter of cairns and banks on a gently sloping, unimproved, area of unenclosed moorland which was edged to the north by an expanse of mire (Fig 38; Pl 72). There was little consistency of monument type; small cairns were few and far between, and there were three unrelated, irregular banks, a possible round cairn (*WG 562*), and two possible structures (Fig 42).

The most clearly defined of the structures (*WG 575*) appears to have been two overlapping putative house platforms, which were remote from the rest of the group. They were internally terraced and had

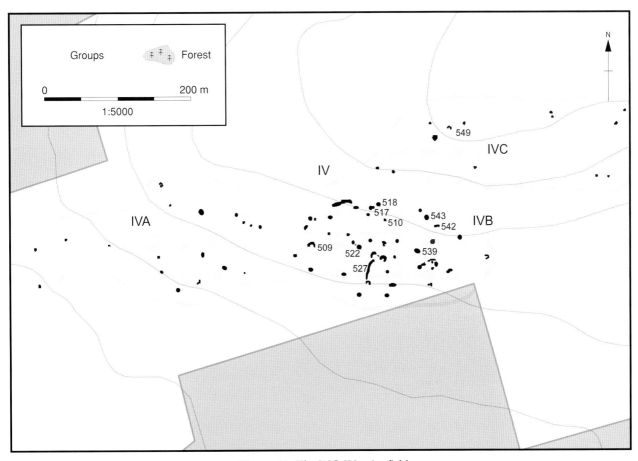

Figure 41: The WG IV cairnfield

95

Plate 72: The area of the WG V cairnfield, looking west

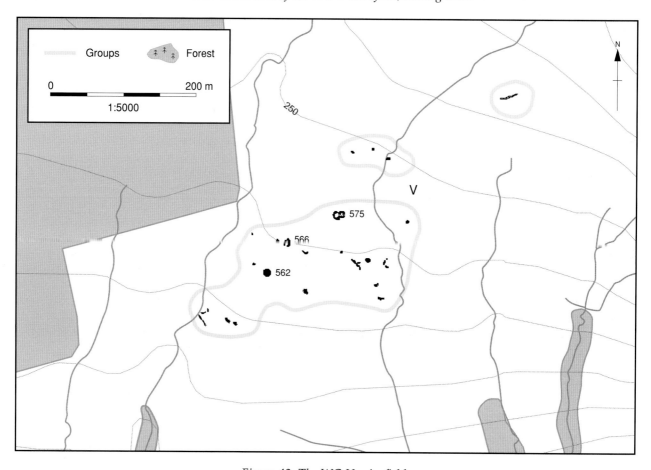

Figure 42: The WG V cairnfield

96

well-defined, prominent banks around the northern sides, although their southern sides were only defined by very slight breaks of slope. The other possible structure (*WG 566*) had a sub-rectangular shape, which was open to the south and had slight internal terracing. Monument *WG 562* was a large, prominent, circular platform (10.3 m in diameter) with well-defined edges. The upper surface was slightly sloping and had a few small hollows set into it. The site group displayed little evidence of any coherent distribution pattern, and no indication of an associated field system.

Whin Garth VI (Gray Borran): monuments *WG 583-609*

Two adjacent cairnfields were identified on the moderate to steeply sloping, well-drained moorland at the foot of Seatallan mountain (Fig 38). The cairnfields were divided by a large area of crag, sporadic outcrop, and brash, which would have been unusable agriculturally.

One of the cairnfields (WG VIA; Fig 43) was located around the edges of a large area of uniformly sloping, well-drained moorland, which had a smoother surface than much of the adjacent moorland. A discontinuous bank (*WG 585*) defined the south-eastern edge of the area, and a narrow band of cairns (*WG 586-92*) marked the upper, north-eastern edge. The cairns were adjacent to the area of outcrop/brash, and as a consequence there was a greater quantity of surface stone in association with them than in the area immediately downslope. At the bottom of bank *WG 585* was a well-drained, natural terrace, but only two cairns were associated with this feature (*WG 583* and *WG 584*). The fact that the bank extended down the whole of one side of this broader area may be an indication that the adjacent area to the west was farmed, even though it contained no cairns. Significantly, the cairns that were present extended in a band across the slope above this putative farmed area.

The other cairnfield (WG VIB) was a small group of cairns found on a small, well-drained, gently sloping natural terrace, which was limited to the north and south by areas of mire. There was some surface stone around the edge of the terrace, but very little within, which may in part be the result of land improvement. The cairns were fairly well defined and had a relatively uniform size (2-3.5 m in diameter).

Whin Garth VII (Thorn Knott): monuments *WG 610-19*

The group comprised a pair of possible roundhouses (*WG 610* and *WG 618*; Fig 43) and a small cairnfield in an area of moderate to steep moorland on the western slopes of Seatallan mountain (Fig 38). The

monuments were at an altitude of between 350 m and 370 m OD and represent one of the highest settlement groups recorded by the LDNPS. The monuments were on natural terraces, set into the slope, with the roundhouses on individual terraces, and the cairnfield on a larger terrace, immediately above the southernmost roundhouse (*WG 610*).

The terrace containing the cairnfield was fairly broad and reasonably flat, although there was a steady increase in gradient towards its forward lip, to the south-west. The ground within it was fairly well drained and had a smooth, turfed surface. On the north-eastern side was a small, flat-bottomed, natural gully, which had expanded the terrace in that direction. The distribution of the cairns was broadly defined by the topography and as a result they formed a fairly tight cluster. The cairns were well-defined and prominent, with rounded profiles.

The terrace containing the southernmost roundhouse (*WG 610*) had a sharply defined forward edge and a steep back-face. Internally, the ground was generally well drained, apart from a localised mire towards the south-western end, away from the roundhouse. This structure (*WG 610*) had the form of a circular ring bank (*c* 5.5 m in diameter), but had no evidence of an entrance. The internal area was slightly terraced, but was also raised a little above the external ground surface and had the appearance of a circular platform. Immediately to the east, and upslope, was a further small terrace containing the small cairnfield.

The terrace containing the northern roundhouse (*WG 618*) was slightly remote from the southern structure and its associated cairnfield, being about 100 m to the north, though at a similar altitude. The terrace was not as well defined, and had a gentle slope, but was well drained and had very little associated outcrop or surface stone. Structure *WG 618* was a uniform, circular turf-covered bank (*c* 6.1 m in diameter). The forward (south-western) edge was slightly raised, its internal area was slightly terraced, and there was no evidence of an entrance, apart from a large stone with an associated slight depression, set into the north-western edge. Both roundhouses were therefore of a similar size, and approximate form, and neither displayed adequate evidence for an entrance. They were also similar in that neither of their respective terraces had any other monuments apart from these roundhouses.

Taken as whole, this site group appears to represent a small but apparently complete farming unit on terraces adjacent to and between parallel becks. Each of the roundhouses and the cairnfield were on separate small natural terraces, which may have been to maximise the available terraced land. However, it is perhaps also

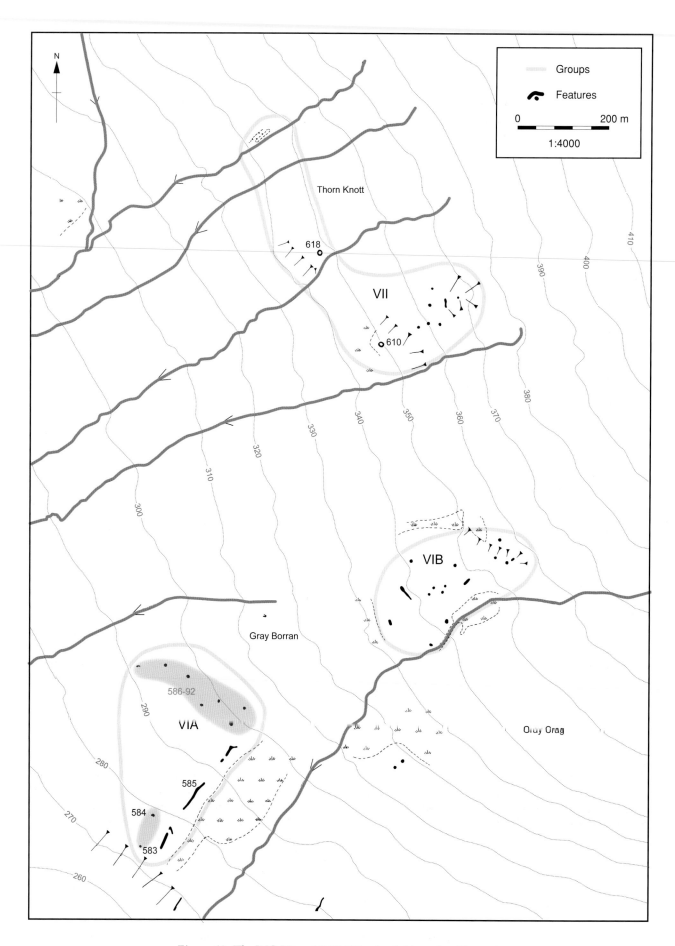

Figure 43: The WG VI and WG VII cairnfields and settlement

significant that the roundhouses were located away from the cairnfield, possibly to separate the domestic and agricultural aspects of the settlement.

Whin Garth VIII: monuments *WG 622-56*
In this area, two small, localised, and spatially remote cairnfields were recorded on an area of gently sloping, though slightly undulating, unimproved, unenclosed moorland (Fig 38). The south-western cairnfield (WG VIIIA; Fig 44) was the smaller and least complex of the two. There were patches of mire in its vicinity, but the extent of the cairns did not appear to have been defined by the local topography. The cairns were moderately defined and some were fairly prominent (*eg WG 627* and *WG 636*). Within the group was a loose scattering of banks or cairn alignments, and it seems to have formed a small, primary type of cairnfield (*Ch 8, pp 328-9*).

The second cairnfield (WG VIIIB) was a relatively compact group of cairns and banks. Although there were localised areas of mire, both within and around the cairnfield, the cairn distribution did not appear to be contained by the visible topography. The cairns were moderately defined and quite prominent and, unlike cairnfield WG VIIIA, there were disproportionate numbers of small cairns and long banks. However, there were few obvious relationships between them and, on the present evidence, they do not appear to define a coherent field system.

Whin Garth IX: monuments *WG 659-72*
In this area, two small, spatially remote cairnfields were discovered on uniformly sloping, unimproved moorland (Fig 38). However, the cairnfields were very different in terms of the size of the component cairns and their concentration.

One of the cairnfields (WG IXA; Fig 44) comprised a small, compact group of moderately defined, low-lying cairns within an island of well-drained, gently sloping land, which was surrounded by rougher, more undulating heather-covered ground. The extent of the island approximately coincided with the extent of the cairn group, and it is possible that this maximised the use of an island of well-drained land that has not changed in extent since the time of the cairnfield's construction. Alternatively, the better land might have been a result of improvement undertaken in the course of the construction of the cairnfield.

The other cairnfield (WG IXB) comprised a group of loosely scattered, large, well-defined and, in some cases, prominent cairns. The largest of these were in a line of three at the eastern side of the group. The central cairn of the three (*WG 671*) had a very well-defined, regular, circular edge and a regular, rounded, prominent, profile (*c* 5 m in diameter, 0.45 m in height).

It was not dissimilar in form to examples of confirmed funerary round cairns, but it was not in a particularly prominent location, and was not sufficiently distinct in form from nearby cairns (*WG 670* and *WG 672*) to be classified with certainty as a funerary monument.

Whin Garth X: monuments *WG 673-88*
This was a rather scattered group of cairns located around the bases of a line of four drumlins and in between two areas of mire (Fig 38); the largest concentration of cairns (*WG 678-80*) was on a small spur between two drumlins, and they were well-defined and typically prominent. However, they were associated with brash deposits and their origin is open to question. Also in the area were two post-medieval stock enclosures; one of these (*WG 674*) was intact, and in places stood to its original height (*c* 1.40 m), but had no evidence of an entrance.

Conclusions
There were two very diverse forms of settlement in the Whin Garth survey area. At one extreme were the small, very localised cairnfields around the higher ground, which were located towards the western side of the area. At the other extreme were the very large cairnfields (for instance, WG I) on the lower ground, and associated complex field systems.

The simple type of settlement (*eg* WG III, WG VI, and WG VIII; Fig 38) appeared to reflect no more than a transient exploitation of the marginal moorland. The primary-type cairnfield (*eg* WG III) was also spatially associated with a burnt mound, a monument which is typically dated to the Bronze Age (O'Drisceoil 1988; Ehrenberg 1990, 41; Neighbour and Johnson 2005), and a watching brief of the area during forest planting recovered four waste flakes of Bronze Age date, but no other artefacts (LUAU 1994c). This, coupled with a limited number of dated parallels for the primary cairnfields (Richardson 1982; Jobey 1981, 35; 1985, 180-4), again of Bronze Age date, would appear to provide reasonable, albeit subjective, evidence to suggest that this cairnfield at least was of Bronze Age date.

In contrast, the WG I complex (Fig 39) was both intensive and permanent; its five phases of field system confirm that it was in use over a considerable period of time, the latest phase having been established by the time of the 1867 First Edition 6" to 1 mile OS map. However, it may not have been in place for very long prior to that date; its walls were very similar to those of the nearby large fell enclosures and it was probably a product of Parliamentary enclosure. The first phase of activity was loosely associated with rectilinear structures that have been identified as shielings, on the basis of the Scale name of the nearby beck and disused farm. The earliest reference to this place-name dates from AD 1365 (Armstrong

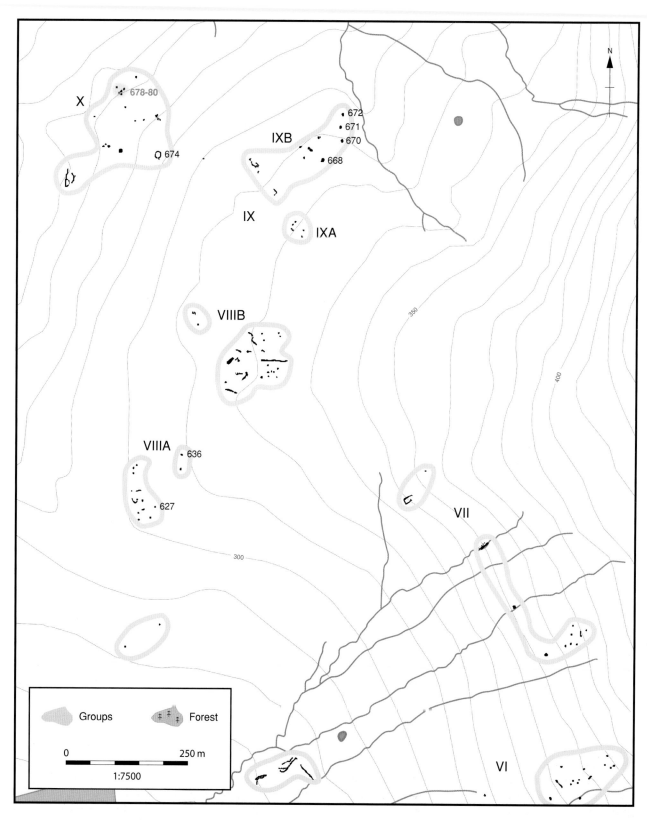

Figure 44: The WG VII, WG VIII, and WG IX cairnfields and field system

et al 1950, 396), which would suggest that there was a transhumant occupation of the site before that date. It is also possible that there were some primary elements of the cairnfield that pre-dated the shielings, and the original clearance of the site may have been considerably earlier than this, potentially even of prehistoric origin. It is, however, more realistic to suggest that Phases 2-5 fit roughly between the two historical dates of 1365 and 1865.

At WG I, it is possible to suggest a simplified sequence of events on the basis of the horizontal stratigraphy discernible. Initially, an area of moorland was partly improved and clearance stone was put into piles. Then, at some time before AD 1365, the area was used for transhumant pasture and shielings were established. This temporary occupation then became more established and a simple field system was created (Phase 1). This then led to a permanent settlement (Scale Farm) and the enclosure of the improved land between the farm and a drove route, or outgang (Guards Lonning; Phase 2). This latter feature then became redundant, and a second farm (Between Guards or Guards End) was established (Phase 3) within its area. This farm acquired and enclosed some of the Scale Farm land, leading to the cultivation of the land on both sides of the Phase 3 walls (Phase 4). Finally, a new field system was established (Phase 5), which largely superseded the old system, and all its gates provided access onto the ridge-top track (Guards Lonning). Scale Farm had also probably been abandoned by this time.

Burnmoor

Burnmoor lies on a ridge between the valleys of the Rivers Esk and Mite, extending to the east up to the western flank of Scafell (Fig 45). The altitude of the moor varies between c 180 m and 330 m OD. The main area of cairnfield and settlement lie on the plateau between the valleys of Miterdale and Whillan Beck, in an area of relatively well-drained, gently sloping land (Pl 73).

Palaeobotanical and archaeological history

Pennington (1970, 72-4 and fig 15a) constructed a pollen diagram from cores taken through the lake sediments of Burnmoor Tarn, to the north-east and downwind of the main groups of small cairns and the five stone circles on Burnmoor (p 111-14). The vegetational history of Burnmoor is well illustrated by this diagram, showing the elm decline at 4229-3653 cal BC (5100±120 BP; K-957), a decline in oak woodland from c 2000 cal BC, and the onset of wetter colder conditions from c 500 cal BC. The decline in the oak forest is of particular interest, as it falls within the period when the stone circles of this area were probably constructed (p 115). Moreover, the presence of an oak forest in the immediate environs of Burnmoor Tarn is further confirmed by the presence of oak leaves in the lake sediment. At the same time, there was an expansion of grassland, and grassland herbs, and the absence of contemporary cereal or weed pollen indicates the existence of an open pastoral landscape. Pennington suggests that deterioration in the climate, illustrated by a reduction in alder pollen and a corresponding increase in that of Coryloids (probably of Myrica (bog

myrtle)), brought an end to the Bronze Age occupation of the uplands from about 1200 BC (Pennington 1970, 72; Pearsall and Pennington 1973, 232). Pennington (1970) recognised a Romano-British clearance episode, dated to cal AD 139–686 (1569±130 BP; NPL-116), associated with cereal pollen. Contemporary with this, and continuing to the present day, was a sharp increase in Calluna (heather) pollen, an indication of the formation of acidic humic soils, bringing a relatively short-lived period of cereal cultivation to an end, perhaps by the seventh century AD. Since then, Burnmoor has been an open, infertile moor, with peat sediments continuing to accumulate in the wetter areas.

The earliest archaeological investigations of Burnmoor were by Mr Wright of Keswick in c 1827, who opened two of the five cairns within the Brat's Hill stone circle (Williams 1856). The stone circles at Brat's Hill and White Moss were recorded on the 1867 First Edition 6" to 1 mile OS map, but neither the groups of small cairns nor the circles at Low Longrigg were shown.

The first detailed survey of the stone circles and some of the adjacent archaeological features was undertaken by Aubrey Burl in the early 1970s (Burl 1976, 93-7). The five stone circles were planned in detail, and the archaeological landscape of Burnmoor was recorded more generally. This survey also plotted the location of some of the principal groups of small cairns, though some of these were interpreted as house platforms and settlements, an interpretation that could not be confirmed by the present survey. Burl (ibid) also investigated the relationship between the stone circles and the groups of small cairns, said then to be a comparatively recently recognised phenomena. He also noted (op cit, 97) that other researchers had argued that these cairns had a ritual function, and in order to explore this he excavated one of the cairns on Low Longrigg (though it is not clear which cairn this was), which confirmed 'its non-sepulchral nature'. In addition, Burl (ibid) also provided a detailed discussion of the nineteenth-century excavations, the interrelationships between the five circles, and their possible significance for astronomical observations.

The stone circles and cairns were noted by the OS Archaeology Division field investigators in the 1960s and 1970s. The earlier of these surveys planned the monuments, but they were only noted on the OS record card (NY 10 SE 12) as being 'scattered over a large area of open moorland'. Most recently, features on Burnmoor were sketched by Nick Higham, in an attempt to show the relationship between 'cairns and the community' (Higham 1986, fig 3.3). The sketch survey shows some of the principal groups and monuments that were recorded in greater detail by the present survey; however, many were not illustrated, only partly depicted, or shown incorrectly.

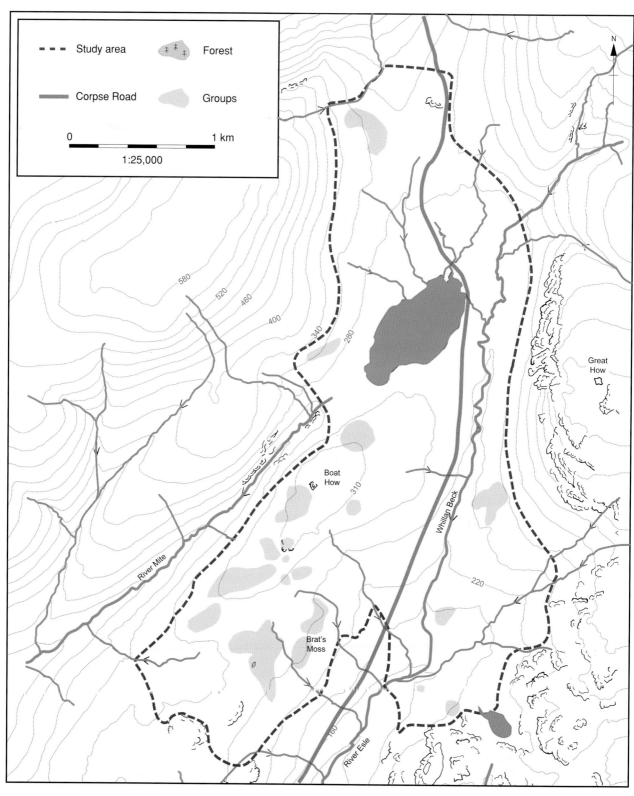

Figure 45: The Burnmoor survey area

The survey area

The survey was undertaken between April and May 1984, covering *c* 5.5 km² of unenclosed moorland (Fig 46). A very dry spring season provided exceptionally good conditions for the observation of features normally concealed by vegetation, and in total *c* 600 monuments, found within 16 site groups, were recorded. The component monuments were mainly groups of small cairns (Fig 47), some of which were characterised by their relationship with stone banks and the five well-documented stone circles (Burl 1976). Smaller cairn groups were also found around Burnmoor Tarn, and on the line of a major col linking Wasdale and Eskdale.

Plate 73: The ridge of Burnmoor, with Burnmoor Tarn in the middle distance

Burnmoor I (Straighthead Gill): monuments *BM 1-44*

A group of small cairns lay on the eastern slopes of Illgill Head, between the 300 m and 330 m contours, with an open aspect overlooking Wasdale Head and facing east towards Scafell (Fig 47). This marked the northern and eastern limit of the zone within which groups of small cairns were abundant; further to the east, the ground rises towards the high fells of the central Lake District. To the south of Straighthead Gill were 41 small cairns and two short lengths of stone bank (*BM 13* and *BM 18*; Fig 48), whilst two

103

cairns (*BM 43* and *BM 44*) lay some distance to the east of the main group. The cairns had an essentially random distribution and there was no evidence of any significant cairn alignments.

Maiden Castle

To the east of the group of cairns at Straighthead Gill was the large round cairn known as Maiden Castle (Fig 47). It was surveyed by the OS Archaeology Division field

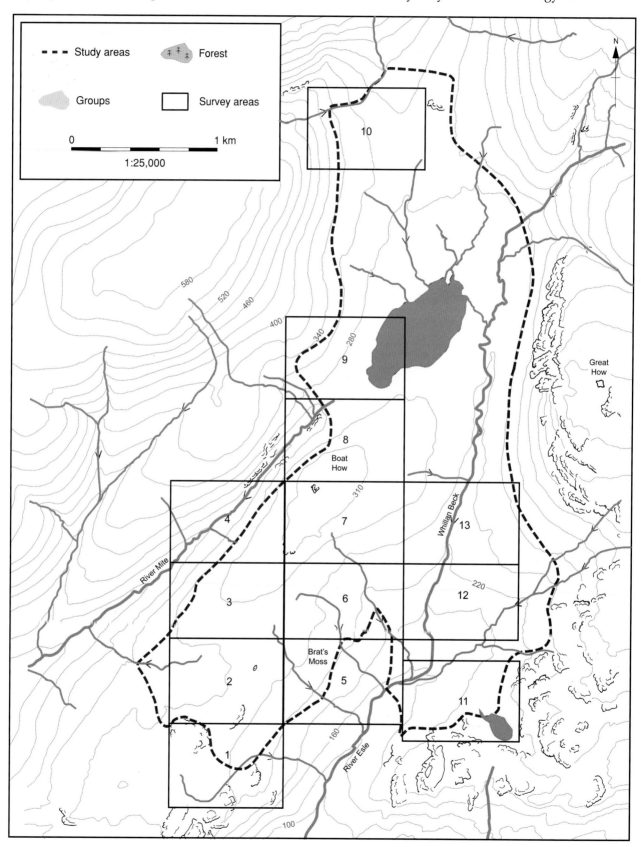

Figure 46: The Burnmoor survey area as planned

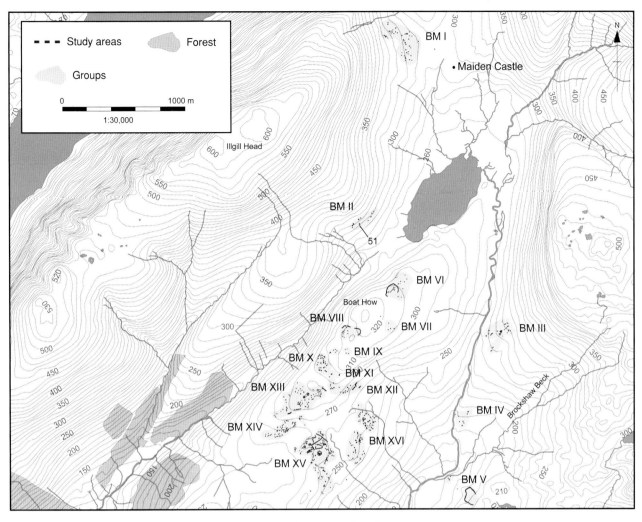

Figure 47: Monument distribution within the Burnmoor survey area

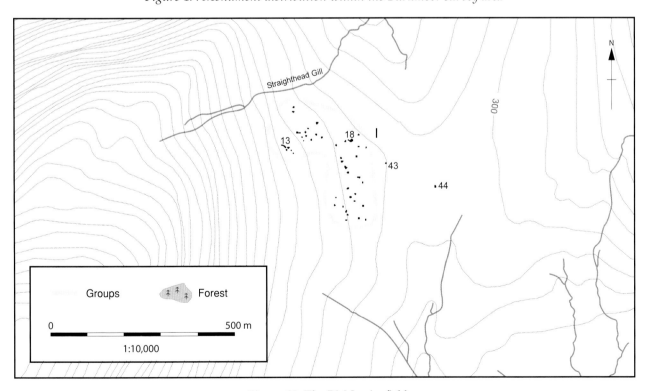

Figure 48: The BM I cairnfield

105

investigator in July 1973, and was described on the OS record card (NY 10 NE 1) as 'A modern sheep stell, now collapsed, built from the residual material of a denuded round cairn on which it now stands. The consolidated base of the latter is still a fairly obvious mound 12 m in diameter and 0.4 m high on the east side, contained by a well-defined peristalith'. Maiden Castle is one of a small number of large round cairns scattered across the area (*Ch 2, pp 44-5*).

Burnmoor II (west of Burnmoor Tarn): monuments *BM 45-54*

This group of small cairns lay on the south-eastern slopes of Illgill Head, between the 290 m and 320 m contours, with an open aspect overlooking Burnmoor Tarn (Fig 47). Eleven small cairns were recorded. With the exception of one (*BM 51*), the group was arranged in two lines of five cairns, both approximately orientated along the contours.

Burnmoor III (south of Lambford Bridge): monuments *BM 56-78*

A group of small cairns lay on the western slopes of Eskdale Fell, above the valley of the Whillan Beck, to the south of Lambford Bridge, between the 240 m and 280 m contours (Fig 47). This area marked the eastern limit of the zone within which groups of small cairns were abundant, as further to the east the ground rises towards the high fells of the Lakeland central massif.

On the rising ground to the east of the Whillan Beck, 25 small cairns were recorded, which were very varied in size. Within the group was a 14.6 m-long stone bank (*BM 59*; Fig 49), at right-angles to

the contours, and an irregularly shaped enclosure (*BM 68*; 15.6 x 14.2 m), which was poorly defined by a bank consisting largely of a scatter of small- and medium-sized stones protruding from the turf. Set in the south-western corner of the enclosure was a small circular depression, enclosed by an ill-defined bank. This was potentially a domestic structure serving the adjacent stock pound.

Burnmoor IV (East of Whillan Beck): monuments *BM 79-86*

This group of small cairns lay on the south-western slopes of Eskdale Fell, between Whillan Beck to the west and Brockshaw Beck to the east, situated between the 180 m and 200 m contours (Fig 47). To the east of the group, the ground rises towards the high fells of the central Lake District. Eight cairns of various sizes were recorded; there were no significant cairn alignments and their distribution was seemingly random.

Burnmoor V (Little Pie): monuments *BM 87-92*

A small group of cairns lay to the south of the Whillan Beck, between the 160 m and 170 m contours, and below the enclosure on Little Pie (Fig 47). This group marked the south-eastern limit of the zone within which groups of small cairns were abundant. Further to the east, the ground rises towards the high fells of the Lakeland central massif. One of the cairns was elongated and three were approximately circular in plan. To the south-east was an isolated, open-ended sub-rectangular structure lying between the 170 m and 180 m contours. Its low wall was quite well defined, and it was possibly a relatively recent bield.

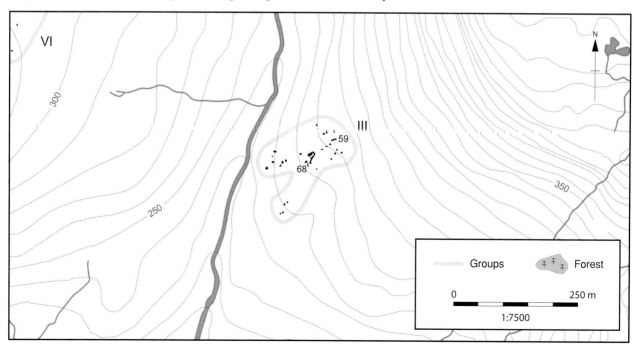

Figure 49: The BM III cairnfield

The monument on Little Pie was a stone-walled enclosure, located on a gentle rise on the southern side of the Whillan Beck valley, below Eel Tarn, between the 180 m and 200 m contours. It was defined by a discontinuous bank, had an irregular shape, was 102 m by at least 133 m in extent, and contained no visible features within its interior. It was probably of ancient date, since its walling was similar in weathering to that of the small cairns. To the south-east, the banks were partly buried beneath peat, and there was a possibility that the enclosure had once been continuous.

Burnmoor VI (Eskdale Moor): monuments *BM 93-116*

An enclosure and a group of small cairns were situated on Eskdale Moor to the north-east of Boat How, between the 300 m and 320 m contours (Fig 47). Much of the site was covered by thick heather, and further surface features may well await discovery. The enclosure was roughly oval in plan, *c* 110 x 82 m in extent (*BM 105*; Fig 50), and was possibly first noted by Burl (1976). The southern length of wall was only very poorly defined on the ground, but was more clearly represented on an aerial photograph (Pl 74). On the east side was a clearly defined entrance. Within the enclosure were three annular features (*BM 109-11*), 3.0-3.5 m in diameter, which were very sharply defined internally, but ill defined externally. They would appear to be robbed cairns, and their small diameters preclude their interpretation as stone-founded roundhouses. Within the enclosure, seven

small cairns were also recorded, all approximately circular in plan.

Beyond the enclosure to the east were a further 11 cairns, which were fairly small in extent. Within this group was a fourth putative robbed cairn (*BM 101*); its diameter of *c* 3.3 m was similar to those within the enclosure.

Most of the cairns were distributed within a broad band that extended north-east/south-west from a point within the enclosure to a point 110 m beyond it, the alignment perhaps being an indication of a former field boundary. The presence of the cairns both within and outside the enclosure could indicate that the two were not contemporary; against this argument, the cairns within the enclosure were more tightly distributed than those outside, which may suggest some relationship. The archaeological potential of this site is particularly high because of the juxtaposition of the cairns and the enclosure, its good preservation partly below later peat, and its proximity to Burnmoor Tarn, with its well-preserved sediments (*p 101*).

Burnmoor VII (Boat How): monuments *BM 117-21*

This group of small cairns lay on the south-eastern slope of Boat How overlooking Burnmoor, only a short distance below the summit, between the 310 m and 320 m contours (Fig 47). Five small cairns were recorded (Fig 50); one was elongated and four were approximately circular in plan.

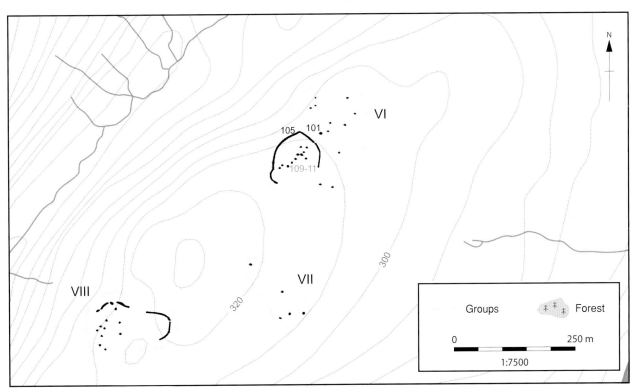

Figure 50: The BM VI-VIII cairnfields and field systems

107

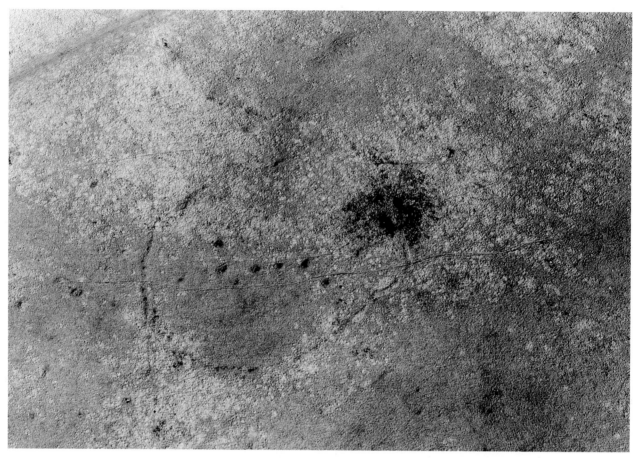

Plate 74: The BM VI cairnfield and enclosure

Burnmoor VIII (Boat How): monuments *BM 122-32*

Partly enclosing the secondary summit of Boat How, between the 310 m and 320 m contours, was an incomplete enclosure and a group of ten small cairns (Fig 50). The enclosure bank showed mainly as an earthwork, with a few stones protruding from the turf (2-3 m wide, 0.2 m in maximum height), and was traceable only on the north and east sides. The ten small round cairns were situated entirely at the west end of the enclosure, and were totally within its likely limits. The absence of any cairns immediately beyond the observed enclosure boundary suggests that they were probably constructed within the enclosure, and were possibly contemporary with it. This group of small cairns was interpreted by Burl (1976, 94, fig 15) as being a settlement with roundhouses, but no roundhouses were identified by the LDNPS, and therefore this interpretation cannot be confirmed.

Burnmoor IX (Boat How): monuments *BM 133-42*

To the south and south-west of the enclosure on Boat How, between the 300 m and 320 m contours, but still above the break of slope, were two further groups of small cairns (Fig 51). The group to the south comprised two cairns, and that to the south-west five cairns. One cairn was elongated and four were approximately circular in plan.

Burnmoor X (South-West of Boat How): monuments *BM 143-70*

To the north and west of Boat How, between the 290 m and 300 m contours, overlooking Miterdale on a sloping terrace below the break of slope around its summit plateau (Fig 47), was a compact group of 27 small cairns, some very poorly defined (Fig 51). Two lengths of stone bank (*BM 169* and *BM 170*), similar in weathering and appearance to the small cairns, were perhaps extant elements of field boundaries. Generally, the distribution of cairns was essentially random. However, within the southern part of the group was an area that was markedly devoid of cairns (bordered by cairns *BM 156-9* and *BM 164-8*), which may reflect an area that had been deliberately cleared, of both stone and cairns, for agriculture.

Burnmoor XI (Low Longrigg North): monuments *BM 171-9*

To the south and west of Boat How, at *c* 290 m OD, and on a sloping terrace below the break of slope, around its summit plateau, was a group of eight small cairns (Fig 51). One was elongated and the rest were approximately circular in plan. To the north of the cairns, on a level area immediately underneath the break of slope and crags below Boat How, were three walls of a structure (*BM 173*; 5 x 7 m; Fig 51). These were composed of large boulders and smaller

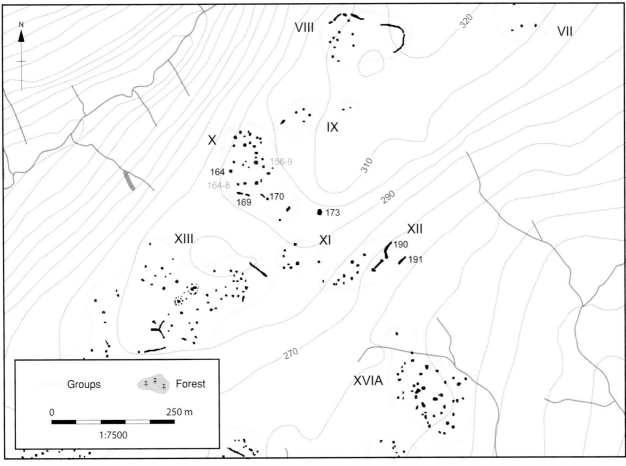

Figure 51: The BM IX-XII cairnfields

stones, and defined the remains of a small building, probably a bield.

Burnmoor XII: monuments *BM 179-91*

A group of 14 small cairns was recorded to the south of, and below, Boat How, between the 260 m and 290 m contours, and overlooking Burnmoor (Fig 47). Most were ill defined and of varied size, the smaller ones being at the south-western end of the group. The group also included three lengths of stone bank (*BM 190* and *BM 191*; Fig 51), which had similar weathering and appearance to the cairns. They were all parallel with each other and were potentially related elements, possibly the surviving fragments of a much larger system. Significantly, though, they were located slightly away from the cairn group.

Burnmoor XIII (Low Longrigg): monuments *BM 192-248, BM 498,* and *BM 49*

Low Longrigg is the gently sloping promontory to the west of Boat How, between the 260 m and 290 m contours, overlooking Miterdale to the north and Burnmoor to the south (Fig 47). The group recorded there included two stone circles, which were planned and described by Burl (1976), and by the OS Archaeology Division field investigator in 1973. However, during the LDNPS, the small cairns

and stone banks adjacent to the stone circles were planned for the first time. The two stone circles (*BM 220* and *BM 221*; Fig 52) were central to the group and were between two clusters of cairns. The positioning of the stone banks and the distribution of the small cairns indicated a spatial relationship with the stone circles.

The limits of the groups of small cairns around the two stone circles were defined on the east and south by two lengths of stone bank (*BM 192* and *BM 248*), similar in weathering and general appearance to the small cairns. The southern stone bank (*BM 248*) incorporated two cairns in its length, reflecting its origins in episodes of clearance.

To the south-west of stone bank *BM 192*, and south of the two stone circles, was a group of 32 cairns (*BM 193-219* and *BM 498-9*), distributed in a *c* 35 m-wide band. This band was generally *c* 25 m to the south of the stone circles and on the same alignment, following the line of the ridge. Only the cairns at the east and west ends of the group extended northwards, seemingly around the stone circles. At the south-western end of the group were two elongated cairns (both numbered *BM 218*) and a circular cairn (*BM 498*), which were aligned, and

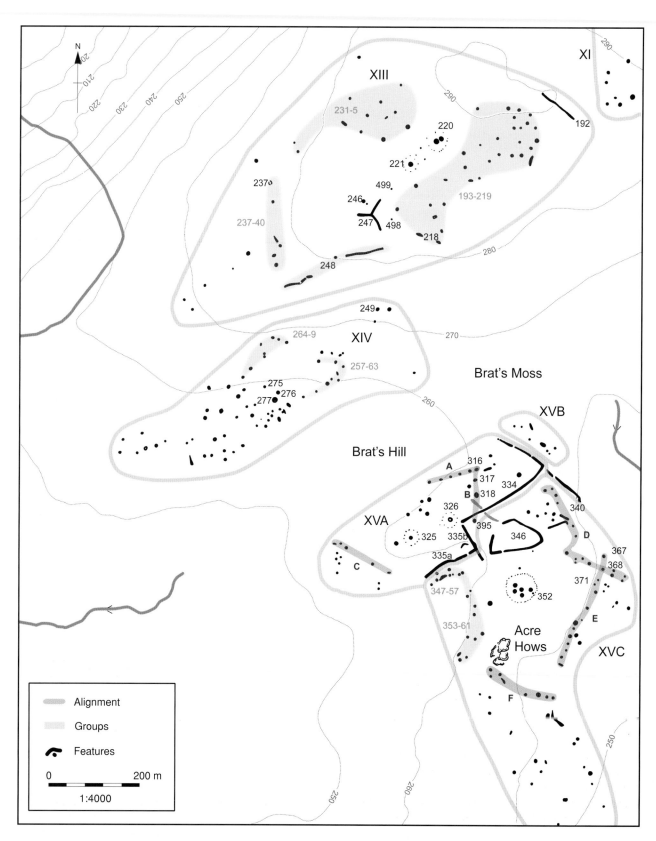

Figure 52: The BM XIII-XV cairnfields and stone circles

apparently of some significance. To the north-west of the stone circles was a second group of 11 small cairns. Their southern limit was at a similar distance from the stone circles to that of the cairns to the south. A regularly defined area immediately around the stone circles was therefore devoid of small cairns, up to 25 m from the outer limits of the two circles. There was a similar absence of small cairns in the zones to the south of the White Moss and Brat's Hill stone circles (BM XV; *p 111*). To the west of

110

circles, and to the north of stone bank *BM 248,* was a large area that was devoid of cairns but edged by banks, or cairns, on all sides (*BM 221* (within the stone circle), *BM 231-5*, *BM 237-40*, *BM 246*, *BM 249*, and *BM 499*). The area may have been a field with clearance stones deposited in piles or banks around it, and was reminiscent of a similar plot defined by cairns at Acre Hows (*BM XV*; *p 113*).

A small cairn found in this site group, near Low Longrigg to the north-east, was also excavated by Burl (1976, 97; *see below*). However, the LDNPS was not able to identify the excavated cairn, unless it corresponds to the hollowed-out cairn, *BM 237*, at the western end of the group.

To the south-west of the stone circles was a bield, with three radiating walls offering shelter to sheep in any wind direction (*BM 247*). It was similar in form to post-medieval bields identified from other LDNPS areas (for instance, *AF 133* on Moor Divock; *Ch 7, p 307*) and is likely to be of a broadly similar date.

To summarise, there was a clear relationship at Low Longrigg between the distribution of the small cairns, lengths of walling, and the two stone circles. The stone circles lay in an area that was devoid of cairns, corresponding to a broad swathe along the ridge, 50 m wide and extending for *c* 250 m. The cairns were either distributed into compact groups on either side of the stone circles, or, along with lengths of stone banks, around a possible rectilinear field, which was to the immediate west of both cairn clusters, and the stone circles.

Burnmoor XIV (Low Longrigg South): monuments *BM 249-307*
In between the two complexes of stone circles, walls, and small cairns at Low Longrigg (BM XIII) and at Brat's Hill (BM XV), was a shallow valley, which contained a small cairnfield group (Fig 52). In this valley there was considerable variation in the soil cover and, in places, areas of glacial drift were close to the surface, whereas elsewhere it was suspected that peat growth might mask some features, and thus prevent a complete delineation of the extent of the cairn groups. The groupings apparent from surface evidence may therefore be illusory, although it could be argued from the overall distribution that the group as a whole may originally have been within an enclosure, of which no trace now remains.

In this area, some 70 small cairns were distributed in a broad band *c* 80 m wide, extending *c* 350 m from south-west to north-east. The southern edge of this group was especially well defined and followed a similar alignment to that of the stone circles to the north at Low Longrigg (BM XIII), and to the south at

White Moss (*p* 111). Within the cairnfield was a sub-rectangular area that was devoid of cairns, but which was delineated by cairns (*BM 257-63*, *BM 264-9*, *BM 275*, and *BM 276*). Although there were no visible stone banks in association with this cairn-free area, it is possible that this was a small agricultural plot, with piles of clearance stone deposited around its perimeter.

Burnmoor XV (Brat's Hill): monuments *BM 308-409*
Brat's Hill
A series of monuments was found around the gently sloping brow of Brat's Hill (Pl 75), which included cairns, stone circles, and enclosures. One group (BM XVA) of small cairns, stone banks, and two stone circles lay on gently sloping ground between the 250 m and 260 m contours, at a similar altitude to those on Low Longrigg, with an open aspect towards the north and north-east (Fig 47). The stone circles were central to the sub-group (Fig 52), and surrounded by cairns and the stone banks. Although the two stone circles (*BM 325-6*; Pl 76) were planned and described by Burl (1976, 93-7), and by the OS Archaeology Division field investigator in 1973, the LDNPS planned the small cairns and walls adjacent to the stone circles for the first time. The cairns and stone circles were enclosed on the east and south by three lengths of stone bank (*BM 334* and *BM 335*), which were *c* 2 m wide, the latter with an entrance on the south side. All were similar in weathering and general appearance to the cairns, although parts of these banks, and their possible continuations, were masked by later peat growth. In contrast to Low Longrigg (BM XIII), there was no clear spatial relationship between the cairns and the stone circles.

A total of 26 cairns lay to the north and east of the enclosure banks. To the north, the group was largely defined by a significant alignment of cairns (A), one of which had possibly been used as a shooting butt (*BM 316*). A further putative alignment extended south, and approximately perpendicular to this first alignment (B); at the south of this possible alignment was a large cairn, which had been incorporated into a later stone bank (*BM 335*). Significantly, this would imply that the stone banks post-dated the cairn alignment.

A small cluster of nine cairns, to the west of the stone circles, was similarly edged by a line of five cairns (C) to the east, which was approximately perpendicular to, and potentially convergent with, the line of stone bank *BM 335*. Also of interest was the alignment of stone banks *BM 334/5*, which had a corner immediately adjacent to the easternmost stone circle (*BM 326*), and appeared to have avoided the stone circle deliberately. Moreover, the alignment of stone bank *BM 335b*, to the south, forms a tangent with the western edge of

Plate 75: BM XV, at Brat's Hill, with stone circles BM 325 *and* BM 326 *(centre)*

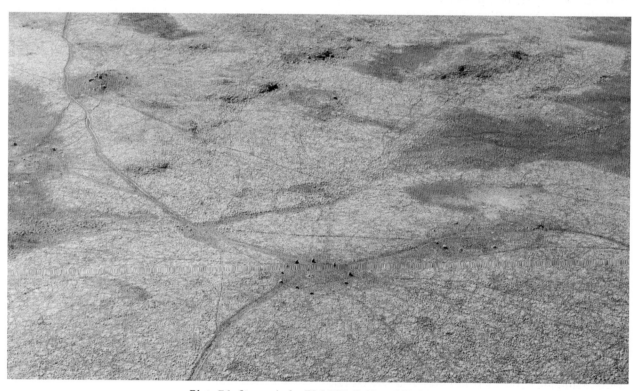

Plate 76: Stone circles BM 325 *(left) and* BM 326

stone circle *BM 352*, to the south, and to the north it forms a tangent with the eastern edge of stone circle *BM 326*. The implication is that these banks respected the stone circles and may, therefore, be later features. The vista from the entrance in bank *BM 335a* was also on the same alignment, which extended to the centre of the easternmost stone circle (*BM 326*). To the east of the stone banks enclosing the Brat's Hill stone circles was a group of eight small cairns, located at *c* 260 m OD (BM XVB). It is possible that these were also part of this group of cairns, although they were separated from it by stone bank *BM 334*.

112

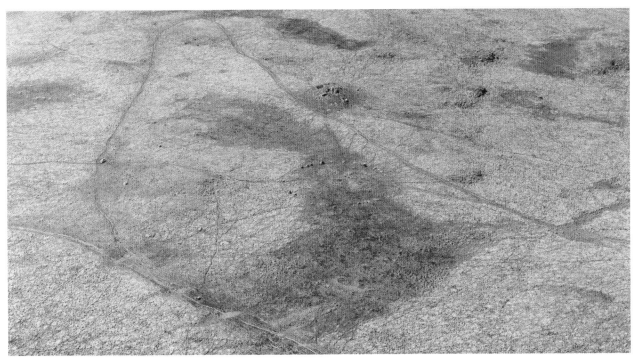

Plate 77: Stone circle BM 352, *looking south towards the outcrop on Acre Hows*

Acre Hows

Acre Hows (Fig 52) is a prominent outcrop giving a good view to the north and east over the expanse of Burnmoor, and to the south over the Whillan Beck and towards Eskdale. The monuments in this area (BM XVC) included a stone circle (*BM 352*), an enclosure (*BM 346*), and bands of small cairns, which were divided from those cairns found on Brat's Hill (*p 111*) by stone banks *BM 334-5*.

The stone circle (*BM 352*) lay on a promontory overlooking Burnmoor, slightly above the 260 m contour; it was the largest of the five stone circles found on Burnmoor, and had an open aspect towards the north and north-east (Pl 77). It was planned and described by Burl (1976, 93-7; Fig 53), and also by the OS Archaeology Division field investigator in 1973. The LDNPS, therefore, mapped the small cairns and walls adjacent to the stone circles. Two of the cairns in the stone circle were excavated by a Mr Wright of Keswick in *c* 1827, revealing 'in the centre of each, under a rude dome composed of five large stones, remains of burnt bones, with fragments of the horns of the stag and other animal remains' (Williams 1856, 226). This would appear to indicate a conventional Bronze Age-type cremation within a simple cist, but these five burial cairns were not necessarily contemporary with the stone circle (Pl 78).

To the north of the stone circle was a slightly irregular, D-shaped enclosure (*BM 346*), which was defined by stone banks, with an entrance on the north-west side. The 2.9 m-wide bank was similar in weathering and general appearance to the adjacent small cairns and stone banks *BM 334-5*, on Brat's Hill (*p 111*). The

interior of the enclosure was entirely devoid of small cairns, or other features. In addition, this enclosure lay within the corner of the *BM 334-5* boundary bank, but had a different orientation and was not necessarily a contemporary feature.

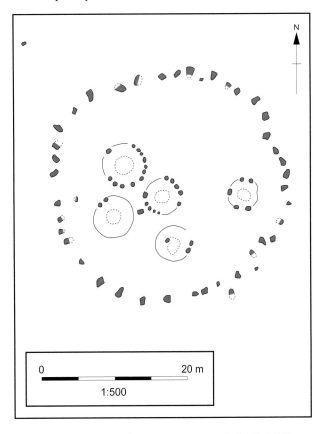

Figure 53: Plan of Burnmoor stone circle BM 352
(after Burl 1976)

Plate 78: Cairns within stone circle BM 352

For the most part, the cairns were arranged around a rectilinear area, or field, that had stone circle *BM 352* at its centre, but otherwise contained almost no cairns. The north-east side of this plot was edged by a narrow band of circular cairns (Alignment D), which extended north-west/south-east and to the east of the D-shaped enclosure (*BM 346*). Within this same area were two lengths of stone bank (*BM 340*), one of which was similarly orientated to the western section of stone bank *BM 335*, found to the west. Given this, it is possible that these banks were related features, and that the enclosure (*BM 346*) sandwiched between them was not a contemporary feature.

The south-eastern side of the putative plot was defined by a significant cairn alignment (E), comprising cairns of different sizes. The south-western side of the plot, to the south of Acre Hows, was defined by a cairn alignment (F) extending across the line of the contours. The western side of the plot was defined by a narrow band of 11 cairns (*BM 353-61*), following the line of the 260 m contour. Finally, to the west of the D-shaped enclosure (*BM 346*), and immediately south of stone bank *BM 335*, were a further nine small cairns. Their proximity to the stone bank suggests a possible relationship.

Further south from Acre Hows, the remaining cairns were spread more randomly over the hillside, albeit in a very broad north-west/south-east band. However, vegetation cover within this area may have prevented identification of additional features associated with the cairn group.

Discussion

Together, the complexes on Brat's Hill form an archaeological landscape of exceptional preservation and importance. The discontinuous form of the visible surface remains indicates that there is the potential for further features concealed by later peat growth, particularly as some of the identified features were only visible in the sustained dry weather of April and May 1984. The relationships between the stone circles, the groups of small cairns, and enclosures are clearly of interest, especially when seen in relation to the northward and southward projection of stone bank *BM 335*. The putative cairn alignment, *BM 316-18*, with *BM 395*, has a possible terminus, with a prominent bulge in stone bank *BM 335*, which could imply an earlier cairn incorporated into a later boundary bank. In any case, the *BM 334/5* stone banks were orientated differently from the cairn alignments, and boundary *BM 335* appeared to divert around cairn group *BM 347-51*. It can thus be argued that these relict boundaries post-date the cairnfield. Furthermore, the alignments of stone banks *BM 334* and *BM 335* respect stone circles *BM 352* and *BM 326* tangentially, which also suggests that the surrounding stone banks post-date the stone circles. Although there was no obvious relationship between the D-shaped enclosure (*BM 346*) and boundaries *BM 334/5*, it is possible that these were also not contemporary features, but instead reflect different phases of the development of the Brat's Hill complex.

The sub-rectangular arrangement of significant alignments of cairns possibly reflects the deposition of cleared stone around a plot of improved ground, or field, which significantly contains almost no cairns. It is interesting to note that the large stone circle, *BM 352,* is in the middle of this plot, but has no direct relationship with any of the components of the cairnfield, or proto-field system. It is seemingly at odds, therefore, with the proto-field system, and it is probable that it was not contemporary with the agricultural phase of activity occurring in this area, as shown by the surrounding cairnfield.

Burnmoor XVI (Brat's Moss): monuments *BM 415-97*

On the south-east slopes below Burnmoor, overlooking the Old Corpse Road and the valley of the Whillan Beck, was a completely separate group of 89 small cairns lying between the 240 m and 260 m contours (Fig 47). The cairns fell into two, possibly distinct, sub-groups within this area.

The first sub-group (BM XVIA; Fig 54) comprised 44 small cairns located within a roughly rectangular area measuring *c* 100 x 50 m. Of these, 14 were elongated and 30 were approximately circular in plan. The cairn distribution was essentially random and there were no significant alignments.

The second sub-group (BM XVIB) was found to the south, and within this group the cairns were more thinly spread. The northern part of the group was a compact cluster of cairns (*BM 456-72*), again with an essentially random distribution. To the south of this, the cairns formed bands. One to the west comprised cairns *BM 473-81*, and the eastern limit to the group was a band of cairns parallel to the contours (*BM 482-8* and *BM 494-6*). Although some degree of linearity was visible, it is not clear that they were sufficiently rationalised to form elements of a field system.

Conclusions

Although the five stone circles on Burnmoor have been repeatedly studied on many previous occasions (*inter alia,* Burl 1976), the LDNPS provided, for the first time, an overview and accurate plan of the archaeology of Burnmoor as a whole. As a result of this work, it is clear that the ritual/funerary function of the stone circles contrasts with the agricultural character of the cairnfields and proto-field system found in this area. For instance, there is no direct relationship between the cairns and the stone circles, and the larger Brat's Hill stone circle (*BM 352*) is anomalously positioned within an agricultural plot defined by cairn alignments. The implication is that these distinct elements were parts of two spatially superimposed, but chronologically separate, landscapes. Certainly, there are indications within some of the site groups of multi-phased activity and

there is an implication that the activity on Burnmoor extended across a broad period of time.

Given these observations, it is possible to construct a very tentative sequence of activity on Burnmoor during the prehistoric period. However, in the absence of scientific dating evidence, the chronology of the area inevitably remains uncertain, and there was probably considerable overlap between the different episodes of activity.

Phase 1: funerary/ritual landscape

The large Brat's Hill stone circle (*BM 352*) is very distinctive and has characteristics of an early monument (*cf* Burl 1976, 60). For example, it is large, open, has a flattened shape, a large number of stones, and also an outlier. As such, it is distinct in form from the other four stone circles in this area, which are much smaller, circular, have limited numbers of stones, and are more typical of the later type of stone circles (*ibid*). Although *BM 352* has five burial cairns within it (Fig 53), these were not necessarily contemporary with the stones and do not provide an indication of the date of this primary monument. Given the potential early date of one element of the ritual/funerary landscape, it may be that the whole landscape was relatively early, however. Furthermore, if it is assumed that the funerary/ritual landscape was not in contemporary use with the BM XV agricultural field system, it is therefore perhaps more likely to pre-date, rather than post-date, the proto-field system. Even if the stone circles did pre-date the BM XV system, this does not exclude the possibility that some of the stone circles were contemporary with the other cairnfield/clearance activity found on Burnmoor.

Phase 2: primary cairnfields

The most basic element of agricultural activity on Burnmoor was a series of small, localised, primary cairnfields, comprising randomly distributed cairns (BM I-IV, BM VIII, BM IX-X, BM XII-XIV, and BM XVI). It is tempting to link this pioneering activity to the early part of the decline in oak woodland, from *c* 2000 cal BC to *c* 500 cal BC (Pennington 1970, 72-4). At the outset of this period, Burnmoor was evidently still a largely wooded environment, and it is possible that the localised groupings of the cairnfields reflect initial clearances within this forest. These areas acted, therefore, as foci for human activity, which may also explain the absence of prehistoric features between the known monument groups.

In some areas, the monument groups appear to have expanded and merged with their neighbouring groups, or clearances, such as at BM XVI, where three distinct concentrations of cairns, linked by lower densities of these features, were recorded. While some groups seemed to be simple random groupings

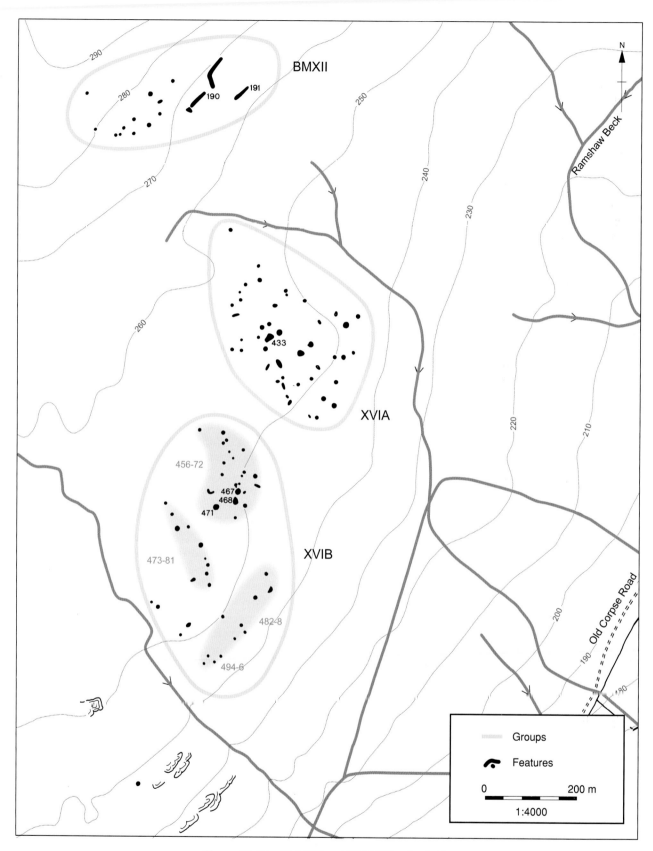

Figure 54: The BM XII and BM XVI cairnfields

of cairns, such as BM XVI and BM X, apparently a product of a single phase of activity, others appeared to reflect more disparate components that potentially indicate more than one phase of activity. For example, an alignment of cairns (BM VI; *p 107*) extending north-east/south-west, on the northern side of Burnmoor, was seemingly truncated by a largely continuous stone bank (*BM 105;* Fig 50), forming a partial enclosure, which was probably unrelated to, and later in date than, the cairn alignment.

Phase 3: proto-field systems
While the majority of the Burnmoor cairnfields are primary in character, there are several (BM XIII-XV), centred on Brat's Hill and Low Longrigg, which display clear indications of linear organisation and the establishment of plot boundaries. These possibly reflect either the rationalisation of primary cairnfields, or represent the establishment of a basic or proto-field system on open ground.

At BM XIV (*p 111*), at the north-eastern end of a group of essentially randomly distributed cairns, was a possible plot defined by alignments of cairns (*BM 257-63*, *BM 264-9*, *BM 275*, and *BM 276*; Fig 52), which suggests secondary development of a primary cairnfield. By contrast, at BM XV, the majority of the cairns were aligned around a large plot centred on the large stone circle (*BM 352*) at this locale. In this instance, the implication is that these features, which formed a proto-field system, were established from the outset, and were later in date than the stone circle. This might suggest that woodland in this area had been partly denuded prior to the formation of the proto-field system, and this may explain the relative absence of randomly distributed cairns, which are normally associated with the clearance of woodland. Indeed, it is also possible that the absence of a primary cairnfield may be a reflection of the initial use of this area as a funerary / ritual landscape, which may in itself have been positioned at the edge of a woodland clearing. This cleared area, and also the stone circle, then became the focus for later agricultural activity.

Phase 4: developed field systems
At BM XV (*p 111*), there are indications of a further phase of the development of the field system, as several stone banks forming parts of a rectilinear field system appear to conflict with, and post-date, the cairn alignments. One notable example of this was stone bank *BM 334*, which extended through a cairn alignment (*BM 316-18*, and *BM 395*), and that also incorporated one of the cairns from this alignment within its fabric. It was also clear that the system of stone banks respected, and post-dated, the stone circles found in this area. In addition to this, an enclosure (*BM 346*) appears then to have been established which, based on its positioning, was probably later than the stone banks. The imposition of later enclosures on an earlier area of agricultural activity was also evident at BM VI (*p 107*), where a partial enclosure (*BM 105*) was seen to cut through a north-east / south-west cairn alignment.

Discussion
It is perhaps worth quoting Burl (1976, 95), who argued, after considering the landscape surrounding the Burnmoor stone circles, that 'surmises on the interconnections of such sites and Brat's Hill or even between themselves is more a matter for the visionary than the archaeologist'. This statement has now, to some extent, been overturned as a direct result of the LDNPS, which has provided a clearer, albeit in some cases speculative, overview of how the Bronze Age sepulchral and agricultural landscapes inter-related in this area. Moreover, as a direct result of the detailed survey work undertaken on Brat's Hill, the significance of this important site has been considerably enhanced.

4

THE SOUTH-WEST FELLS – WEST

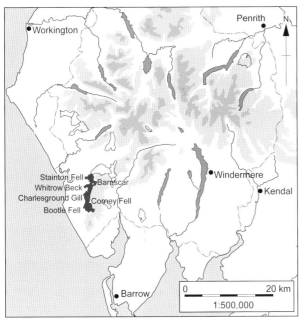

Figure 55: The extent of the survey in the western South-West Fells

The South-West Fells of the Lake District comprise a narrow range of hills defined by the coastal plain to the west and south, the Duddon Valley to the east, and the Esk Valley to the north. The central ridge is formed by a series of low summits rising to a maximum height of 572 m OD at Whitfell, and around the perimeter of this steep-sided central ridge, at an altitude of between 150 m and 250 m OD, is an extended, broad planation terrace, with a gentle surface gradient. The proximity to the coastal plain of this agriculturally viable land made it an appropriate area for extensive marginal settlement, and many prehistoric settlement remains have been identified there, particularly around the western side of the Fells.

In total, the survey programme investigated 23.7 km² of unimproved land extending from Kinniside Common to Wasdale, which was divided into 11 survey areas. The areas on the western side of the South-West Fells (Fig 55) were on Bootle Fell, Corney Fell, Charlesground Gill, Whitrow Beck, Stainton Fell, and Barnscar. Most of these were adjacent to each

other and there are very few areas around the western side of the planation terrace that do not bear evidence of ancient agricultural activity. Parts of this terrace have subsequently been reoccupied by medieval farms and enclosures, in particular around the farms of Stainton (SD 127 947), Woodend (SD 167 963), and High Corney (SD 124 928). However, the majority of the terrace has seen little, if any, reoccupation and the prehistoric settlements have largely been preserved.

Bootle Fell

Bootle Fell is an area of undulating moorland on the west-facing slopes of the South-West Fells, adjacent to the coastal plain (Fig 55). This area is also only 2 km from Barfield Tarn, where palaeoecological sampling demonstrated vegetational disturbance, clearance, and cultivation from the mid-neolithic period onwards (Pennington 1970, 69). The cultivation episode was evidenced by substantial amounts of cereal pollen from *c* 4000 cal BC onwards (*op cit*, 68), which coincided with a sharp reduction in the amount of elm and oak pollen, indicative of forest clearance. A later period of intensive clearance, probably during the Bronze Age, led to permanent and complete deforestation. To a great extent, the palynological events depicted correlate with similar events recorded at Ehenside Tarn (*op cit*, 69), and would therefore appear to be symptomatic of vegetational changes taking place across the coastal plain. However, given the proximity of Bootle Fell to Barfield Tarn, it is likely that many of the sites surveyed were within its airborne pollen catchment, and thus, to an extent, the activity at Bootle Fell will have been reflected in the palynological record. Specifically, the Bronze Age forest clearance episode may equate with activity on Bootle Fell, though not necessarily its complete deforestation.

The terrain of the moor generally had a gentle to moderate gradient, with the notable exception of the Kinmont and Crookley Beck gullies (Fig 56). To the south of the area, there was a sharp increase in gradient, leading up to the summit of Black Coombe.

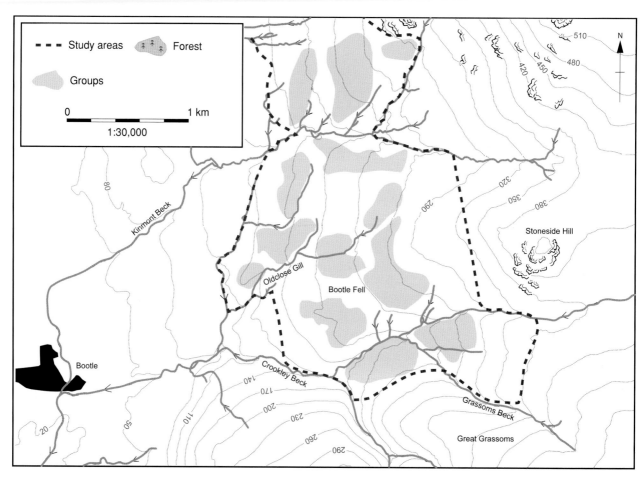

Figure 56: The Bootle Fell survey area

Near the bottom of these steep southern slopes (Great Grassoms) was a medieval field system (BF XI; *p 134*), but otherwise the exposed slopes were found to be archaeologically barren. Towards the east of the survey area, the cairn groups petered out as the altitude increased. The highest group (part of BF X; *p 131*) was found at 345 m OD, but generally the cairnfields and settlements were at altitudes between 160 m and 270 m.

To the north, Kinmont Beck divided the survey area from the large cairnfields on Corney Fell (*p 139*). However, the beck did not appear to have served as a boundary in antiquity, as there were cairnfields of a similar character extending almost up to each side of its gully.

Substantial mires on the fellside may have constrained the extent of some of the cairnfields. An extensive area of mire to the west of BF II and BF III (*pp 123-5*) appeared to have restricted the spread of cairnfields further downslope. Cairnfield groups BF I-III, BF V, and BF VI were distributed around a large area of mire, centred on SD 130 896, and BF II was almost an island, being surrounded by mire on most sides. The limits of the mire did not appear to have changed significantly since the construction

of the cairnfield, because the furthest extent of this generally corresponded to the edges of the poor drainage. However, a few sites were discovered (*BF 251-2*, *BF 257*, and *BF 309* in BF II; *BF 417* in BF III; *see p 125*) in poorly drained land, which may indicate a limited expansion of the mire.

Archaeological history

Although several round cairns on Bootle Fell have undoubtedly been the subject of antiquarian explorations (*eg BF 637* and *BF 804*), there is no published record of any excavations. Some of the cairnfields (BF II, BF III, and BF VII-X) were depicted schematically on the 1900 Second Edition 6" to 1 mile OS map, whilst the settlement on Grassoms (BF XI) was first recorded by Rev James Wilson (1915, 365), who described it as a 'quadrangular area, surrounded by an earthen dyke, faced with stones, having a ditch on the outside'. In 1961, the cairnfields depicted on the 1900 Second Edition 6" to 1 mile OS map were scheduled as Ancient Monuments (now SM32831 and SM32833).

History of settlement on Great Grassoms

There are two historical references to 'Gressholmes', which would seem to be a settlement (BF XI; *p 134*) in an area to the south of Crookley Beck, called Grassoms on an enclosure map of 1857. The earliest, from the

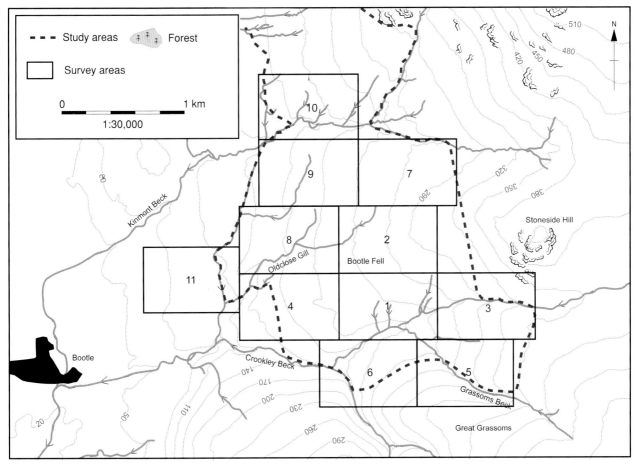

Figure 57: The Bootle Fell survey area as planned

Register of the Priory of St Bees (Wilson 1915, 364-5), was an agreement dated to AD 1252 between John Hodilston, the Lord of Millom, and the Abbot of St Mary's, York. In this document, John Hodilston and his wife agreed to honour an agreement between themselves and the prior of St Bees concerning Gressholmes, and that 'as soon as [they] come to Copeland [they] will have the afore said land, Gressholmes, returned to the abbot and the convent of St Mary's, York'. However, the document then states that if 'he is unable to return the land for some reason, some other land of the same value' would be made over. The second historical reference is from the Millom Courtbook of 1510-23 (CRO D/LONS/W/Millom Courtbook 1510-23, 64). In this, there is a rental of 1510, which includes the text 'a tenement called Gresholmys and Whytehow clos in the hand of the lord because of the said lord remain on that place and protects sheep' (rent 21s 2d).

Gressholmes was still owned by the Lord of Millom in 1510 and, although it is clear that the Priory of St Bees had a claim upon the land, it was not necessarily ever in monastic hands. Although the agreement of 1252 (Wilson 1915) only refers to the land of Gresholmes, the dispute suggests that it was of some value and was therefore probably in

agricultural use. By 1510, a shepherd was resident on the land, which would suggest that the Grassoms settlement pre-dated this rental.

The survey area

The survey was undertaken in May 1987 on 3.5 km^2 of unenclosed moorland (Fig 57). In total, 918 monuments were recorded within 11 site groups (Fig 58). These groups indicated a broad range of activity on the marginal lands, and included some extremely large cairnfields (for instance, BF I and BF II), but also some smaller cairnfields exploiting localised areas of good agricultural land (BF VI and BF VIII). In some areas, there was evidence for the development of a proto-field system, notably on Little Grassoms (BF X). Scattered throughout these groups were some substantial funerary round cairns, and in particular one small, localised, group of funerary cairns, again on Little Grassoms. A medieval field system was also recorded on Great Grassoms, associated with two substantial rectangular houses (BF XI).

Bootle Fell I (Kinmont Beck): monuments *BF 1-182*

A large cairnfield on uniformly sloping moorland was edged to the south and west by mire and

121

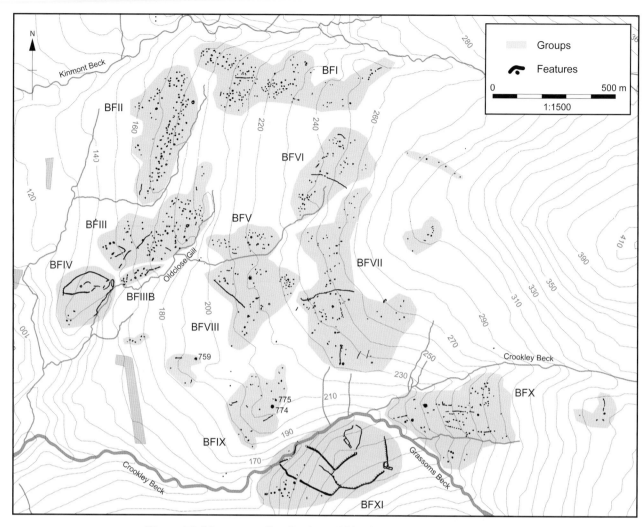

Figure 58: Monument distribution within the Bootle Fell survey area

to the north by the very steep-sided Kinmont Beck (Fig 58). To the east, the cairnfield was not defined by topographical features and a very small concentration of small, clearance-type cairns extended upslope from the main part of the site.

The cairnfield formed three distinct sub-groups. The first (BF IA; Fig 59) comprised a compact cluster of moderately large, well-defined, and occasionally prominent cairns. At the south-east edge of this group was an alignment of eight cairns (A), which may reflect linear stone clearance along a former boundary. At the eastern edge of this group was an unusual type of monument (*BF 30*), which comprised a well-defined mound with an attached semi-circular enclosure. There were no other similar examples on Bootle Fell, although similar monuments were recorded on Stockdale Moor (*SM 423, SM 151,* and *SM 169; Ch 3, pp 75-6*).

The second sub-group (BF IB; Fig 59) comprised a generally small, fairly ill-defined group of cairns, the average cairn size increasing towards the west. A straight, but ill-defined, stone bank ran through the centre of the sub-group (*BF 139*), with cairns *BF 140* and *BF 141* perhaps extending the line of this feature to the east, whilst another possible boundary, with a right-angled bend, was defined by an alignment of cairns (B). This second group was divided from BF IA by a substantial break of slope, with the cairns from each respective group lying immediately adjacent to this topographical feature. Significantly, the cairns from these two groups differed in prominence and, to a lesser extent, size, suggesting that they related to different episodes of stone clearance.

The third group (BF IC; Fig 59) contained fairly prominent and well-defined cairns. There were no obvious alignments and the cairns would appear to have had an essentially random distribution. In addition, the area between the second and third groups was largely devoid of monuments, and the cairns again differed in definition, size, and irregularity of form, suggesting different clearance episodes.

Taken as a whole, although there were only a few stone banks, several cairn alignments did appear

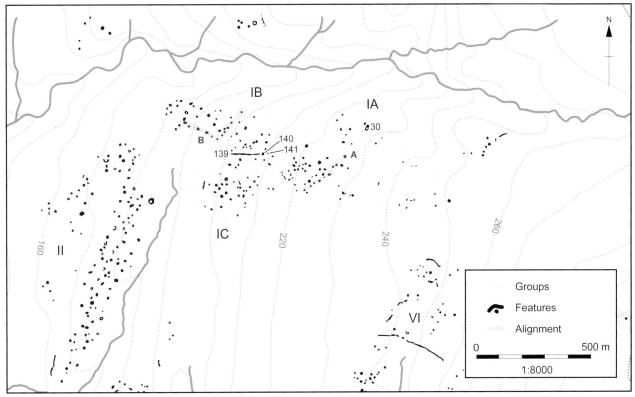

Figure 59: The BF I cairnfield

to define the extent of the cairnfield, and may have corresponded to the lines of former boundaries. For example, the alignment of cairns recorded in BF IA appears to a have defined its south-eastern edge, whilst the alignment recorded in BF IB defined part of the south-western extent of the cairnfield. Stone bank *BF 139* was a more obvious boundary marker, but its alignment was also extended by the position of a number of cairns, which appeared to define the southern extent of one element of the cairnfield.

Bootle Fell II (Damkirk Beck): monuments *BF 183-310*

This monument group comprised a large cairnfield, which was located on a well-drained, long natural ridge (Fig 58), whilst two additional, smaller, groups of cairns were recorded at the base of the ridge (Pl 79).

Within the large cairnfield (BF IIA; Fig 60), located on the ridge, the distribution of cairns was clearly defined by the natural topography, and they were bounded to the east by an area of mire and to the west by a sharp break of slope. There was a more gentle change of gradient at the far northern end of the ridge and a few cairns spread down the hillside. The long ridge was crossed by gullies, created by two small streams, which did not appear to have affected the distribution of the cairns. The size and prominence of the component cairns gradually increased towards the southern end of the ridge,

those at the northern end being generally small, ill defined, and irregular, although a few were moderately prominent. At the far southern end of the cairnfield, the cairns were very prominent (0.5 m in height), very large, and well defined. Despite the size and prominence of the southern cairns, their distribution was comparable to those forming the remainder of the large cairnfield, and they appeared to be large stone clearance cairns, rather than having any other function. There were no obvious cairn alignments within the cairnfield and the distribution was essentially random.

Plate 79: The BF II cairnfield, looking south

123

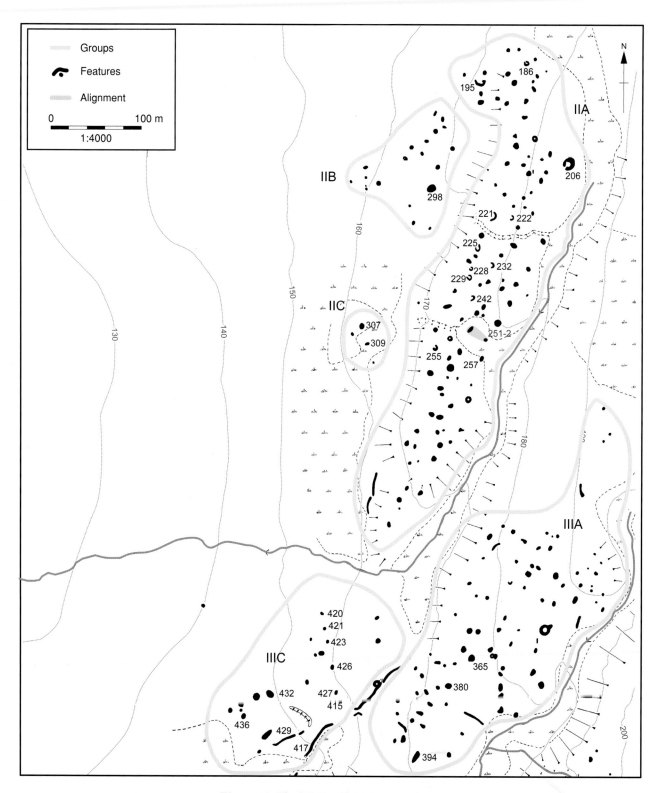

Figure 60: The BF II and BF III cairnfields

In addition to the cairns forming the large cairnfield, ten monuments were identified along the western side of the ridge, which shared a distinctive form. These were all irregular, approximately semi-circular banks of similar size (*c* 5 m across), which all had their open face towards the south-west (*BF 186, BF 195, BF 221, BF 222, BF 225, BF 228, BF 229, BF 232, BF 242,* and *BF 255*). The banks were usually low-lying and often ill defined, and each enclosed an unterraced, rough-surfaced interior. Five were aligned approximately parallel to the western break of slope (*BF 221, BF 225, BF 228, BF 229,* and *BF 242*), whilst the others were interspersed with the cairns of the large cairnfield. There were no other examples of such features elsewhere on Bootle Fell, but the site has a parallel at WG IV, in Whin Garth (*p 94*).

Given their orientation, they are unlikely to have been shelters, nor are they likely to have been grouse butts, as they were not prominent and were grouped closely together. They were, however, reminiscent of a group of semi-circular banks on Hollow Moor (WG IV; *Ch 3, p 94*). A very prominent, oval ring bank (*BF 206*, with an average diameter of 8.7 m) was also recorded at the northern end of the ridge. This ring bank was approximately level and had an eccentric interior. The ground outside the ring was also level and there was no evidence of internal terracing; a large entrance on the south-western side faced into the prevailing winds. Despite the eccentricity of the interior and the orientation, there is a possibility that this was a roundhouse.

Of the two smaller cairn groups found at the base of the ridge, one (BF IIB) comprised a band of generally ill-defined cairns extending west from the base of the ridge, in a localised area of generally well-drained ground. However, close to these small clearance-type cairns, and below the long break of slope, was a very large, very prominent, oval cairn (*BF 298*: 12.6 x 11.9 x 0.5 m). The profile of this cairn was fairly regular and flat-topped, and it appears to have been capped with small stones, in contrast to the larger stones found around its outside. Although not located in a prominent position, it contrasted with the adjacent cairns and may well have been a funerary monument.

The second small cairn group (BF IIC) at the base of the ridge was defined by a small cluster of four cairns, which partly lay within an island of better-drained ground, surrounded by mire. One of the cairns (*BF 309*) was located within the mire, perhaps suggesting a change in the drainage pattern since the construction of the cairns. The cairns were irregular in size, with the largest (*BF 307*) being 6.5 m in diameter, while the others were less than 3 m in diameter.

Bootle Fell III (Oldclose Gill): monuments *BF 311-438*

In a similar way to BF II, immediately to the north (Fig 60), this large cairnfield was also constrained by the local topography, being located on a gradually undulating ridge between two stream gullies. It comprised a large group of cairns at the northern end of the ridge and two distinct, but smaller, groups at its lower, south-western end (Pl 80).

The distribution of the cairns in the main cairnfield (BF IIIA) was essentially random and there were no significant cairn/stone bank alignments. The cairns were generally varied in form and size, although some, towards the southern end of the cairnfield (*eg BF 365, BF 380*, and *BF 394*), were larger and more prominent than those upslope. Despite the size of some of the cairns, they all showed irregularities of shape and form, and were consistent with stone clearance.

Plate 80: The BF IIIA cairnfield, looking north-east

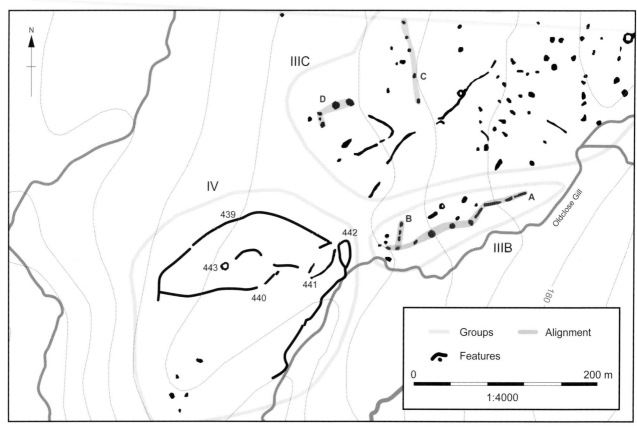

Figure 61: The BF IIIB and BF IV cairnfield and field systems

One of the smaller groups of monuments (BF IIIB) in this area was located on a protruding limb of the ridge, comprising a narrow band of cairns and banks. An alignment of these (A; Fig 61) defined the southern edge of the cairn group, possibly representing a former boundary. A further short cairn alignment (B) was approximately perpendicular to this.

The second small group of monuments (BF IIIC) in this area was located on gentle, sloping ground below and to the west of the main ridge, adjacent to areas of mire. Contained within this group were banks *BF 415* and *BF 417*, which were of dry-stone construction and were probably discontinuous sections of a single wall. This was aligned, in between the main cairnfield (BF IIIA) and the BF IIIB cairn group, along the bottom of a 'dip', which was partly filled by mire. It was orientated towards the terminals of walls in BF IV (*p 128*), had a similar form to them, and may have been a further element of that field system. Attached to the side of wall *BF 415* was a circular structure, with large stones incorporated into the foundations. There was no obvious entrance, though collapsed material had obscured much of the evidence. A similar example (*BF 640*) was recorded in BF VII (*p 129*). An alignment of cairns (C) extended from the north-eastern end of bank *BF 417*, and may have been a further boundary of the field system.

There was a possible independent plot to the west of *BF 417*. This was defined on two sides by the banks of *BF 429*. The downslope bank was irregular in width and profile, and contained no evidence of dry-stone construction; the cross-slope bank had a lynchet-like profile, with evidence of soil slippage from the downslope side. The other two sides of this field were possibly formed by cairn Alignment D, which defined an approximate right-angle. The lack of cairns within the area apparently enclosed by these features suggests that the area may have been used for cultivation.

Discussion

In contrast to the random cairn distribution within the rest of the cairnfield, one of the smaller groups of monuments in this survey area (BF IIIC) had aligned clearance cairns; a dry-stone wall with a possible attached shelter; and a partly enclosed plot, which may have been used for cultivation. Although this group was not necessarily contemporary with the main cairnfield, it may have been a part of the BF IV field system (*see below*), immediately to the south, which contained similar elements.

Bootle Fell IV (Old Close): monuments *BF 439-48*

An irregular field and enclosure were recorded on a gently sloping section of a natural spur formed by two stream gullies (Fig 58); within the field was a small ring bank. The northern and eastern limits of the spur were edged by two long banks, of which one was parallel to Oldclose Gill, and the other followed the line of a natural shelf above an area of mire.

126

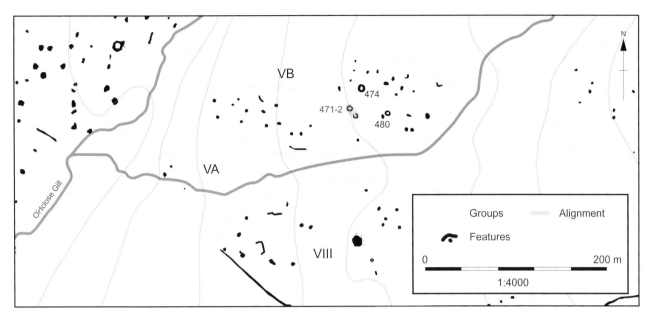

Figure 62: The BF V cairnfield

The field

The field had an irregular shape, defined to the south by banks *BF 440* and *BF 441* (Fig 61), and to the north by the prominent and lyncheted bank, *BF 439*. This was butted by bank *BF 440* and continued to the west beyond the area surveyed. The bank was evidently earlier than *BF 440*, and was also earlier than the field defined to the south by *BF 440*. Banks *BF 440* and *BF 441* were discontinuous, their courses were erratic, and they were occasionally ill defined, in contrast to *BF 439*. At the north-eastern end of the field was a gap between banks *BF 441* and *BF 439*, which was opposite enclosure *BF 442*, probably forming a formal entrance to the field. Within the field there was patchy, narrow, ridge and furrow, aligned east-west, which terminated short of bank *BF 439*. In addition, a length of headland for one of the areas of ridge and furrow was visible at NY 12310 89105. A prominent, annular feature, *BF 443* (9.0 x 8.9 x 0.35 m), was present within both the field and the area of ridge and furrow, which had well-defined outer banks and no obvious entrance. The ridge and furrow was particularly ill defined in the area of this ring feature and, although the stratigraphic relationship between the two elements remains unclear, there was no evidence of a furrow cutting the edge of the ring.

The enclosure

Extending along the western side of Oldclose Gill was a prominent, uniform, and well-defined bank (*BF 442*), which was perhaps a decayed dry-stone wall. At its northern terminus was an enclosure (*c* 30 x 13 m), which was marked by a well-defined, decayed wall, partly revetted into the eastern and northern slope of a spur on the northern side of Oldclose Gill. By contrast, its western side was ill-defined, low-lying, and irregular in form. No obvious entrance was observed, but this may have been obscured by an area of tumble found along the line of the western bank. The interior was approximately level and appears to have been terraced.

Discussion

The field system was associated with ridge and furrow cultivation and had a very different character from that of the adjacent BF III cairnfield. Given this, it is probable that these were not contemporary landscapes. However, there were similarities between this field system and that at BF XI (*p 134*), which also had large fields, defined by continuous banks, an absence of cairns within the fields, with similar small enclosures, and a long boundary parallel to the adjacent stream.

Bootle Fell V: monuments *BF 449-89*

Two small cairnfields were identified on an area of gently sloping, well-drained land, bordered to the south and east by a beck, to the north by an extensive mire, and to the west by the break of slope of the Oldclose Gill gully (Fig 58). The cairnfields were separated by a break of slope and had very distinct characters.

The western cairnfield (BF VA; Fig 62) lay below the dividing break of slope and comprised fairly low, ill-defined cairns with regular rounded profiles. In contrast, the eastern cairnfield (BF VB) was on a slight hillock and comprised cairns that were generally better defined and slightly more prominent. This latter group also included four tightly clustered ring features (*BF 471-2*, *BF 474*, and *BF 480*) in various states of preservation. Ring features *BF 471*, *BF 474*, and *BF 480* had regular outlines, were well-defined internally and externally, and had flat, or terraced, interiors (*BF 471*: 6.8 x 6.3 x 0.25 m; *BF 474*: 7.6 x 7.0 x 0.35 m; *BF 480*:

6.0 x 5.6 x 0.3 m). Significantly, ring features *BF 471* and *BF 480* also had possible entrances and might therefore form the remains of possible roundhouses. Ring feature *BF 472* was only visible as a semi-circular feature, and was not particularly well defined (6.0 x 5.7 x 0.3 m).

Discussion
The concentration of ring features in this survey area was reminiscent of the cairnfield recorded at Birrel Sike, West Cumbria, where there were 39 similar features (Richardson 1982). The excavation of one of these (HC1) revealed that it had been deliberately constructed, with larger stones around the inner and outer edges, and it was interpreted by the excavator as a ring cairn; it produced a radiocarbon date of 2396-1756 cal BC (3670±100 BP; BIRM-1018).

Bootle Fell VI (Levens Moss): monuments *BF 490-554*
In this survey area (Fig 58), two small cairnfields were identified, which were separated by a possible field. The more southerly of the two cairnfields (BF VIA; Fig 63) comprised a compact group of cairns on a natural island of well-drained land, edged to the north, west, and south by extensive mire, and to the east by a sharp break of slope. The cairns were moderately well defined and some were fairly prominent. The distribution was essentially random and it would appear to have been a primary form of cairnfield (*Ch 8, p 328*).

The other, more northerly, cairnfield (BF VIB) was small and compact, and was located at the foot of a substantial break of slope. In general, the cairns were not very prominent, having regular rounded profiles, and were consistent with stone clearance. Stone bank *BF 541* defined the northern edge of the cairnfield and had no obvious relationship with any of the banks of the possible field.

The possible field (BF VIC) lay between the two cairn groups, and had irregularly defined boundaries; to the south, it was edged by a fairly continuous bank (*BF 518*), except where it extended over a sharp break of slope. The western boundary, however, comprised an alignment of very irregular banks (A) and on the eastern side there was only an alignment of four cairns (B), parallel to the western banks.

Only two isolated cairns were identified in the possible field, together with a small rectilinear structure (*BF 519*) set into a substantial break of slope across the middle of this field. The structure had two elements: a small square building (1.8 x 1.7 m); and a partially enclosed courtyard area. The walls of the building survived to a height of seven courses (1.7 m) and, although the floor was partially obscured by collapsed material, it was probably internally terraced. The volume of collapse and the present height of the walls suggest that the structure was roofed. Although its entrance faced west, towards the

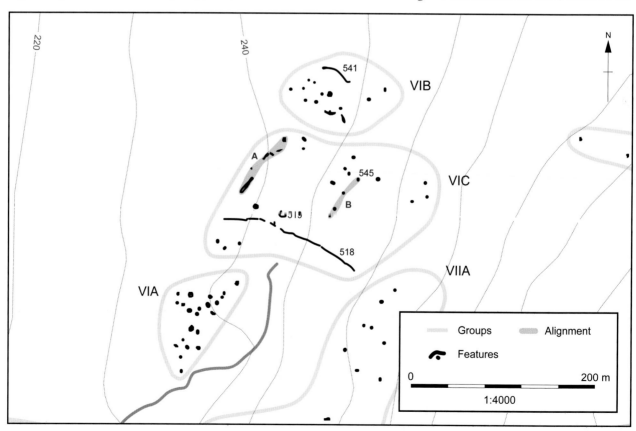

Figure 63: The BF VI cairnfield

128

prevailing winds, it would have been partly protected by the outer wall of the courtyard. The small size of the building suggests that it served only as temporary accommodation and it may have been a shieling, or an elaborate shepherds' bield.

Bootle Fell VII: monuments *BF 555-660*

Several diffuse groups of scattered cairns and occasional banks on gently sloping land were recorded on a natural terrace, positioned between the 240 m and 270 m contours (Fig 58), that was sporadically edged by a break of slope at top and bottom. The terrace was most clearly defined at the northern end, where there were two small, scattered groups of low-lying, clearance-type cairns (BF VIIA; Fig 64). These monuments were for the most part located on the gently sloping terrace between two marked scarp slopes, and there were no associated banks, and little

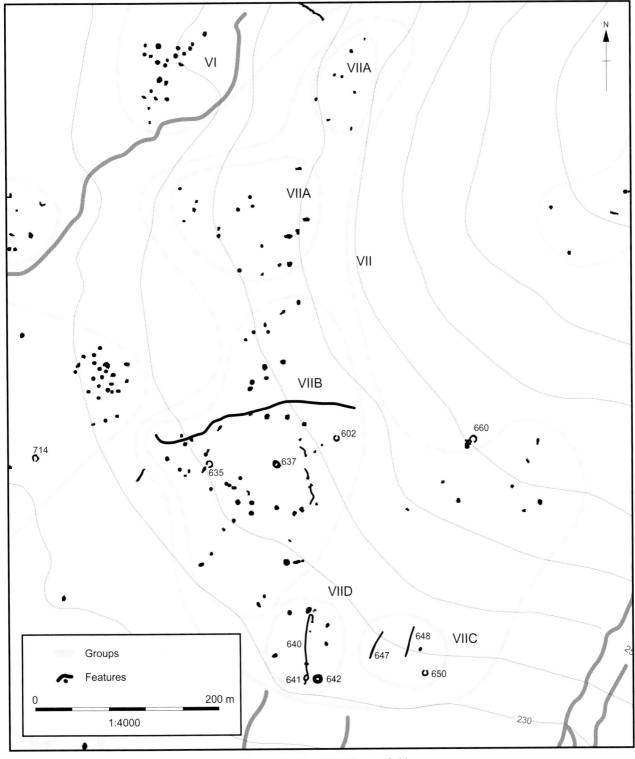

Figure 64: The BF VII cairnfield

discernible pattern to the cairns. This was therefore essentially a primary cairnfield.

In the central part of the site was an amorphous group of cairns, with interspersed funerary monuments and a ring bank (BF VIIB). The cairns were significantly larger and more prominent, but were generally uniform in character and were consistent with stone clearance. Round cairn *BF 637* was situated on the top of a low hillock; it was large, very prominent (0.5 m high), very well defined, and is likely to have been a funerary monument. There were also smaller cairns and a discontinuous bank around the base of the hillock, leaving an area around the central monument that was devoid of cairns. Such a distribution may have reflected a deliberate intention to separate funerary from agricultural activities. Associated with the peripheral cairns were two circular ring features (*BF 602* and *BF 635*), possibly roundhouses, which appeared to be internally terraced.

In the south-eastern part of the site was a series of parallel banks, associated with a ring feature (BF VIIC). The banks (*BF 647* and *BF 648*) were orientated downslope, and may have defined the edges of an arable plot, although neither had lynchet profiles. The ring feature (*BF 650*) was approximately circular, with ill-defined edges, and a wide entrance to the north. It was internally terraced and would appear to represent the remains of a roundhouse.

The final group of monuments (BF VIID) recorded in this area was located on a natural promontory, edged by a break of slope to the south and west. In this area, a wall (*BF 640*) with an irregular enclosure at the northern end (Pl 81), and a large round cairn at the other, were recorded. Wall *BF 640* was continuous, uniform, prominent, and had substantial kerbing. Immediately to the north-east of an enclosure was a short section (*c* 4 m) of low wall foundation, which may represent a limited extension. The enclosure was formed by the butting of an enclosing wall onto the end of the straight wall. Given this, it would seem probable that it was a later feature, set into the middle of the wall and built from stone robbed from its redundant northern section. The enclosure had a slightly irregular shape and an ill-defined entrance to the south. There was a substantial quantity of collapse within it and it was not possible to determine if it had been internally terraced. It was not particularly large (*c* 6.3 x 5.5 m) and perhaps was a small shelter.

The southern end of wall *BF 640* merged with a large, fairly prominent, round cairn (*BF 641*), with a central depression. A similar, but much larger, centrally depressed round cairn was also found adjacent to it (*BF 642*). Neither feature displayed any evidence of an entrance, and their relationship to the wall remains uncertain. The wall contrasted sharply with the stone banks, which were the more usual

Plate 81: Enclosure and attached wall BF 640, *within the BF VII group*

130

form of linear features found on Bootle Fell, and there is a possibility that both it and its associated features were not contemporary with the rest of the BF VII complex.

Bootle Fell VIII: monuments *BF 681-743*

Monument group BF VIII was sharply defined and constrained by the natural topography (Fig 58), being edged to the north by a stream and to the west by an area of mire. There were two sharp breaks of slope, orientated approximately north-south, which divided the area into three blocks of well-drained, moderately sloping land, each of which contained a small cairnfield. The character of each was markedly different, possibly implying different stone clearance episodes and even different agricultural functions.

The more westerly of the cairnfields (BF VIIIC; Fig 65) comprised scattered cairns in an area defined to the west by a mire, to the north by a stream, and to the east by the break of slope. These cairns were limited in number, and varied in size and form.

The more easterly of the cairnfields (BF VIIIA) comprised a relatively large concentration of cairns within a small, sharply defined area, and it was not constrained by the present topography. The component cairns were small, relatively uniform in form, and contrasted with those cairns (BF VIIIB) recorded on the central section of the terrace.

In this central area, the cairns displayed a wide variety of type and scale, and were loosely scattered over the natural terrace. This central group also included two large funerary round cairns (*BF 731* and *BF 717*). Cairn *BF 731* was in a prominent position on a small, low hillock, and was very large (*c* 13.5 m in diameter and 0.5 m high), with evidence for a kerb on the eastern side. Cairn *BF 717* was also in a prominent position at the head of a low promontory, and was also large in size (*c* 10 m in diameter and 0.4 m high). To the east of the central group of monuments, in a relatively isolated location, was a well-defined ring bank (*BF 714*), with a south-west-facing entrance, which may have been a roundhouse.

Bootle Fell IX (Coppycow): monuments *BF 752-94*

Several small cairn groups were identified within an expanse of undulating, erratically drained moorland, which was bordered to the south-west and north-east by extensive mires (Fig 58). The cairns usually coincided with areas that were well drained, within the least undulating terrain, and they were loosely scattered and also varied in size and form. Although there were some short sections of stone bank, these did not appear to relate to each other, and there was no evidence for even a simple field system in this area.

Three round cairns (*BF 759, BF 774,* and *BF 775*; Fig 65) were, however, located on the tops of low hillocks. They were distinctive in terms of size and prominence, and were probably funerary monuments. Cairn *BF 759* had been disturbed by an old excavation trench on the southern side, but otherwise had a regular, circular shape (*c* 10 m in diameter). The other two round cairns were relatively close together on a flat-topped hillock overlooking Crookley Beck. Cairn *BF 774* had a raised flat top (0.5 m high), a regular circular shape (*c* 13 m in diameter), and a well-defined edge, particularly on the southern side, although there was no evidence for a kerb. Cairn *BF 775* was a much smaller and less prominent cairn (7 x 7 x *c* 0.35 m), with a uniform flat top and a very regular, well-defined edge.

Bootle Fell X (Little Grassoms): monuments *BF 800-81* and *BF 889*

An extensive cairnfield was identified on a natural spur, known as Little Grassoms, formed by the confluence of Grassoms and Crookley Becks (Fig 58). Down the length of the spur there was a moderate, uniform gradient and the ground was well drained throughout. However, there were areas with substantial amounts of surface brash, which hindered the identification of some cairns. In this monument group, there were two cairnfields, divided by a small tributary of Grassoms Beck.

The main cairnfield (BF XA) lay to the north of the tributary and appears to have been a product of two very distinct episodes of stone clearance (Fig 66). One of these was represented by randomly distributed cairn (*i*), whilst the other was represented by alignments of elongated cairns (*ii*).

The group of randomly distributed cairns (*i*) was on a gently sloping, natural terrace, edged to the east and west by breaks of slope, and to the north by the edge of the Crookley Beck gully. An abundance of surface brash was present in the area and as a result it may have been lower-quality agricultural land. The cairns displayed considerable variation in size and form; some were fairly large and well-defined (*eg BF 865*), whilst others were small, and associated with the surface brash. Although some cairns were elongated, there was no consistent orientation, and the group was probably a primary type of cairnfield (*Ch 8, p 328*).

The group of elongated cairns (*ii*) was on land with a steeper slope, but with considerably less natural surface brash, representing better agricultural land, at least in the recent past. There were at least five parallel alignments of cairns and stone banks orientated

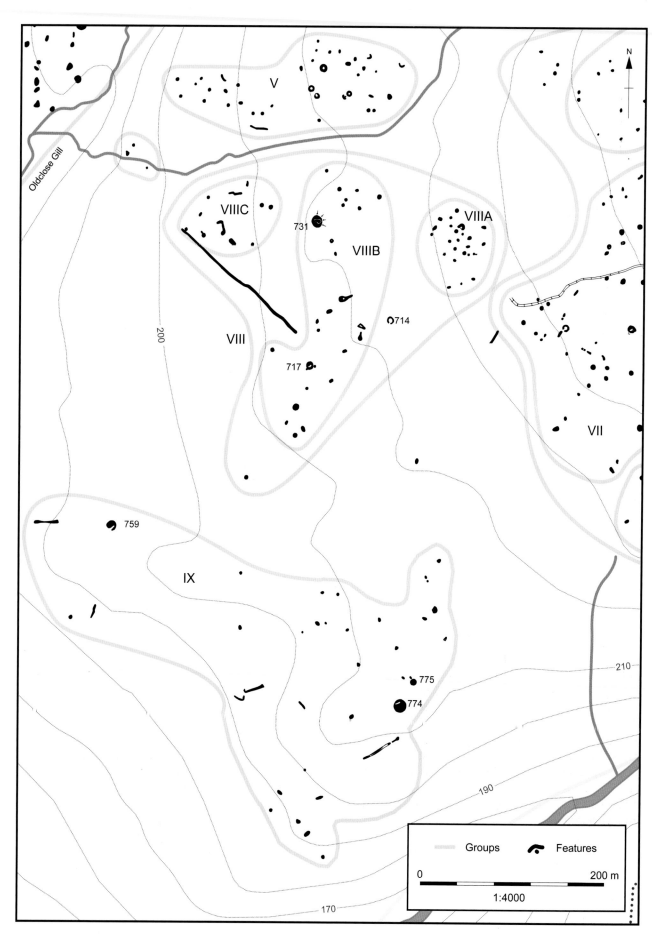

Figure 65: The BF VIII and BF IX cairnfields

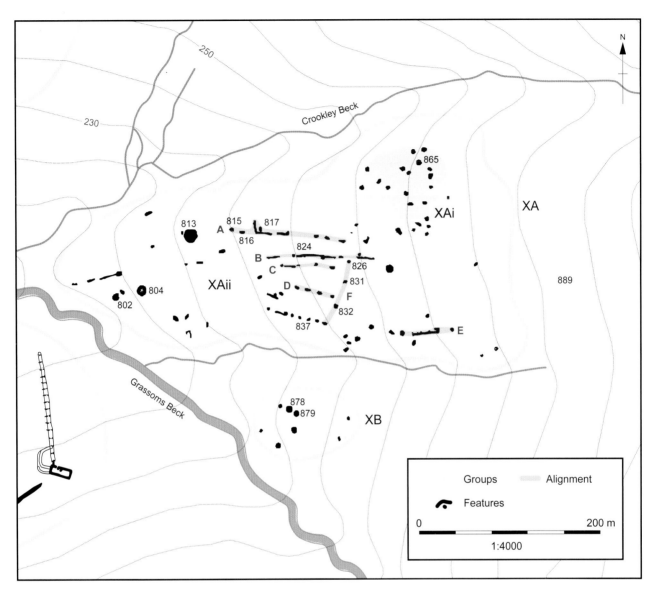

Figure 66: The BF X cairnfields

downslope, which were between 90 m and 130 m in length (Alignments A, B, C, D, E; Fig 66). Many of these cairns were elongated, in the same direction as the alignment. Some alignments also included narrow, ill-defined banks, between the cairns (*eg BF 824* and *BF 817*). Bank *BF 817* had a short, cross-slope section, although the main east-west alignment was continued by cairns *BF 815* and *BF 816*. There was a longer, cross-slope alignment (F) that joined the upper eastern ends of the other alignments. In between the alignments, there was a marked absence of cairns and relatively little surface stone.

The second cairnfield (BF XB) recorded in this area lay to the south of the beck and was small, comprising only eight cairns, although these were above average size and prominence. At least two of them were funerary monuments (*BF 878-9*). The group was very localised, compact, and was situated at the tip of the spur on well-drained, gently sloping ground.

Relatively large numbers of apparent funerary round cairns (*BF 802, BF 804, BF 813, BF 878,* and *BF 879*) were also recorded in both cairnfields. Cairn *BF 804* was very prominent, with a well-defined, regular outline (including traces of a kerb; Pl 82); its profile was fairly regular, although antiquarian excavations had caused a large central depression (10.5 x 8.5 x 0.6 m). This 'excavation' had exposed two upright slabs, at right-angles to each other, which were the remains of a now robbed cist (Pl 83).

Cairn *BF 813* was also a funerary cairn, and was both extremely large and very prominent (14.2 x 14.2 x *c* 1 m; Pl 84). It was well defined, with traces of a kerb along the eastern side, and had a regular profile. An outer bank was just discernible from the main fabric of the cairn, particularly around the eastern perimeter. This may indicate that the monument was a filled-in ring cairn (Pl 85). Furthermore, several similar examples occur in the North West, including one

133

Plate 82: Cairn BF 804, looking north

recorded during the LDNPS at Stainton Fell (*SF 338; p 175*), and also other examples, such as Hardendale cairn (Howard-Davis and Williams 2005), and the cairns at Manor Farm, Borwick (Olivier 1987), and Cefn Bryn (Ward 1988). Round cairns *BF 878* and *BF 879* were immediately adjacent to each other and were similar in form and size (*BF 878*: 6.6 x 6.5 x 0.35 m; *BF 879*: 5.3 x 5.2 x 0.35 m). They were both prominent

Plate 83: An exposed cist within round cairn BF 804

and well defined, with regular circular shapes and profiles, in contrast to the stone clearance-type cairns in the area. However, unlike the other funerary-type monuments on Bootle Fell, these cairns were not positioned on summits, though their position on the ridge of a spur meant that they were clearly visible from within the Crookley Beck valley.

Discussion

The parallel lines, defined by the irregular deposition of cleared stone, recorded in this survey area probably defined a simple field system, marking divisions between plots of agricultural land. The alignment of four cairns at the eastern ends of the east-west alignments possibly marked the upper extent of these plots. The area within had been deliberately cleared of cairns and unwanted surface stone, which would have enabled the unrestricted use of an ard or plough; however, none of the banks had lynchet profiles and hence there was no confirmation that these plots had been cultivated. The widths of the plots were not regular (north to south: 18 m, 10 m, 29 m, and 30 m) but, with the exception of the smallest (10 m), they were comparable in size and shape with the narrow plots of TB XIII on Town Bank (20-30 m wide; *Ch 3, p 60*).

Bootle Fell XI (Great Grassoms): monuments *BF 890-918*

Within this area, in the southern part of the survey area (Fig 58), the recorded monuments reflected two

134

Plate 84: Round cairns BF 813 *and* BF 804, *within the Little Grassoms cluster of funerary monuments*

Plate 85: Cairn BF 813, *looking south*

135

distinct elements: a field system with two farmsteads (BF XIA and BF XIB; Fig 67); and a cairnfield (BF XIC; Pl 86). Despite their spatial association, these diverse elements may not have been contemporary.

Farmsteads and field systems (BF XIA and BF XIB)
The main elements of farmstead BF XIA were a rectangular house (*BF 897*); an attached enclosure; a small field to the east of the house (A*ii*); and a large field to the west (A*i*). Building *BF 897* was a three-roomed structure (18 x 7 m; Pl 87), which had two external entrances into the northernmost cell. Access to the other two cells was via the northern one. Internal terracing only occurred within the smallest room, in the south-east of building, which may have been a sleeping area.

To the north-west of the farmstead was an attached rectilinear enclosure (210 m²) bordered by prominent, well-defined banks. Access to the enclosure was only from the large field to the west (defined by *BF 895*). The downslope bank of the enclosure had a lynchet-like profile, which had resulted from soil slippage.

To the east of building *BF 897* was an irregularly shaped 'field' (A*ii*), defined by regular, prominent stone banks. The land within the 'field' was undulating, with occasional surface stone, and was poorly drained at the northern end. The boundaries were continuous, with the exception of a large gap at the southern end, and it may have served a pastoral rather than an arable function.

The larger 'field' to the west of building *BF 897* (A*i*) was defined by a large bank and ditch, which converged with the stone bank boundary (*BF 896*) of the eastern field. The ditch was on the outside of the bank and presented a greater obstacle to animals outside the field than to those within it. The boundary would thus appear to have been designed to keep animals out rather than contain them. The terrain within the field had a uniform gradient and was well drained.

Farmstead BF XIB was similar in layout to farmstead BF XIA, although its fields and house were larger. The house (*BF 892*: 24 x 9 m; Fig 67) had a single partition wall, which created two unequally sized rooms (west room: 6 x 5.5 m; east room 12.5 x 6 m; Pl 88). There was evidence of dry-stone construction within the outer walls, which stood to a height of 0.5 m, although there were only limited quantities of collapse, suggesting

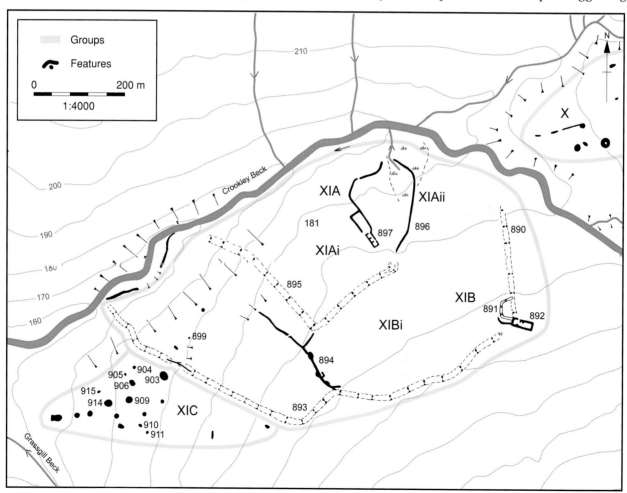

Figure 67: The BF XI settlement and field system

Plate 86: The BF XI settlement and field system at Great Grassoms

Plate 87: The three-celled longhouse, BF 897, and associated plot, at Great Grassoms, looking south-east

Plate 88: Longhouse BF 892, at Great Grassoms, looking south-west

that the stone had been robbed from the walls, or that this was a foundation for a timber superstructure.

Downslope from farmstead BF XIB, a small, approximately rectilinear enclosure (*BF 891*: 160 m^2) was recorded, which was similar to that adjacent to *BF 897*. However, it utilised part of bank *BF 890* as its eastern boundary, its downslope bank did not have a lynchet-like profile, and there was no evidence of an entrance.

Two large banks and ditches (*BF 890* and *BF 893*) extended north and south-west from farmstead BF XIB. The ditches were external and the features were very similar to bank *BF 895*, associated with farmstead BF XIA. Although there was no evidence of a stone facing to the bank, a revetment had been recorded in the early twentieth century (Wilson 1915, 365). Bank *BF 893* extended across the slope for *c* 250 m, then turned sharply downslope; after *c* 25 m, the downslope section became a stream gully and the bank petered out. The stream gully was particularly straight and contrasted with other streams in the area, which had irregular courses. It therefore probably originated as an artificial bank with a ditch draining the adjacent land, and subsequently water erosion had removed the bank and enlarged the ditch.

Bank *BF 893* formed the outer boundary of two large fields divided by wall *BF 894*. The easternmost of these fields (B*i*) was edged to the north by the banks of farmstead BF XIA, although there was a very large gap (92 m) between the end of banks *BF 890* and *BF 896* of farmstead BF XIA. This field contained well-drained land, with a fairly uniform, low to moderate slope, in contrast to the western field, which was much steeper. The dividing boundary (*BF 894*) displayed clear evidence of dry-stone construction and contrasted with the other bank and ditch boundaries. Wall *BF 894* appears to have butted onto a large clearance cairn. On the east side of the wall was a small rectilinear building (6 x 4 m) with an entrance to the south. Two semi-circular platforms also butted onto the side of the wall, with well-defined, regular edges and uniform flat tops.

Cairnfield BF XIC
The cairnfield was located on a natural spur formed by the confluence of Grassgill and Crookley Becks, the ground being relatively gently sloping and well drained. The cairnfield comprised two very distinct types of cairns: ill-defined, low-lying mounds (*eg BF 899*, *BF 904*, *BF 905*, *BF 910*, *BF 911*, and *BF 915*), and large, prominent, well-defined cairns (*eg BF 903*, *BF 906*, *BF 909*, and *BF 914*). The extreme differences between these two types suggest that they were not constructed at the same time and may even have been the result of different activities. The small cairns were typical of stone clearance, whereas the largest cairn (*BF 903*) had a possible kerb and was similar in size and prominence to funerary cairn *BF 804* in BF X (*p 133*), probably having a similar function. The cairns were distributed on both sides of one of the field system boundaries (*BF 893*), with the majority lying to the south-west of it, which suggests that the cairnfield and the field system were not contemporary.

Discussion
The farmsteads were on steep, exposed, and relatively high land. Such terrain has traditionally been associated with pastoralism, but there was evidence that some of the 'fields' were used for cultivation. The small enclosure attached to farmstead BF XIA had a lynchet at the bottom, which was likely to have been the result of soil disturbance (ploughing). A similar enclosure (*BF 891*) was attached to farmstead BF XIB. Although there was no evidence of a lynchet, this enclosure was also more likely to have served an arable, rather than a pastoral, function, as it had no obvious entrance and was defined by a bank with an external ditch. This latter arrangement presented a greater obstacle to animals from outside and may have been dug as a means of excluding stock from this area.

The large fields of both farmsteads BF XIA and BF XIB were defined by broad banks and, again, had external ditches which were inappropriate for the containment of stock. In particular, the large field adjacent to *BF 892* (B*i*) had a very large gap to the north, which would have been difficult to close using temporary fencing. It was, therefore, unlikely to have been used for the containment of stock. By contrast, the field to the east of *BF 897* (A*ii*) had a stone bank and walls, with relatively small gaps, which could be closed easily by temporary fencing. The enclosed ground was undulating, stony, and, in places, boggy. It was unsuitable for cultivation and its probable function was stock control. Moreover, it is documented that there was a shepherd in the vicinity in the sixteenth century (CRO D/LONS/W/Millom Courtbook 1510-23), and this evidence implies that these farmsteads had a mixed agricultural economy.

The two farmsteads were very similar in type and were almost certainly roughly contemporary. However, they were probably not built at exactly the same time, although it is not immediately obvious which was the earlier. A short section of stone bank linked wall *BF 894* to *BF 895* (farmstead BF XIA), but appeared to butt both. Wall *BF 894* seemed to butt on to a corner of bank *BF 893*, yet without its presence there would have been no clear purpose for a corner in bank *BF 893* at this point. Therefore, there is a possibility that, despite their different forms, these features were part of an integral, broadly contemporary field system.

Conclusions
There were two contrasting types of settlement on Bootle Fell: that typified by the cairnfields of BF I and BF II, and the more sophisticated farmsteads at BF IV and BF XI. The cairnfields were typically simple, although some inconsistencies in the pattern reflected various degrees of planning. Cairnfields such as BF II and BF VIII had essentially random distributions of clearance-type cairns, whereas within cairnfield BF I there were alignments of cairns

which appeared to define the edges of the cairnfield. Although the distribution of cairns within the BF I boundary was also essentially random, this may imply a more organised approach to land clearance. At cairnfield BF X, the organised approach had been taken a stage further, since the cairn alignments defined the edges of parallel plots, which contained no cairns or surface stone.

There were several ring features scattered across the moor, although many of these did not appear to have had a domestic origin. The ones that were most probably roundhouses were loosely grouped within the area of BF VII (*p 129*), which was probably a settlement. Four of these were orientated in an east-west line (*BF 660, BF 602, BF 635,* and *BF 714;* Fig 64) and were fairly regularly spaced, between 140 m and 190 m apart. The other roundhouse was associated with a pair of parallel banks, which may have been a simple plot, and there is a possibility that all were integral elements of a small settlement. Three of the roundhouses had south-west-facing entrances (*BF 660, BF 635,* and *BF 714*), while the other two had northerly entrances. They were all between 6.5 m and 8.4 m in diameter and three of them were either internally terraced or on flat ground. Structures *BF 660* and *BF 714* had internal slopes similar to the ground surface outside, which cast some doubt over whether they originally formed domestic dwellings.

Many of the cairnfields were spatially associated with prehistoric funerary round cairns (*eg* cairns *BF 813* and *BF 804* within the BF X cairnfield (Fig 66), and *BF 637* within the BF VII settlement group (Fig 64)) and there is a possibility that the cairnfields were of an approximately similar date. There was undoubtedly farming activity in the area during the latter part of the prehistoric period, as demonstrated by pollen analysis from Barfield Tarn (Pennington 1970, 68-70), which lies only *c* 2 km away from the Bootle Fell survey area. This analysis showed that in this part of the coastal plain there was possible cultivation, in association with clearance and vegetation disturbance, during the later part of the neolithic period, and also vigorous clearance and cultivation leading to total deforestation at the beginning of the Bronze Age (*ibid*). Although the pollen-catchment area of Barfield Tarn may have extended for 15-20 km, meaning that the recorded pollen may have been derived from other areas aside from Bootle Fell, the fact that there was total deforestation probably indicates that there was disturbance of the tree cover throughout the area during the Bronze Age, including on the adjacent fells.

The field systems of BF IV and BF XI clearly contrasted with the cairnfields and appeared to demonstrate a later phase of occupation. One of the main banks in the BF XI farmstead (*BF 893; pp 137-8*) cut through the BF XI cairnfield and seems to have been a later feature (Fig 67). The implication is that there were two contrasting and widely separated phases of occupation on Bootle Fell, and it is probable that both complex field systems date to the medieval period. Indeed, the boundaries of the BF IV field defined an area of ridge and furrow, typical of medieval and later cultivation. Two historical references are also known (*pp 120-1*), from 1252 and 1510, to land called Gressholmes (or Grassoms, BF XI) and, by the time of the later reference, there was a shepherd resident there. In addition, the BF XI structures were medieval in character (Ramm 1970) and it is very probable that this settlement on Great Grassoms was that referred to by these medieval documents.

Corney Fell

The Corney Fell survey area lay in the southern part of the South-West Fells planation terrace, which faces out over the West Cumbrian coastal plain, and was between the Bootle Fell survey area to the south (divided from it by Kinmont Beck) and the Charlesground Gill survey area to the north (Fig 55; Pl 89). It extended up from the enclosed lands around High Kinmont farm, at *c* 150 m OD, to an altitude of *c* 300 m on the lower slopes of the Whitfell ridge (Fig 68). The terrain was open fell and was used only for sheep pasture.

Archaeological history
Cairns on Corney Fell were first recorded on the 1867 First Edition 6" to 1 mile OS map, and were also noted by Collingwood (1923, 268). The cairns were subsequently located, but not planned, by the OS Archaeology Division field investigators in 1963 and 1973.

In addition, a study was undertaken by Jean Ward in 1972 to examine the potential for burials within the Corney Fell cairns, which involved an outline survey of part of the Corney Fell area, in conjunction with the excavation of two of the cairns (Ward 1977). Samples were also taken from the excavations and submitted for phosphorous analysis. This demonstrated that there were no significant concentrations of phosphorous from the most northerly of the two cairns (*p 144*). However, the sample extracted from the second cairn (*p 143*) did contain a significantly higher concentration of phosphorous relative to the background level. On the basis of this, it was tentatively suggested that the second cairn may have contained a burial (*op cit*, 5).

Plate 89: The Corney Fell (foreground) and Charlesground Gill survey areas, looking north

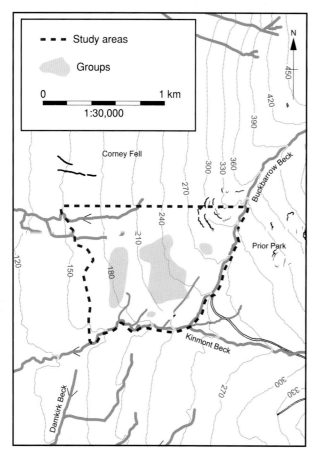

Figure 68: The Corney Fell survey area

The survey area

The survey was undertaken in 1984, covering *c* 4 km² of unenclosed moorland (Fig 69), from which 324 monuments within five site groups (CF I-V) were recorded (Fig 70). The monuments were mainly small cairns, generally located in distinct cairnfield groups, some of which were associated with stone-bank boundary markers, representing elements of field systems. These principal groups are described from west to east.

Corney Fell I (north-west of Kinmont Beck): monuments *CF 1-112*

North-west of Kinmont Beck, a group of 112 small cairns extended in a broad north-south band for *c* 600 m, between the 170 m and 210 m contours (Fig 70). In general, the distribution of the cairns was essentially random, but they were interspersed with a relatively limited number of either stone banks, or linear cairns, that were orientated downslope, suggesting some degree of rationalisation of the primary cairnfield.

The southernmost of these features was a faint lynchet between cairns *CF 2* and *CF 4* (Fig 71), which was orientated north-east/south-west downslope, but otherwise did not incorporate any stone along its length. However, further north was a series of parallel stone banks/linear cairns running down the hillside, which included three long spreads of stone clearance,

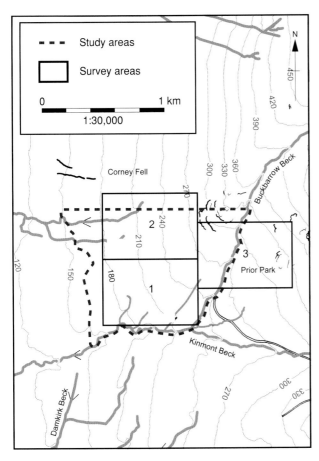

Figure 69: The Corney Fell survey area as planned

or stony banks (*CF 43*, *CF 51*, and *CF 52*). On the line of the largest of these (*CF 43*) were a further two small cairns, which may have represented a downslope continuation of the alignment. Within the centre of the group, a marked concentration of cairns was edged to the north-west by a distinct alignment of eight cairns (A), which again followed the north-west downslope orientation, and may indicate a former boundary. Stone bank *CF 87* was also orientated downslope, but extended east-west at a slight diagonal to the cairn alignment. Several elongated cairns (*CF 97*, *CF 98*, *CF 101*, *CF 102*, and *CF 107*) were also recorded in the northern part of the group, the orientations of which suggested that they had been formed through clearance along two boundaries. The northern limit of the group was also marked by two long stone banks (*CF 112*). Overall, both the cairn alignments and stone banks clearly indicated a degree of linearity within the cairnfield. While they may represent surviving components of a former field system, they appeared to have had little direct relationship with the mainly randomly distributed cairns found in the rest of the cairnfield.

The cairns recorded in this survey area had typically prominent, rounded profiles, *c* 4 m in diameter, and were 0.25-0.4 m in height. There were also limited numbers of relatively large cairns (*CF 80*, *CF 82*, *CF 91*, *CF 93*, *CF 97*, *CF 99*, *CF 101*, and *CF 102*),

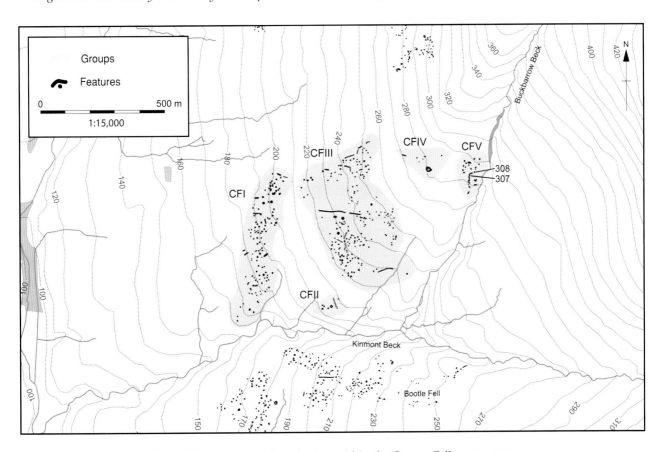

Figure 70: Monument distribution within the Corney Fell survey area

141

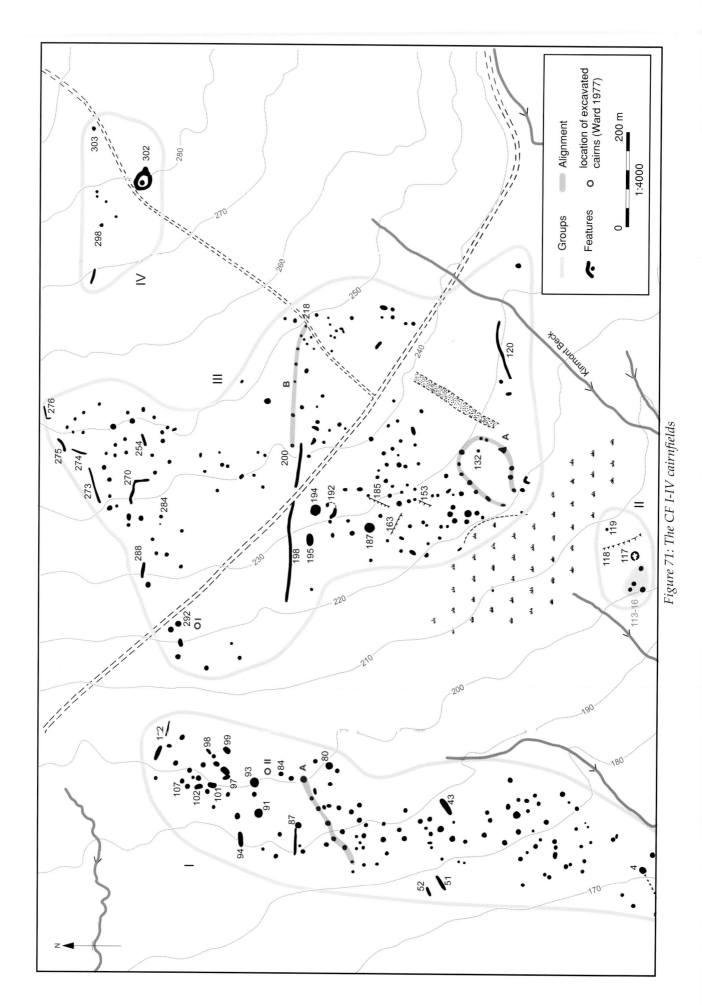

Figure 71: The CF I-IV cairnfields

Plate 90: Cairn CF 93, *looking north*

of which the latter four were not particularly prominent. The others were more scattered, were relatively prominent, standing out from the adjacent cairns, and may have been the product of clearance activity on a greater scale than elsewhere within the group. However, the largest of these, cairn *CF 93*, which was 10.5 m in diameter and 0.45 m in height, may represent a funerary monument (Pl 90). Excavation of a nearby cairn (II) by Ward (1977) in 1972 revealed a sub-ring-type structure, comprising large stones around the edge, with smaller stones in the centre. Also in the centre was a spread of pink and white ash, flecked with charcoal, from which samples were taken for phosphate analysis (*op cit, 3*). The results suggested a high content when compared to the adjacent ground and, as phosphates are typically concentrated within animal/human remains, particularly dung or bones (Renfrew and Bahn 1991), this would suggest the presence of human or animal remains within the cairn. Similar cairns, such as *CF 93* nearby, potentially had the same function.

Corney Fell II: monuments *CF 113-19*

A group of five small cairns, a probable roundhouse, and a lynchet were located on a bluff between a small stream to the north, and Kinmont Beck to the south (Fig 71). In this area the land was relatively flat, between the 200 m and 210 m contours, and was well drained, but was edged by a steeply sloping terrace to

the south-west. An area of mire separated this locale from the CF III site group to the north-east.

Four of the cairns (*CF 113-16*) were tightly clustered and a fifth (*CF 119*) was isolated at the eastern edge of the group. They were moderately prominent, with slightly rounded profiles, and averaged *c* 4 m in diameter. The putative roundhouse (*CF 117*) comprised a well-defined annular bank (9.7 m in diameter) with an internal terraced platform and a west-facing entrance. To the east was a 0.2 m-high lynchet (*CF 118*), extending for *c* 50 m along the line of the contour. It is perhaps significant that the only roundhouse in the survey area was associated with a small number of cairns, and was spatially removed from the main cairn groups, yet was associated with a small area of arable ground, as evidenced by the lynchet.

Corney Fell III: monuments *CF 120-297*

This monument group contained the largest of the Corney Fell cairnfield groups (Fig 71), comprising 177 cairns, stone banks, and occasional lynchets (Pl 91). These monuments extended in a very broad band along the slope to the west of Buckbarrow Bridge, between the 220 m and 240 m contours (Fig 70).

The southernmost extent of the cairn group was edged by an area of mire which divided this group from that of CF II (Pl 92). The majority of the cairns

Plate 91: The CF II cairnfield, looking west

Plate 92: Clearance cairns in the southern part of CF III, looking west, over the wet ground

were between 2 m and 4 m in diameter, and were on average smaller than the CF I cairnfield to the west. Three cairns (*CF 187, CF 194*, and *CF 195; Fig 71*) were significantly larger, up to 11 m in diameter (Pl 93). All three were also very prominent, in marked contrast to their neighbouring cairns, and may have served a funerary function. One cairn within the group (I) had also been subject to excavation and phosphorous analysis (Ward 1977: cairn I). This relatively small cairn was found to comprise larger stones within the centre, but it displayed no evidence of deliberate construction and had no ash or charcoal deposits (in contrast to the other cairn excavated: II; *p 143;*

op cit, 1). The phosphate levels were comparable to the background levels, and there was no evidence to support human burial within this cairn.

As with the CF I cairnfield, the cairn distribution was essentially random, but with some elements of linearity. In the southern part of the group, a curved alignment of cairns (A) defined an 80 x 50 m open area devoid of cairns (apart from cairn *CF 132*), which may have been a small agricultural plot. However, there were no lynchets, or similar earthworks, that might indicate arable activity either within or around the suspected plot. By contrast, further north were three sections of lynchets (*CF 153, CF 163*, and *CF 185*), all at right-angles to each other, which suggest the fragmentary survival of rectangular arable fields or plots.

Further to the north, a line of cairns (B) was on a parallel alignment to a broad, continuous, 1.5 m-wide stone bank (*CF 198*), which appears to have been upcast from an adjacent ditch. The bank and ditch (*CF 198*) extended considerably to the west of the cairn group, had no direct relationship with any of the cairns, and were potentially later features. They had been cut by the construction of the moorland road, which they clearly pre-date.

In the northern part of the cairn group was a further concentration of small cairns (Pl 94), which in terms of

144

Plate 93: Possible funerary cairn CF 194, looking north

Plate 94: The northern part of the CF II cairnfield, looking south

145

their distribution had a well-defined curving eastern edge. Within the group were seven lengths of stone bank (*CF 254, CF 270, CF 288,* and *CF 273-6*) which, for the most part, had uncertain relationships and did not form an obvious or coherent field system. One length of stone bank (*CF 270*) had a right-angled turn and may have defined two sides of a rectangular plot, particularly as the potential area within such a plot was devoid of cairns. There was no clear relationship with any other stone bank. Stone banks *CF 288* and *CF 273-6* were ranged along the north-western side of the cairn group, but they did not have a consistent orientation and were not necessarily parts of a boundary line. To the north was an expanse of similar terrain, which was devoid of cairns until the cairn groups at Charlesground Gill (CG IX; *p 156*) were reached, some 380 m to the north.

Corney Fell IV: monuments *CF 298-303*

At a distance of *c* 200 m to the east of the large CF III cairnfield, on a gently sloping spur to the west of Buckbarrow Beck, was a small cairn group associated with an enclosure (Fig 71). The cairns were not prominent and were small, varying from 2 m to 3.5 m in diameter. Five of the cairns were grouped to the north-west of the enclosure (*CF 302*) and the sixth was further to the north-east.

The enclosure (*CF 302*) was elongated, with broad 3-3.5 m-wide banks (Pl 95), an interior measuring 14 x 11 m, and external dimensions of 22 x 18 m. The banks apparently reflected the collapse of former walls, which were relatively high. It had a narrow entrance, along the slope and away from the cairn group, which was faced with prominent

stones on the external side, and there may have been portal stones. The interior of the enclosure was substantially terraced and it may have been used as a domestic dwelling, rather than as a stock enclosure. Furthermore, in the centre was the very indistinct outline of a circular ring feature, which had the appearance of a small roundhouse. Given the very substantial nature of the outer bank, and the presence of a possible roundhouse, then this would imply that these remains formed part of a small simple enclosed settlement.

Corney Fell V: monuments *CF 304-23*

A group of small cairns and a discontinuous boundary were recorded on fairly level ground, immediately adjacent to the steep gully edge of Buckbarrow Beck (Fig 70), the site lying between the 200 m and 285 m contours. The cairns and enclosure were first recorded in 1979 (Potter 1979, 7). The cairns comprised an irregular, randomly distributed group in the northern, upslope part of the site, and varied considerably in size, with the largest measuring some 14 x 5 m.

In the southern, and lower, part of this survey area was a series of stone banks and circular and elongated cairns, forming an irregular, discontinuous boundary that was, for the most part, orientated north-south. The northernmost part comprised a stone bank (*CF 307*; Fig 70), with a right-angled turn, and cairn *CF 308* was on the line of the east-west extension. Apart from the partially surviving kerb of stone bank *CF 307*, the general extension of banks and cairns followed an irregular line, of varying width, which was clearly discontinuous. In general, the irregular form of this feature was consistent with

Plate 95: Enclosure CF 302, *looking south-west*

the deposition of clearance stone along the line of a former boundary, which would appear to have formed a partial enclosure, edged to the east by the line of the Buckbarrow Beck gully.

Conclusions
The five groups of small cairns and associated features on Corney Fell could be seen as foci for human activity and, although spatially separated, were broadly similar to the monuments recorded in the neighbouring Charlesground Gill (*see below*) and Bootle Fell survey areas (*p 119*).

Groups CF I-III and CF V varied considerably in size but, for the most part, had a broadly comparable character. They were essentially randomly distributed cairnfields, which incorporated linear features indicative of field or plot boundaries. These elements were mainly limited in number and scale. They did not reflect an extensive development of the cairnfield, but seemed to have formed the initial establishment of a field system. The fragmentary survival of lynchets in groups CF I-III were of particular importance, as these demonstrate some arable farming, albeit on a small scale.

Potential settlement remains were also found in two of the monument groups. *CF 117* in group CF II (*p 143*) was a probable roundhouse and, significantly, was associated with a small group of cairns and a lynchet. However, there was no indication of any relationship with the larger CF III group to the north, possibly because cairn remains were not evident within the mire that separated the two groups. The enclosure and very tentative building (*CF 302*) in group CF IV (*p 146*) were distinct in character from the other groups, and the two were not necessarily contemporary.

Occasional large cairns recorded in the cairnfields could simply reflect extensive stone-clearance activity in a particular locale. This was particularly evident in cairns *CF 97* and *CF 101* (*p 141*), which were within a group of similarly large cairns, and formed components of a possible field system. However, there were others (*eg CF 91, CF 93, CF 187*, and *CF 194*; Fig 71) which were significantly larger than their neighbours, did not have any obvious relationship with other cairns, and may potentially have served an alternative, or additional, function. Investigation of one of these (*p 143*) revealed some elements of structure, deposits of ash, and samples with higher than background concentrations of phosphates. This provided potential evidence of a funerary function, although it is not clear whether such burial activity was contemporary with the agricultural activity found in this area, whether the burial cairn was a later or earlier construction, or whether an existing cairn was adapted.

Charlesground Gill

The Charlesground Gill survey area (Fig 72) was on part of the South-West Fells planation terrace between the Corney Fell and Whitrow Beck survey areas (Fig 55). The terrace in this area was not well defined, neither its forward nor back edges being particularly sharp or steep-sided, and most of it was enclosed pasture. The back edge of the terrace was defined by the River Annas, and east of it were the steadily steepening slopes which become the long, central ridge of the South-West Fells. The Annas also served as the western, lower limit of the survey area, and most of the cairnfield groups were on the unenclosed, sloping ground that rises up from the terrace, between *c* 150 m and 310 m OD.

The area had very poor natural drainage, particularly towards the western side of the survey area, where the gradient was more gentle; however, there were also areas of mire on the steeper ground to the east. The cairnfields were mainly on this better drained, steeper and higher ground, but even there they were partly contained by areas of mire and some were on islands of better-drained land within mires (*eg* CG VII; *p 155*). Only two (CG I and CG III; *pp 148-50*) of the nine cairnfield groups were not limited to some extent by surrounding mire and, as a result, they were generally small and localised.

The southernmost site group (CG IX) was only *c* 300 m from part of the Corney Fell (CF III) group (*p 143*). The character of both site groups was broadly similar, and the boundary between the two survey areas was more administrative than actual. The northernmost site group of the Charlesground Gill survey was similarly fairly close to the adjacent Whitrow Beck settlement (*c* 250 m); however, the two site groups were more diverse in form and were not necessarily contemporary.

Archaeological history
The earliest reference to antiquities in this area is from the 1900 Second Edition 6" to 1 mile OS map, which labelled the CG V group as 'Cairns', and this was subsequently repeated in the archaeological inventory of 1923 (Collingwood 1923, 268). In 1961, the CG V site group was scheduled as an Ancient Monument (SM32839) on the basis of the OS mapping, but its quoted grid reference is in error by *c* 700 m, which has resulted in the inclusion of two entries for the same site within the HER for Cumbria. In 1983, Val Turner identified site group CG III from vertical air photographs (LDHER no 2701).

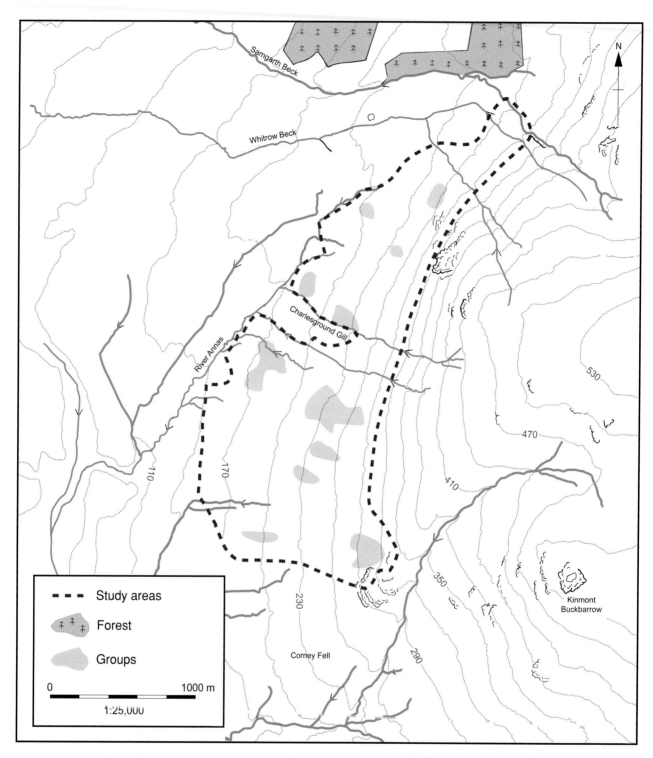

Figure 72: The Charlesground Gill survey area

The survey area

The survey was undertaken in May 1989 over 2.4 km²
of unenclosed land (Fig 73). In total, 281 monuments
were identified in nine site groups (CG I-IX; Fig 74)
within a generally moderately sloping terrain. For the
most part, the groups comprised small cairnfields,
located on isolated areas of well-drained or gently
sloping ground. The notable exception was CG V,
a sizable cairnfield, incorporating very large cairns
and elements of a proto-field system and a small,

cultivated, plot. In addition to these groups, there
were also limited numbers of scattered ungrouped
cairns and banks (*CG 19-29, CG 40-4, CG 76-9*, and
CG 192-4), which are not individually described
within this volume.

Charlesground Gill I: monuments *CG 1-18*

A small cairnfield was identified on a gently sloping,
slightly undulating natural terrace (Fig 74), with crags
and outcrop around the forward apron, and brash

148

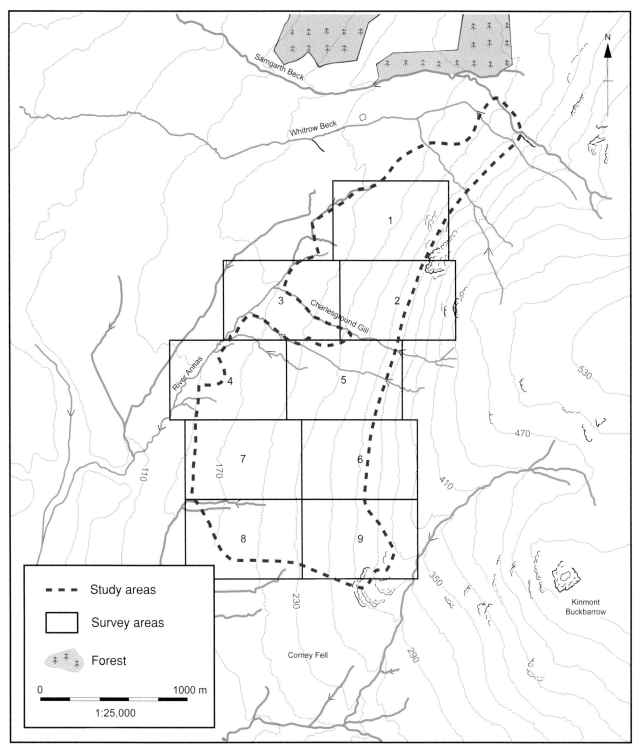

Figure 73: The Charlesground Gill survey area as planned

deposits towards the back, upslope edge. The central part of the terrace was relatively free of surface stone. There was a steep slope below the terrace, which was fairly well drained.

The cairnfield had been positioned to maximise the fairly flat, well-drained ground, but was also contained by the local topography. The cairns were generally small, ill-defined and low-lying, there were no significant alignments, and the group had a semi-random distribution. Away from the main group was a small, semi-circular bank (*CG 18*; Fig 74), which enclosed a fairly flat, stone-free area. The bank was fairly well defined, particularly around the southern external edge, which was marked by a few partly upright stones. This was distinct in form from the clearance-type cairns and was possibly a small structure. Other than this, the site would appear to have formed a primary, undeveloped form of cairnfield (*Ch 8, p 328*).

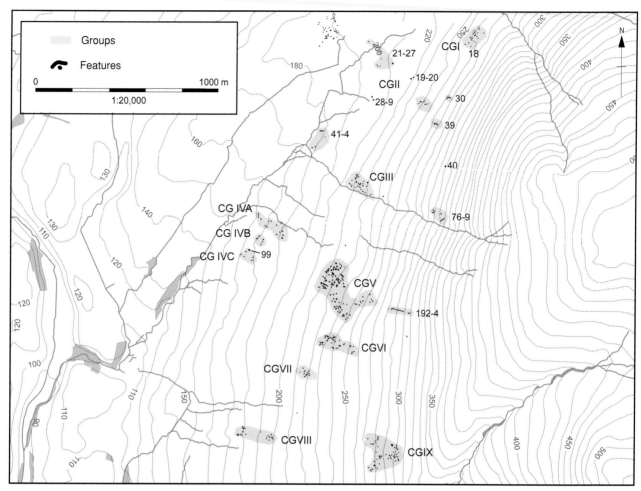

Figure 74: Monument distribution within the Charlesground Gill survey area

Charlesground Gill II: monuments
CG 30-9

A small group of cairns was recorded on well-drained, moderately sloping and slightly undulating ground, the cairns being contained to the north and west by an area of mire (Fig 74). There was relatively little surface stone within the cairnfield, but brash deposits defined the periphery of the area. The cairns were fairly low lying, and some of them were ill defined. Their distribution was essentially random, with no obvious pattern, and it would appear to have been a small, isolated area of stone clearance.

Above and spatially remote from the cairnfield were two, walled, stock shelters (*CG 30* and *CG 39*), whilst a small rectangular building butted the wall of the southernmost shelter. There was no evidence of any relationship between the stock shelters and the cairnfield.

Charlesground Gill III: monuments
CG 45-75

A small cairnfield was located on a gently sloping terrace, which was up to 30 m above the level of the much larger planation terrace (Fig 74). The cairns were largely contained by the local topography and, unlike

many of the cairnfields in this area, their extent was not restricted by poor drainage, as the ground was well drained, both within the cairnfield and beyond.

The cairns were generally well defined and fairly prominent, but were not uniform in size or distribution. They ranged in size from small to moderately large and there was a larger concentration on the more gently sloping ground, towards the forward edge of the terrace (western side). Towards the eastern side of the group, the concentration lessened with the increase in gradient.

Orientated downslope, through the middle of the cairnfield, were two cairn and bank alignments (A and B; Fig 75). Extending across the slope from the top of bank *CG 62* was a negative lynchet (between cairns *CG 62* and *CG 63*), indicating soil disturbance on the downslope side of the lynchet, and it is probable that the lynchet and bank represented two sides of a very small cultivated plot. The cairnfield was slightly larger than some of the smallest, primary types identified in the LDNPS and, by virtue of the alignment and small size of the plot, it appeared to display a slightly greater degree of agricultural complexity.

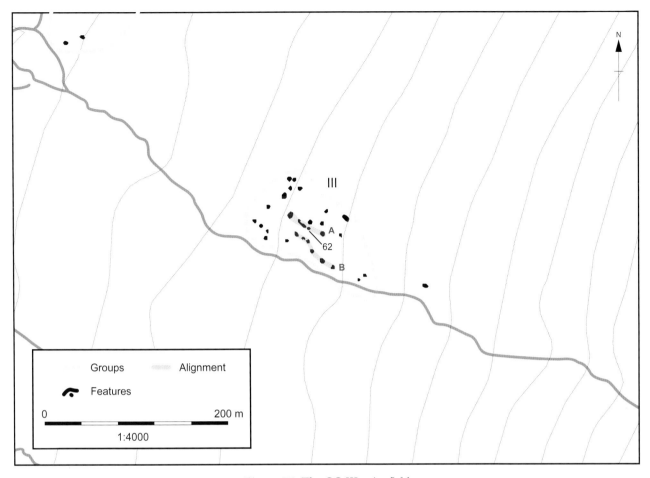

Figure 75: The CG III cairnfield

Charlesground Gill IV: monuments CG 80-104

This monument group comprised three small cairn groups on undulating, but predominantly gently sloping, moorland, near the edge of the planation terrace (Fig 74). This area collects the run-off from the steeper, higher ground to the east and as a result was fairly badly drained. Each of the small cairn groups was on a small island of better-drained land.

The first cairn group (CG IVA) was surrounded by poorly drained ground and, in addition, there were patches of mire within this group of monuments. The ground was generally fairly rough and there were substantial amounts of surface stone throughout the area. The cairns were all small and fairly ill defined, with no obvious pattern.

To the south, a second small group of cairns (CG IVB) was recorded on a well-drained, relatively flat natural terrace. These were generally better defined and larger than those of the other two sub-groups. There was an alignment of cairns along a natural break of slope, which also appeared to have a negative lynchet-like profile, and may be indicative of soil slippage from the area immediately below it.

The third group of cairns identified in this area (CG IVC) lay to the south of CG IVB and was a scattered group located on a gently sloping, undulating area of moorland. There was brash in association with the cairns and mire around the area, particularly on the western downslope side. The cairns were generally low lying and ill defined. The group included a small horseshoe-shaped structure (CG 99), which was open to the west (the source of prevailing winds) and displayed no evidence of internal terracing. It had fairly prominent banks (0.4 m in height) and may have been a bield.

Charlesground Gill V: monuments CG 105-91

This was the largest of the Charlesground Gill site groups (Fig 74; Pl 96), comprising 86 discrete monuments, which formed three distinct groups. Overall, the cairnfield was largely contained by the surrounding topography; to the north and west there was a large mire, to the east a steep scarp slope, and the southern edge was partly defined both by the scarp slope and the mire. In the centre of the area was a very prominent terrace, with a very well-defined forward apron, but a less well-defined back edge, coinciding with a large brash deposit.

151

Plate 96: The CG V cairnfield and proto-field system

Most of the cairns (CG VA; Fig 76) recorded in this monument group were concentrated on the undulating slope to the north of the terrace. This area comprised well-drained land, which was bounded on three sides by mire, and at both the southern and eastern extremities of the group there were also cairns (*CG 152-4*) located within areas of mire. Given this, it seems likely that parts of the surrounding mire had expanded since their construction.

The cairns contained within the main group were generally very large and prominent (up to 0.8 m in height) and were well defined. Those at the northern end, for the most part, had regular, rounded profiles, but those at the higher, south-eastern end were irregular in both profile and shape. It was also apparent that some of the cairns found in this group had been altered and added to. For instance, three cairns had semi-circular bields built into, or on, them (*CG 135*, *CG 140*, and *CG 141*), and one of these (*CG 140*) had a section of bank linking two adjacent cairns. Several had also been merged together by additional stone, and thus had an irregular shape. For example, the large, elongated cairn, *CG 125*, and large cairns *CG 133-6* had been combined into an immense, irregular pile, which contained a very large volume of stone (Pl 97). Two of the four cairns (*CG 133* and *CG 136*) also had a large boulder deliberately placed on top. Although the purpose of

this is uncertain, it is reminiscent of those long cairns recorded on Town Bank (*TB 551* and *TB 564*; *Ch 3, p 57*). There also appeared to be alignments of cairns (A, B, C, and D; Fig 76), which defined the northern, eastern, and southern edges of this group, although, within the cairnfield itself, the cairn distribution was essentially random.

Immediately to the south of the main cairn group was a small plot, defined by banks and cairn alignments (*CG 149* and *CG 151*), whilst a lynchet defined the upper edge and extended into an adjacent area of mire to the south. Bank *CG 149* was very prominent, but also very irregular. Cairns along the line of this boundary had been merged by subsequent clearance stone to form a semi-continuous stone bank. Bank *CG 151* was not as prominent, but generally contained more stone and had a greater uniformity of width. Within the 'plot' was a small bank and associated cairn, and there were some scattered stones. The presence of the lynchet, and the concentration of clearance stone into prominent, parallel banks, would suggest this had been a small cultivated plot.

A second, scattered, group of large, well-defined cairns (CG VB) lay to the south of the main cairn group, on the terrace, edged to the west by the forward scarp, and to the east by an extensive brash deposit. The surface of the terrace was approximately level, well

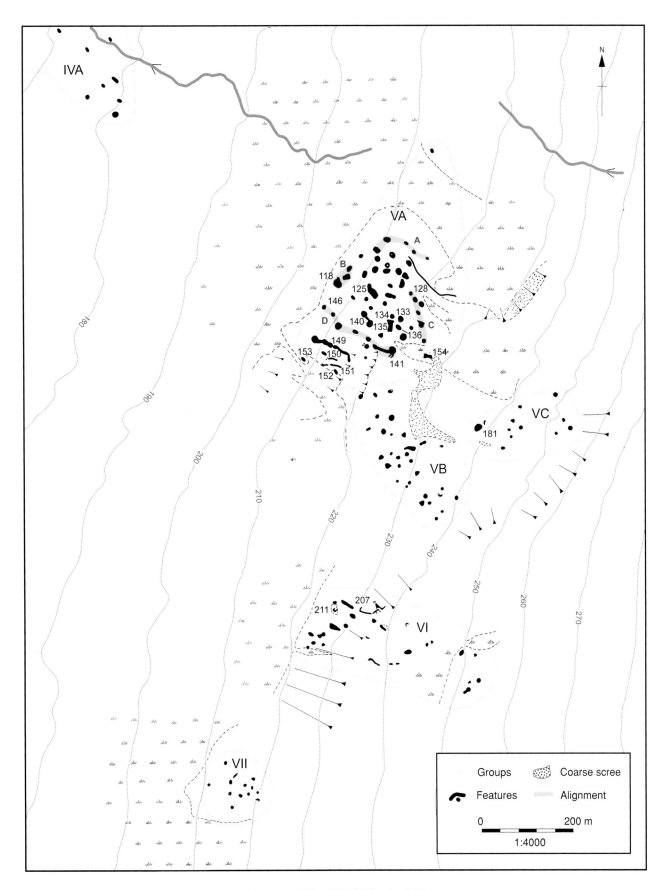

Figure 76: The CG V-VI cairnfields

drained, and had very little exposed stone. The cairns were distributed in a narrow, curved band, the shape of which did not precisely correspond to that of the terrace. Although there were no significant cairn

Plate 97: The large clearance cairns, making up the central part of CG V

alignments, there is a possibility that the forward edge of the terrace had been augmented by positive lynchet formation, perhaps indicating limited cultivation. The cairns were smaller and fewer in number than those found in the main cairn group, indicating that less clearance stone had been removed from this area. This, however, is likely to reflect the greater build-up of soil over the terrace in comparison to the adjacent ground, rather than any difference in agricultural activity between the two areas.

A third, small, scattered group of cairns (CG VC) lay to the east, on uniformly sloping, well-drained ground, edged by a scarp slope to the east, mire to the north, and brash deposits to the west. There was a scatter of surface stone throughout this area and also some larger concentrations. The cairns were markedly smaller, less prominent, and less well-defined than those found in the other cairn groups recorded in this survey area. As there were larger quantities of surface stone in this area than in the adjacent areas, this small amount of cleared stone probably reflected a lower intensity of agricultural activity than elsewhere in the group.

Discussion
The cairns recorded in the main cairn group (CG VA) were both very large and prominent (*c* 6.8 m in average diameter, with an average height of *c* 5.1 m). Some were of an equivalent size to funerary round cairns, with diameters measuring between 7 m and 26 m (Yates 1984b, 34), but these did not stand out significantly from the rest. In some instances, the

cairns had uniform, rounded profiles, but the shapes were often irregular. The largest cairns often had the most irregular form (for instance, *CG 125* and *CG 135*) and appeared to reflect an erratic and unplanned construction, sometimes as a result of the merger of two smaller cairns. These cairns were spatially associated with a cultivated plot and, despite their size, were consistent with stone clearance. The scale of this clearance, coupled with the coalescing of many cairns, would suggest that the cairnfield was the product of an extended episode of agricultural exploitation.

The construction of bields into the large cairns indicated a later phase of activity. However, these were probably only used occasionally or unintensively by medieval or post-medieval herdsmen.

Charlesground Gill VI: monuments CG 195-215
Within this area, a small cairnfield was located on a natural terrace (Fig 74). The forward scarp slope was steep, with an extensive mire at its foot, whilst the floor of the terrace was very gently sloping and also contained a small mire. The main concentration of banks and cairns was on the scarp slope, and there was only a small scatter of banks and cairns on the floor. The latter group was spread on both sides of the mire and there were no banks and cairns on the poorly drained ground (Fig 76). Amongst the monuments on the scarp slope was a small dry-stone wall (*CG 207*) and an associated rectilinear structure (*CG 211*). The wall (*CG 207*) had a Z-shape and survived to five or

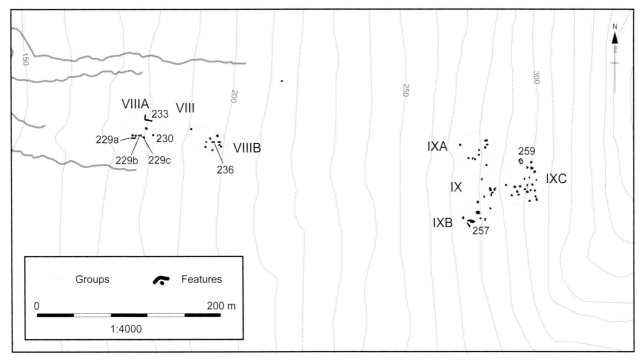

Figure 77: The CG VIII and CG IX cairnfields

six courses in places; extending downslope from it was an irregular bank, which displayed no evidence of dry-stone construction. The structure was three-sided, with its open side towards the north-east, and was a possibly a bield.

Discussion
The cairns in this area were spread over the whole of the scarp slope, not just around the edge, and there were two small structures within this group. It was evident that the steeply sloping ground was in agricultural use and was not simply used as a repository for waste stone. Given the slope, any disturbance of the ground would have resulted in lynchet formation and, as there was no evidence of this, it is probable that the cairnfield was associated with pastoralism.

Charlesground Gill VII: monuments CG 216-27
A small, compact group of cairns was recorded on a small peninsula of well-drained ground, within an extensive area of mire (Fig 76). The isthmus faced towards a scarp slope, and the cairn group was effectively contained by the topography. The cairns were regular in form, with rounded, fairly prominent profiles, and a fairly uniform size (2.8 m in average diameter). The cairnfield would appear to have been the result of a single stone-clearance episode.

Charlesground Gill VIII: monuments CG 229-41
This monument group comprised two small areas of cairns, which were divided by an area of mire (Fig 74). They were located on fairly gently sloping, slightly undulating ground between two streams. There was much poorly drained ground in the vicinity, and both cairn groups were edged by mire to the south.

The more westerly (CG VIIIA; Fig 77) of the two cairn groups was partly edged by mire to the north, and contained cairns which varied in form, size, and definition. Within the group were some short linear banks (CG 229a and CG 233) and a small semi-circular bank (CG 229b: 4.2 m in diameter). There was no evidence of any significant cairn alignments or relationship between the banks that could be indicative of a field boundary. However, in some instances, the banks did have a direct relationship with adjacent cairns. Banks CG 229b and CG 229c were linked to neighbouring cairns by smaller and less well-defined banks and stone alignments. Although the group comprised diverse elements, these were possibly all contemporary.

The second small cairn group (CG VIIIB) recorded in this area was compact, and was largely bounded by the surrounding mire. The cairns in this group were low-lying and small, but fairly uniform, and it is probable that the cairnfield was a product of a single episode of stone clearance. With the exception of cairn CG 236, the cairns were distributed in a D-shaped ring, which had a largely cairn-free centre. The ground within this ring was relatively stone-free, fairly flat, well drained, and of slightly better quality than that immediately outside the ring. It is probable that in this instance the clearance cairns were positioned around the edge of a small area of agriculturally usable ground.

Charlesground Gill IX: monuments
CG 242-81

A relatively large cairn group lay on moderately sloping, well-drained, ground, lying between 270 m and 300 m OD (Fig 74). In this area there was a small, natural terrace, with a well-defined, scarped forward apron. There were also substantial amounts of surface stone, particularly around crags beyond the southern and eastern edges of the terrace. The cairnfield was found to reside both on and at the foot of the terrace, and it could be divided into three distinct sub-groups.

One of the sub-groups (CG IXA; Fig 77) was located on the more gently sloping ground in this locality, at the foot of a scarp defining the terrace. To the east there was a break of slope, and to the west (downslope) the gradient increased. Although the cairns were associated with large amounts of brash, they were generally fairly well defined and prominent, with slightly irregular shapes.

The second sub-group (CG IXB) was also found at the foot of the scarp slope and contained a group of irregular cairns and a sub-rectangular structure. The cairns were associated with substantial brash deposits, and in some instances their definition was poor. Five were elongated and aligned across the slope, the alignment of which appears to have been significant, and may reflect an original boundary. The rectangular structure (CG 257) was a very ill-defined feature but was butted against a prominent curved bank. The interior of the structure had slight internal terracing set into the west-facing slope. It was possibly a small building, or bield.

The third, and largest, sub-group (CG IXC) was located on the top of the natural terrace, and the extent of the cairns was broadly dictated by the topographical constraints of this natural feature. The cairns were generally well defined and fairly prominent, but there were no significant alignments, and the distribution was essentially random. At the northern end of the group, adjacent to the forward terrace edge, was a fairly well-defined, double-celled structure (CG 259: 11 x 7.2 m; Pl 98). There were no obvious corners and it was not clear from the surface evidence whether it had a sub-rectangular or sub-circular configuration. The south-eastern cell was enclosed, with no surface indication of an entrance, and it was internally terraced, slightly below the level of the external ground surface. The north-western cell was three-sided, open to the north-east, and there were no obvious surface indications of internal terracing. The banks were not high (c 0.25 m) and comprised mainly small and medium stones, suggesting that the 'walls' were not very substantial. The structure and the cairns were spatially associated and there is a

Plate 98: Two-celled rectilinear structure CG 259, looking south-west

probability that these were contemporary components of a small agricultural settlement.

Conclusions

The most significant feature within the Charlesground Gill survey area was the poor drainage, which had clearly constrained the areas of agricultural activity. As a consequence, these areas were localised, and often on lesser-quality agricultural land, with steep gradients or significant amounts of surface stone.

The cairnfields were generally small and few displayed any evidence of field systems, or similar features arising from the rationalisation of farming land. Indeed, settlement within this area may well have been transient. The only possible exception to this generalisation was the CG V site group, which again was restricted by the surrounding mire. The component cairns were exceptionally large, apparently the product of extensive stone clearance, and there are several factors which could have led to the clearance of such a volume of stone. For instance, the paucity of farming land may have necessitated a greater intensity of agricultural activity at the site, resulting in substantial amounts of stone being brought to the surface. Alternatively, because much of the surrounding land was covered by mire, the settlement may have been sited on less than ideal ground, with a consequence that there were abnormal amounts of brash and surface stone to clear. Another possibility, which may have resulted in extensive stone clearance, is that the settlement was farmed over an extended period of time. However, it is also possible that the pattern of clearance might have been influenced by a combination of all three of these factors, and it is

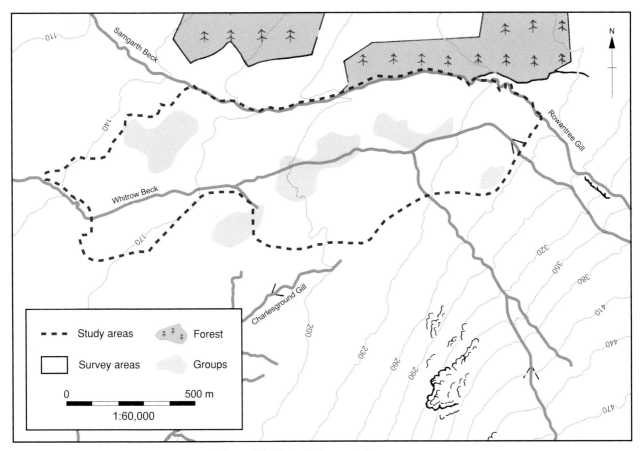

Figure 78: The Whitrow Beck survey area

certainly probable that this settlement had a longer lifetime than the majority of the Charlesground Gill cairnfield groups. Moreover, the presence of cairn alignments, and a small cultivated plot, in association with the typically randomly distributed cairns would suggest that there may have been more than one stage of agricultural activity, and that this site was not as short-lived as other site groups with simpler monuments.

Whitrow Beck

The Whitrow Beck survey area was again located on part of the South-West Fells planation terrace (Fig 55). It was edged to the north by Samgarth Beck, to the east by Rowantree Gill and the steep slopes of Whitfell, to the south by the Charlesground Gill survey area and the enclosed land of High Corney Farm, and to the west by the enclosed land of Grange Farm (Fig 78). The study area extended between 140 m and 250 m OD, but most of the archaeological sites were on the lower, more gently sloping ground (Pl 99). The gentle gradient meant that there were localised areas of poor drainage, particularly to the north of the WB III group, which had limited the expansion of the cairnfield in this direction.

Archaeological history
Cairns and a circular embankment between Samgarth Beck and Whitrow Beck were first noted by Parker in 1904 (Collingwood 1923, 267), and were first plotted on the 1900 Second Edition 6" to 1 mile OS map. The groups of cairns were more precisely located, but not planned, by the OS Archaeology Division field investigators in 1963 and 1973, the revision of the OS record card (SD 19 SW 6) in 1973 describing the enclosure as 'a sub-circular, stone-walled Iron Age/Romano-British homestead containing one stone-founded round house'. A Romano-British bronze penannular brooch was recorded (Fell 1972, 66) from the enclosed settlement (*WB 163*) at Whitrow Beck (*p 164*).

The survey area
The survey was undertaken in April 1984, covering *c* 1.25 km² of unenclosed moorland (Fig 79). In total, *c* 341 monuments, within five site groups (WB I-V), were recorded. The sites comprised cairnfields associated, in some instances, with vestiges of a field system and enclosed settlement (Fig 80), the character of the sites being broadly similar to those recorded in the nearby Stainton Fell (*p 167*) and Charlesground Gill (*p 147*) survey areas. In addition to these groups, there was also a limited number of scattered ungrouped cairns and banks, which are not individually described within this volume.

Plate 99: The Whitrow Beck survey area, looking north-east

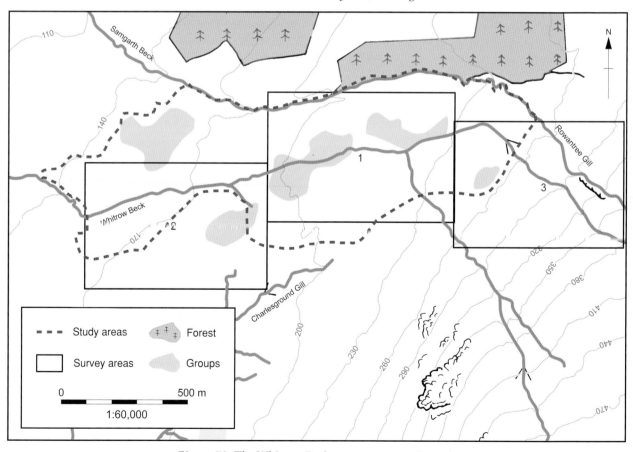

Figure 79: The Whitrow Beck survey area as planned

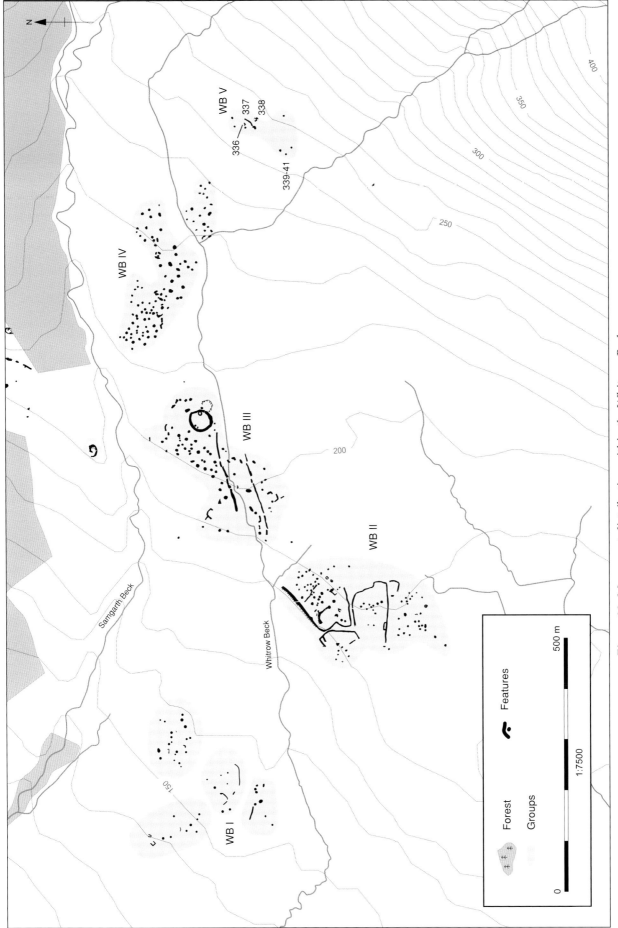

Figure 80: Monument distribution within the Whitrow Beck survey area

WB V

337
338

336

339-41

WB IV

WB III

WB II

WB I

Samgarth Beck

Whitrow Beck

400

350

300

250

200

150

Forest

Groups

Features

0   1:7500   500 m

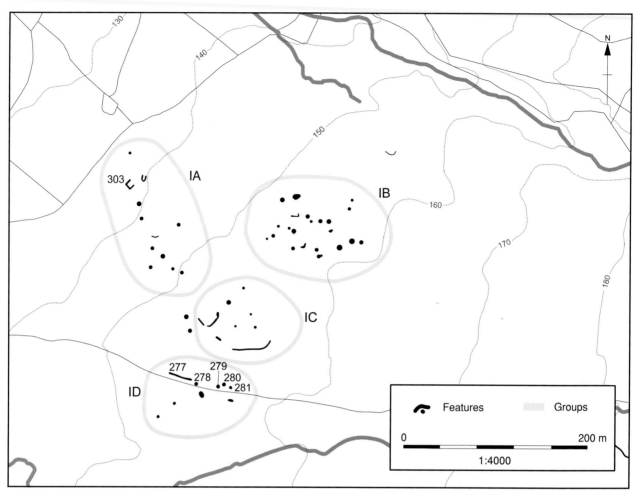

Figure 81: The WB I cairnfield

Whitrow Beck I: monuments *WB 273-332*

This monument group comprised four groups of cairns, which were located on slightly undulating, broadly level ground between the Whitrow and Samgarth Becks (Fig 80). One of these groups (WB IA; Fig 81) was defined by a north-west/south-east linear spread of cairns, which extended up the predominantly gentle slope. They were for the most part well-defined, slightly prominent, mounds with rounded profiles. There was a single, very ill-defined rectangular structure (*WB 303*), which may indicate a subsequent adaptation of a former cairn. Despite the linearity of the spread, there were no definite cairn alignments that would have indicated the line of a field boundary, but the spread was orientated towards the CG I group (*p 148*), which incorporated stone banks, reflecting the lines of former field boundaries. Another closely related, and potentially contemporary, monument group (WB IC) was defined by a loose scattering of cairns, associated with stone banks. The stone banks and one elongated cairn were discontinuous elements of a former field boundary extending around the south side of the cairn group.

The remaining two cairn groups (WB IB and WB ID) recorded in this area were relatively distinct in character and may have been created by different clearance episodes. One of these groups (WB IB) was a compact group of relatively small clearance cairns, which were mainly well defined and, in some instances, fairly prominent. The cairn distribution was markedly more compact than the adjacent groups (WB IA and WB IC), but was grouped around an area that was devoid of cairns and had a relatively well-drained surface. The cairns may thus have reflected clearance of a small plot in the centre of the group. There were no particular alignments that would have been indicative of former field boundaries

The other distinct cairn group (WB ID) was characterised by a small group of loosely scattered cairns, which were relatively well defined and prominent. Four of the cairns (*WB 278-81*) were aligned (east-west) with a section of stone bank (*WB 277*), and together may indicate the alignment of a former field boundary.

Whitrow Beck II: monuments *WB 1-94*

To the south of both the Samgarth and Whitrow Becks, immediately east of an intake of enclosed land, was a field system with associated clearance cairns (Pl 100). The field system comprised three principal fields,

Plate 100: WB II, to the east of the enclosed land

linked by a trackway that also served to separate them (Fig 80). To the south was a group of small cairns, which was not edged by relict boundaries. The fields in part appeared to be an extension of the present-day field pattern to the west, which had an atypical form, comprising a sub-circular 'enclosure,' with a series of fields radiating out from it. The relict field system would appear to have reflected further radial 'arms' of this pattern and it is likely that the modern field system represents the continuity, or even possibly reuse, of the earlier one. The land within the modern field system had been intensively improved and there were no surviving elements of the relict system within it (Pl 100). Although the relict layout had been incorporated into the post-medieval pattern, this did not provide any indication as to the date of origin of the field system, since it is possible that the banks and walls of prehistoric fields were reused at a much later date.

The monuments in this area could be divided into three distinct sub-groups. The first sub-group (WB IIA; Fig 82) comprised a large area of cairns and a field (field 1) which was related to the other two fields, in this area (fields 2 and 3; *see below*), and was aligned towards the D-shaped hub of the modern field system (Pl 100). Field 1 was defined

by a low, continuous stone bank (0.2 m high and up to 2 m wide; *WB 28*). Stones protruding from this bank formed a definite kerb and appeared to indicate dry-stone construction. To the north of this field was a trackway or outgang, which separated it from field 3. It then bifurcated north of field 1 to separate fields 2 and 3. The track opened out towards the east and provided a typical funnel-shaped intake to enable the movement of stock from the open fell into enclosed land. These tracks were orientated towards the centre of the D-shaped hub of the modern field system, which further emphasised the relationship between the relict and modern systems. Butted against the southernmost boundary of field 1 was a small rectilinear structure.

Within the enclosed area, associated with monument sub-group WB IIA, were 13 small cairns (*WB 31-42*), their distribution being similar to a group of cairns (*WB 1-27*) to the south of the field. Significantly, there were no surviving cairns immediately adjacent to the relict field boundary, yet the broad pattern and spread of cairns was similar on both sides of the boundary, and one cairn alignment extended across the boundary (A; Fig 82). The southern end of this alignment was marked by a short, curved section of stone bank

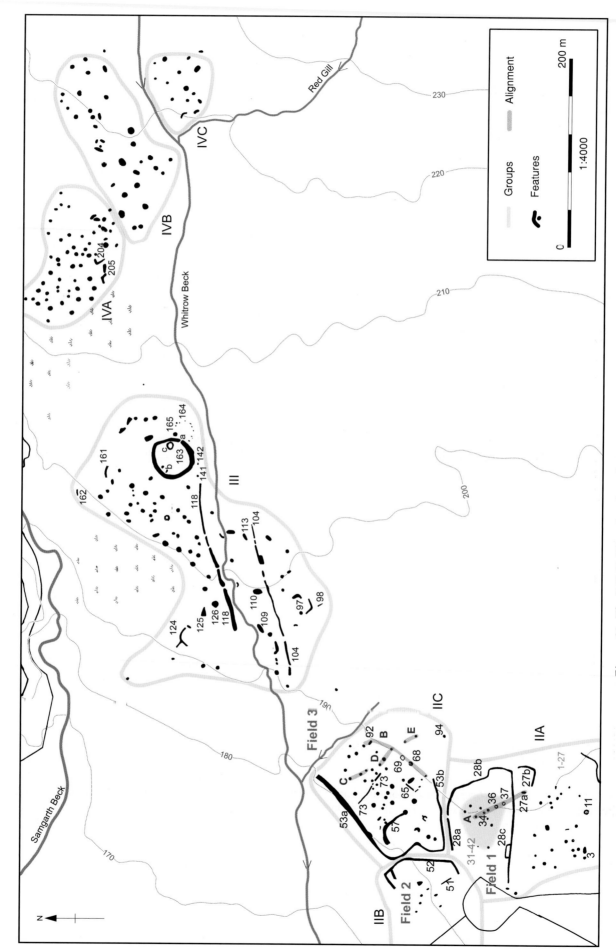

Figure 82: The WB II–IV enclosed settlement, cairnfield, and field systems

(*WB 27b*), and together they may have represented an earlier phase of the field system. The dearth of cairns on either side of the relict walls suggested that the cairnfield pre-dated the construction of the field boundary, and that those cairns immediately adjacent to the walls had been robbed to provide component stones for them. Three cairns with depressions in the centre (*WB 34*, *WB 36*, and *WB 37*) showed clear signs of robbing. At the southern extent of the small cairns was a possible small roundhouse (*WB 11*), with an internal diameter of 2.55 m, although only a few stones, protruding from the turf, marked the position of its wall. It was located at the south-western corner of a rectilinear alignment of cairns, which may have defined an agricultural plot.

The second distinct monument sub-group (WB IIB) comprised part of a field (2) and a group of cairns. Field 2 was defined to the south and east by a low bank (*WB 52*), which was up to 0.2 m high and 2.4 m wide; it incorporated extant elements of a kerb and appeared to have been a relict dry-stone wall. The northern section of this wall was, in plan, a continuation of the modern field boundary to the west. Within the enclosed field were eight small cairns, none close to its edge, and again it is possible that some of the cairns closest to the wall had been robbed to provide stone for it. On the south side of the field was a 3.7 m length of stone bank (*WB 51*), possibly the remnant of a wall, dividing the field into two.

The third monument sub-group (WB IIC) included field 3, which was defined on the east by a stream flowing to the Whitrow Beck, and on the south and west by a low relict wall (*WB 53*), which was up to 0.2 m high and 2 m wide. Its continuation on the north-west side of the field (*WB 53a*) was marked by a lynchet (up to 0.4 m high), which was in plan a continuation of a bank in field 2 to the west. Within the field were 43 small cairns, none close to its edge. However, unlike the other two fields, there did appear to be a relationship between the cairns and the field, as an alignment (B, and possibly *WB 92*; Fig 82) extended northwards from one end of this boundary. There was also a series of cairn alignments (C, D, and E) and stone banks (*WB 73*, *WB 57*, and *WB 65*) within the cairnfield, which were aligned perpendicular, or parallel, to the line of lynchet *WB 53a*. However, as these alignments also corresponded to the orientation of the slope, it was not necessarily an indication of a relationship between the cairns and the lynchet.

Stone bank *WB 73* (0.1 m high and 1.5 m wide) clearly divided the cairns within WB IIC, those to the north-east being markedly smaller than those to the south-west. In the area to the south-west of stone bank *WB 73* was a possible rectilinear structure, defined on three sides by a stone bank or wall (*WB 65*: up to 0.15 m

high and 2.3 m wide). Within the south-western part of the cairn group, a further sub-division comprised a wall and lynchet (*WB 57*: 1.6 m wide, with the lynchet up to 2.1 m high), which extended north-west from a cairn. There was only one cairn (*WB 94*) which was clearly beyond the boundary of field 3. The cairns were generally well-defined and fairly prominent, with rounded profiles. Two of these (*WB 68* and *WB 69*) were distinctive, in that they each had a stone kerb and what appeared to be an enclosing ditch, but they were not significantly larger than the other component cairns.

Discussion

There was no intimate relationship between the cairnfield and the surrounding field boundaries that would have suggested that the cairns were constructed later than these boundaries. Indeed, it would appear that elements of the cairnfield may have been robbed to provide stone for their construction. However, there seemed to be relationships between these two elements, which may indicate that the form of the field system developed from a proto-field system incorporated within the cairnfield. An alignment of cairns forming the south-east side of one of the distinct monument sub-groups (WB IIC) was orientated towards the terminus of wall *WB 53b*, and the cairnfield did not continue beyond lynchet *WB 53a*. Similarly, the cairn alignment within another of the monument sub-groups (WB IIA) extended across wall *WB 28a*, but was orientated towards stone bank *WB 27b*, part of which was aligned on the east boundary of the field.

The evidence would therefore appear to suggest that a radial field system centred on a D-shaped hub was superimposed on, and incorporated elements of, an earlier cairnfield and proto-field system. The radial field system was subsequently partly incorporated into the post-medieval pattern, allowing the survival of its north-eastern half. The date of the cairnfield system remains uncertain, but, if feature *WB 11* could be confirmed as a roundhouse, it would suggest that the earliest phase of the site was of later prehistoric date.

Whitrow Beck III: monuments *WB 95-171*

A group of small cairns, an enclosed settlement, and associated field system were located to the south of the Samgarth Beck and on both sides of, but largely to the north of, the Whitrow Beck, between the 180 m and 210 m contours (Fig 82). There was an open aspect to the west towards the coastal plain, and south-west towards Charlesground Gill.

There were 78 small cairns extending over a distance of 330 m from south-west to north-east. The north-western edge of the cairnfield corresponded to an area of mire, approximately on the line of the 200 m

Plate 101: The WB III enclosed settlement (WB 163, centre right) and cairnfields, looking south

contour (Fig 82). The cairns were generally prominent and well-defined, and included several larger oval or elongated monument (*WB 109*, *WB 110*, and *WB 113* were notable examples). To the north-east of the enclosed settlement was a discrete group of seven cairns. Some of these were elongated, and for the most part they were arranged in a line, which turned from north to north-west. These possibly reflected a former field boundary.

At the southern limit, to the south of the Whitrow Beck, were three lengths of stone bank (two numbered *WB 97*, and *WB 98*), which were possibly bields. An apparent boundary (*WB 124-6*; up to 0.2 m high) comprised an alignment of three cairns and a stone bank, and was aligned north-west / south-east. At the northern extremity of the cairn group were two further structures, one a low, stony bank (*WB 161*: 0.1 m high), whilst the other (*WB 162*; 0.8 m high) was evidently of more recent date.

On either side of the Whitrow Beck were long lengths of stone bank (*WB 104* and *WB 118*) up to 0.4 m high, which varied considerably in width from 1.5 m to 4 m. The banks were parallel and appeared to have been parts of a field system. They did not appear to

have had a direct relationship with the small cairns, which were distributed without any apparent pattern across this area, the orientations of the elongated cairns being typically at right-angles to those of the major stone banks. The northernmost of the banks (*WB 118*) was orientated towards the southern edge of the enclosed settlement (*WB 163*) and the continuation of the line was possibly defined by two cairns (*WB 141* and *WB 142*). There was consequently an implied relationship between the stone banks and the settlement.

The enclosed settlement (*WB 163*; Pl 101) was approximately 40 m in diameter, and defined by a stone wall and bank (up to 0.4 m high and 3 m wide; Pl 102), the entrance being on the south-eastern side. Within the enclosure were two roundhouses and a small cairn. The best-preserved of the roundhouses (*WB 163c*) was near the entrance and was 8 m in diameter and well defined, with a possible entrance, again on its south-eastern side. Only part of the second roundhouse (*WB 163b*) survived. Immediately beyond the entrance of the settlement was a roughly circular area, which was edged by nine orthostats (*WB 164*) and a small circular cairn (*WB 165*). A further five orthostats were incorporated

164

Plate 102: The external wall of enclosed settlement WB 163, *looking east*

into the enclosure wall. This may have been a small stone circle, which would have been partly destroyed by the construction of the homestead, and partly incorporated into its fabric, as evidenced by the presence of the orthostats.

Discussion
The WB III group appears to have incorporated at least two phases of development. The earliest element was the cairnfield, which was arranged in a north-east/south-west linear spread that crossed the line of the Whitrow Beck. The orientation of the cairn group broadly corresponded to the line of an area of mire, which may indicate that the basic drainage pattern of the area had not changed significantly since the prehistoric period. Possibly contemporary with the cairnfield was a putative stone circle (*WB 164*), located on the eastern edge of the cairn group.

The second phase of activity comprised the enclosed settlement and field system. There was an implied relationship between the northern (*WB 118*) of the two long stone banks and the enclosed settlement, suggesting contemporaneity, with both elements appearing to have been imposed on the cairnfield. There is a possibly pertinent parallel at the nearby Barnscar site (*p 188*), where a Romano-British settlement also had a series of parallel-walled

field boundaries extending directly out from it. This field system was also superimposed onto an earlier cairnfield.

Typologically, the enclosed settlement is likely to be late Iron Age or early Roman in date, on the basis of a limited number of parallels from north-west and north-east England (*Ch 2, pp 34-6*). A Romano-British bronze penannular brooch was recovered from the Whitrow Beck enclosure (Fell 1972, 66), which would suggest that the settlement was in use during the Roman period, although it is of course possible that the settlement had an earlier foundation date.

Whitrow Beck IV: monuments *WB 172- 271*
To the east of, and separate from, the WB III settlement group was a further large group of 114 small cairns (Pl 103). These cairns were located to the south of the Samgarth Beck and mainly, but not entirely, to the north of the Whitrow Beck, between the 210 m and 230 m contours (Fig 80). The most prominent feature of this group was its well-defined curving southern boundary, which partly corresponded to the edge of an area of mire to the west. On the northern side, the limit was less sharply defined (Fig 82). There was a degree of linearity to the cairns at the edges of the overall group, which may suggest that the limits of the cairnfield were defined by hard rather than

Plate 103: The WB IV cairnfield, looking south-east

amorphous boundaries. Otherwise, there was no evidence of a field system, and the cairns generally had a random distribution.

The cairns were generally fairly prominent and well defined, but there were differences in overall size. Three broad sub-groups could be defined by their distribution density and their average diameter, and these characteristics may have reflected different episodes of stone clearance. The first sub-group (WB IVA; Fig 82) contained a relatively high density of small cairns, and also two sections of adjacent stone bank, which were possibly fragments of a single structure (*WB 204* and *WB 205*). The second sub-group (WB IVB) was found to the south-east, and its character differed from that of the first group in that it comprised a broad north-east/south-west spread of large, loosely distributed cairns. The third sub-group (WB IVC) was divided from the other two cairn groups by the Whitrow Beck, and although the component cairns were relatively small, they had a compact distribution, as seen in WB IVA.

Whitrow Beck V: monuments *WB 334-41*

To the south-east of the main areas of cairnfield were two small groups of cairns located between the 240 m and 250 m contours (Fig 80). The most southerly of these consisted of three small cairns (*WB 339-41*). The northern group consisted of four small cairns, together with fragments of two possible structures, characterised by wall fragments (*WB 336* and *WB 338*) standing up to 0.6 m and 0.5 m respectively. These two fragments of walling were separated by a stone bank (*WB 337*), which was up to 0.2 m high.

Conclusions

The cairnfields recorded in the Whitrow Beck area appear to reflect discrete plots of agricultural ground, which had been subject to prehistoric land improvement. Their earliest phases indicated a degree of consistency of character, typically with a broad, random distribution of cairns, and only occasional cairn alignments or stone banks. To an extent, the positions of the cairnfields reflected topographical differences; the cairnfields in WB III and WB IV in particular had been constrained by areas of mire. However, these factors did not entirely define the extent of the cairnfields, and there may have been other spatial parameters which constrained the groups, such as areas of dense woodland, which have not survived to the present day.

Two of the cairn groups (WG II and WG III) had later field systems superimposed upon them, while the others had no sign of such development.

166

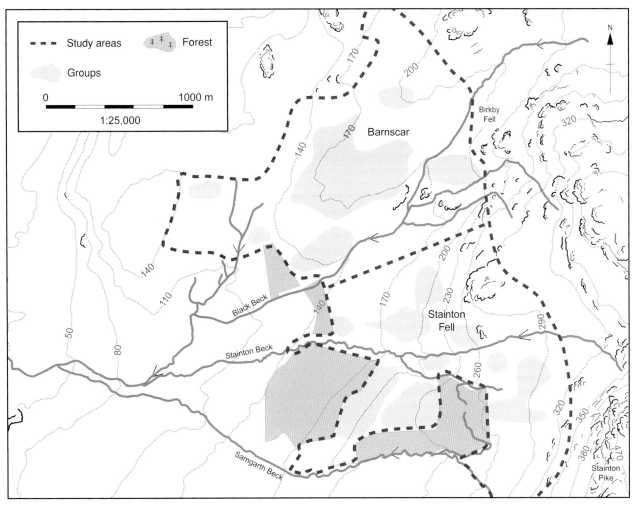

Figure 83: The Stainton Fell and Barnscar survey areas

In particular, WB IV contained a field system associated with an Iron Age/Romano-British settlement. There was no direct link between the two later field systems, although an area of marshy ground and peat formation could have masked any potential linking features. The WB II group is also potentially significant because its field system was adjacent to, and partly overlain by, the enclosed land of the present-day field system, which in this area had the irregular lines, shapes, and sizes that are typically indicative of a field system with an early unplanned origin. Indeed, there was also some correlation between the alignments of the WB II field boundaries and those of the present-day fields, suggesting that to some extent the modern field system developed from the WB II field system. This may either reflect continuity and development of the prehistoric/Romano-British field system, or alternatively, it may reflect the reoccupation of the site at a much later date, entailing the reuse of the existing, albeit decayed, walls of the earlier field system. In either case, it is important, as it provides an insight into the potential processes that led to the formation of modern field patterns in this area.

Stainton Fell

The Stainton Fell survey area encompassed semi-enclosed and unenclosed moorland on the west-facing slopes of the South-West Fells, adjacent to the coastal plain (Fig 55). Although some areas in this landscape were partly enclosed (SF I and SF VI), none of the land had been improved within the recent past. To the north, the survey area was divided from that of the extensive Barnscar settlement (*p 178*) by Black Beck, whilst to the south it was divided from the Whitrow Beck survey area (*p 157*) by Samgarth Beck (Fig 83). The survey was limited to the west by forestry plantation, and the easternmost limit was defined by a sharp increase in gradient, leading up to the summit of Stainton Pike. The highest site group (SF III) was found at *c* 310 m OD, but the main area of cairnfields was within an altitude range of 150-260 m.

The cairnfield groups were generally on gentle or moderately sloping land, and their extent was often defined by local topography. The cairnfields in SF I-II, SF V, and SF VIII were partly defined by the steep

167

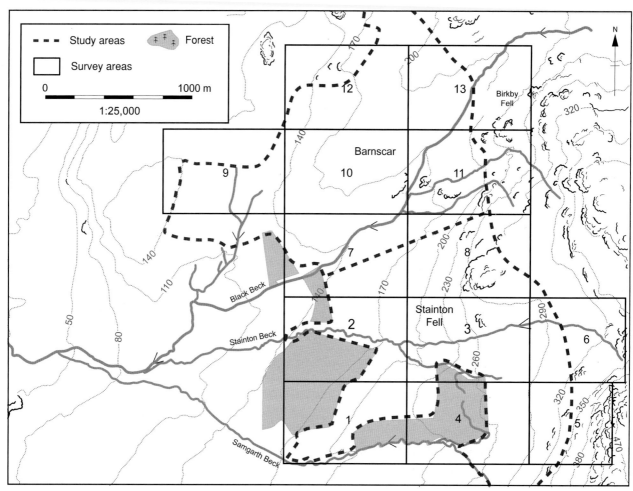

Figure 84: The Stainton Fell and Barnscar survey areas as planned

gullies of Stainton Beck and its tributary, while the cairnfields in SF VI-VII were in an area of gently sloping, poorly drained ground, and were on islands of dry ground surrounded by bog. Within the survey area, there were only two small extents of moderately sloping, well-drained ground, below 280 m OD, that were found not to have cairnfields (between SF IV and SF V, and to the south of SF I). It would thus appear that the fell was fully exploited in antiquity.

There are now large areas of dense, coniferous forest on Stainton Fell, which were planted by the time of the 1956 6″ to 1 mile OS map. The cairnfields in SF I-III and SF VI extended right up to the forest boundaries and it is likely that they also once spread into the areas now covered by forest. The trees were set too close together to allow access, however, and therefore no reconnaissance was undertaken within the forest. It is likely, though, that any sites within had been destroyed by deep ploughing in advance of planting (*Ch 9, p 356*).

Archaeological history

Prior to the present survey, only the SF I cairnfield had been recorded. Ten cairns, corresponding to part of the SF I group (SF IA), including a large long cairn,

SF 2, were shown on the OS Second Edition 6″ map (1900). In 1964, those cairns that were schematically represented on this early map, and circular platform *SF 90*, were scheduled as Ancient Monuments. In 1982, a vertical aerial photographic reconnaissance programme by LUAU identified a further 13 cairns in the SF IA and SF IB cairn groups.

The survey area

The survey was undertaken in April 1988 over 2.6 km² of unenclosed and enclosed moorland (Fig 84). In total, 514 monuments were found within nine survey areas, which comprised a series of extensive cairnfields (SF I and SF II), with associated proto-fields and house platforms (Fig 85). Also within the group were several very substantial funerary round cairns (*SF 2* and *SF 338*), and also a putative long cairn (*SF 363*). In addition to these, there were limited numbers of scattered ungrouped cairns and banks (*SF 175* and *SF 397-408*), which are not individually described within this volume.

Stainton Fell I: monuments *SF 2-116*

The cairnfield in this area (Fig 85) was located within two large fields, which are shown on the 1867 First Edition 6″ to 1 mile OS map. These fields are irregular,

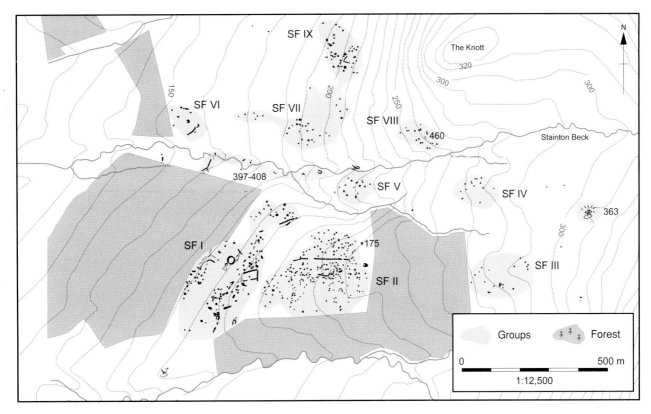

Figure 85: Monument distribution within the Stainton Fell survey area

some of their boundaries having antecedents, and they were denoted as intake on both the First Edition and later mapping. They would thus appear to have been part of a pre-Parliamentary enclosure. The boundaries of these fields clearly overlay elements of the cairnfield and associated boundary banks (*eg SF 35*; Fig 86). The cairnfield in SF I was divided from the SF II cairnfield by a *c* 70 m-wide area that was devoid of cairns (Pl 104). The two cairnfields had clearly contrasting characters, the component cairns of SF I being considerably larger and more prominent than those of SF II. They appear to have been the product of different episodes of stone clearance, although a long, continuous bank (*SF 174*; *p 173*) within the SF II cairnfield was closely aligned with the main boundary of plot *SF 35*, suggesting that some elements of each area may have been in contemporary use.

The ground throughout the SF I cairnfield was well drained and there were only small amounts of surface scree associated with the cairns (Pl 105). They were situated on gently sloping land, although there was a long, steep scarp slope extending through the middle, which divided the cairnfield into two distinct monument sub-groups (SF IA and SF IB; Fig 86).

One of these sub-groups (SF IA; Fig 86) contained a band of cairns positioned along the top of the scarp slope that divided this cairnfield. These cairns

were generally large and prominent, and were distinct from the other cairns in this area, which were significantly smaller. There was also a marked difference in the distribution of the cairns found in the northern and southern parts of this sub-group, with those to the north having an essentially random distribution, whereas those to the south of the *SF 35* banks were mostly aligned with other cairns and banks. Some of the alignments defined the edges of rectilinear areas that were devoid of cairns and were possibly cultivation plots.

In addition to the cairns, *SF 14* created a clear plot within SF IA. This was edged by seven elongated turf-covered banks and a length of stone bank, and was approximately square, enclosing an area of *c* 560 m². Within the plot were only occasional surface stones, and the outer cairns and banks would appear to have been piles of stone cleared from within. A limited amount of soil against the lower cairns of the plot would appear to have been a positive lynchet, suggesting that the plot had been cultivated. A second plot (plot *i*) was found immediately to the south and east of plot *SF 14*, bordered by ten cairns and banks (*SF 11*, *SF 12*, *SF 14-16*, and *SF 21-5*). It was sub-rectilinear and enclosed an area of *c* 1560 m². Beyond were substantial amounts of surface stone, but only occasional stones and no clearance mounds were identified within; it is probable that the plot was cleared and the waste stones deposited around the outside.

169

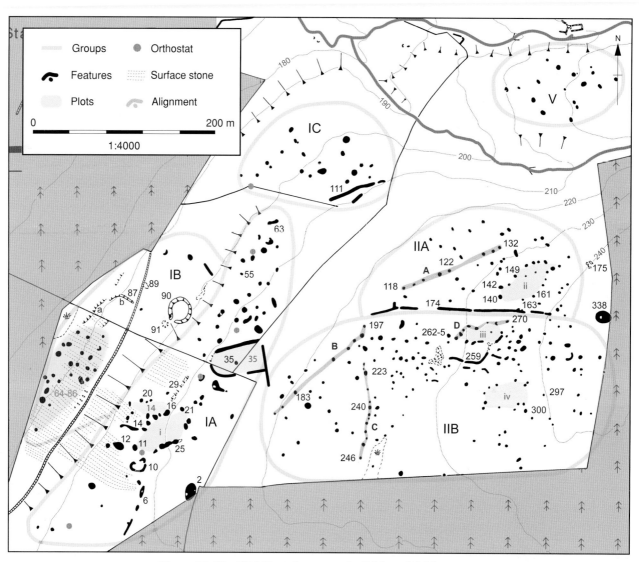

Figure 86: The SF I-II settlement, cairnfield, and field systems

Plate 104: SF I (left) and SF II (right), separated by a narrow area without monuments to the right of the visible modern field boundary (centre left), looking north-east

Plate 105: The well-drained land on which the SF I field system and cairnfield developed

Extending north along the slope from plot *i* was a stone bank with a negative lynchet-like profile (*SF 29*), which had possibly been created by cultivation. The area immediately downslope from the bank, however, had substantial amounts of surface stone and did not appear to have been cleared.

Another plot (*SF 35*) was found within SF IA, which was overlain by modern field boundaries and edged by fairly continuous earth and stone banks. Immediately

to the north of the plot was a compact group of clearance cairns. The plot, however, contained only one small cairn, and relatively small quantities of surface stone, which had apparently being deposited around the edges. The top and bottom boundaries of the area had lynchet-like profiles, and thus the plot had probably been cultivated.

Other features associated with SF IA included faint, narrow ridge and furrow, which was observed on

Plate 106: Large cairn SF 2, *looking south*

the group's western side, extending down the steep scarp slope. It crossed the western boundary of plot *SF 14*, and passed around cairn *SF 20*; none of the cairn alignments followed the same orientation as the ridges and it would thus appear that the ridge and furrow post-dated the cairns and 'plots'. Also to the south-west of plot *i*, an unusual type of enclosure (*SF 10*) was identified. On its western side it comprised a possible rectilinear structure, which was similar in form to a building from Charlesground Gill (*CG 259; p 156*), and extending from this were two very irregular stone banks which converged to form an entrance. The interior of the enclosure was approximately flat, although there was a limited amount of tumble associated with the banks. It was linked to cairn/bank alignment *SF 6* by a faint stone bank, and stone bank *SF 25* also converged, suggesting a relationship.

Another feature contained within SF IA was found to the east, though somewhat remote from the main part of the cairnfield. This was an extremely prominent, large pear-shaped cairn (*SF 2*), with a regular, rounded profile (21 x 11 x 2 m; Pl 106). The stones forming the cairn were mainly medium-sized, but there were some large stones around its south-western edge, which may have been a kerb. There was no evidence of any recent disturbance, as the lichen cover was uniform over all the surface stones.

It was not in a particularly prominent location, but the size, height, shape, and possible kerb would imply that it was a funerary monument.

A north/south alignment of six large orthostats (Fig 86) was also identified in the centre of this monument sub-group, all of which had been crudely worked to produce pointed tops. The distance between the stones was fairly regular, being 75 m, 80 m, 75 m, 90 m, and *c* 100 m respectively. A field wall had been built around the most northerly of these, between 1867 and 1900 (OS First and Second Edition 6" to 1 mile maps), but the stones had little association with the cairns or lynchets. They therefore possibly post-dated the construction of the early plot and were perhaps markers for a pre-Parliamentary enclosure boundary.

The second monument sub-group (SF IB) in this area comprised a group of cairns and a large, circular platform, located below the scarp slope running through the centre of the cairnfield. At the foot of the slope, and extending through the centre of this monument group, was a decayed dry-stone wall, which overlay lynchet *SF 87* and cairn *SF 89*. A truncated part of the wall was shown on the 1867 First Edition 6" to 1 mile OS map, but was not marked on the 1900 Second Edition 6" to 1 mile map. Although both ends of the wall terminated at intersections of the modern field system, it was overlain by one of the modern field walls (also shown on the OS First Edition map), and thus it probably related to an earlier field system, which clearly pre-dated the Parliamentary enclosure boundaries. To the west of the wall was some narrow ridge and furrow, which terminated at a discontinuous, irregular turf-covered bank/headland, parallel to, and about 3 m west of, the decayed wall; this possibly marked the line of an earlier phase of this boundary. Although there was an obvious gap between the ridge and furrow, it was similar in width on either side of the wall, and was potentially a product of a single episode of cultivation. The majority of the cairns formed a compact group (SF 64-86), limited to the east by this turf bank. Many were aligned on the same orientation as the ridge and furrow and there is a possibility that these were either contemporary or had been severely altered by this episode of cultivation.

Several lynchets were also associated with SF IB. These were positioned at its northern end, the lowest of which (SF 87a) related to the ridge and furrow, whereas the upper L-shaped lynchet (SF 87b) was cut by it, and was probably a product of earlier cultivation. L-shaped lynchet SF 87b also defined two sides of a small field, within which there was no ridge and furrow and very little surface stone.

In addition, a large circular platform (SF 90: 27 m in diameter) was partly set into the side of the scarp slope, with a corresponding earthwork built up to create the forward apron of the platform. There appeared to be a greater volume of spoil in the apron, however, than could have been excavated from the slope, suggesting that spoil was brought in from elsewhere. This had resulted in the platform being raised above the external ground surface, and it also served to improve the drainage. By this means, the platform was made level, and contained only occasional surface stones; it had an entrance on the south-western side, defined by large portal stones. As a great deal of effort had been expended in creating a drained, level surface, a domestic rather than an agricultural function can be inferred, and it may have served as the platform for a single large roundhouse, or several smaller structures. It was similar to platform TB 636 recorded in Town Bank (Ch 3, pp 59-60), which also had an enlarged forward apron. Adjacent to the entrance was a much smaller, circular platform (SF 91), set into the slope, which was possibly an individual house platform.

Apart from the two main monument sub-groups within this area, an additional, albeit smaller, monument sub-group (SF IC) was also identified, positioned to the north-east of SF IA. This contained a limited number of clearance-type cairns, but there was no evidence of any ridge and furrow. The cairns had an essentially random distribution, although they were edged to the south-east by lynchet SF 111. The cairn group was separated from SF IA by a 60 m-wide area that was devoid of cairns. However, lynchet SF 111 was aligned with a small, but similar, stub of bank (SF 63) recorded in the northern part of SF IA, and there may have been elements within both groups that were possibly related.

Discussion
A complex sequence of various site types could be discerned in SF I, which indicated a multi-phased occupation of this landscape. The latest elements were the modern field walls, which overlay all other features, yet were built before 1867. The decayed wall that ran through the centre of SF IB represented an earlier phase of this field system, which had certainly gone out of use by 1900 (OS 6": 1 mile map). The turf bank parallel to the decayed wall was probably its precursor, since ridge and furrow was edged by it, and was also contemporary with it. The cairns to the west of the boundary appeared to relate to this ridge and furrow and were either contemporary with it, or were earlier features which had been altered by this later episode of cultivation.

In addition, ridge and furrow cut lynchet SF 87 at the northern end of SF IB and also overlay part of plot SF 14, associated with SF IA. Thus, it is likely that the ridge and furrow also post-dated the other two apparently arable plots found in this area (plot i and SF 35). The randomly distributed cairns to the north were defined to the south-east by field SF 35 and thus may have been contemporary features. Several standing stones also pre-dated a field wall built between 1867 and 1900, but appeared to post-date the construction of the fields and cairns recorded within SF IA.

An early element within this monument group might be a large long cairn (SF 2), which would appear to be a prehistoric funerary monument. However, there was no obvious relationship between it and any other elements of the cairnfield/field system.

Stainton Fell II: monuments SF 117-338
This large, dense cairnfield was on gently sloping, well-drained land (Fig 85), which had been unenclosed moorland until the planting of the surrounding forest, subsequent to the 1956 6" to 1 mile OS map (Pl 107). There were substantial brash deposits, particularly in the southern half of the cairnfield, and a scatter of surface stone throughout. Running through the centre was a decayed wall (SF 174), which defined the northern side of a corridor that was devoid of cairns. The wall appeared to divide the cairnfield into two

Plate 107: The SF II settlement, field system, and cairnfield, hemmed in by modern forestry plantation, looking south-east

distinct sub-groups, but it was not necessarily contemporary with it, particularly as the empty corridor may have been a result of robbing nearby cairns for the construction of the wall. The decayed wall was orientated with the northern boundary of plot *SF 35* in the SF I cairnfield (*p 169*), suggesting links between at least some elements within these monument groups. The component cairns of SF II were significantly smaller and less prominent than those of SF I, and they may represent a different episode of stone clearance.

One of the cairn groups (SF IIA; Fig 86) was located to the north of the dividing boundary (*SF 174*). The cairns in this sub-group were generally small and often ill defined. Many of the cairns were scattered without any clear pattern, although one cairn alignment was orientated approximately north-east/south-west (A) and a possible plot (*ii*) was also edged by 14 cairns (*SF 140*, *SF 142*, *SF 149-61*, and *SF 163*). The area defined by these features contained only two small cairns and limited amounts of surface stone, but no obvious lynchets.

The second cairn group (SF IIB) in this area was positioned to the south of the dividing boundary (*SF 174*), and formed a very large, dense group of small, generally ill-defined, cairns. Their distribution

was similar to that observed within the adjacent group to the north, and a few cairn alignments and three possible plots can be identified, combined with a large number of cairns which did not demonstrate any evident ordering.

One of the cairn alignments (B) marked the western side of SF IIB. This alignment was discontinuous and orientated north-east/south-west, approximately along the contours. In addition, another alignment (C) was recognised in the centre of the cairnfield, aligned approximately north-south, on a convergent course to the first. Close to these alignments were plots *SF 259* and *iii*, which were divided from each other by a line of four cairns. Plot *SF 259* was edged to the south by a stone bank, and to the west by a large deposit of natural surface stone; plot *iii* was edged to the north and east by an alignment of ten cairns (D). Both plots had a negative lynchet at the top and would appear to have been cultivated. There were only limited amounts of surface stone in the plots, which contrasted with the rocky terrain outside, and it would appear that waste stone was cleared to the edges, forming the banks and cairns. Plot *iv* was a rectilinear area defined by an alignment of 11 cairns (E), but there was little evidence to establish if it had ever been cultivated. For instance, there

174

Plate 108: Round cairn SF 338, revealing an in-situ ring bank

were no lynchets at the top or bottom, and the ground within it was slightly undulating. However, it had probably been cleared of surface stone, as the ground within was relatively stone-free when compared to that outside.

At the eastern end of SF IIB, directly in line with bank *SF 174*, a large round cairn (*SF 338*) was also recorded. It was well defined, very prominent, and had a regular, rounded profile (14.5 x 13 x 1.5 m; Pl 108). The south-eastern quadrant of the mound had been robbed, exposing a circular bank around the edge of the cairn, the matrix of which comprised earthfast small stones, contrasting with the soil-free, larger stone matrix of the disturbed mound. It is possible that the bank was an original, pre-cairn, feature, rather than a product of the disturbance, perhaps forming a ring cairn, later capped by a round cairn. This is a well-paralleled type of funerary monument, as at Manor Farm, Borwick (Olivier 1987), Cairn GCRC II (Ward 1988), and Hardendale (Howard-Davis and Williams 2005), and typically dates to the Bronze Age.

Discussion
The character of the cairnfields on either side of dividing wall *SF 174* was very similar; the component cairns were similarly sized, they both included cairn alignments, which approximately followed the contours, and both contained plots defined by lines of cairns. The implication is that they were broadly contemporary and may even have been the product of the same clearance episode. The western end of wall *SF 174* coincided with the western edge of the cairnfield and, similarly, the wall did not extend beyond its eastern edge, suggesting that the wall and cairnfield were related. There was no direct relationship between the cairnfield and the round cairn (*SF 338*), as no clearance cairns were found within a *c* 35 m radius of this monument. This may reflect a deliberate intention to separate the funerary monument from agricultural activities.

Stainton Fell III: monuments *SF 339-63*
This monument group (Fig 85), comprised a small cairnfield, together with a possible funerary long cairn, which were situated on a relatively gently sloping, slightly undulating area of exposed moorland, at the foot of Stainton Pike. The cairnfield was spread around the south-western slopes and summit of a small hillock, the cairns being generally small and not particularly prominent. Their distribution was largely dictated by the local topography and no significant cairn alignments were recognised.

A possible funerary monument (*SF 363*) was an extremely large, long, prominent, oval mound on the summit of a small hillock. Although it may have been an entirely natural feature, it did display elements suggestive of an artificial origin and could therefore have been a natural feature enlarged to form a long cairn. Its western end was very well defined, and it had a regular, rounded profile. It also incorporated two orthostatic stones (*c* 2 m high) set on either side of the centre line, which were reminiscent of portal stones (Pl 109). However, at the eastern end it merged into the natural slope and there were natural outcrops protruding from it. It appeared to contain a soil matrix, rather than stone, which is unusual for Lake District funerary monuments, as demonstrated by numerous upland surveys (*see Ch 1*).

Plate 109: Façade of putative long cairn SF 363

Stainton Fell IV: Monuments SF 364-78
A small, compact cairnfield lay on the moderately sloping ridge of a spur, formed between two streams (Fig 85). The component cairns were fairly small, had rounded profiles, but were not very well defined because of the dense vegetation cover in the area. There were no significant alignments, and the distribution was essentially random. The limits of the cairnfield did not correspond to any present-day topographical features.

Stainton Fell V: monuments *SF 379-96*

The cairnfield comprising SF V was very similar to that found in SF IV, lying on the same moderately sloping ridge and having a similar density (Fig 85). It was limited on its northern edge by a break of slope along the Stainton Beck gully, but otherwise its boundaries did not correspond to present-day topographical features (Fig 86). The cairns were generally larger than those of SF IV, with rounded, only slightly prominent, profiles, but they were otherwise similar. There were no significant cairn alignments and the distribution was essentially random.

Stainton Fell VI: monuments *SF 409-18*

A small cairnfield was located on an island of moderately drained ground, surrounded by areas of mire, on the north side of Stainton Beck (Fig 85). The extent of the cairnfield was contained within the modern field boundaries that were, for the most part, shown on the 1867 First Edition 6" to 1 mile OS map, although a small plantation on the western side had been created by the time of the 1956 OS 6" to 1 mile survey. Two of the cairns were close to the plantation boundary and the cairnfield may have been truncated by associated tree planting. The cairns were varied in form. For

instance, *SF 410* was large and fairly prominent, but had been seriously disturbed, whereas *SF 416* and *SF 414* were small and low-lying (Fig 87). Four of the cairns (Alignment A) were aligned, adjacent and parallel to a modern northern field wall, and the cairnfield did not extend beyond this. Apart from this common alignment, there was no evidence of a relationship between the wall and the cairn alignment, and there was only a slight possibility that the modern boundary line reflected an earlier boundary. At the southern end of the group was a broad bank (*SF 409*), which incorporated extant elements of dry-stone masonry and coincided with the edge of a small mire. It was separated from the main part of the cairn group and was not necessarily a related element.

Stainton Fell VII: monuments *SF 419-52*

The terrain in this area was gently sloping (Fig 85) and there were only occasional deposits of surface stone. However, there was also a thick tussocky grass cover, which limited the definition of the monuments. Two small cairn groups were identified on islands of well-drained land within a large expanse of mire. One (SF VIIA) comprised six, ill-defined, low-lying cairns, whilst the cairns in the

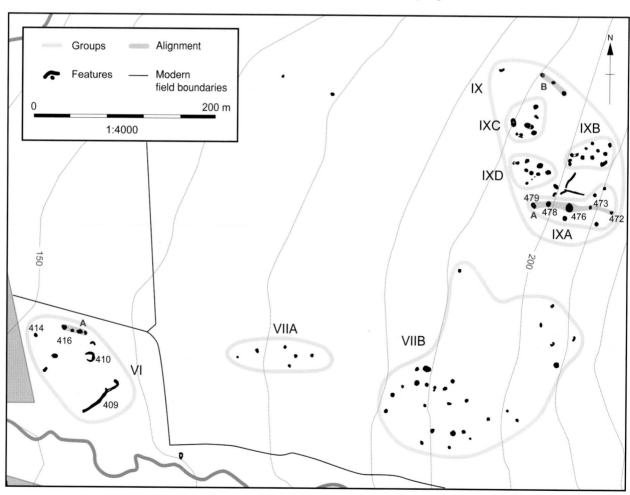

Figure 87: The SF VI-VIII cairnfields

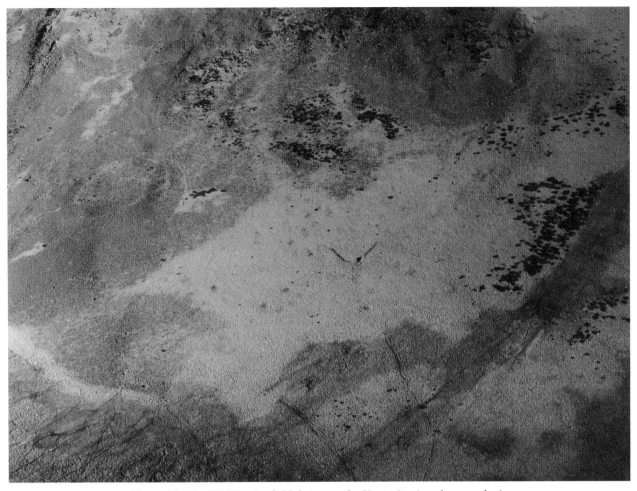

Plate 110: The SF IX cairnfield, between the Knott (top) and areas of mire

other group (SF VIIB) were of various sizes, were not particularly prominent, and were randomly distributed. No cairns were visible within the mire, which may indicate that the present local drainage pattern had not significantly changed since the construction of the cairns.

Stainton Fell VIII: monuments *SF 453-69*

This small cairnfield was located on a moderately sloping area of undulating moorland adjacent to a large crag (Fig 85), with associated scree, although the ground around the cairns was relatively free of surface stone. The cairnfield was limited to the south by the Stainton Beck gully, but otherwise its limits did not correspond to present-day topographical features. The cairns were generally small and occasionally low-lying, but one significantly larger cairn (6 x 4.5 x 0.5 m), comprising stone piled up against an erratic boulder, was clearly also a product of stone clearance.

There were two, possibly significant, cairn alignments orientated downslope, which may have represented the lines of former boundaries. In between and above these alignments was a short section of dry-stone wall (*SF 460*) with collapse on its western side, though this had no clear relationship with the cairn alignments.

Stainton Fell IX: monuments *SF 470-510*

The cairnfield was on well-drained, gentle to moderately sloping land, which was clearly defined by the local topography (Fig 85). The eastern edge was defined by a steep break of slope that led up to the summit of the Knott, and on the north-western side it was edged by a another sharp break of slope, below which was an expanse of bog that also defined the south-western edge of the cairnfield (Pl 110).

The cairns were grouped into four small clusters (SF IXA-D; Fig 87) with open areas of evenly sloping ground in between. The component cairns in three of the clusters (SF IXB-D) were fairly similar, being quite large, well-defined, and prominent. However, the cairns within the remaining cluster (SF IXA) were small, ill-defined, and occasionally low-lying. There were also two possibly significant cairn alignments. These comprised a line of five, regularly spaced, cairns (A; SF IXA) and a line of three cairns (B) at the northern end of the cairnfield. Elsewhere, however, the cairns appeared to exhibit an essentially random distribution.

In the centre of the group was a radial, three-armed, dry-stone structure standing to a height of 0.5 m, that represented the characteristic remains of a post-medieval stock shelter, affording protection from the wind in all directions. These, typically isolated, shelters are a common feature of the Cumbrian fells (for instance, *Ch 3, BM 247; p 111*), and although this shelter was spatially associated with the cairnfield, it is unlikely that they were contemporary features.

Conclusions

Most of the land in the Stainton Fell area that was well-drained, not too steep, or too high, had been exploited agriculturally, as evidenced by the cairnfields, which would indicate that there had been considerable pressure on the land. The cairnfields, however, displayed significant differences of form. Some, for example, were small, compact groups of randomly scattered cairns, with little sense of order (SF III-VIII), but there were also larger cairnfields, which included an element of planning. Although this latter type included substantial numbers of randomly scattered cairns, there were also many clearance cairns arranged in lines, or around possible cultivation plots, with occasional lynchets (*eg* SF I and SF II). In contrast, the larger cairnfields appeared to represent a more organised and intensive approach to stone clearance and agricultural exploitation. However, the broad similarities between the two forms suggest that, in origin, their practices were not dissimilar. The smaller cairnfields were also usually on land of lesser quality, either because of the moderate slopes or because their extents were contained by the local topography. Conversely, the larger cairnfields were on gently sloping ground and were mostly unrestricted by the topography. It is, therefore, possible that their positioning on the better ground encouraged their expansion and development into the more advanced form of agricultural system.

The SF I monument group displayed clear evidence for two main phases of activity. The first phase was represented by two of the cairn groups (SF IA and SF IC) recorded in this area, whilst the later phase was represented by ridge and furrow, associated with the cairns of another of the recorded cairn groups (SF IB), and also by an ephemeral earthen bank. The ridge and furrow is indicative of medieval, or post-medieval, agriculture (*Ch 2, p 30*), and there was a direct relationship between this cultivation and the boundaries shown on 1867 First Edition 6" to 1 mile OS map. Therefore, there is a clear implication that the second phase was relatively late in comparison with the earlier cairnfield phase.

Barnscar

Barnscar (Fig 55) represents the largest and most complex cairnfield recorded in north-west England, its main site group (BS IV) comprising over 610 separate monuments. It is apparent from the surface evidence and the results of antiquarian excavations that there was a multi-phased occupation of this landscape, which at least spanned the Bronze Age and Roman periods.

Barnscar lies on a broad raised terrace between the steep craggy peaks of Birkby Fell and the steep-sided, glacially cut Esk valley to the north-west (Fig 83). Devoke Water and its associated cairnfields (*Ch 5, p 197*) lie on the same natural terrace, about 2 km to the north-east, and to the south of Black Beck were the Stainton Fell cairnfield groups (*p 167*).

The main settlement at Barnscar (BS IV) was on a flat-topped ridge in the middle of the terrace, which was edged to the south-east by Black Beck. There were extensive mires in association with Black Beck, around the edge of the ridge. Three small groups of cairns within poorly drained ground, around the southern and western sides of the cairnfield, may indicate a limited and localised expansion of the surrounding mire. Furthermore, within two of these cairnfields, peat-forming vegetation was not yet dominant, which would imply that the mire expansion was a relatively recent phenomenon. At a third cairnfield, the construction of a stone bank along the slope had restricted the local drainage and had effectively acted as a dam (*p 195*). As a result, blanket peat had formed upslope from it, engulfing five cairns. With the exception of the BS I and BS II monument groups, the cairnfields were on unenclosed land which had not been recently improved.

Palaeobotanical history

Three pollen records exist for the Barnscar area, from a site near to Black Beck and one close to the Knott (OA North 2009a), whilst the third comes from a buried soil located beneath a clearance cairn found at Barnscar (Walker 1965a; *p 179*). Peat inception dates from the first two of these sites, of 3360-3020 cal BC (4490±40 BP; SUERC-4523; Black Beck) and 3370-3090 cal BC (4553±35 BP; SUERC-4524; the Knott), were associated with strong clearance signals in the pollen record (OA North 2009a). This suggested that the landscape at Barnscar and the Knott had been extensively cleared during the neolithic period, very much earlier than the widespread Bronze Age clearance highlighted at Tewit Moss, some 3.5 km to the north-east (*Ch 5, p 203*). This early clearance may also have caused an increase in run-off from

Barnscar, into the Black Beck valley, so initiating peat formation. However, such early clearance may have been temporary, and woodland regeneration may have taken place before the Bronze Age.

This hypothesis is supported, in some measure, by the limited pollen analysis carried out on the buried soil found below an excavated cairn (*BS 190*) in the BS IV monument group (Walker 1965a; *p 182*). This analysis suggested that, prior to the cairn's construction, there was at least a partially wooded landscape of birch, oak, alder, and hazel, with occasional clearings. A sample from the fill of a pit, discovered under the cairn, also contained a large proportion of grasses and herbs, which would suggest partial deforestation had begun by this stage. It can therefore be assumed that the cairn was constructed when the area was still partially forested, although the construction of this and other cairns, and the associated episode of clearance, would have caused considerable disturbance to the local vegetation. Indeed, Walker (1965b, 62) suggested that the apparent evidence for burning of the surface soil, found beneath the cairn, and also the excavation of pits, perhaps during the removal of tree-stumps, may be an indication that the clearance cairns were associated with an episode of deforestation. Walker (*ibid*) further argued that, during this process, the original soil surface of the forest was stripped and deposited in piles, which were subsequently capped by cairns.

In addition to the pollen records from Barnscar, several pollen cores have been taken from the area of Devoke Water. This is some 2.5 km downwind of Barnscar, and the pollen preserved in these cores will reflect in part the past vegetation of the Barnscar area (see the Birkby / Birker Fell survey; *Ch 5, p 197*).

Archaeological history

The earliest documented reference to the Barnscar settlement dates from 1794 (Hutchinson 1794, 562 and 578). This inaccurately described the extent of the settlement, and obliquely referred to the farmstead (*BS 477; p 188*). This farmstead was also shown on the 1867 First Edition 6″ OS map of this area. According to Dymond (1893), the earliest known antiquarian activity on Barnscar was undertaken by Lord Muncaster in about 1885, but there were 'indications of small burrowings of an earlier date which have not been recorded' (*op cit, p 186*). Lord Muncaster excavated at least three trenches within the farmstead and also 'opened' several cairns, within one or more of which were inverted cinerary urns. Clare Fell (*cf* Walker 1965b, 64-5) described two collared urns of uncertain provenance, which may have come from these excavations. Dymond (1893) produced a survey of the Barnscar settlement (BS IV), which was of an exceptionally high standard for the period; however, it only included about half

Cairn excavated by Walker	Survey no
2	*BS 508?*
5	*BS 555?*
8	*BS 422*
9	*BS 411*
10	*BS 190*

Table 3: Cairns recorded by the LDNPS which were excavated by Donald Walker (1965b)

of the associated cairnfield. It does, however, show the cairns that had been opened prior to his survey, and so provides a *terminus ante quem* for these explorations.

Between 1957 and 1958, Donald Walker (1965b) excavated ten cairns from the BS IV site group. In general, these cairns were excavated by the quadrant technique, although in some, only the centres were opened. The present survey recorded ten cairns that had been excavated subsequent to the Dymond survey (*BS 185, BS 190, BS 192, BS 217, BS 222, BS 411, BS 422, BS 453?, BS 503,* and *BS 555;* BS II), and, of these, seven had been excavated using the quadrant technique. However, their positions did not coincide well with Walker's crude location map, and it is only possible to correlate some of Walker's excavated cairns with those recorded by the present survey (Table 3).

A detailed understanding of the results of Walker's excavations is crucial to any discussion of the BS IV monument group. In summary, this work suggested that the majority of the excavated cairns displayed a broadly similar stratigraphy, which appeared to indicate a common construction sequence. The main events of the construction sequence were as follows: the original ground surface was first partly burnt; there was then partial stripping of the surface soil, although soil was retained in the intended centre of the cairn; pits were excavated into the natural subsoil and the excavated soil from the pits was distributed over the area of the intended cairn; the pits became filled with a burnt soil; and finally, rocks collected from the ground surface were piled into a cairn. In addition to the excavation programme, a series of soil samples was collected from beneath one of the cairns (*BS 190*) for palaeobotanical analysis (*see above*).

In about 1957, an excavation was also undertaken in the BS IV farmstead by G de G Sieveking. Although the results of this work remain unpublished, the excavation recovered a Romano-British brooch (C Richardson *pers comm*). Most of the BS IV settlement was scheduled as an Ancient Monument (SM32861) on the basis of the 1900 Second Edition 6″ to 1 mile OS map.

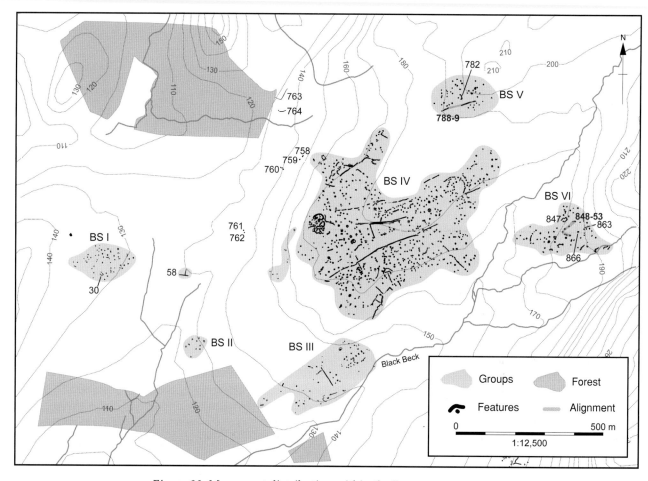

Figure 88: Monument distribution within the Barnscar survey area

The survey area

The survey was undertaken between April and May 1988, over 1.8 km² of unenclosed and enclosed moorland (Fig 84). In total, 875 monuments were found within six site groups (BS I-VI; Fig 88), the primary cairnfield (BS IV) being very extensive, probably representing the largest in Northern England. Associated with it was a platform settlement, a settlement containing roundhouses, a complex enclosed settlement, and field systems, which were linked to each of these settlements. Around the main cairnfield were several smaller cairnfield groups. In addition to these, there were also limited numbers of scattered ungrouped cairns and banks (*BS 58* and *BS 758-64*), which are not individually described within this volume.

Barnscar I: monuments *BS 1-57*

This relatively compact cairnfield was on uniform, well-drained, gently sloping land (Fig 88). Its eastern edge was defined by a sharp break of slope, which had an extensive mire at its foot. Apart from this break of slope, the limits of the site group were not defined by the present-day topography. Both this and the BS II cairnfield were contained within a large field, which is marked on the 1867 First Edition 6" to 1 mile OS map, and was probably a product of the

enclosure movement. However, the land contained was covered by dense, tussocky moorland grass and it had not been improved in the recent past.

The cairns were moderately prominent, with regular, rounded profiles, although they were generally ill defined, as a result of the dense tussocky vegetation cover. There were no significant cairn alignments, and although there were a few banks, these were generally very short and did not appear to have related to their neighbouring monuments. The distribution of cairns and short banks was thus essentially random. It comprised a localised area of ground cleared of stone, which had a form that was very distinct from that of the complex BS IV settlement area to the east, and was probably a product of short-lived occupation. The only distinctive feature was monument *BS 30*, which was an incomplete enclosure, defined by low banks, with a slightly sunken interior.

Barnscar II: monuments *BS 59-68*

This monument group contained a small group of cairns located on gently to moderately sloping land, edged to the west by a steep-sided stream gully (Fig 88). The ground was generally well drained, but was covered by dense, tussocky moorland grass and clearly had not been improved within the recent past.

The cairns were generally low lying and were ill defined because of the vegetation cover. There were no significant cairn alignments and, apart from the break of slope to the west, the limits of the cairnfield were not defined by the present-day topography. The distribution of the cairns appeared to be essentially random.

Barnscar III: monuments *BS 69-138*

The cairnfield in this area comprised two relatively discrete groups of cairns, on an area of gently sloping land below and to the south of the Barnscar ridge (Fig 88). The ground was generally well drained, although both cairn groups were limited to the south-east by slight breaks of slope, with mire at the bottom. The two groups were separated by a *c* 35 m gap, were distinct in cairn size and concentration, and may have been a product of different episodes of stone clearance.

The first cairn group (BS IIIA; Fig 89) was found within a field that is plotted on the 1867 OS First Edition 6″ to 1 mile map and was presumably a product of the enclosure movement. There was a slight difference between the vegetation and ground surface within the field and outside, and there is a possibility that the modern field had been subject to limited improvement. The cairns in this group were well scattered and varied in size and height, those to the east being generally more prominent and larger than those to the west. At the lower (southern) side of the group was a natural

terrace; it contained a curved section of dry-stone wall (*BS 86a*) that was distinct in character from the rest of the monuments in this group. It was not necessarily a related feature and may have been a later bield. Towards the eastern side of the group were also two banks (*BS 91* and *BS 92*) at right-angles to each other; both were fairly well defined and regular in width/profile. Bank *BS 92* was also orientated towards the end of a lynchet-profiled bank (*BS 86b*), lying along the edge of the natural terrace. The area to the west of bank *BS 92* was almost devoid of cairns, yet there was a small, compact group (*BS 93-7* and *BS 99*) immediately to the east of it. In addition, there was a difference in the terrain on either side of the bank, the ground to the west appearing smoother, with greener vegetation, than that to the east. Bank *BS 92* thus appeared to have served as a boundary between two differing types of land use, and it is a possible that the three linear features (*BS 91*, *BS 92*, and *BS 86b*) defined a field which may have been cultivated or improved. Near the upper end of bank *BS 92* was a small semi-circular bank (*c* 4.8 m in external diameter) around a slightly raised, fairly level, circular platform (*BS 102*). It was a deliberate structure, but its small size makes it unlikely that it originally formed a dwelling.

The second cairn group (BS IIIB) in this area was located at the foot of a craggy scarp slope, marking the south-western edge of a ridge, and there were

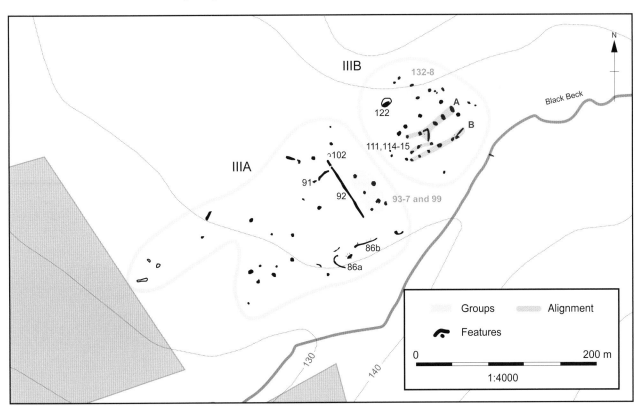

Figure 89: The BS III cairnfield

181

substantial amounts of scree and surface stone associated with its highest cairns (*BS 132-8*). The distribution of the cairns was fairly compact, and they were prominent and well defined. In addition to the cairns, several banks were also recorded beyond the modern field boundary, which varied in size. Many of the cairns and banks were arranged within two parallel alignments (upper alignment: A; lower alignment: B; Fig 89). These appeared to define the sides of a small rectilinear plot, which contained a series of cairns at its western end (*BS 111*, *BS 114*, and *BS 115*), with only occasional surface stones, but no evidence of any top or bottom lynchets. Cairn *BS 122* was somewhat remote from the main part of the group and was significantly larger than the other cairns (11.1 x 10.7 x 0.4 m), although it was not particularly prominent. It was not necessarily a clearance cairn and may not have been a contemporary component of the cairnfield.

Barnscar IV: monuments *BS 139-757*
A very large cairnfield and associated settlement were recorded on a low, flat-topped ridge with gently sloping sides (Pl 111). There were extensive mires to the north and east, and also in association with Black Beck to the south (Fig 88). The limits of the cairnfield coincided either with the edges of these mires, or marked breaks of slope; it would appear, therefore, that the extent of the settlement was largely defined by the local topography.

Within the south-western part of the cairnfield was a small line of crags, with associated scree and brash deposits, but elsewhere within the settlement area there were only occasional surface stones. The ground within the cairnfield was unnaturally smooth and contrasted with the more undulating and rough ground just outside; there is therefore some possibility that the ground was improved in antiquity.

The cairnfield and settlements were exceptionally complex and, for ease of description, these features have been divided into seven separate monument groups (BS IVA-G). Some of the divisions are artificial and do not correspond to original boundaries. As a result, cairn alignments and one of the plots spread over more than one of the monument groups.

Monument group BS IVA
BS IVA (Fig 90) was limited to the south by an irregular and, in places, gentle, scarp slope, below which was a large mire. The cairns petered out towards the south-west, though the ill-defined edge did not correspond to any present-day topographical features. To the north of this monument group was a narrow, *c* 20 m-wide, gap separating it from monument group BS IVC, which was edged by the cairn alignment *BS 349-51*. The cairns at the eastern end of BS IVA were generally smaller and less prominent than their counterparts within BS IVC, and it is possible that the group division reflected an original boundary line.

A long bank, *BS 371*, divided this monument group from BS IVD and BS IVE, to the north (Pl 112). Although the bank was fairly continuous, it displayed

Plate 111: The BS IV settlement, field system, and cairnfield, looking south-east

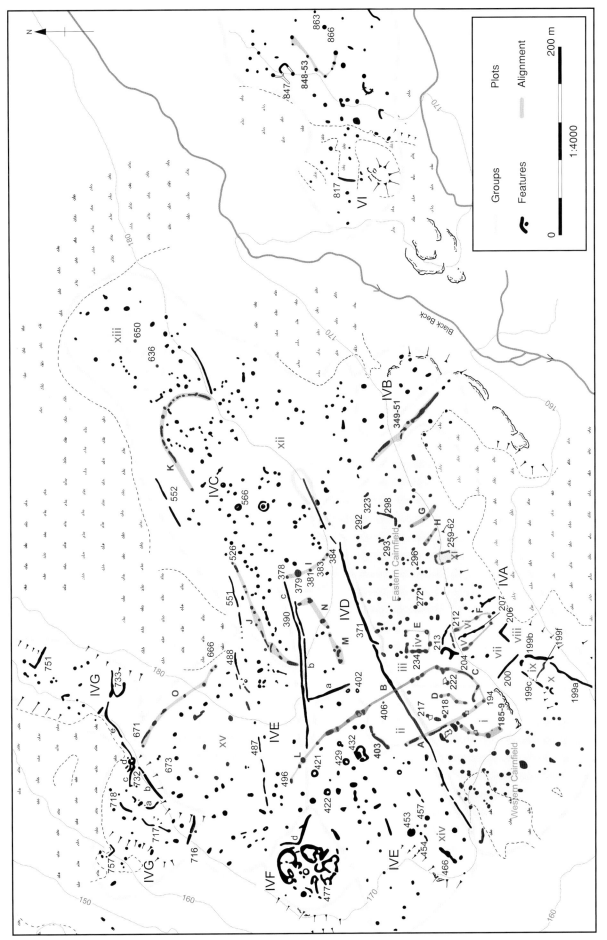

Figure 90: The BS IV unenclosed settlements, complex enclosed settlement, cairnfield, and field systems

183

Plate 112: BS IV, BS IVE (foreground), and BS IVA, separated by bank BS 371 (centre), looking south

substantial variation in form, its eastern end being fairly prominent, with a uniform width, and well defined, with some evidence of kerbing, suggesting that it represented a decayed dry-stone wall. However, in contrast, its western end was ill defined, low-lying, with a negative lynchet profile. Similarly, its relationship with the adjacent cairns varied across its length. For example, at its eastern end, a large concentration of cairns lay to the south, but none to the north, implying that it marked a cairnfield boundary. However, at its western end, there was a concentration of generally uniform cairns on both sides of the bank, and it did not appear to have marked the line of an original boundary in this area. Within BS IVA, there were also distinct and slightly diverse areas of agricultural activity.

The central settlement area comprised a sub-rectangular platform (*BS 213*), with cultivation plots (*i-viii*) extending radially from it, indicating that it had a central and integral role within the surrounding agricultural system. However, *BS 371* was designated the arbitrary northern edge of this monument group, and thus part of the field system was within BS IVD and BS IVE. The platform was defined by three prominent, broad, banks, and had a fairly level interior, the upslope (north-west) side being level with the external ground, but the downslope (south-east) side was about 0.8-1.0 m above the surrounding ground level. It was a large

and prominent earthwork, which provided a measure of its central importance to the settlement, and was similar to, though slightly more prominent than, a platform (*TB 636*) identified on Town Bank, which also had plots extending from it (*Ch 3, pp 59-60*). The platform possibly served as a base for one or more domestic, timber buildings.

The associated agricultural plots were diverse in form and scale. Some were large, but had no evidence of top and bottom lynchets, whereas others were smaller, with clear indications of internal soil slippage. They all appeared to be defined by differing quantities of clearance stone, deposited around their edges. In some cases, this took the form of well-spaced alignments of cairns, and in others the cairns were more closely separated and had been merged to form banks (*eg BS 234*).

The largest of the plots (*ii*) was defined by a pair of long, parallel cairn and bank alignments (A and B), and the eastern side was orientated towards platform *BS 213*, suggesting a relationship. The top of the plot appeared to be defined by bank *BS 403*, although this may also be a component of an alignment within monument group BS IVD (*p 187*). The bottom of the plot appeared to have been defined by a cairn and bank alignment (C), which seemed to respect platform *BS 213*. The area within the plot was free of cairns to the north. However, in the southern section, there

184

were some cairns (*BS 217, BS 218,* and *BS 222*) and a possible significant cairn alignment (D), which may have represented a sub-division of the larger plot. The bottom bank (*BS 204*) had a slight, positive lynchet-like profile, which implies cultivation within this plot, which was bisected by bank *BS 371*, which was probably a later boundary marker.

To the west of the large plot was an open area without cairns, which was edged to the west by cairns *BS 185-9,* and to the east by cairns *BS 191-4 (plot i).* There were no associated lynchets, and the area had not necessarily been cultivated. To the north of rectilinear platform *BS 213* was another plot, edged by alignments of cairns, which had been merged by subsequent clearance (plot *iv*: Alignment E), and this had a slight negative lynchet along its upper boundary. Only one cairn was found within this plot, which had a fairly smooth internal ground surface, implying that it had been cultivated. Between this plot (*iv*) and the large plot to the west (*see above*) was a sub-triangular open area that was devoid of cairns. There were no lynchets associated with this area, so it had probably not been cultivated.

Immediately downslope from the platform was a pair of narrow, parallel plots (*v* and *vi*), defined on the outside by cairns (Alignment F), and divided by a line of merged cairns (*BS 207*). There was a broad linear earthen ridge (with a width of *c* 7 m) down the centre of the eastern plot, with slight furrows on either side. No equivalent feature was identified in the western plot. The top bank (*BS 212*) had a faint, negative, lynchet profile and it is probable that one or both of the plots had been cultivated. To the south of the platform was a pair of adjacent, rectangular plots defined partly by banks *BS 200* and *BS 206* (*vii* and *viii*). The cross-slope section of bank *BS 206* divided the two cultivated plots and had a combined, positive- and negative-lynchet profile.

The final pair of plots (*BS 199;* plots *ix* and *x*) in this central area were divided by an irregular, low-lying bank (*BS 199f*). The downslope bank (*BS 199a*) was very prominent and had a positive lynchet-like profile. The upslope bank (*BS 199c*) was the reciprocal negative lynchet, and the internal ground surface between was fairly smooth, with only occasional surface stones, indicating that the plots had clearly been extensively cultivated. At the south-western end of bank *BS 199c* was a semi-circular, terraced platform. A further small plot (*xi*) was located within the cairnfield on the eastern side of BS IVA, defined by banks and cairns *BS 259-62.* It was 'U'-shaped, and only 20 x 11 m in size.

To the west of the cultivation plots defined by bank *BS 199* was a cairnfield, which contained generally large and well-defined cairns (*BS 139-77, BS 179-89,* and *BS 195-7*), with regular shapes and regular rounded, prominent profiles (Pl 113). They were on average larger and slightly more prominent than

Plate 113: Large clearance cairns in the BS IVA cairnfield

those cairns within the eastern cairnfield found in this survey area (*see below*). They did not appear to be arranged in lines and had an essentially random distribution, being more loosely scattered towards the south-western edge.

To the east of rectangular platform *BS 213*, and its associated cultivation plots, was another cairnfield, containing fairly prominent and well-defined cairns (*BS 239-327*); these were on average smaller than those found in the western cairnfield (*see above*). They did not seem to be randomly distributed, many being arranged in irregular alignments downslope (*eg* G and H). Several elongated cairns were also similarly orientated downslope (*eg BS 262, BS 272, BS 293, BS 296,* and *BS 323*). However, the alignments, for the most part, did not appear to define agricultural plots or boundary lines, and may simply have been arranged to assist the manoeuvrability of an ard or plough. At the eastern end of this cairnfield, there was evidence for a more systematic form of cultivation, within an erratically defined plot (banks: *BS 292, BS 298,* and *BS 293*). The lower bank (*BS 298*) had a distinct, prominent lynchet profile, indicative of soil slippage; however, there was no evidence for a top lynchet.

Monument group BS IVB

A small group of prominent, large, and well-defined cairns was identified at the south-eastern edge of the BS IV group (Fig 90). The group was edged to the south-west by a cairn alignment (*BS 349-51*), to the south-east by a craggy, scarp slope, and to the north-east by an expanse of bog. Although this monument group and the cairnfield (BS IVC) to the north were separated by a gap of only *c* 20 m, they appeared to be distinct in character. The cairns in BS IVB were larger, more prominent, and more loosely scattered than those of the adjacent group, and they were perhaps a product of different stone-clearance episodes.

Monument Group BS IVC

This big group of generally large and prominent cairns was at the north-eastern extent of the BS IV settlement (Fig 90). It was limited to the south-east, east, and north by a large area of mire. To the south, it was separated from the BS IVB cairns by a narrow gap, and to the west it was divided from BS IVD by a short cairn alignment (I) positioned between the ends of two decayed walls (*BS 390* and *BS 371*). The area to the west of the alignment had only occasional cairns, which clearly contrasted with the relatively high density of prominent cairns to the east. There is therefore a possibility that the alignment marked an original boundary line.

The division between monument groups BS IVC and BS IVE, to the west, was marked by an alignment of banks and cairns (J), which extended from decayed wall *BS 390*. The alignment appeared to define an original boundary, as there were no cairns immediately to the north of it, in contrast to the high cairn density to the south. Although there were cairns (BS IVE) to the west of the alignment, they were significantly smaller, less well defined, and less prominent than those to the south-east. Curving stone bank and cairn Alignment K may, indeed, form the eastern end of a field system linked to Alignment J.

There was a marked gap (*c* 16 m) between the cairns of BS IVC and decayed wall *BS 390c*, which would imply that the wall did not define the boundary of the cairnfield. Stone bank *BS 551*, to the north of the cairnfield, similarly showed little direct relationship to the cairns; it had a convergent orientation with cairn Alignment J but was separated by a significant gap (*c* 10 m), even at its easternmost limit.

Within the cairnfield were two distinctive, large semi-enclosed areas that were devoid of cairns and did not contain any mire or other limiting topography. The largest (*xii*) covered an area of *c* 6500 m². It was surrounded by a high density of cairns and was also edged by cairns. At the north-eastern limit of the cairnfield was another semi-enclosed area (*xiii*), of similar size (*c* 5400 m²), edged by an irregular line of cairns. For the most part, there were no cairns to the east of this boundary, but the area within did contain two cairns (*BS 636* and *BS 650*). The ground within these apparent plots did not appear to be smoother or less undulating than that outside. Furthermore, their shapes were distinctly irregular, they were not edged by banks or merged cairn alignments, and there was no evidence of any associated lynchets. They were also quite distinct in form from the agricultural plots within BS IVA.

The component cairns forming the boundaries were generally very large, very well defined, and had prominent, regular, rounded profiles. However, there was a slight reduction in the overall size and prominence towards the north-eastern end of the cairnfield. Within each area there was a degree of uniformity of the size and form, and there were only two cairns which were significantly larger than their respective neighbours (*BS 379* and *BS 566*). Cairn *BS 379* was very large and prominent (7.9 x 7.7 x 0.7 m), with a large, central, irregular depression that would appear to have been the result of antiquarian disturbance, prior to Dymond's (1893) plan. Cairn *BS 566* was a large, well-defined, sub-circular mound (8 x 7.3 x 0.35 m), with a flat-topped, not particularly prominent, profile; a bield had been constructed on its north-western side. Its form and size were very distinct from that of its neighbours, and it may have served a different function.

Monument group BS IVD

This monument group formed a possible sub-rectangular field. Its southern limit was arbitrarily defined as the lynchet-profiled bank, *BS 371*, which separated this monument group from BS IVA. However, the cairns had a similar form and distribution on both sides of the bank and, given this, the bank was probably a later feature. In addition, there was a long cairn alignment (L), which extended north-west through both monument groups from the rectilinear platform, *BS 213*, in BS IVA (*p 184*). The field defining BS IVD was separated from BS IVE by a series of cairns (*p 187*), and bank alignments *BS 402-4* and *BS 390a-c*, which formed its northern and western edges. At the eastern end it was divided from BS IVC by cairn alignment (I), which extended between the ends of banks *BS 390* and *BS 371*.

The parallel banks (*BS 390b/c*), defining the northern edge of the field, were on average about 3 m apart, and they were both continuous and well defined, although the longer bank (*BS 390c*) was also the more prominent. There was evidence of kerbing along the *BS 390c* section, which had probably been a dry-stone wall. The banks were orientated towards the complex farmstead, *BS 477* (BS IVF; *p 188*), and seem to have defined part of a track, which served the farmstead.

Bank *BS 390c* did not appear to define the extent of the adjacent cairnfield (BS IVC) and its western end stopped short of the cairn alignment (L) defining the edge of the BS IVE cairnfield. Apart from a possible line of five cairns (Alignment I) between the terminals of walls *BS 390c* and *BS 371*, the *BS 390* boundary appeared to post-date the adjacent cairnfields.

The ground within the field was fairly smooth, with only occasional surface stone, although this was not significantly different from the ground outside its boundaries. There was no evidence of any associated lynchets, although it was on the summit of the ridge, and thus the ground was almost flat; in consequence, there would have been little soil slippage.

A possible small rectilinear field was sub-divided from the northern part of the larger field. It was defined to the north and west by banks *BS 390a/b*, and the other two sides were defined by cairn Alignments M and N.

Monument group BS IVE

A large area of cairnfield was recorded at the western end of the Barnscar ridge (Fig 90). For the most part, the terrain throughout the group was either flat or gently sloping, but the western end of the ridge was cut by a shallow, east/west gully and there were flat-topped spurs on either side (Pl 114). Farmstead (*BS 477; p 188*) had been constructed on top of the

Plate 114: The complex enclosed settlement, BS 477, and the western part of the BS IVE cairnfield, on the northern spur of the Barnscar ridge

northernmost spur, whilst a small plot was found on the flat-topped southern spur. The gully in between the spurs had a slightly rough surface, with relatively large amounts of surface stone, and the cairns within were relatively small.

The topography largely defined the limits of the cairnfield from the western side through to its north-eastern edge, the northern and western edges coinciding with the moderate scarp slope around the edge of the Barnscar ridge. Immediately below the northern scarp slope was a small settlement (BS IVG; *p 191*), which was distinct in form and location from the main Barnscar cairnfield and settlement. The south-eastern edge of the cairnfield was defined by a cairn alignment (O; Fig 90), which partly coincided with the edge of a mire.

Monument group BS IVE was divided from BS IVD by alignments of both cairns (L) and banks (*BS 402-4* and *BS 390a*). There was also a comparable bank (*BS 487*) aligned east-west through the middle of the cairnfield. This was discontinuous, irregular in width and quantity of stone, and included sections which had a lynchet profile. Significantly, the cairns had a similar distribution and form on either side of this bank, and hence it did not appear to have had a direct relationship with the surrounding cairnfield.

The cairns in the southern part of BS IVE were more varied in size and form than in the other monument groups, and there was an intimate mix of small and large cairns, with little conformity of shape. The largest of these would appear to have been cairn *BS 432*. This was a very irregular, very prominent, elongated mound with an erratic internal depression. It was shown as having been opened on Dymond's plan (1893) and it would appear to have been severely disturbed. The size and elongated form of the mound may be an indication that it was originally a large, very prominent, long cairn. Indeed, there were other large cairns in the area (*BS 421*, *BS 422*, and *BS 429*) which had also been opened prior to 1893, but they were not sufficiently distinct from their neighbours to provide unequivocal evidence of a funerary function. The cairns in the northern part of BS IVE were more uniform in size, and were generally large and well defined, with fairly prominent, rounded profiles.

On the flat-topped spur at the south-western edge of the cairnfield was a possible cultivated plot (*xiv*, defined by cairns *BS 454-7* and *BS 461-6*. Along its upper side, the cairns (*BS 454* and *BS 466*) had been merged by subsequent clearance, and exhibited a negative-lynchet profile. The terrain within the plot was fairly smooth and gently sloping, but was not

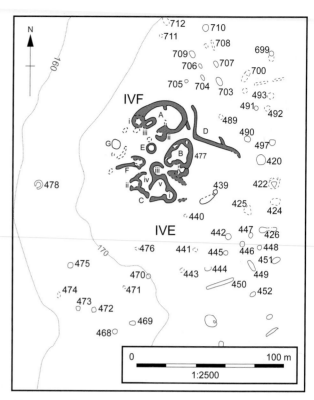

Figure 91: The BS IVF complex enclosed settlement (BS 477)

significantly different from that outside. A much larger semi-enclosed area (*xv; c* 10,000 m²) was found in the northern part of the cairnfield, edged by cairns. There were substantial numbers of cairns outside, but only occasional cairns within this enclosed area, despite the well-drained and uniformly sloping internal terrain. The enclosure had an irregular shape, and because it was not edged by banks, merged cairn alignments, or lynchets, it was very ill defined. Bank *BS 487* passed through the middle of the enclosed area, but there was no indication that they were contemporary features.

Monument group BS IVF

A complex enclosed settlement lay on top of a gentle spur extending from the western side of the Barnscar ridge (*BS 477*; Fig 90). It comprised three enclosure groups (A-C), configured in a radial pattern to form an integral, semi-enclosed farmstead (BS IVF; Fig 91). Each enclosure group comprised one or two large, irregular enclosures, with associated roundhouses. The domestic and agricultural functions of the farmstead were combined within each of these enclosure groups and there was a certain amount of replication between them. There was also considerable similarity between their layout, and they broadly appeared to be self-contained units. This was in clear contrast to the form of enclosed farmstead *AF 203* on Askham Fell (*Ch 7, p 309*), where there was complete integration, with all the roundhouses being grouped together and kept separate from the enclosures, which were also grouped together. The

Plate 115: Enclosure group A in the complex enclosed settlement, BS IVF

differences in design between the two farmsteads possibly reflects differences of social interaction, since the layout of the Askham Fell farmstead suggests a communal domestic arrangement, in contrast to that of farmstead *BS 477*, which appears to have served three fairly independent family units. In addition to the three enclosure groups, there were also a further four, apparently unrelated, structures and banks (D-G).

Enclosure group A
The main enclosure (37 x 22 m) was defined by very broad, regular, and prominent banks containing substantial amounts of stone, divided into two sections by a low-lying, irregular and discontinuous alignment of stones across the centre. The ground within the enclosure was slightly undulating and lay below the external ground level by up to 0.5 m (Pl 115). The main entrance to the enclosure was from the south-west and there were two possible structures, A*i* and A*ii*, on either side of it.

Structure A*i* comprised a prominent ring-bank incorporated into the north-western side of the entrance. It had a moderately defined, circular, internal edge (*c* 4.5 m in internal diameter), but the external edge merged with the enclosure bank and was therefore ill defined. The interior had almost no surface stone, was fairly flat, and was on a similar level to that of the external ground surface, but was raised with respect to the ground level within the enclosure. It was possibly overlain and partly disturbed by rectilinear structure A*iii* (*see below*). The regularity of shape and the prominence of the banks associated with structure A*i* suggested that this was a roundhouse, and whilst there was no evidence of an entrance, this was perhaps obscured by an area of disturbance to the south-east.

Structure A*ii* was an approximately circular bank with an ill-defined and very irregular internal edge. This structure contained large amounts of stone and there were also substantial amounts of stone within its interior, obscuring its base. In addition, a possible entrance could be discerned towards the west. Dymond (1893) described it as a hut and his plan showed it as having been opened.

A third structure, A*iii*, comprised two fairly well-defined parallel banks, with slightly curved ends (10 x 5 m externally). The banks contained large amounts of mainly large and medium stones, and there were some larger stones set into the internal edge, suggesting that they were decayed walls. The interior was relatively flat, but the western end was obscured by some collapse. There was no evidence of an entrance but it may have been obscured by tumble on the western side. It extended into the main enclosure and was built up above the base of the enclosure; it also appeared to have been superimposed onto building A*i* (*see above*). Its elongated form was an incongruous component of the enclosure group and thus it was probably not a contemporary feature.

189

Plate 116: Enclosure group B in BS IVF, looking east

Enclosure group B

This enclosure was large and irregularly shaped, with a very broad external bank (Pl 116). The north-western section was sufficiently wide to accommodate three small hollowed features (the largest had a diameter of *c* 2 m) that had been set into it. The interior of the enclosure was slightly undulating and lay below the external ground level. At the south-west end was a small sub-circular semi-enclosure, which was joined to the main part by a very faint bank. There was no obvious entrance into the enclosure.

On the southern side of the main enclosure was a bank, the width of which varied, that defined an irregularly shaped partial enclosure, open to the west. The feature had been extensively disturbed by the excavation of a large trench (prior to 1893) within the sub-enclosure and, possibly as a result, the interior was irregular and undulating. Dymond (1893) described this sub-enclosure as a hut and his plan indicates that the southern bank had a regular, semi-circular, internal edge. There was no evidence for this curved edge, but it may have become obscured by spoil from the excavations.

Enclosure group C

Enclosure group C comprised two enclosures (C*iv* and C*v*) with three roundhouses (C*i-iii*) incorporated into the edges. Roundhouse C*i* was large, very well defined, and was incorporated into the south-eastern side of enclosure C*v*. It had a large, very broad, prominent bank and a well-defined entrance on the north-western side; its only access was from enclosure C*v*. The interior was approximately level and had a smooth surface. Roundhouse C*ii* was on a raised section of the spur, above the adjacent enclosure, C*iv*. It comprised slightly irregular, moderately prominent banks, with a broad, western entrance. It had been internally terraced, and the

interior was slightly undulating but approximately level. Roundhouse C*iii* was a very large, circular structure, with well-defined, very large, and very prominent banks. It had a very broad, ill-defined, eastern entrance, but no access from enclosures C*iv* and C*v*. It had been substantially terraced internally, and there was a height difference of up to 1 m between the floor and the top of the bank. The surface was slightly undulating and included some large surface stones.

Enclosure C*iv* was an irregularly shaped area between roundhouses C*ii* and C*iii*. Its northern bank was fairly prominent, containing large amounts of stone, and it had a fairly flat, level surface, which appeared to have been internally terraced. Indeed, it was significantly higher than the upper level of C*v*. Access to C*iv* was via C*v*. Enclosure C*v* was the larger of the two, which were divided by a prominent terraced bank. The other external banks of C*v* were generally well defined, broad, and moderately prominent. The interior was gently sloping and slightly undulating, and was at a similar level to the external ground surface. The main entrance was on the south-western side.

Additional structures and banks

In addition to the enclosures, several unrelated features were also recorded in this settlement. These included a bank; a sub-circular structure; an irregular structure; and a round cairn.

The bank (D) was prominent, L-shaped, and contained substantial quantities of stone, had a regular width, and included some larger stones along the edge. It would therefore appear to have been a decayed wall. The eastern section was orientated towards banks *BS 390* (Fig 90), forming a track heading away from *BS 477*, and also the eastern entrance of this farmstead. The northern section was parallel to the external bank of the enclosure, and was separated from this by a distance of *c* 4.5 m. It possibly defined a track around the eastern side of the farmstead and, indeed, was reminiscent of the track around farmstead *AF 203* on Askham Fell (*Ch 7, p 309*).

The sub-circular structure (E) was defined by a very well-defined, flat-bottomed, sub-circular pit (6.8 x 6.5 m), with kerb stones set into the internal face (Pl 117). The interior was approximately level, *c* 0.3 m below the external ground surface, and included bedrock protruding through the turf. There was no visible entrance, and the kerbed edge was unbroken. It was described by Dymond (1893, 180-1) as a roundhouse and was marked on his plan as having been opened. The visible remains were therefore probably the foundations of a structure that had been exposed by excavation.

190

Plate 117: BS 477E, *placed centrally in complex enclosed settlement BS IVF*

The irregular curvilinear structure (F) was a comparatively small feature, located on the summit of the spur. Both its internal and external edges were poorly defined, and the internal edge was also irregular. There were piles of stones in the centre, which had been deposited subsequent to its decay and therefore may be an indication of disturbance. It is possible that an entrance once existed on the eastern side, leading into a corridor (*c* 4 m wide) defined by irregular banks, that fed into the centre of the settlement.

Immediately to the west of the summit, a large, well-defined, and prominent round cairn (G; 6.2 x 5.7 m) was identified. It was not directly related to the farmstead, and was not necessarily a contemporary feature.

Monument group BS IVG

A small, discrete farm unit lay on the north side of the Barnscar ridge (Fig 90), comprising a single roundhouse, incorporated within a simple field system; this was associated with a small, scattered cairn group. The main part of the settlement was on a natural terrace, which had an approximately level, but slightly undulating, surface. The upper, fairly steep, scarp slope divided the settlement from the BS IVE cairnfield, whilst the forward lip was defined by a further scarp slope. To the north-east was an extensive mire, and the extent of the settlement had clearly been constrained by this local topography.

The settlement included four possible plots. The largest of these (*BS 732*: *c* 700 m²) was defined by prominent banks, which containing substantial amounts of stone (Pl 118). The upper boundary contained evidence of a dry-stone structure and had a negative-lynchet profile, the lower bank having an obvious, positive-lynchet profile. The plot appeared to have been extensively cultivated.

Plate 118: Plot BS 732 *of the BS IVG settlement, looking north-east*

Plate 119: Roundhouse BS 732d, *looking east*

To the north-west of plot *BS 732* was an alignment of ill-defined and slightly irregular banks (*BS 716-18*). Banks *BS 717* and *BS 718* appeared to have had positive-lynchet profiles, which would imply soil slippage from the area upslope of the banks.

Below the north-western edge of the terrace was a very small, rectilinear plot (*BS 757*: *c* 100 m²) on moderately sloping ground. It was defined on two sides by an L-shaped bank, to the south by a pair of cairns, and to the north by a break of slope. It was slightly sunken below the external ground level and contained a mire, although this had clearly formed since it was constructed.

Above and to the east of the main terrace was another, less well-defined, terrace. It contained an irregularly shaped plot (*BS 733*), edged by a regular horseshoe-shaped bank, the eastern side of which was defined by a substantial scarp slope. The interior was slightly sunken with respect to the external ground level. This plot was linked to the main settlement by a uniform, prominent bank (*BS 732e*), which was possibly a decayed dry-stone wall, and overlay, and thus post-dated, the plot boundary (*BS 733*). A roundhouse (*BS 732d*) was incorporated into the wall linking the *BS 733* and *BS 732* plots and comprised a very prominent, well-defined, circular bank (Pl 119). The interior was substantially terraced and its only entrance faced towards the north-east, away from the adjacent plot.

On the main terrace, there were only a few scattered, irregular, clearance-type cairns. These were outside the plots, and for the most part unwanted stone seems to have been incorporated within the plot boundaries. There was another small scatter of irregular clearance-type cairns on the two levels of terrace to the north of plot *BS 733*. At the northern end of the terraces, on a moderate slope, was an L-shaped uniform bank (*BS 751*), the bottom section of which had a lynchet-like profile, indicative of soil slippage.

Discussion
The settlements and field systems
Barnscar was a very concentrated, large, and extremely complex cairnfield, associated with three settlements, which were clearly not contemporary. Each settlement had an associated field system and it is evident that the remains were a product of an extended multi-phased development. However, only a limited number of phased relationships could be identified from the survey evidence and it is, therefore, only possible to suggest a crude sequence for the development of the settlements, field systems, and cairnfield (Fig 92).

There were three farmsteads (*BS 213*, *BS 477*, and *BS 732*) associated with the cairnfield, which were all spatially remote from each other. Farmsteads *BS 213* and *BS 732* were both single-structure entities, but otherwise were distinct from each other in form. In contrast, farmstead *BS 477* was much larger and more sophisticated, was very distinct from the other two, and was probably not contemporary with either.

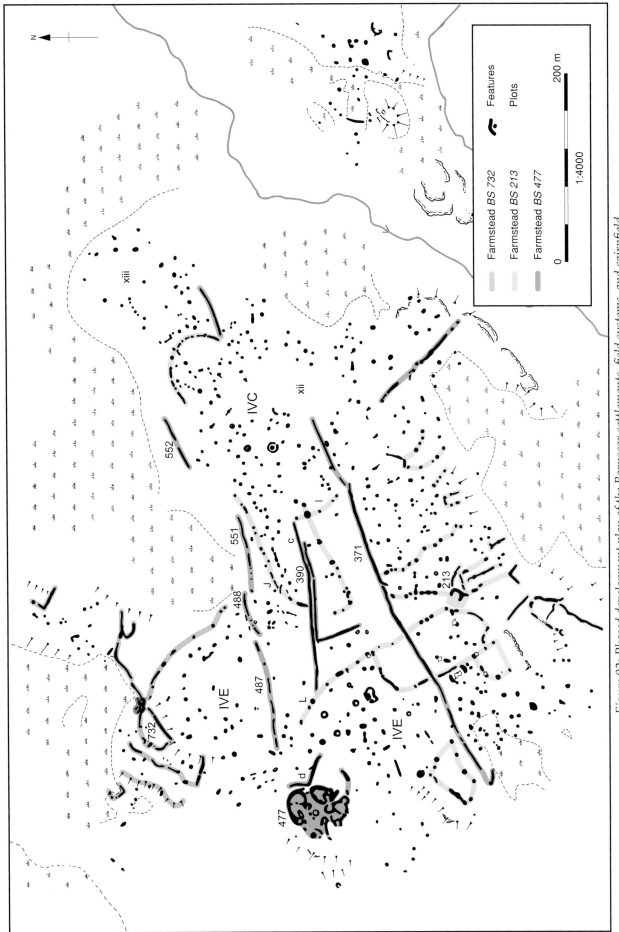

Figure 92: Phased development plan of the Barnscar settlements, field systems, and cairnfield

Farmstead *BS 213* was defined by a sub-rectangular platform and was very basic by comparison with the remains of farmstead *BS 477*. It had a series of cultivated plots radiating out from it, and was clearly an integral and presumably contemporary component of the field system. The elongated cairn alignment that extended north-west from *BS 213* appeared to define an edge of cairnfield BS IVE, since there was a substantial concentration of cairns to the west of the line, but only occasional cairns to the east. It is therefore possible that the platform and the cairnfield were related features.

Farmstead *BS 732* comprised a single roundhouse, also directly related to several cultivated plots. Moreover, a cairn and bank alignment defining the eastern edge of the BS IVE cairnfield was orientated directly towards this structure, suggesting a relationship between the farmstead and the cairnfield.

The most complex of the three farmsteads (*BS 477*) contained up to eight possible roundhouses and was considerably larger than farmsteads *BS 213* and *BS 732*. It also appeared to have been related to a field system, defined by a series of very long, well-defined banks/walls orientated along the ridge (*BS 371*, *BS 390*, and *BS 487-8*). In the centre of the field system was a pair of prominent banks (*BS 390*), which probably defined the edges of a track. This arrangement was aligned with a similar, prominent bank (*BS 477d*; Fig 91), which defined a possible track around the farmstead. The evidence suggests that track *BS 390* served the farmstead and was therefore a contemporary feature. The boundaries of this field system (*BS 371* and *BS 390c*) were prominent and were the most dominant boundaries on the Barnscar ridge, yet, for the most part, they did not appear to have defined the edges of the cairnfields.

The northern bank of the field system (*BS 487*, *BS 488*, and possibly *BS 551* and *BS 552*) was also aligned with the *BS 477* farmstead. It passed through the BS IVE cairnfield, and the semi-enclosed area within this, but there was no indication of any difference in the form or distribution of the cairns on either side of it. However, it did not appear to have bordered the cairns and was also possibly a later feature.

There was a marked gap (*c* 15 m) between wall *BS 390c* and a band of cairns forming part of BS IVC (*p 186*), implying that they were not contemporary. However, the band of cairns was divided by a bank alignment (J), which did not extend up to the wall. The cairn distribution and shape were similar on either side of the bank, suggesting that they pre-dated the bank alignment, and it is possible that this bank was also contemporary with bank *BS 390c*. Significantly, the cairns to the east of the bank were larger and much more prominent than the cairns to the west, implying that those to the east had been added to during a later episode of stone clearance.

Bank *BS 390c* stopped just short of, and apparently respected, a possible cairn alignment defining the eastern edge of the BS IVE cairnfield (L). Given this, it may therefore have post-dated the cairnfield in this area. Decayed wall *BS 371* was similar in form and prominence to bank *BS 390c*, and both of these features were linked by a cairn alignment (I). Unfortunately, the evidence for a relationship between *BS 371* and the adjacent cairnfields was contradictory. For example, at its western end it lay within a scattered group of fairly similar cairns, which had an approximately similar distribution on either side of the bank, whilst in the centre it crossed a pair of long cairn and bank alignments, which defined a possible plot. In both instances, it gave the impression that it was a superimposed feature. In contrast, at the eastern end, the bank appeared to mark the northern edge of a large concentration of cairns and there was an implied relationship. However, it is possible that, in this area, this wall was in fact a later feature, which had been superimposed on the line of an earlier boundary that originally defined the edge of the cairnfield.

Conclusion
Although there was no direct relationship between farmsteads *BS 732* and *BS 213*, both appeared to have been related to the adjacent cairns. By contrast, the apparently later field system orientated along the ridge (Fig 92) had an indirect relationship with farmstead *BS 477* and appeared to overlie, or cross, both these cairnfields and a plot extending from *BS 213*.

Farmsteads *BS 213* and *BS 732*, and their respective field systems, occupy discrete areas, seemingly respecting each other, which may suggest that they were in use at the same time, though that does not necessarily indicate that they had similar foundation dates. The domestic structure with *BS 213* was a house platform, while the other farmstead contained a stone-founded roundhouse. This, on the basis of unreliable typologies, may suggest that *BS 213* was the earlier settlement; however, excavation will be necessary to determine adequately what their chronological relationship is.

There was seemingly some chronological overlap between these two settlement centres, each with comparable cultivated plots, field systems defined by cairn alignments and banks, and also related cairnfields. Later, however, the settlement (*BS 477*) had moved to the top of the ridge and was associated with a large field system orientated along the ridge, which comprised very prominent banks/walls, but which had no direct relationship with the surrounding cairnfields. The unenclosed roundhouse and platform settlements (*BS 213* and *BS 732*) could fit typologically within a Bronze Age context, while the complex enclosed settlement (*BS 477*) is more consistent with a Roman date. Such typologically based chronologies have been compiled from only limited amounts of excavation data, but where there has been more recent excavation of such settlements, incorporating radiocarbon dating (*eg* Johnson 2004), there has been a tendency to extend the date range for these monument types.

Blank areas within the cairnfields
There were also two large, irregularly shaped areas (BS IVC, *xii* and *xiii*) that, whilst lying within the cairnfield, contained no cairns (Fig 92). They were not defined by banks or lynchets and were distinct in form from the plots associated with *BS 213*, which were typically much smaller. The land within these areas did not contain significant quantities of surface stone or mire, and was broadly similar to that of the rest of the cairnfield, suggesting that, to some extent, each area had been improved. It is perhaps significant that the semi-enclosed area (BS IVC*xiii*) was edged for the most part by a single line of cairns, and it is probable that these cairns were a product of stone cleared from within. If the land was exploited, the paucity of associated lynchets would suggest that it was not farmed intensively.

Barnscar V: monuments *BS 765-808*
This monument group included a small cairnfield located on a fairly undulating, moderate slope of a small spur (Fig 88). There was a limited area of mire at the western foot of the spur, but otherwise the extent of the cairnfield was not defined by the present topography. The cairns on the eastern side of the group were fairly well defined and prominent, whereas those to the west were on slightly steeper ground and were smaller, less well defined and generally low lying. There were no significant cairn alignments and the distribution was essentially random. In the centre of the group was a prominent, three-sided bank (*BS 782*), which displayed no evidence of internal terracing (*c* 20 x 1.9-4.0 x 0.35 m), and its function remains uncertain. At the foot of a break of slope, marking the southern edge of the spur, was a fairly regular but low-lying, ill-defined bank (*BS 788* and *BS 789*). To the south of it was a small group of cairns, which were generally smaller than those of the main cairn group.

Barnscar VI: monuments *BS 809-75*
A scattered cairnfield was encountered on an area of slightly raised ground between two streams (Fig 88). Its extent had clearly been constrained by the topography. To the north and south it was defined by mire, to the east by the lower slopes of

a minor, craggy peak, and to the west by a small, steep-sided hillock (Fig 90). To the north of this, a short section of bank (*BS 817*) seems to have acted as a dam, restricting the drainage into Black Beck to the west. The component cairns in the central part of the cairnfield were generally fairly prominent and medium-sized. However, those to the west, in a less well-drained area, were smaller and occasionally ill defined.

Within the cairnfield were two possible plots, which varied in size and form. The smaller plot (*BS 847*: *c* 140 m²) had a rectilinear shape determined by very ill-defined, narrow, and irregular banks; the southernmost bank had a slight lynchet profile. The larger plot (*c* 1600 m²) also had a rectilinear shape, but was defined on three sides by a possibly significant cairn alignment (*BS 848-53*, *BS 866*, and *BS 863*); there was no evidence of any lynchets associated with the plot.

Conclusions
There is no direct dating evidence for the small cairnfields constituting the BS I-III and BS V-VI monument groups, and so any chronological discussion will inevitably centre upon the large settlement represented by BS IV. However, the character of these small cairnfields was similar to that of the earliest phase of the BS IV settlement, and it is possible that they were of a similar date.

The component cairns of the BS IV settlement displayed a marked degree of uniformity of size and form within each locality, and were commonly found around the perimeter of cultivated plots. They appeared, for the most part, to have been a product of stone clearance, as confirmed by Walker's (1965b) excavations of ten of the cairns. The excavated cairns were scattered throughout the cairnfield but, with the exception of two small cairns constructed on boulder clay, they all had a similar stratigraphy. Such a uniformity of construction sequence may be an indication that many of the cairns originated in the same broad phase of stone clearance. Moreover, the palaeobotanical analysis of samples taken from beneath cairn *BS 190* (BS IVA) suggested that its construction was probably associated with deforestation (*p 179*). Such activity has a possible correlation with one of the two episodes of forest clearance recorded in the Devoke Water pollen section (Pennington 1964, 215-9; *Ch 5, p 203*). One of these has been very tentatively dated to the Bronze Age and the other is radiocarbon-dated to the Roman period.

Although the majority of the cairns were a product of stone clearance, there was evidence that some had funerary functions. Dymond (1893, 186) reported that excavations of cairns on Barnscar, undertaken by Lord Muncaster earlier in the nineteenth century, uncovered cinerary urns. A few cairns were significantly larger than their neighbours (such as *BS 379* in BS IVD; *BS 429*, *BS 432*, and *BS 453* in BS IVE; *BS 566* in BS IVC, and possibly *BS 421* in BS IVE; Fig 90), and these could potentially have had a funerary function. Four (*BS 379*, *BS 421*, *BS 429*, and *BS 432*) had been opened prior to Dymond's survey (*ibid*) and may have been the sources of Lord Muncaster's urns. The dating of these cairns is thus dependent upon a pair of unreliably provenanced urns (Walker 1965b, 64-6), which are of middle Bronze Age date. Even assuming the existence of Bronze Age funerary cairns on Barnscar, there are no chronological implications for the wider cairnfield, as they may have been constructed on the ridge prior to its agricultural use. Because of the proximity of Barnscar to Devoke Water, it is likely that any intensive forest clearance would be represented by the two episodes recorded in the palaeoenvironmental record there (*p 203*). Indeed, it is even possible that the early peat inception at Black Beck (*p 178*), dated to the neolithic period, may have been caused by soil erosion resulting from clearance.

From the excavations of funerary cairns, it is evident that there was Bronze Age activity on Barnscar, perhaps coincident with an episode of forest clearance. It would also appear that the Romano-British episode of forest clearance coincided with the later phase of settlement on Barnscar. The character of the early phase of this settlement was very distinct from that of the later phase, and was more consistent with dated examples of Bronze Age settlement (Richardson 1982; Jobey 1981, 35; 1985, 180-4) than of Romano-British examples. It is therefore probable that the earlier phase of settlement was associated with the earliest, possibly Bronze Age, episode of forest clearance. However, the complex enclosed farmstead (BS IVF) is a type normally dated to the Roman period (*Ch 2*, *p 37*), and the finding of a Romano-British brooch within *BS 477* during the excavations by G de G Sieveking (C Richardson *pers comm*) would appear to confirm this date.

5

THE SOUTH-WEST FELLS – EAST

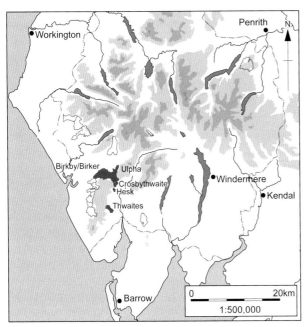

Figure 93: The extent of the survey on the eastern South-West Fells

The eastern side of the narrow range of hills forming the South-West Fells, overlooking the Duddon Valley, and defined by the Esk Valley to the north and the coastal plain to the south, contained the survey areas of Birkby/Birker Fell, Ulpha Fell, Crosbythwaite, Hesk Fell, and Thwaites Fell (Fig 93). Although for ease of description the eastern side of the South-West Fells has been divided from the survey areas on the western side (*Ch 4*), in reality there is a close spatial relationship between the monuments found within the two parts. For instance, the westernmost cairnfield group of Birkby/Birker Fell is close to the large site group of Barnscar (*Ch 4, p 178*) and therefore, to an extent, the division between these survey areas is artificial.

Birkby/Birker Fell (Devoke Water)

Birkby/Birker Fell lies on the high ground to the south of Eskdale and incorporates the upland tarn of Devoke Water. The survey area extended across Birkby and Birker Fells which, for the purposes of the survey, were

divided by the boundary separating the parishes of Muncaster and Eskdale. The survey area was bounded to the north by the enclosed land of Cropple How Plantation and the steep craggy slopes of Brantrake Crags and Garner Bank, to the east by the Ulpha Fell survey area, to the south by Devoke Water, and to the west by the Barnscar survey area (Fig 94). Within these boundaries, an area of gently to moderately sloping undulating ground was interspersed by localised crags, such as Water Crag and Rough Crag. Most of the sites examined by the survey were situated on the more gently undulating moorland between the steep slopes into the valleys, on the north and west, and the higher ground to the south, falling between *c* 170 m and 290 m OD.

Archaeological and palaeoecological history

The monuments on Birkby/Birker Fell include those first noted by Clifton Ward in 1878 (Clifton Ward 1878, 250; Collingwood 1923, 266), who recorded a large number of archaeological sites in this area, during his work for the Geological Survey. It is also possible that he was responsible for supplying information to the OS, which led to the depiction of the groups of small cairns at Devoke Water West and Water Crag on the 1900 Second Edition 6" to 1 mile OS map (Clifton Ward 1878, 241). These same depictions also enabled the sites to be included in the schedule of ancient monuments from the 1950s onwards, and allowed Jim Cherry (1961) to reassess the archaeology of these, and of the adjacent fells.

Cherry's (*ibid*) work was particularly important in expanding the number of known sites. His rapid survey of 16 separate sites extending over the South-West Fells highlighted, for the first time, the great numbers of monuments existing within this area, which were awaiting detailed recording. It also highlighted those areas which might benefit from additional survey. In addition, Cherry, working in conjunction with Bill Fletcher, undertook rescue excavation of a cairn just south of the Devoke Water/Birkerthwaite crossroads (SD 1709 9709), which was prompted by the straightening of the road (Cherry and Fletcher 1964). The cairn measured 3.6 x 4.5 m, and

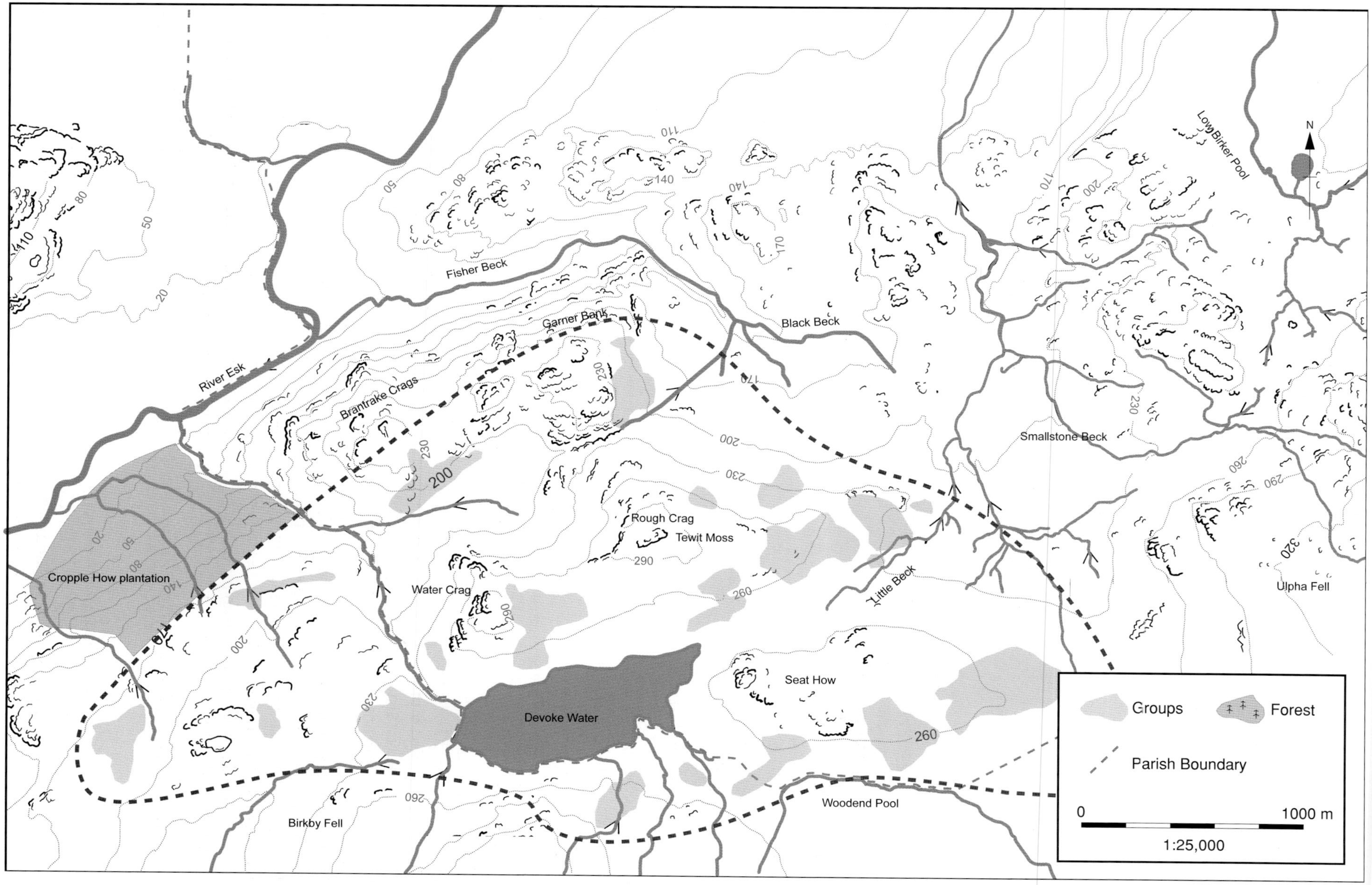

Figure 94: The Birkby/Birker Fell survey area

Low Birker Pool

Ulpha Fell

Smallstone Beck

Little Beck

Seat How

Woodend Pool

Black Beck

Rough Crag

Tewit Moss

Devoke Water

Garner Bank

Water Crag

Fisher Beck

Brantrake Crags

Birkby Fell

River Esk

Cropple How plantation

Forest

Groups

Parish Boundary

1:25,000

1000 m

N

was probably a product of clearance, as no kerbing or internal structures were apparent. During this excavation, a single flint flake was also recovered, but was not sufficiently diagnostic to provide a date for the construction of this cairn.

Further fieldwork by Cherry in 1963 led to excavation at Brantrake Moss (BB VI; SD 151 950) in 1964 (Fell 1970). During this excavation, a field wall (possibly *BB 488*; *p 214*) was examined and this was found to rest on a buried, organic, surface. Subsequent pollen analysis revealed that the wall had been built when deciduous woodland had been cleared for pasture, and possibly cultivation (Pearsall and Pennington 1973). Furthermore, the palynological information was correlated with a pollen diagram for Devoke Water (*op cit*, 234-5) and this suggested that the wall dated to the Roman period.

Devoke Water Cairn Excavation
In addition to the excavation work undertaken in the 1960s, the excavation of a cairn within the BB IX monument group (SD 1671 9770; *p 216*) was carried out in 1985 by the departments of Classics and Archaeology and Geography at Lancaster University. This excavation was undertaken as part of a palaeoenvironmental study, which aimed to reconstruct the environmental context pertinent to the cairnfields found in this area.

The cairn was located at the northern end of the BB IX (Pike How) cairnfield, on an area of very gently sloping ground, and was slightly removed from the main concentration of cairns on the steeper ground to the south. The excavated cairn, although not typical of the monuments found in this group, was selected because, being on flatter ground, there had been a build-up of peat in its vicinity.

Excavation revealed that the current land surface, consisting of a thin band of turf and peat, between 0.02 m and 0.04 m in depth, covered the cairn and extended beyond its limits. The main body of the cairn consisted of a mass of igneous stones, covering an area of 4.5 x 4 m, with a maximum depth of 0.4 m (Fig 95). The body of the cairn overlay a patchy and intermittent buried soil horizon, with a high humic content, which reached a maximum depth of 0.05 m, and from which samples were taken for pollen analysis and radiocarbon dating. The buried soil also sealed the natural boulder clay and extended beyond the limits of the cairn.

The main body of the cairn had neither kerbing, nor internal structure, and seemed to have been a product of stone clearance. Within this, the largest stones, up to 0.6 m across, were concentrated in the south-west quadrant and were, in part, overlain by smaller stones, up to 0.25 m across, which extended to the north-east. This spatial patterning may relate to the primary and secondary clearance of stones from the surrounding fields, with the initial clearance episode being represented by the deposition of the larger stones forming a cairn. This was then followed by the addition of smaller stones to the established cairn, as and when they were encountered during the use of the surrounding land. Moreover, stones thrown onto a cairn in this manner would invariably roll back in roughly the direction from which they had come, resulting in the extension of the monument in that direction. Given this, it can be assumed that the field, or plot of land, associated with this particular cairn was situated to its north-east. Without secure dating evidence, however, it is not possible to determine the dates of the primary and secondary clearance, which may feasibly have occurred days, years, or even hundreds of years, apart.

A single piece of worked flint was recovered from the topsoil immediately to the south-east of the cairn. The piece is the proximal end of a broken blade with a 'gull-wing' profile (Inizan *et al* 1992), which can be indicative, though not necessarily diagnostic, of the neolithic period. The recovery of this piece indicates that prehistoric activity was taking place in the area, but it is not clear whether this activity included the initial clearance, which led to the establishment of the primary cairn. Radiocarbon dates were, however, obtained from material taken from the interface of the buried soil horizon, and the natural boulder clay, found below the cairn (*p 200*), and these date the buried soil horizon to the early medieval period. The positioning of the section through the cairn, however, meant that the sampled buried soil, from which the dates were obtained, only lay below that part formed from the smaller stones. Therefore, the dates only give a *terminus post quem* for the secondary episode of clearance, which may have occurred some considerable time after the initial construction of the cairn.

Pollen diagrams (Fig 96) were created from a sample extracted from the soil sealed by the cairn, and from a sample removed from a sondage, which was dug adjacent to the excavation. The soil sample from below the cairn was extracted from a grey layer, located beneath the mor humus, immediately below that part of the cairn constructed from smaller stones, and the pollen spectra from this suggest a vegetational cover of secondary woodland and grassland. The non-arboreal pollen (herbs) was dominated by grasses and ribwort plantain (*Plantago lanceolata*). Pollen analysis of the peaty mor humus above the till subsoil, within the sondage adjacent to the cairn, demonstrated that the vegetation became more open after the creation of the cairn, with *Calluna* (heather) dominating the plant community. The composition of the pollen spectra from both samples was characteristic of activity dating to the Roman period.

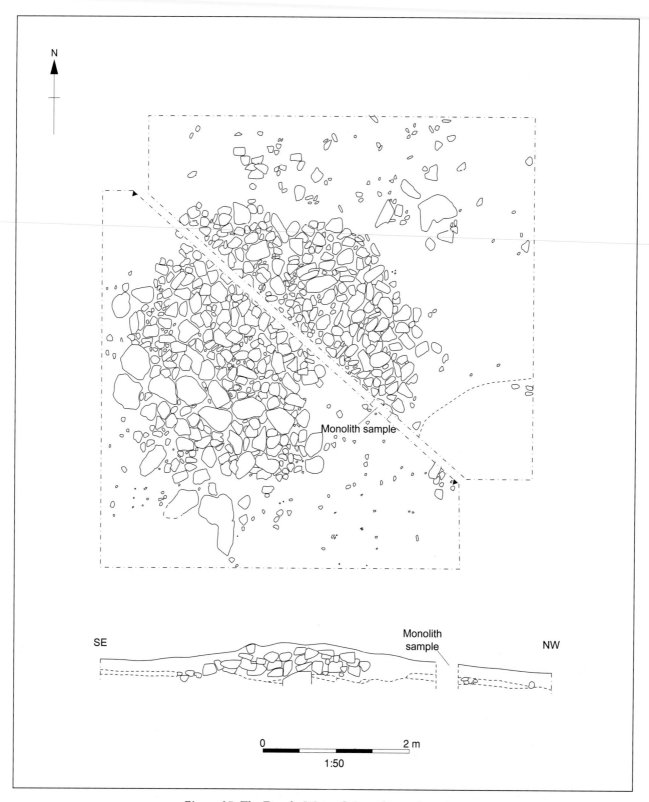

Figure 95: The Devoke Water Cairn: plan and section

A sample from immediately beneath the cairn provided radiocarbon dates from its two humin and humic fractions, which gave respective dates of cal AD 662-979 (1230±70 BP; CAR-911) and cal AD 977-1229 (970±60 BP; CAR-911). In addition, the fine and humic fractions from the mor humus above the till subsoil in the sondage were also dated to cal AD 1019-1279 (890±60 BP; CAR-912) and cal AD 1260-1408 (670±60 BP; CAR-912) respectively. These dates suggest that clearance activity continued into the high medieval period (G Wimble *pers comm*). However, the possibility that the dates were contaminated cannot be discounted, but it is considered that this is unlikely, as both the

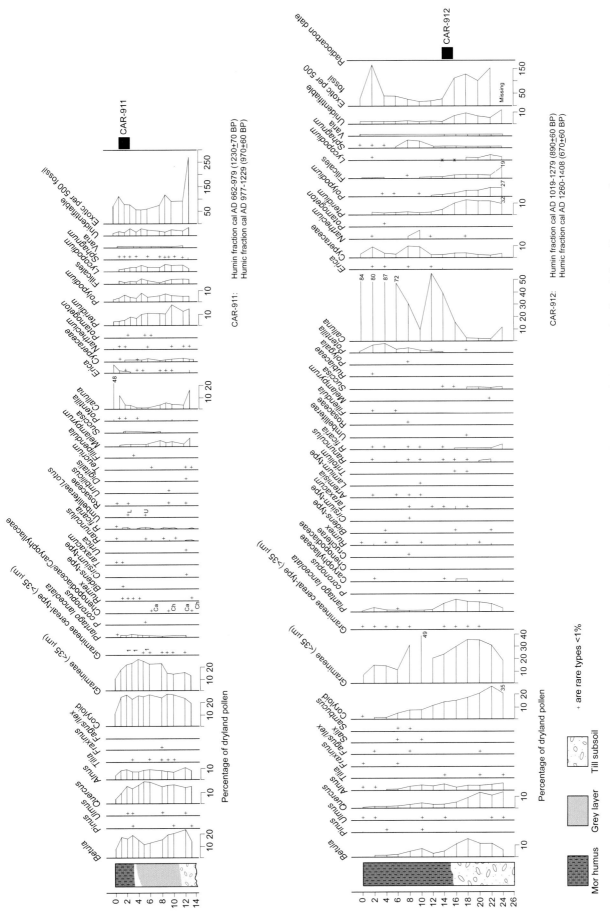

Figure 96: The Devoke Water Cairn: pollen diagrams, from beneath the cairn (top) and the adjacent sondage

201

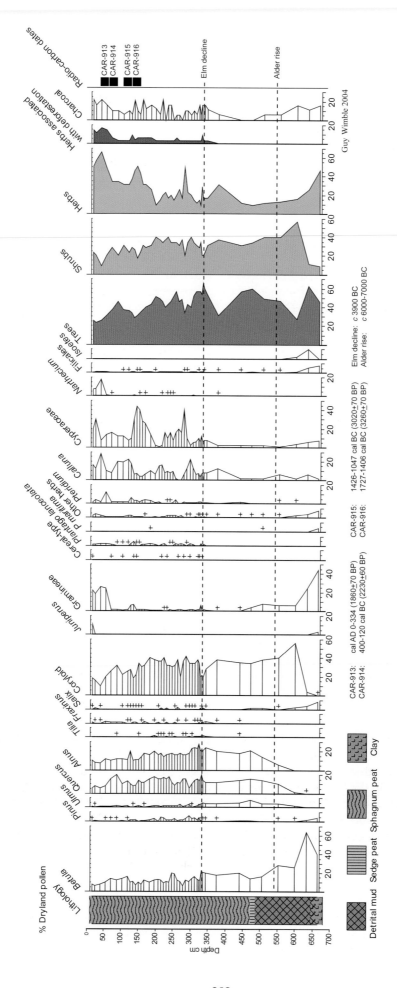

Figure 97: Tewit Moss: pollen diagram

Guy Wimble 2004

Elm decline: c 3900 BC
Alder rise: c 6000–7000 BC

CAR-915: 1426–1047 cal BC (3020±70 BP)
CAR-916: 1727–1406 cal BC (3260±70 BP)

CAR-913: cal AD 0–334 (1860±70 BP)
CAR-914: 400–120 cal BC (2230±60 BP)

Clay

Sphagnum peat

Sedge peat

Detrital mud

humic and the fine fractions showed consistent results in each of the dates.

Vegetational history of Devoke Water and Tewit Moss
Devoke Water, lying at 250 m OD, is an upland tarn 23-4 ha in area and 2 km away from Barnscar (*Ch 4, p 178*). It lies in an area that had been the focus of palynological investigation, and it is possible that the preserved pollen from this area reflects the vegetational history of Birkby and Birker Fells, and also Barnscar, particularly as Devoke Water lies downwind of the latter.

Three complete pollen diagrams directly relate to these areas. Two are from the Devoke Water deposits, one from a marginal core, and the other from deep water, all of which have been published and subsequently discussed by Pennington (1964; 1965b; 1970; 1973; 1991). Material in these lake sediments is likely to have included both atmospheric and water-borne pollen, and thus the preserved pollen would include that derived through drainage into Devoke Water, from the uplands, and also regional atmospheric pollen, which may well have been derived from Barnscar. The third pollen diagram is based on samples extracted from Tewit Moss (Fig 97), approximately 500 m north-east of Devoke Water (G Wimble *pers comm*). At this location, the pollen rain would have been derived from atmospheric deposition and thus it would include both local and regional pollen. This would include pollen from heather (*Calluna*) and sedge (Cyperaceae), which are likely to have been growing on the mire, whilst the pollen from oak (*Quercus*) and elm (*Ulmus*) would have been derived from trees growing on drier land.

Although the top 0.18 m of the Tewit Moss diagram was not analysed, and thus the most recent changes were not recorded, the three pollen diagrams do suggest that there had been continuous sediment deposition since the early Holocene, and thus they contained a complete record of vegetational change. However, prior to the early Holocene, the accumulation rate of sediments differed sharply at the three sites, and thus they are difficult to compare. Those from the deep-water core at Devoke Water were thin, in total less than 0.50 m, seemingly because of the very unproductive nature of the lake. The vegetation cover in the Devoke catchment area evidently prevented soil inwash into the lake, thereby reducing sedimentation (Pennington 1964). The diagrams from the marginal core and Tewit Moss, however, demonstrated a far more rapid rate of sediment accumulation.

The mesolithic period
The three pollen diagrams suggest that in the early mesolithic period (*c* 10,000 cal BC to *c* 6000-5500 cal BC) Devoke Water was initially surrounded by birch and hazel scrub/forest, which then developed into a mixed community, containing increasing numbers of pine, oak, and elm. Sometime between *c* 6000 cal BC and *c* 5500 cal BC, alder migrated into the area, and colonised the wetter parts of the landscape, whilst a mixed deciduous woodland continued to thrive on the drier ground. This regime continued until the late mesolithic period (*c* 6000-5500 cal BC to *c* 4000 cal BC), when the Tewit Moss pollen diagram suggests some changes in the vegetation prior to a decline in elm. In addition, during this period, grass and heather pollen increased and ash (*Alnus*) and lime (*Tilia*) pollen were recorded for the first time (G Wimble *pers comm*). Significantly, ash is a tree found in relatively open woodland and therefore its presence, together with the increasing amounts of heather and grass, suggests a more open woodland canopy than previously recorded.

The neolithic and Bronze Age
The Elm Decline, regionally dated to *c* 4000-3800 cal BC (Walker 2001; Tipping 1994), is recorded in all three diagrams, which allows their correlation. Following the Elm Decline, the accumulation rate of the sediments in the deep-water core from Devoke Water accelerated rapidly; organic muds replaced the earlier minerogenic sediments, reflecting greater productivity. These muds are interrupted by bands of minerogenic material, which Pennington (1964) associated with forest clearance in the water catchment area of the lake; similar minerogenic bands have been recorded at Seathwaite Tarn and Blind Tarn (*ibid*). The earlier minerogenic bands from Devoke Water, together with reductions in oak pollen, probably reflect the permanent change in the uplands from oak woods to acid heathland (Pennington 1964; 1965b; 1970; 1991). Pollen diagrams from Burnmoor Tarn (centred on NY 185 025) and Seathwaite Tarn (centred on SD 253 985) both show this change, and at Seathwaite it has been dated to 1608-920 cal BC (3040±14 BP; NPL 124; Pennington 1970; Callow and Hassall 1969).

The finer resolution of the pollen analysis at Tewit Moss demonstrated a series of small-scale, temporary clearances and burning episodes throughout the neolithic period and Bronze Age, culminating in a major clearance episode, which reached its maximum at 1729-1411 cal BC (3260±70 BP; CAR-916; G Wimble *pers comm*). The values of tree and shrub pollen in these episodes decreased, but those of herbs associated with clearance increased, and these changes in the pollen were also associated with increased values of charcoal. Between these episodes, the values of tree and shrub pollen recovered, suggesting some regeneration of woodland. Contemporary with these clearance episodes, in the Tewit Moss pollen diagram, were increases in heather (*Calluna*) and sedge (Cyperaceae) pollen, suggesting that acidic vegetation became established in the neolithic period, which then became more widespread in the Bronze Age. There are also sporadic records of cereal-type pollen in the Tewit Moss pollen diagram, from the possible Elm Decline to the surface of the moss, but these do not appear to be closely correlated with marked clearance episodes. Furthermore, cereal pollen is difficult to distinguish from some wild grasses, such as *Glyceria* (sweet grasses), which are aquatic or wet ground plants (Andersen 1979).

The Iron Age
Climatic deterioration in the early Iron Age probably brought about the permanent conversion of the higher uplands to the bleak moorlands that characterise the area today (C Wells *pers comm*), with the natural acidification of the upland soils and the growth of heather (*Calluna*) moorland and *Sphagnum* bog (Pennington 1991). However, there was also a partial regeneration of woodland on the drier soils around Devoke Water and Burnmoor Tarn (Pearsall and Pennington 1973, 232). In addition, at Tewit Moss, there was clear evidence that forest regeneration occurred after 1426-1054 cal BC (3020±70 BP; CAR-915), following the major clearance episode of the middle Bronze Age, with rising values of tree and shrub pollen, and falling herb pollen. This, perhaps, indicates that trees were colonising areas of grassland and that there was also an increase of heather moorland on the wetter, more acidic, soils around Tewit Moss.

The Roman period
Higher up the stratigraphic sequence, at Devoke Water, a minerogenic band was sealed by a layer of organic debris, in which there were high concentrations of *Calluna* pollen. Pennington (1964; 1965b; 1970) considered this to be the inwash of organic soils from the surrounding heathland vegetation. The state of preservation of *Calluna* pollen in the debris suggests that it had been redeposited, and because the values of tree pollen were low, it is probable that the organic debris was from deposits which had formed after the elm decline. Moreover, these deposits perhaps related to the development of *Calluna* moorland after the neolithic/Bronze Age clearance of the uplands. Radiocarbon dates of cal AD 148-679 (1585±130 BP; NPL-119) and cal AD 129-666 (1620±130 BP; NPL-120) suggests that this potential clearance episode dates to the Roman period, or immediately after (Callow and Hassall 1969; Pennington 1970). Pennington (1991) also thought that the inversion of radiocarbon dates from the organic debris supported her earlier hypothesis that it had been washed into the lake. This band of organic debris was associated with evidence of cereal pollen in the uplands (Pennington 1970), suggesting cultivation and land use in the environs of Devoke Water in the Roman period, continuing

into the early medieval period. Further support for Romano-British activity also comes from Tewit Moss, where clearance activity expanded sharply after cal AD 0-334 (1860±70 BP; CAR-913). The pollen diagrams indicate that this episode of clearance was as intensive as that during the Bronze Age, but was much longer lived.

Pollen analysis of a layer of peat buried beneath a field bank at Brantrake Moss has further enhanced the evidence for Romano-British activity around Devoke Water (Fell 1970). Two pollen spectra from this layer matched those in two samples from Devoke Moss dated to *c* AD 200 and *c* AD 580 (Pearsall and Pennington 1973, 234-5), thereby dating the wall there to the Roman period or immediately after.

Medieval period
Both at Devoke Water and Tewit Moss, following the Roman period, there was probably a slight and brief regeneration of the woodland, which seemingly dates to the seventh or eighth century AD. However, from the early medieval period onwards, through to the present, the pollen diagrams suggest that the landscape remained cleared, with only some secondary woodland. This reflects the continued grazing of the uplands since this period, but not necessarily intensive farming in the vicinity of Devoke Water. However, the episode of cultivation, indicated by cereal pollen, extended into the early medieval period and would suggest that, at least for part of the second half of the first millennium AD, some local arable farming was practised in this area.

The survey area
The survey was undertaken in 1982 and 1983, and between April and June 1984, covering, in total, *c* 4.5 km² of unenclosed moorland (Fig 98). During the survey, 1038 monuments were recorded within 18 site groups (BB I-XVIII; Fig 99), the monuments being mainly small cairns, generally located in distinct groups, some of which were associated with stone banks, or in some cases enclosures and roundhouses. For the most part, the cairn groups occupied localised areas of gentle or moderately sloping, well-drained ground across a broad open area of moorland.

Birkby/Birker Fell I: monuments *BB 1-78*
A group of small cairns was recorded on the northern slopes of Birkby/Birker Fell to the east of Raven Crag, between the 170 m and 200 m contours, and overlooking Eskdale and Muncaster Fell to the north (Fig 99). The cairnfield was within an area of moderately sloping, generally well-drained, land, with a considerable amount of rock outcrops, which hindered the interpretation of some of the monuments. The cairns fell into two clearly defined sub-groups,

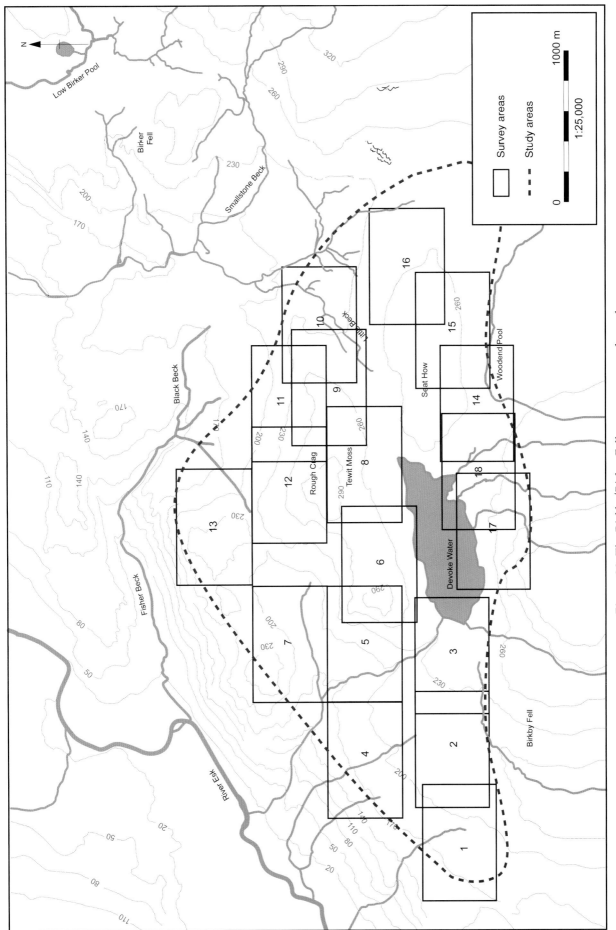

Figure 98: The Birkby/Birker Fell survey area as planned

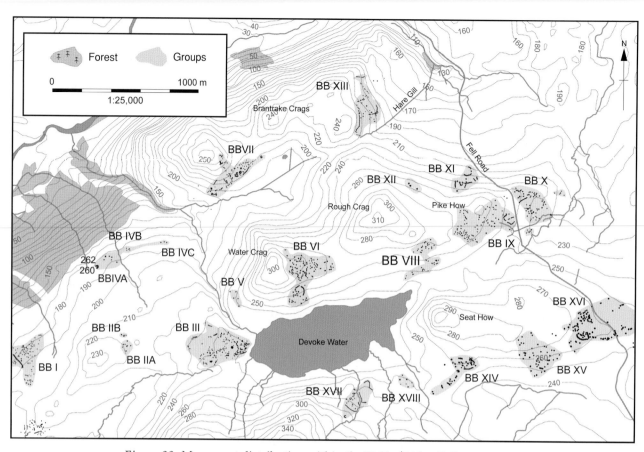

Figure 99: Monument distribution within the Birkby/Birker Fell survey area

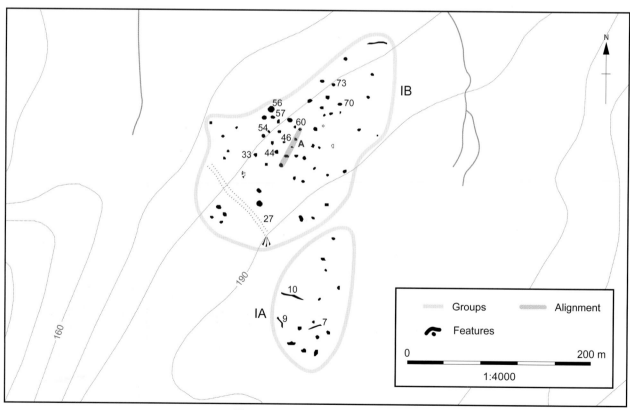

Figure 100: The BB I cairnfield

the division between them roughly corresponding to the 190 m contour (Fig 100).

The first cairn group (BB IA) was the highest and more southerly of the groups, and comprised a loose scatter of small cairns, for the most part found on level ground, where peat growth may have obscured other features. Associated with these were three stone banks (*BB 7, BB 9,* and *BB 10*), of similar appearance and weathering to the cairns. However, there was no interrelationship between these stone banks, or between them and the cairns, and there were no significant cairn alignments. The distribution, even given the presence of stone banks, appeared to reflect essentially random clearance.

The second cairn group (BB IB) was located on the steeper northern slope of this area, below the 190 m contour, and comprised a compact group of generally small and ill-defined cairns, which were for the most part made up of medium and large stones. At least nine of the cairns (*BB 33, BB 44, BB 46, BB 54, BB 56, BB 57, BB 60, BB 70,* and *BB 73*) had evidence of some form of kerbing, which was mostly visible on the downslope sides. The cairns had an essentially random distribution and, while there were some possible cairn alignments in the midst of the group (*eg* Alignment A), other cairns were situated on all sides, and it is not clear if the alignments were significant. This would appear to have been a typical primary-type cairnfield, with cleared stone deposited within small, closely grouped cairns.

Faint traces of narrow ridge and furrow, in some cases cutting cairns, together with the accumulation of hillwash, showed that the cairns lay partly within a later field system or intake. It was also evident that many of the cairns were partly sealed on the upslope side by hillwash. The alignment of the ridge and furrow matched that of the adjacent intake field boundary, suggesting some historical relationship.

Possibly associated with this was a section of hollow-way (*BB 27*), which was orientated downslope and irregularly marked by large stones.

Birkby/Birker Fell II (Black Beck North): monuments *BB 79-91*

A discrete cairnfield of small cairns was situated on a sheltered col between two outcrops of rock, between 210 m and 220 m OD, overlooking Eskdale and Muncaster Fell to the north (Fig 99). The cairns were moderately well defined and between 2.9 m and 5.9 m in diameter. They formed two groups, that to the south comprising eight cairns (BB IIA), which had a loose and essentially random distribution. The northern group (BB IIB) was spatially separated from that to the south and had a much more compact distribution of five cairns. There was no evidence of any significant cairn alignments and the distribution was therefore essentially random; this was a small primary-type cairnfield.

Birkby/Birker Fell III (Devoke Water West): monuments *BB 92-259*

On a prominent, low rise to the west of Devoke Water, slightly above the 240 m contour (Fig 99), was a complex cairnfield comprising substantial numbers of small cairns (138), four large potential funerary cairns, several sections of stone bank, and three putative structures. The site occupied a key position, being an area of level, but well-drained, ground immediately adjacent to Devoke Water, a major upland tarn (Pl 120). It was also on the principal east/west communication line that extended through Barnscar, past Devoke Water, and east via Ulpha Fell to the Duddon Valley.

Plate 120: The BB III cairnfield (foreground), immediately to the west of Devoke Water

The cairns varied enormously in size, condition, and prominence, the smallest being 1.8 m in diameter, and, excepting the four large putative funerary cairns, the largest was up to 7.5 m across. Their distribution for the most part displayed some linearity, and in between the alignments or linear bands of cairns, there were large open areas that were devoid of any monuments.

The most notable of these open areas was defined to the east by a cairn alignment (A; Fig 101), to the north by a short cairn alignment (B), and to the south by a further alignment (C). Only in the south-western corner was this open area not properly defined by cairn alignments. The open area had a sub-circular shape, between 75 m and 80 m across, and although upward of 28 cairns defined its extent, there were only three cairns within it. This was, therefore, potentially an agricultural plot, around which clearance stone had been deposited in piles. Perhaps the most significant aspect was that one of the three cairns within the plot was an extremely large round cairn (BB 185), which had been placed on the highest point of the low rise at the centre of the plot. The cairn was 14.6 m in diameter, 0.9 m in height, had a clearly defined kerb, and almost certainly had a funerary purpose (Pl 121). The presence of a funerary cairn/ritual monument within the centre of what would appear to have been an agricultural plot was certainly unusual but not unique. For instance, on Burnmoor,

the largest of the Brat's Hill stone circles (BM 352; Ch 3, p 113) was also within a clear rectangular plot, defined by clearance cairns.

To the west was a second circular area that was devoid of cairns, defined to the north by a stone bank/cairn alignment (D), to the south by a cairn alignment (E), and an amorphous band of cairns to the east, but was open in the north-western sector. This putative plot had no cairns at all within its interior.

In the south-western part of the group was a less clear, putative plot, defined by both cairn alignments and stone banks (F). Significantly, this also had a large round cairn in its interior (BB 100), which measured 13 x 8 m in plan, and there was a further, albeit smaller, cairn (BB 107) near the northern edge of the plot, which was 6.5 m in diameter and 0.6 m in height.

On the eastern side of the cairnfield was a very compact group of small cairns (BB 235-59), which were for the most part randomly distributed. Associated with this was a possible small roundhouse (BB 240), which was 7 m in diameter, and to the west of this a second possible roundhouse (BB 179) was identified, with a diameter of c 8 m and with an entrance on its north-east side; both had levelled areas internally, that were 4.5 m in diameter.

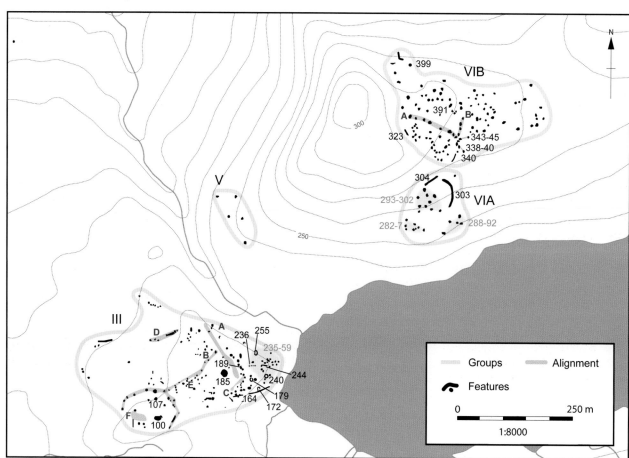

Figure 101: The BB III and BB VI cairnfields

Plate 121: The large round cairn (BB 185) in the centre of a plot within the BB III cairnfield

Two approximately parallel stone banks (*BB 164,* and *BB 244* and *BB 236*) also lay within this group. Built against the inside of bank *BB 164* was a D-shaped structure *(BB 172),* 1.6 m wide, with an entrance on the east side. The northern of the two parallel stone banks consisted of two separate lengths (*BB 189* and *BB 244*), with four stones in alignment (*BB 236*) in the intervening area. Although the two stone banks may have been related, being parallel, there was little consistency of orientation with the cairn alignments, raising the possibility that these were not contemporary components of the cairnfield.

One apparent anomaly within the group was a rectangular building (*BB 255*), just to the north of the cairnfield group. It was 10 m long by 6 m wide, with 0.35 m-high walls, and stood on a rectangular platform, which was terraced into the hillside. It also had an entrance on the western side, away from the terracing. No other structure recorded in this area was constructed in this way, which may be an indication that this was also a later feature, and it may be compared to putative medieval buildings found elsewhere in the region, for instance in Ennerdale (OA North 2003a); it is possible, given its remote location, that this was a shieling or shepherd's hut.

Discussion
The BB III group contained some randomly distributed cairns, but for the most part they were arranged into alignments or bands. There was no evidence of lynchets, an indication of ploughing (*Ch 2*), but, given the level terrain, it would be unusual for lynchets to form. On the other hand, there were open areas, which were probably agricultural plots. The configuration of the cairns would appear to correspond to a proto-field system

(*Ch 8, p 329*), and, given the fact that it was associated with stone-founded buildings, it might be suggested that this was a small settlement which developed from a basic primary cairnfield; this in turn implies a degree of permanence. Unenclosed stone-founded roundhouses are most commonly of later Bronze Age, or even early Iron Age, date, while the classic funerary round cairns would suggest a Bronze Age date (Jobey 1985, 180-4; Haselgrove 2002, 61). In the absence of scientific dating for the site group, it is possible to suggest that this originated as an agricultural settlement in the later Bronze Age.

Superimposed on this was what appears to be a medieval pastoral structure, as indicated by *BB 255*. The pair of parallel walls, *BB 164* and *BB 244,* appeared also to have been a later element, but it is not clear if this reflects a later episode of prehistoric activity, or if it was associated with medieval activity.

Birkby/Birker Fell IV (Cropple How Plantation): monuments *BB 260-74*
This small cairnfield comprised three small cairn groups, extending along the northern slope of Birkby Fell, between the 180 m and 200 m contours, overlooking Eskdale (Fig 99). The most westerly (BB IVA) of the three cairn groups comprised six cairns and a rectangular structure. The cairns were relatively large by comparison with those to the east being between 3.5 m and 8 m in diameter; the largest (*BB 262*) was both relatively prominent, being 0.7 m high, and was well defined. Despite its relatively large size, and the fact that it was within a group of similarly large cairns, it is likely that both it and the rest of the group were clearance-type cairns. The rectangular structure (*BB 260*) was somewhat indeterminate; it was 8 m wide by at least 8 m long, and had three extant sides, being open to the south-

Plate 122: The area of the BB VI cairnfield, looking south-west towards the west end of Devoke Water

west. The walling was similar in weathering and appearance to that of the cairns, but it was slightly removed from the cairn group, and it is not clear if this was contemporary with the cairns.

Beyond the crags to the east lay the second cairn group (BB IVB), which comprised a relatively compact group of five small cairns. These were uniformly smaller than those to the west, being 2.1-4 m in diameter. The third cairn group (BB IVC), was found 200 m to the east and comprised three isolated round cairns. These were between 3.7 m and 5 m in diameter and as such were relatively large.

Birkby/Birker Fell V: monuments *BB 275-79*

A discrete group of five well-spaced small cairns was situated on the western and lower slopes of Water Crag, between the 230 m and 250 m contours (Fig 99); two of the cairns had previously been identified by Jim Cherry (1961, 7). The cairns were relatively large, varying between 3.2 m and 5.3 m in diameter, and they reflected a small isolated episode of clearance, exploiting the gently sloping, well-drained land on the north-west side of Devoke Water (Fig 101).

Birkby/Birker Fell VI (Water Crag): monuments *BB 280-411*

This was a relatively large cairnfield, containing 130 monuments, on the mainly gentle slopes of the

ridge that separates Water Crag from Rough Crag (Fig 99; Pl 122). The cairnfield could be divided into two distinct sub-groups.

The first cairn group (BB VIB; Fig 101), which formed the main body of the cairnfield, was extremely dense and concentrated. It was located on the south-eastern slopes of Water Crag and extended between the 260 m and 290 m contours, though as the gradient increased to the south, there was a noticeable reduction in the density of the cairns. In size, this cairn group extended over 320 m from east to west and 160 m from north to south, and covered much of the gently sloping plateau between Rough Crag and Water Crag (Pl 123). To the west, the limit of the group was marked by the crags below Water Crag and also by a short length of possible stone bank (*BB 323*), *c* 2 m wide, lying at the base of an area of boulders. The ground was generally well drained and smooth, and had the appearance of moderate agricultural land. To the east, most of the cairns were covered by dense heather, whereas those to the west were for the most part devoid of turf and formed visible landscape features. Within this cairn group, the survey recorded 108 cairns, which were generally varied in character, some being extremely large, and prominent, whilst others within the same group were smaller and were less well defined. Many of the larger cairns were up to 0.45 m in height, and as such were relatively prominent. There was at least one cairn which was both prominent, large, and had a regular

Plate 123: Cairns within BB VIB, looking north-east

shape, situated in the northernmost part of the group (*BB 399*); indeed, this was slightly removed from the cairnfield and was possible a funerary cairn.

The cairn distribution within BB VIB appeared to be random, although there were some significant cairn alignments, which appeared to define the edges of an area that was for the most part devoid of cairns. The longest, and southern, of the alignments extended for 110 m and was made up of cairns that were significantly larger than the majority recorded within the cairnfield. As such, even though it was within a large cairnfield, the alignment was distinctive and presumably significant (A). Extending north from the eastern end of this was a second alignment, orientated north-north-east for 47 m, though its line was continued by a short stone bank (B). To the north of these two alignments was a sub-rectangular area (69 x 45 m) that was, except for a single monument (*BB 391*), devoid of cairns. This was very comparable to the putative plots within the BB III cairnfield (*p 207*) and raised the possibility that this had also been used for agriculture. The size of the cairns edging the possible plot may reflect the possibility that they had been enlarged by the addition of clearance stone from the interior of the plot.

At the southern junction of the two cairn alignments was a series of irregular, partly coalescing, stone banks which formed two plus sides of a rectilinear feature (*BB 338-40* and *BB 343-5*). The upper bank had the characteristic break of slope of a negative lynchet, and at the base was a bank (*BB 340*), which had a positive-lynchet profile. Given the apparent evidence for soil slippage within this feature, it is probable that this was a small cultivated plot, measuring some 26 x 16 m in extent.

The second cairn group (BB VIA) in this survey area was smaller in size and was found on a moderate slope to the south of Water Crag, between the 240 m and 270 m contours. It comprised a group of very large, prominent cairns, set within an area of well-drained and possibly improved ground. The cairns all had consistently uniform, rounded profiles and were relatively large by comparison with those found in the other major cairn group located in this area. They typically had diameters of *c* 5 m, were up to 0.5 m high, and their distribution was essentially random. The northernmost cairns were set within a possibly contemporary enclosure, defined by two stone banks (*BB 303* and *BB 304*), which were similar in weathering and appearance to the cairns. An area of ground between the eastern edge of the cairn group and stone bank *BB 303* was potentially farmed ground, being largely devoid of cairns; this was well-drained and had a smooth, grassed surface. In general, the banks seemed to define the cairnfield and thus they would appear to have been parts of the same field system. To the south, yet still within the cairn group, was a second area that was devoid of cairns, lying between the northern cairns (*BB 293-302*) and extending diagonally across the contours, and two small discrete groups of cairns to the east (*BB 288-92*) and to the west (*BB 282-7*).

Discussion
This monument group appeared to define two distinct sub-groups of cairns. The southernmost (BB VIA) contained relatively large cairns, presumably the product of considerable stone clearance, and apparently associated with cultivation within two distinct plots. In contrast, the northern group (BB VIB) was a predominantly random primary cairnfield, although it did contain a small, putative, cultivated plot. There were clear differences between the two groups, both in terms of the character of the component cairns, but also in terms of their distribution and pattern. In general, the two groups would appear to reflect two distinct episodes of clearance, and perhaps also differences in farming practice.

Birkby/Birker Fell VII (Brantrake Moss): monuments *BB 412-98*
A group of small cairns, enclosures, and walls was situated on the lower slopes of Brantrake Crags, between the 190 m and 230 m contours (Fig 99), in a sheltered position overlooking Brantrake Moss, but with views only as far as Water Crag (Pl 124). There were no other groups of small cairns in this valley. Brantrake Moss was possibly open water in the period when the cairns, enclosures, and walls were constructed and used, and there were possible contemporary waterlogged deposits within the sediments of the moss, although later peat digging may have removed much of this material (Pennington 1970, fig 9).

Plate 124: BB VII at Brantrake Moss, looking south towards Water Crag

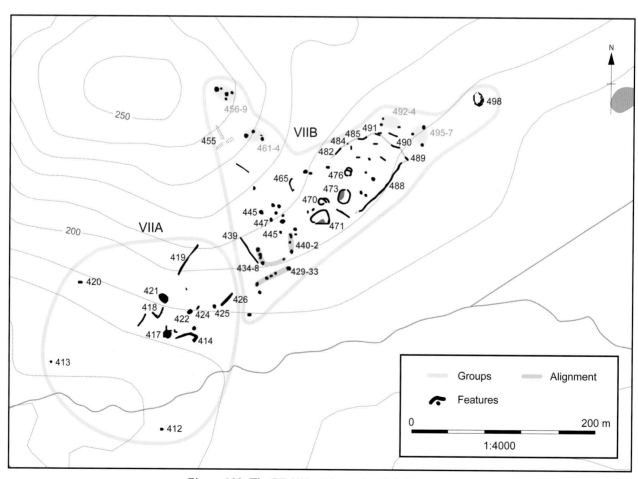

Figure 102: The BB VII settlement and field system

The cairnfields and stone banks

The cairnfield was associated with stock enclosures and roundhouses, which seemed, for the most part, to be contained within a 'field system' defined by short and more elongated sections of stone bank. In terms of the spatial arrangement of the cairns and their character, the cairnfield and stone banks could be divided into two separate monument sub-groups.

With the exception of three more distant cairns (*BB 412*, *BB 413*, and *BB 420*; Fig 102), BB VIIA comprised several cairns and stone banks situated between the 180 m and 210 m contours, on a gently sloping promontory, with steep slopes to the north-east and south-west (Pl 125). The cairns lay within an area defined by a stone bank to the north-east (*BB 439*) and another to the north-west (*BB 419*). Two of the cairns were extremely large (*BB 417* and *BB 421*) and were distinct both in terms of location and size, whereas the remaining features were either sections of stone banks, or were cairns on the lines of stone banks. As such, all would appear to have been components of a field system. The larger of the two large cairns (*BB 417*) was *c* 10 m in diameter, 1 m high, and had an extant stone kerb on the southern side. A bield had been built out of the fabric of the cairn, exposing the upright stones of a rectangular cist, which clearly indicated that this cairn was a funerary monument. The northern large cairn (*BB 421*) was slightly pear-shaped, *c* 9.5 m in diameter, and again

up to 1 m in height; it had an external ditch and there is a probability that this was also a funerary monument.

The principal components of this field system were stone banks *BB 419* and *BB 439*, which defined a predominantly cairn-free area. However, in the southern, lower part of the group was a stone bank (*BB 426*), the line of which was continued by cairns *BB 425*, *BB 424*, and *BB 422*. Collectively, these features would appear to have defined the line of a further north-east/south-west boundary. In addition, there were a further two rectilinear stone banks. One (*BB 418*) was L-shaped and was possibly a former rectangular wall/stone bank. Its walls were 1.3 m wide and they extended from the line of stone bank *BB 419*, which was probably a related component. A second rectilinear stone bank (*BB 414*) was a three-sided structure with a trapezoidal-shaped, which had 1.5 m-wide banks.

The second monument sub-group (BB VIIB) was more extensive than that recorded during an earlier investigation within this area (Fell 1970; *pp 197-9*), with at least 53 cairns recorded. These cairns fell into two main groups, one to the north-east, comprising a loose scatter of very small cairns (with diameters of between 1.5 m and 2.5 m), and one to the south-west comprising a dense concentration of much larger cairns (with diameters of 3.5-4.5 m).

Plate 125: The BB VII settlement and field system, from the opposite site of the valley

Plate 126: Stock enclosure BB 471, *within BB VIIB*

The latter cairns were distributed around an area that was devoid of cairns and may, therefore, have been a small agricultural plot (*BB 434-8, BB 440-2, BB 445,* and *BB 447*). Two much smaller groups (*BB 456-9* and *BB 461-4*) were situated on the slope above the enclosures, between the 220 m and 250 m contours.

Extending around both groups of cairns, and defining monument group BB VIIB, were short, as well as extended, sections of stone bank (*BB 439, BB 465, BB 482, BB 484, BB 485, BB 488, BB 490,* and *BB 491*), which may represent the surviving elements of a continuous field system. A line of cairns (*BB 429-33*) was approximately between banks *BB 488* and *BB 426* (the boundary of BB VIIA), and these cairns may, therefore, have been part of an extended boundary. In some places, the line of the bank (*eg BB 488*) defined the extent of the cairns, but in others the cairns extended beyond the apparent line of the enclosure; hence cairns *BB 495-7* were to the north-east, and outside the enclosure. Given this, there was a possibility that the putative field boundaries were a later element, established around and approximately defining the extent of a cairnfield.

Stone bank/wall *BB 488* was excavated in 1964 (Fell 1970; *p 199*) and the rectangular excavation trench (*BB 489*) was identified during the survey. The excavation revealed that the bank was made up of granite blocks with larger foundation stones set in a black organic soil. Pollen analysis by Pennington suggested that this feature was constructed during the Roman period (*ibid*). The pollen analysis also suggested that the landscape at the time of its construction had been cleared of woodland to allow for mainly pastoral agriculture, but potentially also some cereal cultivation.

Enclosures and roundhouses

Within the central part of the putative field system, within BB VIIB, was a pair of large enclosures, each with an associated roundhouse. The western enclosure (*BB 471*) was roughly triangular in plan, with an entrance on the south side, and maximum internal dimensions of 15.4 x 11.5 m (Pl 126). The 2 m-wide, stone rubble wall of the enclosure still stood to a height of *c* 0.6 m on the interior; tumble on the south side of the interior was possibly building rubble. To the north of this enclosure was a roundhouse with a small annexe to the north-east (*BB 470*; Pl 127). The house had stone rubble walls, *c* 2 m wide and 0.2 m high, with an internal floor area *c* 4.6 m in diameter, and an entrance on the south-east side. The eastern enclosure (*BB 473*) was of oval plan, with a possible entrance on the north-east side, and maximum internal dimensions of 11.5 x *c* 8 m. The stone rubble wall of the enclosure stood to a height of *c* 2 m. The size and irregularity of the shape of both enclosures were consistent with a stock-control function. To the north of this enclosure was a further roundhouse with a small annexe to the north-east (*BB 476*; Pl 128). The house had stone rubble walls, *c* 1.1 m wide and 0.2 m high, with an internal floor area having a diameter of *c* 3.45 m, and entrances on the south-east and north-west sides. Between the two enclosures was an abrupt change of vegetation, from grass to bracken, which may have reflected the sub-surface edge of formerly improved land.

Plate 127: Roundhouse BB 470, *within BB VIIB*

Plate 128: Roundhouse BB 476, *within BB VIIB*

Possible ring cairn

Also located within BB VIIB, to the north-east of the field system, was a possible ring cairn (*BB 498*). This cairn had a diameter of *c* 15m, and was set on a low promontory overlooking the moss. Its external bank was clearest on the south, east, and northern sides, where it was 1.5-2 m wide. The south side was built of massive boulders, each weighing at least half a ton. The

215

north and south walls also marked the limit of a more concentrated area of tumble across the centre of the cairn. There was no indication of internal terracing.

Haematite mine
Close to the two monument sub-groups, on the slope above the enclosures, and between the 230 m and 250 m contours, were abandoned mine workings (*BB 455*), with a trench which was probably the entrance to an adit. Spoil alongside indicated that haematite had been quarried. Below and parallel to the contour was a bank, probably also of quarry spoil. A carefully constructed trackway climbed from Eskdale to reach the mine on the north side of the hill.

Shooting butts
Three shooting butts (*BB 492-4*) were also identified within this area, which had been built in an area of boulder scree, overlooking Brantrake Moss, at the northern edge of the cairnfield.

Discussion
One of the monument sub-groups (BB VIIB) would appear to represent a former field system, approximately defined by stone banks, or possibly walls, which for the most part appeared to define the extent of a cairnfield. Adjacent to this was a comparable area defined by walls/stone banks (*BB 419*, *BB 439*, and *BB 422-6*), which was noticeably devoid of cairns. As such, these two areas would appear to have complemented each other, and they compared with a similar arrangement on Town Bank (TB IV; *Ch 3*, *p 52*, where there were also alternate 'fields' with and without cairns. As with the Town Bank example, it can be suggested that the field areas were to provide two complementary aspects of an agricultural economy, that potentially included some meadowland for the growing of grass for winter fodder.

The field system included two apparent stock enclosures, with associated stone-founded roundhouses, which were within an area of the 'field' that was largely devoid of cairns. Again, this closely matches the situation at TB IV, where there were stone-founded roundhouses, one with an associated stock enclosure, that were set within the cairn-free parts of the field system (*Ch 3*, *p 54*). These features also emphasise that this was a relatively well-established settlement, which was primarily engaged in pastoralism.

The TB IV field system has not been dated, but in terms of its typological development in comparison with other settlements, the site can be considered to be of late Bronze Age, or earlier Iron Age date. However, the Brantrake Moss field system and settlement (BB VII) have been approximately dated by pollen analysis to the Roman period. However, although the main settlement may date from the Roman period, or possibly even a little earlier, the presence of two round cairns (*BB 417* and *BB 421*), and a putative ring cairn (*BB 498*), might suggest that there was also some Bronze Age activity at this site.

Birkby/Birker Fell VIII (Rough Crag): monuments *BB 499-543*
To the south-east of Rough Crag, between the 240 m and 280 m contours, was a group of 45 small cairns, located on gently sloping but undulating ground (Fig 99). This group probably equates with the westernmost of the two groups on Pike How described by Jim Cherry (1961, 8).

The cairns were in two distinct groups, separated by a *c* 50 m-wide natural bench, presently occupied by mire; the absence of cairns on this area of level ground would suggest that it was poorly drained in antiquity. The group was constrained to the north by a craggy knoll, and, although there was no clearly defined topographical limit, an extensive area of mire appeared to mark its southern limit. The cairns were generally ill defined and low lying, typically *c* 0.25-0.35 m high, though some were more prominent. No stone banks were associated and there was little indication of any cairn alignments. This would therefore appear to have been a primary cairnfield, comprising essentially randomly distributed cairns, which in places was constrained by the natural topography.

Birkby/Birker Fell IX (Pike How): monuments *BB 544-637*
A large cairnfield extended along the southern slope of Pike How, comprising 93 small cairns and an enclosure, all situated between the 210 m and 270 m contours (Fig 99). The cairnfield was divided into three distinct spatial sub-groups.

The largest and most densely concentrated sub-group (BB IXA; Fig 103) was located to the south-west, on gently sloping and undulating terrain. The cairns were moderately prominent and generally well defined, although up to 10% were turf covered and ill defined. They were typically 3.5-4.5 m in diameter and up to 0.4 m in height, and were closely packed. No stone banks were identified, nor any significant cairn alignments, and the distribution of the cairns was essentially random. The extent of the cairn group was constrained by crags to the west and east. This was a typical primary-type cairnfield, and included the cairn excavated in 1985 (*p 199*; *c* 20 m north-east of *BB 585*). The excavation demonstrated a secondary episode of smaller clearance stone having been piled up against a primary deposit of larger stones. This secondary deposit spread north-east from the primary core, suggesting that the area being cleared of stone was to the north-east of the cairn, land that was recorded

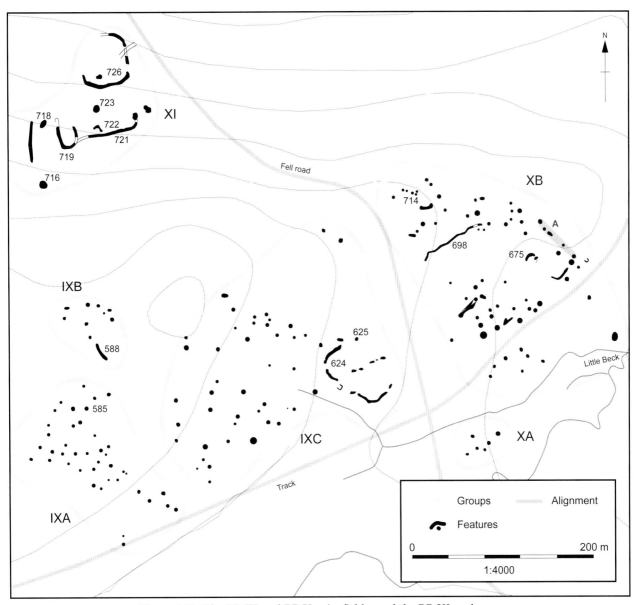

Figure 103: The BB IX and BB X cairnfields, and the BB XI enclosures

as having a relatively smooth surface and was devoid of cairns. It is therefore possible to suggest that this area to the north-east of the cairnfield had been subject to improvement. A radiocarbon assay from the peat beneath the secondary deposit of the cairn produced an early medieval date (*p 200*).

The second sub-group of cairns (BB IXB) was found to the north, and comprised widely scattered, relatively large, cairns positioned on gently sloping land. There were no significant cairn alignments within the group, which was a primary-type of cairnfield. However, there was a length of curving stone bank (*BB 588*), which marked a vegetational boundary and may have defined an area of former improved land.

The third group (BB IXC) formed the eastern part of the cairnfield, and contained a widely scattered group

of cairns, which were fairly prominent, measuring between 3 m and 4 m in size. Generally, this cairn group was located on more gently sloping ground and some of the cairns were within areas of mire, indicating the expansion of poorly drained ground.

Associated with BB IXC, in the angle between the fell road and the track to Birkerthwaite, was also an enclosure (*BB 624*), which had previously been noted by Cherry (1961, 8). Its walls were discontinuous, irregular in thickness, and survived to a height of only one course of boulders. However, in places there were substantial volumes of stone exposed, reflecting the tumble from what must have been substantial walls. The walls formed three sides of a sub-rectangular enclosure which, from north to south, measured *c* 70 m. The fourth side of this enclosure was not identified, but this might potentially have been buried beneath the peat. Extending from the middle of the enclosure was

217

a discontinuous bank / line of cairns, which appeared to reflect an internal boundary. Its western wall extended through an area of extensive outcropping and there were several later shelters incorporated within this. The relationship between the enclosure and the cairnfield was slightly uncertain; the enclosure was at the south-eastern edge of the cairnfield, and there were no small cairns within it. One cairn (*BB 625*), however, appeared to continue the line of the enclosure wall, but this does not necessarily indicate that the enclosure and cairnfield were contemporary.

Birkby/Birker Fell X (Little Beck): monuments *BB 638-715*
An extensive cairnfield lay on the gently sloping terrain to the east of the present-day fell road (Fig 99). This was in part constrained by localised craggy outcrops and an area of mire to the south. It was divided into two main cairn groups, separated by the northern arm of the Little Beck.

The first cairn group (BB XA; Fig 103) contained six small and ill-defined cairns, located amongst areas of mire between the confluence of the tributaries comprising the Little Beck. This small, localised, area of clearance was severely constrained by the surrounding topography.

The second cairn group (BB XB) was located in an area of slightly undulating, but generally gently sloping, terrain on the southern side of a slight spur that extends east from Pike How. The extent of the group was limited to the east by a craggy knoll, and to the north by the watershed between the Black Beck to the north and the Little Beck to the south. There were occasional outcrops within the area and some of the cairns had been deliberately positioned on these to maximise the available good land. Cairns varied from being relatively prominent and moderately large, to being low and ill defined; the larger cairns were, for the most part, in the south-western quadrant of the group. In the northern part of the cairnfield, a short length of stone bank comprised small, elongated, cairns (*BB 714*), and to the east, the edge of the group was defined by a possibly significant cairn alignment (A).

The cairns within BB XB were distributed around a central area that was markedly devoid of monuments, containing only a single sub-circular banked feature (*BB 675*). The northern edge of this area was, in part, marked by a length of stone bank (*BB 698*), which was irregular and discontinuous, but otherwise there did not appear to have been any significant cairn alignments, or banks, defining it. The terrain within the cairn-free area was generally well drained, although there was a small area of poorly drained ground at its southern edge. The surface was not particularly smooth, or stone-free, however, and did not seem to have been improved in antiquity. In general, this would appear to have been a cairnfield, with, for the most part, an essentially random cairn distribution, which had been limited by natural topographical constraints, and had a slightly erratic cairn distribution in order to maximise the better ground.

Birkby/Birker Fell XI: monuments *BB 716-26*
A group of enclosures, cairns, and walls was recorded on the north side of Pike How, overlooking Eskdale, between the 210 m and 250 m contours (Fig 99). Two enclosures were identified, the larger of which was sub-rectangular (*BB 726*; Fig 103), measuring *c* 50 m across, although its north-western side was not identified. The enclosure bank comprised mainly large stones, but rarely survived to more than 1 m in height; the banks were generally irregular and discontinuous, with that on the upper, southern, side being the most prominent. Given the irregularities and discontinuities, and in places lack of volume, these did not appear to reflect the remains of a wall. Within the enclosure was a uniform, gently sloping, almost level area, sharply defined by localised growth of bracken. This had possibly been cultivated, given that its southern bank had indications of a lynchet profile, and much waste stone had clearly been dumped on it.

The smaller enclosure (*BB 719*) was roughly oval in plan (20 x 30 m), its interior also gently sloping and apparently improved. It was linked to a very prominent bank extending along the contours (*BB 721*), which had a sharp break of slope on its downslope side. At its eastern end, the bank turned towards the north, in line with the eastern boundary of *BB 726*, suggesting a relationship between them. Butting against the bank was a rectangular structure (*BB 722*; 9 x 7 m), which had an entrance on the western side.

Within the group were three cairns, of which only one (*BB 718*) had an apparent relationship with the banks / enclosures. The most notable was *BB 723*, which was very prominent, large (6 m in diameter), had medium and large stones protruding, and a fairly regular shape and profile.

Birkby/Birker Fell XII: monuments *BB 727-9*
On a level area of ground on the north-east side of Rough Crag were three isolated, small round cairns (Fig 99). These had an average diameter of 2.7 m, with the largest being 3.8 m and the smallest 1.9 m.

Birkby/Birker Fell XIII (Garner Bank): monuments *BB 730-68*
A group of 31 small cairns, associated walls, and a two-celled structure was situated above Hare Gill on an east-facing slope between the 190 m and 230 m

218

contours (Fig 99). Much of the site was covered by bracken, the limits of which were marked by walls/ stone banks to the north-east and south-west (*BB 765* and *BB 744*; Fig 104).

The key characteristic of the site was that it had stone banks or walls, lynchets, and cairn alignments forming an integrated field system. The longest section of wall (*BB 744/6*) extended north/south and defined the western extent of the site. Its line was approximately continued by a line of cairns (A), and approximately from the end of this cairn alignment was a further alignment, extending east/west (B). Extending north-west/south-east from this alignment was a bank forming a lynchet (*BB 764*), which itself was orientated towards the western terminus of stone bank *BB 765*. A further wall to the south-east, *BB 737*, was orientated towards lynchet *BB 764*, and its western end was orientated towards the *BB 744/6* boundary. Although, quite clearly, there were some considerable gaps within these boundaries, this would appear, in conjunction with the other elements, to have marked the outline of a sub-rectangular field. The area

within this putative field contained an approximate curving alignment of four cairns (C), but otherwise was essentially cairn-free. It is, perhaps, significant that stone bank *BB 744/6* was adjacent, and parallel, to an extended alignment of cairns (A), suggesting that these reflected stone clearance near to, but not on, the line of the *BB 744/6* boundary. Alternatively, bank *BB 744/6* may have been a later element, which had been superimposed onto an extant boundary marked by cairns. On the south side of the site was an alignment of six stones (*BB 730*), marking the south-west limit of the better land, close to a narrow defile leading into the valley of Brantrake Moss.

Abutting curving wall *BB 737*, on the south-east, was a rectangular two-celled structure, terraced into the hillside on a level platform, in a well-sheltered position (*BB 736*). The platform, measuring 20 x 9.5 m in extent, was extremely large compared with the other rectangular buildings recorded during the survey and this, perhaps, suggests that these were simply a pair of stock pounds. However, the site had been deliberately terraced into the slope, which

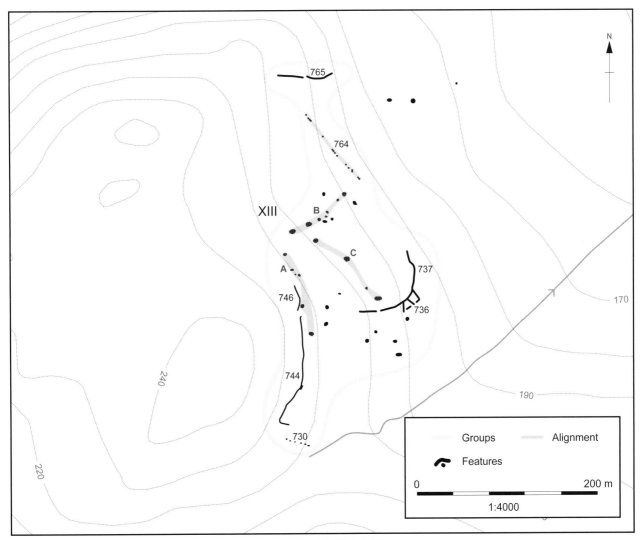

Figure 104: The BB XIII field system

would be unusual for stock pounds, and was more appropriate for a domestic structure. It is thus possible that the platform was originally intended for a timber structure, but had subsequently been developed into its present form.

Birkby/Birker Fell XIV (The Seat: West): monuments *BB 770-811*

A group of 38 small cairns, together with several lengths of stone bank, extended for 360 m from south-west to north-east between the 250 m and 270 m contours to the south of Seat How (Fig 99; Pl 129). The monuments could be divided into two discrete sub-groups.

The first monument sub-group (BB XIVA; Fig 105) comprised a broad band of cairns and two stone banks, which extended south-west/north-east from the main cairn group (BB XIVB). The cairns were low-lying and between 2.5 m and 4 m in diameter. The stone banks (*BB 772-3*), situated towards the western end of the cairn group, were approximately parallel, but about 50 m apart, and the area between was devoid of cairns.

The second monument sub-group (BB XIVB) was larger in size and comprised 31 cairns of varied size and prominence within a broad area that was defined

to the south by a 63 m-long lynchet, and to the north-east by a stone bank (*BB 809*). There was one possible significant cairn alignment (*BB 784-6*), comprising three cairns, of which one was elongated and orientated in the same direction as the alignment, but otherwise the cairns appeared to have an essentially random distribution. Just to the south of the cairns was a sub-circular, internally terraced, bank (*BB 781*), which had an internal diameter of 8 m, and was most probably a terraced platform for a timber structure. Overall, this monument group would appear to reflect a small settlement, incorporating an area of agriculturally improved land, which was contained within partially surviving field boundaries.

Birkby/Birker Fell XV (The Seat: South): monuments *BB 812-85*

A group of 73 small cairns extended for *c* 280 m east to west across the southern slopes of The Seat, between the 240 m and 280 m contours (Fig 99). Most of the cairns were well defined, but were not particularly prominent, and varied in size. The cairnfield divided into two parts, the southernmost comprising a dense concentration of essentially randomly distributed cairns, whereas to the north-east was a large area that was for the most part devoid of cairns (with the exception of cairns *BB 836* and *BB 877*; Fig 105). This was defined to the north and east by what appear to

Plate 129: The area of BB XIV, looking west

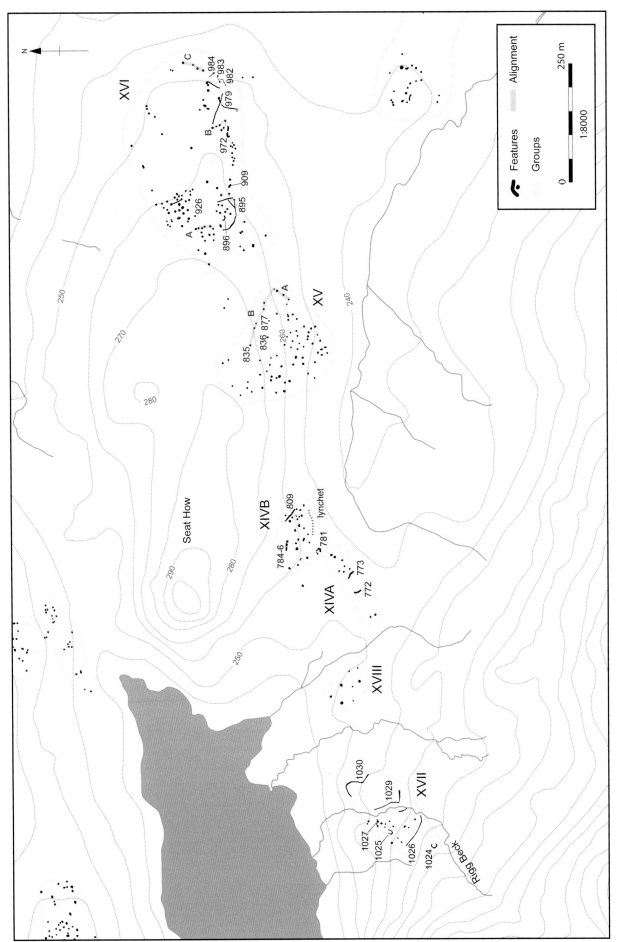

Figure 105: The BB XIV, BB XV, BB XVI, and BB XVII cairnfields and field systems

have been significant cairn alignments (A: south-east; B: north-east). Although the extent of this cairn-free area was not particularly well defined, and there were no stone banks or lynchets associated with it, it is possible that it was a former agricultural plot.

Birkby/Birker Fell XVI (The Seat: east): monuments BB 886-1008

An extensive group of small cairns and stone banks extended for some 520 m, east to west, along the eastern slopes of The Seat (Fig 99), between the 240 m and 270 m contours on either side of the main road from Eskdale to Ulpha (Cherry 1961, 11-12, sites 9 and 9a).

The cairns were generally ill defined and varied in size; peat growth across the cairnfield had masked or partly covered the cairns and, in many instances, their extent was confirmed only by probing. The greatest concentration was in the western part of the site, apparently around a large area devoid of cairns (apart from cairn BB 926), which may potentially have been an agricultural plot. However, as there was peat growth across the whole area, which may have obscured some cairns, the cairn-free area was not necessarily a deliberate creation. Its western edge was defined by a possible cairn alignment (A), but otherwise its extent was defined by a more amorphous, though curving, pattern of cairns. Around the southern side of the area was a 28 m-wide band of cairns that then extended east for a total distance of c 300 m, and was in part marked by short stone banks (BB 972), before turning to the north as a putative alignment (B). There were no cairns on either side of this band and it may have delimited a further plot, albeit less well defined than that to the west.

The eastern limit of the monument group was marked by a further line of cairns and also sections of stone bank (BB 982-4 and Alignment C), extending roughly north to south, although the stone banks were not orientated with the cairn alignment and may therefore have been unrelated. A long east/west bank (BB 979), though, was orientated with the southern terminus of a short section of stone bank (BB 982), suggesting a relationship. Similarly, this bank was orientated with a cairn (also BB 979) at the eastern end of the north/south putative alignment (BB 974-9), which may suggest that these were part of an integrated system. However, it must be stressed that any interpretations of monument distribution are tentative, as there were extensive areas of wetter ground where peat growth may have concealed further cairns and walls. In particular, there was a scatter of cairns to the north and west, which formed no coherent pattern and, because of the peat coverage, may reflect only part of a more complex cairn distribution.

Within the western part of the monument group was one possible half of a D-shaped enclosure (BB 895), with a large and prominent cairn in its south-eastern corner. The northern terminals of the walls were obscured by later peat growth, and it is not known how far they originally extended. The band of cairns to the south of the cairn-free area extended through this partial enclosure, and their distribution did not appear to have been affected by the alignment of walls. It would therefore appear that the partial enclosure was a later feature superimposed onto the cairnfield. Within this partial enclosure was a short length of stone bank that may have represented the fragmentary remains of a small structure (BB 896). However, this bank was on the line of the band of cairns and may have been no more than an extended section of stone clearance, comparable to BB 909 and BB 972, which were also within the east/west aligned band of cairns.

Birkby/Birker Fell XVII (Rigg Beck): monuments BB 1009-29

A group of small cairns, together with associated stone banks, was recorded to the south of Devoke Water, on either side of Rigg Beck, between the 260 m and 290 m contours, and occupying a gently sloping natural terrace (Fig 99). The cairn group comprised 15 cairns, which lay immediately to the west of the beck, and were bounded on the south, upslope, side by a stone bank, following the contour (BB 1026; Fig 105), and on the east by Rigg Beck. All the cairns were approximately circular in plan, none exceeding 5 m in diameter, and most were well defined. At least two also had possible stone kerbs. The cairn distribution was essentially random, and even where there was a section of stone bank (BB 1027), this did not equate with any cairn alignments.

In the centre of the area of cairns was a small enclosure (BB 1025), which was U-shaped in plan, 10 m wide, and at least 14 m long, with gaps, possibly entrances, on each of the two long sides. The wall of the enclosure was 2.5 m wide and 2.2 m high.

To the south of, and over 52 m from, the main bank (BB 1026) was a sub-circular enclosure (BB 1024). Its rubble stone wall was 1.9 m wide and 0.4 m high, with a possible entrance on the east side.

East of the Rigg Beck were two further lengths of walling (BB 1029 and BB 1030), which may have represented two sides of a plot, or enclosure, within which there were no cairns. The wall on the west roughly followed the bank of the beck for most of its length (2 m wide and up to 0.8 m high), delimiting the flatter ground to the east. On the north was a second length of wall (BB 1030), which approximately followed the line of the apron edge of the natural terrace, and together these walls defined the extent of the well-drained level ground forming the terrace.

Birkby/Birker Fell XVIII (Devoke Water South): monuments *BB 1031-8*

South of Devoke Water, close to the 250 m contour (Fig 99), was a group of eight small cairns, which was roughly midway between BB XIV on the western slopes of The Seat, and Rigg Beck (BB XVII). The cairns were all approximately circular in plan and the northernmost three were the largest (5.3-7.5 m in diameter), whereas those to the south were markedly smaller. There were no associated linear features, such as stone banks, and no alignments could be discerned.

Conclusions

The monuments

The Birkby/Birker Fell survey area was for the most part gently undulating fell, lying between the steep valley sides of Eskdale on the north, and the higher and rockier slopes of the hills to the south. Birkby and Birker Fells thus afforded a wide swathe of land suitable for grazing, being a continuation of the natural bench exploited by the Barnscar settlement. Not only did this terrace provide a good area for settlement, but it was also a natural communication route across the South-West Fells; the route from Barnscar to Devoke Water, now marked by orthostats, is of an unknown but ancient origin, and may well have served prehistoric as well as more recent communities.

Looking at the pattern of the cairnfields as a whole, the cairn groups reflected localised exploitation of land since, instead of each merging into each other, there was a regular spatial separation between them; this may indicate deliberate planning to define the land belonging to each farming settlement. This was most noticeable to the south of Devoke Water, where BB XVII, BB XVIII, BB XIV, BB XV, and BB XVI were comparable in form and were potentially contemporary; they extended in an east/west line across the landscape at a distance of 380 m, 420 m, 530 m, and 450 m respectively (Fig 105).

To the north of Devoke Water, the position of farmed areas was dictated more by the topography, and hence the best drained and most gently sloping land had been selected, yet there was nevertheless some degree of uniformity in their spatial separation. Thus BB I was 650 m from BB II, which in turn was 750 m from BB III (Fig 99). BB II was also 600 m from BB IV, which in turn was 850 m from BB VII; BB III was 690 m from BB VI, which was 800 m from BB VIII, 740 m from BB X, and 350 m from BB XI.

The distance between BB VI and BB XI was considerably less than that between the other groups, but was similar to that between the groups to the south of Devoke Water. Although it is clear that there was some degree of consistency between the spatial separation of the sites, it can only be very tentatively suggested that this related to any degree of territorial organisation, as this assumes that the sites were in some degree contemporary.

Devoke Water

The Birkby/Birker Fell survey is of considerable importance, in part because of the broad variety of settlements and cairnfield remains identified, but principally because of the amount of palynological work that has been undertaken within the area from mires such as Tewit Moss, Devoke Water, and from beneath archaeological monuments (*pp 197-203*). These have the potential to inform the development of the landscape and to provide a new perspective on those settlements elsewhere in the region, which do not have such absolute dating. The Devoke Water pollen diagram (Pennington 1970) is significant in that, to a substantial extent, it reflects waterborne, as opposed to aerial-borne pollen. Therefore, the pollen diagram will be biased towards material from the watershed of the lake, rather than the large settlement sites, such as Barnscar, which were within the aerial-catchment area. Within this waterborne catchment area were BB III, BB VI, BB VII, BB XIV, and BB XVII.

The palynological evidence suggests that the earliest clearance activity occurred in apparently short episodes from the neolithic period onwards, culminating in a major clearance episode in the middle Bronze Age (Pennington 1970). The archaeological evidence for this episode of activity is provided by the round and ring funerary cairns at Devoke Water West (BB III; *p 207*) and Brantrake Moss (BB VII; *p 211*), and also the discovery of flint artefacts within the fabric of the excavated cairns at Pike How (*p 199*) and Little Beck (Cherry and Fletcher 1964). From the later Bronze Age onwards, and throughout the Iron Age, there was a period of forest regeneration, potentially reflecting, in part, the climatic decline of the early Iron Age that would have made upland farming uneconomic.

The next major clearance episode occurred from the middle of the Roman period, and was at its height in the later Roman period through to the early medieval period. This episode of clearance would appear to have been reflected at the Brantrake Moss settlement (BB VII; *p 211*), where there was a cairnfield and proto-field system linked to stock pounds and unenclosed roundhouses. On purely typological grounds, the presence of unenclosed stone-founded houses within the settlement would suggest a date range in the later Bronze Age to mid-Iron Age (Gates 1983), yet the pollen sample from beneath the wall on the south side of the field system would indicate a mid-Roman date (Fell 1970; *p 199*). This would suggest either that there had been a reoccupation of an earlier site within the Roman period, or that the tradition of unenclosed settlements continued in some remote areas into the Roman period. The clearance was sufficiently extensive that it became permanent, albeit with some secondary woodland regeneration.

Although there was undoubtedly early medieval activity in the area, the principal evidence for this is from the radiocarbon dates beneath the excavated clearance cairn at Devoke Water (*p 199*), situated in the BB IX (Pike How) monument group (*p 216*). The implications of the date for this cairn are potentially considerable. The cairn was in the northernmost part of a cairnfield, which had no significant alignments, had no evidence of a field system, and had an essentially random distribution. Such a cairnfield can be categorised as a primary type, in that it had not been developed into a proto-field or more rationalised field system. On the basis of typology and some palynological evidence, this is considered to reflect the primary episode of stone clearance following forest clearance (*Ch 8, pp 327-8*), which has most typically been associated with the widespread primary forest clearances of the Bronze Age. In the case of the later first millennium AD date from the Devoke Water cairn, derived from beneath its secondary accumulation of stone, this was a period when the primary forest had been cleared and had not recovered (*Ch 8, pp 327-8*). In this instance, it is therefore probable that there was a substantial time interval between the primary and secondary episodes of clearance, and that the larger, primary, accumulation of material might reflect earlier, Bronze Age, clearance. This is also not out of keeping with the evidence found in other areas of the uplands, where it also appears that some cairns were a product of two, widely separated, episodes of stone clearance (*Ch 6, pp 276-8*). Given this, it is therefore probable that, in addition to the primary phases of clearance, there was also substantial secondary stone clearance and land improvement in the Pike How area during the early medieval period. Unfortunately, on the basis of the available evidence, it is not possible to determine whether the distribution of cairns in this area was a product of this period of activity, or one of the earlier periods of activity, as reflected within the local pollen record.

The palynological and dating evidence from the environs of Devoke Water are of considerable importance in demonstrating that this upland area was subject to land improvement and was farmed over several periods, from at least the Bronze Age onwards. The implication is that the cairnfields in this area were a product of this extended activity, spanning over two millennia. This, in turn, may suggest that other similar cairnfields within the region, which have not benefited from scientific dating, may also have a similarly complex development.

Ulpha Fell

Ulpha Fell lies on the high ground to the west of Dunnerdale and Harter Fell, and to the south of Eskdale (Fig 93). The survey area was bounded to the west by the Birkby/Birker Fell survey area, to the south by the enclosed land above Dunnerdale, and to the east by Harter Fell and Dunnerdale Forest (Fig 106). The boundary between Ulpha Fell and Birker Fell is formed by the parish boundary dividing Ulpha from Eskdale, although this boundary was not used in this survey, as it extended through the middle of an area rich in archaeology, which was included in the Ulpha Fell survey area. Most of the monuments recorded were situated on the more gently undulating moorland, at an altitude range of 180-300 m OD, north of the steep slopes above Dunnerdale, in the Smallstone Beck valley to the east, and south of Birkerthwaite.

Archaeological history
The sites on Ulpha Fell were first recorded on the 1900 Second Edition 6" to 1 mile OS map, and these same depictions were also transferred to the revised edition of the OS map (1920). Cherry (1961) assessed the archaeology of the northern part of the South-West Fells and included within this were several sites falling within the Ulpha Fell survey area. Cherry's (*ibid*) work was particularly important in increasing the number of known sites, and was one of the major catalysts for the work during the 1980s. His survey of 16 separate sites, extending over the South-West Fells, was a rapid identification exercise which, for the first time, highlighted the great numbers of monuments existing and awaiting detailed recording. It also served to raise the question of where additional survey might identify new sites.

The survey area
The survey, undertaken in 1982 and 1983, covering, in total, *c* 4.9 km² of unenclosed moorland (Fig 107), recorded a total of 299 monuments within 13 site groups (UF I-XIII; Fig 108). These, for the most part, were small isolated cairnfield groups exploiting gradually sloping areas of well-drained land. In addition, there was also a D-shaped enclosure

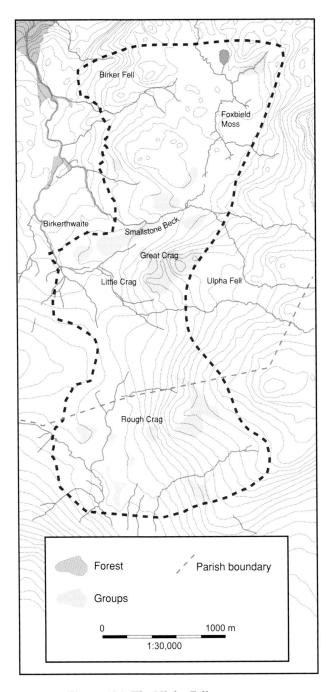

Figure 106: The Ulpha Fell survey area

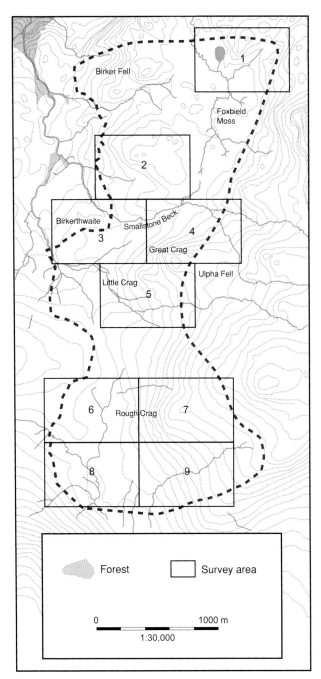

Figure 107: The Ulpha Fell survey area as planned

(UF II), associated with a small number of cairns, and a group of three roundhouses (UF VI), as well as a limited number of scattered ungrouped cairns and banks (*UF 44, UF 68, UF 69,* and *UF 187*), which are not individually described within this volume.

Ulpha Fell I (Birkerthwaite): monuments *UF 9-43*

A group of small cairns extended over 450 m to the south of Birkerthwaite Farm, on level ground between the 210 m and 230 m contours (Fig 108). The field in which most of the sites lay was taken out of the common in the 1960s, and since this time it has been improved and ploughed at least

once (R H Leech *pers obs*). As a result, most of the cairns were in poor condition, many with visible damage from ploughing. The cairns formed two sub-groups, although the lacunae between them may have been artificial, reflecting damage from improvement/ploughing in the western field that contained one of the cairn sub-groups.

The first cairn group (UF IA) contained 14 cairns of varied size and prominence. No significant alignments were seen, but there was a small area within the group that was devoid of cairns. However, this apparent cairn-free area may have been a product of recent land improvement, and therefore

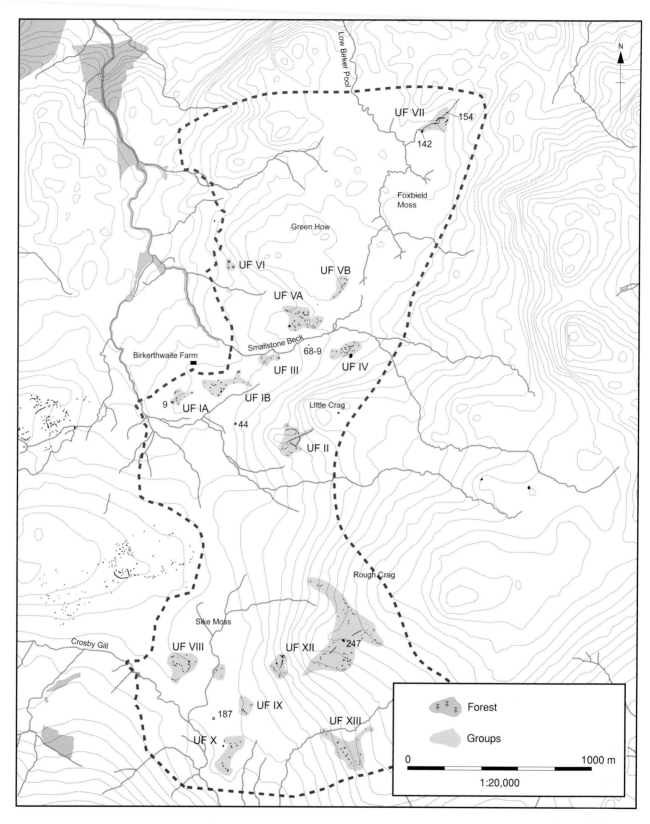

Figure 108: Monument distribution within the Ulpha Fell survey area

may not have any archaeological significance. To the west of this group was a large elongated cairn (*UF 9*, 12.8 x 5.6 x 1.0 m), which was prominent, had a depression in its centre, and was covered by turf. Its shape and definition were irregular, however, and it is possible that it was a natural outcrop.

The second cairn group (UF IB; Fig 109) comprised a group of ill-defined, medium to very large cairns, which lay within a field that had been subject to improvement. The south-western extent of the cairn group extended close to, but no further than, a modern field boundary, raising the possibility that

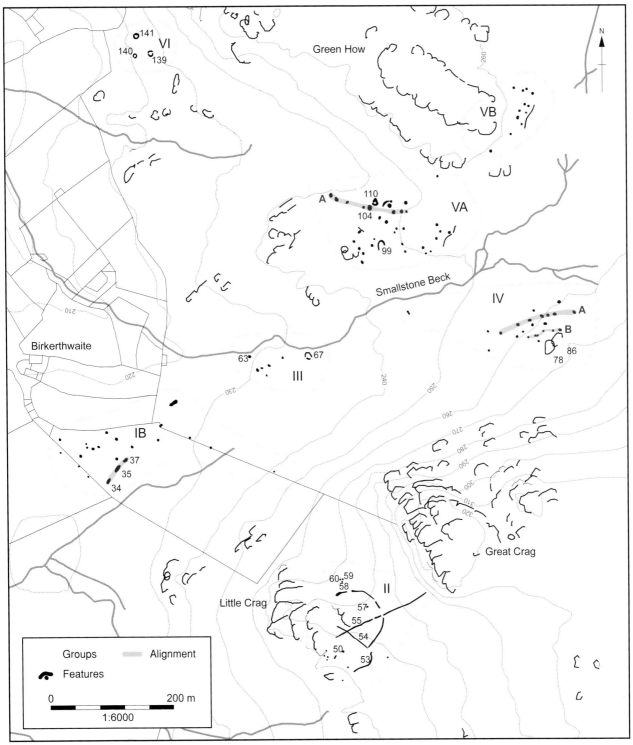

Figure 109: The UF I-VI cairnfields and enclosure

any cairns to the south-west of this boundary had been destroyed by recent land improvement. The medium-sized cairns had no significant alignments, but there was an area within the group that was devoid of cairns, though again this may reflect recent land improvement rather than any original layout. The south-east side of the group was delimited by an alignment of three cairns (11.7 m, 14.7 m, and 8.4 m in length; *UF 34*, *UF 35*, and *UF 37*), their long axes following that of the alignment. These marked the limit of an area of improved pasture, and would therefore appear to have been a product of this episode of agricultural improvement. Their appearance and weathering was similar to those of the other small cairns, which would suggest that they were not of recent origin. However, it is possible, given that they were very distinct in size, character, and location, that they reflect a different episode of clearance activity and one which probably post-dated the episode associated with the medium-sized cairns.

Ulpha Fell II (Great Crag): monuments *UF 45-60*

A D-shaped enclosure, a long boundary wall, and a group of small cairns were situated on the col between Great Crag and Little Crag, between the 270 m and 290 m contours; the site was sheltered from the west by Little Crag (Fig 108).

The D-shaped enclosure (*UF 54*; Fig 109) exploited the flat summit of the col and butted onto the face of Little Crag, utilising it as its western side (Pl 130). The enclosure was of similar plan and altitude to the D-shaped enclosure on Hesk Fell (*HE 46; p 251*), but was slightly smaller in size, its straight, south-west side being *c* 90 m in length, whereas the same side of *HE 46* was 115 m long. The exterior wall was well-defined except where obscured by vegetation, and was similar in appearance and weathering to the groups of small cairns. The interior was devoid of features except for one small cairn (*UF 57*). To the south, one wall (*UF 53*) appeared to extend up to the south-west side of the enclosure, which was crossed by a later wall (*UF 55*; Pl 130) between Great Crag and Little Crag, which related to an intake that extended from the enclosed lands of Birkerthwaite. To the north of the enclosure was a small compact group of three small cairns (*UF 58-60*), and to the south, a further nine cairns were recorded; one was elongated (*UF 50*; 6 x 3.2 m), and the rest were small and circular (1.7-2.8 m in diameter).

The D-shaped enclosure was comparable not only in shape to the Hesk Fell example, but both had an association with small external cairnfields, and were associated with additional walling relating to elements of a putative field system. The only significant difference is that *HE 46* had a building set into each corner, whereas the enclosure at Great Crag had no such associations.

Ulpha Fell III (Smallstone Beck South): monuments *UF 61-7*

A group of six small cairns and an enclosure were situated to the south of the Smallstone Beck, in the flat base of the valley between the 220 m and 240 m contours (Fig 108; Pl 131). The cairns were relatively large and prominent, being between 3.5 m and 5 m in diameter (on average); one cairn (*UF 63*; Fig 109) was 5.1 m long by 4.1 m, had a kerb on the south-east, and four other large boulders around the edges. It was slightly removed from the rest of the group and could potentially be a funerary monument. Four of the six cairns were also aligned, and this may be significant.

To the east of the group of small cairns, and *c* 15 m to the south of the Smallstone Beck, was a well-defined enclosure of sub-rectangular plan (*UF 67*), with walls standing on average 0.5 m high. There were three breaks in the walling, of which one was undoubtedly the original entrance. The height of the surrounding wall, up to 0.8 m in places, and its relatively good condition probably indicated a post-medieval date for the enclosure. Its character contrasted with that of the cairns and there was no indication that it was contemporary with them.

Plate 130: The UF II enclosure (UF 54), from Little Crag

Ulpha Fell IV (Smallstone Beck East): monuments *UF 70-91*

Twenty-one small cairns were situated to the south of the Smallstone Beck, between the 250 m and 270 m contours (Fig 108). The site was on a north-facing slope immediately below a line of low crags, and was separated from the group to the north by the Smallstone Beck and an area of marshy ground. Of the 21 cairns recorded, almost all were well defined, relatively prominent, and large in size. Of the elongated cairns, the longest was 6.6 m, and the circular cairns were between 1.9 m and 5.6 m in diameter, but the majority were at the upper end of the size range. There was a possibly significant alignment, extending in a slightly curved arc along the line of the contours (A; Fig 109), at the northern, lower side of the group. A further, and less convincing, alignment extended in an arc that was parallel to the first, but upslope of it (B). In between, and beyond these two putative alignments, were further scattered cairns, which confused the distribution, and it is not beyond the realms of possibility that these 'alignments' were coincidental patterns within an essentially random distribution.

Ulpha Fell V (Smallstone Beck North): monuments *UF 92-138*

Thirty-nine small cairns and a small enclosure were situated to the north of the Smallstone Beck, between the 240 m and 260 m contours, overlooking Foxbield Moss (Fig 108). These monuments were separated by craggy ground and were divided into two sub-groups, as there was a clear spatial division between the larger group to the south-west, and a smaller group some 150 m to the north-east (Fig 109).

The larger of the monument sub-groups (UF VA) was located south of Green How and comprised 29 small cairns. The cairns varied in size, but those in the higher, northern part of the group were markedly larger than their counterparts to the south. To the north-west was a distinct line of eight cairns (Alignment A), which may have formed a significant alignment. Elsewhere, the distribution appeared to be essentially random, albeit within small localised concentrations. Within the alignment was a large, slightly irregular cairn (*UF 104*; 8 x 7 m) with a central depression; its size and the depression probably reflected later disturbance, probably antiquarian. Adjacent to this was a larger, tear-drop-shaped monument (*UF 110*; *c* 11 x 7 m), containing substantial amounts of stone, with a large central depression, and a gap to the west. This was potentially also a disturbed monument, and its eccentric shape reflected the deposition of spoil; however, there is also a possibility that this was a small structure, with a west-facing entrance. In the southern part of the cairn group was a U-shaped length of wall (*UF 99*), which was *c* 13 m long and may have been part of an enclosure.

Plate 131: The UF III cairn group, to the south of Smallstone Beck, looking south-west

229

The smaller of the monument sub-groups (UF VB) was located on the south-east slopes of Green How, approximately on the line of the 260 m contour, and comprised a group of ten small cairns, some of which were on the edge of a moss. The cairns varied slightly in size, between 2.5 m and 4 m; there were no obvious cairn alignments and their distribution was essentially random.

Ulpha Fell VI (Green How West): monuments *UF 139-41*

On the west-facing slopes of Green How, immediately above the enclosed land (Fig 109), were three probable roundhouses of approximately similar size, and of unknown date. Roundhouse *UF 140* had an average internal diameter of 4.6 m, with a 1 m-wide stony bank, standing to a height of 0.4 m, and a possible entrance to the south-west. The outside edge of the building was mostly obscured by turf or moss, and there were a few large boulders to the north and south of this. A second roundhouse (*UF 141*; Pl 132) had an average internal diameter of 5.6 m, a 1.5 m-wide stony bank standing to a height of 0.6 m, and a possible entrance to the north. The third roundhouse (*UF 139*) had an average internal diameter of 6.3 m, with a 1 m-wide stony bank, standing to a height of 0.35 m, and two possible opposed entrances, to the east and west.

Ulpha Fell VII (Low Birker Tarn): monuments *UF 142-54*

A group, comprising a large cairn, small cairns, stone banks, and roundhouses, was situated between the 240 m and 260 m contours, to the south of the stream south of Tarn Crag, which drains into Low Birker Pool (Fig 108). Further to the east, the ground rises towards Harter Fell and the high fells of the central Lake District. The site marked the north-eastern limit of the zone within which groups of small cairns were abundant.

The western extremity of the site was marked by a well-defined, large, and prominent cairn (*UF 142*; 9 m in diameter and 0.7 m high) on a low promontory extending west into the moss. It had a possible kerb around the edge, and had been hollowed out for use as a later shelter. It was probably a funerary cairn given its size, relative isolation, and prominent location.

With the exception of a single cairn to the north (*UF 154*), the rest of the monuments, comprising stone banks, cairns, and roundhouses, were arranged in a U-shaped linear pattern. Within this U-shaped alignment, there were no cairns, but the ground was relatively smooth and may have been improved. The cairns and the banks

Plate 132: UF VI, including roundhouse UF 141

were low lying and generally ill defined, whilst the two roundhouses had internal diameters of 5-5.5 m and their 1 m-wide walls stood to a height of 0.2-0.3 m. The northernmost was partly obscured by vegetation, but would appear to have had an eastern entrance; the southernmost had a small entrance on the north-east side.

The site group would appear to have comprised a small settlement arranged around an agricultural plot, which had been improved, with the stone produced being deposited to create a series of banks and cairns. If the relationship between the round cairn and the settlement was more than a simple spatial one, then there is an implication that the settlement related to Bronze Age activity.

Ulpha Fell VIII (Sike Moss): monuments *UF 155-79*

Two small groups of cairns were recorded in the area of Sike Moss (Fig 108). The larger, western group (UF VIIIA; Fig 110) was situated on a slight rise between Woodend Pool to the west and the stream draining Sike Moss to the east, between the 220 m and 260 m contours. The cairns were generally low lying and small, and varied from 1.9 m to 3.8 m

in diameter. They were distributed in a sinuous arc around the southern part of the group and a short line of three cairns could be discerned in the northern part (*UF 173-5*). Between these potentially significant alignments was an irregular-shaped area that was devoid of cairns and which may have served as an agricultural plot. On the eastern edge of the area was a well-defined ring feature (*UF 169*) that had an external diameter of 7.5 m, but was low lying, being only 0.25 m high; it had no obvious entrance. While there is a possibility that it was a roundhouse, its insubstantial nature may suggest that it was a clearance cairn, with stone deposited around a former tree trunk, a type identified during the excavations at Birrel Sike (Richardson 1982).

The smaller cairn group (UF VIIIB) was situated 140 m to the east, on the east side of an unnamed stream draining Sike Moss. It comprised four small cairns, which were varied in size, the largest being 5.3 x 3.5 m, whilst the smallest had a diameter of only 2 m. The two easternmost cairns were surrounded by mossland on all sides, and further cairns could potentially have been masked by later peat growth.

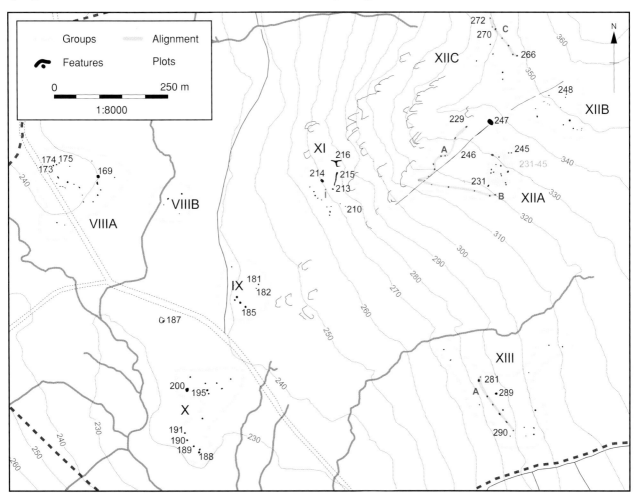

Figure 110: The UF VIII-XIII cairnfields

Ulpha Fell IX (Brown Rigg East): monuments *UF 180-6*

On the better-drained ground, just to the east of Sike Moss, was a group of eight cairns (Fig 108). The four to the south were the largest and most prominent, with the largest having a diameter of 5.8 m (*UF 185*; Fig 110), and two of these had possible kerbs. The two small cairns to the northeast (*UF 181* and *UF 182*) were ill defined. The group included no significant alignments and the distribution of cairns was essentially random.

Ulpha Fell X (Brown Rigg South): monuments *UF 188-201*

A group of small cairns and one larger cairn were located on a low promontory between the 230 m and 240 m contours to the east of Crosby Gill (Fig 108). The monument group comprised two marked concentrations of cairns, which were between 2 m and 3.5 m in diameter and were generally low lying. The southern concentration comprised five cairns, of which four were aligned in a shallow arc (*UF 188-91*; Fig 110), marking the edge of an area of poorly drained ground. The northern concentration had an essentially random distribution. However, most of these stood proud of the boggy ground and one (*UF 195*) was almost concealed by later peat growth. This highlights the possibility that the group included other cairns that had been buried beneath the peat, and hence the distribution may in part have been a reflection of site visibility rather than original design.

The principal monument in this area was a large cairn (*UF 200*), described by Jim Cherry (1961, 13, site 130) as being almost 12 m in diameter, but which was found on measurement to be 8.2 m in diameter and 0.5 m high. The cairn was well defined with a distinct kerb, but the south-eastern part had been disturbed to allow the construction of a bield.

Ulpha Fell XI (Rough Crag West): monuments *UF 202-16*

A further group of small cairns and associated stone banks/walls were recorded immediately to the west of Rough Crag (Fig 108). The cairns were on average 3 m in diameter, moderately prominent, and were for the most part roughly arranged around two sides of a rectangular area that was itself devoid of cairns, perhaps forming a plot (*i*; Fig 110). Slightly remote from the main group of cairns was another (*UF 214*) that was significantly larger than the rest, being 8.6 x 6.6 m, which was both well defined and very prominent, being 0.8 m high. Given its abnormal size, when compared to the rest of the group, it is possible that it had a funerary function.

Spatially associated with the cairns was a series of decayed walls/stone banks, which were one course high and formed of large boulders, some of which were earthfast. The northernmost of these (*UF 216*) formed a three-sided rectangular structure extending from the slope. Continuing the line of this cross-slope bank was a further stone bank (*UF 215*), and beyond that the line was continued by a cairn (*UF 213*). These potentially reflect the relict elements of a field system, and though there was no direct relationship, it is probable that they were contemporary with the cairnfield.

Ulpha Fell XII (Rough Crag East): monuments *UF 217-78*

A group of small cairns, together with one larger cairn, extended over the western slopes of Rough Crag between the 300 m and 360 m contours (Fig 108). The small cairns numbered 58 in total and were found within three spatially discrete sub-groups.

The first sub-group (UF XIIA; Fig 110) comprised a number of moderately prominent cairns, with an average diameter of *c* 3.5 m, which were distributed around a sub-triangular area that was devoid of cairns. This cairn-free area was bounded to the north-west by a north-east/south-west band of cairns (Alignment A), to the south by a significant alignment of cairns (B), and to the east by a randomly distributed block of cairns (*UF 231-45*). The cairn-free area was 1 ha in extent and potentially defined an agricultural plot.

The second cairn sub-group (UF XIIB) was located between the 340 m and 350 m contours. This group was characterised by a number of particularly small and low-lying cairns, on average little more than 2.5 m in diameter, with the smallest having a diameter of 1.6 m. There were no obvious cairn alignments and the distribution would appear to have been essentially random.

The third cairn sub-group (UF XIIC) was the most northerly and comprised well-defined cairns that were on average 3 m in diameter, although one (*UF 270*) was 5.3 m long. All of the cairns were moderately prominent. There was one significant alignment of cairns (C), which was orientated north-west/south-east.

Lying in between the cairn sub-groups was a larger cairn (*UF 247*), which was at least 50 m away from the nearest small cairn. This was well defined (12.9 x 9.9 x 1 m), had a kerb of small stones, a small depression in the centre, and a modern cairn on top. Its size, location, kerb, and height would suggest that it was a funerary monument. In addition to the large cairn, two sections of stone bank (*UF 246* and *UF 248*) formed part of a single boundary that extended through the site. The stone banks were turf covered, *c* 1.5 m wide, and discontinuous in places, but, when combined, could be traced for a total length of 450 m. This boundary was aligned on the large cairn (*UF 247*) and the westernmost stone bank (*UF 246*) butted against it.

Discussion

The archaeological significance of UF XII is emphasised by the interesting sequence of stone banks and cairns. The long boundary (*UF 246/8*) butted against the large cairn and was clearly later. Similarly, it extended directly through the cairnfield at an oblique angle to the northern band of cairns, and cut through the putative plot; there was no physical relationship with any of the cairns and it would appear to have post-dated the abandonment of the cairnfield. The alignment lay at a slightly oblique angle, some 290 m to the south of the parish boundary dividing Ulpha from Birker Fell (Fig 106), which was clearly a territorial boundary of some antiquity, and this configuration suggests that the wall pre-dated the boundary.

Overall, the groups of small cairns centred on large cairn *UF 247*, which was probably a Bronze Age funerary monument. While there was no direct relationship between this monument and the cairns sufficient to confirm contemporaneity, it is probable that the cairn was a major feature in what was probably a prehistoric landscape.

Ulpha Fell XIII (Winds Gate): monuments *UF 279-99*

A group of 21 small cairns lay between the 270 m and 320 m contours on a west-facing slope, *c* 200 m north-east of Winds Gate, and extended *c* 280 m from north to south (Fig 108). There were no associated stone banks or other features. The cairns were prominent, generally well defined, and varied in size (diameters of 3-6 m). There was a north-west/south-east cairn alignment (A; Fig 110), and a band extended east from its southernmost point. This band of cairns/cairn alignment did not reflect a random distribution, but at the same time did not adequately define the extent of a possible plot.

Conclusions

The Ulpha Fell survey area was defined by an arbitrary boundary, which encompassed 13 apparently unrelated cairnfields or settlement groups. These in effect reflect the southern extension of the landscape recorded on Birkby and Birker Fells (*p 197*). The spacing between sites observed on Birkby and Birker Fells could

also be seen when examining the relationships between those further south, at Sike Moss (UF VII), Brown Rigg east (UF IX) and south (UF X), Rough Crag east (UF XI) and west (UF XII), and Winds Gate (UF XIII).

Although the character of the cairnfield groups displayed some considerable similarity, they did not form the constituent parts of a more complex site, such as that identified on Corney Fell or Stainton Fell (*Ch 4, pp 139, 167*). Instead, they appear to have been for the most part small, localised areas of cairnfield where the cairns were randomly distributed, although there were occasionally indistinct areas within the cairnfields that were devoid of cairns. There were rarely more-developed indicators of field systems and at only two of the sites were there apparently domestic structures. In general, they appeared to reflect the spatially localised, and possibly short-lived, areas of improved land associated with primary forest clearance.

Several putative funerary monuments were associated with the cairnfields. These were typically larger, more prominent, and better defined (often with kerbs) than their clearance cairn counterparts; they also were typically located in more remote positions. The classic example was cairn *UF 247* (UF XII; *see above*), which was both large and prominent, had a kerb, and was between three groups of cairns. Further examples were cairns *UF 63* ((UF III; *p 228*), *UF 142* (UF VII; *p 230*), and *UF 200* (UF X; *p 232*), all of which were situated on the same gently sloping ground as the adjacent cairnfield. These appear to demonstrate a practice of burial within the broad confines of settlement/farming areas, contrasting with the alternative tradition of burying the dead on summits or exposed locations.

One other feature of interest was the wall (*UF 248; see above*) between the large cairns on Rough Crag and Brown Rigg south, which had a similar appearance and weathering to the cairns, but clearly post-dated the adjacent cairnfields. The date of this monument is unknown, as it also appeared to have no relation to any medieval farming areas, nor did it relate to the probably historical boundary between Birker and Ulpha parishes. It did not enclose land, or relate to any identified field system, and was thus potentially a territorial boundary. The survey of the Lake District Fells as a whole has provided very little evidence for such features, the only comparable example on the South-West Fells being the long length of walling (*TF 1*) to the west of groups of small cairns on Thwaites Fell (*p 254*).

Crosbythwaite

North and north-west of Crosbythwaite Farm (SD 190 950), on either side of Crosby Gill, were two settlement areas (CT I (Crosby Gill) and CT II (Crosbythwaite), which were on gently sloping ground, both within the extent of Parliamentary enclosures (Fig 111; Pl 133); however, both sites were outside the primary intake of Crosbythwaite and the adjacent Brighouse Farm. The eastern site (CT II) was one of the most complex sites recorded during the LDNPS and would appear to reflect a multi-phased settlement and field system.

Archaeological history
The Crosbythwaite settlement appears to have had a long and multi-phased history. However, the earliest historical indication of activity in the area derives from place-name evidence. The '-by' element of the Crosbythwaite name means village or hamlet, and is primarily of Old Norse origin (Armstrong *et al* 1950). Similarly, the '-thwaite' element of the name means a clearing, and also has an Old Norse origin (*ibid*). The earliest identified documentary record for Crosbythwaite is from the accounts of lands belonging to a Madam Bridget Hudleston (1645-1715) of Millom Castle, who held the Crosbythwaite Farm in 1702 (Jones

1966, 316). The Hodgkinson and Donald map of Cumberland (1770/1) depicted both Crosbythwaite and Brighouse Farms and showed that the road to Eskdale became unfenced immediately north of Crosbythwaite Farm; evidently the area of the Crosbythwaite settlement (CT II) was not within enclosed land at that date. By the time of the 1867 First Edition 6" to 1 mile OS map, however, the site was within the extent of the Parliamentary enclosure. The large field to the south of the settlement is called Brighouse Intake and would indicate that historically the fields containing the CT II site were within the ownership of Brighouse Farm, rather than the nearer Crosbythwaite Farm. The earliest archaeological recording of the Crosbythwaite landscape was by Cherry (1961), who identified CT II as being a 'complicated site', which may have been a 'farm' prior to the present-day farm in this area.

The survey area
The survey, covering 0.95 km², was undertaken in April 1983 (Fig 112), and recorded a total of 370 monuments within two site groups (CT I and CT II; Fig 113). These comprised two settlements, both with field systems, pastoral enclosures, and apparently domestic structures. The Crosbythwaite site (CT II) was an extremely complex multi-phased settlement, incorporating two settlement areas, an interlinked field system, and a series of cultivation terraces.

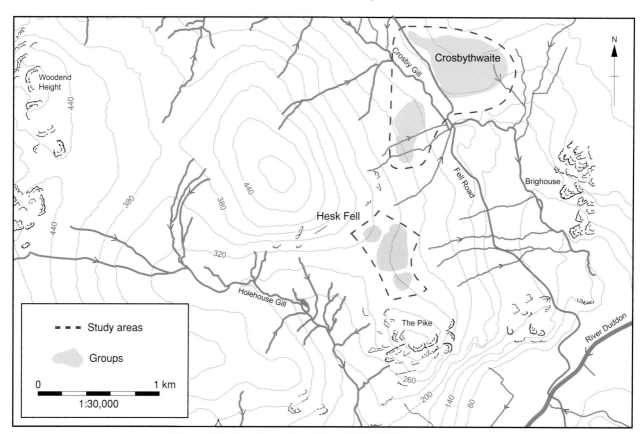

Figure 111: The Crosbythwaite and Hesk Fell survey areas

234

Plate 133: The enclosed land and open fell above Crosbythwaite, looking east

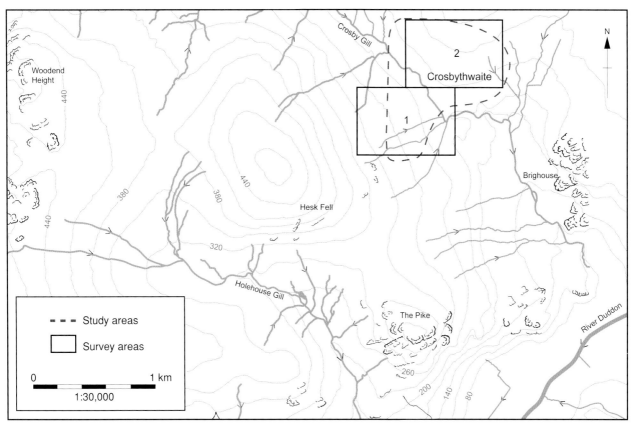

Figure 112: The Crosbythwaite survey area as planned

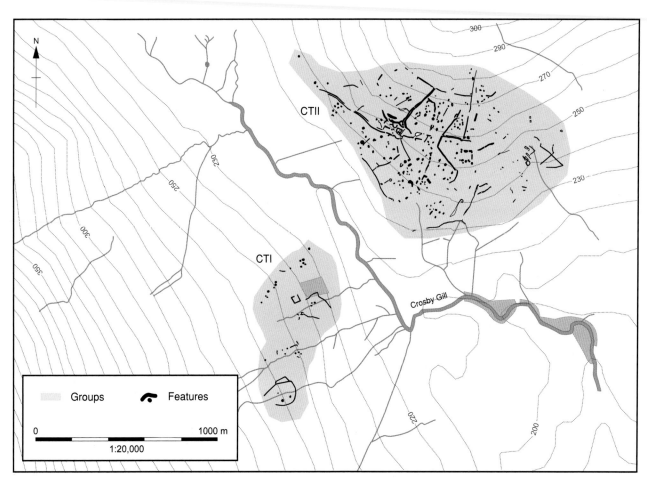

Figure 113: Monument distribution within the Crosbythwaite survey area

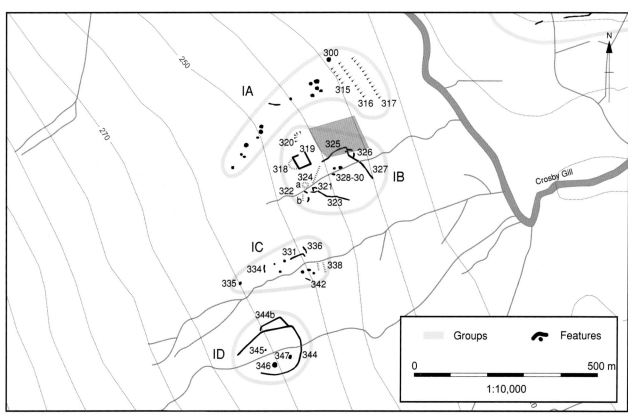

Figure 114: The CT I settlement and cairnfields

The survey area was originally part of the Ulpha survey area (*p 224*), hence the site numbers sequentially follow those of Ulpha Fell; however, the sites were very distinct in terms of location and character, and have therefore been described separately. In addition to these groups, there were also a few scattered ungrouped cairns and banks, which are not individually described within this volume.

Crosbythwaite I (Crosby Gill): monuments *CT 300-47*

This site group contained four distinct monument sub-groups, which lay between the 230 m and 270 m contours on an east-facing slope to the west of Crosby Gill (Fig 113). The first monument sub-group (CT IA; Fig 114) was located to the north of a modern plantation and comprised 14 small cairns extending in an east/west band down the slope. The cairns varied in size (with diameters of 3.5-6.5 m), with the largest being at the base of the slope. Just below these was a series of probable lynchets set along the slope (*CT 315-17*), and associated with these lynchets was a single clearance cairn (*CT 300*).

The second monument sub-group (CT IB) was found to the south, upslope of the plantation, and comprised two building platforms of similar size (*CT 318* and *CT 320*). The northernmost platform (*CT 320*) was rectangular (9.2 x 8.8 m) and was terraced into the slope; the southern platform (*CT 318*) was well defined by banks to the west and south (10.8 x 7 m), with a short section of wall surviving in the north-west/north-north-west corner. Platform *CT 318* was immediately adjacent to an approximately square stock enclosure, with an entrance on the north side (*CT 319*); the walls were composed of rubble contained between two faces of large stones, a constructional technique normally associated with medieval or post-medieval structures (LUAU 1997f). Running through the stock enclosure was a stone drain.

To the south of the building platform, and also associated with this second monument sub-group, was a large, slightly irregularly shaped enclosure (*CT 323-5*), which had an open side to the south-east. The southern side (*CT 323*) was turf covered, the north-western side (*CT 324*), being ill defined, survived as a terrace edge, but to the north it comprised a wall foundation of boulders (*CT 325*), generally one course high, with a similar appearance and weathering to the nearby small cairns. The modern course of the beck cut this latter section. Towards the centre of the enclosure were three small cairns (*CT 328-30*). On the north-eastern side of the enclosure was a small, subsidiary half-circular enclosure, with a possible entrance to the north-east (*CT 326*), and opposite, inside the main enclosure, was a rectangular terraced platform, with large boulders in the outer bank (*CT 327*). The enclosed area measured 10 x 5.5 m, with an entrance

on the south-east side. At the south-western corner of the enclosure was a series of building platforms (*CT 322*). The northernmost of these was a well-defined square platform (*c* 8 x 6 m), defined by a terrace to the north and west, and a bank to the south and east (*CT 322a*). To the south, and set against the northern platform, was a second platform (*CT 322b*), with an oval plan, partly defined by terraced banks, but also by two sections of wall. A further structure (*CT 321*) was in the south-west angle of the main enclosure, just below terrace *CT 322b*. This possibly pre-dated the enclosure, thus accounting for a kink in the enclosure's plan at this point, which was defined by a 1.5 m-wide wall, that had a possible entrance to the east. A beck now flows through *CT 321*, which has eroded the physical remains of this monument.

The third monument sub-group (CT IC) lay some 200 m to the south-west of CT IB, and was characterised by cairns and fragments of walling, close to a second stream descending to Crosby Gill. Seven small cairns and four apparently unconnected sections of stone bank were recorded, the two sections of stone bank to the west (*CT 334* and *CT 331*) being made up of relatively large boulders, while those to the east were constructed of smaller stones (*CT 336* and *CT 342*). To the south was a possible building platform (*CT 338*), measuring 7 x 4.1 m in extent, which was set into the slope, with an apron to the east.

A further 200 m to the south was the fourth monument sub-group (CT ID), which comprised a large D-shaped walled enclosure (*CT 344*; 86 x 65 m). The 1.3 m-wide walls were of weathered medium to large boulders protruding through the turf, and masonry was exposed on the north-west and south-east sides; there was a broad entrance to the west. On the north side was an annexe (*CT 344b*), which was of similar construction and dimensions to the main enclosure, and also had an entrance to the west. Inside the main enclosure were three small cairns (*CT 345-7*). The size and shape of the enclosure were very similar to those of the D-shaped enclosure at Little Crag (UF II; *p 228*), which measured *c* 90 x 70 m and was also associated with cairns. The only significant difference between the two enclosures was the annex associated with that at Crosbythwaite (*CT 344*).

Crosbythwaite II (Crosbythwaite): monuments *CT 350-648*

The CT II monument group was extremely complex (Fig 113), and for ease of description it has been divided into discrete areas, for the most part based around a field system centred on the westernmost settlement found in this area (Fig 115). However, this field system had been imposed onto a series of earlier remains, and therefore the division of the descriptive areas is essentially arbitrary for the earlier periods.

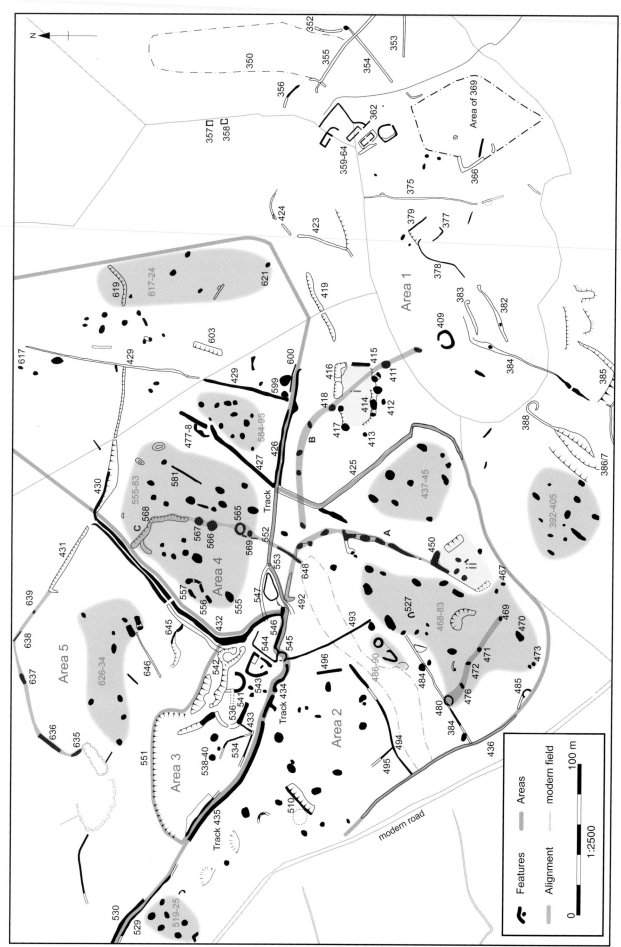

Figure 115: The CT II settlements and field system

238

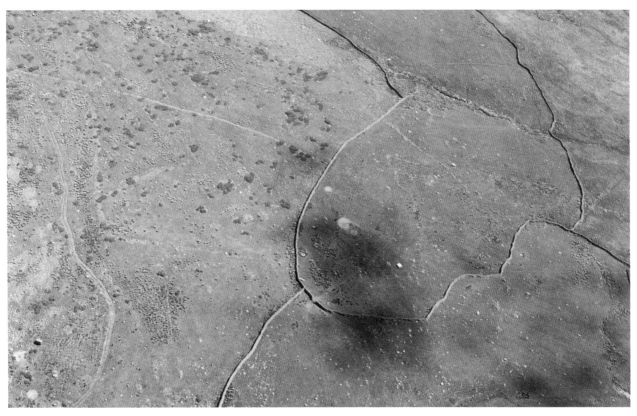

Plate 134: The CT II field system, and the eastern part of the site (Area 1)

Area 1 (*CT 350-424*)

Area 1 was the eastern part of the site, centred on a settlement composed of rectilinear structures (*CT 359-64*), and includes what was apparently an associated field system (Pl 134). It was bounded to the west by a field (Area 2) relating to the western settlement (Area 3) and was defined by a line of boundary banks (*CT 425*) and cairns (*CT 467, CT 469, CT 470,* and *CT 473*). Further north, it was edged by the north-eastern field (Area 4) of the western settlement, defined by boundary bank *CT 426*, and a line extending to the south of the southernmost cairn within that group (*CT 621*).

The area comprised a series of mainly north-east/south-west cultivation terraces that appeared to form a coherent system, extending out from the settlement (*CT 359-64*). For the most part, the boundaries were walls, but in the eastern part of the area was a system of banks/ditches (*CT 352-6*), which followed a comparable orientation.

The rectilinear settlement

Towards the north end of Area 1 was one of the better-preserved farmstead complexes in Cumbria (Fig 116). The settlement was located on a raised area on the side of a shallow gully immediately adjacent to its spring. Two of the houses (*CT 359* and *CT 361*) were overlain by the walls of the extant field system, and clearly the settlement had been abandoned by the time this was established.

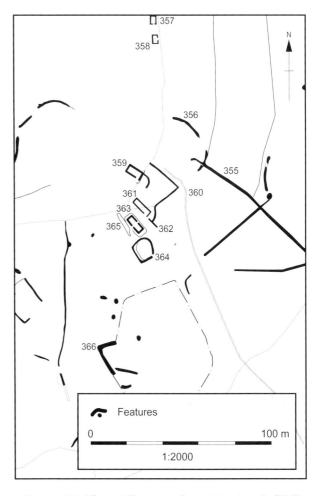

Figure 116: The rectilinear settlement in Area I, CT II

239

The central feature was a house (*CT 363*; 10 x 4.2 m) set on a raised rectangular platform (Pl 135). Its 0.8 m-thick foundations were of massive boulders, and it had centrally placed, opposing doorways. To the north-east were two further buildings of similar construction; the nearer (*CT 361*) had similar dimensions, but an entrance close to the south-west angle. The building beyond (*CT 359*) also had an entrance at the south-west angle, but its primary cell was slightly smaller (9 x 4.7 m), although it appears to have had an extension to the south-east. To the south was a sub-rectangular stone-walled and heavily terraced enclosure and possible putative building platform (*CT 364*), with an entrance in the south-east corner (Pl 136). Given its heavy terracing, it is probable that this was a platform for a building, the maximum dimensions of which were 9 x 7 m.

Extending around the eastern side of the settlement was the wall of a rectilinear 'courtyard' (*CT 362*), and a further bank on the western side (*CT 365*) would appear to have defined, at least in part, the western side of this 'courtyard'. A single sherd of thirteenth-/fourteenth-century pottery, part of a jug, came from a molehill 13 m to the east of *CT 364*.

To the north of the main settlement were two further rectilinear structures, immediately adjacent to a current field boundary (*CT 357-8*; Fig 115). They were very similar in form, built of dry-stone masonry walls in moderately good condition, and were both relatively small (*CT 357*: 4.9 x 3.6 m; *CT 358*: 5.0 x 3.5 m). They were spatially remote from the Area 1 field system, and their relatively

Plate 135: House CT 363, *in the rectilinear settlement, looking north*

small size distinguished them from the structures of the rectilinear settlement. There is therefore a possibility that they provided temporary, or transhumant, accommodation, and were not necessarily contemporary with the main settlement.

Plate 136: Terraced platform CT 364, *in the rectilinear settlement*

The northern field system

To the north-east of the small stream adjacent to the settlement was a series of banks and ditches forming the boundaries of a coherent field system. The primary boundary (*CT 355*) was parallel to the stream, the field system to the south-west of the settlement (*CT 366*), and also to the 'courtyard' boundary (*CT 360*). In addition, the stub of a bank extended south-west from bank *CT 355* towards the eastern angle of the 'courtyard', and then in a curve (*CT 356*) towards the present-day field boundary; this potentially would have defined a small field extending north from the 'courtyard'. This field system clearly related directly to the adjacent settlement. Extending north from boundary bank *CT 355* was an area of broad ridge and furrow (*CT 350*; Fig 115), although no headland was discerned.

The southern field system

To the south of the farmstead, the limits of an area of ridge and furrow (*CT 369*; Fig 115) and a boundary wall (*CT 366*) marked the extent of a small field, parallel to the northern field system, and approximately orientated on a further field to the west of the settlement (*CT 379*). Between these two putative fields was a long, relict boundary wall (*CT 375*), which was orientated at an oblique angle to the two small fields and extended up to the present-day field boundary. This wall was almost certainly a later element of the landscape and possibly a predecessor to the present-day field system.

The small field to the south-west of the settlement was defined by two walls (*CT 377* and *CT 379*) and had a lynchet along its upper side (Pl 137). This was linked to a series of cultivation terraces (*CT 382-4*) to the west by curvilinear wall *CT 379*, which was composed of massive stones. Terraced bank *CT 382* was in line with wall *CT 379*. In general, the walls of this small field comprised substantial amounts of large stones, but very few cairns were found within its vicinity, suggesting that the walls were being used to absorb cleared stone. The terraces comprised a series of parallel strips with smooth, improved, once-cultivated land in between. Clearance stone had been deposited in substantial mounds along the terrace edges. Extending from the uppermost terrace was a long bank (*CT 384*), which converged with a large rectangular cultivation terrace (*CT 385*) at the southern edge of the complex; this latter feature had a very smooth interior and had clearly been substantially improved/cultivated.

Parallel to, and to the west of, large terrace *CT 385* was a series of parallel strips (*CT 386/7*) which, for the most part, extended across the contours. The upper end of terrace *CT 386* curved around a small circular terraced platform (*CT 388*), which had almost certainly been a building.

Immediately to the west of cultivated strips *CT 386/7* was a group of 12 large cairns (*CT 392-405*), which were mostly orientated downslope. The cairns reflected localised clearance and had an uncertain relationship

Plate 137: Plot CT 377, *looking south-east, with the lynchet (foreground) along its upper side*

241

with the adjacent terraces. There was a substantial gap between this cairn group and those in Area 2, and they did not appear to reflect contemporary clearance episodes.

The northern cultivation terrace

To the west of the rectilinear settlement was a large rectangular terraced platform edged by substantial banks, incorporating large cairns (*CT 414-17*), which suggested considerable amounts of clearance, with material being deposited around the outside of the terrace. The surface of the terrace was smooth, and stone free, clearly having been subject both to improvement and cultivation. Around its outside were a few additional cairns (*CT 411-13* and *CT 418*). Considerable effort had clearly been employed in creating and clearing the terrace, particularly as it formed a relatively small plot (*i*), which contrasted with a nearby terrace (*CT 425*) that edged a much more substantial field. Given its size and the effort involved in its construction, it probably indicates kitchen-garden-type cultivation. Extending east from the upper bank (*CT 416*) was a further lynchet (*CT 419*) that itself fed into bank *CT 424* (Fig 115). This curved downslope, and was orientated with the 'courtyard' boundary of the rectilinear settlement (*CT 362*). Lynchet *CT 419* was parallel to terraces *CT 382* and *CT 383*, and it is tempting to speculate that both this and the terraced plot (*CT 414-17*) were components of a field system that related to the rectilinear settlement.

Platform/roundhouse CT 409

To the west of the settlement was a small sub-circular embanked enclosure (*CT 409*), roughly 13 m in diameter, with an entrance on the northern, upper side; it had an internally raised, levelled platform and was probably constructed for domestic purposes (Pl 138). As all other elements within Area 1 were consistent with medieval cultivation, or were related to the rectilinear settlement (with the possible exception of cairns *CT 392-405*), this platform formed something of an anomaly, in that it had the characteristics of a prehistoric structure. It may potentially, therefore, be an indication of earlier activity in this area.

Area 2 (*CT 425* and *CT 437-529*)

Area 2 (Fig 115) was defined by field boundaries that extended from the western settlement (Area 3). The northern edge of the area was marked by track *CT 435*, leading west from the Area 3 settlement towards Eskdale, and also the east/west track that led eastwards (*CT 552*). The eastern boundary was a large terraced bank (*CT 425*) that merged into a modern field wall to the south, the southern boundary being defined by the limit of a cairn group (*CT 468-83*), and the western side was defined by a long lyncheted bank (*CT 436*), which was approximately parallel to the modern road. The archaeology in Area 2 was made up of several discrete elements, which included cairn groups; stone banks; cultivation plots; and long boundary banks.

Eastern cairn group

The easternmost cairns (*CT 437-45*) were extremely large and prominent, forming a discrete group on the basis of their character and spatial extent. They were situated below and to the south of a major terraced bank (*CT 425*) and it is perhaps significant that there was no spread of cairns on the north-eastern side

Plate 138: Roundhouse CT 409, looking north-east

of this feature. The ground in the vicinity of the cairns was relatively smooth, and devoid of surface stone, although part of the area was covered with gorse. It is possible that the large size of the cairns reflected the deposition of clearance stone brought up by the cultivation of the land downslope of terraced bank *CT 425*. The essentially random distribution of the cairns would appear at odds with the terraced field in which they were found, and the considerable effort that had been employed to improve this land. One possibility is that the cairns pre-dated the bank, but had been enhanced by later land improvement. If this was the case, it would imply that the area to the north-east of terrace *CT 425* had been cleared of cairns to allow cultivation on the land above it.

Central cairn group
Within the central part of Area 2 was an amorphous distribution of cairns (*CT 468-83* and *CT 486-90*), both large and small. To the north-west, the distribution was, in part, limited by a natural rubble spread, and to the south it stopped well short (*CT 469*, *CT 471*, *CT 472*, and *CT 476*) of the western field boundary (*CT 436*). The eastern side of the cairn group was defined by a long stone bank, formed by substantial cairns (Alignment A) extending north-east from an apparent plot (*CT 450; ii*). These cairns created an extended curving path terminating at the boundary extending east from the Area 3 settlement area (*CT 492*). A further, very putative, cairn alignment (B) extended from this primary stone bank into Area 1, close to the division between Areas 3 and 4, and terminated at platform *CT 409* in Area 1 (*p 242*). It is therefore possible that cairn Alignment B linked platform *CT 409* with the cairn group in Area 2.

Also within the central cairn group were three annular features that could potentially have been roundhouses, of which the most clearly defined was *CT 480*, which had a diameter of 7.5 m, with an entrance to the south-west. It was internally terraced and therefore was almost certainly a domestic structure. Further north-east was a second annular feature (*CT 527*), also internally terraced but less well defined, and in the southern part of the group was a third sub-circular feature (*CT 485*), from which the lyncheted bank (*CT 436*) extended.

Western cairn group
The cairn group to the west of the rubble spread was of a much lower density than the central group, although there was one small group of six cairns (*CT 519-25*) in the north-western part, which was relatively compact. As with the central group, there was considerable variation in the size of the cairns, but many were large, reflecting the considerable amounts of land improvement in the area.

Rectilinear field system
Extending across the centre of Area 2 was a series of parallel stone banks (*CT 484*, *CT 494-6*, and *CT 510*), which appeared to form a coherent field system, although they varied in definition, as is typical of many of the stone banks recorded during the survey. Banks *CT 484* and *CT 494* extended north-east from lynchet boundary *CT 436*, towards bank *CT 493*, which led to a putative roundhouse (*CT 545*) in the western settlement (Area 3; *see below*). The two parallel banks (*CT 484* and *CT 494*) were set perpendicular to *CT 436*, whilst bank *CT 493* was parallel to this, and together they created a rectangular pattern to the field system, defined ultimately by *CT 436* and apparently also by bank *CT 425*. Significantly, the banks, particularly *CT 484*, overlay cairns and also a putative roundhouse (*CT 480*), and were therefore later components of this landscape.

Area 3 (*CT 530-53*)
Area 3 comprised the western settlement and the focus for the field system within Areas 2, 4, and 5 (Fig 115). It was situated on level ground at the foot of a substantial scarp slope; the area was in part a natural terrace, but may have been enhanced by a build-up of material along the line of the tracks (*CT 434* and *CT 435*) on the forward apron of the terrace. The area was defined naturally to the north by the scarp slope (*CT 551* and *CT 542*), which had in part been cut back to allow for a hollow-way (*CT 432*) to extend north-east from the settlement. The terrace and scarp slope extended down to the line of a trackway (*CT 434-5*), which ran through the settlement, with a substantial bank on the downslope side.

The nucleus of the settlement was a three-sided enclosure (*CT 543*; Fig 117) situated at the junction of the trackways leading from the east, north, and west. The entrance was to the east, opening onto the main north/south hollow-way (*CT 432*). The enclosure was internally terraced and its external walls were 1.5 m wide and prominent. Within the enclosure were the foundations of a small rectangular structure, and possibly a second structure in the north-east corner, defined by a possible rubble spread.

To the east of both this and the north/south track was a level area (*CT 544*), possibly a field, bounded by the foundation of a terraced stone wall on the west and the terraced bank bounding Area 4 to the east. At the southern edge of this area was a circular, internally terraced, ring bank, probably a roundhouse (*CT 545*). Its entrance led onto the north/south trackway (*CT 432*) and it was at the head of an east/west trackway (*CT 434-5*) leading from the north-west of Eskdale (*p 244*).

Field *CT 544* defined the eastern extent of a yard, which was edged by scarp slope *CT 542* to the north,

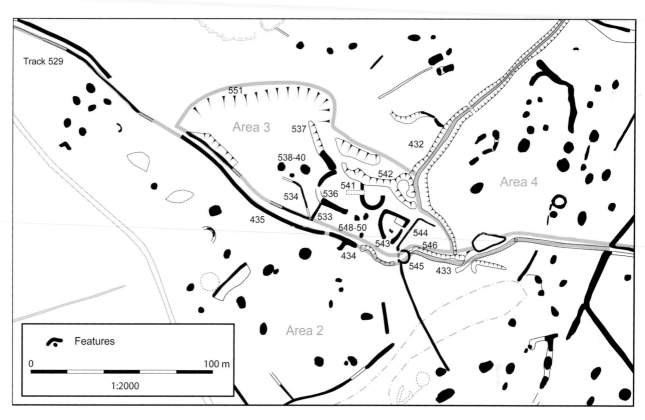

Figure 117: The western settlement, Area 3, CT II

banks *CT 533* and *CT 536* to the west, and the terraced track, *CT 434*, to the south. Enclosure *CT 543* was at the eastern end of this area and the rest of the area was occupied by cairns, stubs of wall, and a semi-circular structure (*CT 541*), butting against the northern scarp slope. This latter structure was not internally terraced and was very wet; it thus did not seem to have been for domestic purposes, but could potentially have been used for stock control. Set into the western side of the yard (overlying *CT 536*) was a modern sheepfold, which had disturbed the surrounding structures and also confused their interpretation. Set above the yard was a sub-circular terraced platform (*CT 542*), which had an entrance opening out onto north/south hollow-way *CT 432*. West of the sheepfold, and bounded by the trackway to the south (*CT 435*) and the scarp slope to the north (*CT 551*), was an area that was seemingly an enclosed field adjacent to the settlement. The only features recorded there were a fragment of wall (*CT 534*) and three clearance cairns.

The trackway west of the settlement
The trackway (*CT 434-5*) leading from the north-west entered the fields to the west, and was clearly visible between two low stone banks or walls for a distance of *c* 240 m west of the settlement. The trackway had been terraced into the slope and, particularly in the area adjacent to the settlement, there was a marked break of slope to the south. It seemingly terminated at the entrance to roundhouse *CT 545*, where it

converged with hollow-way *CT 432* from the north (*p 243*). The relationship between this track and that to the east remains uncertain, but it potentially extended initially south via a gap between putative roundhouse *CT 545* and bank *CT 434*. A further possible section of trackway zig-zagged up the scarp slope to the north of the settlement, above terraced platform *CT 542*, leading from the yard area up to Area 5 (*p 246*).

Area 4 (*CT 555-625*)
Area 4 was defined for the most part by the boundaries that extended from the western settlement (Area 3), forming a rectangular field (Fig 115). The western boundary was the hollow-way (*CT 432*), which opened out onto the open fell, and from there a former head dyke extended east (*CT 430/619*), defining the northern side of the field. The hollow-way (*CT 432*) was one of the more substantial components of the landscape and allowed for the movement of stock from the settlement onto the open fell (Pl 139). The eastern extent of the area was not defined by a field boundary, but has been taken as the easternmost extent of a group of cairns and banks (*CT 617-24*). The southernmost extent of the field was the east/west track (*CT 426* and *CT 552*) extending from the settlement in Area 3.

Within the field were substantial numbers of cairns, which varied in size, but generally were large and indicated considerable clearance activity from the immediate locale. The westernmost group of cairns (*CT 555-83*) had an erratic and apparently random

Plate 139: Hollow-way CT 432, leading from the western settlement (Area 3; centre), looking south

distribution. Furthermore, this distribution was not precisely constrained by the boundaries of the field, and therefore there was no obvious contemporary relationship between two. Extending through the cairn group was what was possibly a significant cairn alignment (Alignment C), which may have reflected a former boundary. Its uppermost section was a lyncheted bank (*CT 568*), which extended from the hollow-way (*CT 432*) and curved round to the south; its line was continued by cairns *CT 566-7*, *CT 569*, and stone bank *CT 648*, which terminated at stone bank *CT 450-9* in Area 2. This putative boundary crossed trackway *CT 552*, suggesting that it pre-dated this feature. One of the monuments within the alignment was a circular, internally terraced, platform (*CT 565*), which was perhaps a building platform. In the western part of the cairn group, a series of conjoined cairns (*CT 556* and *CT 557*) was identified, which enclosed a terraced area that may have been a small plot.

The central cairn group comprised a compact area of much smaller cairns (*CT 584-95*), the distribution of which was apparently constrained by adjacent boundary bank *CT 427*, although their precise relationship with this bank is uncertain. The eastern cairn group was a much more amorphous scatter, generally smaller and less well defined than their

counterparts in the central and western groups. The cairns extended in a north-west/south-east line up the fell and, significantly, this took them across the head dyke boundary (*CT 430*) defining the upper limit of the Area 4 field, which would suggest that the cairns pre-dated the field.

While the principal features defining the extent of Area 4 and the apparent field were hollow-way *CT 432*, head dyke *CT 430*, and trackway *CT 426/552*, there were also additional boundary banks which had an uncertain relationship with those of the field. The most substantial was *CT 427*, which was a very substantial terraced bank, and was a continuation of *CT 425* to the south. It was parallel to the line of hollow-way *CT 432*, but did not extend as far as head dyke *CT 430*, so some uncertainty remains as to the relationship with the field. The northern section of the boundary was parallel and equally spaced from two other lyncheted banks within the area (*CT 581* and *CT 603*), raising the possibility that they were related. A further boundary bank (*CT 429*) extended north from trackway *CT 426*, but overlay a cairn (*CT 599*) at its southern end, cut through head dyke *CT 430*, and also extended through the eastern cairn group. It would, therefore, appear to be one of the later features within the area.

The latest feature in the landscape was clearly the modern field boundary, which extended north-west/south-east through the area and linked into a common head dyke that was part of the extant pattern of Parliamentary field enclosure along the north side of Dunnerdale. However, since this boundary was not depicted on the 1900 Second Edition 6" to 1 mile OS map, it clearly had a twentieth-century construction date, and was therefore not constructed as part of the Parliamentary enclosure movement. Despite its relatively late date, it was ruinous and survived only as a foundation.

Trackway CT 426/552

Substantial trackway *CT 426/552* defined the southern part of the field in Area 4. To the east of bank *CT 427* it was revetted, with a substantial drop on the downslope side, but to the west it was more indistinct, extending above terrace *CT 553*, although it seemed to have diverted around both sides of an indistinct, sub-triangular platform (*CT 547*). The line to the south dropped down between terraced banks *CT 434* and *CT 492* and it was there orientated on roundhouse *CT 545*. The northern element of *CT 426* followed along the northern side of platform *CT 547*, before leading down terrace edge *CT 600*. These sections of track contrasted markedly with the well-constructed trackway (*CT 435*) to the west of the settlement, which was integral to the field system and settlement. Instead, the eastern track (*CT 552*) diverted awkwardly around and over components of the western settlement and its field system and may, therefore, have post-dated these features. The eastern section also appeared to cut through boundary terrace *CT 427*, which was of uniform construction on both sides of the track. The only feature it appeared to be contemporary with was north/south wall *CT 429*, which was clearly a late feature in the complex.

Area 5 (*CT 626-47*)

Area 5 lay to the north of Area 3 and formed a field defined by boundaries extending from this settlement (Fig 115). The field was edged to the east by hollow-way *CT 432*, which then turned to the north-west to form a head dyke (*CT 431*). The extension of the head dyke was defined by a curved alignment of cairns and stone banks *CT 635-9*, the former butting onto a large outcrop to the west. The southern extent of the field was defined by the scarp slope dividing it from the settlement, and also western trackway *CT 530*. The interior of the field had been improved, and was gently sloping, smooth ground, with relatively little surface stone, edged by substantial breaks of slope (*CT 551*). Inside were fragments of walls (*CT 646*), lynchets (*CT 645*), and at least ten cairns (*CT 626-34*).

Conclusions
CT I

The complex sequences that seem to have underlain CT I were not easily discerned, and, in addition, the four monument sub-groups identified in this area (CT IA-D; Fig 114) were very different in character, and were not necessarily contemporary. For instance, D-shaped enclosure *CT 344* (*p 237*) comprised well-defined continuous walling, and was clearly for stock, and this was distinct in character from the more erratic enclosure (*CT 323-5*) found to the north (in CT IB; *p 237*). This enclosure was defined by a stone bank and was associated with up to five sub-circular and sub-rectangular building platforms (*CT 321*, *CT 322a*, *CT 322b*, *CT 326*, and *CT 327*; Fig 114); it would therefore appear to have formed a small settlement. Similarly, the cairn groups in CT I had a marked linear spread and had no direct association with the other groups. Significantly, the northernmost cairn group (CT IA), was spatially associated with strip lynchets, which are more typical of medieval cultivation, but it is not known if these were contemporary with the cairns.

D-shaped enclosure *CT 344* also had a marked similarity to a D-shaped enclosure (*UF 54*) to the north, on Ulpha Fell (*p 228*). Both were of similar shape and size, with enclosure *UF 54* having a long axis 90 m long, whilst the long axis of enclosure *CT 344* measured 86 m. Both enclosures also incorporated walls, as opposed to stone banks, neither had any associated buildings, and both had an association with small numbers of cairns. There was also a similarity between these two enclosures and the slightly larger D-shaped enclosure (*HE 46*) found on Hesk Fell (*p 251*), although the Hesk Fell enclosure differed slightly, in that it had structures set into its corners. Given their similarities, all of these enclosures were almost certainly originally used for stock control. They also appear to form a distinct type, and may have been broadly contemporary, though none has been excavated and their precise date is unknown. The *UF 54* enclosure, however, was overlain by the wall of a squatter-type intake extending from the primary ring garth of Birkerthwaite and, as such a wall is likely to be a later medieval or more probably post-medieval feature, then it is evident that this enclosure was older than the intake.

CT II

CT II was, with the possible exception of Barnscar (*Ch 4, p 178*), the most complex settlement site recorded by the LDNPS programme, and, indeed, of any known in the region more generally. Its complexity derives from what was evidently multi-phased activity, presumably over an extended period of time. An attempt has been made to rationalise this complexity and the remains have been tentatively arranged into five broad phases of activity (Fig 118). This development is presented from the earliest identified activity through to the present, and an attempt has been made to fit this into a chronological sequence.

Phase 1

The earliest phase of activity would appear to be represented by the cairns and their associated components, which comprised roundhouses (*CT 480* and *CT 565*) in Areas 2 and 4, a cultivated plot (*CT 450*), and also some long stone banks created by elongated cairns. There was, however, considerable commonality between this and the field divisions of Phase 2 (*p 248*), in part because the cairns had been adapted and enlarged over the life of the field system, and also because the cairns and associated stone banks appeared to relate to a precursor of the western settlement. In effect, Phases 1 and 2 are subdivisions of the extended life of the settlement and, as a consequence, defining a coherent relationship between them is difficult.

In Area 2, the cairns and a roundhouse (*CT 480*) were overlain by a series of field boundaries that extended from a long lynchet (*CT 436*), making up the south side of the Area 2 field, and the same boundaries

extended up to the southern side of the western settlement. Although the cairns clearly pre-dated parts of the field system, they did not necessarily pre-date all of this system. Also, in Area 2, a long stone bank (Alignment A) did seem to have a relationship with the cairns. This stone bank was lyncheted on its upper side and led to a terraced bank that converged with roundhouse *CT 545* in the area of the western settlement. This would indicate that there may have been a relationship between the cairns and the original western settlement; however, this boundary was not apparently contemporary with the adjacent terraced bank (*CT 425*) that formed a component of Phase 2. One possible cairn alignment (B) also extended from this stone bank (Alignment A) into Area 1, through the area of a terraced plot (*CT 414-17*), and converged with large roundhouse *CT 409* (*p 242*). Although this was defined by only a limited number of cairns, it would conveniently link the roundhouse to the cairnfield, the roundhouse being otherwise an incongruous element within a later field system (Phase 4, *p 248*).

In Area 4, an arcing stone bank/cairn alignment (C; *p 245*), extending from Area 2, seemingly terminated at hollow-way *CT 432*. The southernmost part of this alignment seemed either to cut stone

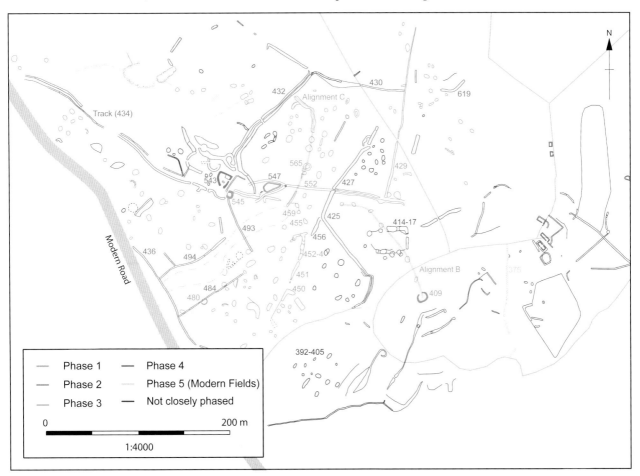

Figure 118: Phased development plan of the CT II settlements and field system

bank *CT 459* (Alignment A) or merge with it, but the precise relationship was uncertain. The fact that the northern end of this cairn alignment extended towards hollow-way *CT 432* raises the possibility that there was a return for the enclosure bank that followed the line of the later hollow-way. In this case, it would suggest that the hollow-way had its origins in Phase 1 but, as there was no hard evidence for this, it has been included in Phase 2. With a few notable exceptions, the cairn distributions did not appear to match the Phase 2 boundaries, notably in the eastern cairn group of Area 4, which extended north beyond the former head dyke (*CT 430/619*).

Phase 2
The Phase 2 remains include those monuments that formed a coherent field system, and also a number of inter-related monuments. However, although taken together these monuments do seemingly create a field system, it is entirely possible that some of the monuments had their origins in Phase 1. Those boundaries extending from the western settlement, unless they were clearly of Phase 1, have been defined as Phase 2, including the western track (*CT 434/5*), the southern field system (*CT 436*, *CT 484*, *CT 493*, and *CT 494*), hollow-way *CT 432*, and the associated former head dyke (*CT 430*). A greater problem is the phasing of bank *CT 425/7*, which did not directly relate to any of the other boundaries and had no direct link with the western settlement. However, its northern section (*CT 427*) was parallel with hollow-way *CT 432*, its lower section was parallel with boundaries *CT 436* and *CT 493* of the southern field system, and it turned towards *CT 436*, and hence was probably a component of this field system.

The western settlement contained two possible domestic structures, one an unenclosed roundhouse (*CT 545*; Fig 117) and the other a more complex rectilinear structure, within a sub-triangular enclosure (*CT 543*). These two very different structures almost certainly reflect different periods of settlement and, given that there were two different phases of field system, both converging on the western settlement area, it is possible that there was also multi-phased settlement within Area 3.

The relationship between Phases 1 and 2 is certainly anomalous. For example, terraced bank *CT 425* did not directly relate to nearby stone bank *CT 450-5* (Alignment A), although an interconnecting bank (*CT 456*) did partially link the systems. There were several large cairns below the bank, but none above, which may suggest that the distribution of the cairns was constrained by this terraced boundary. However, the land above may have been deliberately cleared of cairns for cultivation, and certainly the ground surface there was smooth and stone-free, as if had been subject

to land improvement. Similarly, a concentration of cairns was noted below the upper terrace (*CT 427*) but there was a marked absence above. At present, it is not possible to establish reliably whether the cairns preceded the terraced bank or were built after it, and thus the cairns have not been phased.

Both the Phase 1 and 2 field systems focused on the western settlement (Area 3). It is therefore tempting to postulate that each of the two domestic structures there (*CT 545* and *CT 543*), which were of very different character, related to a different phase of the field system. It is probable that rectangular structure *CT 543* related to Phase 2, and that the roundhouse (*CT 545*) was part of the earliest activity, particularly as several other unenclosed roundhouses within the LDNPS were found to have had a direct relationship with cairnfields.

Phase 3
The Phase 3 remains within the complex comprised two linear features. These had an orientation distinct from those of Phase 2, and would thus appear to have been a separate element of the field system. The track to the east of the western settlement (*CT 552*; Fig 115) diverted awkwardly around platform *CT 547* and cut through lynchet *CT 434*, suggesting that it postdated this feature. Similarly, at its eastern end, it cut through bank *CT 427*. Extending north from this track was a long wall (*CT 429*) that was also clearly a later component, as it passed through the cairns in Area 4 and cut the line of the former head dyke (*CT 430/619*). Although these elements clearly postdated the Phase 2 field system, they did not have a point of contact with any elements of the Phase 4 system (*below*).

Phase 4
The remains within Area 1 for the most part appear to have formed a coherent field system (Fig 115) relating to the rectilinear settlement (Fig 116). This comprised a series of terraced plots and strip fields that were either inter-related or had parallel orientations. Although there were associated cairns, they were for the most part few and far between. The notable exceptions were cairns *CT 392-405*, which formed a discrete localised group and were adjacent to one of the terraced banks, although it is not clear if they were contemporary or they related to the Phase 1 monuments found to the west of a rubble spread. Accordingly, the cairns have not been phased.

Although there was a relatively clear internal relationship within the Phase 4 monuments, there was relatively little direct interaction between these field components and those of the earlier phases, allowing a relationship to be established. One possible relationship suggests that the tentative cairn alignment

(B) leading towards large roundhouse *CT 409* predated terraced plot *CT 414/17*. The terraced plot, in any case, lay within an improved field defined to the south-west by large terraced bank *CT 425*, and as such would have severely restricted the area for cultivation within the field defined by *CT 425*. This does not make sense if they were contemporary, but perhaps suggests that the terraced plot was a later insertion which, in turn, implies that this field system post-dated Phase 2.

Phase 5
The final phase of activity is defined by the Parliamentary enclosures, and earlier field boundaries that make up the present-day field system. These boundaries clearly overlay elements of all previous phases of activity. In addition to the boundaries shown on the modern OS 1:10,000 maps, there was also wall foundation *CT 375*, which had an oblique orientation to that of the Phase 4 field system and butted against the modern field boundary.

Chronology of occupation
The roundhouses associated with Phase 1 would suggest a prehistoric or, at the latest, a Roman date for this phase, if the dating of the Brantrake settlement on Birkby Fell (BB VII) can be extended to this area (*p 211*). The second phase of activity in the western settlement, that apparently associated with the triangular enclosure containing the rectilinear building (*CT 543*), cannot be dated with any precision, as these monuments do not fit with any defined typological forms. However, the sequence of development clearly culminated in the Phase 4 settlement, which can be dated to the medieval period by virtue of the typological form of the rectilinear houses and by the fortuitous finding of thirteenth-/fourteenth-century pottery in a molehill in its immediate vicinity. At present, the possible date range for Phases 1-3 must therefore span the whole of the first millennium BC and the first millennium AD. There was evidence for the retreat of settlement in the late medieval period to its present limits, and so, with the abandonment of the medieval settlement (Phase 4), the highest farms became Crosbythwaite and Brighouse (*c 0.5 km from Crosbythwaite), both of which are still inhabited.

Hesk Fell

The survey area (Fig 93) contained a large D-shaped enclosure with an associated cairnfield on a moderately sloping col between the summits of Hesk Fell and The Pike (Fig 111), formed by the diffluent passage of a glacier across the watershed between the Holehouse and Crosby valleys. The monuments were not concentrated in the centre of the col, but just downslope, to the north-east.

The whole survey area was contained within enclosed, but unimproved, land. The ground was generally well drained, but it was adjacent to a large area of mire at the bottom of a natural bowl on the eastern side of the col. The turf cover was fairly thin and occasional exposed brash outcrops were scattered over the area.

Archaeological history
The D-shaped enclosure and associated cairnfield were added to the archaeological record only relatively recently. The earliest description of the site was by Cherry (1961, 14-15), who described the enclosure as oval, with an associated group of cairns, including one that had sustained earlier excavation (HE 15; *p 250*). Although the site is shown on modern mapping from 1977, it was not shown on earlier OS maps.

The survey area
The survey was undertaken in May 1984 over 0.15 km^2 of enclosed rough pasture land (Fig 119). In total, 78 monuments were found within three site groups, which comprised two cairnfields and a large D-shaped enclosure with associated corner structures, as well as other enclosures (Fig 120). Further cairnfield groups were observed *c* 300 m to the east of the monuments, but these were beyond the boundaries of the survey.

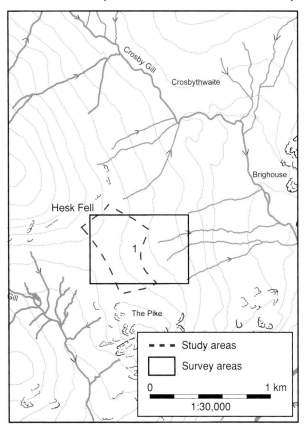

Figure 119: The Hesk Fell survey area as planned

249

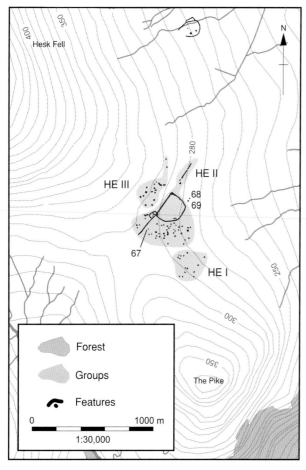

Figure 120: Monument distribution within the Hesk Fell survey area

In addition to these groups, there were also limited numbers of scattered ungrouped cairns (*HE 67-9*), which are not individually described within this volume.

Hesk Fell I: monuments *HE 1-43, HE 50-2, HE 67*, and *HE 70-4*

A randomly scattered cairnfield was recorded on the low to moderate slopes at the eastern edge of the col (Fig 120). The ground was moderately well drained, but there were localised areas of poor drainage between the cairns. The cairnfield was divided into four distinct sub-groups, which reflected both the topography and separate episodes of clearance.

The first cairn group (HE IA; Fig 121) was small, and contained a scattered group of cairns, lying at the southernmost limit of the cairnfield. These varied in size and form, with rounded profiles, and they were moderately well defined. There were sporadic brash outcrops in the area and some of the cairns appeared to be superimposed on these natural outcrops.

The second cairn group (HE IB) was also small, but formed a compact group, which lay on moderately

well-drained ground. The cairns varied in form and size and were moderately well defined. They were, however, associated with sporadic brash outcrops, and it is a possible that some of these may have been augmented by clearance stone.

To the north lay the third cairn group (HE IC). This was separated from HE IB by a marked dip, which had less well-drained ground at its base, implying that the gap between the two cairn groups reflected the poor quality of this land. The cairns in HE IC were identified on gently sloping, moderately drained ground to the south of a D-shaped enclosure (*HE 46e* in HE II; *p 251*). The cairns were fairly prominent and well defined, with rounded profiles. However, in this group, they were significantly smaller and less prominent than those of an adjacent group to the west (HE ID; *see below*), and there was also a distinct gap between the two groups. The cairn group extended close to the southern boundary of the large enclosure (*HE 46e*) but did not cross it, which would suggest that either the distribution of the cairns respected the enclosure, or that any cairns within it had been robbed to create the enclosure wall. Cairn *HE 15* was extremely large and prominent, and was markedly larger than the surrounding cairns. It had a hollowed centre, which was irregular in shape, and this probably reflected antiquarian disturbance. Its size may be an indication of a funerary function; however, this may in part have been attributable to the redistribution of spoil around the main body of the cairn as a result of potential antiquarian excavation (*p 249*).

The fourth cairn group (HE ID) was found to the west of HE IC, and contained relatively large cairns, with prominent rounded profiles. They were markedly larger and more prominent than those of the adjacent group (HE IC), the two groups being separated by a distinct gap. These cairns were, however, generally smaller than those of the HE III cairnfield to the north-west, which were very loosely scattered, but were nevertheless substantial. There is an implication that the cairns in HE IC, HE ID, and HE III reflected different episodes of clearance. The cairns within HE ID also included some very large stones, which may have represented *in situ* natural material. This may, in turn, suggest that clearance stone had been deposited against natural blocks to maximise the available land. The cairns were distributed in a north-west/south-east band, and those at the north-western end were noticeably smaller than those to the south-east. A small group of three cairns (*HE 50-2*) matched this alignment but lay to the north-west of boundary *HE 44*. If these cairns were a part of the clearance episode reflected by HE ID, then it would suggest that boundary *HE 44* was a later feature.

250

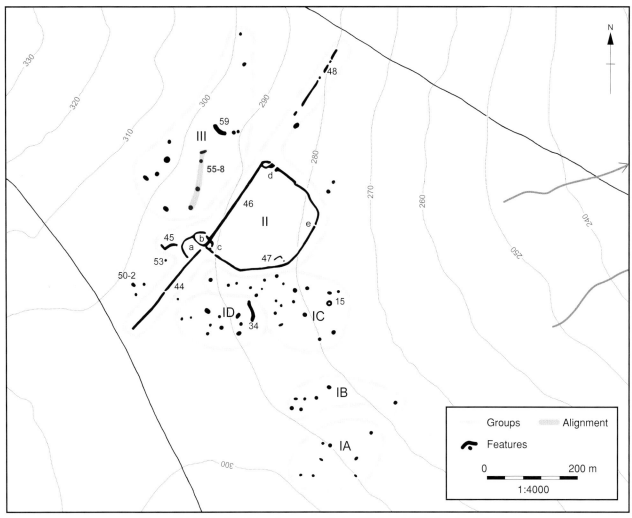

Figure 121: The HE II enclosure, and the HE I and HE III cairnfields

Hesk Fell II: monuments *HE 44-8*

This site group comprised a D-shaped enclosure (*HE 46*; Fig 121), two associated smaller enclosures (*HE 46a* and *HE 46b*), and a pair of boundary banks (*HE 44* and *HE 48*; Pl 140). These boundaries were long, fairly continuous, prominent, turf-covered banks with rounded profiles. Although only a few stones protruded, on the evidence of their uniformity, they were probably decayed dry-stone walls. These boundary walls extended north-east/south-west from the western (upper) side of the D-shaped enclosure (*HE 46e*) and stopped just short of the modern field walls, with no evidence of any continuation beyond them. If there was a relationship between the historical and modern boundaries, it would suggest that the latter were in part a fossilised survival of an earlier field system.

The D-shaped enclosure (*HE 46*)

A large enclosure (*c* 114 x 86 m) covered an area of *c* 9100 m², with small buildings set into the south-western and north-eastern corners (*HE 46c-d*). Its shape was formed by the construction of a semi-circular enclosure onto a straight boundary wall,

and this indicates that the enclosure post-dated this boundary. The enclosure comprised a prominent, uniform, continuous dry-stone wall, with external revetting and small stone packing. The walls were up to three courses high in places, and the entrances survived well, with only limited collapse obscuring the gaps, and with substantial blocks of masonry acting as revetments on either side.

The interior of the enclosure comprised moderately sloping, well-drained ground, which did not appear to have been improved, and it did not contain any definite cairns. There were, indeed, natural outcrops within the interior and there was no evidence that this area had ever been cultivated. A small L-shaped wall (*HE 47*), composed of a line of very large boulders, was also identified towards the south-east corner. It may have been a decayed rectangular structure, although there was no evidence of any internal terracing. Despite the relatively narrow entrances to the enclosure, which were more appropriate for use by humans than stock, its function was consistent with controlling stock, and this may explain the unimproved internal ground, and the continuous, prominent enclosing walls.

South-western building

A very well-defined, semi-rectilinear building (*HE 46c*), was set into the corner of the D-shaped enclosure (Pl 141). It had an apsidal north-eastern end and the north-western wall had been built against the enclosure wall. At this point, the wall had a double thickness, and it is evident that the building post-dated the enclosure. Although the structure was substantially decayed, the volume of collapsed stone was not particularly great, when compared to that of the enclosure wall, which may indicate either that stone had been robbed from the site or that the stone walls never extended to full roof height.

There was clear evidence of internal terracing within the building and it was also evident that it once had a domestic function. The entrance was to the east, into the D-shaped enclosure but, unlike the other building found within the enclosure (*HE 46d*; *see below*), there was no adjacent entrance leading directly out from the enclosure. Therefore, access to the structure was only possible via the enclosure itself.

Northern building

Building *HE 46d* was set into the corner of the main enclosure, and had prominent dry-stone walls, with an abundance of associated collapse (Pl 142). There was an entrance on the north-eastern side leading beyond the enclosure rather than into it, which contrasted with the southern structure (*HE 46c*). An apparent butt join between the west wall and the D-shaped enclosure suggested that the structure was a later addition. Internal terracing was evident, but it was

not as clear as that recorded within the other building (*HE 46c*) found within the enclosure.

Northern sub-enclosure (*HE 46b*)

Sub-enclosure *HE 46b* was constructed against the principal north-east/south-west field boundary (*HE 44*). It had an oval shape, the southernmost arc of which was incorporated into the *HE 46/44* boundary wall. The definition of the banks at the interface between these two features was poor, and consequently it was not possible to establish the precise relationship between them. The sub-enclosure had a single entrance on its north-eastern side, which used a prominent outcrop as its northern portal. Elsewhere, the enclosing bank had a dry-stone fabric core. There was no evidence of internal terracing and it does not appear to have had a domestic function.

Southern sub-enclosure (HE 46a)

Enclosure *HE 46a* was formed by the construction of a sub-circular arc of bank butting against the north-eastern enclosure, and wall *HE 44*; a gap between them was probably an entrance. The bank incorporated an exposed stone revetment in its north-eastern section. The interior was not terraced, but a slight hollow was seen near the north-eastern corner of the enclosure. This enclosure, and also the adjacent sub-enclosure (*HE 46b*; *see above*), probably functioned as stock enclosures.

Hesk Fell III: monuments *HE 54-66*

This was a loose scatter of cairns to the north-west of the D-shaped enclosure (*HE 46* in HE II), which was edged by a steep, craggy scarp slope immediately

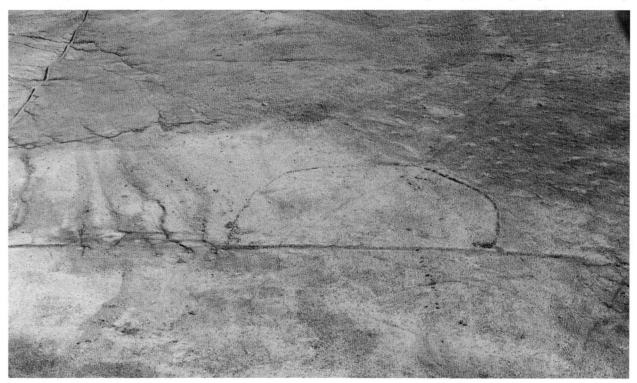

Plate 140: The Hesk Fell enclosure (HE 46) and its associated boundary banks

Plate 141: Structure HE 46c, set into the south-western corner of the D-shaped enclosure

Plate 142: Structure HE 46d, set into the north-west corner of the D-shaped enclosure

to its north-west. The cairns were on gently sloping, moderately drained ground, although there were localised areas of poor drainage between them. Generally, the cairns were fairly prominent and well defined, with rounded profiles, and were in marked contrast to the component cairns of HE I. Within them, there was a possible north-east/south-west alignment (*HE 55-8*; Fig 121). One of the cairns (*HE 59*) was also elongated, though it did not share the same orientation as the possible cairn alignment.

Conclusions

Two apparently distinct elements could be discerned in the Hesk Fell survey area. These comprised the cairnfields (HE I and HE III) and the D-shaped enclosure (*HE 46e*), with its associated boundary walls and enclosures, the relationship between them being slightly ambiguous. If the cairnfields pre-dated the enclosure, it would be reasonable to expect to find some cairns within the latter, but only one dubious cairn was identified within the enclosure's interior. However, it could be argued that any cairns in the vicinity of the enclosure would have been robbed to provide stone, and hence there would be no cairns in its immediate surroundings. Perhaps the most interesting aspect of the distribution is that the HE IC cairn group had a basic east/west distribution, which extended beyond the enclosure and therefore did not simply match its shape. Such a linear distribution would not necessarily extend north into the enclosure, and the adjacent section of the enclosure appeared to have been curtailed, in a way that matched the alignment of the cairnfield. This could suggest that the shape and extent of the enclosure had been modified to exclude the cairns.

A small group of cairns (*HE 50-2*), which formed a limited cluster to the north-west of wall *HE 44*, also provided evidence for a sequence of activity. The cluster was directly in line with the linear spread of the HE ID cairn group, and the component cairns were comparable in size and form to those on the southern side of the wall. It can be argued, therefore, that this small cluster was a northern outlier of the HE ID cairns and that, similarly, cairn *HE 53* was an outlier of the cairns found in HE IC. If this were the case, it would suggest that boundary *HE 44* was constructed through an extant cairnfield. Stratigraphically, the boundary was the earliest element in HE II, and therefore it would suggest that the activity associated with this, and the D-shaped enclosure, post-dated the cairnfield.

In terms of chronology, the cairnfields had a broadly primary character and could potentially be prehistoric in date. Although the enclosure had a very distinctive character, there are no dated parallels in the region; however, the boundary associated with the enclosure appeared to respect two boundaries that are still in use, and one building within the enclosure had a sub-rectangular shape. It is therefore possible that it was either medieval in date or was used at that time.

Thwaites Fell

Thwaites Fell lies on the south-eastern side of the South-West Fells (Fig 93), within a col between the low summits of Lath Rigg to the west, and Barrow summit to the east; on either side of the col are the valleys of Black Beck, to the south, and Logan Beck to the north (Fig 122). To the west of Lath Rigg, the terrain extends up towards the main South-West Fell ridge, extending south from Buck Barrow towards Black Coombe. The col is an area of gently sloping, and generally well-drained, unimproved moorland, constrained by enclosed farmland to the north, by enclosed, and now forested, land to the east, and by enclosed land filling the Black Beck valley to the south. The fell extends from 130 m to over 540 m OD, but within this altitudinal range most of the archaeological sites were on the lower and more gently sloping ground, centred on the col, between the 200 m and 330 m contours.

Archaeological history

Cairns on Thwaites Fell were first recorded on the 1900 Second Edition 6" to 1 mile OS map. Subsequent enhancement of the OS record is outlined in individual cases below. Otherwise, there has been little previous archaeological research in this particular area, in contrast to the other South-West Fell survey areas, to the west and north.

The survey area

The survey was undertaken in April 1984, covering *c* 2 km² of unenclosed moorland (Fig 123). A total of 327 monuments was recorded within five site groups (TF I-V; Fig 124). The monuments were mainly small cairns, which for the most part lay within a broad band that extended north-north-west/south-south-east, following the line of the contours. Within this band were discrete groupings of cairns, which are described from north to south.

Thwaites Fell I (Hodgewife Well): monuments *TF 1-7*

To the north of the spring at Hodgewife Well, and centred on the source of the adjacent stream, was a group of six small cairns and a long discontinuous stone bank, located on fairly level ground between the 300 m and 310 m contours (Fig 124). The cairns were mainly grassy mounds, with some stones protruding, and were typically 4-5 m in diameter. They were not tightly grouped and, apart from the apparent pairing of cairns *TF 3* and *TF 4*, and cairns *TF 5* and *TF 6* (Fig 125), there was little pattern in the distribution. The only notable cairn was *TF 2*, which was significantly larger (8 m in diameter), higher (0.5 m high), had a rounded profile, and was better defined than the rest of the group. It was remote from the others, which raises the possibility that this had a different function (possibly funerary) from the other cairns in this area. It also had an off-centre depression, which is probably indicative of antiquarian disturbance, but no records of any such investigations survive.

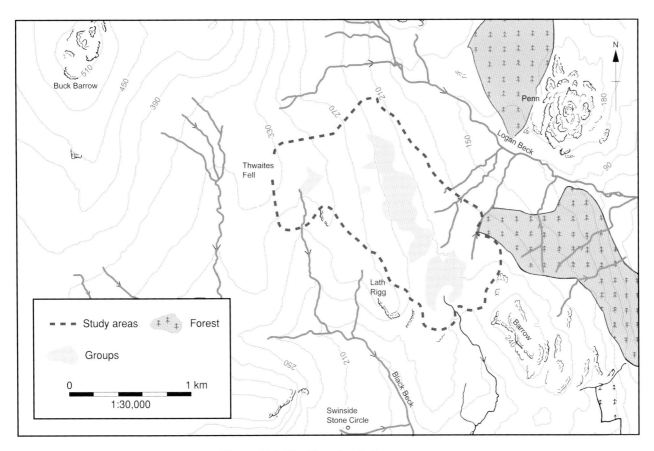

Figure 122: The Thwaites Fell survey area

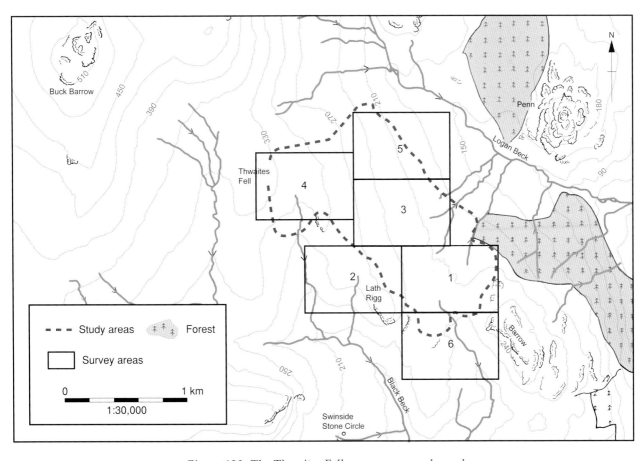

Figure 123: The Thwaites Fell survey area as planned

255

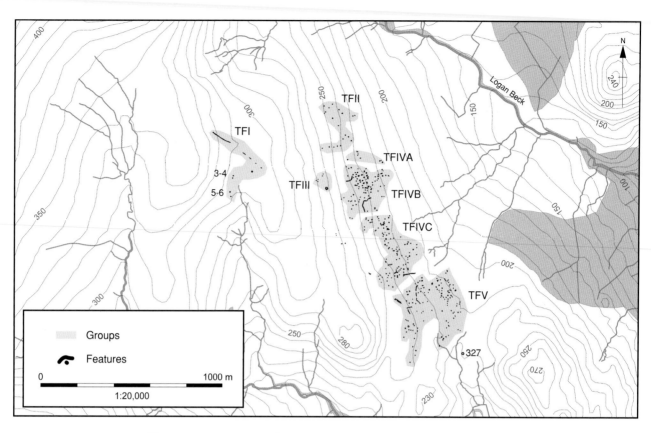

Figure 124: Monument distribution in the Thwaites Fell survey area

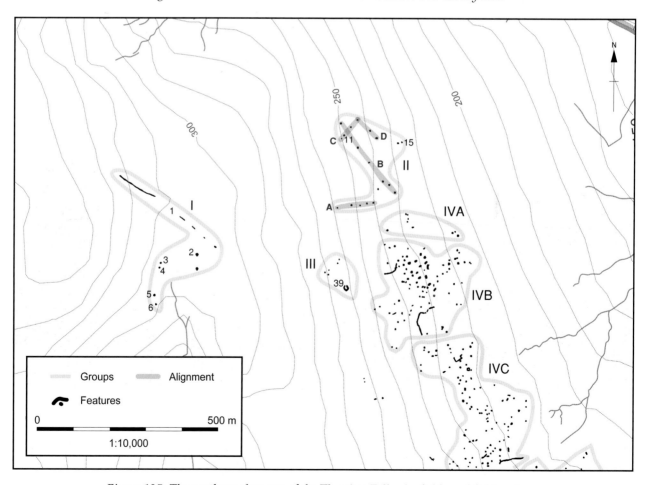

Figure 125: The northern elements of the Thwaites Fell cairnfields and field systems

256

To the north of the cairns, and with no obvious association, was a discontinuous 1-3 m-wide stone bank or wall (*TF 1*), which could be traced over a distance of at least 350 m. Though rarely higher than 0.1 m, it was for the most part clearly visible in the short grass. In plan, it appears to have been aligned westwards, towards the summit of Buck Barrow, and eastwards, on the Barrow summit.

Thwaites Fell II (Logan Beck): monuments *TF 8-26*

A group of 18 small cairns was located on the east-facing slope of Thwaites Fell between the 210 m and 260 m contours, above the valley of Logan Beck (Fig 124). The majority of the cairns were ill-defined, low grassy mounds with protruding stones, varying from 2.7 m to 5.0 m in diameter, and typically less than 0.2 m in height. This cairn group had a generally low density, which was in marked contrast to that of TF IV, immediately to the south, where the cairns were very closely packed; it may be significant that a marked gap of *c* 60 m existed between TF II and TF IV.

No stone banks were associated with the cairns; however, several apparently significant cairn alignments were visible. Alignment A (Fig 125) was orientated east/west (downslope) and was *c* 100 m long, and Alignment B was orientated north-west/south-east and was *c* 208 m long. Significantly, the east/west alignment appeared to point towards the southernmost cairn of the north-west/south-

east alignment, suggesting that they were related, possibly being two sides of a large field. Two further, much smaller, alignments (C, measuring 66 m long, and D, measuring 70 m long) formed two sides of a rectangular plot. Of the 18 cairns in this group, only two (*TF 15*) did not clearly form part of any alignment, and it would seem that the group was the surviving surface manifestation of a former localised field system.

Thwaites Fell III: monuments *TF 34-9*

A group of five small cairns and a possible roundhouse were recorded on moderately sloping ground, between the 260 m and 270 m contours, to the east of, and above, TF IV (Fig 124). The cairns were small, low-lying, ill-defined, grassy mounds with protruding stones.

The putative roundhouse (*TF 39*; Fig 125; Pl 143) was located on a natural terrace to the south of, and remote from, the cairns. It was relatively well defined, with an enclosing grassy bank with stones protruding, and had a possible entrance on the northern side. The bank was sub-circular, being slightly elongated (16 x 13 m externally, and 8 x 6.5 m internally) and was not particularly prominent, being only 0.2 m high. Although this feature had several attributes akin to a roundhouse, its location on the side of one of the steeper sections of slope, and its remoteness from the cairnfield, does cast some doubt over this interpretation.

Plate 143: Putative roundhouse TF 39, *looking south*

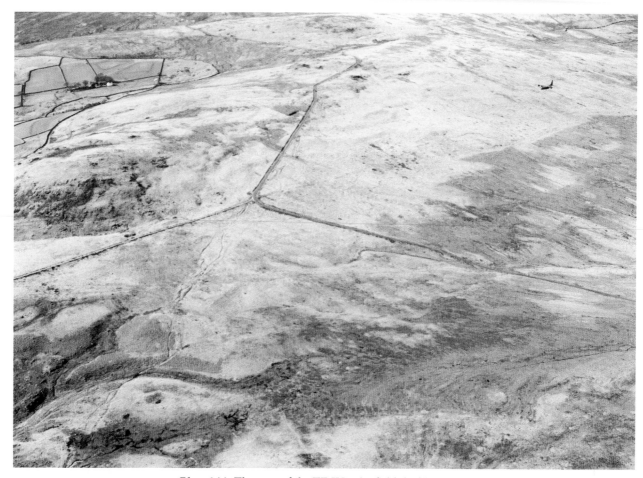

Plate 144: The area of the TF IV cairnfield, looking west

Thwaites Fell IV (West of Smallthwaite Forest): monuments *TF 27-33* and *TF 40-222*

Within this survey area (Fig 124), over 182 monuments were recorded, which comprised extensive groups of small cairns and associated stone banks, together forming a cairnfield (Pl 144). This cairnfield extended in a north-north-west/south-south-east band, following the contours, for a distance of *c* 700 m, and it faced east over the valley of Logan Beck and the Duddon Valley. The cairnfield was divided into three, spatially discrete, monument sub-groups.

The first sub-group (TF IVA; Fig 125) formed a small group of cairns that were spatially remote from the other monument groups. This included four small cairns, set close together in an arc, and five further cairns, of mixed size and character, scattered up to 120 m from the main cluster.

The second monument sub-group (TF IVB; Fig 126) was larger in size and contained 80 cairns, with associated walls and sections of stone bank, which were closely packed, mainly between the 210 m and 250 m contours. The monument distribution displayed two clear, albeit merged, patterns. The first was characterised by a densely packed sub-elliptical concentration of very large cairns (*TF 43-71*

and *TF 86-91*), the largest measuring 8.6 x 6 m in size, with a very substantial height of 0.6 m (*TF 52*). The distribution of these monuments seemed to be essentially random, but two short, parallel alignments (*TF 60-3* and *TF 48*, and *TF 51-3* and *TF 56*) were discerned, and there was also a section of stone bank (*TF 47*; 38 m long and 2.5 m wide), which appeared to be a western extension of the northernmost of the two alignments. Given that they were parallel (north-east/south-west), and that there was an association between one alignment and the stone bank, it is probable that they were significant, perhaps indicating the positions of boundaries.

The second pattern of cairns evident within TF IVB was defined by a long, narrow band of cairns (A), which extended north-east/south-west diagonally across the slope and crossed the southernmost part of the sub-elliptical group. These cairns contrasted with the others recorded in this area, being formed predominantly of small cairns, typically between 2.5 m and 4 m in diameter, which were between 0.1 m and 0.2 m in height. The fact that they extended in a linear spread, and that they were so much smaller, would suggest that they were a product of a different episode of stone clearance from the other cairns, despite being spatially associated. Although these cairns were within

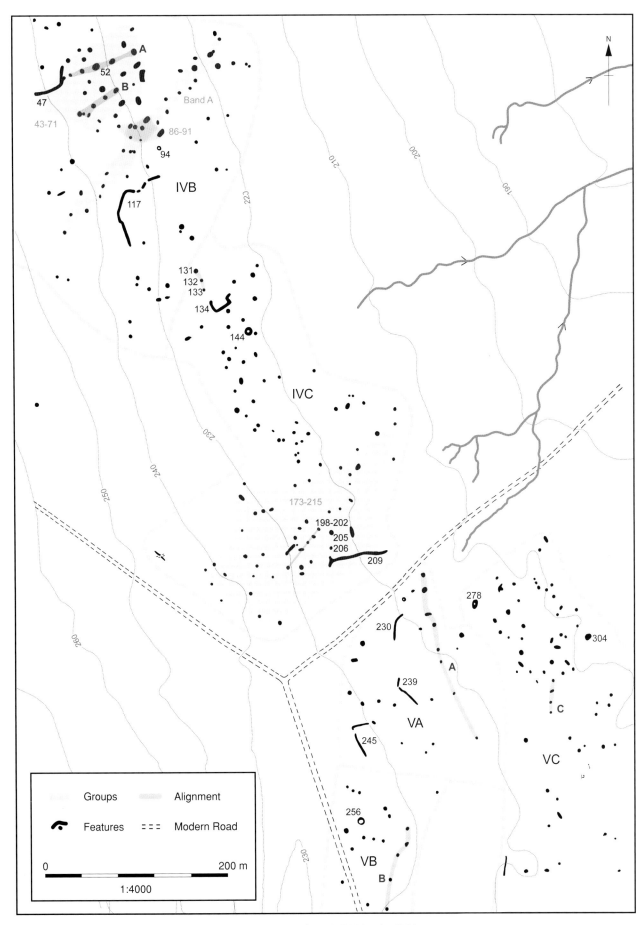

Figure 126: The TF IV-V cairnfields

Plate 145: Round cairn TF 144, within TF IV

a narrow band (*c* 15 m wide, but 260 m long), there was little evidence for definitive cairn alignments that may have been indicative of former field boundaries. Adjacent to the band of cairns was a small bield (*TF 94*), its walls standing three courses high, which was probably of relatively recent date. A discontinuous stony bank (*TF 117*; up to 0.5 m high and 2.9 m wide) also followed an erratic course, in part parallel to the narrow band of cairns, but also extending southwards. It defined the western part of an area which was notably devoid of small cairns, and as such could potentially have defined part of a field.

The third monument sub-group (TF IVC) comprised 96 small cairns, with associated stone banks, which extended as an elongated band for *c* 400 m from north to south, for the most part along the slope, and mainly between the 210 m and 250 m contours. At the southern end was a general east/west spread of tightly packed small cairns (*TF 173-215*). A marked gap of *c* 90 m, which was occupied by the modern fell road, separated this sub-group from the TF V cairnfield (*see below*). The majority of the cairns were small, ill-defined, grassy mounds, with protruding stones, and varied from 2.5 m to a maximum of 5 m in size. The notable exception was the large annular monument (*TF 144*) located in the northern part of the group, which had a diameter of 8.25 m, was fairly well-defined, and had a large central depression, probably indicative of robbing (Pl 145).

In general, the cairn distribution within TF IVC was random and there were relatively few significant alignments. There was, for example, a line of five cairns in the southern part of the group (*TF 198-202*), although the elongated cairns within this were not orientated along its line, and it is probable that the alignment was fortuitous rather than deliberate. By contrast, there was a small alignment of three cairns (*TF 131-3*) that continued the line of an ill-defined rectilinear stone bank (*TF 134*), and which would appear to have been a significant alignment. The stone bank defined three sides of a rectangle and, along with the boundary implied by the cairn alignment, may potentially have formed part of a small plot. At the southern edge of the group was a 68 m-long, ill-defined, east/west-orientated stone bank (*TF 209*). Two cairns (*TF 205* and *TF 206*) continued the line of a north/south stub of the bank, and may suggest a significant alignment, though, on the basis of only two cairns, it is difficult to interpret this as an agricultural plot.

Thwaites Fell V (Lath Rigg): monuments *TF 223-327*

A large group of 104 small cairns, with associated walls and fragments of enclosures, extended for *c* 480 m from north to south, along the slopes of Thwaites Fell, mainly between the 210 m and 240 m contours (Fig 124). To the north, the limit was marked by the road across Thwaites Fell, and on the south it was marked by the steeper and rockier ground to the north of the farm of Thwaite Yeat. The cairnfield was divided into three distinct sub-groups.

The first sub-group (TF VA; Fig 126) was characterised by a loose scattering of cairns, and incorporated cairn alignments and stone banks, which would appear to have been the vestiges of a field system. The majority of the cairns were small, ill-defined mounds with protruding stones. They were typically circular, although a few were elongated in plan, and were between 2.5 m and 4.5 m in size, and about 0.2 m in height, their form being consistent with clearance cairns. A marked north / south alignment was formed by cairns of various size and form (A), perhaps a result of erratic clearance on the line of a former boundary. Extending erratically, and in places parallel to, this alignment, were two discontinuous stone banks (*TF 230* and *TF 239*), which were only 0.1 m in height. Between these two putative boundaries was an open area, containing only three cairns, which may have been a plot. A further putative plot lay at the south-western edge of the monument group, defined by two stone banks (*TF 245*) set at right-angles to one another. However, the southern and eastern sides of this possible plot did not survive as surface evidence.

To the south-west, a small group of relatively small and low cairns (typically 3 m in diameter and 0.2 m in height) was recorded, forming the second monument sub-group (TF VB). There was, however, one cairn (*TF 256*) which was in very marked contrast to the others in this group, having a diameter of 8 m and a height of 0.6 m. This cairn also had a severely disturbed centre, probably indicative of antiquarian investigation. It was fairly well defined and, given its size and prominence, it is possible that it had a funerary function. For the most part, the distribution of the small cairns was essentially random, although one possible north-north-east / south-south-west alignment of five cairns (B) was recorded.

The third monument sub-group (TF VC) comprised the main concentration of cairns found in this area. These were very varied in size and shape, the smallest having diameters of no more than 2.5 m, whilst the largest had diameters of 7 m. Although many of the cairns were round, substantial numbers were also elongated, and they did not have consistent orientations. The largest cairn (*TF 278*) was elongated, measuring 9 x 5 m, but had an irregular sub-rectangular shape, was not particularly prominent, and its function remains uncertain. A further large cairn (*TF 304*) was more circular and

Plate 146: Ring cairn TF 327

261

slightly more prominent (7.4 x 6.1 x 0.4 m). The cairn distribution was for the most part random, and they were tightly packed, although one possible significant alignment of four cairns (C) was visible. Further south, the cairns were less densely packed, with no obvious distribution pattern.

Possibly the most significant individual monument on Thwaites Fell was a large annular cairn (*TF 327*; Fig 124), which lay to the south and was remote from TF VC (Pl 146). It was on a natural spur with a broad vista to the south, overlooking the Black Beck valley, and the Swinside stone circle (SD 172 882) was only 1 km to the south-west of this site (Fig 123). Cairn *TF 327* was between 12 m and 13 m in diameter and the external banks were very prominent, being up to 0.5 m high. Several prominent stones were visible around the inside of this, which appeared to be an internal kerb, and there was no sign of a gap, indicative of an entrance; the interior of the monument was relatively flat. By virtue of its position and isolation from the cairnfield, its internal kerbing, size, and general form, it would appear to have been a ring cairn, and typologically this would fall into the 'kerbed ring cairn' category as defined by Lynch (1972).

Conclusions

The Thwaites Fell cairnfield was one of the larger groups of cairns on the South-West Fells. From north to south, it comprised a broad band of small cairns that extended for over 1 km along the contours of the fell, with no clear breaks between the individual monument groups and sub-groups (Fig 124). There were substantial differences of size and prominence between the component cairns of the groups, however, with those of the southernmost groups (*eg* TF VC) being markedly smaller than those of TF IVB, to the north. For the most part, the cairns exhibited a broadly random distribution, although there were distinct indications of linearity within their distribution, and occasional stone banks, that suggest the beginnings of the rationalisation of the cairnfield into fields. The most notable example of this was in the TF II group (*p 257*), where there were relatively few cairns, but almost all were within clearly defined alignments; interestingly, although this presented the best case for a proto-field system, there were no stone banks or more continuous linear features within it.

One of the more enigmatic features was the long discontinuous boundary bank/wall (*TF 1*; Fig 125) to the north-west of TF I, which extended for more than 350 m, and was remote from the main cairnfield. It displayed similarities of general form and linearity with a long boundary bank (*UF 246*) that extended past Rough Crag, on Ulpha Fell (*p 233*), for a distance of 455 m. This latter bank cut through cairnfields and was clearly a later feature. Similarly, bank *TF 1* displayed little direct relationship with the cairnfield and was probably also a later feature.

Despite the extensive cairnfield remains, there were few direct indicators of habitation, a feature not uncommon within the context of the less-developed cairnfields, such as on Corney Fell, Bootle Fell (*Ch 4*), and Stockdale Moor (*Ch 3*). The only possible structure was *TF 39*, which was an irregular sub-circular feature, 16 x 13 m in size (TF III; *p 257*). However, this was located on one of the steepest sections of slope, away from the main cairnfield, which was not a typical location for a contemporary domestic structure.

It was quite typical within cairnfields to find larger funerary-type cairns mixed in with their smaller clearance counterparts, and in this respect Thwaites Fell was no exception. However, the numbers of clearly defined funerary monuments were relatively low. Three putative round cairns were defined on the basis of their relative size, prominence, and regularity of shape (*TF 2*; Fig 125, *TF 144*, and *TF 256*; Fig 126). Cairn *TF 2* (TF I; Fig 125) was within a very loosely scattered group, so much so that it cannot be said to have had a direct association with other cairns; the other two cairns were closely mixed in with smaller cairns (in TF IVC and TF VB; Fig 126). What made these cairns distinctive is that they were unusually large and stood out from their immediate neighbours, yet, interestingly, there were some comparable cairns within the TF IVB monument group, but these clearly formed a tight group of large clearance cairns. All three of the putative funerary cairns had central depressions, indicative of antiquarian disturbance; whether anything was found in the course of these explorations has not, however, been documented.

Commonly, round cairns were sited in prominent locations, with a wide, open, vista, and in this respect none of these putative round cairns had distinctive settings, although there is generally a good vista from any point on the slope on which they were found. In contrast, the obvious ring cairn within the group (*TF 327*; Fig 124) was in a very prominent position on a spur overlooking the Black Beck valley. Few classic ring cairns were recorded during the LDNPS, but this was one of them, with an internally kerbed edge, a prominent outer bank (without an entrance), and a diameter of 14 m. Ring cairns have been explored on numerous occasions throughout the country and typically date to the mid-second millennium BC (*Ch 2, pp 41-4*); it is therefore likely that this monument had a comparable date. The relative proximity, however, between this annular funerary monument and the Swinside stone circle, dated to the neolithic period (Burl 1976), and only *c* 1 km to the south-west, may be coincidental rather than a deliberate design feature, as a low bluff blocks any line of site between the two monuments.

6

THE SOUTHERN AND CENTRAL FELLS

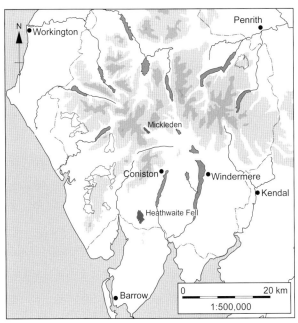

Figure 127: The extent of the surveys in the Southern and Central Fells

While the majority of the survey work undertaken by the LDNPS programme examined the marginal lands adjacent to the west Cumbrian coastal plain, the opportunity was also taken to investigate archaeological landscapes within the southern and central parts of the Lake District, providing a comparison with those on the western seaboard (Fig 127). It was recognised that southern Lakeland was an upland terrain that had not previously been subject to any systematic study and its archaeological resource had not been adequately characterised.

Within the Southern and Central Fells, two specific areas were considered by the LDNPS. One of these comprised Heathwaite Fell, which was known to contain a settlement landscape centred on Pewet Tarn (HF IX; *p 272*), the only portion of the Southern Fells to be considered by the LDNPS, an area of the Lake District that extends south from the high peaks of the Old Man of Coniston into the Furness peninsula. The fells are defined to the west by the Duddon Valley and estuary, and to the east by Coniston Water and the valley of the River Crake. At the northern end of the range, where the Southern Fells merge with the Central Fells, they are steep, exposed craggy mountains, with a maximum height of 801 m OD (Old Man of Coniston). Further south, the fells are lower (*c* 300 m OD), and comprise more rolling, rounded, hills, and a significant proportion of them have been enclosed. The extant early human settlement remains are generally scattered on the marginal, moderately sloping land throughout the lower fells. Settlements and funerary monuments have been identified across Torver High Common (LUAU 1994a), at the base of the Old Man of Coniston, and also on Torver Low Common, to the west of Coniston Water (LUAU 1995).

The other area selected for survey was the Mickleden Valley, in Great Langdale. Significantly, this area is situated at the foot of the summits containing many of the most significant axe-factory groups, and the survey of the settlement and field system in the base of the valley was undertaken as an adjunct to the axe-factory survey (Claris and Quartermaine 1989). The intention of this survey was to examine whether there was any correlation between the remains in the valley with the axe-factory sites on the adjacent valley sides. In the event, it was recognised that the activity in the valley post-dated the axe-factory working and that there was no relationship between the landscapes, and as a consequence the Mickleden Valley survey was not published alongside that for the axe factories (*ibid*). Indeed, the observed pattern of activity evident in the Mickleden Valley is typical of that seen in the valleys of the Central Lake District, which seem to have relatively few early prehistoric settlement areas, by contrast with the western valleys of Wasdale (OA North 2009c), Eskdale, and Ennerdale (OA North 2003a), which do. Furthermore, the terrain of the Central Lake District is such that the land would only sensibly have been farmed if more viable areas around the periphery of the Lake District had already been occupied. It is perhaps significant, therefore, that the survival of archaeological remains at the head

263

of the Mickleden Valley is only because the land in this area was too marginal to have justified the expansion of the enclosure into the area. Moreover, the archaeological landscapes that are found within remote valleys, such as the Mickleden Valley, are, perhaps inevitably, very different from those found elsewhere within the Lake District (Bevan *et al* 1991), and provide an important adjunct to the survey evidence obtained from the western marginal lands.

Heathwaite Fell

Heathwaite Fell (Fig 127) is an expanse of undulating moorland immediately adjacent to an area of coastal mire (White and Heathwaite Mosses), which formed following an early Holocene transgression that was at its peak during the period 7060-6707 cal BC (7995±80 BP; HV-3362; Hodgkinson *et al* 2000, 34).

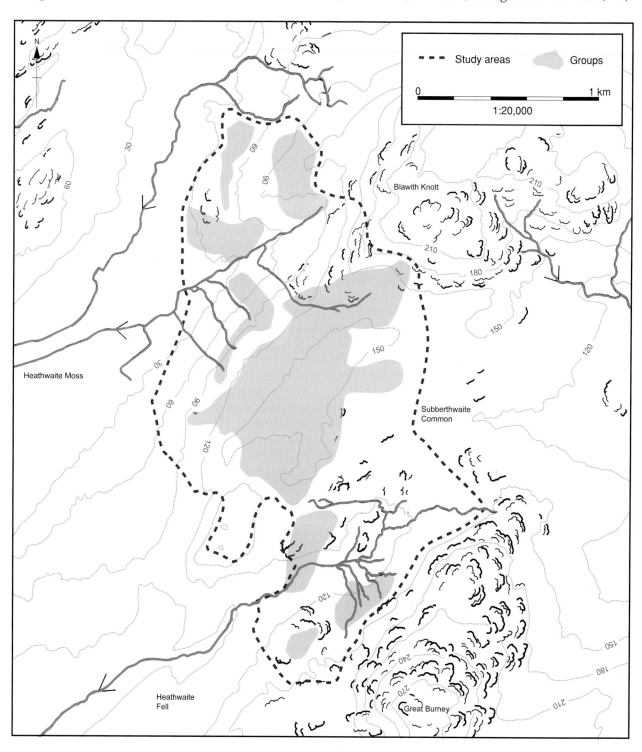

Figure 128: The Heathwaite Fell survey area

A further brief transgression affected the Duddon estuary around 4400-3600 cal BC (5277±120 BP, Q-85; 5015±100 BP; HV-34600; *ibid*). However, a palaeoecological core from White Moss showed that the mire was above sea level by the Bronze Age, but was subject to extensive periods of flooding, particularly during the early Roman period (Wimble 1986).

The main areas of settlement were on a raised, undulating plateau at an altitude of 120-170 m OD (Fig 128). This plateau rises above the coastal mire quite steeply and is limited to the north and south by the peaks of Blawith Knott and Great Burney. In places, the soil is fairly thin and there are substantial amounts of surface stone, particularly below the plateau, in the northern part of the survey area; in extreme cases, this confused the definition of clearance cairns.

The plateau was formed by the passage of an ice sheet which, on its departure after the last ice age, left irregular depressions across the landscape that became small tarns (Pennington 1978). Within the survey area, there were nine such tarns that still contained water, but were in various stages of silting up, and many had become basin mires. On the southern side of Blawith Knott, there was a semi-circular cirque (or cwm), carved from the hill by glacial action, which was filled by peat, but was originally also a tarn. Around the bowl, there were some small cairnfields (HF IV; *p 268*), although it is not known if the tarn had standing water at the time of their construction. It is clear, however, that there has been some expansion of the mires since the construction of the cairns. For instance, monuments *HF 368-70* and *HF 372* in HF IX (*p 272*), and monuments *HF 504* and *HF 510* in HF XIIA (*p 279*), were within areas of bog, but as these were relatively isolated examples, it may be that the drainage of the area has not changed significantly.

By contrast, the pattern of vegetation in the general area appears to have undergone substantial changes since the Bronze Age, according to the pollen diagrams for the nearby White Moss (Wimble 1986). Originally, the area was covered by mixed forest, comprising mainly oak, alder, and hazel. However, between *c* 1200 cal BC and 950 cal BC, a well-defined clearance episode has been recognised, which was followed by a period of forest regeneration. A further clearance episode occurred between *c* 450 cal BC and the end of the first millennium BC, which was again followed by a period of forest regeneration. Towards the end of the Roman period (*c* cal AD 350), until about cal AD 800, there was another, less-marked, episode of forest clearance, and, from *c* cal AD 1100, extensive clearance led to the almost complete deforestation of the surrounding land, and there was no subsequent regeneration. Because the area of White Moss is large, the pollen recorded in these cores represents both the regional and local vegetation, presumably including that from

around the settlements on Heathwaite Fell. Therefore, it is possible that one or more of the clearance episodes recorded in the pollen diagrams relates to activities associated with these settlements.

Archaeological history

The earliest recorded antiquarian activity at Heathwaite dates from 1842 (Evans 1842, 114-15), when it was reported that there were two stone circles 'within a short distance of each other', called the Giant's Graves (*HF 113* and probably *HF 117*; *pp 268-70*). Evans undertook excavations in the spring of 1842 and found charred bones in the centre of each, with those in the northern circle covered by a thin, flat stone. In the southern circle, Evans also found fragments of a stone ring, one inch in diameter.

The Pewet Tarn settlement (HF IX; *p 272*) was first recorded on the 1850 6" to 1 mile OS map, which showed the main field boundaries and an area of cairns to the north of the settlement. The earliest description of the settlement itself was in 1877 (Clifton Ward 1878, 254-5), followed in 1889 by Swainson-Cowper's work (1893, 397-9, 402-7), mapping the Stone Rings enclosure (*HF 530*; *p 280*) and the Pewet Tarn farmstead (*HF 330*; *p 273*). He recorded the house platforms on the southern edge of the settlement (*HF 405-12*) but interpreted them as 'slinger's platforms'. In 1953, the area around the Pewet Tarn settlement and the cairns to the north was scheduled as an Ancient Monument (SM34990), on the basis of the archaeological detail shown on the 1919 6" to 1 mile OS map.

The survey area

The survey was undertaken between April and May 1987 on unenclosed moorland (Fig 129). In total, 530 monuments were found within 13 survey areas, revealing significant evidence of prehistoric and medieval activity (Fig 130). Although it covered only 3.75 km² of these expansive fells, it provided a good indication of the archaeological potential of the area. There were numerous small- and moderate-sized cairnfields within the study area, but, in addition, there was a very substantial medieval settlement (HF IX; *p 272*) associated with large pastoral enclosures and an extensive field system, within which there was evidence of ridge and furrow cultivation. In addition to these groups, there was also a limited number of scattered ungrouped cairns and banks (*eg HF 148, HF 160-2, HF 170-4,* and *HF 467-8*), which are not individually described within this volume.

Heathwaite Fell I (Thwaite): monuments *HF 1-17* and *HF 78-86*

Within HF I (Fig 130), five small, relatively isolated monument sub-groups were recorded, which lay on the top and southern slopes of Thwaite spur, to the south-west of Blawith Knott.

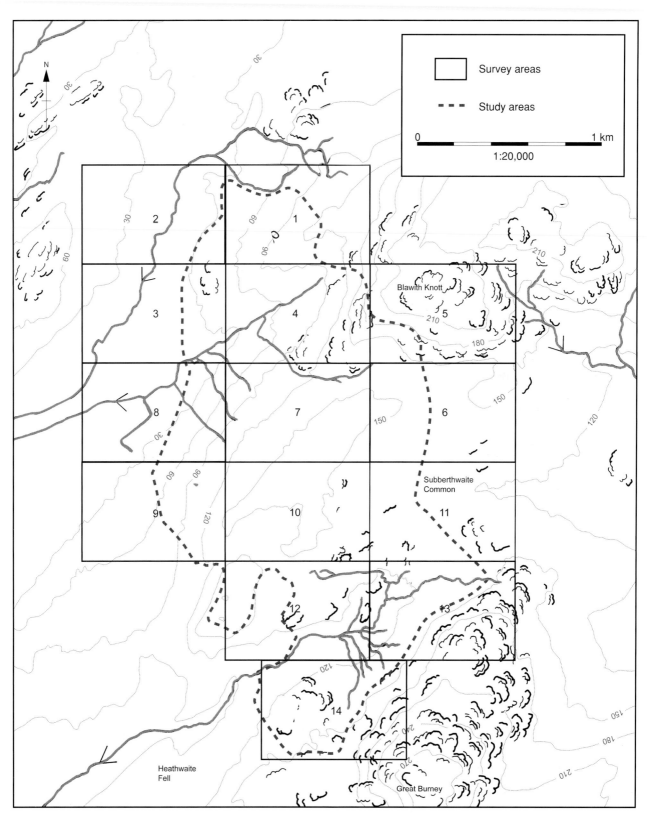

Figure 129: The Heathwaite Fell survey area as planned

The first monument sub-group (HF IA; Fig 131) comprised a loose scatter of low, ill-defined mounds on top of the spur, where the land was well drained and had a generally low, but slightly undulating, gradient. There were substantial amounts of brash protruding from the turf cover, which confused the definition of the cairns, and some of these mounds may have been natural.

The second and third monument sub-groups were located within large natural bowls, termed nivation hollows (Ballantyne and Harris 1994), set into the

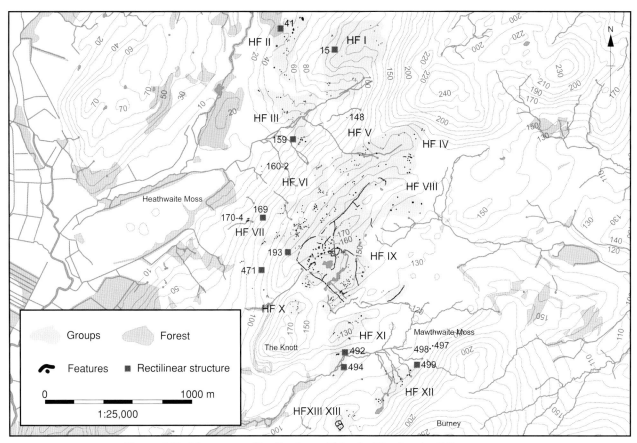

Figure 130: Monument distribution within the Heathwaite Fell survey area

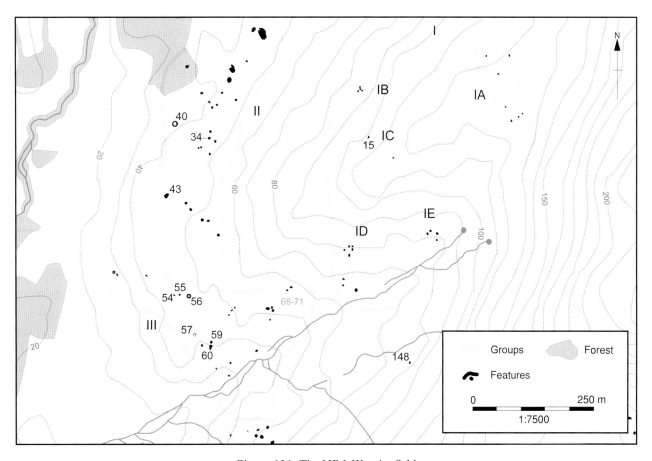

Figure 131: The HF I-III cairnfields

267

steep slope of the Thwaite spur, which had formed as a result of ice action. These bowls had relatively flat bases and offered reasonable protection from south-west to north-easterly winds. The smaller, northernmost hollow had a compact group of four small, though prominent, cairns (HF IB), which were probably a result of stone clearance. Within the larger, southernmost bowl, there was a small, three-sided, dry-stone-walled structure (HF 15; HF IC), and the lack of evidence for a fourth wall suggests this possibly served as a shelter. The fourth and fifth monument groups (HF ID and HF IE) comprised two small, compact cairnfields on the southern slopes of the Thwaite spur, containing small, generally low-lying, field clearance-type cairns.

Heathwaite Fell II (Spunham): monuments HF 18-50

A scattered group of small cairns was recorded on a natural terrace at the foot of the Thwaite spur, in an area of slightly undulating and generally well-drained ground (Fig 130). Numerous brash deposits covered the ground and some of the cairns appeared to have been built on top of them, thereby confusing their definition, since these cairns were generally low lying and ill defined. Three sites were clearly artificial and contrast with the rest of the group. Monument HF 34 (Fig 131) was a roughly oval terrace set into a slight slope, with a corresponding mound of spoil on the downslope side. The 'floor' was approximately flat and it may have been a platform for a structure. Monument HF 40 was a well-defined, roughly circular, ring bank, with mainly small stones protruding from the turf cover. There was slight evidence of internal terracing, but no sign of an entrance. This lack of entrance, when coupled with the small size of the stones, inappropriate for dry-stone construction, suggests that it was not a domestic structure, but may well have formed a ring cairn of the type found at Birrel Sike (Richardson 1982). Monument HF 43 was a distinctive, large, oval cairn, contrasting with the adjacent, small, ill-defined cairns, and thus it probably had an alternative function.

Heathwaite Fell III (Beck Gilla): monuments HF 51-73

An ill-defined group of scattered cairns was identified on a very undulating terrace, edged to the east by the Thwaite spur and to the west by the steep slope that drops to the raised mire of Heathwaite Moss (Fig 130). The ground was fairly well drained, although there were sporadic, exposed brash deposits which confused the definition of some cairns (especially HF 54 and HF 55; Fig 131), which had been constructed adjacent to this.

There did not appear to be a significant pattern to the distribution of the cairns, although cairns

HF 68-71 did form a more compact grouping. Most of the cairns were small, fairly low-lying, ill-defined features, and were consistent with stone clearance. There were, however, also two possible roundhouses (HF 56 and HF 57) in this area. Monument HF 56 was a circular bank (c 5.5 m in diameter), which had an entrance to the north-east defined by possible portal stones on either side. Monument HF 57 was a sub-circular platform terraced into a steep, east-facing, slope (5.5 x 4.5 m), with an approximately level floor. It was fairly small by comparison with examples from Northumberland, where a sample of 25 house platforms had an average diameter of 9.8 m (Gates 1983), but it possibly supported a very small structure.

On the opposite side of a steep, rocky gully were two large funerary cairns (HF 59 and HF 60), situated close together. Cairn HF 60 was a large, prominent, regular pear-shaped mound (10 x 4 x 0.5 m), which mainly comprised small stones on the surface. It was well defined and there were indications of a kerb on the eastern side. Cairn HF 59 was only about 3 m upslope from HF 60. It had a circular shape and was smaller (5 x 4 x 0.35 m), but otherwise had a similar form. The size, shape, and possible kerbing of HF 60 were suggestive of a long cairn used for funerary purposes and, by association, HF 59 may have had a similar function. The cairns were positioned part way down a moderate slope, despite the fact that there were prominent hillocks in the vicinity. It would therefore appear that the prominence of the location was not an important factor in the siting of the cairns.

Heathwaite Fell IV (Blawith Knott): monuments HF 87-117

The monuments in this site group were distributed around a small, semi-circular cirque (Fig 130), the bottom of which was filled by an oval bog, originally a tarn. The monuments could be separated into two groups of cairns, associated with a limited number of isolated sites.

The first cairn group (HF IVA; Fig 132) was located to the north of the bog within the bowl of the cirque, and three of the sites (HF 87-9) were on a small natural terrace, about 20 m above the level of the bog. The cairns were generally small, low lying, and were often associated with exposed brash deposits, which confused their definition. Another monument (HF 94) was also discovered in this area, though this was slightly removed from the cairn group. This monument was defined by an irregular, sub-circular, flat-bottomed terrace set into the south-facing slope of the bowl, about 8 m away from the edge of the bog. It was about 7 m across and may have been a platform for a structure.

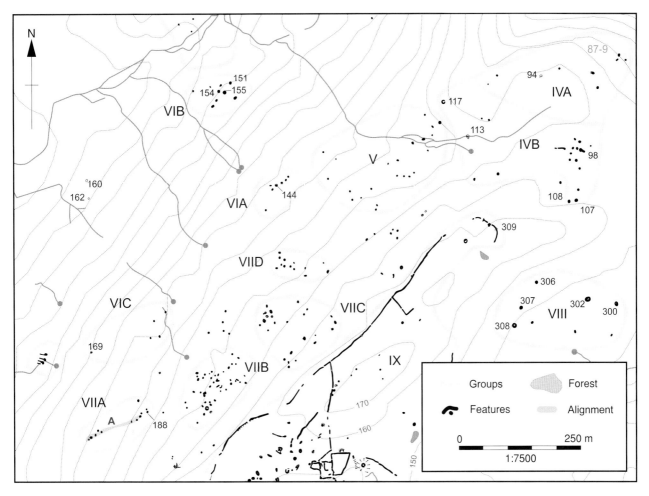

Figure 132: The HF IV-VIII cairnfields

The second group of monuments (HF IVB) was located to the south of the bog, on well-drained, fairly flat ground. The cairns in this group clearly contrasted with those found in the adjacent group, in that they were regular, well defined, and fairly prominent. Some of the cairns were also large (*eg HF 98*, *HF 107*, and *HF 108*), particularly at the northern end of the group, where they had a compact distribution. However, they displayed irregularities that are consistent with stone clearance.

A severely disturbed ring monument, known as Giant's Graves (*HF 113*), was also identified at the western tip of the cirque, and about 85 m to the north-west was another ring feature (*HF 117*), positioned on a raised natural terrace. Monument *HF 113* was a roughly circular bank (10 x 8 m), edged around the southern side by upright kerb stones, and a large orthostat was recorded on the north-western side, with a smaller one to the south-east (Pl 147). Given these features, it is likely that it originally had a funerary function. Extending south-east from the large orthostat was a linear excavation, cut through the middle of the monument. Monument *HF 117* was only slightly prominent, being a circular bank (*c* 8.5 m in diameter), which appeared to be kerbed

both internally and externally by small stones that only just protruded through the turf cover. There was a large slab adjacent to an entrance on the eastern side of the ring, which may have been a portal stone. In the middle was a circular depression, which was probably the result of disturbance. A small modern cairn had been built within the depression in order to prop a large flat stone upright.

Discussion

Evans (1842) described the excavations of two stone circles, which he called Giant's Graves, that apparently lay adjacent to each other. Monument *HF 113* was undoubtedly one of these, particularly as it was labelled Giant's Graves on the 1919 OS 6" to 1 mile map, whilst the other was most probably *HF 117*, which had a limited number of kerb stones and so could have been confused with a stone circle. Furthermore, in both cairns, excavation trenches were visible. Evans (*ibid*) recorded that there was a flat stone covering charred bones in the northern cairn, and in the central depression of monument *HF 117*, a flat stone had recently been propped upright, which may correspond to this feature. The discovery of cremated bone from the ring features would also appear to confirm that

Plate 147: HF 113, the Giant's Graves funerary monument

they were funerary monuments. These essentially form hybrids between the classic forms of ring cairn and stone circle, and according to Lynch's (1972; 1979) classification of Welsh ring monuments, monument *HF 117* would be classed as a 'kerbed ring cairn', and monument *HF 113* probably as a 'complex ring cairn' (*Ch 2, p 41*). There also appear to have been differences of approach in terms of the siting of the monuments; *HF 117* was very prominent, on a raised natural terrace, which was clearly visible from far around, whereas *HF 113* was on a gentle slope beneath some low crags.

Heathwaite Fell V: monuments *HF 118-40* and *HF 287-99*

A scattered cairnfield was identified on moderately sloping, undulating terrain below the main Heathwaite Fell plateau (Fig 130). The component cairns were generally small, low lying, and were consistent with stone clearance. They were loosely distributed across the open fell and extended north-eastwards as far as the two funerary monuments (*HF 113* and *HF 117*; Fig 132) in HF IV. A 100 m-wide area was devoid of cairns, separating the south-western edge of this cairnfield from the HF VII cairnfield, further along the slope. The cairns of HF VII were, in any case, much more closely grouped than those of HF V, and it is probable that these cairnfields were the result of different episodes of clearance.

Heathwaite Fell VI: monuments *HF 141-47, HF 150-9*, and *HF 165-8*

Three small groups of cairns were identified in this monument group, which were located within nivation hollows, set into the moderate to steep slope found to the north-west of the Heathwaite Fell plateau (Fig 130). The first group (HF VIA; Fig 132) comprised a small collection of cairns located on a natural terrace. There were steep, craggy slopes around three sides, which provided shelter from south-westerly to north-easterly winds, and the base of the terrace was relatively flat, although there were scattered patches of bog throughout. The cairns were well defined, fairly prominent, and were regularly shaped, but were nevertheless typical of field clearance. However, monument *HF 144* had a ring form and was probably a disturbed round cairn, which was irregularly defined on its inside edge.

The second cairn group (HF VIB) was fairly compact and was located in a relatively flat-bottomed, bowl-shaped hollow set into the moderate slope of the moor. Within the hollow, the land was fairly well drained, had little surface stone, and was better agriculturally than that found outside of the hollow. Some of the cairns (*HF 151, HF 154*, and *HF 155*) were fairly prominent, but many of them were ill defined. They were consistent with stone clearance, and the area would appear to have been a small patch of cleared agricultural land.

The third cairn group (HF VIC) comprised four small, scattered, clearance-type cairns, which were positioned in the bottom of a bowl-shaped nivation hollow, with steep slopes to the north, east, and south. Within this hollow was also a circular area of bog, which may originally have been a tarn.

Heathwaite Fell VII: monuments *HF 177-285*
A relatively large cairnfield was recorded on a terrace immediately to the north-west of the main plateau (Fig 130). The terrace was essentially flat, but undulating in places, and was generally well drained. To the south-east the ground rose towards the plateau, and to the north-west a steep gradient dropped towards Heathwaite Moss. The undulations of the terrain served to divide the cairnfield into four sub-groups, with each sub-group occupying an area that was relatively flat and free of outcrop and brash deposits. This cairnfield contrasted with that forming the adjacent HF V, in that the cairns were tightly grouped, whereas those in HF V were loosely distributed. Thus, they may reflect different episodes of field clearance, being separated by a 100 m-wide area devoid of cairns.

The first cairn sub-group (HF VIIA; Fig 132) comprised 15 small cairns that were not particularly prominent, which were associated with some brash deposits. Significantly, eight of the cairns were aligned (Alignment A), and since this is unlikely to have been simply coincidence, it may represent the deposition of cleared stone along the line of a former boundary.

The second cairn sub-group (HF VIIB; Fig 132) was located on a relatively flat part of the terrace. The component cairns were tightly grouped, and ranged in form from the typical small, low-lying and ill-defined cairns (*eg HF 203-6*; Fig 133) to large, prominent cairns (*eg HF 201* and *HF 212*). Cairn *HF 201* (7 x 6.5 x 0.4 m) had a well-defined, regular shape and profile; around its northern edge was a low bank, and there were larger stones around the other edges. It did not display the normal, erratic construction characteristics of clearance cairns and may therefore have had an alternative function, but this was the only cairn that may not have resulted from simple stone clearance. At the northern end of the group, cairns *HF 228-30* were linked by a break of slope, which defined three sides of a potential plot (270 m²) that was lower than the level of the adjacent moorland. This was probably a result of soil slippage and may indicate ground disturbance caused by cultivation. With this exception, the cairnfield appeared to have had an essentially random distribution, typical of the primary type of cairnfield.

The third cairn sub-group (HF VIIC; Fig 132) was defined by a compact cluster of cairns (*HF 247-56*; Fig 133) and a loose scatter to the south (*HF 257-70*), which were separated from HF VIIB (*see above*) by a line of large craggy outcrops. The clustered cairns were on a gently sloping, well-drained part of the terrace, many of the cairns being fairly large and generally well defined. By contrast, the scattered cairns were spread across an undulating terrain with an abundance of outcrop and brash deposits, and were generally low lying and ill defined.

The fourth cairn sub-group (HF VIID; Fig 132) was a relatively compact cluster of cairns on a slightly undulating part of the terrace, which contained some brash deposits. Many of the cairns were ill defined and irregular, and were consistent with stone clearance. The only exception to this generalisation was cairn *HF 285* (Fig 133), which was located in a prominent position, on top of a small hillock, away from the main group. It was relatively large (6.5 x 3.8 x 0.4 m), prominent, and was well defined.

Discussion
The cairnfield in this area contained cairns that had a very basic form and an essentially random distribution pattern, spread across an undulating, rocky terrain. With the possible exception of the potential plot (*HF 228-30*; HF VIIB), there was no evidence of any field system, typical of the cairnfields on Heathwaite Fell, and no evidence of any cultivation. The substantial gap between the edge of the cairnfield and the north-western boundary of the settlement at Pewet Tarn (HF IX, *p 272*) indicated that they were unrelated systems (Fig 133).

Heathwaite Fell VIII (Long Rigg): monuments *HF 300-8*
A scattered group of very large cairns was recorded on gently undulating ground on the main plateau (Fig 130). The land was generally well drained, but also included some mire-filled hollows. Large blocks and ridges of craggy outcrop protruded from the landscape, but there were no surface brash deposits. The land was being used for silage production and was of better agricultural quality than that found in many of the other survey areas.

Five cairns were over 6.5 m in diameter (*HF 300, HF 302*, and *HF 306-8*; Fig 132) and most of the component cairns were fairly prominent. The largest, cairn *HF 302* (11.1 x 8.8 x 0.6 m), had a regular, oval shape and a central depression, which was a result of disturbance. Cairn *HF 308* (9 x 7.5 x 0.7 m) also had a central depression, which may have been a result of antiquarian disturbance. They were not typical of stone clearance mounds, but the surface evidence did not allow any firm alternative interpretation.

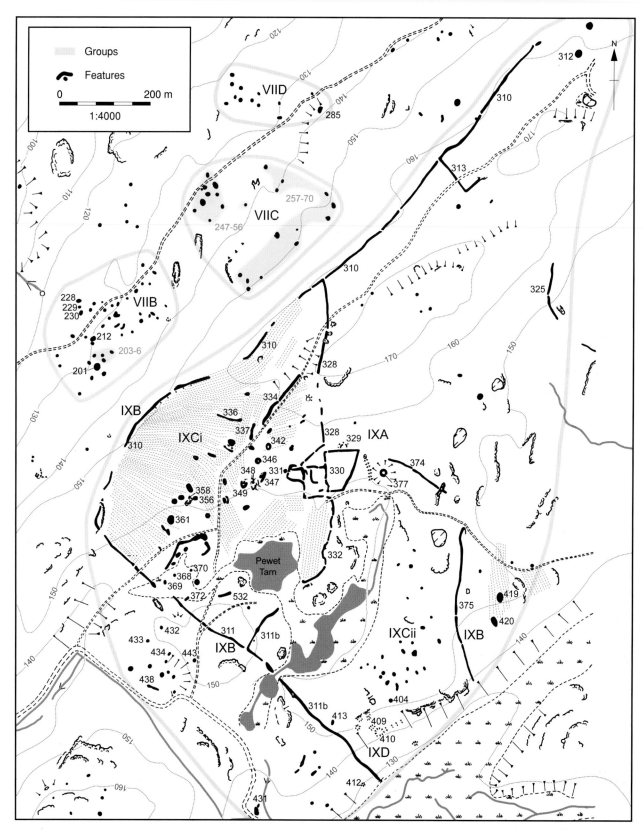

Figure 133: Parts of the HF VII cairnfield and HF IX (Pewet Tarn) settlement and cairnfields

Heathwaite Fell IX (Pewet Tarn): monuments *HF 309-443*

In this area, a complex site group was recorded which was located on a raised section of the main plateau (Fig 130), edged on the north-western side by a gently sloping, long ridge, orientated north-east/south-west, with a steep slope descending on the far (northern) side (Pl 148). The south-eastern side of this raised area was marked by a steep, craggy slope that dropped down to a large, mire-filled hollow. The terrain was

272

Plate 148: The HF IX (Pewet Tarn) settlement and field system, looking south

gently undulating, with occasional craggy outcrops throughout, and relatively few exposed brash deposits. Areas of low ground were filled with tarns and mire, but the adjacent land was often well drained. To a limited extent, the mire appears to have expanded since the construction of the cairns, as it had encompassed monuments *HF 368-70* (Fig 133).

The survey area contained a diversity of elements and types of monument, reflecting multi-phase occupation. The most characteristic was a farmstead (HF IXA), central to the group, from which a series of field boundaries radiated, defining an extensive field system (HF IXB; Pl 148). Both within and outside this were cairnfields (HF IXC), and, set into the southern slope of the raised section, there was a group of possible house platforms (HF IXD).

The farmstead (HF IXA)

The farmstead (*HF 330*) was located on a gentle, south-facing slope and comprised a series of interlinked, rectilinear enclosures (*i-v*; Fig 134). The biggest of these (*i*) was a very large, quadrilateral field/enclosure, bounded by dry-stone walling up to 1.6 m in height. The land within it was rough pasture, although a small break of slope at the top, north-eastern, corner may have been caused by soil slippage. There were three possible entrances associated with this enclosure. The first was found between enclosures *i* and *ii*, which was well defined with possible side portals. The second was a very crude aperture between enclosures *i* and *iii*, whilst the third was represented by a further crude

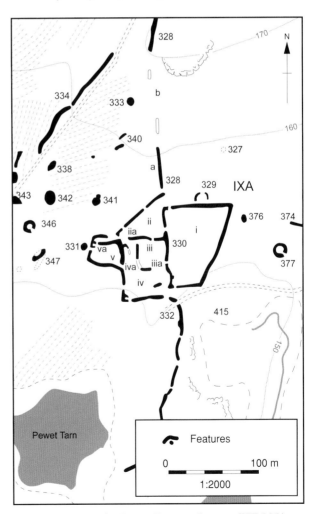

Figure 134: The Pewet Tarn settlement (HF 330)

273

gap at the south-western corner of the enclosure. The western wall was butted by wall *iia*, and at its southern end was built on top of a ridge of outcropping stone; as a consequence, it followed a slightly erratic line.

Enclosure *ii* was clearly a later element, formed by the construction of the north-west wall to enclose an area between enclosures *i* and *iii*. The land within it was rough pasture, apparently unimproved. Enclosure *iii* was a small, irregularly bordered area in the north-eastern corner of enclosure *iv*. The slope within it was gentler and more uniform than that of the adjacent enclosures (*i*, *ii*, and *iv*) and the ground appeared to have been improved; there was a negative lynchet from wall *iia* and a corresponding positive lynchet formed the lower boundary. It would thus appear to have been a cultivated plot. Enclosure *iv* was essentially a square field containing plot *iii* in the north-eastern corner. The enclosed land was fairly rough, rocky, and apparently unimproved.

A large entrance to the settlement complex was located between the south-west corner of enclosure *i* and wall *HF 332*. From the outside, there was a convergence of these walls towards the entrance, which may have been a deliberate construction feature in order to funnel stock into the enclosure.

In the south-west corner of *iv* was a very small structure (1 x 2 m), comprising a small stub of bank extending from the north-south wall, within which there was a deep hollow. Another small, rectilinear, three-sided enclosure was butted against wall *iva* (*c* 4.5 x 2.2 m), which only stood to about two courses high, with little associated collapse. The ground within sloped uniformly, with no sign of artificial levelling; it is therefore unlikely that it was a dwelling.

The land within enclosure *v* has clearly been improved; there was a sharp break of slope down from the northern, upper, wall, and a gradual decrease in gradient towards the south, culminating in an approximately level area adjacent to the bottom wall. A small, three-sided enclosure, similar to that in the south-western corner of *iv*, butted onto the western wall of *v* (2 x 3 m). The continuation of the western wall curved to the east and a possible narrow enclosure had been formed between it and wall *va* (width 1.5 m). The ground within it sloped steeply and was covered by tumble; the enclosing walls comprised small and occasional medium stones, and there was no evidence of any dressed stone. Its narrow shape, lack of internal terracing, and the small stones of its walls do not suggest that it was a dwelling, although its function was not evident.

The boundaries of the enclosures to some degree all displayed evidence of dry-stone construction and it

is apparent that they were walls rather than banks. However, they also appear to have been used for unwanted surface stones; the wall between enclosures *i* and *iii*, and wall *va*, were thicker (*c* 1.7 m and *c* 1.8 m) than strictly necessary and some intact sections of wall *iva* between enclosures *iv* and *v* were over 2.2 m thick. The latter wall stood to a height of *c* 1.5 m and must have absorbed large amounts of clearance stone, which probably originated from the improved land of enclosure *v*, rather than the unimproved land of enclosure *iv*.

No obvious dwellings were recognised within the enclosures, but immediately to the north of enclosure *i* was a semi-circular platform (*HF 329*: 9.5 x 6.5 m) set into the moderate slope, with remains of walling around the inner edge of the terrace. This would appear to have been a small domestic structure.

Taken as a whole, there appears to have been a diversity of agricultural activities represented within this farmstead. Enclosures *i*, *ii*, and *iv* were probably used to contain stock, since they contained essentially unimproved agricultural land, and the entrance to *iv* may have been designed as a funnel. In contrast, enclosures *iii* and *v* contained improved land and top and bottom lynchets, and they would thus appear to have been cultivated, although probably for different types of crop from those produced on areas of ridge and furrow beyond the farmstead (*see below*). The enclosures also appear to have been the product of more than one phase of construction; wall *iia* butted the north/south wall of enclosure *i*, implying that field *iv* post-dated larger enclosure *i*. Wall *iiia* butted onto wall *iia*, confirming that the small cultivated plot, *iii*, was a later feature than enclosure *iv*, which contained it. Finally, the north-western bank of enclosure *ii* appears to have butted wall *va* and therefore post-dated enclosure *v*.

Field system (HF IXB)
A series of banks and walls was centred on the enclosures (*see above*), and although there were substantial gaps, these defined the approximate boundaries of two, or possibly three, large fields (Fig 133; Pl 148).

The south-eastern field was defined by boundaries *HF 332*, *HF 311*, *HF 374*, and *HF 375*, and enclosed an area of about 5.3 ha. Bank *HF 332* extended directly out from the southern wall of enclosure *iv*, and bank *HF 374* was orientated in line with the northern boundary of enclosure *i*, and hence the field clearly related to the farmstead. The southern edge of the field was defined by a sharp, craggy break of slope with a large area of mire at the bottom. Within it was a long tarn with an extensive area of mire around it. To the south-east was a well-drained ridge, which had a cairnfield on it (*p 276*) and some very faint, narrow ridge and furrow, orientated north/south (Pl 149).

Plate 149: Ridge and furrow and walls on the north side of Pewet Tarn

The western field was defined by boundaries *HF 328*, *HF 310*, and *HF 311*, and *HF 332*, and enclosed an area of about 5.7 ha (Fig 133). Bank *HF 328* extended out from the north-western boundary of enclosure *ii* and thus this again appears to have related to the farmstead (Fig 134). The terrain within it was poorly drained around Pewet Tarn, but elsewhere was well drained and had a fairly uniform, gentle gradient. It contained a relatively large cairnfield (*p 276*) and extensive ridge and furrow, which did not extend beyond the limits of outer boundaries *HF 310* and *HF 311* (Fig 133; Pl 150); on the upslope side of bank *HF 310*, there was a broad lynchet. The pattern of the ridge and furrow had been severely compromised by the essentially random distribution of cairns and, in places, there was a change of orientation every 50 m or so to avoid them. The only area where there was a uniform pattern of ploughing was in the north-western part of the field, where there were no cairns.

The area to the north-east of the farmstead had also been cultivated, as indicated by occasional patches of faint ridge and furrow along a gentle ridge and on uniformly sloping land to the east of boundary *HF 375*. However, the surviving banks only partly enclosed the area; boundaries *HF 328*, *HF 374*, and *HF 310* limited the area to the south, west, and north-west, but to the east there was only a 62 m-long bank (*HF 325*), which may or may not have been a survival of a longer boundary.

Another smaller field was possibly defined by boundaries *HF 310*, *HF 313* (Fig 133), and *HF 309* (Fig 132). During the survey, no boundaries were observed linking the eastern end of bank *HF 313* with the southern end of bank *HF 309*, although the 1919 6″ to 1 mile OS map showed a continuation of *HF 313* which passed to the south of a small tarn. On top of a small hillock, within this possible small field, some faint ridge and furrow was visible.

Substantial variations in the form of the boundaries were observed. The northern section of *HF 310* was generally prominent, with large amounts of stone, and displayed clear evidence of dry-stone construction, whereas the southern section (south of the junction with *HF 328*) was ill defined, discontinuous, very irregular, and displayed no evidence of structure. Boundary *HF 311* was generally a stone bank, yet at the north-western end it incorporated a 3 m section of dry-stone wall. Boundary *HF 332* was a substantial wall, which stood up to 1.5 m in places and was up to 2.5 m thick. This had a significantly large proportion of small stones, which was not ideal for dry-stone construction, and it is probable that the wall was built to absorb large amounts of clearance stone. By contrast, boundary *HF 311b* represented the continuation of wall *HF 332* on the opposite side of a narrow mire, yet it was irregular, discontinuous, ill defined in places, and displayed no evidence of structure.

Plate 150: The walls, stone banks, and ridge and furrow of HF IXB

When considering the remains of this field system as a whole, those sections of boundary that did not display evidence of structure had probably never been walls, particularly as there were no foundation stones. Furthermore, it can also be assumed that these foundations were not robbed, as there were abundant, alternative sources of stone around, found within the cairns, brash deposits, and outcrop. The large gaps within the boundaries imply that, by themselves, they did not control stock, and their irregularities and discontinuities suggest that they were a product of field clearance. The sections of dry-stone wall, particularly *HF 332*, incorporated substantial amounts of stone, and it is possible that wall construction was used as a means of absorbing large quantities of cleared stone where necessary.

Cairnfields (HF IXC)

The tarns and mires in the centre of the site group divided the cairnfield into two discrete bands (HF IXC*i* and HF IXC*ii*; Fig 133). The north-western cairnfield (HF IXC*i*) was mainly within the western field, but it also extended to the south-west and was clearly not constrained by its boundaries. The distribution of the cairns was essentially random and there were no alignments associated with the ridge and furrow. Instead, the pattern of ridge and furrow had clearly been disrupted by the need to avoid the inconveniently positioned cairns. Even when the linear banks and

cairns were approximately orientated with the line of the ridge and furrow, there was sometimes still a need, as with *HF 336*, for the plough to divert around the end of the feature. This implies that the cairns pre-dated the ridge and furrow.

The size and character of the cairns varied substantially, depending on which side of field boundary *HF 311* they were positioned. Cairns *HF 431-4* lay outside the field and were generally small, low lying, and ill defined, whereas the cairns inside the field were often large, very prominent, and very well defined. Despite the differences, they all appear to have been a product of stone clearance; they usually had irregular shapes and were often deposited on top of outcrops to maximise the amount of land available for agriculture (*eg HF 347-9, HF 356, HF 358,* and *HF 361*). The difference in scale probably reflects the fact that earlier cairns were added to by stones raised from later cultivation. Another form of stone clearance was possibly represented by sections of bank that contained substantial amounts of stone, yet displayed no evidence of dry-stone construction, and did not relate to any of the field boundaries (*eg HF 334, HF 336-7, HF 372, HF 438,* and *HF 532*).

Monuments *HF 342, HF 346,* and *HF 377* were ring features with prominent, thick outer banks, and deep, internally revetted central hollows that extended far below the external ground level (*HF 377*: bank 0.9 m high (from top of bank); 1.4 m deep; *c* 4 m in diameter internally). Two appeared to have been adapted from former cairns (*HF 342* and *HF 346*) and two had entrances (*HF 346* and *HF 377*). They were located on either side of the farmstead (Fig 134) and may have had a relationship with it. At least one of them (*HF 377*) displayed similarities of form to potash and kilnwood kilns (Davies-Shiel 1974); it was cut into a moderately steep bank, was internally revetted, and had an aperture at ground level (Pl 151). However, its size (8 m in diameter) was more comparable to the latter type of kiln, as these were typically larger than those used to produce potash.

The south-eastern cairnfield (HF IXC*ii*) was partly within the southern field, but also extended beyond its boundaries (*HF 311* and *HF 375*). There was ridge and furrow in association with the cairns, though it was not possible to ascertain any direct relationship between them. However, there were no obvious cairn alignments along the line of the ridge and furrow, and it did not appear to have been influenced by the distribution of the cairns.

The component cairns were generally small, but the height and definition varied throughout the cairnfield. The average height within the southern field was slightly greater than that of the cairns outside the field system (to the south-west of *HF 311b*), but the difference was not as marked as within the northern cairnfield (HF IXC*i*). There were two long

cairns, however, which, in terms of their size and height, clearly contrasted with the others (*HF 419*: 11 x 7 x *c* 0.5 m, and *HF 420*: 11 x 5.7 x 0.38 m). Both had regular, rounded profiles and *HF 420* had a well-defined pear shape. The adjacent ridge and furrow diverted around the cairns and, while they may have been enlarged by the addition of stone brought up by the plough, there is a possibility that they were funerary monuments.

At the north-eastern end of the field system, within a possible field defined by boundaries *HF 310*, *HF 313*, and *HF 309* (Fig 132), there was a large round cairn (*HF 312*: 8 x 7.5 x 0.35 m) on a slight promontory, which dropped sharply away on the northern side. It had a possible kerb around the northern edge and an irregular, internal depression, which was slightly off centre; the irregularities may be an indication of disturbance. It was remote from either cairnfield, was found in a prominent location, and it may have been another funerary monument.

Platforms (HF IXD)
Set into the steep slope that defined the south-eastern edge of HF IX was a group of circular and oval platforms (Fig 133). They varied in size from 2.5 m (*HF 412*) to 8.4 m (*HF 410*) in length, and also varied in form. Monument *HF 410* had a bank around its forward edge, thus creating a hollow rather than a level platform, whilst monument *HF 409* had a long, narrow, ledge-like shape (6.2 x 2.5 m), rather than the normal sub-circular platform. No evidence of combustion

Plate 151: Putative potash kiln HF 377

was observed on the platforms, a characteristic feature of charcoal burning, and, despite the irregularities, these were most probably platforms for domestic structures. Although they were mostly grouped within the southern field, platform *HF 412* lay to the south-west of bank *HF 311b*, and their distribution was not apparently constrained by the field boundaries. They were spatially associated with the southern cairnfield (HF IXC*ii*) and there was a similar group of platforms on the opposite side of a mire-filled gully, which was also spatially associated with small cairns (HF XI; *see below*). There is thus a reasonable possibility that the two groups of platforms were broadly contemporary.

Discussion
The farmstead lay at the centre of the field system, all three internal field boundaries converging upon it, with wall *HF 332* merging into the southern wall of enclosure *iv* (HF IXA; Fig 134); it is therefore a reasonable assumption that the farmstead and field system were in contemporary use. The ridge and furrow was edged by the field boundaries (*HF 310-12*; Fig 133) and none was observed to the north, west, or south of the field system. Although ridge and furrow was recognised to the east of the two fields, there is a case for suggesting that this was contained within a third, less well-defined field. It is therefore a probability that the ridge and furrow was also broadly contemporary with the field system.

Both cairnfields (HF IXC*i* and HF IXC*ii*) extended beyond the boundaries of the field system and, with the exception of the cairnfield within the western field, they were similar in character to the other cairnfields on Heathwaite Fell, which were not spatially associated with field systems (HF IV-VII, *pp 268-71*, and HF X, *p 278*). The pattern of the ridge and furrow in the western field had been severely disrupted by the seemingly random distribution of the cairns, and erratic changes of orientation had been made to avoid one or more of them. The cairns were not aligned along the ridge and furrow, and some of the elongated cairns and banks (*eg HF 336* and *HF 334*) would have disrupted the movement of the plough. Although the distribution of the cairns suggests that they pre-dated both the ridge and furrow and the field system, their character and form within the fields contrasted with those outside; the former were much larger, more prominent, and were sometimes orientated in the direction of the cultivation. The most probable explanation for this apparent contradiction is that the cairns pre-dated the ridge and furrow, hence the distribution, but had subsequently been enlarged and extended through the addition of further waste stone, which had been brought to the surface during the later cultivation of this area.

Although the main group of platforms lay within the southern field, platform *HF 412* was outside. These were similar to a group of platforms on the opposite side of a narrow valley (HF XI; *see below*), which was far beyond the extent of the field system. It is therefore likely that the platforms were not contemporary with the field system, but they might have had a relationship with the southern cairnfield (HF IXC*ii*), since they were spatially associated with this.

There thus appears to have been at least two phases of occupation on this raised section of the plateau. The earliest phase is represented by the cairnfields and possibly also by the platforms, and the second phase is indicated by the farmstead and its associated field system.

Heathwaite Fell X (The Knott): monuments *HF 444-56*
A small cairnfield lay on a very undulating, rocky bench half way up The Knott (Fig 130). The ground was well drained, but there were large outcrops and occasional brash deposits throughout. The cairns were generally small, though occasionally prominent, and were consistent with stone clearance. They were often located adjacent to outcrops or brash deposits, probably in order to maximise the best ground for agriculture.

Heathwaite Fell XI (Knott End): monuments *HF 476-96*
The monuments in this group were scattered across an undulating, rocky hill and an adjacent mire (Fig 130) and these, based on their distribution, could be divided into two distinct sub-groups. The more northerly sub-group (HF XIA; Fig 135) comprised a limited number of small, clearance-type cairns, adjacent to three circular platforms (*HF 483-5*), set into the steep, north-facing slope. The platforms were between 2 m and 4 m in diameter and were generally ill defined. The internal surfaces were not particularly level but clearly contrasted with the slope of the hillside. They were similar in form to the platforms on the opposite side of the valley (HF IXD, *pp 277-8*), but were generally smaller. In addition to the cairns and platforms, this monument group also contained a prominent ring bank (*HF 476*: 6 m in diameter) located at the bottom of the hill, adjacent to a mire. Its external edge was well defined, but the internal edge was ill defined and irregular. There was no evidence of internal terracing and no obvious entrance, and this, coupled with its relatively isolated position, suggests that it may have been a ring cairn.

The other monument sub-group (HF XIB) comprised four small, irregular cairns (*HF 487-90*) on a rocky bench near the top of the hillock; two small rectilinear structures (*HF 492* and *HF 494*); a short, broad, prominent stone bank (*HF 493*); and a small bridge (*HF 495*).

Heathwaite Fell XII (Mawthwaite Moss): monuments *HF 497-521*

Within this group, the monuments were located on a narrow section of moderately well-drained ground, forming an interface between the steep craggy slopes of Burney peak to the south-east and the poorly drained ground of Mawthwaite Moss to the north-west (Fig 130). The terrain was slightly undulating,

but approximately level, with occasional outcrops and exposed brash deposits, mainly on the south-eastern side. The monuments formed two small cairnfields, each having a distinct character, which to an extent reflects the terrain on which they were constructed.

One of the cairnfields (HF XIIA; Fig 135) was located on undulating, fairly rocky, terrain. It had few

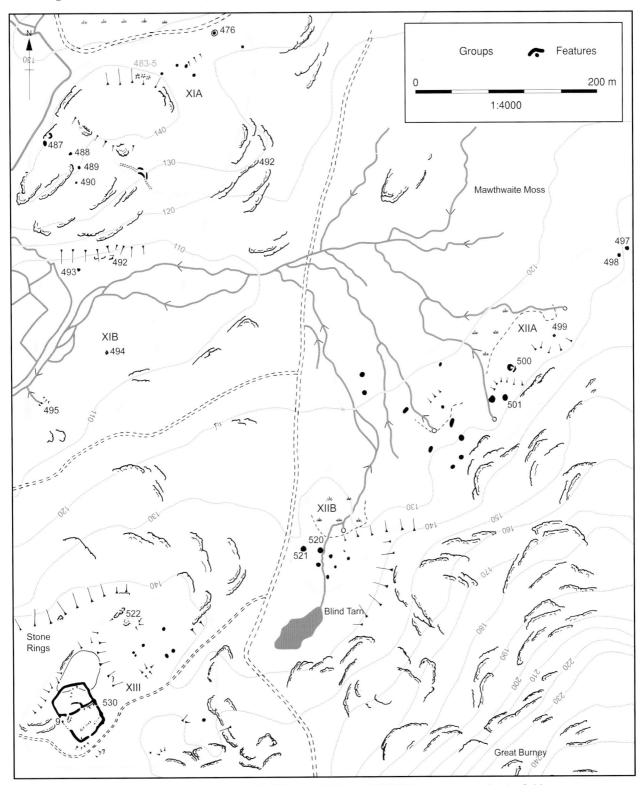

Figure 135: The HF XI and HF XII cairnfields, and HF XIII enclosure and cairnfields

component cairns, scattered over a wide area, which were generally fairly large, only slightly prominent, and well defined. However, within this cairnfield were four large and prominent round cairns, which contrasted with the other, more typical clearance cairns, and may have had an alternative function. These included cairns *HF 497* and *HF 498*, which were remote from the rest of the group to the north-east, and cairns *HF 500* and *HF 501*. These latter two cairns had both been disturbed, but originally had heights extending up to *c* 0.5 m.

The other cairnfield in this area (HF XIIB) was positioned on well-drained, generally level ground in a natural bowl set into the steep north-western slopes of Burney peak. The cairns formed a tight cluster on either side of a small stream. They varied in size and, although the majority were small and not particularly prominent, two moderately large cairns (*HF 520* and *HF 521*) were contained within this cairnfield.

Heathwaite Fell XIII (Stone Rings): monuments *HF 522-30*

This monument group comprised a large enclosure (*HF 530*) on the gently sloping top of a steep-sided hill, and a small group of cairns, with a structure to the north-east of the hill (Fig 135). The ground on top of the hill and around the eastern and southern sides was uneven, with numerous outcrops and occasional brash deposits. However, a large, natural terrace lay immediately below and to the north-west of the hill, which had a very flat surface with no outcrop or brash deposits. No ridge and furrow or other archaeological features were observed on the terrace, but the uniform, levelled surface may be an indication of systematic soil disturbance caused by cultivation.

The component cairns were scattered across well-drained, but undulating, ground at the foot of the hill and were generally, small, irregular, and ill defined. A structure (*HF 522*), remote from the cairns, was also identified, and this comprised a regular, circular, platform set into the gentle slope of a small, natural terrace. The curved edge of a low crag formed the southern external edge, and the internal edge was defined by a curved line of medium to large stones and a very slight bank. It had a north-easterly entrance.

Enclosure *HF 530* (Pl 152) had a roughly rectangular shape and was divided into two similar-sized parts. The ground in both was generally undulating and rocky. The outer boundary survived as a bank with a uniform width, but displayed limited evidence of dry-stone construction on the northern and eastern sides, which signifies that it was originally a wall. The present bank survived to a fairly uniform height

of only *c* 0.3 m, and there was likely to have been only sufficient stone for a relatively low wall. Three entrances through the outer bank into the southern part of the enclosure were identified, but no direct external access was apparent into the northern part of the enclosure. However, there was a possible entrance on its south-western side, which could have been used to funnel stock into either the northern or southern parts of the enclosure. It comprised a bank opposite the entrance, which, if extended with a gate, would have closed off the southern part and forced stock through the entrance into the northern part of the enclosure. Similarly, blocking off the entrance to the northern part of the enclosure with a gate would force stock into the southern part.

Discussion
The land within the enclosure was similar to that outside and did not appear to have been improved. An entrance on its south-western side would have been appropriate for controlling the movement of animals, and the enclosure probably served to corral stock. It was built on rough, undulating ground on the top of a hill, despite there being a flat, well-drained terrace immediately adjacent. This may be an indication that the terrace was used for a more appropriate function, such as cultivation.

The only evidence for a domestic structure, in association with the enclosure, was the single, small building (*HF 522*) below the summit of the hill. This was comparable in form to monument *HF 329* in the Pewet Tarn settlement (*p 274*), which also had elements of a circular stone structure set onto a platform, and similarly was the only such structure associated with the stock enclosures and fields of the HF IX farmstead.

Conclusions
The Heathwaite Fell cairnfields were very basic in character; they comprised randomly distributed cairns that did not appear to be aligned, and there were no stone banks specifically relating to the cairns. The only possible exceptions were three cairns (*HF 228-30*; Fig 133) located along the line of a small lynchet. Some of the cairnfields were relatively large (*eg* HF VII), while others were quite small (*eg* HF XIIB), yet they all appeared to have the same essential character (with the exception of HF IXC*i*, which may have been altered subsequently; Fig 133). There is, therefore, a possibility that they all date to approximately the same period.

The cairnfields outside the HF IX field system were not associated with ridge and furrow, while those inside the field system appear to have pre-dated the ridge and furrow. The basic form of the cairnfields contrasted with known medieval examples

Plate 152: The HF XIII (Stone Rings) enclosure (HF 530), on the top of a small hill

(*eg* WG I; *Ch 3, p 83*) and there is a probability that they corresponded to one of the earlier clearance episodes, rather than that of post-AD 1100 recorded in the White Moss pollen diagram (Wimble 1986). There was later prehistoric activity on Heathwaite Fell, as evidenced by the Giant's Graves ring cairns (HF IV; Fig 132), and forest clearance in the general area has been recorded for the latter part of the Bronze Age (*ibid*). It is therefore tempting to relate the cairnfields tentatively to this early clearance episode.

The HF IX field system clearly defined the limits of the ridge and furrow, and both elements were likely to be in contemporary use. Typically, ridge and furrow was a feature of medieval or post-medieval cultivation (Bowen 1961, 48-9; Hall 2001), and it is therefore likely that the field system coincided with the post-AD 1100 episode of forest clearance (Wimble 1986). However, although these field systems may be a product of medieval or post-medieval activity, no concerted documentary research seems yet to have been undertaken, to draw together the relevant sources, which might aid in the interpretation of the Heathwaite Fell monuments, and specifically the farmstead and field systems at HF IX (A Winchester *pers comm*).

Scattered across the moor were nine small, rectilinear dry-stone structures (*HF 15, HF 41, HF 159, HF 169, HF 193, HF 471, HF 492, HF 494,* and *HF 499*; Fig 130), which, generally, were not spatially associated with the other sites recorded in this area. The only exception to this was structure *HF 193*, which was near two small cairns. The structures were also often located adjacent to topography that provided some protection from the elements; thus, structure *HF 15* was set within a nivation hollow, structure *HF 41* was located between two crags, and structures *HF 169* and *HF 471* were adjacent to west-facing crags. The structures all had approximately similar sizes, some 2.5-5 m in length, and had similar rectangular shapes. Four of them were four-sided structures, but the rest had open sides, which were not necessarily all a result of subsequent decay. They were probably bields, shepherds' huts, or even shielings, and their lack of association with other settlement remains may be an indication that they represent a separate, and less intensive, period of pastoral activity on Heathwaite Fell. The settlement remains therefore appear not only to reflect two widely separated periods of intensive farming activity, but also a sporadic use of the area for upland pasture.

Mickleden

Mickleden (Fig 127) is one of two feeder valleys to Great Langdale, formed through glaciation, with a classic U-shaped cross-section, with very steep sides, and a correspondingly flat base. The sides of the valley are covered with coarse scree and are too steep to have accommodated any settlement, or formalised agricultural activity (Fig 136). However, across the upper slopes on the south-eastern side are the remains of extensive neolithic axe factories, which exploited a band of volcanic fine-grained tuff that outcrops at an altitude of over 600 m OD (Claris and Quartermaine 1989). Drumlins and general morainal drift occupy the extreme north-western valley head, but elsewhere the terrain is generally well drained and mostly level, although the turf cover throughout the valley floor is relatively thin. The ground had sufficient agricultural viability to enable the establishment of a formalised farming landscape across the valley floor (Pl 153), and a rich relict agricultural landscape, comprising a basic field system and cairnfield, survived in the unenclosed sections of the valley. Although there were considerable scree and morainal deposits associated with the sites, field systems had been constructed around the periphery of the drumlins and scree.

Previous palaeobotanical and archaeological investigation

The earliest survey of this area was undertaken as part of the 1862 First Edition 6″ to 1 mile OS mapping, and although this did not show any cairnfields, it did record two stock enclosures (*MB 1* and *MB 136; p 294*). The earliest descriptive record of settlement remains in the area dates from 1877, when Clifton Ward (1878, 254) referred to cairns and some old walled enclosures in the bottom of the Mickleden Valley. In the latter half of the twentieth century, Tom Clare (1980) undertook a schematic survey of the cairnfield, which was presented in an unpublished management evaluation of the axe factories. He identified a rectilinear structure (*MB 92*) in MB IV (*p 290*), and suggested that two monuments (*MB 12* in MB II (*p 288*) and *MB 116* in MB VI (*p 293*)) represented funerary kerbed cairns.

Since this latter survey, the area has been subject to considerable archaeological investigation, which has provided a new macroscopic perspective upon the formation of the valley landscape. The National Trust undertook an historic landscape survey of Great Langdale, which examined the physical and documentary evidence for the development of settlement (Bevan *et al* 1991). This was completed in tandem with a detailed topographical survey of the Mickleden cairnfield by the Lancaster University Archaeological Unit and the National Trust, as

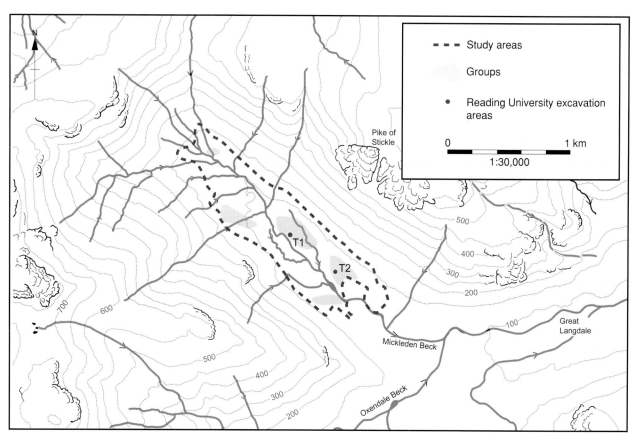

Figure 136: The Mickleden Beck survey area, with the location of the excavation trenches

Plate 153: The MickledenValley, at the head of Great Langdale, looking north-west, with enclosed land in the valley bottom

part of the LDNPS programme. This topographical survey was undertaken alongside a survey of the neolithic axe factories (Claris and Quartermaine 1989), and, following on from the Mickleden survey, a palaeobotanical investigation was undertaken by Reading University as a part of a broader study of the nearby axe factories (Bradley and Edmonds 1993). Indeed, the palaeobotanical history of Great

Langdale has benefited from a considerable amount of pollen analysis of cores from Blea Tarn, Angle Tarn, Langdale Combe, Red Tarn Moss, and Thunacar Knott (Pennington 1965b; 1970; 1973; 1975; Walker 1965a; Bradley and Edmonds 1993). The earliest episode of forest clearance identified from the Blea Tarn and Angle Tarn cores dates from *c* 3000-2000 cal BC, with a peak at about 2500 cal BC (Pennington 1970). The percentages of grass and herb pollen increased with altitude, suggesting that forest clearance expanded down from the summits. A further episode of clearance was identified in a core from Langdale Combe, which was dated to 2029-1667 cal BC (3510±70 BP; OXA-2180; Bradley and Edmonds 1993). This clearance episode continued to the point of peat formation, which in that locality started to form during the later Bronze Age.

Excavation and palynological investigation at Mickleden

Excavation and palynological investigation, undertaken by Reading University's Department of Archaeology, investigated two stone banks (*MB 25* and *MB 70*; pp 288, 292), which extended across the valley, through the excavation of two separate trenches (Fig 136). Trench 1 (Fig 137), across bank *MB 25*, measured 8 x 2 m, and indicated that the bank had a stone core with no formal structure, although there was an impression that the larger stones were peripheral to a small stone core. The excavation demonstrated that a lynchet had formed against the north-western side of the bank, although it was not confirmed whether this was a product of natural or human agency. Trench 2, across bank *MB 70*, measured 10 x 2 m, and revealed a similar irregular stone structure.

Two pollen samples were also taken from Trench 1. Sample A was taken at a depth of between 140 mm and 240 mm, and Sample B at a depth of between 200 mm and 280 mm. Both were at the level of an old ground surface exposed within the section. Only one pollen sample was taken and processed from Trench 2 (Sample C: 260-280 mm), which was from beneath stone bank *MB 70*. The pollen diagram was constructed by calculating each pollen species as a percentage of total pollen (including spores), and the resulting pollen diagram (Fig 138) shows the pollen recorded in all samples.

In Sample A (Trench 1), herb pollen predominated, with relatively limited percentages of tree and shrub pollen, the woodland being mixed, mainly containing *Betula* (birch), *Quercus* (oak), and *Alnus* (alder). Significant numbers of pastureland plants were represented (*Plantago lanceolata* (ribwort plantain), Compositae (dandelion and daisy family), and Ranunculaceae (buttercup family)), but only very limited amounts of plants associated with arable activities (*eg* Cruciferae (cabbage and cress family)).

There is a significant proportion of *Calluna* (heather), by comparison with the other samples, which would suggest a shift towards a heathland environment. There was also a significant increase in Filicales (ferns), which were probably growing on open land near to the sample site. Charcoal was present in fairly large quantities, which may attest to human clearance activity.

In Sample B (Trench 1), a predominance of herb pollen was again seen, by comparison with trees, shrubs, and spores. The grass percentages were extremely high, and significant proportions of *Plantago lanceolata* and Ranunculaceae would suggest that there was an open pastureland environment at the time of deposition. *Cerealia* (cereals) was present in significant quantities, together with *Matricaria T* (mayweed / German chamomile), *Plantago major/media* (hoary plantain), and Compositae *Cichorium*-type (includes dandelions, chicory, and hawkweeds), which may be an indication that arable farming was being undertaken alongside the primarily pastoral economy. Compared with Sample C (*see below*), there was a marked increase in heathland plants, Cyperaceae (sedges), *Pteridium* (bracken), and *Calluna*.

In Sample C (Trench 2), the percentages of herb pollen were very low by comparison with Samples A and B (*see above*). The grasses were significantly reduced and there was a marked increase of shrubs, particularly *Corylus*-type (hazel). The proportion of *Polypodium* (polypodies) was very high compared with the other samples; this grows on or near trees, and its spores are very large, so it is unlikely to have travelled very far. This, together with the *Corylus*-type pollen, would indicate a wet woodland environment, although the presence of Graminae (grasses), *Plantago lanceolata*, and Ranunculaceae would suggest clearance activity and the beginnings of pasturage.

Sample C reflects a very different botanical environment from that seen in Samples A and B; it was a predominantly wet woodland environment in conjunction with limited evidence of clearance, whereas the other two samples reflect a predominantly pastoral landscape, with an indication of limited cultivation. These environmental differences appear to reflect differing stages of clearance. Sample C demonstrated an early stage of clearance, whereas Samples A and B demonstrate a later stage, when the environment had been extensively cleared and a mixed farming economy was being practised.

The low percentages of *Ulmus* (elm) would suggest that the pollen was deposited after the elm decline, regionally dated to *c* 4000-3800 cal BC (Walker 2001; Tipping 1994), and at nearby Blea Tarn, to 4217-3530 cal BC (5020±120 BP; K958; Pennington 1970).

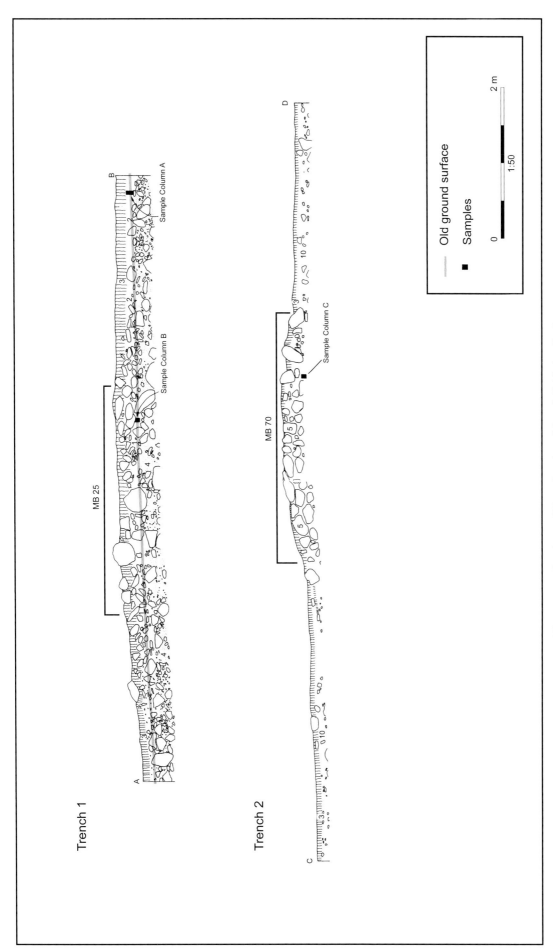

Figure 137: Sections of Trenches 1 and 2 at Mickleden Beck

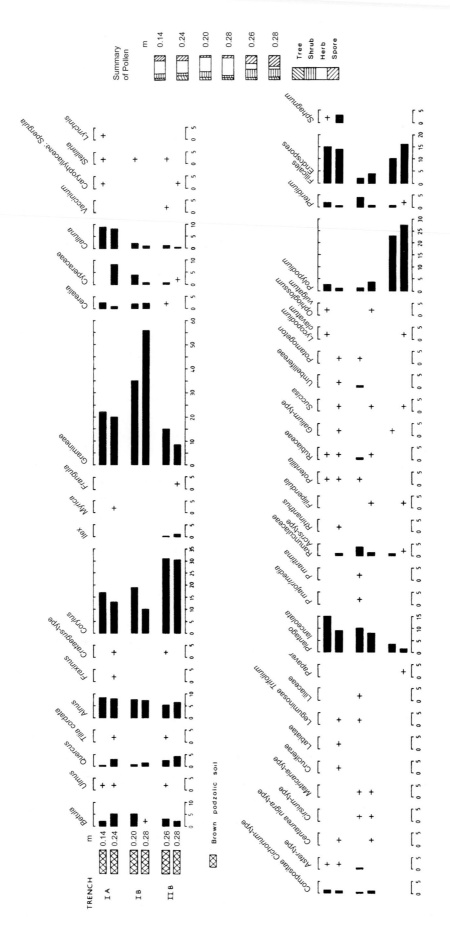

Figure 138: Mickleden Beck: pollen diagram

286

There was also a notable absence of *Pinus* (pine), and this was in line with Walker's (1965a) research, which suggested that *Pinus* had decreased virtually to extinction in the drier areas of the Langdale region (in Godwin's Zone VIc, in the earlier mesolithic period (Godwin 1975)), and was only reintroduced into this area during the seventeenth century AD. The presence of cereal pollen is also significant, as it indicates that cultivation was being practised in the environs of the stone banks. Furthermore, this cultivation might date from the Roman period onwards, as cereal pollen within an upland context is rare prior to this period, but appears during the Roman period at upland sites, such as Burnmoor and Devoke Water (Pennington 1970; *Ch 3, p 101*; *Ch 5, p 203*). It would therefore seem probable that the diagram fits between the onset of cultivation in the Lakeland highland zone in the Roman period and the seventeenth-century reintroduction of pine.

Survey area

The survey was undertaken intermittently between June and September of 1984 and 1985, when weather conditions prevented high-altitude work on the axe factories. However, summer working meant that some of the sites, particularly along the valley sides, were obscured by considerable bracken growth, and as a consequence, there is a possibility that occasional, peripheral monuments were not recorded. The survey area comprised 0.6 km² of unenclosed, valley bottom land (Fig 139) from which 140 monuments were identified within six site groups (Fig 140).

The extent of the survey area was defined to the north, west, and east by the steep valley sides, and to the south-east by enclosed farmland. No survey was undertaken within the enclosed fields because land improvement had resulted in the destruction of any settlement remains, and the corresponding construction of some extremely large, relatively recent, clearance cairns. Visitor pressure has also both directly and indirectly resulted in damage to monuments; for example, some of the cairns at the south-eastern end of the survey area were robbed in 1984 to provide metalling for the adjacent valley track (J Quartermaine *pers obs*). Pedestrian and vehicle erosion along this track had also resulted in damage to walls and stone banks, mainly within the MB III group (monuments *MB 19, MB 25, MB 26, MB 41,* and *MB 47; p 289*), and drainage operations had resulted in damage to some of the monuments.

Mickleden I: monuments *MB 2-10*

A small cairnfield lay between 160 m and 170 m OD on an undulating, relatively gently sloping terraced area on the south-western side of the Mickleden Valley (Fig 140). It comprised seven cairns and an approximately semi-circular stone bank (*MB 4*; Fig 141), forming an arc on the west side of a drumlin. Monument *MB 5* was a seemingly modern ring of stones within this arc, its stones not being set in the ground, but instead situated lightly on the grass. The cairns (*MB 2, MB 3,* and *MB 6-10*) were partly turf-covered, of an average height of 0.4 m, and

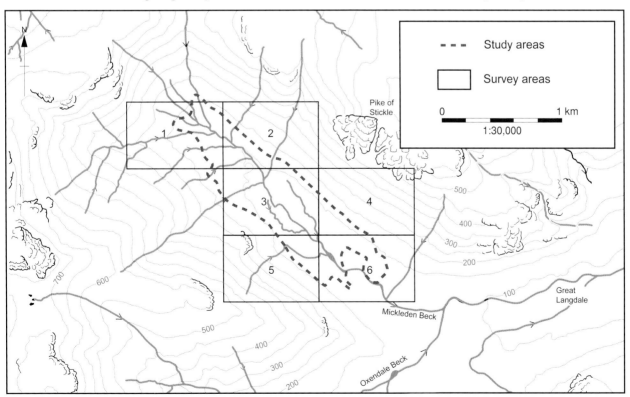

Figure 139: The Mickleden Beck survey area as planned

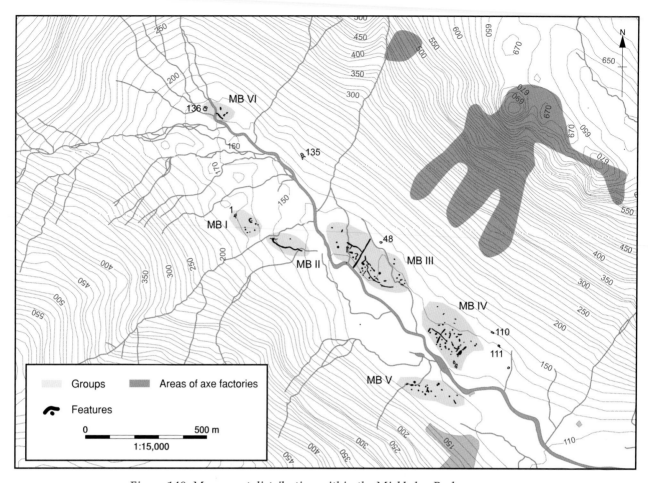

Figure 140: Monument distribution within the Mickleden Beck survey area

had some evidence of disturbance, the stone bank (*MB 4*) and one of the cairns having been built against natural features to maximise the available ground for agriculture. The cairn group was not directly associated with a field system and it would appear to have been a primary form of cairnfield.

Mickleden II: monuments *MB 11-12*

A continuous, decayed wall (*MB 11*) and a kerbed cairn (*MB 12*; Fig 141) were recorded on a gently sloping area of cleared pastureland bounded by streams on three sides (Fig 140). Wall *MB 11* effectively acted as the fourth side of an enclosing quadrilateral that linked two parallel streams; there was no evidence of a continuation on the opposite sides of each stream. This enclosed land was mostly clear of loose stones, was well drained, and is relatively good-quality pasturage. The wall, in places, was over 1 m high and included sections of intact dry-stone masonry.

The wall had no direct relationship with a small circle of about 20 stones defining the external kerb of a cairn (*MB 12*; Pl 154). There was an internal, slightly raised scatter of stones, with evidence of a slight depression, or disturbance, just south-east of the centre. The stones stood to a height of 0.25 m, and the plan was slightly oval, measuring 4 x 3 m on each axis. This

form corresponds to Lynch's (1979, 5) kerbed cairn monument type, which she defined as 'being between 3 m and 5 m' and having 'inappropriately large kerb stones'. On the basis of excavated Scottish examples, they are typically dated to the later Bronze Age (Ritchie *et al* 1975). Despite the spatial association, there is no evidence of a relationship between either of these sites and the nearby MB I cairnfield.

Mickleden III: monuments *MB 13-57*

A cairnfield and associated field system were recorded on the flat valley bottom on the north-east side of Mickleden Beck (Fig 140). To an extent, the distribution of the cairns was dictated by the topography, as four drumlins defined a northern edge to the group. Cairnfields MB III-IV were broadly similar in form, but were localised and separated by a 160 m-wide cairn-free gap (Fig 142). The land between the two could have been used for agriculture and the topography of the terrain did not appear to explain the evident separation between them.

The most significant element of the group was the field system, comprising a long, cross-valley wall (*MB 25*), and a series of stone banks meandering along the valley (*MB 19*, *MB 26*, *MB 27*, and *MB 37-41*). The cross-valley wall (*MB 25*) was considerably

288

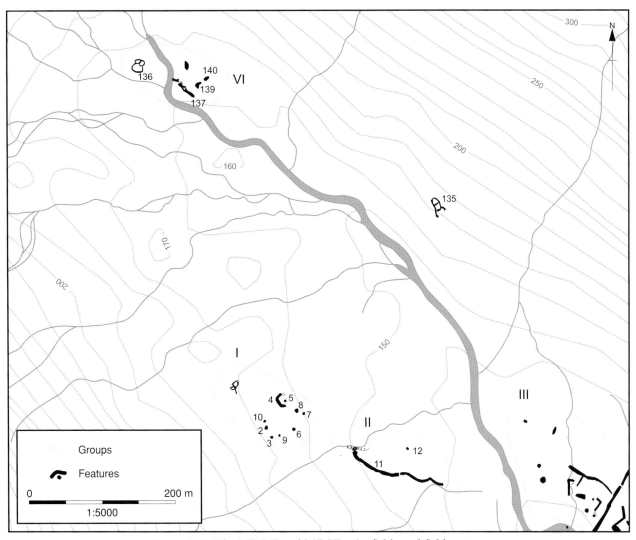

Figure 141: The MB I-II and MB VI cairnfields and field systems

Plate 154: Kerbed cairn MB 12

decayed, but was broadly continuous and up to 0.5 m in height (Pl 155). It contained a considerable volume of stones, perhaps therefore a decayed dry-stone wall, and was targeted for excavation by Reading University (*p 284*). By contrast, the stone banks that extended along the valley were low, discontinuous, and irregular in volume of stone and width. In places they included cairns within their overall lines (*eg MB 26, MB 39,* and *MB 41*). Their form was more consistent with stone clearance, perhaps deposited against former boundaries.

The stone banks appeared to have defined two very irregular and discontinuous lines along the valley. That to the south was defined by banks (*MB 20, MB 24,* and *MB 37-41*), whereas that to the north was defined by banks / cairns (*MB 19, MB 26, MB 27,* and *MB 42*). There was a clear relationship between the cairns and the stone banks, particularly as cairns were incorporated into stone banks (*eg MB 42*) and an alignment of cairns (A) was orientated with a dog-leg in stone bank *MB 37*. However, there was no direct relationship between wall *MB 25* and either the cairns or the stone banks; its only possible relationship was with stone bank *MB 19*, which stopped 2.5 m short of wall *MB 25*. Wall *MB 25* extended considerably beyond the extent of the

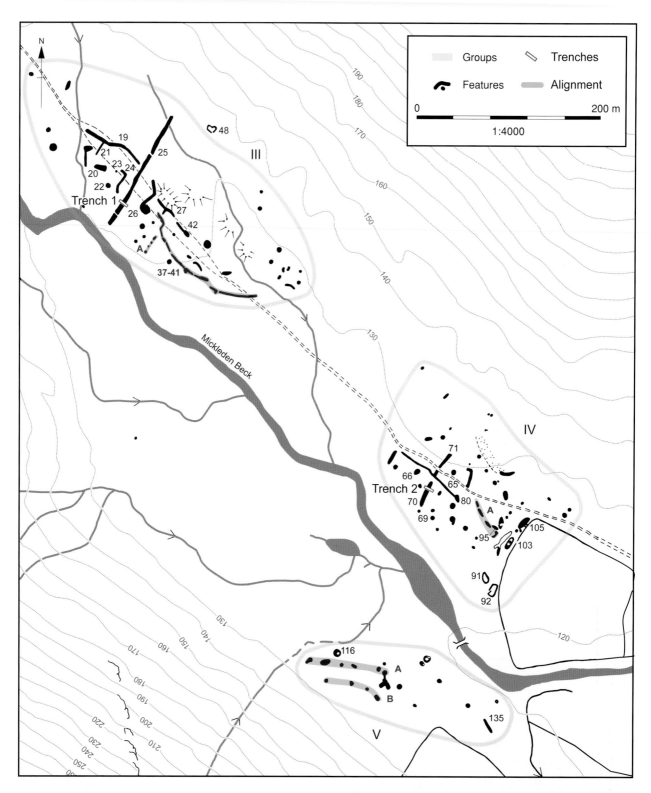

Figure 142: The MB III-V field systems

cairnfield group, was very different in form to the boundary features within the main group, and was not necessarily a contemporary feature.

Mickleden IV: monuments *MB 58-109*

A cairnfield and associated field system was located in the valley bottom on the north-eastern side of Mickleden Beck (Fig 140). The cairns were generally well defined, prominent, and, in some instances, were fairly large (Pl 156). Notable amongst these was cairn *MB 66* (Fig 142), which was pear-shaped, large, and prominent (8.2 x 6.9 x 0.6 m). This cairn had also been disturbed, but otherwise had a rounded profile. Despite their size and prominence, none of the cairns was sufficiently distinctive to justify interpretation as a funerary monument.

Plate 155: Walls MB 25 *(foreground) and* MB 19, *within MB III, looking north-west*

Plate 156: The MB IV cairnfield, looking south

The field system was composed of discontinuous and generally irregular stone banks. The main stone bank (*MB 65*) was orientated along the valley, was extremely low-lying (a maximum of *c* 0.1 m high), and contained minimal amounts of stone. A further stone bank orientated along the valley comprised four elongated cairns (*MB 86-8* and *MB 95*). The stone bank across the valley (*MB 70-71*), which was trenched by Reading University (*p 284*), was wider, had a relatively large volume of stone (Pl 157), and butted the much narrower *MB 65* stone bank. The stone banks were closely associated with cairns; for instance, stone bank *MB 65* terminated at a large cairn (*MB 80*), cairn *MB 69* was directly in line with stone bank *MB 70*, and, to an extent, the cairn distribution was defined by stone banks. It would thus appear that the cairns and the stone banks were contemporary features.

The south-eastern end of the site group had been truncated by the later enclosure wall, which is shown on the 1862 First Edition 6" to 1 mile OS map.

There were, however, some significant surviving monuments adjacent to this dry-stone wall. Cairn *MB 105* was a long mound of exposed stone in an area of closely cropped grassland. Its maximum height was only 0.26 m, but the centre had been extensively disturbed. Despite its poor condition, both the outline and orientation were well defined. Set on top of the mound was a small, semi-circular ring of stones, which butted the modern field wall and was clearly a later feature. Mound *MB 103* was similar in shape and size to *MB 105*, and similarly had been extensively disturbed.

Two structures (*MB 91* and *MB 92*) were located slightly apart and to the south of the main group. Monument *MB 92* was a single-celled, rectilinear structure (Pl 158), comprising a turf-covered external bank with a stone core (0.4 m high). It had a single entrance, with an inward turning terminal to the bank on the west side. Adjacent to it was a pear-shaped bank of medium-sized stones (*MB 91*), enclosing an area that was free of stones (Pl 159). It was very well

Plate 157: MB 71, *looking towards Pike of Stickle and the axe factories*

Plate 158: MB 92, *looking east*

Plate 159: Pear-shaped structure MB 91, *looking east*

defined and may have been a structural feature. These two possible structures were spatially remote from the main group, and also variant in form. It is therefore possible that they were not contemporary elements, but may have had more in common with other rectilinear structures scattered throughout the valley (p 294).

Mickleden V: monuments *MB 113-34*

A small cairnfield lay on a natural terrace on the south-western side of Mickleden Beck (Fig 140). The group included only a very short stone bank

(*MB 135*; Fig 142) at the eastern edge of the site, but there were two alignments of elongated cairns orientated in the direction of this alignment (A and B). There is therefore an implication that the cairns were constructed along the line of a former boundary.

The cairns were generally well defined, although some displayed evidence of disturbance, and for the most part they were consistent with stone clearance. Cairn *MB 116* was distinctive in terms of its relative size (6.2 x 6.0 x 0.5 m), prominence, and its regular form, but a funerary interpretation cannot be attributed on the basis of these surface characteristics alone.

Mickleden VI: monuments *MB 137-40*

A series of irregular stone banks and occasional cairns was recorded at the head of the Mickleden Valley, to the east of the beck (Fig 140). The terrain was undulating, but the group was located on one of the few localised areas with level ground. The main stone bank (*MB 137*; Fig 141) was short, wide, and contained a considerable amount of stone. Banks *MB 139* and *MB 140* were aligned on the eastern end of bank *MB 137*, and apparently reflect a considerable amount of clearance stone deposited against an L-shaped boundary.

Stock enclosures and domestic structures

Several irregular stock enclosures and domestic structures were scattered around the edge of the valley bottom (Fig 140). Three of the enclosures (*MB 1*, *MB 135*, and *MB 136*) were located at about the 170-180 m contour, part way up the valley sides and mostly adjacent to drumlins. They had masonry standing to a height of 1.5 m and were multi-celled. Enclosure *MB 136* comprised three cells, of which one may have had a domestic function. This monument would appear to have been multi-phased and possibly developed from an original circular pound. The condition and form of the stock enclosures would indicate a post-medieval date, although it is possible that the original phase of enclosure *MB 136* may have had an earlier origin.

In addition, another three smaller, and more decayed, structures were located further down the valley side (at about 130-140 m OD). Enclosure *MB 48* was also a stock enclosure, but was considerably more decayed and smaller than the others (Fig 140). In contrast, monuments *MB 110* and *MB 111* may have had a domestic function. Monument *MB 110* was a dry-stone structure incorporating two cells, one of which was a stock enclosure, whilst the other appeared to have been a sub-rectangular building, although there was no surviving evidence of an entrance. Monument *MB 111* was a rectilinear, single-celled structure with apertures at both ends, more consistent with a domestic function than stock control. None of the structures related to the areas of cairnfield and field system, but would appear to reflect a later episode of pastoral activity within the valley.

Conclusions

The combined evidence from both the extant remains and palaeobotanical analysis suggest that the Mickleden monuments were the product of more than one phase of agricultural activity. The palaeobotanical core from Langdale Combe (Bradley and Edmonds 1993), above the valley, identified an intensive Bronze Age clearance episode, probably reflecting activity in the immediate locality of the core site; small stone structures, possibly relating to transhumance, have also been found at Langdale Combe. These were sealed by peat and therefore must be earlier than the onset of peat formation (*op cit*, 140). However, the source of the pollen may also include the adjacent valley bottom (Moore *et al* 1991, 15). The identification of a kerbed cairn (*MB 12*; Fig 141) is an indication that at least some parts of the valley bottom were cleared of forest during the Bronze Age, and this confirms that there was activity within the valley at this time. The random nature of the cairns within the main cairnfield groups (MB III-V; Fig 140) suggest these were primary cairnfields, which in other areas have been ascribed to the prehistoric period (*eg* Stockdale Moor; see *Ch 3*). However, this does not necessarily exclude the possibility of a primary forest clearance episode at a later date.

There was also evidence of later activity within the valley, with rectilinear and even boat-shaped structures (*MB 91*, *MB 92*, *MB 110*, and *MB 111*) that might date to the medieval period. Indeed, a parallel for structure *MB 92* was a medieval structure (*BF 892*) found on Bootle Fell (*Ch 5*, *p 136*). However, these probable medieval features had no direct relationship with the cairnfields, and they were also all distinct in form from the individual elements of the adjacent cairnfields. It is therefore possible that in the Mickleden Valley there was a multi-phased occupation, and that prehistoric farming areas were reused during the medieval period. Such a reuse would inevitably involve a certain amount of adaptation of the earlier features, as well as the construction of new boundary markers and domestic structures. The pollen analysis from beneath the stone banks in the MB III-IV monument groups (*pp 288-90*) unfortunately had ambiguous results, but did suggest a very broad date range for this activity, falling between the start of the Roman period and the seventeenth century AD.

7

THE EASTERN FELLS

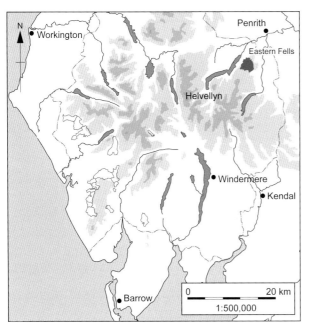

Figure 143: The extent of the survey on the Eastern Fells

The Eastern fells are defined to the west by the Troutbeck and Ullswater valleys, which separate them from the Helvellyn massif (Fig 143). On this western side, the fells are steep, exposed, craggy mountains, which rise to 828 m OD (High Street). Extending north, east, and south from High Street are radial valleys, which contained most of the later settlement in the region (Kentmere, Longsleddale, Swindale, Haweswater, and Bannerdale). Towards the east, the fells are lower (*c* 300 m OD), more rolling, with rounded hills, which eventually merge with the lower lands of the Lowther valley.

The area has been investigated by three landscape survey programmes, which have examined a significant proportion of the lower, easternmost fells. These include the Shap and Askham survey, which examined localised areas around Ralfland Forest, Knipe Moor, and the north side of Haweswater. This survey was undertaken as part of the LDNPS programme, but was published separately (Turner 1986; 1991). The second was undertaken for the Lake District National Park Authority and the North West Water Authority and examined over 85 km² of

enclosed and unenclosed land within the Haweswater Estate (LUAU 1997c). The third survey focused on marginal land on Askham Fell, and the results of this work form the basis of this chapter.

Taken together, the surveys across the Eastern Fells discovered that the extent of early settlement was generally scattered on marginal, moderately sloping land throughout the lower fells, and that it comprised prehistoric, Roman, and medieval settlement remains, each centred on different foci. The prehistoric settlements survived as localised cairnfields, scattered throughout the marginal fell, whilst Roman settlement was focused in the north and west, near to High Street, where the Roman road from the southern Lake District crossed the high fells towards the fort at Brougham (Margary 1973). In contrast, the medieval settlement was typically contained within the valleys and the area around Shap Abbey.

Askham Fell

Askham Fell forms a gently sloping col between Heughscar (north) and Loadpot (south) Hills, on a ridge dividing Ullswater from the Lowther Valley (Fig 144). It forms a natural communication route between the two valleys and has been used as such since the prehistoric period (*cf* AF VII; *p 305*). The survey area encompassed slightly undulating, unenclosed moorland, which was edged to the north, west, and east by enclosed land, and to the south-west by an arbitrary line corresponding approximately to the 360 m contour.

There are extensive mires and areas of poor drainage, mainly around the central flat area of the col, near Pulpit Holes. These areas were generally devoid of archaeological monuments, which were mostly located on the slightly higher, better-drained, ground. There was only evidence for limited change to the drainage pattern in localised areas, notably the small mire in cairnfield AF IC, which encompassed parts of banks *AF 35*, *AF 37*, and *AF 38* (*p 301*), and may have expanded since the construction of the cairnfield.

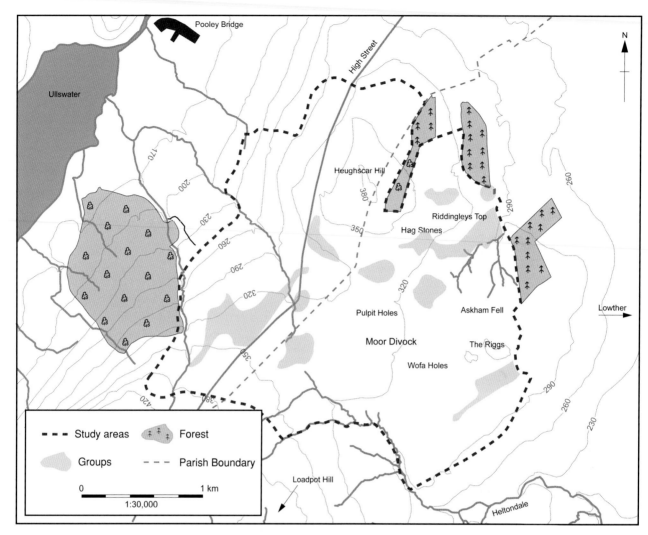

Figure 144: The Askham Fell survey area

The solid geology of the region is limestone, and consequently the area is pock-marked with sink holes. The main concentrations of these are in the central, flatter parts of the col (Pulpit Holes and Wofa Holes), but there are other occasional, scattered sink holes throughout the area. Some were either formed, or have expanded, relatively recently. For instance, bank *AF 213* (near Heugh Scar, *p 298*) lay on the edge of a line of sink holes and had partly collapsed into them, probably as a result of their expansion. A small sink hole was also identified in the middle of stone avenue *AF 121* (*p 305*), with the orthostats forming the avenue being positioned on either side of its edges, whilst a grouse butt was found collapsing into an adjacent feature.

On the higher parts of the fell, mainly around Heughscar Hill, limestone pavement is exposed in patches, with only thin turf cover over more extensive, adjacent areas. The land is of limited agricultural quality, but it was able to support two early, although not contemporary, farmsteads (*AF 203* and *AF 206*, *pp 309-11*). Areas of pavement existed within their outer banks, but that within farmstead *AF 203* was slightly below the

external ground level and had probably been exposed as a result of grazing, or other forms of erosion. It has been demonstrated that in some areas, notably around Malham Tarn, sheep grazing can lead to a reduction in turf cover over the limestone pavement (Sweeting 1974, 56-9), hence the land quality around the farmsteads may have been better in antiquity than at present.

Archaeological history

The earliest recorded antiquarian activity on Moor Divock, which is a part of Askham Fell (Fig 144), was an excavation of round cairn *AF 130* (*p 306*) by Canon Simpson in about 1861, which discovered an adult inhumation contained in a slightly off-centre cist (Taylor 1886, 335-6). Possibly at about the same time, Canon Simpson also excavated round cairn *AF 119* (*p 305*), in which he found a cremation within an inverted urn (Simpson 1883; Taylor 1870, 165).

The Moor Divock monuments were also depicted on the 1863 First Edition 6" to 1 mile OS map, which showed the most prominent of these monuments. These included High Street (*AF 1, p 299*); The Cockpit (*AF 86, p 302*); the Cop Stone (*AF 115, p 305*); and the

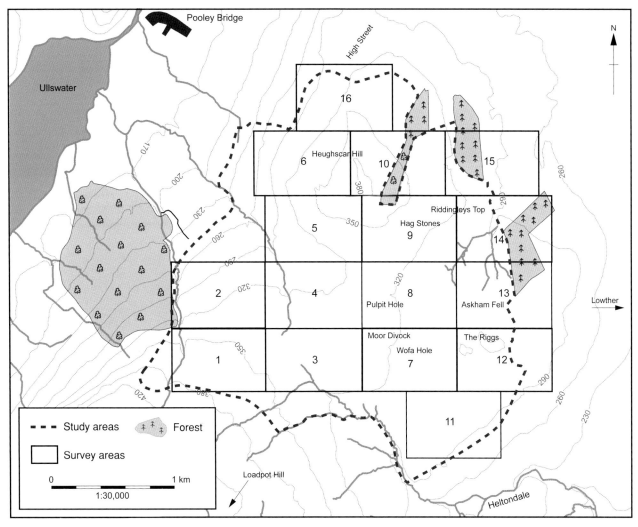

Figure 145: The Askham Fell survey area as planned

tumuli found at AF VII (*p 305*). The following year, in 1866, Canon Greenwell and Michael Taylor excavated in cairn circle *AF 117* (*p 305*), where they uncovered the cremated remains of an adult in association with a Food Vessel (Greenwell 1877, 400-1). Taylor (1886, pls I-IV) produced individual plans of monuments *AF 86, AF 115, AF 117, AF 119, AF 122,* and *AF 130,* and also recorded stone avenue *AF 121,* but in a more continuous form than was observed during the present survey. There was no depiction of the sink hole, which is presently on the line of the stone avenue.

In 1933, after approximately a 50-year hiatus, Spence (1934) initiated a new wave of interest in Askham Fell, undertaking a basic survey of the Threepow Raise cairnfield (AF II). The following year, he reported on the excavation of three cairns from the same cairnfield (Spence 1935a), the positions of two of which were tentatively identified by the LDNPS (*pp 301-2*). No burials were found and the description of one of the cairns, in particular, appears to indicate that it had been for clearance. In the same year he undertook a basic survey of the 'Romano-British' and 'medieval' settlements (*AF 203* and *AF 206, pp 309-11*)

on Skirsgill Hill (Spence 1935b), and two years later the RCHM(E) (1936, 21-8) published a more detailed plan of the *AF 203* enclosed settlement. Between 1938 and 1943, Hay (1938; 1943; Collingwood 1937) identified a second crossing point of High Street (*AF 5*) over Elder Beck, in addition to that marked on the OS maps near The Cockpit.

The more substantial monuments on Askham Fell have been scheduled as Ancient Monuments on the basis of the 1899 6" to 1 mile OS map. These include the individual funerary monuments of AF VII, The Cockpit stone circle (*AF 86, p 302*), three monuments from the Threepow Raise cairnfield (AF II), and also the area between two Romano-British-type enclosed settlements on Skirsgill Hill (AF X; *p 309*). However, the adjacent settlement, *AF 206* (*p 311*), was not included on the list of scheduled monuments in this area.

The survey area

The survey was undertaken in May 1988 on 5.5 km^2 of unenclosed moorland (Fig 145), recording 221 monuments which formed 12 monument groups

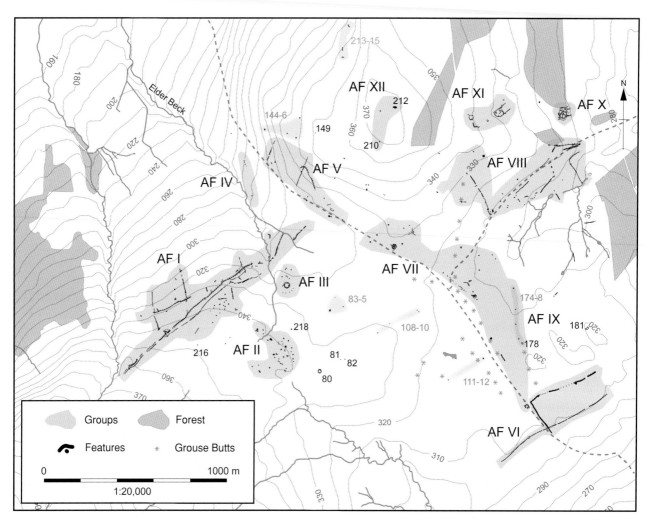

Figure 146: Monument distribution within the Askham Fell survey area

(Fig 146). Askham Fell displayed more variety in the character of its monuments and landscapes than any other of the areas considered during the LDNPS programme. These varied from a section of Roman road, with associated field system (AF I), to a line of prehistoric funerary monuments extending across the moor (AF VII) and a substantial stone circle, known as The Cockpit (*AF 86, p 302*). There were also cairnfields (AF II) and more scattered groups of cairns and associated stone banks (AF IV-V), but nothing of the complexity found in West Cumbria. Two diagnostic settlements were surveyed on the eastern side of the study area, one a complex enclosed settlement (*AF 203, p 309*), and nearby an enclosed settlement containing a rectilinear house (*AF 206, p 311*). In addition, there were abundant remains of post-medieval mineral extraction and lime working.

There were about 36 small, round cairns (*eg AF 81-5, AF 108-12, AF 144-6, AF 149,* and *AF 216;* Fig 146) and banks (*AF 213-15*; Fig 146) scattered across the moor which were not incorporated into groups or cairnfields, and displayed no relationship to any other monuments. They have not been described here

(details are contained within the archive and LDHER). In addition to the numbered sites, there were also some late post-medieval/industrial monuments, which were scattered across the moor. Although these were often in the proximity of site groups, they were clearly not related, including grouse butts, lime kilns, and evidence for quarrying.

Grouse butts

In the course of the survey, 27 grouse butts were recorded on Askham Fell, and apart from one in the Wofa Holes area, all of these were arranged in lines. There were four lines of butts radiating south-east, north, south-west, and west from a well-built, central butt near the junction of two tracks (Fig 146). To the south-west of the main fell track was a further line of six butts, facing south-west into the area of the Wofa holes. They varied in form, some being simple curved banks with only limited evidence of internal revetting, whereas others had complete circular plans with well-constructed entrances. They were all on the south-eastern side of the parish boundary between Askham and Barton, which also serves as the boundary between two estates.

298

Lime kilns

Two lime kilns (*AF 147* and *AF 181;* Fig 146) and associated quarries were recorded within the survey area, and another just outside, at NY 4829 2354. Kiln *AF 147* lay on the western slope of Askham Fell and was linked via a charging ramp to the main Pooley Bridge/Helton track. It was built into a terrace and comprised a partly decayed, rectilinear, dry-stone structure set into a moderate slope. The single bottom aperture was arched and in good condition (1.1 m high), but the top charging aperture was blocked, and its precise width remains unknown.

Kiln *AF 181* lay on relatively gently sloping ground and was partly set into a large, irregular, artificial mound on top of a relatively low natural rise. It comprised a rectilinear, masonry draw kiln, with a single firing chamber standing to a height of 4.65 m, with an arched base aperture, 1.85 m high, and a 3.5 m-wide top aperture. The lime output was transported via 20 m of hollow-way to a track that led onto the Helton road.

These were typical examples of the draw kiln, which first appeared during the eighteenth century and was constructed in large numbers during the eighteenth and nineteenth centuries (Johnson 2002; LUAU 1989, 8-11). The earlier of the two kilns was probably *AF 147*, since, despite the fact that both were marked on the 1863 First Edition 6″ to 1 mile OS map, *AF 147* was described as an 'Old Limekiln' and had presumably fallen out of use by that date.

Quarrying

Extensive areas of opencast extraction were identified across the moor, which were not related to the lime kilns. The quarrying was linear in shape and was found on a broad line that extended from the west side of Heughscar Hill (NY 484 234; Fig 144) via the Hag Stones area to south of the Riggs (NY 499 218), apparently following a mineral vein. Only small sections of quarry (near the Hag Stones) were shown on the 1863 First Edition 6″ to 1 mile OS map, implying that most of the extraction took place after that date.

Askham Fell I (High Street): monuments *AF 1-38, AF 100,* and *AF 219*

This monument group was located on gently sloping ground on the edge of the Ullswater valley (Fig 146). It was generally well drained, but there were occasional, localised patches of mire scattered throughout the area. It contained two diverse elements: a section of Roman road, with associated banks; and a small cairnfield.

Roman road (AF IA)

A 1180 m-long section of the High Street Roman road (*AF 1* and *AF 5*; Fig 147) was located within this survey area. Beyond the visible south-western end of the road was an area of thick peat and, despite extensive ground reconnaissance, no continuation was observed. The north-eastern end of the Roman road section appeared to merge with a modern track, which probably defined the continuing line of the road. The surviving section was not entirely continuous and its form varied throughout its length. The best-preserved section, between NY 4764 2219 and NY 4792 2224, comprised a well-defined, fairly regular, flat-topped *agger,* with an irregular, discontinuous ditch only on the south-eastern (upslope) side, cutting through the *agger* in two places to allow for drainage. The *agger* was on average about 4 m wide and up to 0.5 m above the bottom of the ditch. By contrast, at the south-western end (between NY 4738 2176 and NY 4755 2192), the road could only be seen as two parallel ditches, between 7 m and 9.5 m apart, with no evidence of an *agger*.

As the road approached the gully of Elder Beck, it became increasingly damaged as a result of water erosion; the ditches increased in size and the *agger* became a round-profiled, central bank that eventually disappeared completely into a large water-worn gully, at the bottom of which was a localised area of mire. It would appear that the road and ditches affected the drainage pattern of the area on the western side of Elder Beck, and the gully and localised mire may have formed since the road was constructed.

A possible ford crossing Elder Beck was recognised at NY 481742 22350 by Hay (1943), the road (*AF 5*) running diagonally up the eastern side of the gully, being a narrow, ill-defined track, partly sunken into the slope. Some 40 m to the east of the beck, the road took the form of a low bank with a slight ditch on the upslope side.

A series of banks was also recorded, which were either orientated parallel to the road, or terminated close to it. However, although these banks clearly respected the line of the road, they may have post-dated its construction. Stone bank *AF 2* was 430 m long, discontinuous, and irregularly defined, orientated approximately parallel to the Roman road. It apparently merged into bank *AF 3*, but because of the poor definition at this point, it was not possible to determine the relationship between the two monuments. Banks *AF 3* and *AF 4* were similar in form, displaying large amounts of stone, of similar width and prominence, and were probably component parts of a single feature. Bank *AF 4* displayed evidence of kerbing and may have been a wall, and part of it was also found to overlie the Roman road, suggesting that it post-dated its use.

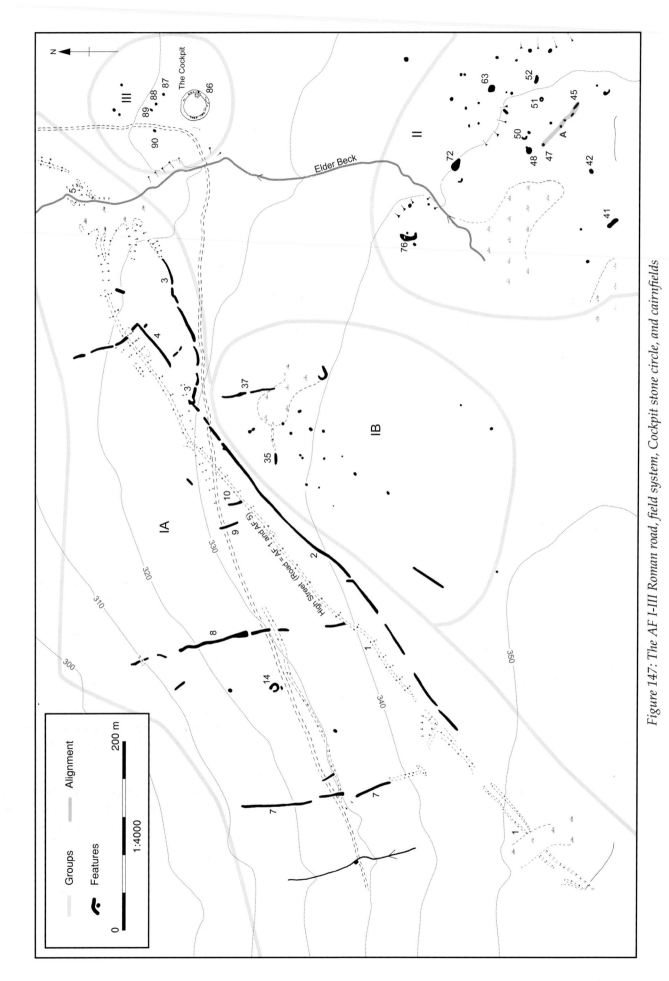

Figure 147: The AF I-III Roman road, field system, Cockpit stone circle, and cairnfields

Extending downslope from the road was a series of parallel, discontinuous, irregular stone banks (*AF 7-10*), similar in form to *AF 3* and *AF 4*, and possibly a result of the casual dumping of clearance stone along field boundaries. Banks *AF 8* and *AF 10* butted the Roman road and therefore post-dated its construction. In between banks *AF 7* and *AF 8*, there was an ill-defined, low, circular bank (*AF 14*), which had slight internal terracing and an entrance on its south-western side. Although this monument was very indistinct, it is possible that it formed the remains of a roundhouse.

The cairnfield (AF IB)

A cairnfield to the east of the road comprised small, generally ill-defined, cairns, which displayed no significant alignments and had an essentially random distribution. At the northern end of the group were two stone banks, set perpendicular to each other (*AF 35* and *AF 37*), but separated by a localised, dense mire that obscured any possible relationships. Bank *AF 37* was approximately parallel to banks *AF 8* and *AF 10*, was orientated towards the end of bank *AF 3*, and hence it may have been related to the banks recorded close to the Roman road (*see above*). Stone bank *AF 35* had a slight lynchet-like profile, which may be indicative of soil slippage in the area to the north.

Discussion

The recorded line of the Roman road (*AF 1*) differed by up to 80 m from the line of the road depicted on the 1863 First Edition 6" to 1 mile OS map, which appears to have been copied onto all subsequent OS mapping. Despite careful reconnaissance, no sign of a road was observed along the OS line. Hay (1943) also reported difficulty in identifying the road, but suggested that there was evidence of 'foundation work' in the area of the cairnfield. Although the line of the road depicted on OS mapping may be an inaccurate representation, it is also possible that a second road line once took advantage of a higher and easier crossing of Elder Beck (near The Cockpit), but has subsequently become obscured by peat and vegetation cover. The related banks (*AF 2-10*) appeared to define the boundaries of a crude field system, laid parallel to the Roman road. Given that they either crossed the road or butted it, they clearly post-dated its construction. As the Roman road was used as the framework of the field system, it must have been a fairly dominant feature in the landscape at the time the fields were laid out and may even have been in partial use. If there was a second, higher line of Roman road, however, it never served as a guideline for the fields, and as such, must not have been a long-lived feature.

Askham Fell II (Threepow Raise): monuments *AF 39-77* and *AF 80*

In this area, a cairnfield was recorded on undulating ground, with some of the cairns at the northern end being on the moderately sloping sides of a small gully (Fig 146). The ground was largely well drained, but there were mires in the vicinity. The component cairns were generally fairly small and those to the north were often ill defined. An alignment of five cairns and banks (A; Fig 147) followed the top of a low rise, but otherwise the cairn distribution appeared to have been determined by the local topography. In addition to the smaller cairns, there were limited numbers of larger and more prominent cairns. One of these latter cairns (*AF 48*) stood on the highest part of Threepow Raise, and was a well-defined monument (7.1 x 6.2 x 0.55 m), with a prominent, rounded profile and some large stones around its south-western edge, which appear to have been the remains of a kerb. An excavation into its eastern side had exposed a long, flat, upright stone, which may have been the side of a cist. This putative feature was off-centre and may have been a satellite burial.

On the western side of the cairnfield were two fairly isolated cairns (*AF 41* and *AF 42*). Cairn *AF 41* was located on a slight rise between two areas of mire and was large and prominent, with a slight dumb-bell-like shape (12.2 x 4.4 x 0.35 m). Large upright stones were visible along its south-western edge, which appeared to be elements of a kerb. Cairn *AF 42* was similarly large, prominent, and well defined (5.3 x 4.7 x 0.5 m).

A large crescent-shaped bank (*AF 76*) was also recorded, though this was remote from the cairnfield and was not necessarily a related feature. It contained large amounts of stone and may have been a semi-circular wall. A small bield had been built from the decayed structure at its northern end.

To the south-east of the cairnfield was a remote ring feature (*AF 80*; Fig 146) on a broad, flat area of well-drained ground. It comprised a low, uniform, circular stone bank with a large gap in the northern quadrant, the internal ground level being similar to that outside (19.5 x 1.5 m (width of bank) by 0.2 m). Its function was unclear, although it bore some resemblance to the basic stone ring form of ring cairn (Lynch 1972, 61-4).

Discussion

For the most part, the cairns in AF II were consistent with stone clearance, and this appears to have been confirmed by the excavation of a 3 m-diameter cairn (Spence 1935a, tumulus 2, 67), which revealed a simple pile of large boulders on and partly within a natural subsoil. Unfortunately, Spence (*ibid*) did not describe the location of 'Tumulus 2' precisely within the cairnfield, and it is thus not possible to relate it to any particular cairn recorded by the present survey. Fortunately, the dimensions of the two other cairns (Tumuli 1 and 3) that Spence (*ibid*) excavated do correlate with the survey data. For instance, Spence's 'Tumulus 3' corresponds to monument *AF 51*, the excavation of which revealed a pile of boulders on a subsoil containing pockets of charcoal, which were interpreted as the 'remains of brushwood' (*ibid*). Although the excavator believed this to have been a funerary monument (*ibid*), the description is more consistent with the construction of a clearance-type mound on top of burnt and cleared scrubland.

Spence's 'Tumulus 1' appears to relate to cairn *AF 50*, and this may have had a different function. For example, it stood on the gentle summit of Threepow Raise, and its excavation revealed two adjacent flat boulders, one set upright, the other laid horizontally. The excavation was not able to establish if this was a cist (*op cit*, 66); however, the adjacent large cairn (*AF 48*) had evidence for a kerb and had also been the subject of antiquarian activity, revealing the side of a possible cist. It would thus appear that the Threepow Raise cairnfield comprised two distinct elements; small clearance-type cairns around the lower slopes, and a small number of funerary cairns on the gently sloping tops.

Askham Fell III (The Cockpit): monuments *AF 86-93*

This monument group comprised the stone circle known as The Cockpit and some associated cairns, which were located in a well-drained, gently sloping area close to a natural ford across the Elder Beck (Fig 146). The stone circle (*AF 86*; Fig 147; Pl 160) comprised an annular, stone bank, with 27 large standing and recumbent stones set for the most part into the internal face of the bank (31.5-32.8 m in average diameter; Fig 148). The width of the bank was not uniform, being particularly broad around the north-eastern side. The highest stone stood about 0.95 m high, although some of the recumbent stones were over 1.9 m in length; some stones may have been removed, as there was a notable gap around the north-north-western side. Taylor (1886, 337-8) reported a cairn incorporated into the north-western edge, but this seemed to correspond to a line of five recumbent stones and would appear to be a result of collapse rather than a deliberate feature. Another cairn on the north-eastern side appeared to correspond to a slight mound (*ibid*), which was recorded as part of the present survey. A rectangular alignment of stones butting onto the inside of the bank (*c* 5 x 5 m) was recorded on the south-eastern side, which lay in an area of rushes and was therefore ill defined. Only limited amounts of stone were in association with this feature, but it appeared to mark an area distinct from the rest of the stone circle, similar in form and size to the rectangular enclosure within Castlerigg, near Keswick (Waterhouse 1985, 95-8). Apart from this feature, the internal area was flat and at a similar level to the ground outside.

Beyond the southern perimeter of the stone circle was an arc of five orthostats (between 1.2 m and 0.4 m in height), which had radii from the centre of the stone circle of 38.5-45 m. On the opposite side was an arc of four small cairns (*AF 87-90*; Fig 147), which had radii from the centre of the circle of between 35 m and 51 m.

Plate 160: The Cockpit stone circle, AF 86

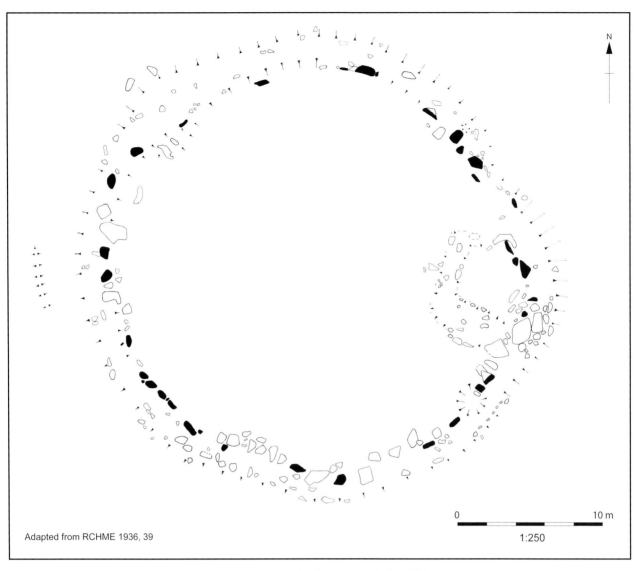

Adapted from RCHME 1936, 39

0   10 m

1:250

Figure 148: The Cockpit stone circle, AF 86

Discussion

Burl's (1976, 59-61) analysis of chronological traits in Cumbrian stone circles suggested that The Cockpit was a later, rather than an earlier, monument, principally because the stones were set within a low embankment. However, the present survey appeared to show a significant number of traits defined by Burl as 'early' (*op cit*, 60). For instance, its diameter was greater than 27 m, it had more than 20 stones, a flattened shape, and some of the now recumbent stones were over 1 m high. Whether the five orthostats to the south of the circle were parts of a concentric outer circle or were outlying stones is, however, open to debate.

Askham Fell IV: monuments *AF 94-9* and *AF 148*

A very small group of cairns and a bank were recorded on the moderately well-drained slopes between Elder Beck and the main fell track (Fig 146). An alignment of four small cairns (A; Fig 149) was orientated towards cairn *AF 148*, on a line parallel to the track. There were

no other cairns in association with these four and the alignment possibly reflects stone clearance along a former boundary.

Askham Fell V: monuments *AF 101-07* and *AF 138-43*

A group of banks and cairns was identified on well-drained, moderate, slopes to the north of the main Pooley Bridge/Helton track (Fig 146). These were divided into two apparently unrelated monument sub-groups.

Associated with the first monument sub-group (AF VA; Fig 149) was a large, slightly prominent round cairn (*AF 103*: 10.6 x 9.5 x 0.3 m). It had a regular, well-defined edge but an irregular profile, as a result of extensive robbing, and a small mound to the west (also *AF 103*) was probably spoil from this excavation. The cairn was found to be approximately in line with the alignment of prehistoric funerary monuments recorded in AF VII (*p 305*). It is therefore possible

303

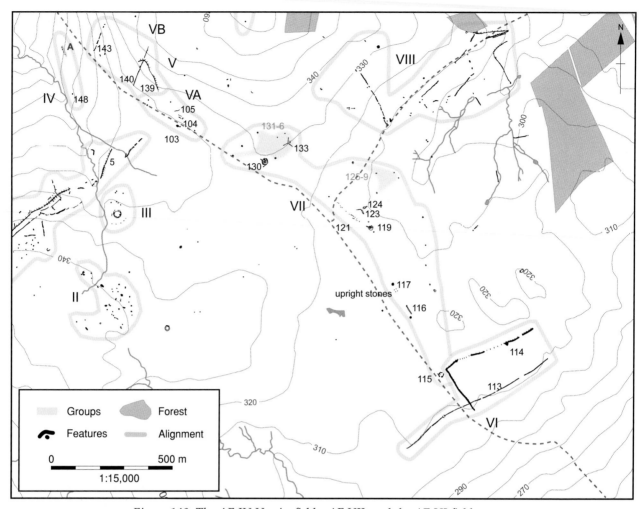

Figure 149: The AF IV-V cairnfields, AF VII, and the AF VI field system

that it was another funerary cairn and that it was the most north-westerly of those observed in the alignment.

Also contained within AF VA was a series of low-lying, ill-defined, parallel banks (*AF 104* and *AF 105*), located to the north of and parallel with the track. Although they were associated with brash deposits, there is a possibility that they were lines of cleared stone, superimposed on natural deposits.

The second monument sub-group (AF VB) included two parallel stone banks (*AF 140* and *AF 143*), which were positioned *c* 200 m apart. Both were ill defined, discontinuous, and irregular, and displayed no evidence of dry-stone construction; they thus appeared to have been a product of stone clearance along boundary lines. Their common orientation lay diagonally across the slope and was not apparently dictated by the local topography, perhaps marking the edges of a 200 m-wide field. Some very faint ridge and furrow was also identified in the area, which partly crossed the northern end of bank *AF 140*. This bank was aligned with the northern section of the Roman road (*AF 5; p 299*) and, although the precise course

of the road through the AF V area was not identified, there remains the possibility that the orientation of the bank was determined by its line. Bank *AF 139* was a large, prominent, bank, with a ditch along the upslope side, cutting bank *AF 140*, and itself crossed by some ridge and furrow near its southern end.

Askham Fell VI: monuments *AF 113-14*

These were two prominent linear earthworks, which delimited a substantial area of unimproved land (Fig 146); however, they had very different forms and were not necessarily contemporary. Bank *AF 113* (Fig 149) was a long, fairly uniform, and prominent stone bank, which possibly represented a decayed dry-stone wall. In contrast, monument *AF 114* was a well-defined, very deep, ditch, which was bounded by banks on both sides. It was clearly not intended for drainage, as it went over the top of a low rise, and had no feeder or outlet drains.

Bank *AF 113* was orientated approximately parallel to the Helton/Scales road, whilst ditch *AF 114* comprised two lengths set perpendicular to each other, one parallel to bank *AF 113*, the other apparently cutting it. Although bank *AF 113*, and probably also ditch

AF 114, appear to have served as boundary markers, neither related to the adjacent modern field walls. Ditch *AF 113* was also cut by a narrow section of possible nineteenth-century quarrying, suggesting they were not modern. However, the uneroded condition of the earthworks would suggest that they were not of any great antiquity.

Askham Fell VII: monuments *AF 115-37*

The main element recorded in this area was a line of large, prehistoric, funerary monuments (*AF 115*, *AF 117*, and *AF 119*; Fig 149), and a 'stone avenue' (*AF 121*), approximately parallel to the modern track between the Lowther and Ullswater valleys (Fig 144).

The funerary monuments

The funerary monuments were arranged in a line, at the southern end of which was the Cop Stone, a large orthostat set into the south-eastern side of an irregular, discontinuous, low-lying, ring bank (*AF 115*; Pl 161). The orthostat was *c* 1.7 m high and unworked, leaning over to one side, but still very stable, indicating that a considerable proportion of the stone remained beneath the ground. The bank was approximately circular, was very narrow, and

included only four medium-sized stones protruding from the turf. Taylor (1886, 326-7) reported that there used to be ten recumbent stones located around the bank. The internal area of the ring bank was approximately level, but was pock-marked and generally uneven. Some irregular depressions were identified around the bank and in the circle, which were not shown on Taylor's (*ibid*) plan, and these probably represent antiquarian disturbance. The recumbent stones around the bank were small by comparison with the Cop Stone itself, a situation comparable to that at the Giant's Grave (*HF 113*) on Heathwaite Fell (*Ch 6, p 269*), which comprised a ring bank and a single large monolith. It is possible, therefore, that this was a variant form of ring cairn.

Another of the funerary monuments (*AF 117*), known as the Ring of Thorns, formed an impressive, compact cairn circle (as defined by Lynch (1972, 62-3)), comprising ten, large, closely spaced orthostats positioned around the edge of a round cairn (diameter of the stone ring: 6 m; diameter of the cairn: 10 m; Pl 162). There was no evidence for an entrance. In the centre was a substantial depression, not shown on Taylor's (1886, pl v) illustration, which was apparently created following Greenwell's excavation in 1866 (Greenwell 1877, 400). Given this, the depression was probably a product of that excavation. During this excavation, a Food Vessel was discovered, within a layer of sand, beneath which were the remains of a cremated adult (*ibid*).

A third funerary monument within this line of monuments comprised a very large (17 x 15 x 1.4 m), prominent, slightly oval-shaped round cairn (*AF 119*), which stood on top of a gentle rise (Pl 163). Near its western end was a line of three very large orthostats orientated north-south, the central stone having an approximately rectangular profile, perhaps having

Plate 161: The Cop Stone, AF 115

Plate 162: The Ring of Thorns cairn circle, AF 117

Plate 163: Orthostats on top of round cairn AF 119, looking south-west

been crudely worked. The surface of the cairn was pock-marked with three large, irregular depressions and other smaller undulations, indicating extensive antiquarian disturbance. Indeed, one exploration by Canon Simpson (1883), opposite the largest orthostat, revealed a cremation within an inverted urn. Extending west-north-west from the cairn was an ill-defined spur, orientated towards stone avenue *AF 121* and round cairn *AF 130* to the north-west (*see below*). On the north-eastern side were two further, smaller protuberances.

The last funerary monument (*AF 130*) found in this line of monuments is known as White Raise Cairn. This was an approximately circular, very large and prominent cairn (22 x 17.9 x *c* 1.8 m), which had three stone banks extending tangentially from its main body. The matrix of the cairn comprised stones of all sizes, with only a very small soil component. Its upper surface had been severely disfigured by antiquarian disturbance. This had led to the creation of small hollows and mounds of spoil across the surface of the monument, and it was difficult to determine original features from this later disturbance. Slightly south-west of its centre was an open and empty cist (1.25 x 0.6 x 0.4 m; Pl 164) with an adjacent limestone capping slab, which was no longer *in situ*, and there were also substantial mounds of spoil around it. This cist was exposed by Canon Simpson (1883), who found it to contain a crouched inhumation burial, perhaps unsurprising, as it is typical in size to the cists containing inhumations from south-west Scotland (which have an average of 1.14 x 0.66 m; Yates 1984a, 24-5).

Plate 164: Exposed cist within round cairn AF 130

The largest of the tangential banks extending from the body of cairn *AF 130* was orientated south-west. It was moderately prominent and had some larger stones along the edge, which may have been an indication of dry-stone construction. A second bank extended north-north-west tangentially along the edge of the cairn, but was never divorced from it. The third bank extended towards the north-west, continuing the line of funerary monuments in this area. It was not particularly prominent, and was much less well defined than the south-west bank. There were significant amounts of turf over the banks, and these were well decayed, thus apparently not of recent date. However, the vegetation obscured any relationships between the banks and the cairn.

The 'stone avenue'

The 'stone avenue' (*AF 121*) comprised two approximately parallel alignments of stones, on a line between round cairns *AF 117* and *AF 130* (length of avenue: *c* 122 m; maximum height of stones: 0.45 m). In the northern line were 15 irregularly spaced stones, and the southern line comprised seven stones. Many were clearly orthostats, but others had no obvious longitudinal axis, and were not necessarily upright. The northern line appeared to have been interrupted by a sink hole, which may have formed or expanded since the construction of the stone alignments. Further stones were recorded to the west of the sink hole, but, though these were larger than their eastern counterparts, they were not as well aligned.

The number of stones recorded was fewer than previously seen by Taylor (1886). In particular, no stones were observed between cairn *AF 119* and cairn circle *AF 117*, although this may reflect greater vegetation cover than actual destruction. The small size of the stones, the extensive bracken cover in the area, and possibly some limited disturbance resulted in the existence of the avenue being questioned by the RCHM(E) survey (1936), and it has also subsequently been reported as no longer existing by both Waterhouse (1985, 117) and Burl (1993, 47). However, the feature can still be seen, and it provides significant evidence of the interrelationship between the diverse funerary monuments found in this area.

Other monuments

Apart from the funerary monuments and 'stone avenue', several other monuments were recorded in this monument group. These included a 37 m-long bank (*AF 116*), positioned between the Cop Stone (*AF 115*) and cairn circle *AF 117*. This bank was orientated directly towards the cairn circle, but only approximately towards the more distant Cop Stone. It was not particularly prominent, but was uniform in width, and kerbed, and it would appear to have been a decayed wall. A short distance to the south of cairn circle *AF 117*, and in line with wall *AF 116*, a rectangular configuration of four upright stones was recorded. These were first identified by Taylor (1886, 330-2) as being part of the stone avenue.

In addition to these monuments, groups of scattered small cairns (*AF 125-9* and *AF 131-6*) were also discovered, which bore no apparent relationship to the alignment of the funerary monuments. Monument *AF 133* was a stock shelter, comprising three walls radiating outwards from a central point, thus providing shelter from winds of all directions. It was a post-medieval type, examples of which are commonly found on the Cumbrian Fells (*eg BM 247, Ch 3, p 111*). Decayed walls *AF 123* and *AF 124* may have been a similar type of shelter, and the south-western end of wall *AF 124* had possibly been robbed to construct a small bield on its north side. However, it was orientated towards a 120° bend in wall *AF 123* and, if joined, the combined monument would have had a three armed, radial form.

Discussion

Although there were natural rises or hillocks in the vicinity of these funerary monuments, they had not been used, the cairns being instead located along a very deliberate line, parallel to the present track. In addition, they were associated with a series of linear features, which were not only on the line but orientated along it. These features included wall *AF 116*, the spur/bank extending from *AF 119*; stone-avenue *AF 121*; and the north-west bank extending from *AF 130*. These funerary monuments were clearly related by the alignment, and were probably relatively contemporary. Round cairns (*eg AF 119* and *AF 130*) in northern England typically date to the early Bronze Age (Yates 1984b, 2-4) and the presence of a Food Vessel within cairn *AF 117* would suggest that the 'cairn circle' also dated from that period. This alignment exceeded the normal laws of coincidence and it is probable that the features were linked by a prehistoric routeway, which utilised the natural communication route over a col between the Lowther and Ullswater valleys; in addition, or perhaps alternatively, it may have served as a boundary line.

Askham Fell VIII: monuments *AF 157-73* and *AF 184-202*

This monument group comprised a series of discontinuous stone banks and a possible field between a long band of quarrying and a long, east-west scarp edge at Riddingleys Top (Fig 146). The terrain was mainly gently sloping, well-drained land. The monuments in this area could be divided into two distinct sub-groups.

The dominant feature of the first monument sub-group (AF VIIIA; Fig 150) was a long, fairly straight, but discontinuous, stone bank (*AF 162*), which extended from a natural depression, at its north-west end, to a series of banks and a partial enclosure (*AF 161a*) at its south-eastern end. The

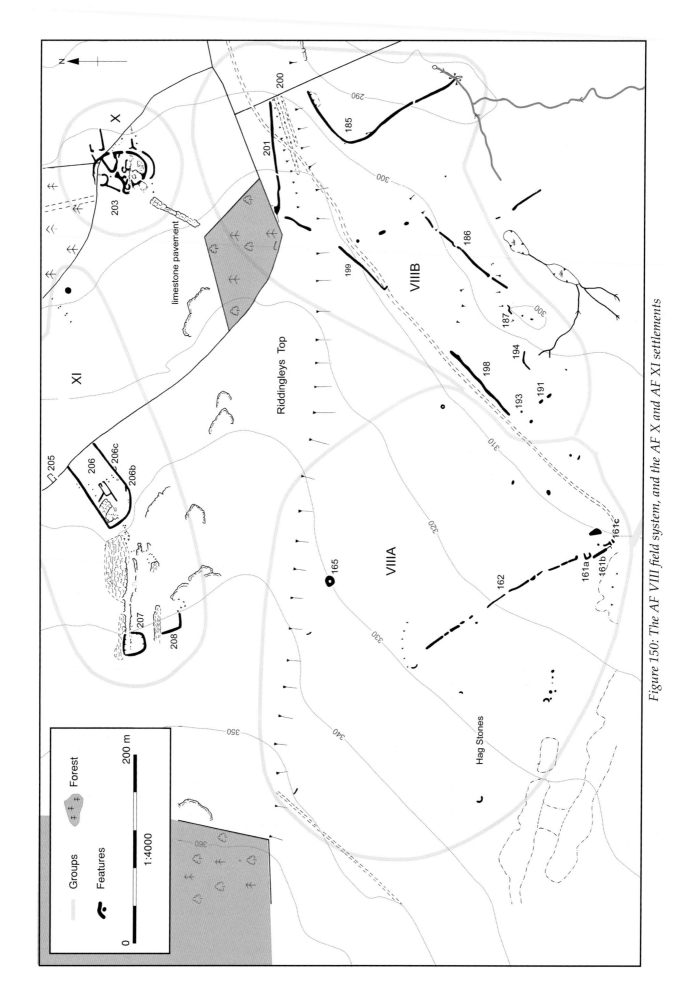

Figure 150: The AF VIII field system, and the AF X and AF XI settlements

308

bank contained only limited amounts of stone, and was irregular in width, and it was possibly formed as a result of casual stone clearance along a boundary. The partial enclosure (*AF 161a*) had decayed dry-stone walls on three sides (6.3 x 6.1 x 0.55 m), with the open side towards the east, away from the prevailing winds; it was therefore possibly a bield. Extending south-east from this was a broad bank (*AF 161b*) with a T-shaped bank (*AF 161c*) adjacent to its southern end. These defined the sides of a narrowing corridor, and had some characteristics typical of a complex entrance.

A round cairn (*AF 165*), located at the foot of the long, east-west scarp, was also included within AF VIIIA, even though it was found in a fairly remote location. It was large, well defined, very prominent, and had a regular, slightly elongated, circular shape (9.9 x 8.3 x 0.75 m). A central depression was the result of antiquarian exploration, but otherwise it had a regular profile. Its relative isolation and deliberate, substantial, form would suggest that it was a prehistoric funerary monument.

The second monument sub-group (AF VIIIB) included a possible field, which was partly defined by banks and alignments of cairns. The upper boundary was represented by two prominent and broad stone banks (*AF 198* and *AF 199*). Bank *AF 198* was particularly uniform in width and stone quantity, and was perhaps a decayed dry-stone wall. The north-east end of bank *AF 199* was linked to a lower field boundary (*AF 186*) by a line of three, elongated cairns, which were all aligned perpendicular to the adjacent boundaries. Bank *AF 186* had a regular width, but was not a prominent feature. It was parallel to the top boundary, on the other side of a gully, and appeared to end on top of a low rise. The south-eastern corner of the field was very poorly defined, with banks *AF 187* and *AF 194* following the edge of a low scarp and a small mire. The line upslope, linking with bank *AF 198*, was possibly represented by cairns *AF 191* and *AF 193*. The land within these putative boundaries was of poor agricultural quality, being unimproved, fairly steep in places, and containing a small gully. However, it is not unknown for field boundaries to enclose low-quality land (for instance, the southern field of HF IX, on Heathwaite Fell; *Ch 6, pp 274-6*) and it is a possible that this land acted as pasturage rather than being cultivated.

A possible continuation of the line of stone bank *AF 199* extended beyond the edge of the 'field' and linked with an east-west stone bank (*AF 201*). This latter bank was both prominent and had a regular

width and height, with a ditch on its downslope side, in clear contrast to stone bank *AF 199*. It was overlain by two modern field walls, but no continuation of the bank was observed beyond the western field wall because of dense vegetation cover. The bank was observed to continue beneath the eastern modern wall and thus beyond the extent of the survey area. Its full extent was therefore not established. Just below bank *AF 201*, and at the foot of a long break of slope, was a pair of parallel ditches (*AF 200*), but no corresponding banks. They were deep, with well-defined, sharp edges, and their condition suggested that they were not of great antiquity. However, they were overlain by the modern enclosure wall, which was built about 1840 (Spence 1935b, 64-5). Although the ditches and the bank converged at an acute angle, their stratigraphic relationship was not clear.

Below the scarp edge was a long stone bank (*AF 185*), which at the top was orientated along the contours, approximately parallel to the pair of ditches (*AF 200*). It turned downslope and there was markedly less well defined; large boulders had been placed against its eastern side, probably as a result of stone clearance. At the north-east end, it had been partly undercut by a small quarry. The land within the bank had a steep but uniform gradient and occasional surface stones.

Askham Fell IX: monuments *AF 174-8*
Adjacent to the line of funerary monuments (AF VII, *pp 305-7*) was a long, scarp slope orientated approximately north-south, falling away to the west (Fig 146). On top of the scarp was a line of five, well-separated cairns (*AF 174-8*), mostly fairly small and slightly irregular, with the exception of cairn *AF 178*, which was fairly large, moderately defined, and prominent (7.7 x 5.5 x 0.5 m). It had a central disturbance and a smaller adjacent mound was possibly spoil from this excavation. As a result of the disturbance, the cairn had an irregular profile and shape, but its form was more consistent with a funerary monument than a clearance cairn.

Askham Fell X: monument *AF 203*
Enclosed settlement *AF 203* was one of a pair of such settlements located on Skirsgill Hill, although the other (RCHM(E) 1936, 24-6) was not recorded by the LDNPS, as it lay outside the survey area (at NY 4995 2325). The *AF 203* (Fig 150) settlement was on gently sloping, slightly undulating ground, with extensive limestone outcrop in the vicinity (Pl 165). Just to the south-west of the settlement was an elongated section of limestone pavement, and within the settlement was a small, crag outcrop, which divided it into two sections, with exposed pavement in the southern sub-enclosures.

Plate 165: The complex enclosed settlement, AF 203, *looking north-west*

The settlement comprised an outer bank enclosing a series of sub-enclosures and possible structures (*a-k*; Fig 151). The external bank was an integral element of the settlement, sub-enclosures being butted against it and buildings set into its corners. However, on the western side, the bank appeared to divert around one of the structures (*a*). The width of the bank was relatively uniform throughout (*c* 2.5 m) but there was a marked variation in height and definition; around the southern section, large revetment stones were seen in the external face, providing evidence of dry-stone construction. This also formed the most prominent section, but its maximum height was only 0.35 m with respect to the external ground level. The north-western section was very low-lying, ill defined, and appeared to butt onto sub-enclosure *g*. The settlement was divided into three sections, each with independent access from the outside, although there was no access between the southern and middle sections.

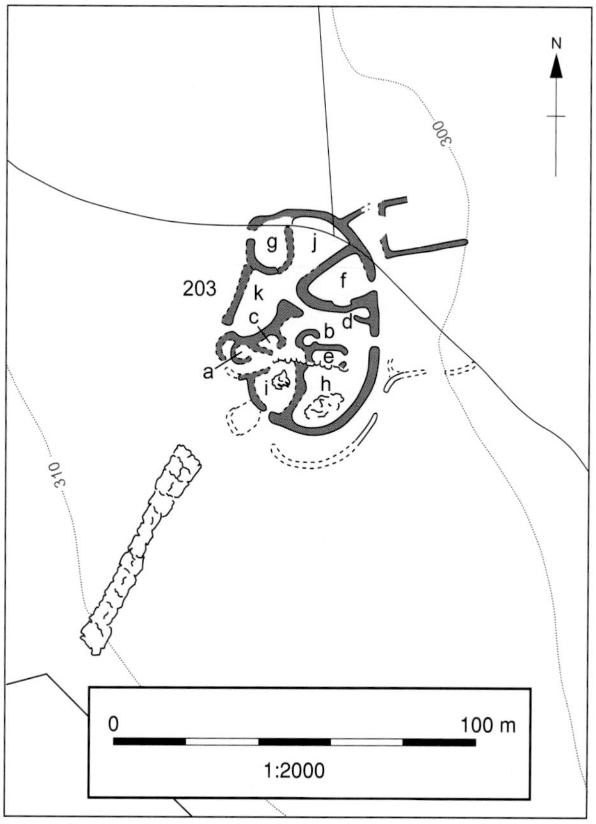

The southern section

The southern part of the settlement was divided from the middle section by a 1 m-high crag, and comprised two adjacent sub-enclosures (*h* and *i*), divided by an irregular, ill-defined bank. An entrance through the outer bank led into sub-enclosure *i*, but there was no obvious break in the dividing bank and no visible access into sub-enclosure *h*. The sub-enclosures were relatively large and fairly irregular, perhaps intended for stock control. Limestone pavement had been exposed in the sub-enclosures, below the external ground level, as a result of severe erosion, possibly by stock.

The central section

In the central part of the settlement, five structures (*a-e*) were recognised, which all had entrances facing onto an irregular courtyard, allowing access to the main entrance through the outer bank. There was no access to the southern section and only a small entrance into the northern section (via sub-enclosure *k*).

Structure *a* was fairly regular and circular, with a flat, internal area terraced into the slope (internal diameter: 4.2 m). Structure *b* was small, circular, and generally ill defined, the internal surface being approximately

Figure 151: The layout of enclosed settlement AF 203

level, but fairly bumpy. Structure *c* was very ill defined and irregular, set into the southern side of the dividing bank between the middle and northern sections, whilst structure *d* was small and circular, set into a corner between the external bank and the boundary of sub-enclosure *f*. It had a slight internal hollow. Structure *e* was relatively large and rectilinear, adjacent to the crag which separated the middle and southern sections. The internal surface had been slightly terraced into the slope and was approximately level.

There were also indications of a possible cambered track extending eastwards from the main entrance into the central section. The northern edge of this track was defined by a break of slope, whilst its southern edge was marked by an ill-defined bank.

The northern section
In the northern part of the settlement, four large, irregularly shaped sub-enclosures (*f*, *g*, *j*, and *k*) were surveyed, their access being from the outside via well-defined entrances. The exception was sub-enclosure *j*, which was essentially an extension of sub-enclosure *k* and had no independent access. The sub-enclosures contained ground that was approximately flat, but slightly undulating, and they were generally at a lower level than the adjacent central section. Like the sub-enclosures of the southern section, their form suggested a stock-control function.

Discussion
The settlement appears to have been designed to utilise the enclosed land as efficiently as possible, but at the same time to separate the accommodation from agricultural activity. Access to the central, domestic, section was independent of the other two, apart from a small entrance into sub-enclosure *k*. Access to the sub-enclosures was generally from the outside of the main enclosure and was mutually independent of each other. Although this was a practical arrangement in agricultural and domestic terms, it was not defensive, and it seems likely that this apparently enclosed design was not a response to deteriorating political conditions. This type of enclosed settlement is generally dated to the Roman period (*Ch 2, p 37*).

Askham Fell XI: monuments *AF 204-09*
An enclosed, rectilinear farmstead (*AF 206*; Fig 150), with a pair of associated small enclosures (*AF 207* and *AF 208*), was recorded on gently sloping and well-drained land to the west of AF X. However, there were substantial amounts of exposed limestone pavement throughout the area and also within the settlement (to a height of 0.4 m). Although some of the pavement may have become exposed subsequent to its construction, a few of the banks (*eg AF 207*) were built at the edge of exposures, and a track was also edged by the pavement. Clearly, therefore, parts of the pavement had already been exposed when the settlement was built.

The enclosed farmstead (*AF 206*; *c* 2830 m^2) comprised an outer bank and a single, central house (Pl 166). The bank was regular in width and height, and displayed occasional evidence of dry-stone construction, apparently being a decayed wall. The

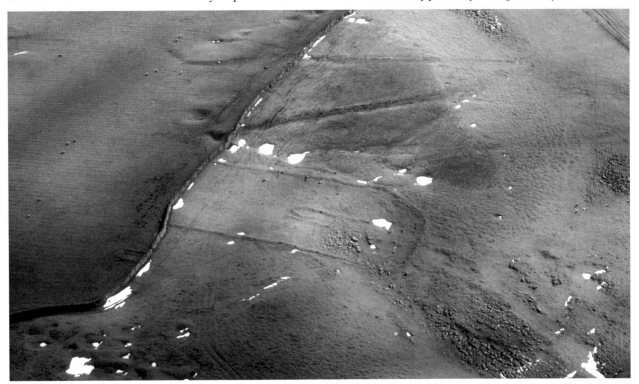

Plate 166: Enclosed settlement AF XI, with its rectilinear house

north-eastern section of this wall was beneath a modern field boundary, built around 1840 (Spence 1935b, 64-5). In the north-west side was a possible gap, but it contained ill-defined vestiges of the bank and thus it is likely to have been a result of later disturbance, as opposed to an entrance. There were no other visible gaps within the outer wall, and it is probable that the main entrance to the enclosure was via the north-eastern side, opposite the entrance to the house, but this had become obscured during the construction of the modern field wall. Two, small, semi-circular structures (*b* and *c*) butted onto the south-eastern side of the outer wall, neither of which was internally terraced. The house was a regular, rectangular structure (15.1 x 7.9 x 0.35 m), comprising decayed, but well-defined, outer walls (Pl 167). There was an entrance in the north-eastern side, defined by a large portal stone on one side, and the internal area was terraced into the slope, being fairly flat.

Extending westwards from this enclosed farmstead was a sunken track, defined on its northern and southern sides by the edges of limestone pavement. Although it exploited a natural feature, it appears to have been expanded in places. In some places this expansion was undertaken in order to create a continuous corridor, whilst in other places the expansion related to stone quarrying. The track was also crossed in some areas by low-lying lines of outcrop, which would not have restricted pedestrian or animal traffic, but would have prevented the use of vehicular traffic.

The sunken track led into enclosure *AF 207*, which had prominent and continuous outer banks, but only one entrance (26 x 26 x 0.5 m). The enclosure could have served to control stock and the sunken track would therefore have enabled the movement of stock into it. Near to this enclosure was a three-sided, rectilinear plot (*AF 208*), defined by prominent, uniform banks on two sides, and the edge of limestone pavement on the other. There was no evidence of a bank on the eastern side. The internal area had no exposed stone, but was slightly undulating.

To the north of the enclosed settlement (*AF 206*) was a small rectangular building (*AF 205*; 9.5 x 5.5 m), also in part overlain by the modern field wall. It was in a much better condition than the structure in *AF 206*, with dry-stone masonry throughout, well-built corners, and a well-defined entrance in the south-western wall. Despite their spatial association, the differences in condition may be an indication that they were not contemporary.

Discussion

The enclosures, sunken track, and farmstead appear to have been related elements of a single settlement. The form of the enclosed farmstead clearly contrasted with that of the nearby enclosed settlement (*AF 203, p 309*) and was seemingly of a later date. The *AF 206* building was similar to examples on Bootle Fell (*BF 892* and *BF 897*; *Ch 4, p 136*), which have been dated by historical sources to the period between AD 1250 and 1510. The farmstead was also similar to one on Cock Law (Ramm 1970, 46-7), which had

Plate 167: The longhouse in AF 206, *looking south*

312

rectangular structures in the centre of a rectilinear enclosure. Excavation of the latter farmstead by Kate Hodgson produced a seventeenth-century pipe bowl, and it would thus appear that the form of the AF XI farmstead is consistent with either a medieval or early post-medieval date.

Askham Fell XII: monuments *AF 210-12*

A group of three apparently unrelated cairns was recorded on Heughscar Hill (Fig 146). The terrain was well drained and gently sloping, with extensive exposures of limestone pavement throughout. Cairn *AF 212* was not particularly prominent, but was large, approximately pear-shaped, and had a regular, rounded, profile (18.6 x 8.7 m). It was in a prominent position near the highest point of the hill and was possibly a funerary monument. Parish boundary posts had been set into this cairn, and also cairn *AF 210*, to the south of *AF 212*.

Conclusions

Askham Fell is on a natural communication route between the Ullswater and Lowther valleys, following the line of a col between Heughscar Hill to the north and the ridge of Loadpot Hill to the south (Fig 144). The line was followed by a significant alignment of large Bronze Age monuments (*AF 115, AF 117, AF 119,* and *AF 121; pp 305-7*), which included round cairns, ring cairns, standing stones, and a stone avenue. In a number of instances, the standing stones, associated with some of these monuments, are precisely in line with other funerary monuments, emphasising the deliberate nature of the alignment. The significance of the alignment is examined further in *Chapter 8* (*pp 345-9*).

Another communication route across Askham Fell (High Street) was established at least by the Roman period, linking the Roman forts at Ambleside and Brougham (Margary 1973). It was built along the top of the ridge between these valleys, exploiting the line of the high ground, crossing Elder Beck just below The Cockpit Stone Circle (*p 302*), and then crossing over Heughscar Hill in a direct line towards Brougham. The Roman route may have continued in use for a substantial period of time, as field systems in its proximity appear to have butted against, and generally respected, the line of the road. Sections of the Roman road, to the west of the study area (LUAU 1997c), are represented by a hollow-way, which suggested that the road was used extensively in the medieval period,

once the metalled surfaces of the road had degraded, as, indeed, is indicated by its name (Smith 1967).

Possibly one of the earliest monuments on Askham Fell was the Cockpit stone circle (*AF 86; p 302*), which displayed some of the earlier characteristics of such monuments (Burl 1976, 60). It stood immediately adjacent to a natural ford across Elder Beck, slightly higher than the Roman crossing, which may suggest that a route along the ridge was in use prior to the Roman period. There are notable examples of Roman roads adopting the line of prehistoric routeways, particularly in upland areas, where these routes are in part dictated by the topography. In eastern Snowdonia, a Roman road from the fort of *Canovium*, on the Conwy, extended westwards towards the fort of *Segontium* (at Caernarfon) across an area of rugged terrain, at Bwlch y Ddeufaen (OA North 2004b). This line is closely associated with prehistoric funerary monuments, including the Cerrig Pryfaid stone circle, as well as standing stones and round cairns. The implication is that the Roman road followed the line of an earlier routeway that had been marked by prominent monuments (*see Chapter 8, p 349*).

Parallels for sepulchral landscapes

The presence of the putative ancient crossroads on Askham Fell will have encouraged activity in the environs, despite the rough nature of the terrain. This may in part explain the results of the survey, which appear to show that the fell was used unintensively, and possibly sporadically, from the prehistoric period through to the present. The presence of a small primary cairnfield (AF IB; *p 301*) appears to indicate a prehistoric presence, in addition to the sepulchral activity principally associated with the routeway. The activity in the area during the Roman period is not only in the form of the road, but also in the occupation of the enclosed settlement on Skirsgill Hill (*AF 203*). The nearby small farmstead (*AF 206*) possibly dates from the medieval period, and stock shelters *AF 123* and *AF 133* reflect a post-medieval unintensive, pastoral use of the fell.

More recently, the fell was a source of limestone used in the production of lime for agricultural purposes, evidenced by lime kilns *AF 147* and *AF 181* (*p 299*), and this was quarried more extensively along a mineral vein. During the same period, the moor was in use for game shooting, evidenced by the lines of grouse butts across the eastern part of the fell.

Plate 168: The Burnmoor peat scales

8

THE DEVELOPMENT OF THE LANDSCAPE

The Aims of the LDNPS

Management aims

The LDNPS, conceived in the early 1980s, was the first of many upland surveys which have sought to record the vast, and nationally important, archaeological resource preserved in the marginal lands of Northern England. Its primary aim was to enable the management of this resource by enhancing the Historic Environment Record and by initiating a programme of scheduling by English Heritage. The impact of developments and changes of use have been dramatically reduced as a result of the documentation of this archaeological resource, and most of the landscapes have now been protected as Ancient Monuments as a result of English Heritage's Monuments Protection Programme (*cf* Darvill and Fulton 1998).

The limitations of the survey from a management perspective, however, were that, certainly for the earlier surveys, the recording was targeted on cairnfields. There was consequently an over-emphasis on these important landscapes, and the more peripheral archaeological features and landscapes were not recorded to the same level. While post-medieval monuments within the areas of the cairnfields were undoubtedly recorded, those outside the core survey areas were not necessarily mapped, or if they were, it was to a lower level of detail. A case in point is at Burnmoor, where a comprehensive record was made of the cairnfields and stone circles, but the important post-medieval/medieval peat scales on the southern side of the study area (Pl 168; Winchester 1984) were omitted from the survey.

Similarly, the earlier surveys in the programme exclusively examined the unenclosed moorland because this was where there was the best survival of archaeological landscapes. However, they ignored the lower enclosed moorland, which also contained archaeological landscapes, and, from a management perspective, is where there is the greatest potential for agricultural improvement, and developmental impact;

consequently, these areas were where there was the greatest need for archaeological recording.

These limitations were, to an extent, rectified within the later surveys, which defined more extensive areas of investigation and produced a much fuller record of the archaeological resource within them. A case in point was that one of the last of the surveys, at Whin Garth (*Ch 3, p 81*), was specifically targeted on an archaeological landscape within enclosed land, which had been severely affected by agricultural improvement.

Academic aims

The secondary aim of the survey was to gain an improved understanding of the archaeology of the marginal uplands and, in this respect, it had a considerable advantage over the identification surveys that have succeeded it (for instance, the Haweswater Estate Survey; LUAU 1998a). The later identification surveys were able to use GPS technology, which provided quick and easy locational recording of landscapes, and it became possible, therefore, to undertake wide and extensive surveys of vast tracts of moorland. While this provided an invaluable management tool, the monuments were identified and located but not recorded in detail, limiting the opportunity for appropriate analysis. As a consequence, the level of detail and the wide expanse of the recording reflected within the LDNPS programme has only rarely been repeated in the North West. Moreover, the dataset from the LDNPS programme includes some of the most important archaeological landscapes in the region, recorded at a level that has enabled detailed analysis of both their form and development. This, in turn, has led to a greater understanding of the exploitation of the marginal fells over the course of four millennia.

The only major limitations of the LDNPS were that, as the earlier surveys were specifically targeted on cairnfields, these are unduly represented within the dataset. While such landscapes are a common feature of the uplands of West Cumbria, their over-emphasis within the dataset is a slightly artificial artefact of the survey methodology (*see above*), and this over-emphasis creates an exaggerated impression that all exploitation of the marginal lands resulted in the creation of cairnfields.

Function and Origin of Cairnfields

Cairnfields are common over large tracts of marginal land, on Cumbria's Western and South-West Fells, and were clearly an important manifestation of the agricultural exploitation of these lands, and the function of the individual cairns as depositories of unwanted stone is now generally accepted (*Ch 2, pp 27-8*). However, the circumstances that prompted their construction, and the nature of the agricultural activity practised on the associated land, are still subjects of controversy. Dimbleby (1961) has suggested a pastoral function largely on the basis of the paucity of cereal pollen from pollen cores in the vicinity of cairnfields. By contrast, it has been argued, notably by Yates (1983) and Fleming (1971), that they belong with arable agricultural practices. To an extent, the debate has been clouded by an assumption that all cairnfields are broadly similar, roughly contemporary, and reflect a consistent agricultural strategy. The evidence from the present survey, however, would suggest that cairnfields have diverse origins, are not necessarily contemporary, and indicate varied farming practices. There is therefore an element of truth on both sides of the argument.

Arable cairnfields

There can be little doubt that some cairnfields were a product of arable practices, reflecting accumulations of waste stone brought up by the ard, or plough. Indeed, during modern agricultural practice, stone is still routinely pushed to the sides of fields, whilst during the latter half of the last century, cultivation cairnfields were still created in areas such as Scotland (Graham 1956, 23). Similarly, an historical date for some of the Scottish cairnfields has also been suggested (Edwards 1977) by an excavation of a group of small cairns in Aberdeenshire that lay astride cultivation ridges. During this study, Edwards (*ibid*) identified significant amounts of arable weed pollen (Chenopodiaceae (Goosefoot family) and *Artemisia* (Mugwort)), and radiocarbon dates from strata associated with the cultivation ridges produced a date of cal AD 339-760 (1495±95 BP; UB-2084). Similarly, the present survey provided evidence of medieval cairnfields that served arable agriculture, as one of the cairnfields at Town Bank (TB XII) comprised a series of elongated cairns positioned along the edges of cultivation terraces (*Ch 3, p 60*). The cairns were aligned, for the most part, along the forward edge of the terraces, and there was an evident association between the terracing and the cairns (Fig 152). This monument group was also associated with a small, rectilinear, dry-stone structure, which is closely comparable with the medieval type of simple farmstead, or shieling (Ramm 1970). There is, therefore, an implication that the associated cairnfield and terraces were similarly of medieval date.

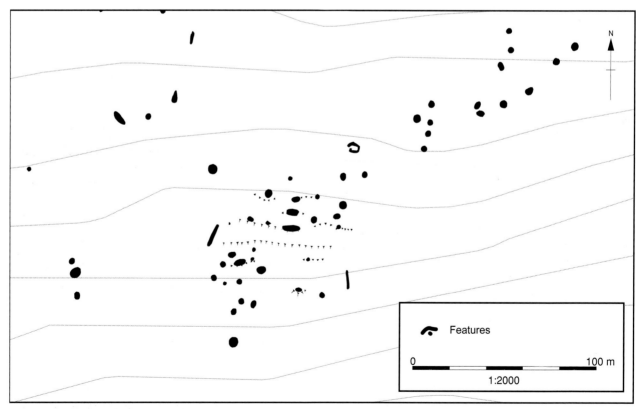

Figure 152: TB XII, putative medieval cultivated terraces associated with elongated cairns, and a possible medieval farmstead or shieling, on Town Bank

Random cairnfields

In contrast to the arable cairnfields, there are considerable numbers of these monuments where the distribution of the cairns is essentially random, and there is no evidence of a field system, associated lynchets, or indeed other evidence for cultivation. Such a distribution would undoubtedly restrict the movement of an ard, or plough, and Yates (1984b) has therefore suggested that any cultivation within them may have been undertaken using a spade. While this may be valid for very small cairnfields, many of those apparently randomly distributed are extremely large (eg Barnscar; *Ch 4, p 178*), covering up to 0.25 km^2, and it seems highly unlikely that these were cultivated by hand. Although there are occasional lynchets, indicative of cultivation, within field systems that are associated with random cairnfields, invariably the cultivated area is remote from the cairnfield. This is clearly demonstrated by the TB IV radial field system on Town Bank, which had four partly enclosed 'fields' (*Ch 3, pp 52-4*). The easternmost and middle fields enclosed the cairnfields, which were of average size for the Stockdale Moor / Town Bank area (TB IVA: *c* 24,000 m^2, and TB IVC: *c* 13,500 m^2; Fig 26). The remaining two 'fields' were largely devoid of cairns, but contained roundhouses (*TB 236* and *TB 303*). Attached to one of the 'field' boundaries, and associated with two roundhouses, was a small plot (974 m^2), which had a very prominent negative lynchet at its top, and an equally prominent positive lynchet at the bottom. These lynchets provide unequivocal evidence of cultivation within the plot, yet the much larger adjacent cairnfields displayed no equivalent evidence of lynchets, or any soil slippage. Both the cairnfields and the plot were directly related to the radial field system boundaries and thus it may be inferred that they were all broadly contemporary. Activity within the cairnfields was apparently being undertaken at the same time as cultivation, but was clearly less intensive than the cultivation within the plot, and extended over a considerably larger area.

The evidence would suggest that the agricultural activity within the cairnfields was not cultivation, in the same sense as that practised within the plot, and is more likely to be related to a pastoral agriculture, such as that related to the growing of hay. It is also possible that, in these areas, the ground between the cairns was cleared of stone to encourage the growth of grass for winter fodder, and to facilitate the cutting of the grass (Barnatt 1987, 410). For instance, in this latter case, any sizable surface stones could potentially damage a fragile sickle during the cutting of a short crop such as grass (Askew *et al* 1985, 19). Although this spatial association between cairnfield and cultivated plot is most clearly demonstrated by the TB IV example, a similar association was observed in many of the other cairnfields recorded during the LDNPS. For instance,

at Barnscar (BS IV), a series of cultivated plots (*BS 199* and *BS 206*; *Ch 4, p 185*) related to an early radial field system and were apparently contemporary with the adjacent cairnfields but, again, the character of these small plots was very different from that of the cairnfields, and their agricultural functions clearly contrasted with those of the cairnfields.

The lack of evidence for cereal cultivation in the pollen record of the area similarly suggests that pastoral activities were prevalent during the second millennium BC. Indeed, as early as 1961, Dimbleby (1961, 127) noted the significant absence of cultivation weeds from upland cores, and suggested that pastoral agriculture was being practised during the Bronze Age. A similar situation has been identified in many other Bronze Age upland clearances throughout northern Britain, and there is a general indication that they 'were mainly for pastoral purposes rather than cultivation' (Askew *et al* 1985, 16). However, no substantial cairnfields have been identified within the primary pollen catchment areas of many of the sites selected for palaeobotanical analysis, and there is thus no direct correlation between the palaeobotanical evidence and the field systems. A more direct relationship exists at the Burnmoor Tarn pollen core site (Pennington 1970, 72), where a decrease in the mixed oak forest, with a corresponding expansion of grasslands, in the mid-second millennium BC has been recognised. In this instance, the vegetational change probably reflects clearance and associated farming undertaken at the large Burnmoor cairnfield, less than 1 km away (*Ch 4; p 101*), towards the source of the prevailing winds. Significantly, no cereal or weed pollen was recorded, which led Pennington (1970, 72) to suggest that this was a reflection of 'pastoral land use in the uplands' during the Bronze Age.

Random cairnfields, exhibiting a basic form, are one of the most common prehistoric agricultural features of the uplands, but despite this, they appear to be an incongruous and almost unnecessary feature within the open, upland, agricultural landscapes with which they are associated. Their component cairns seemingly would have restricted the use of the plough / ard and the slight improvement in grazing potential does not seem to justify the considerable effort of removing surface stones. The explanation for this apparent dichotomy must be that, in reality, their origin is associated not with the open moorland of today, but with localised Bronze Age woodland clearings. Within this context, the landscape would have comprised localised forest clearings, the ground would have been uneven, and pock-marked with surface rock (Askew *et al* 1985, 19), and there would have been large craters following the removal of tree stumps. Considerable land improvement would have been necessary to make the land usable, for even basic agriculture, and any

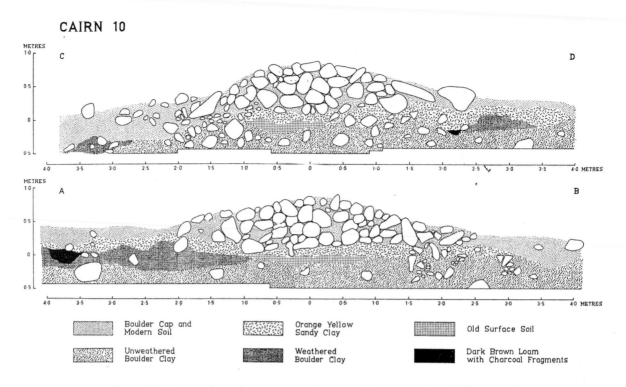

CAIRN 10

Boulder Cap and Modern Soil

Unweathered Boulder Clay

Orange Yellow Sandy Clay

Weathered Boulder Clay

Old Surface Soil

Dark Brown Loam with Charcoal Fragments

Plate 169: Section through the excavated cairn at Barnscar (after Walker 1965b)

works that improved the grazing potential would be considerably less labour intensive than further forest clearance. It seems to have been within this context that the primary cairnfields were constructed.

Palaeobotanical analysis from beneath excavated cairns of Barnscar (Pl 169; Walker 1965b; *Ch 4, p 178*) has also shown that the construction of the cairns was integral to the process of forest clearance; indeed, considerable forest clearance took place after the construction of the excavated cairns. The excavations showed that the original ground surface had been burned in parts, therefore implying that fire was used as part of the forest-clearance process. There were pits left following this process, which were potentially tree throws, and this raises the possibility that either the tree stumps were dug out, a very laborious process, or that the trees were felled by cutting the roots, in which case the root ball would have come out with the tree. In either instance, the resultant pits were then filled with soil and charred rocks, and a cairn was constructed over the top, from surface stone. Given this, it is therefore possible that, in part, the random distribution of cairns, in the most basic form of cairnfield, was largely dictated by the random position of the original trees found within these landscapes, and that the construction of the cairn was the final stage of a land-improvement process, which was primarily concerned with the levelling of the disturbed forest floor. Pastoral activity would then have taken place during and shortly after the forest clearance process. As there would not have been sufficient time for worm action to produce a topsoil, to cover the exposed

surface stone (Yates 1983, 342), there was a need for this surface to be removed. Indeed, in this context, it is credible that the clearance of surface stone would have been required within the localised clearings as a prerequisite to pastoral agriculture. Furthermore, many of the primary cairnfields have discrete limits that do not correspond to any changes in present-day topography, and their extent possibly relates to the size and shape of the original forest clearing.

Dating the Landscapes

Although the LDNPS, and other subsequent management surveys (*Ch 1, p 18*), have recorded a very substantial number of upland landscapes, both within the Lake District and elsewhere in the North West, this process has not usually involved excavation, or targeted pollen analysis, that would help to provide a detailed and precise chronology for the development of these landscapes. As a consequence, chronology is reliant, to a great extent, on the dating evidence associated with comparable monument types and landscapes found in other regions, particularly the North East, where there is an enormous body of comparative evidence, largely due to the work of George Jobey (*inter alia*; Jobey 1968; 1981). Naturally, this raises a number of issues, such as the influence of regionality and monument currency, whereby greater conservatism in areas such as the North West might have resulted in the continuity of use of particular monument types. It is also possible when dealing

318

Plate 170: Roundhouse BB 476, *at Brantrake Moss, looking south-east*

with a basic monument type, such as a clearance cairn, that this could have been created during any episode of land improvement, whether this be ancient or more recent in origin. For example, although traditionally cairnfields are attributed to the Bronze Age, palaeoenvironmental analysis of material beneath a clearance cairn within a randomly distributed cairnfield at Devoke Water (BB IX) produced early medieval radiocarbon dates (*Ch 5, pp 199-200*). Again, near Devoke Water, at Brantrake Moss (BB VII; *Ch 5, p 211),* a small cairnfield, and simple field system, were associated with unenclosed stone-founded roundhouses (Pl 170), which on traditional grounds would suggest a date range in the later Bronze Age to mid-Iron Age (*cf* Gates 1983). However, at this site, a pollen sample from beneath a wall on the southern side of the field system may suggest that this settlement dates to the mid-Roman period (Fell 1970). This date might, in turn, suggest that the unenclosed stone roundhouse had a greater longevity in this part of Britain than elsewhere. Significantly, these examples, which challenge perceived chronological wisdom, also demonstrate that, more generally, there is a need for intrusive exploration of those landscapes recorded during the LDNPS, coupled with programmes of scientific dating, in order to revise and rationalise the chronology of upland occupation.

Datable clearance episodes for some of the cairnfields are, however, potentially reflected in nearby palaeoenvironmental sample sites. For instance, the Burnmoor cairnfields are close to Burnmoor Tarn, from where Pennington (1970, 72-4) identified a Bronze Age clearance episode dating from *c* 2000 cal BC, which extended up to *c* 1200 cal BC, with a further episode of clearance in the Roman period (*Ch 3, p 101*). Similarly,

at Devoke Water, and the adjacent Tewit Moss, there was a series of small-scale, temporary, clearances and burning episodes, dating to the neolithic and Bronze Age, which culminated in a major clearance episode in 1729-1411 cal BC (3260±70 BP; CAR-916; *Ch 5, p 203*). This was followed by forest regeneration from the later Bronze Age onwards and throughout the Iron Age. At White Moss, near to Heathwaite Fell (Wimble 1986; *Ch 6, p 265*), there was a clearly defined clearance episode in the later Bronze Age, at *c* 1200-950 cal BC, followed by a period of forest regeneration, and then a further clearance episode between *c* 450 cal BC and the end of the first millennium BC.

While there are clear differences between the individual sites and areas, it appears that all parts of the Lake District witnessed episodes of forest clearance during the Bronze Age, which lessened drastically in the Iron Age. In most areas, there was also a reoccupation of the marginal land in the late Iron Age, or Roman period, with some continuity into the early medieval period. These apparent episodes of early clearance and upland land use therefore probably provide the chronological context for those monuments that were recorded during the course of the LDNPS.

Cairnfield chronology
The characteristics of this basic form of randomly distributed cairnfield are largely attributable to its origin in forest clearings (*pp 327-8*), and its chronology will similarly relate to periods of intensive forest clearance. It is also a type of cairnfield which appears to relate to pioneer agriculture (*pp 327-30*). Given this, it is therefore more likely to relate to the earlier of the two, principal, clearance episodes identified

from upland pollen cores (Bronze Age and Roman). Furthermore, the permanent change in upland oak forest during the Bronze Age appears to be limited to areas where cairns are in abundance (Pennington 1970, 72). There is thus an implication that intensive Bronze Age clearance and pastoral land use was associated with the cairnfields, and this has largely been confirmed through excavation. For instance, radiocarbon dating appears to confirm that many of these primary cairnfields originated during the Bronze Age; material from beneath a clearance cairn on Millstone Hill in Northumberland (Jobey 1981) produced a date of 2283-1754 cal BC (3640±90 BP; HAR-1942), and excavated clearance cairns from Shaugh Moor, Dartmoor, produced radiocarbon dates of 1875-1459 cal BC (3350±70 BP; HAR-2221), 1932-1497 cal BC (3400±90 BP; HAR-2285), and 1933-1529 cal BC (3430±80 BP; HAR-2219; Wainwright *et al* 1979). From the Lake District, a small cairn excavated at Birrel Sike, between Town Bank and Stockdale Moor (Richardson 1982), produced a date of 2299-1740 cal BC (3640±100 BP; BIRM-1063). Similarly, the association of funerary round and ring cairns in many of the Lake District cairnfields suggests that they also date to the second millennium BC. However, a single radiocarbon date from a clearance cairn at Chatton Sandyford, Northumberland (Jobey 1968), of 3896-3373 cal BC (4840±90 BP; GAK-1507), provides evidence that limited forest and stone clearance activity pre-dated the Bronze Age, at least in some parts of the country. This is reinforced by peat inception dates from the Barnscar area of 3360-3020 cal BC (4490±40 BP; SUERC-4523) and 3370-3090 cal BC (4553±35 BP; SUERC-4524), associated with strong pollen signals, suggesting an episode of neolithic woodland clearance (OA North 2009a; *Ch 4, p 178*).

Although it would appear that the practice of clearing stone into randomly distributed cairns was originally a part of the forest clearance process, and was undertaken to enable pastoral rather than arable practices, this does not exclude the probability that land originally intended for grazing was subsequently cultivated. A notable example of this was at Pewet Tarn on Heathwaite Fell (*Ch 6, pp 272-3*), where a medieval farm (HF IXA) was superimposed on an earlier cairnfield, which was then reused for medieval ridge and furrow cultivation (Fig 133). The boundaries of the farm did not coincide with that of the cairnfield, and its centre was clearly not coincident, providing no evidence of continuity. However, it is perhaps significant that in the medieval reuse of the land the farmers also reused the earlier form of clearance, the small clearance cairns from the first phase of land improvement being substantially enlarged, reflecting stone brought up by ploughing (Pl 171). The configuration of the ridge and furrow was severely disrupted and constrained by the positions of the cairns,

Plate 171: Ridge and furrow diverting around the cairns of the HF IX field system on Heathwaite Fell

which clearly pre-dated the ploughing; however, as the cairns were extended, they became linear, following the line of the ridge and furrow. This provides a classic example of an instance where the reoccupation of a previously farmed landscape entailed similar work practices, but in two widely differing periods.

The Development of Upland Settlement

Alongside agricultural landscapes, the associated dwellings of the farmers were also recognised during the survey, and it is appropriate to discuss the development of these within the context of the LDNPS dataset. To an extent, these have already been discussed in *Chapter 2*, and so, accordingly, the character of change rather than the individual monument types will be discussed here. It is intended that the typological development of the settlement form should be examined, but it is recognised that individual monument types were in use over an extended period, and considerable chronological overlap between them is likely.

Timber structures
The most basic primary cairnfields are, for the most part, not associated with any dwellings, but this does not necessarily indicate an absence of settlement remains, as it is possible, indeed probable, that the earliest structures were constructed of organic materials, which have not survived as surface features. Given the assumption that the primary cairnfields were associated with the initial clearance of the forests, then the most abundant raw material for building would have been the recently felled trees, and it is therefore not too surprising that stone structures are rarely associated with primary cairnfields. Whether or not the earliest dwellings were timber roundhouses, or no more than simple

Plate 172: Small roundhouse beneath a larger shieling, at Stephenson Ground

tent-like structures, cannot be addressed without the benefit of excavation, which has only rarely been undertaken within the context of the cairnfields in the North West. Even when excavation has been undertaken within cairnfields in other regions, these have typically concentrated on the upstanding remains (for instance cairns and banks) rather than those areas with a lack of surface features, which could contain the evidence for timber structures. One exception to this is at Stephenson Ground, in the Duddon Valley, where a timber roundhouse, with a diameter of 4 m, was identified by chance beneath a medieval shieling (Pl 172). Significantly, there was no surface expression to indicate the presence of the roundhouse, which was dated to the early Bronze Age on the basis of ceramic and lithic artefacts (Thorpe 1994). This chance discovery highlights the possibility of timber buildings and structures within many of the primary cairnfields, but given the nature of these structures, and their lack of visible surface remains, they would be difficult to identify unless large-scale excavation was undertaken across a primary cairnfield.

The one circumstance that can produce physical surface evidence for timber structures is when they have been constructed on a slope, and there is a need to terrace the ground to make a level platform for the structure (Pl 173). In normal circumstances, there is a preference to use level ground, where available, for buildings, unless such ground is unavailable (*ie* the whole field system or cairnfield was set on a slope), or what level ground there is has been used for agriculture. A notable example of this is at Heathwaite Fell, where structures (*HF 405-12*; *Ch 6, pp 277-8*) were deliberately sited on the sloping ground at the edge of a flat/gently sloping ridge top, which contained a cairnfield, the presumption being that the better ground had been given over to agriculture. The other possibility is that, in some instances, the buildings were constructed on sloping ground to aid their drainage, making the floor drier than if the structure had been built on level ground.

Such platforms are varied, both in form and size, some of the smaller examples being associated with small primary cairnfields. For example, platform *BS 102* is associated with a simple cairnfield near, but remote from, the main Barnscar complex (*Ch 4, p 181*), whilst platform *HF 57* is adjacent to a very small primary cairnfield on Heathwaite Fell (HF III; *Ch 6, p 268*). However, the majority of recorded platforms were larger and were often associated with complex cairnfields. Notable examples of this were platform *TB 445*, associated with the TB VIII field system (Town Bank; *Ch 3, pp 55-6*), which was immediately adjacent to a stone-founded roundhouse (*TB 444*), suggesting that, in some instances, platforms for timber buildings were broadly contemporary with their stone-founded counterparts, or even preceded them. The larger platforms, which acted as the base for a very large structure or multiple structures, were also always associated with complex field systems, the notable examples being platform *BS 213*, which was central to the large Barnscar cairnfield and field system (BS IVA; *Ch 4, p 182*), and platform *TB 636*, within the cultivated TB XI field system on Town Bank (*Ch 3, pp 59-60*).

The timber house platforms bridge the gap between the most basic agricultural exploitation and the more sophisticated field system, and clearly overlap in chronology with the stone-founded roundhouse, though the earlier examples would appear to be earlier than the stone houses within the LDNPS dataset. Looking outside the region, particularly to the North East, the dated examples are from the later Bronze Age. For example, the excavation of the unenclosed platform site of Green Knowe, Peeblesshire, produced a series of radiocarbon dates with calibrated means between the twelfth and fourteenth centuries BC (Jobey 1980), whilst the settlement at Standrop Rigg, Northumberland, produced a single date of 1050±80 cal BC (3000±80 BP; HAR-3538; Jobey 1983). These dates fall within the broad range for unenclosed settlement (1500-100 BC; Jobey 1985; Haselgrove 2002), but are at the earlier end of the range for stone-founded roundhouses (*p 322*).

Plate 173: Terraced platform TB 291, on Town Bank (TB IV), looking south-east

Stone roundhouses

The stone-founded roundhouse was probably the most common form of domestic structure identified during the LDNPS. These were normally fairly substantial and, for the most part, were larger than the individual house platforms. Their association is typically with the more developed field systems, rather than the primary cairnfield, although there are occasional exceptions, such as the two small roundhouses (*WG 610* and *WG 618*) at Thorn Knott (WG VII at Whin Garth; *Ch 3, p 97*), which were associated with a very small undeveloped cairnfield group, and roundhouse *TB 1* on Town Bank (*Ch 3, p 50*), which had only two cairns in association. Both in terms of the structures and their association, these stone-founded houses appear typologically more developed than timber ones, but it is apparent that there was considerable overlap between these and timber roundhouses. Indeed, in practice, their construction may have been dictated as much by the availability of raw materials as by a change in fashion.

Dating evidence for unenclosed settlements, for the most part, has again come from the North East, and includes both lowland and upland examples. However, the distinction between timber and stone-founded structures is, in this context, somewhat irrelevant, because the availability of the raw material takes on a greater emphasis in determining the form of the structure. The evidence would suggest that there was an extended occupation of such settlements between *c* 1500 cal BC and *c* 100 cal BC (Haselgrove 2002, 60-3), but there is little evidence of any continuation into the Roman period. It is difficult to establish whether this compares with the practice in the North West, given the absence of scientific dating there. There is a potentially significant site at Brantrake Moss (BB VII on Birker/Birkby Fell), where a pair of unenclosed structures (*BB 470* and *BB 476*; *Ch 5, p 214*; *Pl 170*) were associated with a field system, that has been shown to overlie deposits containing pollen of Romano-British character (Fell 1970), though without the benefit of scientific dating, this cannot be regarded as a reliable indicator of Roman date. If this date is confirmed, it would suggest that there was continuity of occupation, potentially including the unenclosed roundhouses, into the Roman period. Whether this was an isolated example, or symptomatic of a more conservative trend in the North Western uplands, cannot be determined reliably, given the present absence of dated interventions at the early upland settlements. It is interesting to note, however, that most of the upland pollen diagrams in Western Cumbria (*cf* Pennington 1970) include a Roman clearance episode, but there are very few complex enclosed settlements in the area, of the type normally ascribed to the Roman period (*pp 36-7*), although there are substantial numbers of unenclosed settlements.

Simple enclosed settlements

Conventionally, the typological development has been thought to be from unenclosed roundhouses to simple enclosed settlements, and that this indicates a need to incorporate defence within the design. This is reflected at Banishead, near Coniston Old Man, where a simple D-shaped enclosed settlement, containing a single roundhouse, incorporated a natural sheer crag as part of its defences (Fig 153; LUAU 1994a). The presence of a prominent bank, potentially topped by a palisade, and an accompanying external ditch would have provided an effective primary level of defence, but its construction would have entailed considerable effort for the small number of families accommodated by it, and seems therefore to be an indicator of a period of hostility and/or political instability. On the basis of excavated examples from the North East, it would appear that the transition from unenclosed to enclosed settlement, for the most part, took place in the late Bronze Age/early Iron Age, and extended throughout the Iron Age (Jobey 1985, 183; Gates 1983, 141; Haselgrove 2002, 61). However, although enclosed settlements seem generally later than unenclosed settlements, there seems to have been considerable overlap, both types being occupied throughout the Iron Age. The only dated example from the North West is the Glencoyne Park 6 settlement, at Matterdale, which has three roundhouses (Hoaen and Loney 2003; 2004; *Ch 2, p 35*), one of which has been dated to the Roman period, and an external ditched boundary dating to the early Iron Age. As such, this settlement was probably founded in the early

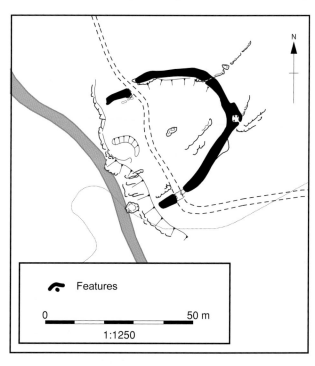

Figure 153: The simple enclosed settlement at Banishead, Torver High Common

Iron Age, but was then occupied for an extended period of time, encompassing both the Iron Age and Roman period.

Only two examples of this type of enclosed settlement were identified in the LDNPS dataset (*WB 163* at Whitrow Beck; *Ch 4*, *p 164*; and *TB 805* on Town Bank; *Ch 3*, *p 64*), and the detailed relationship between the unenclosed and enclosed types cannot therefore be established definitively for the North West. However, potentially significantly, a further simple enclosed settlement was identified at Thornholme, on the opposite side of the Worm Gill valley from the Town Bank example (Fig 154; Crawford and George 1983). The Town Bank example was an isolated settlement, without any direct relationship with any form of field system, or cairnfield, suggesting that it had a purely pastoral economy. Significantly, there was nearby (*c* 40 m away), but otherwise unrelated, a field system which was directly linked to an unenclosed settlement (*TB 748-51*; *Ch 3*, *p 63*). While it could be argued that the enclosed settlement (*TB 805*) used the field system associated with the unenclosed settlement (*TB 748-51*), it is perhaps unusual that, in the course of such an

exploitation, no element of the field system, or even a trackway, was constructed to the enclosed settlement and the fields, in contrast to the unenclosed settlement, where the banks of the field system extended directly out from the roundhouses. The impression provided by the survey evidence is that, at this site, there was a dramatic change, with the abandonment of the unenclosed settlement, and its apparently mixed economy, to be replaced by a defended settlement reliant on a pastoral economy. While it is tempting to relate such a transition to social upheaval, prompted by the climatic decline of the early Iron Age, a certain degree of caution must be applied, given that no excavation evidence is available, and the chronological differential between the settlements has been inferred rather than being based on empirical data. Indeed, the establishment of the simple enclosed settlement may reflect a reoccupation of the site, long after the abandonment of the unenclosed settlement.

At Whitrow Beck, there is no indication of an earlier unenclosed settlement, but the very evident simple enclosed settlement (*WB 163*; WB III; *Ch 4*, *p 164*) is spatially associated with a cairnfield and elements

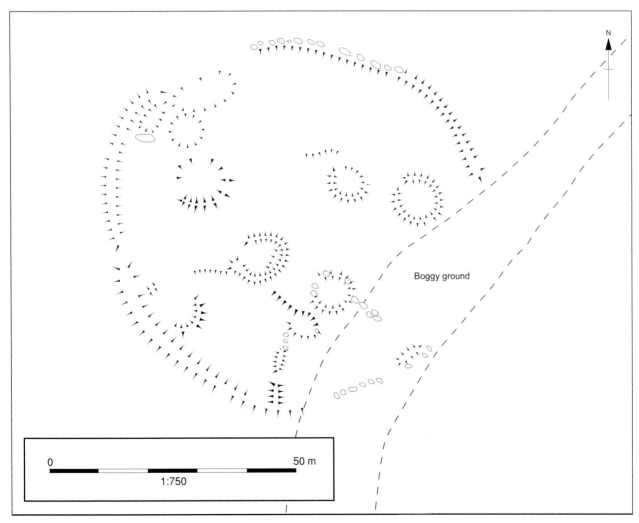

Figure 154: The Thornholme simple enclosed settlement, to the south of Town Bank (after Crawford and George 1983)

of a proto-field system (*WB 104/118*). Given that there are cairnfield groups all across this area, which are unrelated to this or any settlement, the cairnfield probably reflects a phase of land improvement that pre-dated the settlement. However, the proto-field system comprised two long, parallel, banks, of which one converges with the edge of the enclosed settlement. This seems to mirror the situation at Barnscar (BS IV; *Ch 4, p 182*), where one of the two long, primary, banks/walls of a field system (*BS 390*) converged with the edge of a complex enclosed settlement (*BS 477*). This field system post-dates an earlier field system and cairnfield, and by implication it may suggest that the Whitrow Beck enclosed settlement, and field system, indicates a superimposition onto an earlier cairnfield.

The general paucity of simple enclosed settlements in the LDNPS dataset would appear to accord with the palaeobotanical evidence, which suggests that, in most upland areas of the North West, there was a regeneration of woodland during the Iron Age (*Ch 1, pp 10-11*). This evidence may also provide corroborative evidence for an abandonment of the marginal uplands during a period of poor climatic conditions. However, this period of deterioration was seemingly restricted to the early Iron Age, as there are good indications of upland woodland clearances in the latter part of this period (Wells 2003), which may imply that the simple enclosed settlements reflect a return to the fells.

Complex enclosed settlements

The complex enclosed settlement is an obvious typological development from the simple enclosed settlement. It still incorporates circular stone-founded houses within an enclosing bank, but there are significant differences (Pl 174), notably a much

greater emphasis on agriculture rather than defence (*Ch 2, pp 36-7*). They always contain sunken stock pounds, which, along with the roundhouses, fill the available space within the enclosure. Instead of having a single well-defended entrance, multiple entrances all around the enclosure bank are visible, agriculturally a very practical development but defensively a liability. Simple enclosed settlements were usually either circular, or occasionally of more irregular shape, when they utilised a natural topographical feature to enhance their defence (for instance, at Banishead, Torver High Common; LUAU 1994a; Fig 153). However, complex enclosed settlements can be sub-circular, square, or rectangular (*eg* Ewe Close; Collingwood 1908; Broadwood settlement, Ingleton; Johnson 2004; Fig 155), and in some instances fairly irregular.

When compared with the simple enclosed settlement, the complex enclosed settlement is one of the more common types of upland monument, but perhaps significantly was a relatively uncommon element within the LDNPS dataset, with only two examples identified during the survey (*BS 477; Ch 4, p 188*; and *AF 203; Ch 7, p 309*). This type of settlement seems to predominate in the eastern part of Cumbria; the RCHM(E) survey of Westmorland (RCHM(E) 1936), and the surveys of the Haweswater Estates (LUAU 1997c), Lowther Park (LUAU 1997e), and Hartley Fold (OA North 2003b), all on the eastern side of the Lake District, abound with examples, but they are relatively rare in the western part of the Lake District, where most of the LDNPS programme was undertaken. The distribution pattern also differs from that of the simple enclosed settlement, which, although a relatively rare monument, is more common in the western part of the Lake District (for

Plate 174: The complex enclosed settlement at Askham Fell (AF 203)

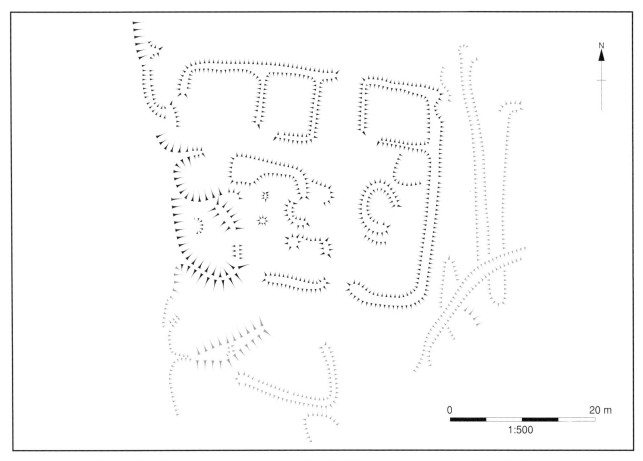

Figure 155: The Broadwood complex enclosed settlement, near Ingleton, North Yorkshire

instance, *WB 163* at Whitrow Beck; *Ch 4, p 164*; *TB 805* at Town Bank; *Ch 3, p 64*; a settlement in Ennerdale; LUAU 1998c; and a settlement at Banishead, Torver High Common; LUAU 1994a).

The complex enclosed monument is typically dated to the Roman period, from the small assemblage of Roman-period finds recovered from a limited number of excavations (*Ch 2, pp 36-7*), and their proliferation on the eastern side of the Lake District may suggest that their inhabitants were exploiting the abundant market stemming from the major north/south Roman military supply route, running up the eastern side of the Lake District (Shotter 1996). By the same token, one of the few western enclosed settlements, at Barnscar (*BS 477*; *Ch 4, p 188*), is not far from the Roman fort at Ravenglass.

The apparent dearth of simple enclosed settlements in the Lake District would also suggest that there was a relatively limited population in the uplands during the Iron Age, and to an extent this indeed may be the case if there was an abandonment of the marginal lands during this period. The palaeobotanical evidence indicates regeneration of woodland during the early part of the Iron Age, implying that the land was no longer farmed (Wells 2003). However, in the later Iron Age, there were climatic improvements, and there are

good indications of woodland clearance, which imply that the uplands were reoccupied during this period (*ibid*; Wimble *et al* 2000). However, the limited number of simple enclosed settlements that have been identified do not adequately reflect the implied increase of activity across the upland zone, and this raises the possibility that the more numerous complex enclosed settlements had their origins in the Iron Age.

Although excavation at the complex enclosed settlements has consistently produced a small number of Roman finds (*eg* Ewe Close; Collingwood 1908), it must be stressed that, in the North West, the Iron Age and the early medieval periods are largely aceramic, so any dating reliant on artefacts will inevitably be biased towards the Roman period. Radiocarbon dating would undoubtedly eliminate this bias, but very few excavated settlements have been subject to scientific dating. The notable exception is an enclosed settlement at Broadwood, near Ingleton, North Yorkshire (Fig 155), which produced a radiocarbon date of 88 cal BC- cal AD 66 (2010±28 BP; KIA 22910) from material found beneath the main external bank of the enclosure, which indicates a late Iron Age foundation for this settlement (Johnson 2004). Other radiocarbon dates from this site include those of cal AD 69-221 (1883±27 BP, KIA22911) and cal AD 22-210 (1914±29 BP, KIA 22912) from material associated with the main roundhouse. In addition, second- to fourth-century pottery was recovered from this settlement which, when taken in conjunction with the radiocarbon dates, suggests occupation extending from the late Iron Age through to the end of the Roman period. However, although this site appears to have been occupied for an extended duration, it is only one example of this settlement type that has been subject to excavation, and there is an urgent need to undertake further excavation work, complete with scientific dating, to clarify the chronology of these distinctive settlements.

Rectilinear houses

A later form of settlement contained the rectilinear house, which is usually found unenclosed, although there was one example (*AF 206*) on Askham Fell which was in the centre of a rectangular enclosure (*Ch 7, p 311*; Pl 175). This type of building ranges from the isolated small, single-celled structure that is little more than a bield, to the large multi-celled structure linked to extensive field systems. The date range is also very considerable, apparently extending from the early medieval period to the sixteenth century, and beyond, in the form of the vernacular cross-passage house (Brunskill 1974; *Ch 2, p 38*). To an extent, the differences reflect the level of permanence of the structure; transhumant dwellings (shielings) are invariably single celled, and relatively small by comparison with contemporary permanently occupied houses, unless they have subsequently developed into permanent settlements. A case in point is at Scale Farm on Whin Garth, where a 30 m-long three-celled house (*WG 442*;

Plate 175: Rectilinear house AF 206 *within its enclosure, on Askham Fell*

Ch 3, p 91) developed from a single-celled structure, near which were several much smaller rectilinear structures (*c* 10 m long; *eg WG 206*), that were potentially shielings. The differences in complexity also presumably reflect the date of the structures, because the more permanently established farmhouses within the landscape tend also to be the later ones.

All of the rectangular houses identified within the LDNPS dataset were related to some form of field system or agricultural remains. Some were associated with cultivation terraces and would have had an economy more dependent on arable agriculture, such as those associated with the small Town Bank house (*TB 706; Ch 3, p 60*), and the large Crosbythwaite settlement (*CT 359-64; Ch 5, p 239*), as well as the settlement found at Ennerdale (LUAU 1998c; Pl 176). Others, although associated with a cairnfield, appear to display some evidence of arable farming, although it seems that the economy was primarily pastoral. Notable examples include the putative Whin Garth shielings (*eg WG 206*), which lay within a cairnfield, but with ridge and furrow visible between the cairns (*Ch 3, p 83*). At Mickleden Beck, such a settlement (*MB 337*) was associated with a cairnfield and field system; pollen analysis undertaken beneath one of the principal boundary banks revealed a predominantly pastoral economy, but some pollen in one of the samples was typically associated with arable practices (*Matricaria T* (mayweed/German camomile), *Plantago major/media* (hoary plantain), and Compositae *Cich* (includes dandelions, chicory, and hawkweeds)), suggesting a more mixed economy (*Ch 6, p 284*).

The majority of the rectilinear houses identified by the LDNPS were within the area of earlier remains, but though there were occasional overlaps between their respective field systems, their foundations were seemingly independent, suggesting a reoccupation of the site, rather than any degree of continuity. A case in point is at Crosbythwaite (CT II), where there was a clearly defined, and apparently medieval, settlement (Area 1), that was seemingly located deliberately to the south of an earlier settlement and its related field system (*Ch 5, p 239*). Although the field systems overlapped, the settlement centres were clearly separated and there was no reuse of the earlier field system. An interesting example was also identified at Askham Fell, where an enclosed medieval settlement, containing a rectilinear structure (*AF 206*), was some 260 m away from a complex enclosed settlement (*AF 203*), of a type presently dated to the Roman period (*Ch 7, pp 309-11*). Despite their proximity, their respective field systems extended in diametrically opposite directions, and their proximity was seemingly more inadvertent than an indication of continuity of occupation.

Plate 176: A double-walled stone longhouse in Ennerdale

Prehistoric Agricultural Development in the Lake District

Within recent years, there have been several attempts to model the development of later prehistoric upland farming systems from primary clearance to the formation of established field systems. These studies are inevitably based on the uplands, because these areas provide the best evidence for survival of field systems at various stages of development, through their fossilisation in these marginal landscapes. The model produced by Fowler (1983, 128-9), based on the typology of Feachem (1973), specifically concentrated on the origin of fields. In this model, five types of 'field' were envisaged. These included:

Type A: irregular, amorphous cleared area, characterised by cairns, but without obvious lynchets or field boundaries;

Type B: irregular but generally rectangular fields, characterised by clearance cairns, lynchets, walls, or stone lines, and sometimes burials, located in mountainous country;

Type C: elongated or geometric fields related to axial lines, which are generally characteristic of south-west Britain;

Type D: roughly square or rectangular fields, akin to many 'Celtic fields' found on the chalk downs, and common in the 'Highland zone';

Type E: somewhat irregular but markedly oblong fields, characteristic of the Pennines and north-west England, but with regional variants, mainly from the Roman period.

While this model represented an invaluable primary stage in developing a typology of fields, it was limited by the amount of upland survey data then available within specific regions, and consequently was based on regional variations evident within different upland landscapes, as opposed to genuine developmental variation. This evident regional variation can distort the typological picture and therefore a single regional context should be used to define the development of agricultural systems, so eliminating the inevitable confusion between transitional forms of field and selected regional forms. Whilst this clearly presents a logical ideal, it is only recently that sufficient data within a single regional context have been available. The generation of major surveys, such as that presented in this volume, and also that undertaken across Bodmin Moor (Johnson and Rose 1994), have enabled a more systematic approach to analysing landscape development.

Another pertinent landscape model for the development of upland farming systems was based on environmental evidence rather than archaeological field observation (Askew *et al* 1985, 19-21). This model outlined the agricultural techniques and stages that lead from the original clearance to the established ploughed field. In a similar way to Fowler's (1983, 128-9) model, this also proposed five separate stages:

Stage 1: conversion of forest to pasture: this process resulted in forest clearings, pock-marked with surface rock and tree stumps, the surface of which would be uneven. The removal of forest resulted in the immediate loss of substantial amounts of plant nutrients and bases, while the continued use of the land for pasture would increase the loss of such bases;

Stage 2: conversion to meadow: there is significant evidence that, initially, animal fodder was collected, probably using sickles, which were more appropriate for the harvesting of hay than cereals (Reynolds 1981). A scenario is envisaged in which clearance cairns would need to be constructed to remove surface stones, which would otherwise damage sickles during the cutting of a short crop such as grass;

Stage 3: the introduction of 'garden' plots: these are defined as small, irregular areas cultivated by hand. The techniques for hand cultivation would have ranged from spade digging to the use of hoes or digging sticks;

Stage 4: ard technology necessitates the use of larger, squared fields, because of the need for cross-cultivation. Obstructions to the movement of the ard, such as cairns or prominent rocks, would be moved to the edge of the plots;

Stage 5: mouldboard plough cultivation: the introduction of the mouldboard plough, which was prevalent from the early medieval period onwards, freed the farmer from the problems of dealing with surface vegetation, because the plough produced soil inversion (Behre 1981). Early plough teams tended to be very long and were cumbersome to turn, and therefore the fields tended to be long and narrow, with aratral curves. Ploughing with single blade ploughs naturally produced ridge and furrow.

Although this model does not give a typology of relict landscapes, it does provide an invaluable framework with which to categorise and establish significant developmental forms of the agricultural system, such as those found within the Lake District.

A revised model for the development of upland settlement

In their present form, none of the models discussed provide a direct correlation with the varied extant field systems of the Lake District. The construction of a revised model, based largely on these earlier ones, is therefore proposed to define the development of prehistoric upland agricultural systems in the region. This provides for the typological development of regionally distinct agricultural systems, in conjunction with the technique-orientated model of Askew et al (1985). It will attempt to show how Cumbrian prehistoric field systems have developed from the original clearances through to their eventual abandonment, or integration into later permanent field systems, and it will try to define each typological form with the introduction or adaptation of agricultural techniques. The more complex field systems invariably show that they developed over an extended period, with different elements of the system being added at different stages, though in their earliest form, these were often little more than a group of random cairns. In addition, these differing elements reflect a move towards more permanent and established occupation and farming techniques.

This model is based on analysis of the relict landscapes of the Lake District which, when they were abandoned, became fossilised at their most advanced stage of development. It is often difficult to discern precisely the forms of earlier landscapes, so this analysis is dependent on a range of landscapes being abandoned at various stages of development. Those primary cairnfields established on poor-quality land will inevitably have been abandoned before they could be expanded or developed. Thus, an impression is gained from the archaeological record that all primary cairnfields were small and located on poor ground, although the reality is more likely that many primary cairnfields will have developed into more advanced agricultural systems.

Primary cairnfield (basic meadowland)

The primary cairnfield was the most common form of this type of activity identified by the LDNPS. It can be defined as a simple cairnfield, comprising essentially randomly distributed cairns, with no evidence of stone banks, cairn alignments, or other elements of a proto-field system. There is never any contemporary association with ridge and furrow or lynchets, although there are several instances where ridge and furrow cultivation has been undertaken during a later phase of use, notably at Heathwaite Fell (HF IX; Ch 6, p 272). They have not been found in association with visible domestic structures, although there is one exception, where a cairnfield at Charlesground Gill (CG IXC) was spatially associated with a medieval type of rectilinear structure (CG 259; Ch 4, p 156). This structure was, therefore, either a later feature, or this particular primary cairnfield was uncharacteristically of post-Roman origin.

The primary cairnfields were often small. On average they comprised only about 15-18 cairns, although the smallest contained only three monuments and the largest comprised 40; none of the largest cairnfields identified can be classified as primary. Many of these primary types lay on very poor agricultural ground, sometimes in only a small hollow or small bench (*eg* SM IX (Stockdale Moor; *Ch 3, p 80*) and CG I (Charlesground Gill; *Ch 3, p 148*); SF IX (Stainton Fell; *Ch 4, p 177*) and BF VIIIA (Bootle Fell; *Ch 4, p 131*); and HF IB (Heathwaite Fell; *Ch 6, p 268*)), which inevitably restricted the size and potential for development. Such sites would inevitably have been abandoned before they could develop into proto-field systems (*see below*), and the archaeological record therefore provides an unrepresentative indication of the scale of these original cairnfields.

The extent of the primary cairnfield was often defined by the edge of mires (*eg* SF VII, BF IA, BF VIA, CG II, and CG VA; *Ch 4*), although differences in the drainage pattern did not necessarily correspond to changes in topography. Moreover, the instances of coincidence between mire edge and the extended cairnfields was so common that this probably indicates that, in most cases, the drainage pattern had not changed significantly since the construction date of the cairnfield (C Wells *pers comm*).

Typologically, the primary cairnfield corresponds to Fowler's (1983, 128) Type A, and would appear to reflect pioneer agriculture following forest clearance; the small, tightly constrained extents of these cairnfields would possibly equate with those of the original forest clearings. This typological form also seems to be similar to stages 1 and 2 of the Askew *et al* (1985) model, where the basic cairnfield is the result of first forest clearance, and then limited land improvement to create meadowland that can be used to produce hay for winter fodder. However, on the evidence of Barnscar (Walker 1965b), there was probably not a long interval between forest clearance and stone clearance. The palaeobotanical record there shows that forest clearance continued to be undertaken after the construction of cairns, and that pits were the result of the loss of the tree stumps.

Proto-field system
Within the Lake District, the proto-field system, in its most simple form, was an adaptation of the primary cairnfield, stone banks, or alignments of cairns, denoting attempts to demarcate and rationalise the land for agriculture. In some instances, they were associated with stone-founded roundhouses and small cultivated plots (*eg* CG V (Charlesground Gill; *Ch 4, p 151*), pointing to a degree of established settlement and the introduction of mixed-farming practices. However, the significant characteristic of a proto-field system is that there is no all-encompassing, rationalised, system, and that essentially it represented a modified primary cairnfield. In its simplest form, it appears as a random (primary) cairnfield with the addition of cultivated plots, or a few stone banks indicating the emergence of boundary demarcation (*eg* BS VI (Barnscar), SM VI (Stockdale Moor), BF I (Bootle Fell), and WG VII (Whin Garth); *Chs 3 and 4*). However, in more developed examples, the erratically defined boundaries marked the limits of areas which were largely devoid of cairns and seem to be the most primitive form of fields. The most basic example is found within monument group SM IV (Stockdale Moor), which was almost indistinguishable from the primary form of cairnfield, apart from some short sections of stone bank (*SM 365, SM 424,* and *SM 434; Ch 3, p 74*) and a significant cairn alignment. These delineated a large, sub-triangular area that was devoid of cairns, and essentially formed a proto-field.

A typical example of a proto-field system can be found on Bootle Fell (BF III; *Ch 4, p 125*). Many of the cairns there had a generally random distribution, but the cairnfield included roundhouses, significant cairn alignments (*eg* Alignment A; Fig 61), and stone banks (*eg BF 415/396*), which suggests that the original primary cairnfield had been modified and rationalised. Cairn Alignment B divided two areas that were largely devoid of cairns and may have been small, poorly defined plots. No all-embracing field system could be discerned within the cairnfield, but there were indications of the emergence of discrete, independent plots. The SF II cairnfield on Stainton Fell is another typical example of a proto-field system (*Ch 4, p 173*). This large cairnfield was mainly random in character, but had some developed elements, including two adjacent cultivated plots (*SF 259*), a few erratically defined cairn alignments, and a single, very prominent wall/stone bank (*SF 174*), which extended across the cairnfield, but was not part of an integral field system. The original cairnfield had then been adapted to incorporate the rationalised elements of a field system, and to introduce small-scale cultivation without affecting the original primary, pioneer, character of the area. Examples of proto-field systems are also found beyond the Lake District. These include those from the East Moors of the Peak District, where they have been classified as Class B field systems (Barnatt 1987, 399), and examples from the North York Moors, where the cairnfields of Iron Howe and Bumper Moor show random cairn distributions, with stone banks uncomfortably imposed on top (Spratt 1990; Hayes and Rutter 1964).

The agricultural techniques practised within the large proto-fields appear to have been similar to those of the primary cairnfield, albeit with a more organised and rationalised approach. Typically, lynchets were not found within the proto-fields (plot *SF 259* on Stainton Fell is one of the exceptions; *Ch 4, p 174*), many of which included significant numbers of random cairns. Again, the character of the fields potentially related to the procurement of winter feed. They were essentially meadows, and the original boundaries were possibly for the purpose of stock control, to segregate areas for hay from those of general pasturage. However, the establishment of small 'garden' plots at some of the sites was a significant innovation, which demonstrates the introduction of very basic, small-scale, arable, or horticultural, techniques within an overall pastoral economy. It indicates that the settlement had become more permanent and established in nature, a logical progression from the original pioneer-style agriculture. In this respect, the proto-field system relates to Askew *et al's* (1985, 20) stage 3 of agricultural development, whereby hand-cultivation techniques would be utilised to produce a small crop. However, those cultivated plots that were incorporated within the proto-field system were relatively rare and small when compared with the extent of the adjacent cairnfields. It is thus clear that the mixed-farming practices were still substantially biased towards the pastoral economy.

Cairn-field-system (mixed-farming land)
The development of a cairnfield system represents a change of emphasis from the random cairnfield towards an all-embracing field system. The field system extended across all or a significant part of the cairnfield, and the distribution of the cairns had a direct relationship with the field boundaries. Although the cairn groups still retained an essentially random distribution within specific areas, their extent was strictly dictated by the field system. Often the field system incorporated 'garden' plots, as an integral element, and these were directly related to a stone-founded roundhouse, or house platform. Although most of these field systems have developed from primary cairnfields, they have been changed and expanded so extensively that they have lost their original primary character, and are therefore distinct from the proto-field systems, which may have been an earlier stage in their development (*see above*).

The classic example of the cairn-field-system is found on Town Bank (TB IV; *Ch 3, p 52*), where there was a series of co-axial-type fields defined by long, continuous stone banks, orientated downslope, and associated with a cairnfield. There, some apparently randomly distributed cairns were contained by field boundaries (*eg* TB IVA and TB IVC), whilst others appeared to be 'garden' plots (*eg* TB 243), or had garden plots within them (*eg* TB IVB and TB IVD), and some contained apparent roundhouses (*eg TB 236, TB 241,* and *TB 303*). Significantly, although considerable cairnfields formed part of the complex,

these were only discrete elements within an all-encompassing field system. Other notable examples include two cairnfield systems from Barnscar (BS IVA and BS IVG; *Ch 4, pp 182, 191*), a field system at Brantrake Moss (near Devoke Water; BB VII (Birkby / Birker Fell); *Ch 5, p 211*), and the Town Bank (TB III) complex (*Ch 3, p 50*). Although, at first sight, these latter examples appear very different, they did display the same basic characteristics. The TB III complex, for instance, had a single large field defined by stone banks (*TB 72, TB 74-5, TB 77-8,* and *TB 80;* Fig 25), with roundhouses incorporated into the outer banks. The internal area was relatively free of features, but a small 'garden' plot (*TB 60*) and cairnfield were identified immediately outside this field.

On Burnmoor, at Acre Hows (BM XVC; *Ch 3, p 113*), there is an example of a cairnfield system in which the component cairns had been incorporated, for the most part, into an irregular field system. Stone bank *BM 335* defined the southern edge of the cairnfield, but more significantly, a large rectilinear field surrounded the large Brat's Hill stone circle (*BM 352*). The field boundary was defined by cairn alignments (D, E, and F; Fig 52), and any other cairns lay outside this field. Again, the field system was the dominant feature of the complex, but the cairnfield was still an integral element, albeit defined by the field system.

This form of cairnfield system is not unique to the Lake District, and there are several examples from other upland regions of Britain. The site at Muir of Gormack (RCAHMS 1990, 69), for instance, is similar to that at Town Bank (TB IV), in that it has the elements of an earlier system partly contained by an all-embracing field system, which had become, by the time of abandonment, the dominant element of the archaeological landscape. Another comparable example is found at Big Moor Central in the East Moors of the Peak District (Barnatt 1987, 397), where a co-axial field system developed out from areas of random cairnfield. In some instances, the cairns at this site have been incorporated into the stone boundary banks, and in others the fields have been sited away from the main concentrations of cairns, leaving alternate areas of cairnfield and cairn-free fields; this compares with the arrangement at TB IV (*Ch 3, p 52*). Another example is the remarkable Danby Rigg cairnfield, on the North York Moors, which is huge in its extent, even when compared to those examples from the Lake District, having upward of 1000 cairns (Spratt 1990, 110; Harding and Ostoja-Zagorski 1994; Pl 177). This cairnfield clearly incorporates elements of a probable co-axial field system, which has been superimposed onto the cairnfield, and that in some respects is similar to the TB IV system. It also contains elements of an earlier, scattered, pattern of field boundaries that have little direct relationship with the

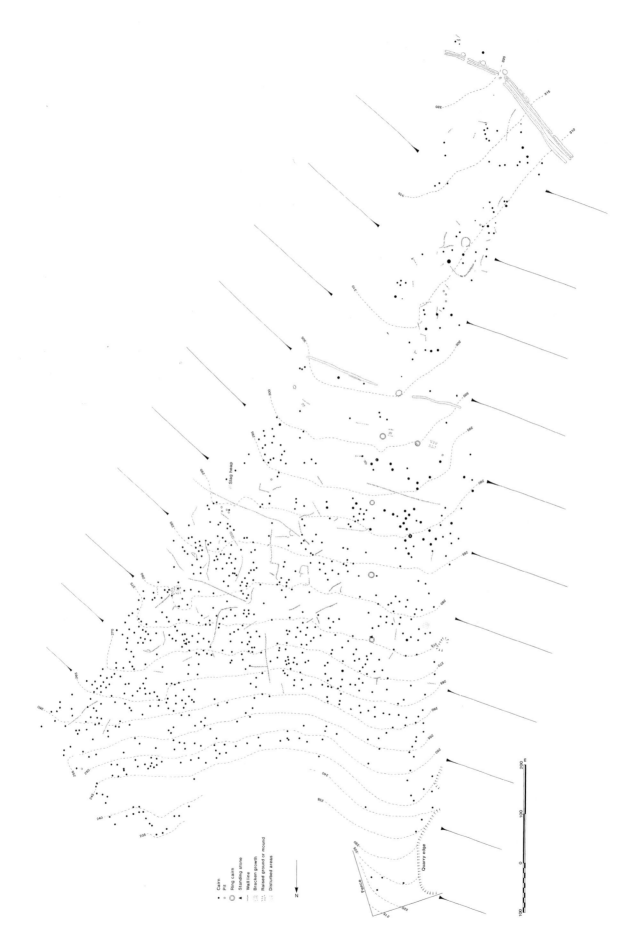

Cairn
Pit
Ring cairn
Standing stone
Wall line
Bracken growth
Raised ground or mound
Disturbed areas

N

Slag heap

Quarry edge

Fence

200 m

100

0

100

Plate 177: The huge cairnfield on Danby Rigg, overlain by a probable co-axial field system (Harding and Ostoja-Zagorski 1994)

co-axial boundaries, and appear to be the remains of an earlier proto-field system. As such, the Danby Rigg site shows its development from primary cairnfield improvement to co-axial field system.

The Lake District form of cairn-field-system is broadly similar to Fowler's Type B field (1983, 128). Although it is considerably more rationalised and ordered than the typologically earlier proto-field system, the agricultural methods do not appear to have been particularly different. For example, the TB IVA cairnfield on Town Bank appears to have been used as a meadow for winter fodder, and the only agricultural distinction from the proto-field system seems to be that these had a greater emphasis on small-scale cultivation, as almost all of the cairnfield systems have 'garden' plots (eg BS IVA (Barnscar); Ch 4, p 182). The agriculture exhibited in these systems appears to have been a balanced mixed economy and, again, would appear to relate to Askew et al's (1985, 20) stage 3 of agricultural development, which incorporates the introduction of 'garden' plots.

Cultivated field system
The cultivated field system represents a dramatic departure from the typologically earlier cairnfield system. The prime characteristic in this seems to have been an over-riding emphasis on the field pattern, rather than the cairnfield. They usually contained only limited numbers of cairns, which are invariably aligned and located in relation to the field boundaries. The fields are regular in shape, devoid of cairns, and their boundaries often incorporate lynchet profiles, suggesting cultivation. There is no evidence of the ridge and furrow typically associated with mouldboard-plough cultivation (Askew et al 1985, 21) and it is likely that most fields relate to ard cultivation. The field systems are invariably associated with stone-founded roundhouses, or even developed farmstead complexes, and there is a clear indication that it formed a part of an established permanent settlement.

The classic example from the Lake District uplands is the TB XIII field system on Town Bank (Ch 3, p 61), which had a series of regular-sized, rectilinear, fields defined by banks with lynchet-profiles. No cairns were identified within the fields, although small numbers were aligned along the upper edge of the field system (TB 792, TB 794, and TB 796) and elsewhere, in relation to the field boundaries. The internal surfaces of the fields were relatively smooth but displayed no evidence of ridges formed by cultivation. The fields were up to 100 m in length and had an average width of 32 m; their large area would have precluded the possibility of hand cultivation, and thus they were likely to have been cultivated by ards. No large random cairnfield was associated and the agricultural emphasis was on cultivation rather than pastoralism.

The fields were directly associated with two complex farmsteads, comprising roundhouses and attached sunken enclosures. This direct relationship with developed farmsteads, rather than simple unenclosed structures, would perhaps suggest a chronology that relates more to the later Bronze Age, or early Iron Age, rather than the earlier Bronze Age (p 324).

The paucity of cairns and other associated features around the fields may imply that the TB XIII field system did not develop from a primary cairnfield but, instead, had been constructed from the outset in this developed form. In this respect, the nearby TB XI cairnfield and field system was in marked contrast; it also displayed many of the characteristics of the cultivated field system, such as fairly regular, narrow fields defined by banks and elongated cairns (TB 625-38; Ch 3, p 60), no random cairnfield, and again, an emphasis upon large-scale cultivation. However, it also included an enormous complexity of peripheral features, particularly banks, which did not relate directly to the field system, and were possibly adapted components from an earlier phase of use; this suggests that this field system was in use for much longer than the TB XIII system.

A few other examples of this form were recognised in the LDNPS dataset, notably TB VIII (Ch 3, pp 55-6). However, this example is relatively small and has little of the complexity seen elsewhere, perhaps because climatic decline and the corresponding upland abandonment deterred such development. This type of field system is, however, much more common in other upland areas of Britain. In North-East Perthshire, for instance, such systems have been identified at Drumderg (RCAHMS 1990, 44; Fig 156), Drumturn Burn (op cit, 47-9), and the Hill of Cally (op cit, 52-3), which display a similar emphasis on basic cultivation; they have rectilinear or irregular field systems incorporating lynchets, and there is a corresponding paucity of associated cairnfields. Other equivalent examples would appear to be the co-axial field system at East Moor on Bodmin Moor (Johnson and Rose 1994, 62-3), Gleniron Fell in South-West Scotland (Yates 1983, 349-51), and White Meldon in Peebleshire (Feachem 1973, 338 and 340). Several comparable examples have also been recorded on the East Moors of the Peak District, notably at Beeley Warren South (Barnatt 1987). In this example, which is closely comparable to the TB XIII system, the co-axial field system includes a series of strip fields, associated with a low density of cairns, which are mostly within the field boundaries.

This emergence of the regulated field system broadly corresponds to Fowler's (1983, 128) Types C and D. The development of agricultural practices within fields is the most important aspect of this typology,

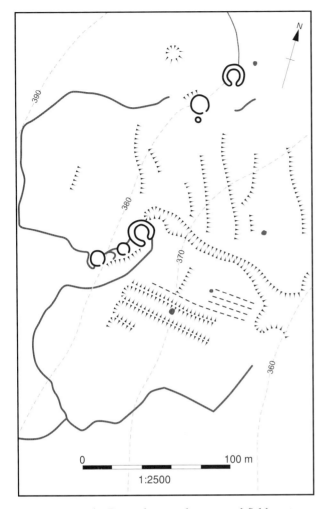

Figure 156: The Drumderg settlement and field system, Perthshire (after RCAHMS 1990, 44)

the shape of the fields being of lesser significance, and more attributable to regional variation than to the evolution of the field systems. This stage of agricultural development in the Lake District clearly relates to Askew *et al's* (1985, 20) stage 4 (ard cultivation). The paucity of cairns and stones within the plots, coupled with the lynchet-profiled boundaries, would appear to confirm the use of an ard-style cultivation technique. However, in the Lake District, the fields are often not square, as would be expected if cross-cultivation techniques were being practised (*op cit*, 20).

The fossilisation of prehistoric fields within later field systems is a possible indicator of continuity of settlement and makes the link between this typological development and its adaptation in the subsequent millennia. Unfortunately, such fossilisation is only rarely identified, but nevertheless is extremely significant. Williamson (1987) has demonstrated the existence of early field systems in East Anglia, which are broadly orientated north-south, bear little relation to the medieval pattern of settlement, and ignore medieval parish boundaries. More significantly, the field patterns are cut by a Roman road and clearly

demonstrate the continuity of pre-Roman field systems through to the present day (*ibid*). In the uplands of south-west Britain, some classic examples of fossilisation have been recorded, notably the settlement at Little Siblyback and, to a lesser extent, Garrow Tor (Johnson and Rose 1994, 60 and 109), where elements of the early field system were incorporated within the boundaries of later fields. However, such evidence of fossilisation does not necessarily indicate direct continuity, as the prehistoric boundaries were sufficiently substantial to encourage their reuse during any reoccupation.

Within the LDNPS dataset, there is little evidence of direct continuity beyond the Roman period, and where medieval settlements were located on sites previously occupied in the prehistoric period (*eg* HF IX (Heathewaite Fell); *Ch 6, p 272*), they appear to reflect the reuse of a favoured place, rather than any actual continuity. For example, at Barnscar (BS IV; *Ch 4, p 182*), the initial prehistoric settlement was also occupied in the Roman period, when there was considerable adaptation of the earlier field system, but there was no evidence of any medieval or later settlement. To an extent, the apparent lack of continuity reflects the strategy of the LDNPS, which placed a greater emphasis upon the examination of unenclosed moorland landscapes than enclosed lands. However, there is also not inconsiderable evidence that most of the prehistoric settlements were ultimately abandoned before they became fossilised into later systems. The intensity of later settlement and farming activity can also obscure and destroy evidence of former settlement. The Crosbythwaite settlements (CT II; *Ch 5, p 237*) provide the best evidence for continuity in the LDNPS dataset, but the character of the original site had been so altered during the medieval period that it is difficult to distinguish possible continuity from a later reoccupation.

Conclusions
Typology
The typological model presented here attempts to define the development of a prehistoric upland agricultural settlement from its earliest pastoral, pioneer occupation of virgin forest, to the formation of established cultivated settlements. In its most schematic and simple form (Fig 157), it depicts the development of an idealised single system, from undisturbed forest, into a cultivated field system, a process which could have extended over a considerable period of time. In this hypothetical example, the initial forest clearance is shown to develop into a rationalised field system, the forest around the settlement being progressively cleared. This development has been closely linked with the change from pastoral to mixed-agricultural practices.

333

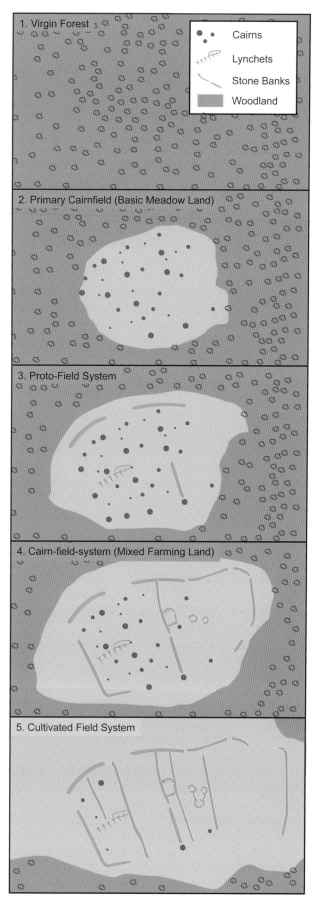

1. Virgin Forest

Legend:
- Cairns
- Lynchets
- Stone Banks
- Woodland

2. Primary Cairnfield (Basic Meadow Land)

3. Proto-Field System

4. Cairn-field-system (Mixed Farming Land)

5. Cultivated Field System

Figure 157: Schematic depiction of the development of a prehistoric field system

The most basic primary cairnfields were essentially pastoral in function, and there is no evidence of associated cultivation features. These small random cairnfields reflect unintensive agricultural practices and could potentially have been a product of transhumance. As the agricultural system became more established, so the land was rationalised and a proto-field system developed. This included cultivation features, which suggests that arable farming was being practised on a limited scale, in conjunction with traditional pastoral activities. By the third stage - the cairnfield system - mixed-farming practices had developed further, with a greater emphasis upon cultivation. The practice of early mixed farming would appear to be confirmed by the TB IV monument group on Town Bank, where evidence was recovered to suggest that the cairnfield was in contemporary use with a cultivated plot, and was not just a relict element of an earlier phase of farming (*Ch 3, pp 182-8*). In the final stage of development, a form of settlement and field system existed that was more reliant on arable farming-practices, and, where observed, the cairns that were associated with such systems were left only around the edges of the cultivated plots.

Although it appears to be a clearly defined typological development relating to the agricultural exploitation of the uplands in the Lake District, this is not necessarily chronologically sequential. For example, small primary cairnfields may have been in contemporary use with more advanced cultivated systems, and, indeed, could potentially even have been satellite-farming areas for the more established settlements. However, the more developed systems do display features, such as stone-founded roundhouses, which are characteristic of the later Bronze Age in northern Britain (Jobey 1985, 180-4), suggesting some chronological dimension to the observed typology.

Distribution

The distribution of the field systems and cairnfields around the Lake District is potentially very significant, and has considerable implications for understanding the development of prehistoric settlement across Cumbria. However, as with most studies into site distribution, the limitations of the datasets must be recognised to ensure that the defined distribution does not merely reflect areas that have been investigated (Fig 158). The LDNPS programme specifically targeted known cairnfields, and so the study has highlighted some of the most substantial and significant of these in Cumbria, but the extent of these survey areas is relatively small, given the extent of the uplands of the Lake District. These areas in isolation are not, therefore, representative of the overall settlement character across the county, or indeed within the National

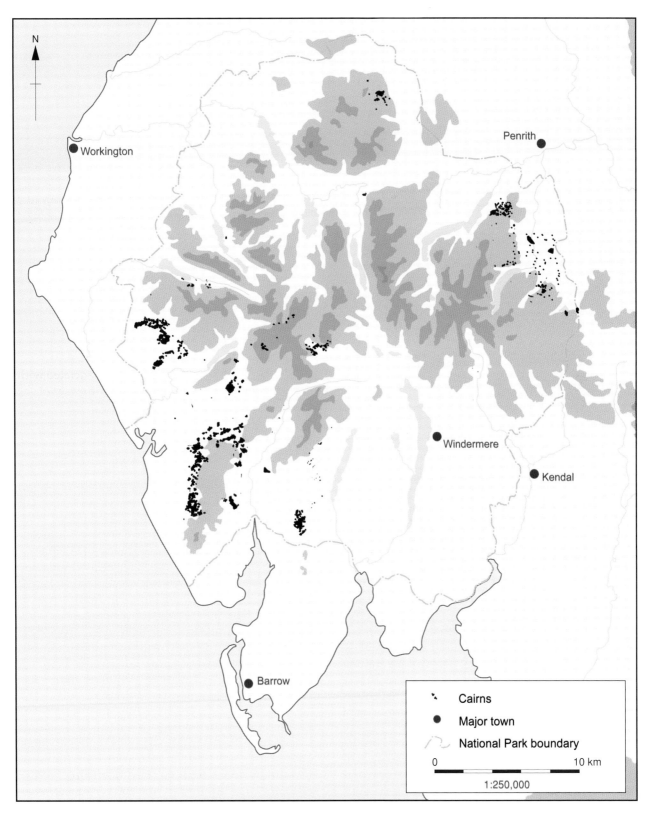

Figure 158: Distribution of cairnfields in the Lake District

Park. Extensive areas of identification survey have subsequently been undertaken across substantial areas of the Lake District (*Ch 1*; Fig 3), however, and these, in conjunction with the Cumbria HER, provide a more balanced representation of the overall settlement pattern.

The general character of the cairnfields is, for the most part, demonstrated by these subsequent surveys, which show that there are occasional cairnfields across much of the Lake District, but, with a few notable exceptions, most of these are relatively small, and usually have less than ten cairns. These small

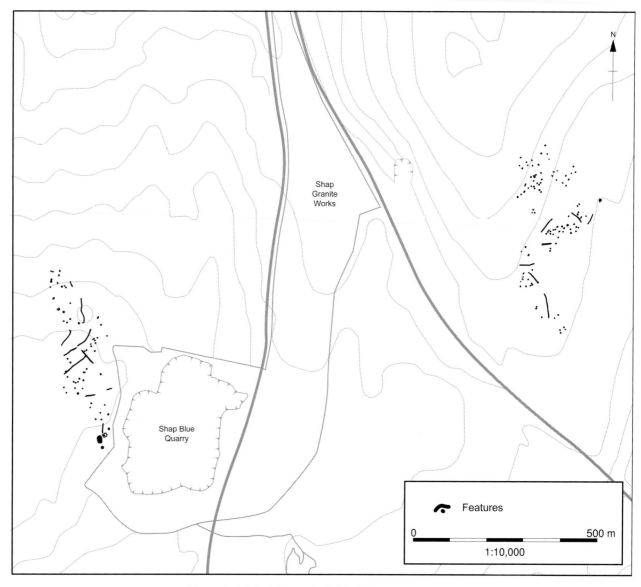

Figure 159: The Shap cairnfields (after Turner 1991)

cairnfields are rarely associated with any field systems, typically have a random distribution, and seemingly reflect a localised and transient improvement of the uplands, typified by the small cairnfields of Torver High and Blawith Commons (LUAU 1994a; LUAU 1995). There are, of course, occasional exceptions, most notably the large cairnfields found at Shap (Fig 159), but this, in its relative isolation, actually highlights the contrast with, and significance of, the vast expanses of cairnfields across the western margins of the Lakeland Massif. These large cairnfields may have started out in the same manner as the small cairnfields seen elsewhere in Cumbria, being formed as a result of unintensive exploitation of the woodlands, which created a small clearing that potentially related to short-term, or transhumant, activity. Presumably, the small cairnfields were exploratory workings within the woodland, because they were not subsequently developed or expanded, and were a small *ad hoc* attempt, potentially by a single family group, to

work new ground. However, in West Cumbria, these areas continued to be used, expanded, and ultimately rationalised into field systems, and hence their ultimate surviving character is very distinct from the smaller examples seen elsewhere in the county.

The distribution of the large cairnfields is significant in that they, for the most part, exist on the marginal uplands immediately adjacent to the flat West Cumbrian coastal plain (Fig 160). The marked concentration of these cairnfields is such that, during the survey, it was possible to predict, with a reasonable degree of confidence, where cairnfields would be found, on the basis that any area of well-drained, gently sloping, land, between 150 m and 300 m OD, and facing towards the coast, would contain a cairnfield.

The implication of this apparent patterning is that the cairnfields reflect some degree of expansion

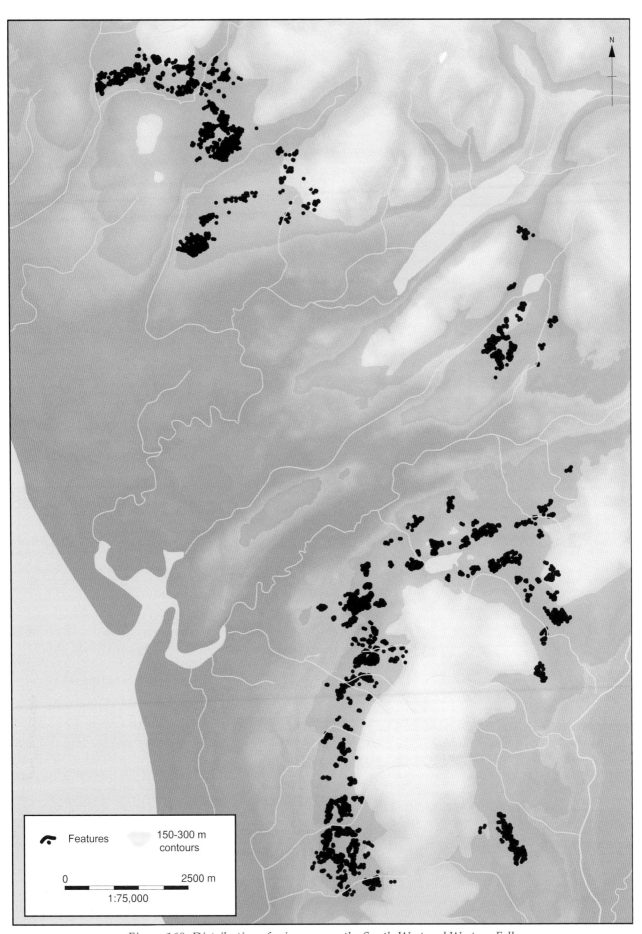

Figure 160: Distribution of cairns across the South-West and Western Fells

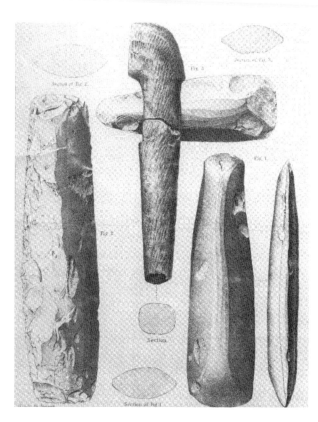

Plate 178: Rough-out and polished Langdale axes from Ehenside Tarn, West Cumbria

out from the coastal plain, and are a symptom of extensive settlement and activity in this lowland area. Indeed, there is a very well-documented pattern of early farming and settlement across the coastal plain

that dates back to at least the mesolithic period, best represented by Eskmeals and Williamson's Moss (Bonsall 1981; Bonsall *et al* 1986; 1989) and at the site uncovered during excavations ahead of the Carlisle Northern Development Route (OA North 2011a). This latter site also had continuity, or reoccupation, in the neolithic period and Bronze Age, and closely mirrors the settlement site of Ehenside Tarn in terms of its lithic assemblage (Darbishire 1873; Pl 178). This is strongly reinforced by the identification of extensive mesolithic to Bronze Age lithic assemblages from fieldwalking of the coastal plain (Cherry and Cherry 1986) and from palaeobotanical evidence (Pennington 1975; Walker 2001), which indicates very early cultivation around the Solway, as well as early woodland clearances. Taken as a whole, this evidence appears to suggest that the coastal plain was an area of considerable early activity, and that settlement developed initially out from the coastal margins in the mesolithic period, but extended throughout the coastal plain during the subsequent neolithic period and Bronze Age.

It must be stressed, however, that the coastal plain is a finite topographical area, defined by the shore on one side and the hills and mountains of the Lake District on the other, and at its narrowest it is now only 1.5 km wide (Pl 179). Given this, any expansion across the coastal lands would inevitably have been constrained by the surrounding topography. Therefore, with an increasing population and the exhaustion of the lowland soils, it is, perhaps,

Plate 179: The narrow coastal plain of western Cumbria, edged to the east by the Lake District mountains

inevitable that there would ultimately have been some expansion off the narrow plain and onto the uplands, which climatically were not so 'marginal' in the Bronze Age.

The initial exploration may have been small-scale in nature and might have been confined to forest clearance for transhumance, from populations primarily resident on the coastal lands. Increasing pressure over time, however, would perhaps have led to the continued development and expansion of the marginal lands, and, to judge by the extensive remains of cairnfields and field systems across much of the these lands, it would appear that such pressure for expansion was considerable. Moreover, examination of the distribution of the cairnfields shows that most of the usable land across the South-West Fells was utilised at some stage (Fig 160).

Even though activity on the marginal lands may only have been peripheral, in comparison with the intensive farming and settlement in the lowlands, the fact that the coastal areas continued to be farmed over subsequent millennia resulted in either the loss or obscuring of early settlement remains. It is perhaps ironic, therefore, that the marginal nature of the uplands has led to the above-ground survival of a series of remains relating to prehistoric activity, which represent some of the best indicators of prehistoric farming in the area, and, for that matter, in the entire region.

Size

The size (Fig 161) and complexity of a cairnfield may be an indicator of the intensity of activity, but, alternatively, it may reflect the duration in which the cairnfield was in use. It is, perhaps, significant that the largest of all the cairnfields, at Barnscar (Table 4), has three settlement centres, two unenclosed, apparently of later prehistoric date, and also a complex enclosed settlement, which has produced a Roman fibula (*Ch 4*, *p 179*). There are also at least two independent phases of field system, superimposed on a cairnfield that probably pre-dated the field rationalisation. The earliest activity at the site is uncertain but, given that there was intensive woodland clearance from the neolithic period and that the latest activity was apparently of Roman date, the site was seemingly exploited for an extended period of time (*Ch 4*, *pp 195-6*). The apparent complexity at Barnscar may therefore reflect considerable longevity of use, even if the two known episodes of clearance were divided by a period of abandonment.

Although any consideration of the longevity of occupation within those sites examined during the LDNPS is severely restricted by the absence of scientific dating, the size of the individual cairns within the cairnfields may also be a reflection of longevity. For instance, an initial cairn constructed as part of the primary land improvement exercise might then have been built up as a result of a continuing, or even sporadic, process of stone clearance; one such example is the cairn excavated at Devoke Water, within cairnfield BB IX (Birker/Birkby Fell; *Ch 5*, *p 216*), which was found to have been a product of multiple episodes of clearance activity. This measured 4.5 x 4 m, was 0.4 m high, and was larger than average, even within its immediate cairnfield. Excavation indicated that it was the product of more than one phase of clearance, with the initial episode comprising large stones, and later activity being represented by smaller stones, which had enlarged the cairn in a north-easterly direction. A potential neolithic flint flake was found within its immediate vicinity, and an early medieval radiocarbon date was obtained from peat located immediately underneath the enlarged portion of the cairn. This radiocarbon assay did not, therefore, necessarily date the primary episode of construction, but probably provides a *terminus post quem* for the subsequent episode of clearance.

Small, undeveloped primary-type cairnfields often have small, relatively low cairns, which might suggest that stone clearance was an ongoing process. Furthermore, if the land had been worked for only a short period of time, then the cairns would not have developed significantly in size. An example of this was found at Threepow Raise on Askham Moor (AF II; *Ch 7*, *p 301*), which was a small, undeveloped, cairnfield, where many of the cairns were less than 2.5 m in diameter, and less than 0.25 m in height. These cairns were certainly small, particularly when compared with those from Barnscar (BS IV; *Ch 4*, *p 182*), which were up to eight-times larger, and which were presumably a product of continued clearance activity over an extended period.

Although cairn size may reflect the duration of clearance, there are also other factors that may have contributed to their size, not least of which was the amount of surface stone, and the stone content of the soil, at the time of the creation of the cairnfield. Some areas, for example, would have required relatively little improvement to enable grazing, because there was relatively little surface stone. Hence, this would have led to the establishment of small-sized cairns. However, other areas, with larger expanses of surface stone, would have required more clearance activity, which would have led to the creation of larger cairns. This is potentially reflected in a marked size variation of cairns within individual cairnfields, which, although common, is very obvious at TF V on Thwaites Fell, where the diameters of the cairns ranged from 2.5 m to 7.4 m (*Ch 5*, *p 260*).

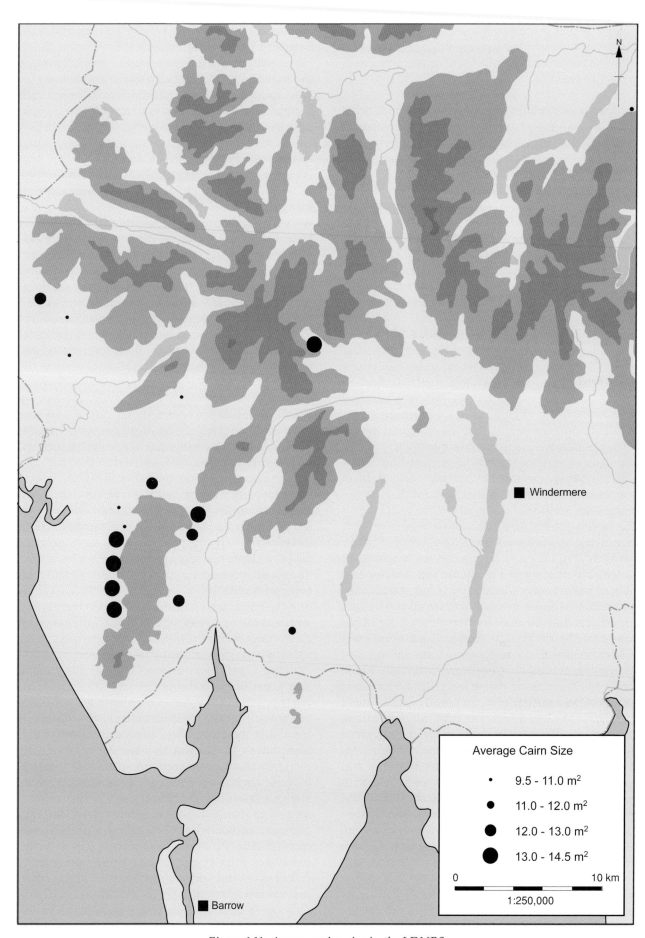

Figure 161: Average cairn size in the LDNPS

Survey area	Average area of cairn (m²)	Average diameter of cairn (m)
Askham	9.63744	3.50
Barnscar	10.70454	3.68
Birker and Birkby Fell	12.53815	3.99
Bootle Fell	13.49522	4.1
Burnmoor	10.81714	3.71
Charlesground Gill	13.24179	4.10
Corney Fell	14.01691	4.22
Crosbythwaite	13.94329	4.21
Heathwaite Fell	11.31315	3.79
Hesk Fell	12.79803	4.03
Mickleden Beck	14.26466	4.26
Stainton Fell	10.47239	3.65
Stockdale Moor	9.73520	3.52
Thwaites Fell	12.68026	4.01
Town Bank	12.06732	3.91
Ulpha Fell	12.400	3.96
Whin Garth	9.99250	3.56
Whitrow Beck	13.53019	4.14

Table 4: Average cairn size for each of the survey areas

Perhaps the most significant factor that affects cairn size, however, is the type of activity being undertaken within the cairnfield. Cairns that were initially established to allow pastoral activities would have grown slowly, reflecting relatively little subsequent ground disturbance, whereas those associated with cultivation activities would have had an accelerated growth, as they became the repositories for stone brought up by the plough, or ard. This link between cultivation and cairn size is demonstrated at monument group HF IX on Heathwaite Fell, where the cairns were associated with ridge and furrow, were within a walled field system, and were extremely large (*Ch 6, p 272*; Pl 171). For instance, within this monument group, the typical cairn had a diameter of *c* 7 m, and was up to 0.8 m in height, whilst there was one example that measured 11 x 6 m in extent, and was 1.1 m in height. This markedly contrasted with cairns that were part of the same broad cairnfield, but which lay outside the medieval field boundary, and were not associated with ridge and furrow cultivation. In contrast, these cairns had diameters of *c* 2 m and were *c* 0.2 m in height. However, given the shape and distribution of the cairns within the HF IX group, it is probable that all were part of the same original cairnfield but, at a later date, probably during the medieval period, a field system was established that extended over part of it. Subsequently, the cairns

within this area were reused to consume stone brought up during episodes of medieval, or later, ploughing. The considerable difference between the sizes of the cairns, within what was essentially a single cairnfield, is an indication of the very considerable impact that a subsequent phase of cultivation and clearance can have upon cairn size.

Co-axial field systems

While there are relatively few large cairnfields elsewhere in the Lake District, prehistoric co-axial field systems are known, such as that found at Little Asby on the eastern fells of the county, adjacent to the Eden Valley (OA North 2009d; Fig 162). At this site, an extensive field system is associated with several stone-founded domestic settlements and large stock pounds (*ibid*). It is also notable that, in some areas, the large co-axial field systems are rarely associated with cairnfields. For example, across the marginal lands above Dyffryn Nantle, in Western Snowdonia, there is a large complex of co-axial field systems, for the most part associated with unenclosed settlements, and the cairnfields, where identified, are very small and widely dispersed (OA North 2006). Similarly, at Little Asby, there is an absence of cairnfields (OA North 2009d). At Town Bank, the co-axial field systems within the TB XIII monument group (*Ch 3, p 60*) are associated with a very small number of cairns, and there are larger cairnfields elsewhere on the Town Bank ridge, but essentially this association is rare. Similarly, there are some co-axial field systems within the Peak District (*eg* Beeley Warren; Barnatt 1987, 397) associated with cairnfields, which were probably surviving elements of an earlier phase of activity. Essentially, these two types of agricultural landscape appear to reflect different, and more probably chronologically distinct, patterns of agricultural activity, and, as with Danby Rigg in North Yorkshire (Spratt 1990, 114; Pl 177), the co-axial field system appears to be a later, almost independent superimposition onto the earlier cairnfield.

The cairnfields seemingly reflect a primary improvement of marginal land that was previously occupied by woodland, and initially may have been a product of unintensive, predominantly pastoral exploitation. In contrast, the co-axial field systems reflect a more intensive, largely arable, working of land that had already been cleared of trees. For example, at Town Bank (TB XIII; *Ch 3, p 60*), it appears that an area of marginal land was initially subjected to primary woodland clearance, which led to the creation of cairnfields. This area was then further developed, resulting in the formation of larger cairnfields, which were rationalised through the adoption of field systems. This process finally led to the creation of a highly organised arable co-axial field system, which was established either directly on an area of primary clearance, or on an adjacent site. Although

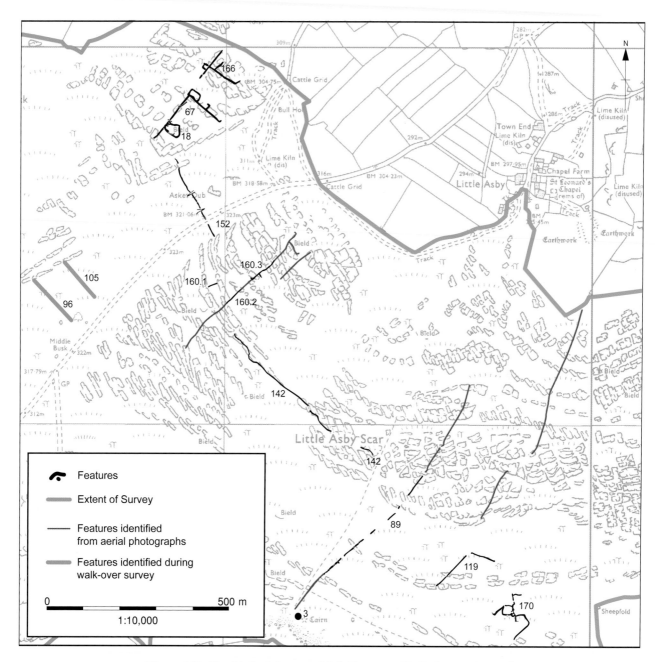

Figure 162: The Little Asby co-axial field system (© Ordnance Survey)

at Town Bank there is clear evidence for typological development, unfortunately, without the benefit of scientific dating, it is not possible to determine the duration of this sequence, or the degree of continuity it might contain.

Funerary and Ceremonial Monuments

One of the more common features in the Lake District landscape were funerary monuments, which have been identified, to some extent, in almost all of the survey areas and, in some instances, such as on Askham Fell, they make up a substantial part of the archaeological landscape. As a class of

monument they are significant, in part, because they relate only to neolithic and Bronze Age activity, and are some of the most diagnostic yet datable monuments in the landscape. Their relationship with the other components of the landscape is also of considerable interest, be it direct or indirect. The survey areas were targeted upon cairnfields and settlement remains, however, and thus any funerary monuments identified were inevitably going to be close to agricultural landscapes. The more remote funerary monuments, standing on promontories and hill summits, were, for the most part, outside the survey areas, but these potentially comprise a significant proportion of the global range of prehistoric funerary monuments in the Lake District National Park.

Plate 180: Long cairn TB 564, within the TB X cairnfield on Town Bank

The relationship between funerary monuments and the landscape varied enormously. Of the limited number of long cairns identified (*Appendix 2*), most appear to be remote from the cairnfields and to be set in locations that were not topographically distinct, neither on any particular high points nor at sites with pronounced vistas. A case in point is the large Sampson's Bratfull cairn (*SM 435*) on Stockdale Moor (*Ch 3, p 71*), which stands in the bottom of a small, shallow gully, and is up to 120 m from the nearest cairn. Similarly, the large putative long cairn on Stainton Fell (*SF 363; Ch 4, p 175*) is in a remote position, at a relatively high altitude, but does not have a particularly clear vista. The exception to this generalisation is the group of long cairns (*TB 564*, *TB 591*, and *TB 536*) on Town Bank (TB X; *Ch 3, p 57*), which were located within an extensive cairnfield. These putative long (or pear-shaped) cairns, particularly *TB 564*, were very well defined, large, prominent, and incorporated elements of kerbs (Pl 180). However, these monuments do not satisfy the criteria for a long cairn, as defined by Masters (1984), particularly as they fall below his minimum length criteria (15 m), and it has been suggested that they could reflect an 'architectural cross over' between long and round cairns (Evans 2008, 72). In addition, if these monuments date to the neolithic period, then their relationship with the surrounding cairnfield is uncertain. At Town Bank, three of the long cairns (*TB 526, TB 541*, and *TB 564*) were aligned parallel to the linear elements of a proto-field system (*TB 524, TB 547-8, TB 570-4*), although it must be admitted that this orientation was directly downslope and does not necessarily indicate a contemporary relationship (*Ch 3, p 57*). At this site, the putative stone bank/cairn alignment, *TB 527*, and cairns *TB 542-4* appeared to cross through this alignment of long cairns, and also to avoid long cairn *TB 541*; this would imply that at least one element of the proto-field system post-dated the long cairns.

Round cairns are quite often situated on summits or exposed positions with good outlooking vistas, and it is evident that they were intended to provide good

Plate 181: The large round cairn on the summit of Simonside, Northumberland

Plate 182: Round cairn BB 185, *standing on a low summit to the west of Devoke Water*

views, or were positioned in order to be seen on the skyline from some distance away (Pl 181). Sometimes these monuments are isolated from any cairns or field systems, such as the round cairn, *HF 312*, at the end of the Long Ridge spur on Heathwaite Fell (*Ch 6, p 277*). In the majority of recorded examples, however, some spatial association was recognised between these and a cairnfield or field system. A good example of this is the line of three large round cairns positioned on the low, raised, summit of Stockdale Moor (*SM 436-8; Ch 3, p 71*), which provides a good vista to the north. Given this, it is evident that their positions related to this specific topographical context, yet there are other cairns all around these monuments. A substantial cairnfield (SM II) lay to the east, and there was a rectilinear alignment of cairns (*SM 300-1, SM 303-4*, and *SM 306-10*) to the west of the largest of the round cairn (*SM 436*), yet for the most part there were no small cairns within their immediate environs. This suggests that there may have been a *cordon sanitaire* around the round cairns, into which clearance activity did not penetrate.

This was more clearly illustrated at the western end of Devoke Water, where a large round cairn (*BB 185*; Pl 182) stands on the summit of a low raise and, though it lay within the centre of the BB III cairnfield, there seemed to be a deliberate, *c* 30 m-wide, gap around it, within which there were only three small clearance cairns (*Ch 4, p 208*). A further example was identified at the SF II cairnfield on Stainton Fell, where a large round / filled ring cairn (*SF 338*) was aligned with a long boundary bank (*SF 174*), yet an area with a radius of *c* 30 m around it contained no small cairns (*Ch 4, p 173*). It therefore seems likely that the round

cairns in both of these areas pre-dated the cairnfields, and, though the cairnfields were constructed around them, the sepulchral / ritual significance of these monuments was recognised and respected, such that an area of 'good' agricultural land was set aside as, in effect, 'holy ground'. This pattern of veneration is, to an extent, reinforced by the cairnfields on the East Moors of the Peak District, where it has been argued (Barnatt 1987, 411) that ceremonial monuments are most typically associated with the earliest phases of cairnfield development, which may be a product of early Bronze Age occupation (Barnatt 2000).

Interestingly, at Burnmoor, there was also an apparent *cordon sanitaire* around the five stone circles on the summit of Brat's Hill (*Ch 3, p 111*). This was most clearly represented at monument *BM 352*, the largest of the

Plate 183: Stone circle BM 352, *on the summit of Brat's Hill, Burnmoor*

stone circles, which stands at the centre of a large sub-rectangular plot that was markedly devoid of cairns, a distribution that clearly enhanced the self-evident majesty of the stone circle (Pl 183). The implication is that the circles either pre-dated, or were contemporary with, the earliest phase of clearance, and the proto-field system that developed around it.

Significantly, the distribution of round cairns in the Lake District differs from that identified in Northumberland, where, for the most part, cairns are not found on summits, but instead on prominent topographical features on hillsides (Field 1999). Although these may have a wide vista, the highest ground within an area does not seem to have been exploited; rather, springs or streams seem to have been important. Such a situation was recognised by a survey undertaken at Simonside, Northumberland, which was specifically intended to examine a rich funerary landscape, and recorded 25 funerary round cairns from an area of only 4.3 km² (Hedley and Quartermaine 2004). Of these, five had been sited very deliberately on the edges of topographical features, such as crags or scarp slopes, clearly intending to provide a wide vista, in preference to natural summits, seemingly because vistas were not as widespread on the adjacent summits. However, the great majority, 20 cairns, were located within a very restricted area (0.13 km² in extent) on the lower slopes of Simonside, and these cairns seemed to have been arranged, for the most part, in lines.

In the Lake District, the number of summit cairns (Mendus 2001) is considerably outnumbered by round cairns located either on lower slopes or low rises; however, they are quite often found on some form of promontory that has an enhanced vista. Where the LDNPS examples seem to differ from those in Northumberland is that there is little evidence of these monuments having a specific association with streams or springs.

The distribution and context of ring cairns appears to be in slight contrast to that of round cairns; in particular, these are only occasionally found on high points with a marked vista. The classic example of such a limited outlook is the Giant's Graves complex ring cairn (*HF 113*) on Heathwaite Fell (*Ch 6, p 269*), which comprised a substantial kerb around an embanked ring, with a single prominent orthostat. Although in the broad vicinity of round cairn *HF 312*, it is not in a prominent position, being near the bottom of a stream gully. In general, this topographical context seems to have been the norm for ring cairns, although there are some exceptions, such as the Thwaites Fell ring cairn (*TF 327*), which stands on a natural spur adjacent to a beck, and has an extensive southerly vista, looking down the Black

Plate 184: Ring cairn SM 36, within the Monks Graves group (SM VII) on Stockdale Moor

Beck valley (*Ch 5, p 262*). It is therefore interesting to note that, while the positions of round cairns identified by the LDNPS programme did not seem to have been associated with a water source, as identified in Northumberland (Field 1999), the ring cairns, to some extent, did.

One of the more significant ring cairn groups is that at Monk's Graves, on Stockdale Moor, (SM VII; *Ch 3, p 78*), which comprises funerary monuments, both round cairns and two ring cairns (*SM 36* (Pl 184) and *SM 38*) on the highest part of the site, and a concentration of small clearance cairns, for the most part in the lower part of the site group. There is no evidence of a *cordon sanitaire* around these funerary monuments, and several clearance-type cairns were located fairly intimately with them. However, there did seem to be a clear size differential between the groups of cairns on the upper and lower parts of the site, and it would appear that these reflected differing episodes of construction. Although the precise chronological relationship between the groups cannot be established without scientific dating, the superficial impression is that the group of funerary cairns, forming a cemetery, was superseded by a cairnfield, but in this instance the funerary nature of the monuments was either not recognised or respected, and the area of agricultural activity was allowed to surround the funerary cairns completely.

Askham Fell

The pattern of distribution of funerary cairns cannot be examined without considering the Askham Fell landscape, where the funerary monuments are, intriguingly, not found in 'typical' locations (*Ch 7, pp 342-3*). For instance, one of the more clearly defined topographical features in this landscape is the long, elevated, ridge of Riddingleys Top (Fig 150), from which there is a magnificent view to the south-west

Plate 185: The Cockpit stone circle, AF 86, on Askham Fell

Plate 186: Round cairn AF 130, one of the large cairns on the line of the stone avenue on Askham Fell

and across to High Street. It is therefore not very surprising that there should be a round cairn (*AF 165*), of apparently funerary function, associated with this topographical feature; however, the cairn stands at the base of the ridge, rather than at its summit.

Askham Fell has some of the most dramatic funerary monuments recorded in the course of the LDNPS: the largest stone circle (The Cockpit; *AF 86*; Pl 185); the largest monolith (The Cop Stone; *AF 115*; one of the largest round cairns (White Raise Cairn; *AF 130*;

Pl 186); and the only stone avenue (*AF 121*) recorded during the survey. Askham Fell also has some of the most dramatic topography, with hills, such as Heughscar overlooking Ullswater, having vistas that extend as far as the Caldbeck Hills to the north-west. The funerary monuments, however, were found on the lowest slopes of the fell, specifically on a natural col forming the lowest natural crossing

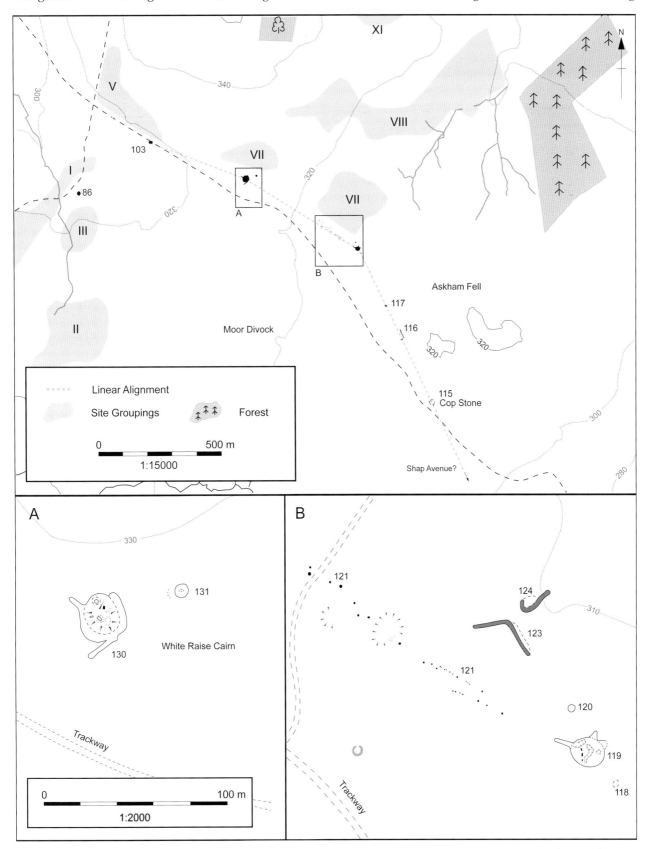

Figure 163: Askham Fell, showing details of cairns AF 130 *and* AF 119, *on the line of the avenue* (AF 121)

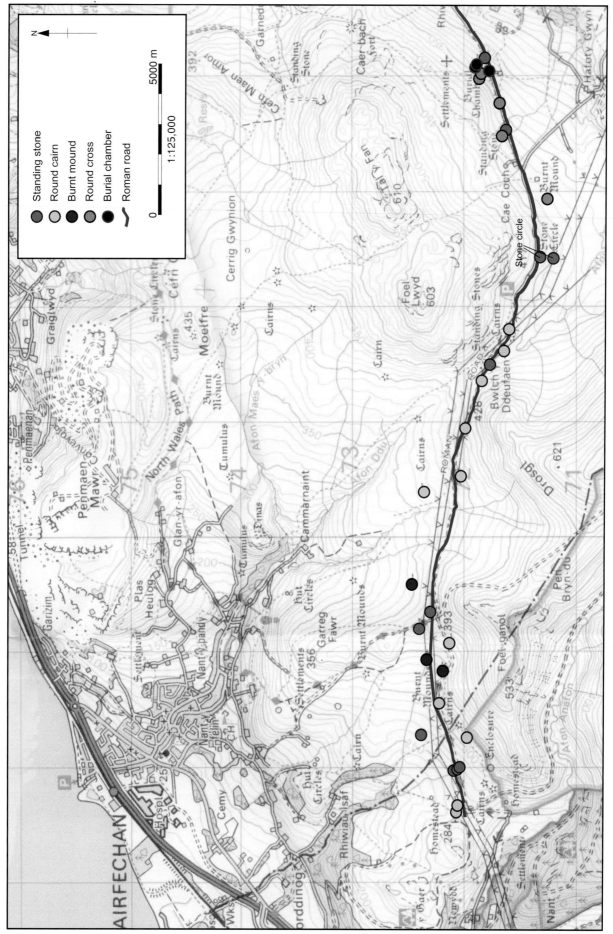

Figure 164: *Bwlch y Ddeufaen, showing prehistoric monuments clustered along a natural routeway* (© *Ordnance Survey*)

348

point between Ullswater and the Lowther Valley. The monuments were all linked by a very clearly defined alignment, linking round cairns, ring cairns, large orthostats, and significantly also a stone avenue (Fig 163). While the alignment is unequivocal, its purpose is less so. In comparable examples from elsewhere, such as at Bwlch y Ddeufaen (OA North 2004b; Fig 164), the alignment of monuments is on a natural communication line, which, in the case of Bwlch y Ddeufaen, extends along a valley and over a col. It is therefore reasonable to assume that, in this instance, the line of monuments was marking a communication route. A further parallel for the Askham Fell landscape is found at Penmaenmawr, in Eastern Snowdonia, which is *c* 2 km to the north of Bwlch y Ddeufaen, and is just above the neolithic Graiglwyd axe-production site (*ibid*). The complex consists of six stone circles, three round cairns, three kerbed cairns, and a standing stone, which are spread out over the top of a spur extending up to the North Welsh coast; there is, however, no direct relationship between the sepulchral landscape and the nearby axe-factory site. This approximate alignment may similarly indicate an ancient routeway that may have been adopted so as to avoid the lower coastal route, which may have been impassable in antiquity.

In other instances, there are examples of lines of funerary cairns on historical boundaries, notably on the western edge of the North York Moors, at Sutton Bank, where the boundary lines extend between the sources of rivers and a cliff face (OA North 2004c). These boundaries are also marked by large banks and ditches, which were possibly constructed or enhanced in the medieval period, indicating that the boundaries had considerable longevity. However, these could not have represented communication routes, as the alignments of monuments extended up to a vertical cliff.

Given the characteristics of the landscape, particularly the col, it is probable that the alignment of the various Bronze Age monuments on Askham Fell (AF VII; *Ch 7, p 305*) did indeed reflect an ancient communication line, but it is possible that such a line was also adopted as a territorial boundary. A similar example occurs on Skipwith Common, to the south of York, where an area of low and very wet land, that is today waste, was crossed by two prehistoric boundaries, marked by multiple lines of earthen banks and ditches (OA North 2010c). One of these boundaries has an ancient trackway, now called Sandy Lane, immediately parallel to it, and this raises the possibility that this was a boundary line that was followed by an early communication route.

However, although the monument group at Askham Fell might simply have marked a line of communication, it is also possible that it held a greater, ritual, significance. For example, because many of the avenues led from a stone circle towards water, Aubrey Burl has suggested that stone avenues served to link 'major ritual centres with lesser but vital elements such as rivers or mortality' (1993, 72). In this respect, it could be comparable to the Avebury avenue. If it was a linear ritual landscape, it is perhaps significant that, although cairnfields are found close to the Askham Fell avenue (for instance, on Threepow Raise; AF II; *Ch 7, p 301*), these were at some distance from the cairn/stone alignment, and there was no evidence for any expansion of agricultural activity into this 'ritual corridor'. Significantly, the large stone circle, The Cockpit (*AF 86*; Pl 185), although not part of the main alignment, stands at the natural fording point of Elder Beck, suggesting that it may have marked another communication route that would have extended along the ridge.

The alignment of funerary monuments extends for 1.45 km, but seemingly terminates to the south-east at the Cop Stone (*AF 115*; Fig 163). It was reported by Taylor (1886, 342), however, on the evidence of local oral history, that there may have been a continuation between the end of the Shap Avenue at Rosgill to the south, and the Cop Stone. Certainly, the north-westernmost section of the Shap Avenue (Burl 1993, 47-9), up to Rosgill (Thompson 1983, 138), is orientated towards the Cop Stone and, bearing in mind the damage that has been inflicted upon the Avenue within the last few centuries, it is possible that a further section extending across enclosed farming land has also been destroyed. The Shap Avenue, like that on Askham Fell, links a series of funerary monuments and stone circles, a feature paralleled elsewhere in Britain, as well as in Brittany (Burl 1993). It is, perhaps, also significant that a ring cairn has been recorded at Inscar (NY 5287 1930; Turner 1991), on the approximate line between the Cop Stone and the western end of the Shap Avenue. It is therefore possible that a major avenue or communication route extended for at least 12 km from Hardendale to the shores of Ullswater, linking a considerable number of funerary monuments.

9

THE CHANGING LANDSCAPE

Land Use

The LDNPS programme was set up to examine some of the more extensive landscapes, that have survived for up to 5000 years on the marginal uplands of the Lake District. Their survival is attributable to unintensive agricultural use, mostly rough grazing, that has been prevalent since the sites were abandoned. However, there have been progressive changes in how the land has been used since the enclosure movement of the eighteenth and nineteenth centuries, when substantial areas of this marginal landscape were enclosed (Pl 187; Whyte 2003). This opened up the potential for land improvement, resulting in the obscuring, or even destruction, of the archaeological landscapes that had previously being undisturbed.

Almost certainly, many ancient landscapes have been lost to such improvements, though the precise amount of loss is difficult to quantify, particularly as antiquarian records typically only note the loss of major monuments, such as stone circles or avenues. Notable examples of this are those antiquarian accounts which record the breaking up of the stones forming the Shap Avenue for use in buildings, and also the clearance of land for enclosure in the late eighteenth and early nineteenth centuries (Nicholson and Burn 1777; Hall 1824).

In more recent years, the evidence for land improvement has become both recognisable and quantifiable, though the level to which land is improved depends largely on its status. For instance, marginal areas, which remain unenclosed, are almost exclusively used for summer grazing

Plate 187: The eighteenth/nineteenth-century parliamentary enclosures near Whin Garth, in the Western Fells

by the surrounding farms, and usually by dint of commoners' rights. This terrain is the most immune from change of use, or improvement, and, perhaps not surprisingly, this type of land is where there is the best survival of archaeological remains. By the same token, it is this type of landscape that was for the most part targeted by the LDNPS programme.

The enclosed but unimproved moorland was taken out of the open fells in the eighteenth and nineteenth centuries as a means of controlling grazing rights (Whyte 2003). This type of land is typically elevated and remote from many communication routes, such as roads or tracks, and hence has not been subject to improvement. Nowadays, it tends to be used for summer grazing, but usually by a single farmer, who either owns or rents the land. However, such enclosed land that is not subject to commoners' rights is at risk from improvement or change of use, which inevitably has a negative impact on the archaeological resource. It is this land type which has been most subject to changes of use, and many of the forestry plantations in the Lake District National Park are within the large fields formed as part of the parliamentary enclosure movement.

Land that was enclosed as part of this enclosure movement, but which has been improved, is typically at the outer reaches of the farmed land. It comprises land enclosed into large, straight-sided fields, that are generally smaller than those of the unimproved, but enclosed, moorland. This land is subject to intensive farming practices, and tends to be used for year-round grazing, and for producing grass crops and silage. Because the landscapes were enclosed within only the last few hundred years, they still retain some extant archaeological landscapes within those fields that have not been ploughed, a notable example being the cairnfields at Whin Garth (WG II; *Ch 3*; *pp 93-4*), which are now within enclosed land. Correspondingly, activity in these fields poses the greatest threat to the surviving archaeological landscapes, since these are also most subject to modern improvements.

The historical enclosures around farms tend to comprise small, irregular fields, which have mostly been enclosed since the establishment of the farms, but in some cases pre-date them. These are the areas that have been most intensively improved, either for grazing or arable farming, and as a result there is typically only a very limited survival of visible archaeological landscapes in these areas, although it always remains a possibility that buried remains will survive. Because there is little visible survival of archaeological remains there, any future improvement to this land will have only a limited impact upon the totality of the archaeological resource.

Threats to the Resource

During the course of the LDNPS fieldwork programme, increased concern was expressed for the future survival of archaeology in the English uplands and, in 1986, Timothy Darvill (1986a; 1986b) drew together the available information on the archaeological resource in the uplands of Britain, and listed the principal threats that it faced. These threats included agricultural land improvement; mineral extraction and quarrying; forestry; natural erosion; erosion caused by visitors; and pressure from public utilities and the military.

In the intervening years since Darvill's (*ibid*) study, there have been several major changes, both to land management and the nature of the threats to the upland archaeological resource. Many of the changes have been beneficial and were occasioned, in part, by the higher profile of upland archaeology, which was achieved as a result of Darvill's (*ibid*) work. Since the 1980s, several important studies have also been published, which have helped to raise understanding of both the significance and fragility of upland archaeology. These include Andrew Fleming's (1988) work on the Dartmoor reaves, various inventory volumes produced by the Royal Commission on the Ancient and Historical Monuments of Scotland (*eg* RCAHMS 1990; 1997; 2007), the *Uplands Archaeology Initiative* of the Royal Commission on the Ancient and Historical Monuments of Wales (*eg* Leighton 1997; Silvester 2011), an investigation into the condition of the upland peats and the threats to their survival (OA North 2009a), and numerous upland management surveys, both in the Lake District (*Ch 1*), and elsewhere (*eg* Topping 1989b).

In addition, conservation management of the archaeology of the uplands has been facilitated by the appointment of archaeological staff in the majority of the English National Parks, and also in some Areas of Outstanding Natural Beauty. This increase in staffing has also taken place in other local authorities with responsibility for upland areas, and the scope and content of Historic Environment Records have improved significantly since the 1980s.

These developments have taken place in the Lake District as well, where the National Park Authority now employs two archaeologists, and knowledge of the archaeological resource has been improved greatly through projects such as the LDNPS and the development of the Lake District Historic Environment Record (LDHER). There is now, therefore, a much better understanding of the significance, extent, and condition of the archaeological resource in the Lake District uplands. However, while some of the threats listed by Darvill (1986a; 1986b) have receded, others have taken their place. In this sense, there remains a need to extend information on both the nature and condition of the archaeology of the Lake District, and to manage the current and future threats to its survival.

The state of archaeology in the Lake District uplands

In 2008, the condition of archaeological sites in the Lake District was assessed through the *English Heritage Scheduled Monuments at Risk Survey* (English Heritage 2008) and the *Lake District Monuments at Risk Survey,* carried out by the Lake District National Park Authority (LDNPA) and its volunteer service. The English Heritage survey established that the Lake District National Park has the greatest number (65) of high-risk monuments in the North West, the majority of which are on upland pasture and threatened by bracken infestation (*ibid*; Fig 165).

The Lake District Monuments at Risk Survey is carried out every five years, in order to provide information on the archaeological resource for the Lake District National Park Partnership's *State of the Park* report (Lake District National Park Partnership 2005), and has extended the condition survey to the entire 273 Scheduled Monuments in the National Park. The resultant data are provided to English Heritage, for Heritage at Risk monitoring, and are also used for targeting conservation resources through agri-environment schemes and other sources of grant aid.

This survey has confirmed the widespread problem of bracken infestation, particularly on many of the extensive areas of prehistoric remains recorded by the LDNPS, as have other comparable studies elsewhere (*eg* ADAS and OA North 2009).

The Lake District Historic Environment Record

The LDHER is the official database of archaeological and historical sites in the Lake District and is the source of information for advice and decisions on planning and land management in the National Park. At present, *c* 30% of the Lake District National Park has been subject to archaeological survey, and the results of both the *Monuments at Risk Survey* and the LDNPS have been incorporated in the LDHER. However, it is anticipated that the record will expand considerably in the future, as further surveys are completed.

Current threats to the archaeological resource in the Lake District

Many of the threats listed by Darvill (1986a; 1986b) applied to the Lake District when the LDNPS was undertaken, and included agricultural land improvement; mineral extraction and quarrying; forestry; natural erosion; erosion caused by visitors; and pressure from public utilities. However, the situation is now somewhat different from that in the 1980s, and there have been changes in the nature of threats to the upland archaeological resource, including different objectives for upland farming, and the need to combat the effects of climate change.

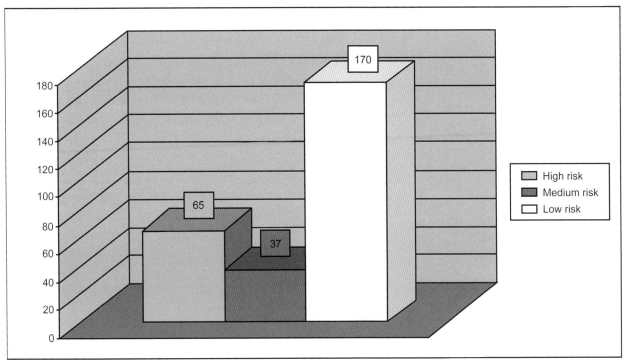

Figure 165: Scheduled Monuments at Risk in the Lake District National Park in 2006

Upland agriculture

For most of the twentieth century, government agricultural policy in the uplands was chiefly concerned with food production. Government intervention in agricultural production began during the First World War, and the Ministry of Agriculture and Fisheries was established in 1919 (Condliffe 2009). In the late 1930s, with the prospect of another World War, the Ministry of Food established guaranteed prices and markets for farmers, and, for the first time, financial subsidies were made available for sheep farming and the improvement of upland soils (*ibid*). As a result, self-sufficiency in food production rose from 40% in 1937 to 60% by 1945 (*ibid*). The recognition during the Second World War of the desirability of a strong agricultural sector led to the establishment of a permanent post-war policy on agriculture, and resulted in a period of significant financial support for farmers, which lasted until the 1980s (*ibid*). Key milestones included the Hill Farming Act (1946), which established grants of up to 50% for the improvement of hill-farming land through the use of fertilisers and land drainage.

Between the 1940s and 1980s, a succession of Hill Farming and Agriculture Acts underpinned a system of grant schemes and livestock subsidies for hill farmers who, in turn, had to maintain good levels of estate management and husbandry (*ibid*). Financial incentives for production were further increased as a result of the UK's entry into the European Economic Community (EEC) in 1972. This led to large increases in the numbers of grazing stock in the uplands, particularly sheep, with a marked rise from 1980, following an EEC initiative to address a shortfall in mutton and lamb meat in Europe (*ibid*). Although the intensively grazed uplands, with their reduced vegetation cover, enabled the clearer detection of archaeological remains, undoubtedly many archaeological sites in the uplands were damaged during this period of intensive agricultural production. For instance, land drainage, which was actively encouraged, often included the digging of drainage channels, known as 'grips', on peat moorland, to improve the land for sheep grazing and grouse shooting, and these channels could damage both below- and above-ground archaeological remains (ADAS and OA North 2009), whilst the intake of peripheral land at lower altitudes often resulted in the clearance of archaeological remains. In addition, the injudicious placing of feeders and salt licks also caused damage to the archaeological remains found at certain archaeological sites.

Within the areas covered by the LDNPS, examples of damage to the archaeological resource can be found at Whin Garth, near Scale Farm (*Ch 3, p 91*), where huge modern clearance cairns have been created within the fields as a result of twentieth-century land improvement (Pl 188), with the concomitant loss of earlier small clearance cairns. Furthermore, in the 1980s, there was also considerable damage at Whin Garth caused by vehicles moving across the historical field systems, as well as severe erosion around feeding troughs, which were often directly placed on archaeological remains (Pl 189). Intensive twentieth-century land improvement at Mickleden Beck has similarly resulted in the destruction of parts of the cairnfield (*Ch 6, p 287*).

Plate 188: One of the large modern clearance cairns at Whin Garth, constructed as part of a programme of land improvement in the late twentieth century

Plate 189: Part of the WG I cairnfield at Whin Garth, with vehicular damage and scars around feeding troughs clearly visible

The intense grazing pressure, dating to the latter half of the twentieth century, also led to soil erosion, as a result of a reduction in vegetation cover, and was a particular problem in the uplands, where there are typically only thin turf deposits over archaeological sites. Indeed, in the Lake District, the detrimental effects of soil erosion were noted at some of the sensitive Langdale axe-production sites, where the survival of deposits of scree and production waste is dependent on the maintenance of a thin covering layer of turf (LUAU 1994b). Moreover, selective grazing by sheep, without the balancing effect of cattle, has contributed to an increase in bracken cover at many upland sites, which is also damaging to archaeological remains (*p 358*).

During the early 1980s, the balance of upland farming objectives was changed, and significantly these changes included conservation of the natural environment (Condliffe 2009). For example, the Wildlife and Countryside Act of 1981 gave greater protection to Sites of Special Scientific Interest (SSSI), of which there are many in the uplands, and the Agriculture Act of 1986 established the Environmentally Sensitive Area agri-environment scheme (ESA), which provided financial incentives for farmers to maintain both the natural and historic environment. Under the ESA, grants became available for the protection of archaeological features and restoration of historic farm buildings at a rate of 80% of costs (Ministry of Agriculture, Fisheries and Food 1994). The Lake District ESA was established in 1993 and included most of the National Park. Its principal aim was to maintain and enhance the landscape, wildlife, and historic value of the area by encouraging beneficial agricultural practices, which was to be achieved through a series of measures, including improving the quality of grassland, heather moorland, and small-scale woodland, as well as the conservation of archaeological features and historic farm buildings. While great numbers of historic farms buildings were conserved through the Lake District ESA, partly because they had a practical benefit, very few archaeological projects were achieved, as a result of the requirement for a 20% contribution towards costs from the farmer.

The Lake District ESA also initiated the current trend towards a significant reduction of sheep numbers on the fells, in order to improve local biodiversity. This trend was massively boosted in 2001 with the outbreak of Foot and Mouth disease, which resulted in huge sheep losses in the county, and even led to some farms abandoning sheep farming altogether. As a consequence, vegetation in parts of the Lake District uplands has begun to recover from years of overgrazing. However, the effect on the condition of archaeological remains has been mixed. The reduction of erosion resulting from increased vegetation cover is clearly beneficial, but the natural succession towards bracken, scrub, and then tree cover could eventually have a detrimental effect on archaeological remains.

The emphasis on improvement of biodiversity, including further reductions in grazing and the encouragement of new native woodland in the Lake District uplands, has been increased in the agri-environment scheme that has replaced the ESA. The Environmental Stewardship Scheme was introduced in 2005 and has two tiers: Entry Level and Higher Level. The main objective of the scheme remains improvement of local biodiversity, but the incentives for protection and conservation of archaeological features have been much improved, with the introduction of a system of Historic Environment Record consultation by applicants, and a 100% grant level for archaeological projects. In 2009, the Lake District National Park Authority began the Environment Land Management Service (ELMS), with Natural England and the National Trust, to offer a service for developing selected Higher Level scheme applications. Historic environment information and advice is one of the added-value benefits of this approach, and several successful archaeological conservation schemes have been implemented.

Mineral extraction and quarrying

At the time the LDNPS was carried out, the last working mineral mine in the Lake District, at Force Crag in Coledale, was about to close, although several working slate quarries remained in the Lake District fells, which are still in production, and the historically significant site at Honister has been reopened for production. However, mining and quarrying in the Lake District National Park is tightly controlled through development management, and these operations are unlikely to pose a significant threat to upland archaeology in the future.

Forestry and woodland

Although extensive larch plantations were established in parts of the Lake District from the late eighteenth century onwards, the first large-scale commercial conifer plantations in the area were those established around the Thirlmere reservoir in 1908 (James 1981). Following the establishment of the Forestry Commission in 1919, the British uplands saw a massive expansion of woodland planting in order to replace the timber used during the First World War, and to create a strategic reserve for the future (ibid). In the Lake District, this led to the establishment of large plantations, including Whinlatter in 1919 and Ennerdale in 1925 (ibid). The perceived damage that this caused, both to the scenic beauty of the area and to the tradition of Herdwick sheep grazing on

the fells, led to strong opposition from an alliance of influential protestors. For example, in 1934, the Forestry Commission purchased land around Hardknott, at the head of the Eskdale and Duddon Valleys, and the storm of protest that this engendered, led in part by the newly formed Friends of the Lake District, resulted in a landmark agreement in 1936, under which the Forestry Commission would not pursue commercial forestry within the core of the Lake District (Symonds 1936; Cousins 2009, 41-59).

The Forestry Commission's conifer plantations had caused considerable damage to those archaeological features which were within areas that were planted. This is particularly evident around Irton Pike, Wasdale, the Hollow Moor/Losca plantations, near Whin Garth, and in Ennerdale (Pl 190), where archaeological survey has located the extensive remains of both prehistoric and medieval features within the forestry plantations (Ch 3, p 82; Spence 1937; LUAU 1998c). Although the 1936 agreement protected large swathes of the Lake District uplands, piecemeal planting of open fell by the Forestry Commission continued until the early 1990s. One of the last examples was an extension to the Blengdale Forest, at Whin Garth. The new plantation in this area included part of a cairnfield, but at least, in this instance, the archaeology was subject to a survey prior to the planting, and a watching brief during the work (LUAU 1994c).

In 1985, the Forestry Commission adopted a Broadleaved Policy, which recognised the importance of broadleaved woodland over conifers (Forestry Commission 2003). The removal of tax benefits in 1988, which had driven the growth of private-sector plantations, reinforced the move away from new conifer plantation. In the National Parks, an accord between the National Park Authorities and the Forestry Commission was signed in 2002, which gave even further emphasis to native woodland and the importance of the cultural landscape (Forestry Commission 2002). In the Lake District, in addition to the cessation of the new planting of open fell, this has led to the conversion of conifer plantations to broadleaf woodland (for example in the upper Duddon Valley) and the conservation of archaeological sites within plantations.

Although the threat to archaeological sites in the uplands from conifer planting has receded, recent moves towards the establishment of new native woodland, to increase biodiversity in the uplands, and to combat the effects of climate change (p 357), may provide a new challenge. There is also an agreed national policy amongst the agencies responsible for strategic land management to increase woodland cover in the uplands, up to a target of 25% cover by 2060 (Natural England 2009). This will have

Plate 190: An enclosed settlement in Ennerdale, possibly Romano-British, which has been cleared of trees

significant implications for the Lake District, where possibilities include an increase of up to 50% of woodland cover in the National Park. In some cases, the establishment of new native woodland will involve planting while, in others, all that will be needed is fencing to exclude grazing stock, to allow natural vegetation to regenerate. However, any archaeological features within these new native woodland areas will be at risk from damage from root growth in the medium to long term. All new native woodland schemes will, therefore, have to be assessed for their potential archaeological implications, and measures taken to avoid damage, through avoidance of archaeology where possible, and the selective management of sites which cannot be excluded from woodland areas.

Climate change

A potentially significant long-term threat to the upland landscapes of the Lake District, and their historic environment, is from climate change. It is becoming increasingly accepted that recent human activity is having an impact on climate, and that, in the future, changes in temperature, rainfall, sea levels, and the magnitude and frequency of extreme weather will increase. For example, evidence from the UK Climate Impacts Programme (1998) has shown that the climate is likely to become warmer and wetter in winter, and hotter and drier in summer. Rainfall intensity will probably increase, and extreme events, such as heat-waves and storms, may increase in frequency and

severity. The floods in north-west Cumbria in the winter of 2009 have provided a stark indication of the immense damage that can arise from extreme weather, whilst in the very dry summer of 2003 there were two major outbreaks of fire in northern Britain, which had a direct effect on several archaeological landscapes. The first, on Anglezarke Moor, in South Lancashire, caused extensive disturbance to the overlying peat and both exposed and damaged the underlying archaeological remains (OA North 2009a). The second, on Fylingdales Moor in North Yorkshire, burnt off the vegetation and shallow organic soils over an area of 2.4 km^2, exposing rich archaeological remains, including cairnfields, prehistoric funerary remains, including cup and ring-marked stones (Pl 191), and

Plate 191: Rock art on Fylingdales Moor, North Yorkshire, revealed by a catastrophic moorland fire in 2003

the subtle surface features normally obscured by the turf (Stone and Horne 2003). While this has provided a remarkable opportunity to study these landscapes, it has also exposed them to the effects of water and wind erosion, which put them at considerable risk of wholesale destruction.

Natural England has undertaken a series of pilot studies of the likely effects of climate change for four 'Character Areas' in England, one of which is the Cumbria High Fells (Natural England 2008). This study has identified several possible impacts of climate change, which could also have a detrimental effect on archaeology. These include an increase in the risk of peat and bracken fires as a consequence of increased temperature and lower rainfall in summer; increased erosion resulting from higher winter rainfall; and erosion of peat soils due to drying out, which could lead to the exposure and disturbance of buried archaeological deposits.

One of the proposed responses to these threats is to manage the landscape so that it is more resilient to climate change. This links into the wider issue of the management of 'ecosystem services', which is primarily concerned with the protection of the key natural features of the uplands, such as water supply, carbon storage, and flood protection. The 'ecosystem services' approach is encapsulated in Natural England's vision for the English Uplands for the period up to 2060 (Natural England 2009), which also includes a recognition of the importance of the historic environment. However, the implications of the current management of ecosystem services for the condition of archaeological sites in the uplands are both positive and negative.

The principal elements of upland management, which can be utilised to make the landscape more resilient to climate change and to protect key ecosystem services, are a general reduction in levels of grazing; introduction of new types of livestock, including native cattle; an increase in native woodland cover through natural regeneration and planting; and protection of upland peat landscapes. The general effect of these is to engender a more robust vegetation cover of shrubs and woodland which, in turn, improves soil stability and reduces erosion. Whilst, in some instances, this can have a beneficial effect for archaeological conservation, the overall effect can be detrimental. For instance, whilst better vegetation cover decreases the potential for erosion, increases in shrub and tree cover can obscure archaeological remains, and cause damage to sub-surface deposits through root action.

This type of management has been introduced through agri-environment schemes such as Environmental Stewardship, and its implications for archaeological

remains have, in some cases, led to special protective measures. For example, on Dartmoor, 14 *Premier Archaeological Landscapes* (PALS) have been designated in order to ensure that, where this type of land management is under consideration, archaeological significance is taken into account, and these have also been defined in *The Vision for Dartmoor* (Dartmoor National Park Authority 2006). The agencies responsible for *The Vision for Dartmoor* have agreed that, within the PALs, the management requirements of historically important features, especially archaeology, will take precedence over that required for ecology. In many cases, this will require periodic cutting and removal of vegetation on archaeological features.

A comparable scheme in the Lake District is the *Wild Ennerdale Project*, established in 2002, with a vision 'to allow the evolution of Ennerdale as a wild valley for the benefit of people, relying more on natural processes to shape its landscape and ecology' (www. wildennerdale.co.uk/vision.html). Within this valley, which is rich in both prehistoric and medieval remains, much of the management has concentrated on replacing the extensive conifer plantations of the Forestry Commission with native woodland, and replacing sheep grazing with cattle. This has had the effect of reducing bracken cover in some areas, though special provision, in the form of manual clearance, has been necessary on selected archaeological sites, in order to prevent damage from the increase in shrub- and tree vegetation.

Bracken

A significant risk to archaeological sites in the uplands of the Lake District is bracken growth (Pl 192). Bracken both obscures archaeological remains and causes damage through its extensive root system (rhizomes), which, as research excavation has demonstrated, can disrupt soil profiles and damage archaeological deposits, particularly in thin upland soil horizons (Gerrard 2001; Pl 193).

Although bracken has always been a component of the upland vegetation community in the Lake District, it has increased in recent years. This increase is principally due to the cessation of the harvesting of bracken for potash production and animal bedding, overgrazing by sheep, and the reduction of cattle grazing on the fells, as the trampling of bracken by cattle reduces its growth.

Bracken growth can be inhibited through a variety of methods, including bruising, cutting, and spraying with herbicide (SEARS 2008). Bruising and cutting has to take place over a minimum of five years, with two cuts in the first year, in order to reduce growth. This is, therefore, a relatively labour-intensive process,

Plate 192: Bracken growth over a cairnfield below Stickle Pike, in the Duddon Valley

Plate 193: Bracken rhizomes infesting a medieval site at Tonguesdale Moss, Eskdale

Plate 194: Small-breed cattle (Galloways) grazing in the Great Moss below Scafell

and one which does not entirely eradicate bracken. Spraying is expensive, relatively difficult to carry out, and can also cause harm to other vegetation. However, recent experiments have indicated that the use of small herds of cattle, such as Galloways, can keep bracken growth at bay, through trampling (Pl 194). This has been demonstrated through the *Wild Ennerdale Project* (http://www.wildennerdale. co.uk/), in an area where there are archaeological remains, and significantly, the relatively small number of cattle, and the size of the grazing area, ensured that damage has not been caused to the archaeological sites in this area. Given this, the use of cattle on the fells appears to constitute a more sustainable method of bracken control and is one that can be effectively pursued through agri-environment scheme agreements. The Lake District National Park Authority is also carrying out a programme of bracken reduction on Scheduled Monuments and other archaeological sites, with assistance from its volunteer service.

Recreation

The Lake District presently receives over 12 million visitors each year and this inevitably has an impact on the area. One of the most obvious effects is the high volume of car traffic at peak holiday times, and the traffic jams that can occur. Many visitors come to the Lake District to engage in recreational activities in the fells, including walking, fell running, mountain biking, and motorised activity (motorbikes and 4 x 4 vehicles). All of these can cause damage to the land surface and to archaeological remains, but, in practice, despite the open access to the fells established by the Countryside and Rights of Way Act (2000), they are largely confined to established, linear, Rights of Way. These footpaths, bridleways, and byways are often of historical interest in their own right, and remedial works to combat erosion will often include restoration of traditional surfacing, such as stone pitching. However, there are a few cases where archaeological remains of earlier periods are crossed by these routes and, where this occurs, remedial conservation and possibly route diversion can reduce the impact. Furthermore, archaeological damage which could be caused by activities that take place away from established routes, for example in the case of organised motorbike trials, can be avoided by informed planning of routes and consultation with the Lake District National Park Authority. Unorganised motorised activities can, of course, cause damage and are particularly difficult to control.

Plate 195: Footpath repairs on The Band, August 2000, looking towards Mickleden and Great Langdale

The principal example in the Lake District of where footpath erosion has caused severe damage to prehistoric remains is at the extensive remains of neolithic axe-production sites in the central Lake District Fells. These sites extend in the main from the Langdale Pikes to Glaramara (Claris and Quartermaine 1989) and, due to the fragile nature of both the archaeological deposits and the turf or peat that generally covers them, they can be severely affected by heavy footpath use. This has led to a programme of footpath repairs and diversion which incorporates the recording and protection of these important sites (Pl 195). A further development has been the production of a *Heritage Partnership Agreement for the Lake District Central Fells Neolithic Stone-Axe factories*, which has established a framework of consents for the various types of footpath repairs that are required (English Heritage 2006).

Conclusion

The successful management and protection of the rich archaeology of the Lake District uplands will depend on the availability of good data. Detailed information on the location, extent, character, and condition of archaeological remains is essential for the Lake District National Park Authority to be able to provide advice to planners, land managers, and the general public. Damage to archaeological features can be avoided by influencing land-management strategies, recreational activities, and conservation projects. Archaeological information needs to be curated in, and made available through, the LDHER. Further survey work, building on the success of the LDNPS, together with regular monitoring visits to assess condition, will also be required (*see below*).

The most pressing threats to upland archaeology are likely to come from the necessary steps that are being taken to improve local biodiversity, and to combat the effects of climate change. The adverse effects of some of the changes in the uplands resulting from this, including growth of scrub and trees, can be avoided, partly through the strategic planning of environmental improvement schemes, and partly through targeted management of those individual sites which are located within scrub or woodland areas. The control of bracken is also a key issue, and will be pursued through agri-environment grant schemes and using volunteer assistance.

The Future

The LDNPS programme has demonstrated that the marginal lands of the Lake District were subject to a complex agricultural development during the later prehistoric period, which, in places, reflected intensive activity and the formation of settlement. The survey has also demonstrated the wealth of archaeological remains within the upland landscapes of this area and the potential for further archaeological and palaeoenvironmental research. The programme of survey only examined a fraction of the Lake District uplands, however, and, although there have been numerous other surveys (*Ch 1, p 18*) following the completion of the LDNPS fieldwork, there is still a considerable need for further survey and research. Moreover, ideally, this work should be geared towards providing scientific dating for the rich and intricate archaeological landscapes of the area, and also refining the links between the archaeological and palaeoenvironmental evidence. In this respect, the LDNPS should be regarded as the starting point for future programmes of research, rather than an end in itself.

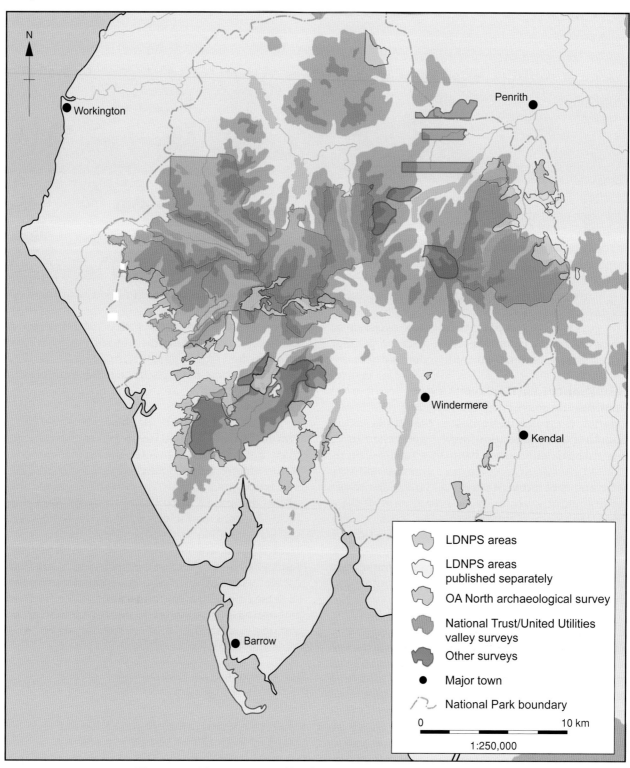

Figure 166: The areas covered by the LDNPS and subsequent surveys

Existing survey work and its limitations

The surveys undertaken as part of the LDNPS programme, and the subsequent identification surveys, extend across 750 km² (Fig 166). Although this coverage is in itself impressive, it still only equates to 32.9% of the total area of the Lake District (2280 km²), and demonstrates that there is still a need for additional archaeological survey within the uplands of the National Park. However, even within the areas that have been examined, the majority of the work comprises a basic level of identification, in which individual monuments are merely depicted as a single 'dot' on a map, whilst only the outer limits of whole archaeological landscapes are mapped.

Whilst this information is adequate for informing the management of an upland landscape, which was the principal objective of these identification-type surveys, it does little to further an understanding of the development of either specific or wider landscapes. In this respect, in order to comprehend fully the history and development of particular landscapes and the wider areas in which they are situated, the more detailed landscape surveys undertaken during the LDNPS, and also a limited number of later surveys, such as those of the High and Low Torver Commons (LUAU 1994a; 1995), are of the utmost significance. Inevitably, therefore, our understanding of how the Lake District landscapes have developed is biased towards the western side of the Lake District, where the majority of the LDNPS recording was undertaken.

Potential for further research

Identification survey

Despite their limitations for the analysis of landscapes, identification surveys have brought a new awareness of the character and complexity of the archaeological resource within the National Park, and they provide the mainstay of landscape management, which is seeking to preserve the archaeological remains for the future. The importance of this type of work cannot be under-estimated, as, without it, the extent, location, and significance of monuments and landscapes must remain unknown. This information also enables the protection of significant archaeological landscapes from the threats represented by changes in land use (*p 351*). Typically, such surveys increase the number of recorded monuments by as much as a factor of ten, and can reveal whole new archaeological landscapes. Given this, any area, particularly of marginal land, that has not been subject to survey potentially contains significant archaeological monuments and landscapes that have yet to be discovered. There is, therefore, a need for more identification surveys, which should concentrate on the peripheral areas of the Lake District uplands, where there is the greatest potential for significant remains, and particularly the marginal, enclosed, lands, as these are under the greatest threat from land improvement. Furthermore, this strategy fits with Initiative 2.2 for the prehistoric period in the *Research Agenda and Strategy* for north-west England (Hodgson and Brennand 2007, 33), which highlights the need to direct investigation towards 'areas of high potential, such as the fell-edge intakes and areas of high-grade agricultural land that are currently being ploughed'. Potentially, such areas should include:

- the northern margins of the Lakes, centred on Bassenthwaite, Derwent Water, and Threlkeld;

- the Caldbeck Fells;

- Eskdale;

- the southern margins of the Eastern Fells, centred on Troutbeck, Kentmere, and Longsleddale.

Detailed survey

The inherent principle behind the identification surveys is that they should serve as the forerunner to more detailed surveys. This has been the case in several instances, notably a series of detailed surveys which were undertaken of individual sites that had previously been recorded in outline by the *Haweswater Identification Survey* (LUAU 1997c). However, for the most part, the extensive areas of identification survey undertaken across the Lake District have yet to be subject to more detailed surveys and, within these, there are some very important archaeological landscapes which warrant more detailed recording to allow an adequate understanding of their form and development. This is in keeping with Initiative 2.3 for the prehistoric period in the *Research Agenda and Strategy* for north-west England (Hodgson and Brennand 2007, 33), which highlights that 'there is a need to move towards more intensive surveys, beyond simply acknowledging the existence of a site, that will enable the building of integrated interpretations of these archaeological landscapes'. Notable sites that would warrant detailed survey include areas that have been subject to identification survey and some that have not. These include:

- Aughertree settlement and field system, in the Caldbeck Fells;

- Threlkeld cairnfield and settlement;

- Lambling Knott and Rannerdale settlements and field systems, in Buttermere.

Palaeoenvironmental analysis

Alongside the results of the LDNPS programme, extensive palaeoenvironmental studies across the uplands, by researchers such as Winifred Pennington (*inter alia* 1970; 1973; 2003) and Walker (1965a; 1966; 2001), have also demonstrated that the marginal lands of the Lake District were subject to a complex agricultural development during the later prehistoric period. Although the specific research interests of these researchers, rather than the archaeological resource, determined the selection of sites, they have provided a valuable body of palaeoenvironmental data, which enhances the known archaeological record. However, many of these studies remain scientifically undated, and the interpretation of the data is biased towards the history of vegetation and past climatic conditions.

Following the recommendations proposed in the *Research Agenda and Strategy* for north-west England, there is a need for the reinterpretation and radiocarbon dating of existing material, together with the detailed analysis of sediment sequences near to known prehistoric sites, such as have been identified during the LDNPS (Hodgson and Brennand 2007, 36). One potential programme of work might therefore focus on those landscapes that contain significant archaeological remains, such as Town Bank, Askham Fell, and Torver High Common. In these areas, the identification of suitable sediment sequences from OS mapping, documentary sources, and a programme of coring is one potential avenue for future research. In addition, the early studies of material from Langdale Coombe (Walker 1965a) and the North Basin of Thirlmere (Pennington 1970) need to be reassessed and the material dated, which would extend the body of evidence presented by Richard Chiverrell (2006). Future landscape survey in the Lake District should also include a palaeoenvironmental element, as this, when combined with survey data, has the potential to increase greatly knowledge of settlement patterns, as well as natural and anthropogenic vegetational changes, and the impact of the climate on the evolving landscape of the Lake District.

Peatlands

The recent Upland Peats programme (OA North 2009a) aimed to identify the potential for archaeological remains surviving beneath the extensive peatlands that cover the higher ground of the Lake District, and northern England more generally. This work targeted four areas in the North West, of which one was the South-West Fells of the Lake District, including Barnscar, where it confirmed that, although for the most part the peatlands have been relatively static, remains of the cairnfield did extend beneath the peat cover. Palaeoenvironmental work associated with this programme also demonstrated that peat inception

dating to the neolithic period was associated with clearance activity, which has considerable implications for an understanding of the Barnscar cairnfield. Furthermore, the programme has highlighted that there is a need to undertake archaeological survey in areas of peatland, and that recording methods will need to be tailored to the identification of the sub-peat resource.

Excavation

After nearly 20 years of intensive survey work throughout the Lake District, it is now possible to recognise the extent and the enormous significance of particular archaeological landscapes. However, only educated assumptions can be made regarding the development of these landscapes, given the lack of excavation and associated scientific dating. Indeed, the way in which certain cairnfields and field systems developed over time, how they related to each other, and how they related to the environment, as reflected in the pollen record, is very uncertain because of the absence of a securely dated chronological framework. There is, therefore, a clear need for a programme of archaeological excavation targeting elements of a landscape, in order to address some of the key outstanding questions generated by landscape surveys such as the LDNPS. Furthermore, this accords with Initiative 2.5 for the prehistoric period in the *Research and Agenda Strategy* for north-west England (Hodgson and Brennand 2007, 33), which emphasises the need to undertake palaeoenvironmental analysis alongside archaeological excavation. However, it must be stressed that, as the layout and form of many of the upland sites is evident from surface remains, there is no need for large-scale wholesale, destructive, excavation. Instead, targeted sampling of key relationships by excavation could examine selected monuments, and elements of these monuments, in order to provide appropriate stratigraphical and chronological information. The emphasis should therefore be on the excavation of small trenches in a large number of sites, rather than large trenches examining a limited number of sites, as such an approach would contribute more dramatically to an understanding of the wider landscape. The key is being able to obtain adequate organic samples within each trench sufficient to enable radiocarbon dating. One such programme has been carried out in the Duddon Valley (Duddon Valley Local History Group and Lake District National Park Authority 2009), which surveyed a wide landscape and then undertook excavations, with associated palaeoenvironmental survey, on two ring cairns (Pl 196).

One of the most informative programmes of excavation undertaken to date has been that on a series of cairns by Donald Walker (1965b) at Barnscar, which used palaeoenvironmental analysis to link the processes of cairn construction into a vegetational context. Whilst this demonstrated that

Plate 196: Research excavations in progress, of two ring cairns, near Seathwaite Tarn in the Duddon Valley

the cairns were a part of the process of woodland clearance, it also highlighted how important it is to undertake a programme of palaeoenvironmental research in conjunction with any excavation programme, and hence this provides a guide for future research methodology.

Indeed, all of the cairnfield groups across the Lake District would benefit from scientific dating, and representative clearance cairns should be examined to establish both the date of construction and also if, and when, these cairns were enhanced. A selection of key monuments from within each site group should also be examined to establish the internal development of individual cairnfields or settlements. In addition, a selection of discrete site types across the whole region should be considered to establish their relationship to one another. Ultimately, the aim should be to establish a framework that will allow a new insight into the development and decline of upland occupation and exploitation of the Lake District.

Conclusion

Although the LDNPS programme was originally conceived in the early 1980s, the results of this work have been able to alter radically our perception of the development of settlement and society across the uplands, and even, to an extent, in the lowlands, of Cumbria. It is, perhaps, a testament to the significance of the landscapes and the survey results that this work has created many more questions about the development of agriculture, settlement patterns, and the impact of climate change than it has provided answers. The programme has highlighted that there is enormous potential for future research into the landscapes of the Cumbrian uplands, and it is anticipated that this survey data, from the second millennium AD, will serve as the basis for research that will take us firmly into the third millennium.

GLOSSARY

Aratral ridge and furrow	A distinctive curving of the ridge and furrow (sometimes s-shaped, other times bow-shaped) on medieval strips of cultivated land, made by medieval ploughmen turning their long teams of oxen as they approached the headland at the end of the field.
Ard	A simple prehistoric type of plough, which typically breaks up a narrow strip of soil. Ard marks can often be seen on excavation of late prehistoric and Roman sites, demonstrating early arable farming.
Bield	A northern vernacular term for a small shelter for persons and, in some instances, stock. It was typically a crude dry-stone structure without a roof. It was designed to protect from the wind and wind-borne elements; examples are often three-sided or semi-circular, with the open side away from the prevailing winds. In some instances, it can be little more than an adaptation of a topographical feature, such as a crag, and comprises a small section of walling to improve the wind protection of the natural feature.
Brash	A mass of fractured rock that has been weathered *in situ*. These natural deposits of small to large frost-fractured stones are often exposed through the turf in localised patches and, in some circumstances, have a similar appearance to artificially constructed cairns.
Cirque	The regional names for this glacial feature are cwm or corrie. It is a large hollow with a very steep or sheer backwall but, on the open side, there is only a low lip. It often contains a sub-circular tarn or mire (such as at HF IV on Heathwaite Fell). They were formed by the continued glacial erosion of nivation hollows (*see below*); these hollows became catchment areas for snow and ice, which flowed out through the open side as a glacier. With time, the glaciation processes deepened and expanded the hollow.
Col	A pass or saddle between two mountain peaks; it provides the easiest crossing point of a chain of mountains or hills. The North West regional name for this topographical feature is hause.
Cord Rig	A form of very narrow ridge and furrow earthworks, typically of late prehistoric date, and most commonly found in upland areas. They are normally around 1 m wide, no more than 0.15 m high, and are believed to be produced using a spade.
Devensian	The most recent glacial stage, culminating in a brief interstadial (Windermere interstadial LDeII), followed by a final cold period (the so-called 'Younger Dryas' or Loch Lomand Stadial, LDeIII). The end of the cold conditions at around 10,000 cal BC (*c* 10,000 BP) marked the opening of the Flandrian age.
Diffluent	Flowing apart or off, particularly in the context of the movement of a glacier from one valley to another.
Draw Kiln	A stone kiln, particularly for lime, designed to maintain a continuous burn. They are typically set into a slope, and have a cone-shaped firing chamber, with the open end at the top; this tapered to a small aperture at the base, from where the lime was drawn, and which provided a limited draught for the kiln's slow burn. A mixture of coal and limestone was fed from the top, and a burning zone was maintained in the centre of the kiln by controlling the amount of lime drawn from the bottom.

Drumlin	An elongated, rounded hill or hillock formed as a glacier recedes, leaving large mounds of glacial drift. They typically form in fields, and a group of them characterises the head of the Mickleden Valley, Great Langdale.
Eutrophication	The natural or artificial enrichment of freshwater habitats by inorganic nutrients (*eg* nitrates or phosphates) promoting excessive algae growth.
Flandrian	Chronozones of the present interglacial stage in Britain, dating from *c* 10,000 cal BC (*c* 10,000 BP) to the present. (See Holocene).
Holocene	The present interglacial stage in Britain, dating from *c* 10,000 cal BC (*c* 10,000 BP) to the present.
Kilnwood Kiln	A large kiln, similar to a potash kiln, comprising a circular open chamber, with an aperture at the base for firing. They were intended to dry wood, producing kilnwood for other industrial uses, which was free of sap, the use of which ensured much higher firing temperatures. Lengths of timbers were set across the top of the kiln and a fire at the base provided slow drying. These kilns are believed to be associated with the medieval lead industry (Davies-Shiel 1974, 37-44).
Mire	Peat-producing ecosystem, which develops in areas of abundant water supply.
Moraine	These are glacially formed accumulations of unconsolidated debris either on a valley floor, from material carried as the glacier advanced, or on the sides where material has fallen from the valley walls. Moraines comprise a mixture of fine silt, stones, and large boulders, which are typically rounded and worn. Some moraines existed on the glacier's surface and were deposited as piles of debris as the glacier melted.
Nivation Hollow	These are formed during glaciation, when ice forms in a hollow or slight irregularity on a hill-side, which is then eroded into hollows / bowls; in so doing, they trap more ice and snow and the process is enhanced. Given adequate time and suitable conditions, they can evolve into cirques (*see above*). The most common location is on the northern side of hills, which are protected from the sun (for instance, HF I, on the north side of the Thwaite spur, on Heathwaite Fell).
Radiocarbon dating	A method of dating ancient organic material. The technique involves the measurement of amounts of radiocarbon remaining in organic matter. Calibrated radiocarbon dates have been converted to calender years and are distinguished by the use of the suffix 'cal BC' or prefix 'cal AD'.
Peat	Partly-decomposed organic material formed in areas of permanent waterlogging.
Planation terrace	These are nearly flat surfaces formed by fluvial, wind, and marine erosion processes, which have been formed into terraces as a result of subsequent glacial cutting so that they form a large natural step. Large, flat, but raised, planation terraces extend around the South-West Fells, and were exploited for settlement and agriculture.
Ridge and Furrow	Cultivation earthworks formed by plough action and typically of medieval or post-medieval date - see *Chapter 2, p 30*.
Rhizomes	This is a characteristic horizontal stem of a plant that is usually found underground, sending out roots and shoots from its nodes. If a rhizome is separated into pieces, each piece may be able to give rise to a new plant, and has the capacity for considerable propagation. Many archaeological sites are severely affected by the rhizomes of bracken, which damage the underlying stratigraphy.

Sink hole   A roughly conical depression formed by the solution (Doline) and/or collapse of underlying limestone strata. Although they often drain water into subterranean passages, they can close and become filled with bogs.

Shieling   A small transhumant structure, most commonly found in upland contexts - see *Chapter 2, p 38.*

APPENDIX 1

SURVEY METHODOLOGY

Reconnaissance

In the first instance, the sites were located using oblique and vertical aerial photographs, where available. Although this technique identified the major site groups, ground reconnaissance was required to identify all individual monuments and surface features. Each survey area was systematically searched by 'fieldwalking' along traverses spaced at approximately 20 m intervals.

Ground Survey

Since the start of the survey programme in 1982, the introduction of increasingly sophisticated survey equipment prompted developments in the survey techniques used. This has resulted in improved productivity and accuracy.

Control
In the first two years of the programme, when only a theodolite was available, the survey control was established by resection, using co-ordinates for topographical detail extrapolated from 1:10,000 OS sheets. From 1984 onwards, with the introduction of Electronic Distance Measuring (EDM) equipment, a network of control stations within each survey area was established by traverse to an accuracy of ±0.2 m. The network was tied into the OS National Grid by traverse or triangulation from trigonometric pillars on adjacent mountain summits, using co-ordinates purchased from the OS. This latter survey process was usually undertaken to an accuracy of ±0.25 m, so that each survey station was better than ±0.45 m with respect to the National Grid.

Detail
Prior to the introduction of add-on EDM equipment in 1984, the archaeological detail was surveyed either by stadia tacheometry or using an optical telemeter – a crude and bulky optical distance-measuring device, which had a maximum range of only 70 m. The use of an EDM considerably improved survey efficiency by comparison with stadia tacheometry, which was slower and required substantial numbers of station set-ups. The survey data were processed manually by entering them into a small portable computer, and the resulting computed National Grid co-ordinates were then manually plotted at a scale of 1:1000 onto A1 drawing film sheets. The survey was drawn up in the field with respect to survey points, which had been marked on the ground by bamboo canes. In 1989, the processing of the survey data was significantly improved by the introduction of total-station equipment, which could output the survey data in a digital format. The data were stored in a small logging computer, which processed them and sent the output co-ordinates to an electronic plotter. The equipment was not only faster to use, but also eliminated human error, reducing the need for field checking.

Plan Production

The pencil plans brought back from the field only included topography local to the archaeological detail, since it was not found to be expedient to survey more remote topography. The background topographical detail and contouring was thus enlarged from 1:10,000 OS plans using a planvariograph, and was then inked up with the archaeological mapping at a scale of 1:1000. Comparisons between topographical detail accurately surveyed with reference to the National Grid and the enlarged OS map detail revealed discrepancies that were generally better than ±6 m, representing the accuracy of the OS map base. All the survey drawings have been digitised and incorporated into the GIS, which forms part of the LDHER.

Site Description

Using standardised forms, each archaeological monument was measured and described according to a set of guidelines which ensured a uniform descriptive record. The site descriptions were subsequently input into a computerised database for inclusion within the Cumbria Sites and Monuments Record, and later transferred to the LDHER.

APPENDIX 2

PREHISTORIC MONUMENT TYPES IN THE LDNPS

Pastoral Enclosures

No	NGR	Length	Width	Shape
CT 344	SD 1853 9486	85 m	69 m	D
HE 46	SD 1841 9410	115 m	90 m	D
HF 530	SD 2538 8618	61.5 m	44 m	Rectangular
TB 6	NY 0924 1013	32 m	23 m	Sub-oval
TB 72-80	NY 9027 9833	179 m	122 m	Oval
TB 649	NY 7395 9869	122 m	98 m	Sub-triangular
UF 54	SD 1848 9772	97 m	70 m	D

Possible Unenclosed Roundhouses

Average diameter: 9 m   Associated with field systems, % of total: 63%   Associated only with cairnfields, % of total: 23%

No	NGR	Diameter	Orientation	Association Fields	Association Cairnfield
SM 591	NY 09942 07805	14 m	east	Yes	Yes
SM 838?	NY 09770 10208	5.8 m	-	-	Yes
TB 1	NY 09450 10025	8.9 m	-	-	Yes
TB 73	NY 09017 09980	7.8 m	-	Yes	-
TB 76	NY 08987 09798	9.9 m	-	Yes	-
TB 236	NY 09068 09435	14.5 m	south	Yes	Yes
TB 241	NY 09041 09396	9 m	west	Yes	Yes
TB 265	NY 08926 09360	12 m	south-east	Yes	Yes
TB 294	NY 08860 09439	11.5 m	east	Yes	-
TB 296	NY 08851 09441	9 m	-	Yes	-
TB 303	NY 08851 09396	9 m	south-west	Yes	-
TB 444	NY 08274 09540	11 m	north-west	-	-
TB 462	NY 08205 09428	9.5 m	-	Yes	-
TB 475	NY 08450 09369	11 m	-	Yes	-
TB 679	NY 07280 09855	12.5 m	-	Yes	-
TB 750	NY 07115 09808	9.5 m	west	Yes	-
TB 802	NY 07016 09823	13.7 m	east	Yes	-
TB 837	NY 06704 09720	9.2 m	west	Yes	Yes
WG 610	NY 12351 06620	c 6 m	-	-	Yes
WG 618	NY 12288 06750	c 6 m	-	-	Yes
BM 101	NY 18008 03670	c 5 m	-	Yes	Yes
BM 110	NY 17964 03637	c 4 m	east	Yes	Yes
BM 111	NY 17971 03637	c 4.5 m	north-east	Yes	Yes
BM 109	NY 17960 03628	c 4 m	north-east	Yes	Yes
BF 206	SD 12750 89828	c 12 m	south-west	-	Yes

No	NGR	Diameter	Orientation	Association Fields	Association Fields
BF 415	SD 12540 89270	c 7 m	-	Yes	-
BF 602	SD 13395 89044	6.2 m	north	-	Yes
BF 635	SD 13258 89014	7.1 m	south-west	-	Yes
BF 650	SD 13491 88794	6.3 m	north	Yes	-
BF 714	SD 13067 89024	8.2 m	south-south-west	-	-
CF 117	SD 12975 90204	8.5 m	west	-	Yes
CG 259	SD 13358 91268	c 7 m	north-east	-	Yes
WB 11	SD 13023 93417	c 5.8 m	south	Yes	Yes
BS 732d	SD 13382 96104	c 8.4 m	east	Yes	-
BB 179	SD 15178 96870	c 8 m	north	Yes	Yes
BB 240	SD 15210 96878	c 8 m	-	Yes	Yes
BB 470	SD 15145 98047	c 9 m	south-east	Yes	Yes
BB 476	SD 15170 98077	c 7.8 m	south	Yes	Yes
UF 139	SD 18148 98653	c 9.1 m	north-west	-	-
UF 140	SD 18146 98622	c 6.3 m	south-west	-	-
UF 141	SD 18172 98625	c 9 m	east	-	-
UF 148	SD 19312 99405	c 5.3 m	east	Yes	-
UF 150	SD 19303 99425	c 4.8 m	west	Yes	-
CT 409	SD 19068 95432	c 12.9 m	north	-	-
CT 480	SD 18831 95428	c 6.7 m	west	Yes	Yes
CT 545	SD 18859 95541	c 7.5 m	west	Yes	-
TF 39	SD 1731289932	15.2 m	north	-	Yes
TF 327	SD 18505 89060	12.2 m	-	-	Yes
HF 40	SD 24964 88671	10 m	-	Yes	-
AF 14	NY 47659 22150	9.8 m	north-west	Yes	-

House Platforms

No	NGR	Length	Width
TB 82	NY 09045 09841	29 m	19 m
TB 265	NY 08926 09360	14 m	10 m
TB 291	NY 08880 09460	21 m	20.5 m
TB 445	NY 08284 09539	7 m	6 m
TB 636	NY 07445 09820	25 m	25 m
TB 679	NY07290 09847	14.4 m	13.5 m
TB 688	NY 07318 09784	8.8 m	8.2 m
SF 90	SD 13517 94491	27 m	27 m
SF 91	SD 13543 94447	8.3 m	8.2 m
BS 213	SD 13493 95747	15 m	10 m
CT 409	SD 19071 95432	13 m	13 m
CT 565	SD 18944 95571	8.3 m	7.5 m
HF 329	SD 25368 87344	9.5 m	6.5 m
HF 405	SD 25388 87053	4 m	3 m
HF 406	SD 25409 87060	6 m	4 m
HF 407	SD 25396 87054	4 m	3 m
HF 408	SD 25385 87044	4 m	4 m
HF 409	SD 25401 87043	6.2 m	2.5 m
HF 410	SD 25408 87040	8.4 m	8.4 m
HF 411	SD 25447 87027	5.5 m	4 m
HF 412	SD 25390 86983	2.5 m	2.5 m
HF 522	SD 25431 86271	4 m	4 m

Simple Enclosed Settlements

No	NGR	Length	Width
WB 163	SD 1339 9386	47 m	42 m
TB 805	NY 6980 9880	37 m	35 m

Complex Enclosed Settlements

No	NGR	Length	Width
AF 203	NY 4978 2312	62 m	45 m
BS 477	SD 1327 9591	66 m	53 m

Possible Long Cairns

No	NGR	Length	Width	Height	Shape
SM 435	NY 09840 08050	25.5 m	13.5 m	1.7 m	Trapezoidal
SM 732	NY 10150 07750	14.4 m	7.4 m	1.1 m	Oval?
TB 526	NY 07683 09946	14 m	7.0 m	0.4 m	Rectangular
TB 536	NY 07640 09925	11.0 m	8.0 m	0.7 m	Trapezoidal
TB 551	NY 07602 09892	8.5 m	4.5 m	0.8 m	Oval
TB 564	NY 07638 09870	14.2 m	8.5 m	0.9 m	Trapezoidal
TB 591	NY 07757 09875	10.2 m	7.0 m	0.45 m	Trapezoidal
HF 60	SD 25029 88230	10 m	4.0 m	0.50 m	Trapezoidal
HF 420	SD 25533 87156	11.0 m	5.7 m	0.4 m	Trapezoidal
SF 363	SD 14780 94620	27.0 m	13 m	c 1.3 m	Trapezoidal
AF 212	NY 48879 23181	18.6 m	8.7 m	-	Trapezoidal

Possible Ring Cairns

The typology defined is after Lynch (1972)

No	NGR	External Diameter	Entrance	Type	Cairnfield Association
SM 36	NY 09998 09769	10.2 m	-	Stone Ring	Yes
SM 38	NY 10004 09790	8.2 m	-	Kerbed Ring	Yes
SM 105	NY 10430 09630	11.9 m	-	Stone Ring	-
SM 493	NY 0934 0796	12.9 m	-	Stone Ring	-
SM 496	NY 0956 0787	17 m	Yes	Kerbed Ring	-
HF 113	SD 25630 87964	9.0 m	?	Kerbed Ring	-
HF117	SD 25579 88034	8.5 m	Yes	Kerbed Ring	-
BF 354	SD 12725 89335	11.5 m	-	Stone Ring	Yes
BF 474	SD 12992 89290	7.3 m	-	Small Ring	Yes
BF 471	SD 12979 89269	6.5 m	-	Small Ring	Yes
BF 472	SD 12985 89261	5.9 m	?	Small Ring	Yes
BF 480	SD 13019 89263	6.0 m	-	Small Ring	Yes
AF 80	NY 48478 21788	19.5 m	Yes	Stone Ring	-
AF 115	NY 49600 21605	c 20 m	?	Kerbed Ring?	-
AF 117	NY 49405 21962	10 m	-	Cairn Circle	-
SA 107	NY 50144 19752	c 7 m	-	Small Ring	-
TF 327	SD 18055 89058	c 12.5 m	-	Kerbed Ring	-

Stone Circles

No	Place Name	NGR	Diameter	No of Stones	Internal Cairns
BM 220	Low Longrigg	NY 1710 0280	21.7 m	15	2
BM 221	Low Longrigg	NY 1710 0270	15.2 m	9	1

No	Place Name	NGR	Diameter	No of Stones	Internal Cairns
BM 325	White Moss	NY 1730 2400	16.6 m	14	1
BM 326	White Moss	NY 1730 0240	16.2 m	11	1
BM 352	Brat's Hill	NY 1760 0230	30.4 m	40+	5
AF 86	The Cockpit	NY 4827 2224	32.8 m	21	0

Round Cairns

No	NGR	Length	Width	Height	Kerbed
TB 293	NY 8860 9451	8.6 m	8.4 m	1.25 m	Yes
TB 518	NY 7680 9986	13.5 m	7.5 m	0.4 m	-
TB 541	NY 7659 9904	12 m	6 m	0.5 m	-
TB 803	NY 7020 9845	18.9 m	17.5 m	1.7 m	Yes
SM 24	NY 9787 9870	7.5 m	4.5 m	0.4 m	-
SM 34	NY 9948 9750	5.4 m	4.7 m	0.2 m	Yes
SM 39	NY 1001 0977	7 m	5 m	0.4 m	Yes
SM 41	NY 1003 0981	4.7 m	4.5 m	0.3 m	Yes
SM 151	NY 9525 9082	11.9 m	8.0 m	0.3 m	-
SM 169	NY 9615 8940	12.3 m	9.2 m	0.4 m	-
SM 382	NY 9485 8465	9.3 m	8.2 m	0.6 m	-
SM 422	NY 9630 8270	14.5 m	6.6 m	0.3 m	-
SM 423	NY 9665 8262	10.7 m	8.7 m	0.3 m	-
SM 436	NY 1017 8310	14.2 m	13.9 m	1.9 m	-
SM 437	NY 1023 0813	11.1 m	11 m	1.1 m	-
SM 438	NY 1023 0804	8.1 m	7.6 m	0.4 m	-
WG 671	NY 1191 0772	4.5 m	4.5 m	0.45 m	-
BF 30	SD 1321 8998	5.5 m	5 m	0.25 m	Possible
BF 298	SD 1259 8980	9 m	8.5 m	0.5 m	-
BF 637	SD 1333 8901	9.5 m	8.5 m	0.5 m	-
BF 641	SD 1336 8878	5.0 m	5.0 m	0.4 m	-
BF 642	SD 1337 8878	9.6 m	9.2 m	0.4 m	-
BF 717	SD 1297 8897	10.4 m	9.7 m	0.4 m	Yes
BF 731	SD 1298 8912	13.7 m	13.1 m	0.5 m	Possible
BF 759	SD 1276 8880	10 m	10 m	0.5 m	-
BF 774	SD 1308 8861	13 m	12.5 m	0.4 m	-
BF 775	SD 1309 8864	7 m	7 m	0.3 m	-
BF 802	SD 1362 8857	7 m	6.5 m	0.35 m	-
BF 804	SD 1365 8856	10.5 m	8.5 m	0.6 m	Yes
BF 813	SD 1370 8862	14.2 m	14.2 m	1 m	Possible
BF 878	SD 1381 8843	6.6 m	6.6 m	0.35 m	-
BF 879	SD 1382 8843	5.3 m	5.2 m	0.3 m	-
BF 903	SD 1317 8831	10.6 m	7.3 m	0.45 m	Yes
BF 909?	SD 1313 8828	8.7 m	8.0 m	0.45 m	-
BF 914?	SD 1311 8828	10.2 m	8.0 m	0.4 m	-
CF 91	SD 1270 9061	8.5 m	8.5 m	0.3 m	-
CF 93	SD 1273 9062	10.5 m	10.5 m	0.4 m	-
CF 187	SD 1300 9049	10 m	8.0 m	0.4 m	-
CF 194	SD 1302 9055	11 m	11 m	0.6 m	-
CF 195?	SD 1299 9055	13 m	7 m	0.4 m	-

No	NGR	Length	Width	Height	Kerbed
SF 2	SD 1357 9427	21 m	11 m	2.02 m	Yes
SF 338	SD 1402 9446	14.5 m	13 m	3.5 m	Yes
BS 379	SD 1357 9591	7.9 m	7.7 m	0.7 m	-
BS 421?	SD 1336 9590	9.1 m	8.7 m	0.35 m	-
BS 429?	SD 1338 9587	7.2 m	6.6 m	0.4 m	-
BS 432	SD 1339 9585	17 m	17 m	-	-
BS 453	SD 1330 9582	7.6 m	6.5 m	0.6 m	-
BS 566	SD 1364 9598	8 m	7.3 m	0.35 m	-
BB 100	SD 1496 9680	13 m	8 m	0.5 m	-
BB 185	SD 1510 9695	14.65 m	14.65 m	0.9 m	Yes
BB 399	SD1560 9740	4.75 m	4.75 m	0.4 m	-
BB 417	SD 1498 9791	0.82 m	0.82 m	1.0 m	Yes
BB 421	SD 1498 9794	7.5 m	7.5 m	1.0 m	-
UF 63	SD 1830 9814	5.1 m	4.1 m	0.35 m	Yes
UF 142	SD 1918 9935	9 m	9 m	0.7 m	Yes
UF 200	SD 1811 9607	8.2 m	8.2 m	0.5 m	Yes
UF 214	SD 1840 9651	8.6 m	6.6 m	0.8 m	-
UF 247	SD 1877 9664	12.9 m	9.9 m	1 m	Yes
HE 15	SD 18544 94034	6.6 m	6.6 m	0.6 m	-
TF 2	SD 169 900	8 m	8 m	0.5 m	-
TF 144	SD 176 898	8.25 m	8.25 m	0.3 m	-
TF 256	SD 179 893	7.9 m	7.9 m	0.6 m	-
HF 59	SD 2503 8824	4.5 m	4 m	0.35 m	-
HF 144	SD 2523 8786	6 m	6 m	0.4 m	-
HF 312	SD 2526 8712	8 m	7.5 m	0.35 m	Yes
HF 419	SD 2553 8718	11 m	7 m	0.5 m	-
HF 497?	SD 2601 8669	6 m	6 m	0.5 m	-
HF 498?	SD 2599 8667	5.5 m	5.5 m	0.4 m	-
HF 500?	SD 2588 8653	5 m	5 m	0.7 m	-
MB 12	NY 2648 6683	4.0 m	3.0 m	0.2 m	Yes
AF 48	NY 4822 2187	7.1 m	6.2 m	0.55 m	Yes
AF 103	NY 4852 2258	4.6 m	4.4 m	0.25 m	-
AF 119	NY 4931 2218	17 m	15 m	1.4 m	-
AF 165	NY 4934 2290	9.9 m	8.3 m	0.75 m	-
AF 178	NY 4957 2194	7.7 m	5.5 m	0.5 m	-

Starfish Cairns

No	NGR	Length	Width	Height	Spurs
SM 739	NY 1015 0775	14.4 m	7.4 m	0.7 m	4
AF 119	NY 4931 2218	17 m	15 m	1.4 m	Possibly 5
AF 130	NY 4888 2244	22 m	17.9 m	1.8 m	3

Burnt Mounds

No	NGR	Length	Width	Height
WG 696	NY 0978 0626	15 m	14 m	0.8 m

APPENDIX 3

RADIOCARBON DATES IN THE TEXT

(Dates are calibrated using Ox Cal v4.1.7 (Bronk Ramsey 2011; Atmospheric data from Reimer *et al* 2009))

Location	Calibrated date	Radiocarbon Age (BP)	Lab Code	Authority
White Moss	7060-6707 cal BC	7995±80 BP	HV-3362	Hodgkinson *et al* 2000
Monk Moors	5986-5384 cal BC	6750±155 BP	BM-1216	Bonsall *et al* 1986
Williamson's Moss	4460-4338 cal BC	5555±40 BP	UB-2545	Bonsall *et al* 1986
White Moss	4351-3801 cal BC	5277±120 BP	Q-85	Hodgkinson *et al* 2000
White Moss	4037-3638 cal BC	5015±100 BP	HV-34600	Hodgkinson *et al* 2000
Burnmoor	4229-3653 cal BC	5100±120 BP	K-957	Tauber 1966
Plasketlands	3985-3712 cal BC	5090±60 BP	GU-2572	Bewley 1993
Seamer Moor	3978-3652 cal BC	5030±90 BP	NPL-73	Manby 1970
Blea Tarn	4217-3530 cal BC	5020±120 BP	K-958	Pennington 1970
Plasketlands	3958-3535 cal BC	4940±90 BP	GU-3573	Bewley 1993
Williamson's Moss	4224-3355 cal BC	4925±165 BP	UB-2711	Bonsall *et al* 1986
Langdale Combe	3772-3530 cal BC	4870±50 BP	BM-2625	Bradley and Edmonds 1993
Chatton Sandyford	3896-3373 cal BC	4840±90 BP	GAK-1507	Jobey 1968
Plasketlands	3706-3379 cal BC	4810±60 BP	GU-2571	Bewley 1993
Langdale Combe	3517-3103 cal BC	4590±50 BP	BM-2627	Bradley and Edmonds 1993
The Knott, Barnscar	3370-3090 cal BC	4553±35 BP	SUERC-4524	OA North 2009a
Black Beck, Barnscar	3360-3020 cal BC	4490±40 BP	SUERC-4523	OA North 2009a
Skendleby	3516-2624 cal BC	4410±150 BP	BM-191	Manby 1970
Stainton	2870-2570 cal BC	4110±35 BP	SUERC-32717	OA North 2011a
Drigg	2480-2280 cal BC	3960±50 BP	GU-5885	OA North 2010b
Drigg	2460-2230 cal BC	3900±50 BP	GU-5884	OA North 2010b
Aldingham	2290-2020 cal BC	3740±40 BP	SUERC-1855	The Morecambe Bay Archaeological Society 2006
Stainton	2280-1630 cal BC	3720±35 BP	SUERC-32714	OA North 2011a
Stainton	2020-1450 cal BC	3270±35 BP	SUERC-32715	OA North 2011a

Location	Calibrated date	Radiocarbon Age (BP)	Lab Code	Authority
Birrel Sike	2396-1756 cal BC	3670±100 BP	BIRM-1018	Richardson 1982
Birrel Sike	2299-1740 cal BC	3640±100 BP	BIRM-1063	Richardson 1982
Millstone Hill	2283-1754 cal BC	3640±90 BP	HAR-1942	Jobey 1981
Aldingham	2140-1910 cal BC	3640+35 BP	SUERC–1856	The Morecambe Bay Archaeological Society 2006
Manor Farm, Borwick	2466-1533 cal BC	3630±170 BP	HAR-5626	Olivier 1987
Langdale Combe	2029-1667 cal BC	3510±70 BP	OXA-2180	Bradley and Edmonds 1993
Weird Law	1974-1523 cal BC	3440±90 BP	NPL-57	Mac Laren 1967
Shaugh Moor	1956-1513 cal BC	3430±90 BP	HAR-2220	Walker and Otlet 1985
Shaugh Moor	1933-1529 cal BC	3430±80 BP	HAR-2219	Wainwright *et al* 1979
Shaugh Moor	1920-1524 cal BC	3430±80 BP	OxA-2127	Howard-Davis and Williams 2005
Shaugh Moor	1932-1497 cal BC	3400±90 BP	HAR-2285	Wainwright *et al* 1979
Hardendale	1869-1515 cal BC	3360±60 BP	OxA-1834	Howard-Davis and Williams 2005
Shaugh Moor	1875-1459 cal BC	3350±70 BP	HAR-2221	Wainwright *et al* 1979
Whitestanes Moor	1874-1414 cal BC	3310±90 BP	GAK-461	Scott-Elliott and Rae 1965
Manor Farm	1739-1399 cal BC	3270±80 BP	HAR-5658	Olivier 1987
Tewit Moss	1729-1411 cal BC	3260±70 BP	CAR-916	**This Vol** *p 202*
Shaugh Moor	1736-1321 cal BC	3240±80 BP	HAR-2214	Walker and Otlet 1985
Sparrowmire Farm	1678-1410 cal BC	3240±50 BP	AA 34789 / GU-8449	Heawood and Huckerby 2002
Duddon Valley	1540-1400 cal BC	3180±30 BP	POZ-24044	Duddon Valley Local History Group and Lake District National Park Authority 2009
Duddon Valley	1430-1250 cal BC	3070±35 BP	POZ-24036)	Duddon Valley Local History Group and Lake District National Park Authority 2009
Morecambe Bay sites	1446-1052 cal BC	3055±65 BP	CAR-552	Chiverrell 2006
Seathwaite Tarn	1608-920 cal BC	3040±140 BP	NPL-124	Pennington 1970
Tewit Moss	1426-1054 cal BC	3020±70 BP	CAR-915	**This Vol** *p 202*
Sparrowmire Farm	1408-1126 cal BC	3020±50 BP	AA-34791 / U-8447	Heawood and Huckerby 2002
Claggan	1386-1128 cal BC	3008±40 BP	SRR-285	Ritchie *et al* 1975
Angle Tarn	1050±80 cal BC	3000±80 BP	HAR-3538	Jobey 1983
Claggan	1297-980 cal BC	2925±50 BP	SRR-284	Ritchie *et al* 1975

Location	Calibrated date	Radiocarbon Age (BP)	Lab Code	Authority
Glencoyne	1105-835 cal BC	2810±50 BP	Beta-171115	Loney and Hoaen 2000
Tewit Moss	400-120 cal BC	2230±60 BP	CAR-914	**This Vol** *p 202*
Baldhowend	375 cal BC-cal AD 65	2120±80 BP	Beta-123084	Loney and Hoaen 2000
South-west Cumbria	345 cal BC-cal AD 69	2065±60 BP	CAR-695	Dumayne-Peaty and Barber 1998; Wimble *et al* 2000; Chiverrell 2006
Broadwood	88 cal BC-cal AD 66	2010±28 BP	KIA-22910	Johnson 2004
Broadwood	cal AD 22-210	1914±29 BP	KIA-22912	Johnson 2004
Broadwood	AD 69-221	1883±27 BP	KIA-22911	Johnson 2004
Tewit Moss	cal AD 0-334	1860±70 BP	CAR-913	**This Vol** *p 202*
Baldhowend	cal AD 179-408	1745±40 BP	GU-9336	Loney and Hoaen 2000
Devoke Water	cal AD 129-666	1620±130 BP	NPL-120	Callow and Hassall 1969; Pennington 1970
Devoke Water	cal AD 148-679	1585±130 BP	NPL-119	Callow and Hassall 1969; Pennington 1970
Burnmoor Tarn	cal AD 139-686	1569±130 BP	NPL-116	Pennington 1970
Aberdeenshire	cal AD 339-760	1495±95 BP	UB-2084	Edwards 1977
Bryant's Gill	cal AD 619-875	1320±60 BP	RCD-434	Dickinson 1985
Devoke Water	cal AD 663-963	1230±70 BP	CAR-911	**This Vol** *p 201*
Simy Folds	cal AD 665-979	1210±80 BP	HAR-4034	Coggins *et al* 1983
Simy Folds	cal AD 687-993	1170±70 BP	HAR-1898	Coggins *et al* 1983
Bryant's Gill	cal AD 691-997	1170±70 BP	HAR-8067	Newman 2006
Devoke Water	cal AD 977-1229	970±60 BP	CAR-911	**This Vol** *p 201*
Devoke Water	cal AD 1019-1279	890±60 BP	CAR-912	**This Vol** *p 201*
Devoke Water	cal AD 1260-1408	670±60 BP	CAR-912	**This Vol** *p 201*

BIBLIOGRAPHY

Primary Sources

CRO(C) D/LONS/W/Millom Courtbook 1510-23, 64 Millom Courtbook of 1510-23

Hodgkinson, J, and Donald, T, 1770/1 Map of Cumberland

PRO MAF 1/2 1857 Enclosure map of Bootle Fell

Ordnance Survey 1850 6″ to 1 mile, First Edition, Lancashire sheet 7

Ordnance Survey 1862 6″ to 1 mile, First Edition, Westmorland sheet 25

Ordnance Survey 1863 6″ to 1 mile, First Edition, Westmorland sheet 7

Ordnance Survey 1867 6″ to 1 mile, First Edition, Cumberland sheet 73

Ordnance Survey 1867 6″ to 1 mile, First Edition, Cumberland sheet 78

Ordnance Survey 1867 6″ to 1 mile, First Edition, Cumberland sheet 79

Ordnance Survey 1867 6″ to 1 mile, First Edition, Cumberland sheet 83

Ordnance Survey 1867 6″ to 1 mile, First Edition, Cumberland sheet 85

Ordnance Survey 1899 6″ to 1 mile, Second Edition, Westmorland sheet 7

Ordnance Survey 1900 6″ to 1 mile, Second Edition, Cumberland sheet 83

Ordnance Survey 1900 6″ to 1 mile, Second Edition, Cumberland sheet 85

Ordnance Survey 1900 6″ to 1 mile, Second Edition, Cumberland sheet 86

Ordnance Survey 1919 6″ to 1 mile, Third Edition, Lancashire sheet 7

Ordnance Survey 1920 6″ to 1 mile, rev edn, Cumberland sheet 83

Ordnance Survey 1926 6″ to 1 mile, Third Edition, Cumberland sheet 73

Ordnance Survey 1926 6″ to 1 mile, Third Edition, Cumberland sheet 78

Ordnance Survey 1956 6″ to 1 mile, rev edn, Cumberland sheet 83

Secondary Sources

ADAS, and OA North, 2009 *Conservation of the historic environment in England's uplands*, unpubl rep

Andersen, S T, 1979 Identification of wild grass and cereal pollen, *Danmarks Geologiske Undersøgelse, Årbog*, **1978**, 69-92

Andrén, A, 2005 Behind heathendom: archaeological studies of Old Norse religion, *Scot Archaeol J*, **27 (2)**, 105-38

Armstrong, A, Mawer, A, Stenton, F, and Dickins, B, 1950 *The place-names of Cumberland*, Engl Place-Name Soc, **21**, Cambridge

Askew, G P, Payton, R W, and Shiel, R S, 1985 Upland soils and land clearance, in D Spratt and C Burgess (eds), *Upland settlement in Britain: the second millennium and after*, BAR Brit Ser, **143**, Oxford, 5-33

Ballantyne, C K, and Harris, C, 1994 *The periglaciation of Great Britain*, Cambridge

Barfield, L, and Hodder, I, 1987 Burnt mounds as saunas, and the prehistory of bathing, *Antiquity*, **61**, 370-9

Barker, M, 1934 Tumuli near Carrock Fell, *Trans Cumberland Westmorland Antiq Archaeol Soc*, n ser, **34**, 107-12

Barnatt, J, 1987 Bronze Age settlement on the East Moors of the Peak District of Derbyshire and South Yorkshire, *Proc Prehist Soc*, **53**, 393-418

Barnatt, J, 2000 To each their own: later prehistoric farming communities and their monuments in the Peak, *Derbyshire Archaeol J*, **120**, 1-86

Barnes, F, and Hobbs, J L, 1950 Newly discovered flint chipping sites in the Walney Island locality, *Trans Cumberland Westmorland Antiq Archaeol Soc*, n ser, **50**, 30-42

Behre, K E, 1981 The interpretation of anthropogenic indicators in pollen diagrams, *Pollen et Spores*, **23**, 226-45

Bellhouse, R L, 1991 The Roundclose: a recessed platform in Eskdale, *Trans Cumberland Westmorland Antiq Archaeol Soc,* n ser, **91**, 119-26

Bennion, H, Monteith, D, and Appleby, P, 2000 Temporal and geographical variation in lake trophic status in the English Lake District: evidence from (sub) fossil diatoms and aquatic macrophytes, *Freshwater Biol,* **45**, 394-412

Bevan, W, Stanley, N, and Webster, A, 1991 *Great Langdale: Vol 1, history of land use,* National Trust, unpubl rep

Bewley, R H, 1993 Survey and excavation at a crop-mark enclosure, Plasketlands, Cumbria, *Trans Cumberland Westmorland Antiq Archaeol Soc,* n ser, **93**, 1-18

Blake, B, 1959 Excavations of native (Iron Age) sites in Cumberland, 1956-58, *Trans Cumberland Westmorland Antiq Archaeol Soc,* n ser, **59**, 1-14

Bonsall, C, 1981 The coastal factor in the mesolithic settlement of north-west England, in B Gramsch (ed), *Mesolithikum in Europa: Proceedings of the second International Symposium on the mesolithic in Europe,* VEB Deutscher Verlag Wissenschaften, Potsdam, 451-72

Bonsall, C, Sutherland, D, Tipping, R, and Cherry, J, 1986 The Eskmeals project 1981-85: an interim report, *Northern Archaeol,* **7/1**, 3-30

Bonsall, C, Sutherland, D G, Tipping, R M, and Cherry, J, 1989 The Eskmeals project: late mesolithic settlement and environment in north-west England, in C Bonsall (ed), *The mesolithic in Europe,* Edinburgh, 175-205

Bowen, H C, 1961 *Ancient fields,* London

Bradley, R, and Edmonds, M, 1993 *Interpreting the axe trade: production and exchange in Neolithic Britain,* Cambridge

Bronk-Ramsey, C, 2011 *OxCal 4.1 Manual,* C14.arch. ox.ac/oxcal/OxCal.html

Brunskill, R W, 1974 *Vernacular architecture of the Lake Counties,* London

Burgess, C, 1985 Population, climate and upland settlement, in D Spratt and C Burgess (eds), *Upland settlement in Britain: the second millennium and after,* BAR Brit Ser, **143**, Oxford, 195-230

Burl, A, 1976 *The stone circles of the British Isles,* Newhaven and London

Burl, A, 1993 *From Carnac to Callanish: the prehistoric stone rows and avenues of Britain, Ireland and Brittany,* Newhaven and London

Callow, W J, and Hassall, G I, 1969 National Physical Laboratory radiocarbon measurements VI, *Radiocarbon,* **II (I)**, 130-6

Cherry, J, 1961 Cairns in the Birker Fell and Ulpha Fell area, *Trans Cumberland Westmorland Antiq Archaeol Soc,* n ser, **61**, 7-15

Cherry, J, and Cherry, P J, 1973 Mesolithic habitation sites at St Bees, Cumberland, *Trans Cumberland Westmorland Antiq Archaeol Soc,* n ser, **73**, 47-66

Cherry, J, and Cherry, P J, 1986 Prehistoric habitation sites in west Cumbria: part IV, the Eskmeals area, *Trans Cumberland Westmorland Antiq Archaeol Soc,* n ser, **86**, 1-18

Cherry, J, and Cherry, P J, 1987 *Prehistoric habitation sites on the limestone uplands of Eastern Cumbria,* Cumberland Westmorland Antiq Archaeol Soc, Res Ser, **2**, Kendal

Cherry, J, and Fletcher, W, 1964 Cairn on Birker Moor, rescue dig, *Trans Cumberland Westmorland Antiq Archaeol Soc,* n ser, **64**, 373

Chiverrell, R C, 2006 Past and future perspectives upon landscape instability in Cumbria, *Reg Environ Change,* **6**, 101-14

Clare, T, 1980 *Interim note on a study of the Langdale axe factory sites,* unpubl rep

Claris, P, and Quartermaine, J, 1989 The neolithic quarries and axe factory sites of Great Langdale and Scafell Pike: a new field survey, *Proc Prehist Soc,* **55**, 1-25

Clifton Ward, J, 1878 Notes on archaeological remains in the Lake District, *Trans Cumberland Westmorland Antiq Archaeol Soc,* 1 ser, **3**, 241-63

Coggins, D, Fairless, K J, and Batey, C E, 1983 Simy Folds: an early medieval settlement site in Upper Teesdale, Co Durham, *Medieval Archaeol,* **27**, 1-26

Collingwood, R G, 1937 Two Roman mountain roads, *Trans Cumberland Westmorland Antiq Archaeol Soc,* n ser, **37**, 1-12

Collingwood, W G, 1908 Report on an exploration of the Romano-British settlement at Ewe Close, Crosby Ravensworth, *Trans Cumberland Westmorland Antiq Archaeol Soc,* n ser, **8**, 355-68

Collingwood, W G, 1923 An inventory of the ancient monuments of Cumberland, *Trans Cumberland Westmorland Antiq Archaeol Soc*, n ser, **23**, 206-76

Condliffe, I, 2009 Policy change in the uplands, in A Bonn, T Allot, K Hubacek, and J Stewart (eds), *Drivers of environmental change in the uplands*, Oxford, 59-89

Coombes, P M V, Chiverrell, R C, and Barber, K E, 2009 A high-resolution pollen and geochemical analysis of late Holocene human impact and vegetation history in southern Cumbria, England, *J Quat Sci*, **24 (3)**, 224-36

Cousins, J, 2009 *Friends of the Lake District: the early years*, Lancaster

Crawford, G, and George, C, 1983 *An archaeological survey of Copeland*, Cumbria County Council Planning Department, unpubl rep

Crone, A, and Mills, C, 1988 Lochportain linear clearance cairn, North Uist, *CEU/AML Ann Rep*, Edinburgh, 32-3

Daniel, G F, 1950 *Prehistoric chamber tombs of England and Wales*, Cambridge

Darbishire, R D, 1873 Note on discoveries in Ehenside Tarn, *Archaeologia*, **44**, 273-92

Dartmoor National Park Authority, 2006 *The Vision for Dartmoor*, < http://www.dartmoor-npa.gov.uk/aboutus/news/au-geninterestnews/au-2006-archive/au_visionlaunchnews>

Darvill, T, 1986a *The archaeology of the uplands: a rapid assessment of archaeological knowledge and practice*, London

Darvill, T, 1986b *Upland archaeology: what future for the past?*, London

Darvill, T, and Fulton, A, 1998 *The Monuments at Risk Survey of England 1995, Main Report*, Bournemouth and London

Davies-Shiel, M, 1974 A little known late medieval industry, part II: the ash burners, *Trans Cumberland Westmorland Antiq Archaeol Soc*, n ser, **74**, 33-64

Dickinson, S, 1985 Bryant's Gill, Kentmere: another 'Viking' period Ribblehead?, in J Baldwin and I Whyte (eds), *The Scandinavians in Cumbria*, Edinburgh, 83-8

Dimbleby, G W, 1961 The ancient forest of Blackamore, *Antiquity*, **35**, 123-8

Duddon Valley Local History Group, and Lake District National Park Authority, 2009 *Ring cairns to reservoirs: archaeological discoveries in the Duddon Valley, Cumbria*, Kendal

Dumayne-Peaty, L, and Barber, K E, 1998 Late Holocene vegetational history: human impact and pollen representativity variations in northern Cumbria, England, *J Quat Sci*, **13**, 147-64

Dymond, C W, 1893 Barnscar: an ancient settlement in Cumberland, *Trans Cumberland Westmorland Antiq Archaeol Soc*, 1 ser, **12**, 179-87

Edwards, K J, 1977 Excavation and environmental archaeology of a small cairn associated with cultivation ridges in Aberdeenshire, *Proc Soc Antiq Scotland*, **109**, 22-9

English Heritage, 1988 *Monuments Protection Programme simple monument class description: burnt mounds*, London

English Heritage, 2006 *Heritage Partnership Agreement: Central Lakeland neolithic stone axe factories, prehistoric ring cairns and medieval shielings*, unpubl rep

English Heritage, 2008 *Scheduled Monuments at Risk North West*, London

Ehrenberg, M R, 1990 Some aspects of the distribution of burnt mounds, in M A Hodder and L H Barfield (eds), *Burnt mounds and hot stone technology: papers from the second international burnt mound conference, Sandwell, 12th – 14th October 1990*, Sandwell, 41–58

Eskdale and District Local History Society, 2008 *Walking in the footsteps of Mary Fair: an archaeological reconsideration of a group of ancient remains near Eskdale Green and on Muncaster Fell*, Eskdale Green

Evans, F, 1842 *Furness and Furness Abbey*, Ulverston

Evans, H, 2008 *Neolithic and Bronze Age landscapes of Cumbria*, BAR Brit Ser, **463**, Oxford

Eyre, S R, 1955 The curving plough strip and its historical implications, *Agricult Hist Rev*, **3**, 80-94

Feachem, R W, 1973 Ancient agriculture in the highland of Britain, *Proc Prehist Soc*, **39**, 332-53

Fell, C I, 1970 A settlement at Brantrake Moss, north of Devoke Water, *Trans Cumberland Westmorland Antiq Archaeol Soc*, n ser, **70**, 287-9

Fell, C I, 1972, *Early settlement in the Lake counties*, Clapham

Field, D, 1999 Barrows, cairns and harmony in the prehistoric landscape of Northumberland, in P Frodsham, P Topping, and D Cowley (eds), 'We were always chasing time', papers presented to Keith Blood, *Northern Archaeol*, **17/18**, 35-8

Field, J, 1993 *A history of English field names*, Harlow

Fleming, A, 1971 Bronze Age agriculture on the marginal lands of north-east Yorkshire, *Agricult Hist Rev*, **19**, 1-24

Fleming, A, 1988 *The Dartmoor Reaves: investigating prehistoric land divisions*, London

Fletcher, W, and Fell, C I, 1987 Stone-based huts and other structures at Smithy Beck, Ennerdale, *Trans Cumberland Westmorland Antiq Archaeol Soc*, n ser, **87**, 27-36

Forestry Commission, 2002 *An accord between the Association of National Park Authorities and the Forestry Commision*, http://www.forestry.gov.uk/pdf/nat-parks-accord.pdf/$FILE/nat-parks-accord.pdf

Forestry Commission, 2003 *The management of semi-natural woodlands. 3 Lowland mixed broadleaved woods: practice guide*, Edinburgh

Fowler, P, 1981 Wildscape to landscape: enclosure in prehistoric Britain, in R J Mercer (ed), *Farming practice in British prehistory*, Edinburgh, 9-54

Fowler, P, 1983 *The farming of prehistoric Britain*, Cambridge

Frodsham, P, and Waddington, C, 2004 The Beamish Valley Archaeology Project, 1994-2002, in P Frodsham (ed), *Archaeology in Northumberland National Park*, York

Gates, T, 1981 Excavations at Hallshill Farm, East Woodburn, Northumberland, *Univ Durham Newcastle Archaeol Rep*, **5**, 7-9

Gates, T, 1983 Unenclosed settlement in Northumberland, in J Chapman and H Mytum (eds), *Settlement in Northern Britain 1000 BC-1000 AD*, BAR Brit Ser, **118**, Oxford, 103-48

Gerrard, S, 2001 The Dartmoor archaeology and bracken project, *PAST*, **37**, 8-10

Godwin, H, 1975, *The history of the British flora*, 2nd edn, Cambridge

Goudie, A, 1983 *Environmental change*, 2nd edn, Oxford

Graham, A, 1956 Cairnfields in Scotland, *Proc Soc Antiq Scotland*, **90**, 7-23

Greenwell, W, 1877 *British barrows: a record of the examination of sepulchral mounds in various parts of England*, Oxford

Grinsell, L V, 1953 *The ancient burial mounds of England*, London

Hall, D, 2001 *Turning the plough: Midlands open fields, landscape character and proposals for management*, Northampton

Hall, G, 1824 Carl Loft's at Shap, Westmorland, *Gentleman's Mag*, **94/1**, 3

Halliday, G, 1997 *A flora of Cumbria*, Lancaster

Harding, A , and Ostoja-Zagorski, J, 1994 Prehistoric and early medieval activity on Danby Rigg, North Yorkshire, *Archaeol J*, **151**, 16-97

Harris, J, 1984 A preliminary survey of hut circles and field systems in south-east Perthshire, *Proc Soc Antiq Scotland*, **114**, 199-216

Haselgrove, C, 2002 The later Bronze Age and the Iron Age in the lowlands, in C Brooks, R Daniels, and A Harding (eds), *Past, present and future: the archaeology of Northern England*, Durham, 49-70

Hay, T, 1938 Ullswater notes, *Trans Cumberland Westmorland Antiq Archaeol Soc*, n ser, **38**, 42-7

Hay, T, 1943 The ford over Elder Beck, *Trans Cumberland Westmorland Antiq Archaeol Soc*, n ser, **43**, 25-7

Hayes, R H, and Rutter, J G, 1964 *Wades causeway: a Roman road in North-East Yorkshire*, Scarborough Dist Archaeol Soc Res Rep, **4**, Scarborough

Heawood, R, and Huckerby, E, 2002 Excavation of a burnt mound at Sparrowmire Farm, Kendal, *Trans Cumberland Westmorland Antiq Archaeol Soc*, 3 ser, **2**, 29-49

Hedges, J, 1975 Excavation of two Orcadian burnt mounds at Liddle and Beaquoy, *Proc Soc Antiq Scotland* (1974-5), **106**, 38-98

Hedges, R E M, Housley, R A, Bronk Ramsey, C, and Van Klinken, G J, 1994 Radiocarbon dates from the Oxford AMS system: Archaeometry Datelist 18, *Archaeometry*, **36/2**, 337-74

Hedley, I, and Quartermaine, J A, 2004 Simonside from prehistory to present, in P Frodsham (ed), *Archaeology in Northumberland National Park*, York, 338-49

Higham, N, 1986 *Northern counties to AD 1000*, Harlow

Hindle, B P, 1984 *Roads and trackways of the Lake District*, Ashbourne

Hoaen, A, and Loney, H, 2003 Later prehistoric settlement in Matterdale and Hutton parishes: recent survey results, *Trans Cumberland Westmorland Antiq Archaeol Soc*, 3 ser, **3**, 51-65

Hoaen, A, and Loney, H, 2004 Bronze and Iron Age connections: memory and persistence in Matterdale, Cumbria, *Trans Cumberland Westmorland Antiq Archaeol Soc*, 3 ser, **4**, 39-55

Hodgkinson, D, Huckerby, E, Middleton, R, and Wells, C E, 2000 *The lowland wetlands of Cumbria*, Lancaster Imprints, **8**, Lancaster

Hodgson, J, 2007 Burnt mounds in the Lake District, Cumbria, in C Burgess, P Topping, and F Lynch (eds), *Beyond Stonehenge: essays on the Bronze Age in honour of Colin Burgess*, Oxford, 204-12

Hodgson, J, and Brennand, M, 2007 The prehistoric period research agenda, in M Brennand (ed), *Research and archaeology in north west England: an archaeological research framework for north west England: Vol 2, research agenda and strategy*, Archaeol North West, **9**, Manchester, 31-54

Hodgson, N, Stobbs, G, and van der Veen, M, 2001 An Iron-Age settlement and remains of earlier prehistoric date beneath South Shields Roman fort, Tyne and Wear, *Archaeol J*, **158**, 62-160

Horne, P, and Oswald, A, 2000 *A probable neolithic causewayed enclosure on Green How, Cumbria*, Archaeol Investigation Rep Ser, **AI/19/2000**, unpubl rep

Howard-Davis, C, and Williams, J H, 2005 Excavations on a Bronze Age cairn at Hardendale Nab, Shap, Cumbria, *Archaeol J*, **161** (for 2004), 11-53

Huckerby, E, and Wells, C, 1993 Recent work at Solway Moss, Cumbria, in R Middleton (ed), *North West Wetlands Survey annual report 1993*, Lancaster, 37-42

Huntley, B, 1993 Rapid early-Holocene migration and high abundance of hazel (*Corylus avellana L*): alternative hypothesis, in F M Chambers (ed), *Climate change and human impact on the landscape*, London, 205-14

Hutchinson, W, 1794 *The history of the county of Cumberland*, 2 vols, Carlisle

Inizan, M L, Roche, H, and Tixier, J, 1992 *Technology of knapped stone*, Cercle de Reserches et d'Etudes Prehistoriques, Meudon

James, N D G, 1981 *A history of English forestry*, Oxford

Jecock, M, Lax, A, and Dunn, C, 2003 *Elterwater gunpowder works, Cumbria: an archaeological and historical survey*, Engl Herit Surv Rep Ser, **AI/9/2003**, unpubl rep

Jobey, G, 1962 An Iron Age homestead at West Brandon, Durham, *Archaeol Aeliana*, 4 ser, **40**, 1-34

Jobey, G, 1964 Enclosed stone built settlements in north Northumberland, *Archaeol Aeliana*, 4 ser, **42**, 41-64

Jobey, G, 1966 Homesteads and settlements of the frontier area, in C Thomas (ed), *Rural settlement in Roman Britain*, CBA Res Rep, **7**, London, 1-14

Jobey, G, 1968 Excavations of cairns at Chatton Sandyford, Northumberland, *Archaeol Aeliana*, 4 ser, **48**, 4-50

Jobey, G, 1980 Unenclosed platforms and settlements of the later 2nd millennium BC in northern Britain, *Scot Archaeol Forum*, **10**, 12-26

Jobey, G, 1981 Groups of small cairns and the excavation of a cairnfield on Millstone Hill, Northumberland, *Archaeol Aeliana*, 5 ser, **9**, 23-43

Jobey, G, 1983 Excavation of an unenclosed settlement on Standrop Rigg, Northumberland, and some problems related to similar settlements between Tyne and Forth, *Archaeol Aeliana*, 5 ser, **11**, 1-21

Jobey, G, 1985 The unenclosed settlements of Tyne-Forth: a summary, in D Spratt and C Burgess (eds), *Upland settlement in Britain: the second millennium and after*, BAR Brit Ser, **143**, Oxford, 177-94

Jobey, G, and Tait, J, 1966 Excavations on palisaded settlements and cairnfields at Alnham, Northumberland, *Archaeol Aeliana*, 4 ser, **44**, 5-47

Johnson, D, 2002 *Limestone industries of the Yorkshire Dales*, Stroud

Johnson, D, 2004 *Excavation of Broadwood Enclosure, Thornton in Lonsdale, North Yorkshire: report on the excavation of a Romano-British enclosure and 17th-century lime kiln*, Ingleton

Johnson, N, and Rose, P, 1994 *Bodmin Moor: an archaeological survey, volume 1: the human landscape to c 1800*, Engl Herit Archaeol Rep, **24**, RCHM(E) Suppl Ser, **11**, London

Jones, G P, 1966 Two Hudleston and Senhouse account books, *Trans Cumberland Westmorland Antiq Archaeol Soc*, n ser, **66**, 312-38

Kinnes, I, 1979 *Round barrows and ring ditches in the British neolithic*, Brit Mus Occ Pap, **7**, London

Lake District National Park Partnership, 2005 *State of the Park report*, www.lakedistrict.gov.uk/caringfor/state_of_the_park

Lamb, H H, 1977 *Climate: past, present and future, volume 2: climate history and the modern world*, London

Lamb, H H, 1981 Climate from 1000 BC to 1000 AD, in M Jones and G Dimbleby (eds), *The environment of man: the Iron Age to the Anglo-Saxon period*, BAR Brit Ser, **87**, Oxford, 53-65

Lambert, J K, 1989 *Charcoal burners and wood cutters of the Furness Fells 1701-1851*, unpubl MA thesis, Univ Liverpool

Leech, R H, 1982 *An assessment of the sites and monuments records for Cumbria and Lancashire*, unpubl rep

Leech, R H, 1983 Settlements and groups of small cairns on Birkby and Birker Fells, Eskdale, Cumbria: survey undertaken in 1982, *Trans Cumberland Westmorland Antiq Archaeol Soc*, n ser, **83**, 15-26

Leighton, D, 1997 *Mynydd Du and Fforest Fawr: the evolution of an upland landscape in south Wales*, Aberystwyth

Lofthouse, C, 1997 *Coniston Copper Mines: archaeological survey report*, RCHM(E), unpubl rep

Loney, H L, and Hoaen, A W, 2000 Excavations at Baldhowend, Matterdale, 1998: an interim report, *Trans Cumberland Westmorland Antiq Archaeol Soc*, n ser, **100**, 89-103

LUAU, 1989 *The 'Langcliffe Quarry' limeworks, Settle: an archaeological survey of the site and Hoffman limekiln*, unpubl rep

LUAU, 1994a *Torver High Common survey report*, unpubl rep

LUAU, 1994b *Langdale erosion research programme project report*, unpubl rep

LUAU, 1994c *Blengdale forest plantation, Cumbria: archaeological watching brief*, unpubl rep

LUAU, 1995 *Torver Low and Blawith Commons: archaeological survey*, unpubl rep

LUAU, 1997a *Forest of Bowland, Lancashire: archaeological survey*, unpubl rep

LUAU, 1997b *Thirlmere Estate, Cumbria, archaeological survey*, unpubl rep

LUAU, 1997c *North West Water Haweswater Estate, Cumbria: archaeological survey*, unpubl rep

LUAU, 1997d *Lowther Estate, Cumbria, archaeological survey*, unpubl rep

LUAU, 1997e *Lowther Park, Cumbria: detailed archaeological survey*, unpubl rep

LUAU, 1997f *Sellafield Tip Extension, Cumbria: Evaluation Report*, unpubl rep

LUAU, 1998a *Haweswater Estate, Cumbria: Phase 4 detail survey*, unpubl rep

LUAU, 1998b *Thirlmere Estate, Cumbria, detail survey*, unpubl rep

LUAU, 1998c *Ennerdale Forest archaeological survey: final report*, unpubl rep

LUAU, 1999 *Hampsfield Allotment, Whitbarrow and Brigsteer Woods, Cumbria: assessment survey*, unpubl rep

LUAU, 2000a *Analysis of post-Bronze Age deposits at Littlewater, Cumbria*, unpubl rep

LUAU, 2000b *Nidderdale AONB, North Yorkshire: archaeological survey*, unpubl rep

LUAU, 2000c *Miterdale and Giggle Alley Forests, Cumbria: archaeological assessment survey*, unpubl rep

Lund, J, and Southwell, C, 2002 *An archaeological monitoring report for The Great Langdale Valley*, National Trust, unpubl rep

Lynch, F M, 1972 Ring cairns and related monuments in Wales, *Scot Archaeol Forum*, **4**, 61-80

Lynch, F M, 1979 Ring cairns in Britain and Ireland: their design and purpose, *Ulster J Archaeol*, **42**, 1-19

Lynch, F M, 1993 *Excavations in the Brenig Valley; a mesolithic and Bronze Age landscape in north Wales*, Cardiff

MacLaren, A, 1967 Recent excavations in Peebleshire, *Proc Soc Antiq Scotland*, **99**, 93-103

Manby, T, 1970 Long barrows of northern England: structural and dating evidence, *Scot Archaeol Forum*, **2**, 1-27

Margary, I D, 1973 *Roman roads in Britain*, 3rd edn, London

Masters, L, 1973 The Lochhill long cairn, *Antiquity*, **47**, 96-100

Masters, L, 1984 The neolithic long cairns of Cumbria and Northumberland, in R Miket and C Burgess (eds), *Between and beyond the walls*, Newcastle, 52-73

Mendus, A, 2001 *A survey of late neolithic and Early Bronze Age summit and ridge top cairns in West Cumbria*, unpubl BA diss, Univ Sheffield

Middleton, R, 1985 A survey of the old copper works, Coppermines Valley, Coniston, *Trans Cumberland Westmorland Antiq Archaeol Soc*, n ser, **85**, 273-4

Middleton, R, Wells, C, and Huckerby, E, 1995 *The wetlands of North Lancashire*, Lancaster Imprints, **4**, Lancaster

Ministry of Agriculture, Fisheries, and Food, 1994 *Environmentally Sensitive Areas Scheme: environmental objectives and performance indicators for ESAs in England*, London

Moore, P D, Webb, J A, and Collinson, M E, 1991 *Pollen analysis*, 2nd edn, Oxford

Moseley, F (ed), 1978 *The geology of the Lake District*, Yorkshire Geol Soc Occ Pap, **3**, Leeds

National Trust, 2000 *Wasdale Head: an historic landscape survey*, unpubl rep

Natural England, 2008 *Responding to the impacts of climate change on the natural environment: the Cumbria High Fells, a summary*, unpubl rep

Natural England, 2009 *Vital uplands: a 2060 vision for England's upland environment*, Newcastle upon Tyne

Needham, S, 1996 Chronology and periodisation in the British Bronze Age, *Acta Archaeologica*, **67**, 121-40

Neighbour, T, and Johnson, M, 2005 A Bronze Age burnt mound in lowland Cumbria: excavations at Garlands Hospital, Carlisle, 1997, *Trans Cumberland Westmorland Antiq Archaeol Soc*, 3 ser, **5**, 11-24

Newman, R M, 2006 The early medieval period resource assessment, in M Brennand (ed), *The archaeology of North West England: an archaeological research framework for north west England: volume 1, resource assessment*, Archaeol North West, **8**, Manchester, 91-114

Nicholson, J, and Burn, R, 1777 *The history and antiquities of the counties of Westmorland and Cumberland*, 2 vols, London

O'Drisceoil, D A, 1988 Burnt mounds: cooking or bathing?, *Antiquity*, **62**, 671-80

OA North, 2002 *Grassguards and Hardknott Forest, Cumbria: archaeological assessment and survey report*, unpubl rep

OA North, 2003a *Ennerdale Valley historic landscape survey*, unpubl rep

OA North, 2003b *Hartley Fold Estate survey, John Strutt Conservation Foundation, Cumbria*, unpubl rep

OA North, 2004a *Site 123, Harrison Coombe, Great Langdale*, unpubl rep

OA North, 2004b *Uplands Initiative Field Projects 2003-4: Eastern Snowdonia (North) survey report*, unpubl rep

OA North, 2004c *Roulston Scar, Sutton Bank, North Yorks: assessment and watching brief report*, unpubl rep

OA North, 2005a *St Catherine's, Windermere, Cumbria: historic landscape survey report*, unpubl rep

OA North, 2005b *Stickle Tarn, Great Langdale, Cumbria: archaeological survey report*, unpubl rep

OA North, 2006 *Uplands Initiative Field Projects 2005-6: Nantle to Beddgelert survey area*, unpubl rep

OA North, 2007a *Paddy End dressing floors, Coniston Copper Mines, Cumbria: archaeological survey report*, unpubl rep

OA North, 2007b *Lowther Castle gardens, Cumbria: archaeological survey report*, unpubl rep

OA North, 2007c *Borrowdale, Cumbria: historic landscape survey*, unpubl rep

OA North, 2009a *Upland Peats: managerial assessment, final report*, unpubl rep

OA North, 2009b *Buttermere, Cumbria: historic landscape survey, volume 1*, unpubl rep

OA North, 2009c *Land at Nether Wasdale, Cumbria: historic landscape survey report*, unpubl rep

OA North, 2009d *Little Asby Scar and Sunbiggin Tarn Common, Eden District, Cumbria: detailed archaeological survey report*, unpubl rep

OA North, 2010a *East Coniston woodland, Cumbria: historic landscape survey report*, unpubl rep

OA North, 2010b *Drigg burnt mound, Cumbria: assessment report and updated project design*, unpubl rep

OA North, 2010c *Skipwith Common – Phase 3, North Yorkshire: airfield and archaeological landscape survey report*, unpubl rep

OA North, 2011a *Stainton West (Parcel 27 North) CNDR, Cumbria: post-excavation assessment*, unpubl rep

OA North, 2011b *Carlisle Northern Development Route, Cumbria: post-excavation assessment*, unpubl rep

Oldfield, F, 1969 Pollen analysis and the history and land use, *Advancement of Science*, **25**, 298–311

Olivier, A C H, 1987 Excavation of a Bronze Age funerary cairn at Manor Farm, near Borwick, north Lancashire, *Proc Prehist Soc*, **53**, 129-86

Palmer, C, 1985 *Evolution of a landscape: Town Bank, Kinniside Common, Cumbria*, unpubl BA diss, Univ Durham

Parker, C A, 1904 *The Gosforth District: its antiquities and places of interest*, Kendal

Pearsall, W H, and Pennington, W, 1973 *The Lake District*, London

Pennington, W, 1964 Pollen analyses from the deposits of six upland tarns in the Lake District, *Phil Trans Royal Soc London, B*, **248**, 205-44

Pennington, W, 1965a Appendix, in J Cherry, Flint-chipping sites at Drigg, *Trans Cumberland Westmorland Antiq Archaeol Soc*, n ser, **65**, 82-5

Pennington, W, 1965b The interpretation of some post-glacial vegetation diversities at different Lake District sites, *Proc Royal Soc London, B*, **161**, 310-23

Pennington, W, 1970 Vegetation history in the north-west of England: a regional synthesis, in D Walker and R G West (eds), *Studies in the vegetational history of the British Isles*, London, 41-79

Pennington, W, 1973 Pollen analysis at the Langdale axe chipping site, *Trans Cumberland Westmorland Antiq Archaeol Soc*, n ser, **73**, 43-6

Pennington, W, 1975 The effect of neolithic man on the environment in north-west England: the use of absolute pollen diagrams, in J G Evans,

S Limbrey, and H Cleere (eds), *The effect of man on the landscape: the Highland zone*, CBA Res Rep, **11**, London, 74-86

Pennington, W, 1978 Quaternary geology, in Moseley 1978, 207-25

Pennington, W, 1981 Record of a lake's life in time: the sediments, *Hydrobiologia*, **79**, 197-219

Pennington, W, 1991 Palaeolimnology in the English Lakes - some questions and answers over fifty years, *Hydrobiologia*, **214**, 9-24

Pennington, W, 1997 Vegetational history, in Halliday 1997, 42-50

Pennington, W, 2003 Evidence from the tarns of vegetation, soils, climate and human settlement, in E Haworth, G de Boer, I Evans, H Osmaston, W Pennington, A Smith, P Storey, and B Ware (eds), *Tarns of the central Lake District*, Kendal, 20-8

Pennington, W, and Lishman, J P, 1984 The post-glacial sediments of Blelham Tarn: geochemistry and palaeoecology, *Arch Hydrobiol*, **69** (suppl), 1-54

Potter, B, 1903 *The tale of Squirrel Nutkin*, London

Potter, T W, 1979 *Romans in north-west England*, Cumberland Westmorland Antiq Archaeol Soc, Res ser, **1**, Kendal

Prehistoric Society, 1981 *National priorities for prehistoric archaeology*, London

Quartermaine, J, 1989 Interim results of survey work on Stockdale Moor and Town Bank, west Cumbria, *Trans Cumberland Westmorland Antiq Archaeol Soc*, n ser, **89**, 25-31

Rackham, O, 1980 *Ancient woodland*, London

Radley, J, 1966 A Bronze Age ring work on Totley Moor, and other Bronze Age ring works in the Pennines, *Archaeol J*, **123**, 1-26

Ramm, H G, 1970 Shielings, farmsteads and stack stands in the northern Border Country, in H G Ramm, R W McDowall, and E Mercer (eds), *Shielings and bastles*, RCHM(E), London, 1-57

Reimer, P J, Baillie, M G L, Bard, E, Bayliss, A, Beck, J W, Blackwell, P G, Bronk Ramsey, C, Buck, C E, Burr, G S, Edwards, R L, Friedrich, M, Grootes, P M, Guilderson, T P, Hajdas, I, Heaton, T J, Hogg, A G, Hughen, K A, Kaiser, K F, Kromer, B, McCormac, F G, Manning, S W, Reimer, R W, Richards, D A, Southon, J R, Talamo, S,

Turney, C S M, van der Plicht, J, and Weyhenmeyer, C E, 2009 IntCal09 and Marine09 radiocarbon age calibration curves, 0-50,000 years cal BP, *Radiocarbon*, **51(4)**, 1111-50

Renfrew, C, and Bahn, P, 1991 *Archaeology: theories, methods and practice*, London

Reynolds, P, 1981 Deadstock and livestock, in E Mercer (ed), *Farming practice in British prehistory*, Edinburgh, 97-122

Richardson, C, 1982 Excavations at Birrel Sike, near Low Prior Scales, Calder Valley, Cumbria, *Trans Cumberland Westmorland Antiq Archaeol Soc*, n ser, **82**, 7-27

Ritchie, A, 1970 Palisaded sites in north Britain: their context and affinities, *Scot Archaeol Forum*, **2**, 48-67

Ritchie, J N G, Thornber, I, Lynch, F, and Marshall, D N, 1975 Small cairns in Argyll: some recent work, *Proc Soc Antiq Scotland*, **106**, 15-38

RCAHMS (Royal Commission on the Ancient and Historical Monuments of Scotland), 1990 *North-East Perth: an archaeological landscape*, London

RCAHMS (Royal Commission on the Ancient and Historical Monuments of Scotland), 1997 *Eastern Dumfriesshire: an archaeological landscape*, London

RCAHMS (Royal Commission on the Ancient and Historical Monuments of Scotland), 2007 *In the shadow of Bennachie: a field archaeology of Donside, Aberdeenshire*, London

RCHM(E) (Royal Commission on Historical Monuments (England)), 1936 *An inventory of the historical monuments in Westmorland*, London

Rogers, P, 2000 Ring and boulder cairns on the Langdale and Grasmere Fells, Lake District National Park, *Archaeol North*, **17**, 16-18

Rollinson, W, 1996 *A history of Cumberland and Westmorland*, London

Scott-Elliott, J, and Rae, I, 1965 Whitestanes Moor (Sites 1 and 80) – an enclosed cremation cemetery, *Trans Dumfriesshire Galloway Natur Hist Antiq Soc*, **42**, 51-60

SEARS, 2008 *Bracken control: a guide to best practice*, Natural Scotland, Edinburgh

Shotter, D C A, 1996 *The Roman frontier in Britain*, Preston

Silvester, R J, 2011 *Mynydd Hiraethog, the Denbigh Moors: discovering upland heritage*, Aberystwyth

Simpson, C, 1883 Stone circles near Shap, Westmorland, *Trans Cumberland Westmorland Antiq Archaeol Soc*, 1 ser, **6**, 176-82

Smith, A H, 1967 *The place-names of Westmorland: volume 1: introduction, river and lake names, road names, the Barony of Kendal*, Engl Place-Name Soc, **42**, Cambridge

Smith, G H, 1978 Excavations near Hadrian's Wall at Tarraby Lane 1976, *Britannia*, **9**, 19-56

Smith, I F, 1974 The neolithic, in C Renfrew (ed), *British prehistory*, London, 100-36

Spence, J, 1934 An early settlement on Moor Divock, *Trans Cumberland Westmorland Antiq Archaeol Soc*, n ser, **34**, 45-9

Spence, J, 1935a A note on tumuli on Threepow Raise, Moor Divock, *Trans Cumberland Westmorland Antiq Archaeol Soc*, n ser, **35**, 66-8

Spence, J, 1935b An early settlement near Askham, *Trans Cumberland Westmorland Antiq Archaeol Soc*, n ser, **35**, 61-5

Spence, J, 1937 Bolton Wood enclosure, *Trans Cumberland Westmorland Antiq Archaeol Soc*, n ser, **37**, 43-8

Spence, J, 1938 Ancient enclosures on Town Bank, Kinniside, *Trans Cumberland Westmorland Antiq Archaeol Soc*, n ser, **38**, 63-70

Spence, J, 1939 Ancient remains in Ennerdale and Kinniside Parish, *Trans Cumberland Westmorland Antiq Archaeol Soc*, n ser, **39**, 31-5

Spratt, D (ed), 1990 *Prehistoric and Roman archaeology of north-east Yorkshire*, London

Stone, J L, and Horne, P D, 2003 *Fylingdales Moor, North Yorkshire, survey report*, Engl Herit, **AER/07/2003**, unpubl rep

Sturdy, D, 1972 A ring cairn in Levens Park, Westmorland, *Scot Archaeol Forum*, **4**, 52-5

Swainson-Cowper, H, 1893 The ancient settlements and earthworks of Furness, *Archaeologia*, **53 (2)**, 389-426

Sweeting, M, 1974 Karst geomorphology in north-west England, in A C Waltham (ed), *The limestones and caves of north-west England*, Newton Abbot, 46-78

Symonds, H H, 1936 *Afforestation in the Lake District*, London

Tauber, H, 1967 Investigations of the mode of pollen transfer in forested areas, *Rev Palaeobot Palynol*, **3**, 277-86

Taylor, J J T, Jones, M D H, Innes, J B, and Oldfield, F, 1987 *Little Hawes Water project*, Univ Liverpool, unpubl rep

Taylor, M W, 1870 On the vestiges of Celtic occupation near Ullswater, and on the discovery of buried stone circles by Eamont side, *Trans Cumberland Westmorland Antiq Archaeol Soc*, 1 ser, **1**, 154-68

Taylor, M W, 1886 The prehistoric remains on Moordivock, near Ullswater, *Trans Cumberland Westmorland Antiq Archaeol Soc*, 1 ser, **8**, 323-47

Tennyson, A Baron, 1830 *Poems, chiefly lyrical*, London

The Morecambe Bay Archaeological Society, 2006 Evaluation of a burnt mound, Aldingham, Cumbria, *Trans Cumberland Westmorland Antiq Archaeol Soc*, 3 ser, **6**, 17-27

Thom, A, 1967 *Megalithic sites in Britain*, Oxford

Thompson, M W, 1983 *The journeys of Sir Richard Colt Hoare, 1793-1810*, Gloucester

Thorpe, I J N, 1994 *The Stephenson Ground survey project: write-up of a talk to the Cumberland and Westmorland Antiquarian and Archaeological Society*, unpubl doc

Thorpe, I J N, and Ball, P, 1994 *Stephenson Ground survey project 1994: interim*, unpubl rep

Tipping, E, Thacker, S A, Wilson, D, and Hall, J R, 2008 Long-term nitrate increases in two oligotrophic lakes, due to the leaching of atmospherically-deposited N from moorland ranker soils, *Environmental pollution*, **152**, 41-9

Tipping, R, 1994 Williamson's Moss: palynological evidence for the mesolithic-neolithic transition in Cumbria, in J Boardman and J Walden (eds), *Cumbria field guide*, Quat Res Assoc, Oxford, 104-27

Topping, P, 1989a The context of cord rig cultivation in later prehistoric Northumberland, in M Bowden, D Mackay, and P Topping (eds), *From Cornwall to Caithness: some aspects of British field archaeology*, BAR Brit Ser, **209**, Oxford, 145-57

Topping, P, 1989b Early cultivation in Northumberland and the Borders, *Proc Prehist Soc*, **55**, 161-79

Turner, V E, 1986 Shapbeck stone circle, *Trans Cumberland Westmorland Antiq Archaeol Soc*, n ser, **86**, 248-50

Turner, V E, 1987 Results of survey work carried out in the Caldbeck Fells, Cumbria, *Trans Cumberland Westmorland Antiq Archaeol Soc*, n ser, **87**, 19-26

Turner, V E, 1991 Results of survey work carried out between the Shap and Askham Fells, Cumbria, *Trans Cumberland Westmorland Antiq Archaeol Soc*, n ser, **91**, 1-11

UK Climate Impacts Programme, 1998 *Changing by degrees: the impacts of climate change in the north west of England*, Manchester

Wainwright, A, 1955 *A pictorial guide to the Lakeland Fells: being an illustrated account of a study and exploration of the mountains in the English Lake District, Book one: The Eastern Fells*, Kentmere

Wainwright, G, Fleming, A, and Smith, K, 1979 The Shaugh Moor project: first report, *Proc Prehist Soc*, **45**, 1-33

Walker, D, 1965a The post-glacial period in the Langdale Fells, English Lake District, *New Phytol*, **64**, 488-510

Walker, D, 1965b Excavations at Barnscar, 1957-58, *Trans Cumberland Westmorland Antiq Archaeol Soc*, n ser, **65**, 53-65

Walker, D, 1966 The Late Quaternary history of the Cumberland lowland, *Phil Trans Roy Soc London, B*, **251**, 1-210

Walker, D, 2001 The dates of human impact on the environment at Ehenside Tarn, Cumbria, *Trans Cumberland Westmorland Antiq Archaeol Soc*, 3 ser, **1**, 1-20

Walker, A J, and Otlet, R L, 1985 Harwell radiocarbon measuresments IV, *Radiocarbon*, **27 (1)**, 74-94

Ward, A H, 1988 Survey and excavation of ring cairns in south-east Dyfed and on Gower, West Glamorgan, *Proc Prehist Soc*, **54**, 153-72

Ward, J, 1977 Cairns on Corney Fell, west Cumberland, *Trans Cumberland Westmorland Antiq Archaeol Soc*, n ser, **77**, 1-6

Waterhouse, J, 1985 *The stone circles of Cumbria*, Chichester

Webster, R A, 1972 Excavation of a Romano-British settlement at Waitby, Westmorland, *Trans Cumberland Westmorland Antiq Archaeol Soc*, n ser, **72**, 66-73

Wells, C, 2003 Environmental changes in Roman north west England: a synoptic overview of events north of the Ribble, *Trans Cumberland Westmorland Antiq Archaeol Soc*, 3 ser, **3**, 67-84

West, T, 1780 *A guide to the Lakes, in Cumberland, Westmorland, and Lancashire*, 2nd edn, London

Whitehead, P G, Barlow, J, Howarth, E Y, and Adamson, J K, 1997 Acidification in three Lake District tarns: historical long term trends and modelled future behaviour under changing sulphate and nitrate deposition, *Hydrology and Earth System Sci*, **1**, 197-204

Whyte, I, 2003 Wild, barren and frightful; Parliamentary enclosure in an upland county: Westmorland 1767-1890, *Rural Hist*, **14 (1)**, 21-8

Williams, B, 1856 On some ancient monuments in the county of Cumberland, *Proc Soc Antiq London*, 1 ser, **3**, 224-7

Williamson, T, 1987 Early co-axial field systems on the East Anglian boulder clays, *Proc Prehist Soc*, **53**, 419-31

Wilson, J (ed), 1915 *The register of the Priory of St Bees*, Surtees Soc, **194**, Durham and London

Wimble, G, 1986 *The palaeoecology of the lowland coastal raised mires of South Cumbria*, unpubl PhD thesis, Cardiff Univ

Wimble, G, Wells, C E, and Hodgkinson, D, 2000 Human impact on mid- and late Holocene vegetation in south Cumbria, UK, *Vegetation Hist Archaeobot*, **9**, 17-30

Winchester, A J L, 1984 Peat storage huts in Eskdale, *Trans Cumberland Westmorland Antiq Archaeol Soc*, n ser, **84**, 103-15

Winchester, A J L, 1987 *Landscape and society in medieval Cumbria*, Edinburgh

Wordsworth, W, and Coleridge, S T, 1798 *Lyrical ballads*, London

Yates, M J, 1983 Field clearance and field survey: some observations and an illustration from south-west Scotland, in F Hammond and T Reeves-Smyth (eds), *Landscape archaeology in Ireland*, BAR Brit Ser, **116**, Oxford, 341-56

Yates, M J, 1984a Groups of small cairns in Northern Britain: a view from south-west Scotland, *Proc Soc Antiq Scotland*, **114**, 217-35

Yates, M J, 1984b *Bronze Age round cairns in Dumfries and Galloway: an inventory and discussion*, BAR Brit Ser, **132**, Oxford

INDEX

394